X Window System User's Guide

Volume Three

X Window System User's Guide

---

for X11 R3 and R4 of the X Window System

by Valerie Quercia and Tim O'Reilly

O'Reilly & Associates, Inc.

Printing and Revision History

Sept. 1988:	First Edition
July 1989:	Second Edition. Revised to reflect Release 3.
Oct. 1989:	Minor corrections.
May 1990:	Third Edition. Revised to reflect Release 4.

Small Print

ISBN 0-937175-14-5

[10/91]

Table of Contents

3 Using the twm Window Manager 33

4 The xterm Terminal Emulator 49

5 Font Specification 79

Figures

Examples

Tables

Preface

By convention, a preface introduces the book itself, while the introduction starts in on the subject matter. You should read through the preface to get an idea of how the book is organized, the conventions it follows, and so on.

In The Preface:

Preface

The X Window System™ is a network-based graphics windowing system for workstations. It was developed by MIT, and has been adopted as an industry standard. The *X Window System User's Guide* describes window system concepts and the application programs (clients) commonly distributed with Version 11, Release 4 of X. Because some commercial X systems still reflect X11, Release 3, we highlight important differences between the two.

Assumptions

This book assumes that X has already been installed on your system, and that all standard MIT clients are available. In addition, although X runs on many different types of systems, this book assumes that you are running it on a UNIX® system, and that you have basic familiarity with UNIX. If you are not using UNIX, you will still find the book useful—UNIX dependencies are not that widespread—but you may occasionally need to translate a command example into its equivalent on your system. The book also assumes that you are using a 3-button pointer, and that the operation of the *twm* window manager is controlled by the *system.twmrc* file from the MIT X11 distribution (if this is not the case, the book provides information that will allow you to understand how *twm* is configured on your system).

This book has been written for both first time and experienced users of the X Window System. First-time users should read the book in order, starting with Chapter 1.

Experienced users can use this book as a reference for the client programs detailed here. Since there is great flexibility with X, even frequent users need to check on the syntax and availability of options. Reference pages for each client detail command-line options, customization database (resource database) variables, and other detailed information.

Organization

The book contains the following parts:

Part One: Using X

Preface
Describes the book's assumptions, audience, organization, and conventions.

Chapter 1: An Introduction to the X Window System
Describes the basic terminology associated with the X Window System: server, client, window, etc. The most important X clients are described.

Chapter 2: Getting Started
Shows the basics of using X: starting the server and creating the first terminal window; starting the window manager; adding additional windows; exiting. This chapter is tutorial in nature: you can follow along at a workstation as you read.

Chapter 3: Using the twm Window Manager
Describes how to use the *twm* window manager. This client is used to manipulate windows on the screen.

Chapter 4: The xterm Terminal Emulator
Describes how to use the *xterm* terminal emulator, the most frequently-used client. Certain aspects of *xterm* operation described in this chapter, such as scrolling and "copy and paste," are common to other applications as well.

Chapter 5: Font Specification
Describes the somewhat complicated font naming conventions and ways to simplify font specification, including wildcarding and aliasing. Describes how to use the *xlsfonts*, *xfd*, and *xfontsel* clients to list, display, and select available display fonts. Since the available fonts and font naming conventions changed radically from Release 2 to Release 3, this chapter also reviews these changes.

Chapter 6: Graphics Utilities
Explains how to use the major graphics clients included with X, notably the *bitmap* editor.

Chapter 7: Other Clients
Gives an overview of other clients available with X, including window and display information clients, the *xkill* program, and several "desk accessories."

Part Two: Customizing X

Chapter 8: Command Line Options
Discusses some of the command line options that are common to most clients.

Chapter 9: Setting Resources
Tells how to use create an *Xresources* file, or other file, to set resources for client applications. This chapter also describes how to use *xrdb*, which saves you having to maintain multiple *.Xresources* files if you run clients on multiple machines.

Chapter 10: Customizing the twm Window Manager
Describes the *.twmrc* file by showing the default file shipped by MIT, and then examining the purpose and syntax of entries. Explains various techniques for revising the *.twmrc* file to modify existing menus and create new ones. A revised *.twmrc* file is also offered for users to copy.

Chapter 11: Setup Clients
Describes how to set display and keyboard preferences using *xset* and how to set root window preferences using *xsetroot*. Demonstrates how to redefine the logical keynames and pointer commands recognized by X using *xmodmap*.

Part Three: Client Reference Pages

Extended reference pages for all clients.

Part Four: Appendices

Appendix A: System Management

Appendix B: The uwm Window Manager

Appendix C: The OSF/Motif Window Manager

Appendix D: Standard Cursors

Appendix E: Release 3 and 4 Standard Fonts

Appendix F: xterm Control Sequences

Appendix G: Standard Bitmaps

Appendix H: Translation Table Syntax

Glossary

Index

Bulk Sales Information

This guide is being resold by many workstation manufacturers as their official X Window System documentation. For information on volume discounts for bulk purchases, call O'Reilly & Associates, Inc., at 800-338-6887 (in California, 800-533-6887), or send e-mail to linda@ora.com (uunet!ora!linda).

For companies requiring extensive customization of the guide, source licensing terms are also available.

xshowfonts.c

The source to *xshowfonts.c*, which is printed in Appendix E, is also available free from UUNET (that is, free except for UUNET's usual connect-time charges). If you have access to UUNET, you can retrieve the source code using *uucp* or *ftp*. For *uucp*, find a machine with direct access to UUNET, and type the following command:

```
uucp uunet\!~uucp/nutshell/Xuser/xshowfonts.c.Z yourhost\!~/yourname/
```

The backslashes can be omitted if you use the Bourne shell (*sh*) instead of *csh*. The file should appear some time later (up to a day or more) in the directory */usr/spool/uucppublic/yourname*.

To use *ftp*, *ftp* to *uunet.uu.net* and use *anonymous* as your user name and *guest* as your password. Then type the following:

```
cd nutshell/Xuser
binary (you must specify binary transfer for compressed files)
get xshowfonts.c.Z
bye
```

The file is a compressed C program.

Acknowlegements

This guide is based in part on three previous X Window System user's guides, one from Masscomp, which was written by Jeff Graber, one from Sequent Computer Systems, Inc., and one from Graphic Software Systems, Inc., both of which were written by Candis Condo (supported by the UNIX development group). Some of Jeff's and Candis's material in turn was based on material developed under the auspices of Project Athena at MIT.

Most of the reference pages in Part Three have been adapted from reference pages copyright © 1988, 1989 the Massachusetts Institute of Technology, or from reference pages produced by Graphic Software Systems. Refer to the "Authors" section at the end of each reference page for details. Other copyrights are listed on the relevant reference pages.

Permission to use these materials is gratefully acknowledged.

This guide was primarily developed using the MIT sample server on a Sun-3™ Workstation, with additional testing done on a Sony NEWS™ workstation running Sony's X implementation, a Visual 640 X Display Station™, and an NCD16™ Network Display Station.

We are grateful to Sony Microsystems for the loan of a Sony NEWS workstation and to Visual Technology Incorporated for the loan of a Visual 640 X Display Station. We appreciate the support of these manufacturers in helping us develop complete and accurate X Window System documentation.

We'd also like to thank the Open Software Foundation for permission to reprint the *system.mwmrc* file in Appendix C, *The OSF/Motif Window Manager*. Special thanks to Elizabeth Connelly of OSF for arranging this.

Special thanks is given to Dave Curry for his expert technical and editorial support.

We'd also like to thank others on the staff at O'Reilly & Associates who helped significantly with the book. Jean Marie Diaz wrote the chapters discussing *twm*, tested examples throughout the book, and provided extensive technical support. Sue Willing coordinated the production effort and the design of illustrations. Donna Woonteiler and Peter Mui indexed the book. Linda Mui, Adrian Nye, and Dan Heller provided valuable technical support. Chris Reilley created the illustrations, many of which were adapted from illustrations done by Laurel Katz and Linda Lamb for previous editions of this guide. Sue Willing, Donna Woonteiler, Colleen Urban, and Chris Reilley prepared the camera-ready copy. Edie Freedman designed the cover for the X Window System series and directed the design of illustrations for this guide.

We'd also like to thank Jim Fulton and Keith Packard of the MIT X Consortium for their technical support and review comments on the book.

Despite the efforts of these people, the standard authors' disclaimer applies: any errors that remain are our own.

Font and Character Conventions

The following typographic conventions are used in this book.

Italics are used for:

- new terms where they are defined.
- file and directory names, and command and client names when they appear in the body of a paragraph.

`Courier` is used within the body of the text to show:

- command lines or options that should be typed verbatim on the screen.

is used within examples to show:

- computer-generated output.
- the contents of files.

`Courier bold` is used within examples to show command lines and options that should be typed verbatim on the screen.

`Courier italics`	are used within examples or explanations of command syntax to show a parameter to a command that requres context-dependent substitution (such as a variable). For example, *`filename`* means to use some appropriate filename; *`option(s)`* means to use some appropriate option(s) to the command.
Helvetica	is used to show menu titles and options.

The following symbols are used within the *X Window System User's Guide*:

[ ]	surround an optional field in a command line or file entry.
$	is the standard prompt from the Bourne shell, *sh*(1).
%	is the standard prompt from the C shell, *csh*(1).
name(1)	is a reference to a command called *name* in Section 1 of the *UNIX Reference Manual* (which may have a different name depending on the version of UNIX you use).

Part One:

Using X

Part One provides an overview of the X Window System and concepts, and describes how to use the most important programs available in the X environment.

1

An Introduction to the X Window System

This chapter describes the features of a typical X display, while introducing some basic window system concepts. It also provides an overview of the X Window System's client-server architecture and briefly describes the most commonly used clients.

In This Chapter:

1 An Introduction to the X Window System

The X Window System, called X for short, is a network-based graphics window system that was developed at MIT in 1984. Several versions of X have been developed, the most recent of which is X Version 11 (X11), first released in 1987.

X11 has been adopted as an industry-standard windowing system. X is supported by a consortium of industry leaders such as DEC, Hewlett-Packard, Sun, IBM, and AT&T that have united to direct, contribute to, and fund its continuing development. In addition to the system software development directed by the X Consortium, many independent developers are producing application software specifically for use with X. Because X11 is a relatively new standard, much of this application software has yet to be released.

First, we'll take a look at a typical X display and consider some general system features. Then we'll discuss what distinguishes the X Window System from other window systems. We'll also briefly consider some of the more important programs included in the standard distribution of X.

Anatomy of an X Display

X is typically run on a workstation with a large screen (although it also runs on PCs and special X terminals, as well as on many larger systems). X allows you to work with multiple programs simultaneously, each in a separate *window*. The display in Figure 1-1 includes five windows.

The operations performed within a window can vary greatly, depending on the type of program running it. Certain windows accept input from the user: they may function as terminals, allow you to create graphics, etc. Other windows simply display information, such as the time of day or a picture of the characters in a particular font, etc.

The windows you will probably use most frequently are *terminal emulators*, windows that function as standard terminals. The terminal emulator included with the standard release of X is called *xterm*. Figure 1-1 depicts three *xterm* windows. In an *xterm* window, you can do anything you might do in a regular terminal: enter commands, run editing sessions, compile programs, etc.

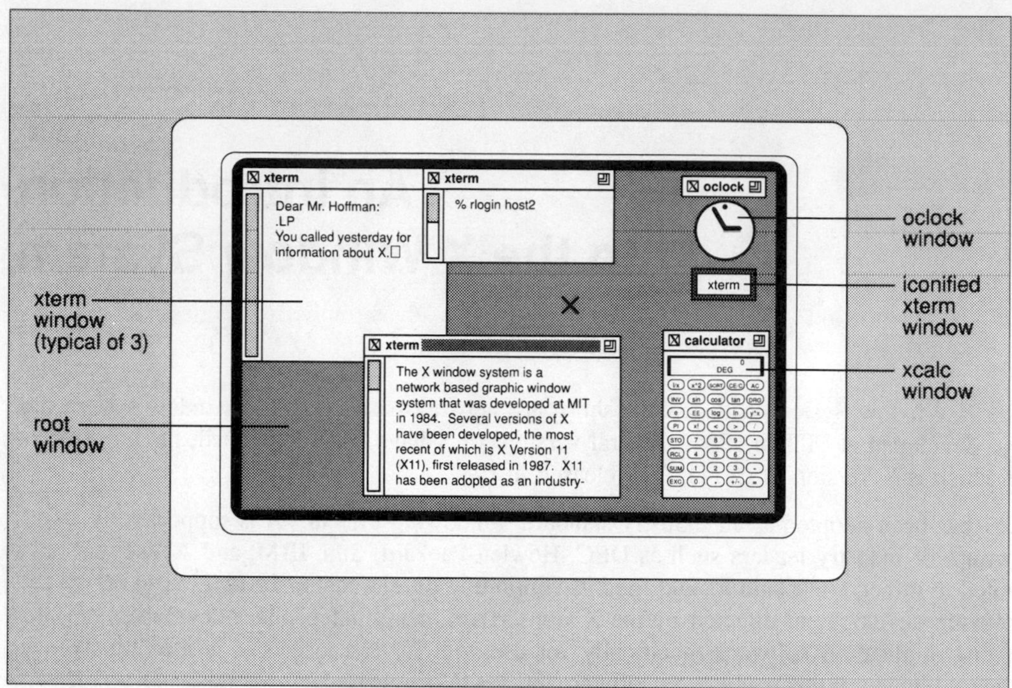

Figure 1-1. X display with five windows and an icon

The display in Figure 1-1 also includes two other application windows: a clock (called *xclock*) and a calculator (*xcalc*).

The shaded area that fills the entire screen is called the *root* (or *background*) window. One of the strengths of a window system such as X is that you can have several processes going on at once in several different windows (perhaps on different machines). For example, in Figure 1-1, the user is logging in to a remote system in one *xterm* window and is editing a text file in each of the two other *xterm* windows. (As we'll see in Chapter 4, *The xterm Terminal Emulator*, you can also cut and paste text between two windows.) Be aware, however, that you can only input to one window at a time.

Windows often overlap each other much like sheets of paper on your desk or a stack of cards. Note that overlapping does not interfere with the process run in each window.

One of the main features of X is a type of program called a *window manager*. The window manager controls the general operation of the window system, allowing you to change the size and position of windows on the display. You can reshuffle windows in a window stack, make windows larger or smaller, move them to other locations on the screen, etc. In short, it is the window manager that controls the "look and feel" of the X Window System.

In Release 4, the X Consortium provides a window manager called *twm*. (*twm* originally stood for "Tom's window manager," in honor of its developer, Tom LaStrange. However, it has since been renamed the "tab window manager." Earlier releases supported a window manager called *uwm*, "universal window manager.") Notice that each window on our typical display has a horizontal bar that spans its top edge. This feature is known as a *titlebar*, mainly because it contains a text description of the window. (Generally, this is the application name, but as we'll see later, you can often specify an alternate title.) The titlebar is provided by *twm* and is one of this window manager's hallmarks.

In addition to displaying title text, the titlebar provides some of the functionality of the *twm* window manager. Using the mouse or other pointer device, you can click on various parts of the titlebar to manipulate the window. Manipulating a window with the titlebar is described in detail in Chapter 3, *Using the twm Window Manager*.

If you are using another window manager, the X display may have a different look and feel. (Though you can run a window system such as X without a window manager, this severely limits the system's power and flexibility, since there is no easy way to change the size and position of windows on the display.)

Also pictured in Figure 1-1 is an *icon*. An icon is a small symbol that represents a window in an inactive state. The window manager allows you to convert windows to icons and icons back to windows. You may want to convert a window to an icon to save space on the display or to prevent input to that window. Each icon has a label, generally the name of the program that created the window. The icon in Figure 1-1 represents a fourth *xterm* window on the display. Icons can be moved around on the display, just like regular windows.

The contents of a window are not visible when the window has been converted to an icon, but they are not lost. In fact, a client continues to run when its window has been iconified; if you iconify a terminal emulator client, such as *xterm*, any programs running in the shell will also continue.

All X displays require you to have some sort of pointer, often a three-button mouse, with which you communicate information to the system. As you slide the pointer around on your desktop, a cursor symbol on the display follows the pointer's movement. For our purposes, we will refer to both the pointer device (e.g., a mouse) and the symbol that represents its location on the screen as pointers. Depending on where the pointer is on the screen (in an *xterm* window, in another application window, on the root window, etc.), it is represented by a variety of cursor symbols. If the pointer is positioned on the root window, it is generally represented by an X-shaped cursor, as in Figure 1-1. If the pointer is in an *xterm* window, it looks like an "I" and is commonly called an *I-beam cursor*.*

A complete list of cursors is shown in Appendix D, *Standard Cursors*. Some of the most common cursor shapes are shown in Figure 1-2. As we'll see later, some applications allow you to select the cursor to use.

*Even though the actual image on the screen is called a cursor, throughout this guide we refer to "moving the pointer" to avoid confusion with the standard text cursor that can appear in an *xterm* window.

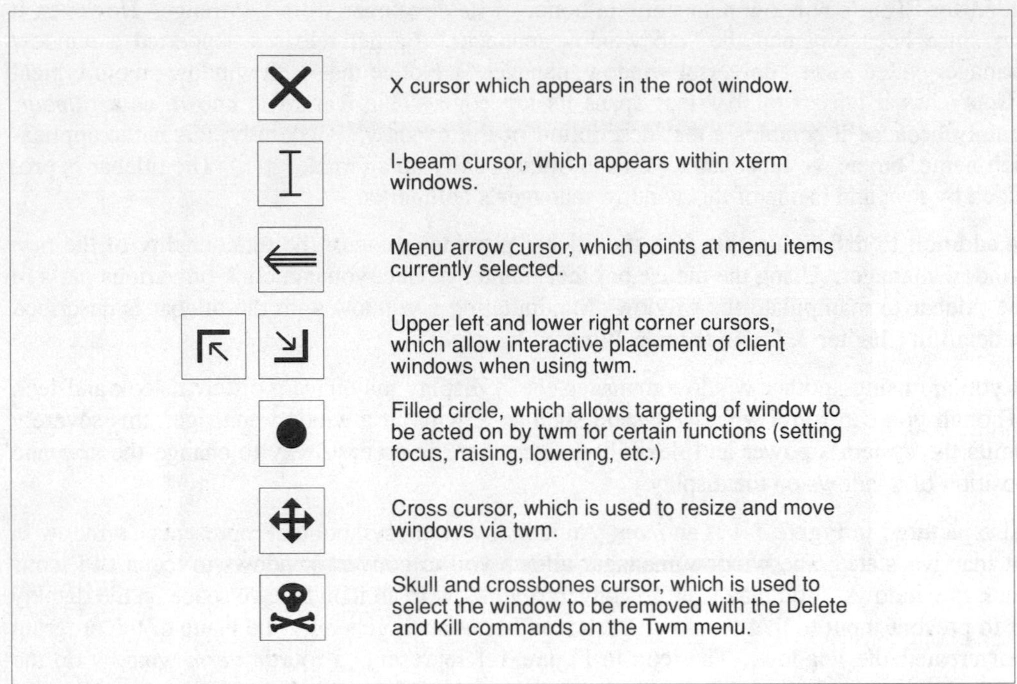

X cursor which appears in the root window.
I-beam cursor, which appears within xterm windows.
Menu arrow cursor, which points at menu items currently selected.
Upper left and lower right corner cursors, which allow interactive placement of client windows when using twm.
Filled circle, which allows targeting of window to be acted on by twm for certain functions (setting focus, raising, lowering, etc.)
Cross cursor, which is used to resize and move windows via twm.
Skull and crossbones cursor, which is used to select the window to be removed with the Delete and Kill commands on the Twm menu.

Figure 1-2. Some standard cursors

You use the pointer to manipulate windows and icons, to make selections in menus, and to select the window in which you want to input. You can't type in an *xterm* window unless you place the pointer in that window, as in Figure 1-3.

Directing input to a particular window is called *focusing*. You must be sure that the pointer rests in the desired window before you begin typing. The window border (if present) and text cursor are also highlighted when the pointer is in that window. The highlighting is a characteristic of *xterm*: other applications may not highlight display features.

The fact that input focus automatically follows the pointer is a default characteristic of the *twm* window manager. Other window managers require you to click on a window to focus input on that window. These two window manager focusing styles are commonly referred to as "real-estate-driven" (or "pointer focus") and "click-to-type."

The most important thing to recognize is that the position of the pointer is very important to a real-estate-driven window manager like *twm*. If something doesn't work the way you expect, make sure that the pointer is in the right place. After you use X for a while, awareness of pointer position will come naturally.

Be aware that it may take a moment for the input focus to catch up with the pointer, especially on slower machines. If you type right away, some keystrokes may end up in the window you left rather than in the new window. This is really a bug and happens because of the additional overhead involved in complex window managers like *twm* or *mwm*. It doesn't happen if you are using a simpler window manager like *uwm*.

Figure 1-3. Focus on an xterm window

The pointer is also often used to display menus. Some X programs, notably *twm* and *xterm*, have menus that are displayed by keystrokes and/or pointer button motions. Unlike some window systems, which allow you to "pull down" menus from a menu bar that is always displayed, *twm* (and most X clients) support "pop-up" menus, which are displayed at the current pointer position. In addition to keyboard keys and pointer button motions, the location of the pointer also plays a role in displaying menus. For example, *xterm* menus can only be displayed when the pointer is within an *xterm* window. Figure 1-4 shows a *twm* menu called Twm, which is displayed by placing the pointer on the root window and holding down the first pointer button.

You generally display this menu by moving the pointer to the root window and pressing and holding down the first pointer button. In Figure 1-4, the arrow next to the menu title represents the pointer. As you drag the pointer down the menu, each of the menu selections is highlighted. Regardless of the program, you generally select a menu item by dragging the pointer down the menu, highlighting the item you want, and releasing the pointer button.

With other programs, particularly several other window managers, you can display a menu simply by placing the pointer on a particular part of the window, e.g., a horizontal bar across the top.

A final note about the X display: in X, the terms *display* and *screen* are not equivalent. A display may consist of more than one screen. This feature might be implemented in several ways. There might be two physical monitors, linked to form a single display, as shown in Figure 1-5. Alternatively, two screens might be defined as different ways of using the same

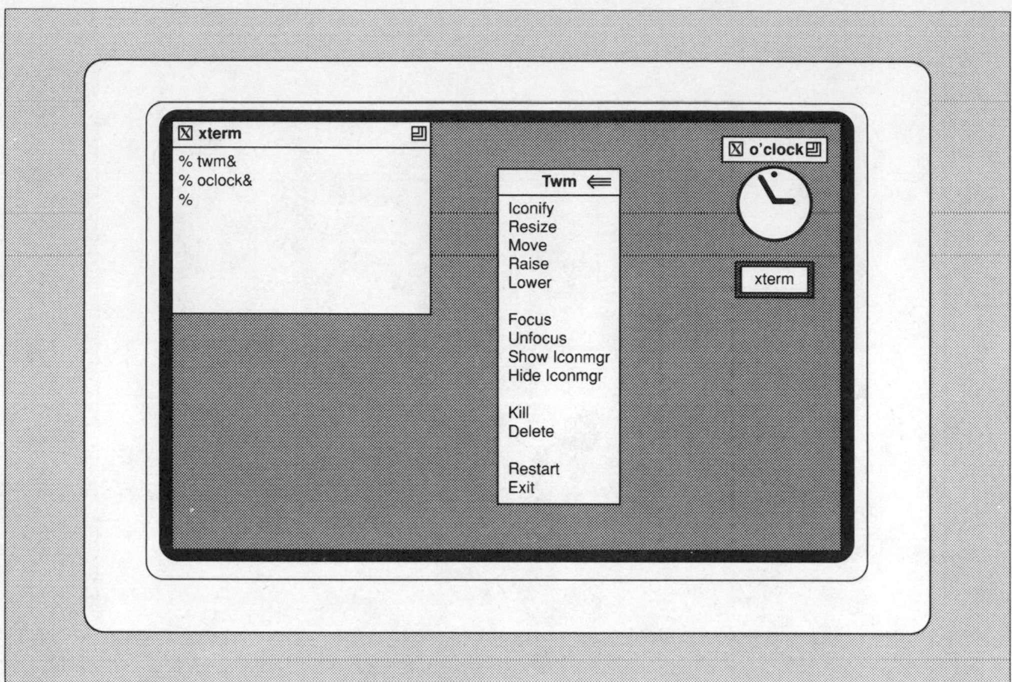

Figure 1-4. Twm menu on the root window

display. For example, on the Sun-3/110 color workstation, screen 0 is black and white, and screen 1 is color. By default, windows are always placed on screen 0, but you can "scroll" between the two screens with the mouse, or place a client window on screen 1 by specifying the screen number in the `-display` option when starting the client. (See Chapter 8, *Command Line Options*, for more information on the `-display` option.)

X Architecture Overview

Most window systems are *kernel-based*: that is, they are closely tied to the operating system itself and can only run on a discrete system, such as a single workstation. The X Window System is not part of any operating system but is instead comprised entirely of "user-level" programs.

The architecture of the X Window System is based on what is known as a *client-server* model. The system is divided into two distinct parts: *display servers* that provide display capabilities and keep track of user input, and *clients*, application programs that perform specific tasks. On a more basic level, the server acts as an intermediary between client application programs and the local display hardware. The client programs make requests (for information, processes, etc.) that are communicated to the hardware display by the server.

Figure 1-5. A display made up of two physical screens

This division within the X architecture allows the clients and the display server either to work together on the same machine or to reside on different machines (possibly of different types, with different operating systems, etc.) that are connected by a network. For example, you might use a relatively low-powered PC or workstation as a display server to interact with clients that are running on a more powerful remote system. Even though the client program is actually running on the more powerful system, all user input and displayed output occur on the PC or workstation server and are communicated across the network using the X protocol. Figure 1-6 shows a diagram of such a network.

There is another less obvious advantage to the client-server model: since the server is entirely responsible for interacting with the hardware, only the server program must be machine-specific. X client application programs can be ported easily from system to system.

The X Display Server

The X display server is a program that keeps track of all input coming from input devices, such as the keyboard and mouse, and input from any other clients that are running. As the display server receives information from a client, it updates the appropriate window on your display. The display server may run on the same computer as a client or on an entirely different machine.

Servers are available for PCs, workstations, and even for special terminals, which may have the server downloaded from another machine or stored in ROM.

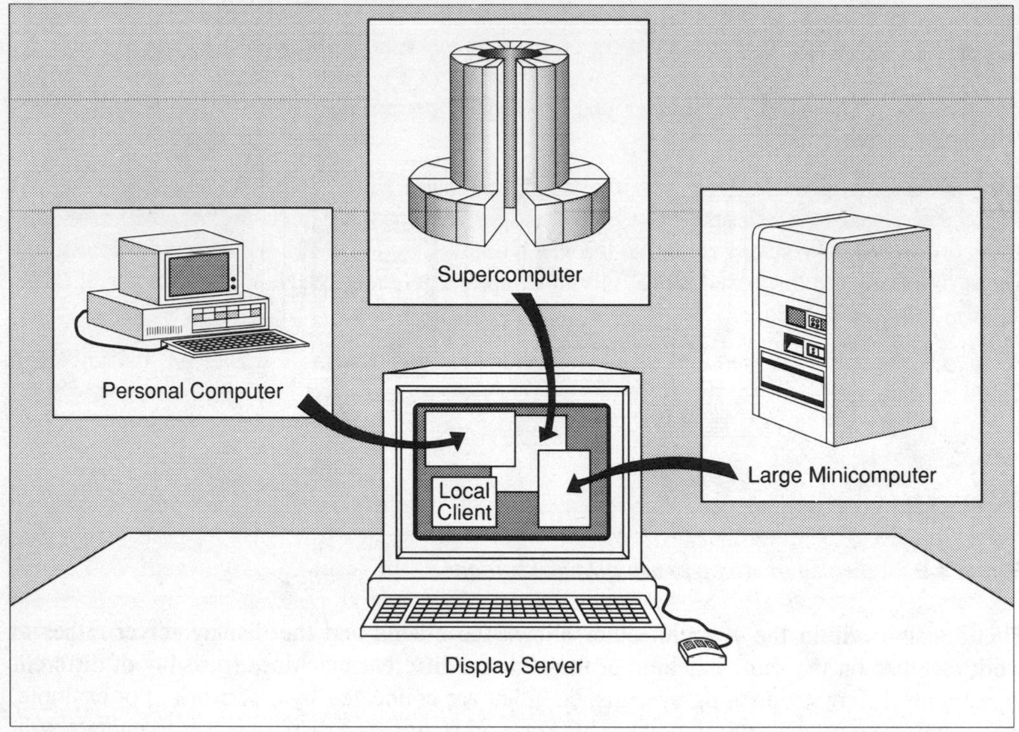

Figure 1-6. A sample X Window System configuration

Clients

X allows you to run many clients simultaneously. For example, you could be editing a text file in one window, compiling a program source file in a second window, reading your mail in a third, all the while displaying the system load average in a fourth window.

While X clients may display their results and take input from a single display server, they may each be running on a different computer on the network. It is important to note that the same programs may not look and act the same on different servers since there is no standard user interface, since users can customize X clients differently on each server, and since the display hardware on each server may be different.

Several of the more frequently used client programs are discussed in the following paragraphs.

The Window Manager

The way a kernel-based window system operates is inherent in the window system itself. By contrast, the X Window System concentrates control in a window manager, several of which are available. The window manager you use largely determines the look and feel of X on a particular system.

The window manager shipped with the standard release of X from MIT is called *twm*. As we've discussed, *twm* allows you to move and resize windows, rearrange the order of windows in the window stack, create additional windows, and convert windows into icons, etc. These functions are discussed more fully in Chapter 2, *Getting Started*, and Chapter 3, *Using the twm Window Manager*.

Prior to Release 4, the standard window manager shipped with X was *uwm*, the *u*niversal *w*indow *m*anager. *uwm* has been superceded by *twm* because the latter has been made compliant with the X Consortium's *Inter-Client Communication Conventions Manual* (ICCCM), introduced at Release 3.

The ICCCM contains standards for interaction with window managers and other clients. It defines basic policy intentionally omitted from X itself, such as the rules for transferring data between applications, for transferring keyboard focus, for installing colormaps, and so on. As long as applications and window managers follow the conventions outlined in the ICCCM, applications created with different toolkits will be able to coexist and work together on the same server.

Because *uwm* does not comply with the standards outlined in the ICCCM, it has been moved to a directory of user-contributed clients in Release 4, where it is still available for those who wish to use it. However, *uwm* is no longer officially supported by the X Consortium, and it should probably not be the window manager of choice. If you are still using *uwm*, Appendix B, *The uwm Window Manager*, discusses getting started with and customizing this window manager.

In this guide, we assume you are using *twm*. Several other window managers, such as *mwm* (the Motif™ window manager), *awm* (Ardent™ window manager), *rtl* (tiled window manager, developed at Siemens Research and Technology Laboratories, RTL), and *olwm* (the OPENLOOK™ window manager) are also widely used.

mwm is discussed in greater detail in Appendix C, *The OSF/Motif Window Manager*.

If the *twm* window manager has been customized at your site or you are using a different window manager, many of the concepts should still be the same. However, the actual procedures shown may well differ. See Chapter 10, *Customizing the twm Window Manager*, for a discussion of how to customize *twm*.

The xterm Terminal Emulator

X11 itself is designed to support only bitmapped graphics displays. For this reason, one of the most important clients is a terminal emulator. The terminal emulator brings up a window that allows you to log in to a multiuser system and to run applications designed for use on a standard alphanumeric terminal. Anything you can do on a terminal, you can do in this window.

xterm is the most widely available terminal emulator. *xterm* emulates a DEC® VT102 terminal or a Tektronix® 4014 terminal. You can display both types of windows at the same time, but only one is active at a time.

Since you can bring up more than one *xterm* window at a time, you can run several programs at once. For example, you can have the system transfer files or process information while you focus your attention on a text-editing session. Multiple *xterm* processes allow you to display interactions in separate windows on your screen. See Chapter 2, *Getting Started*, and Chapter 4, *The xterm Terminal Emulator*, for additional information.

The Display Manager

The display manager, *xdm*, is a client that is designed to start the X server automatically (from the UNIX */etc/rc* system startup file) and to keep it running. (X can also be started manually, as described in Chapter 2.) In its most basic implementation, the display manager emulates the *getty* and *login* programs, which put up the login prompt on a standard terminal, keeping the server running, prompting for a user's name and password, and managing a standard login session.

However, *xdm* has far more powerful and versatile capabilities. Users can design their own sessions, running several clients and setting personal resources (such as keyboard, pointer, and display characteristics). You can also customize special *xdm* files to manage several connected displays (both local and remote) and to set system-wide X resources (for example, client default features). Resources are discussed in Chapter 9, *Setting Resources*. See Appendix A, *System Management*, for a discussion of how to set up and customize the display manager.

Other X Clients

The following is a brief list of some other clients commonly included with X.

xclock	Displays the time of day continuously either in digital or in analog form.
bitmap	Allows you to change your pointers, icons, and background window pattern.
xcalc	Provides a scientific calculator on your display.
xset	Allows you to set various display and keyboard preferences, such as bell volume, cursor acceleration, screen saver operation, and so on.
xwd	Dumps the contents of a window into a file.

xpr Translates an image file produced by *xwd* to PostScript® or other formats, suitable for printing on a variety of printers.

xfd Displays the contents of a font on the screen.

For additional information on these and other clients, refer to Chapter 5, *Font Specification*, Chapter 6, *Graphics Utilities*, Chapter 7, *Other Clients*, Chapter 11, *Setup Clients*, and to the reference page for each client in Part Three of this guide. As more commercial and user-contributed software is developed, many more specialized programs will become available.

Customizing Clients

Most X clients are designed to be customized by the user. A multitude of command line options can be used to affect the operation of these clients. More conveniently, default values for each option can be stored in a file (generally called *.Xresources* or *.Xdefaults*) in your home directory. If you are running clients on multiple machines, a program called *xrdb* (X resource database manager) should be used to store your defaults in the server so that you don't need to maintain an *.Xdefaults* file on each machine.

There is a separate customization file for the *twm* window manager, called *.twmrc*, which is also kept in your home directory.

Client customization is described in Part Two of this guide.

2

Getting Started

This chapter shows you how to begin working if X is already running on your system and how to start the X server manually if X is not running. It also provides preliminary instructions for starting the window manager, twm, *and the* xterm *terminal emulator.*

In This Chapter:

2
Getting Started

This chapter introduces the basics of using X: starting the server and creating the first terminal window; starting the window manager; adding additional windows; exiting. While it is written as a tutorial, you do not necessarily have to follow along at a workstation.

Before you can begin using the X Window System, you must do three things:

- Start the X server.
- Start at least one instance of the *xterm* terminal emulator.
- Start a window manager. (Though you *can* run X without a window manager, this is fairly limiting.)

Depending on how X is configured on your system, some or all of these steps may be performed for you automatically. First, this chapter explains how you can tell if X is being started automatically and how to begin working if it is. Then this chapter describes how to start X manually. Later sections show you how to exit from an *xterm* window and how to start additional client programs.

If X is Being Started Automatically

Depending on how X is being run on your system, the initial screens you see and the way you log in will be slightly different.

If you log in at a prompt displayed on the full screen, your workstation may automatically start the server and open up the first *xterm* window. If this is the case, your screen should then look something like Figure 2-1.

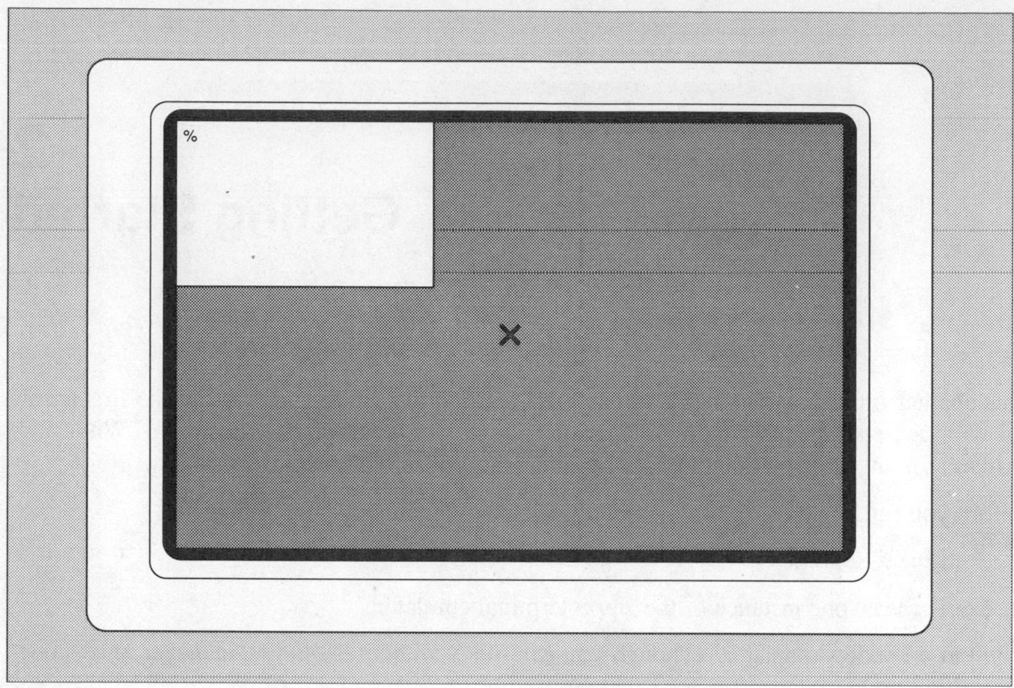

Figure 2-1. Workstation with login xterm window on the root window

If the display manager, *xdm*, is running X on your system, you may see a window similar to Figure 2-2 when you turn on your terminal.

Log in just as if you were using a standard alphanumeric terminal. The screen should then display the first *xterm* window, as in Figure 2-1.

Without any user customization, the display manager executes a standard login "session," providing the first *xterm* window *and* starting the window manager. If the window manager is running, you will see a titlebar on your window, displaying the name of the window ("xterm").

If the *twm* window manager is running, skip to the section "Starting a Second xterm Window" later in this chapter for information on starting additional windows and other clients. If the window manager is *not* running, skip to the section "Bringing Up the Window Manager" later in this chapter for instruction on how to start it.

On BSD 4.3 systems, there is another method to bring up X automatically (from the */etc/ttys* system file). This method has been phased out in Release 4. However, if your system is set up to use this method, when the power is turned on, your workstation should automatically start the server and open up an *xterm* window in which you can log in. If this is the case, your screen should look something like Figure 2-3.

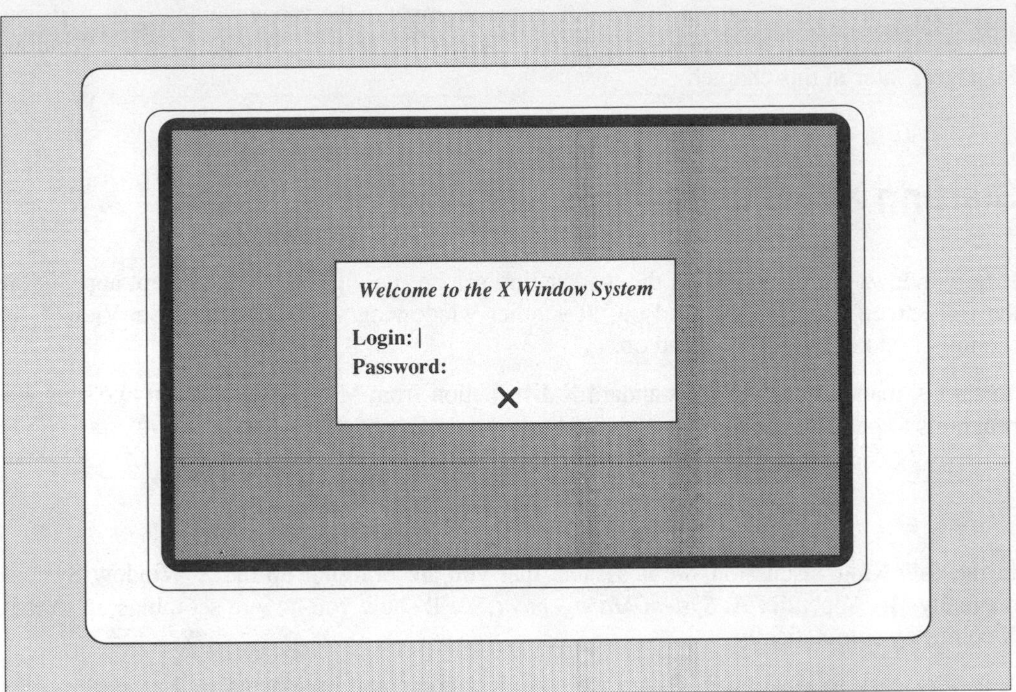

Figure 2-2. xdm login window

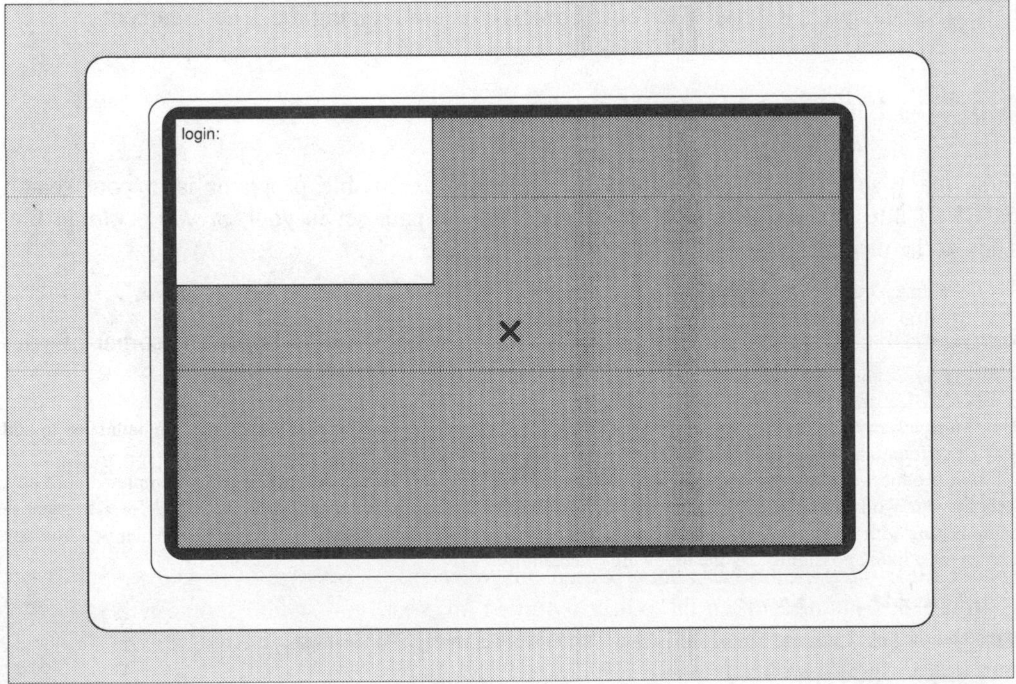

Figure 2-3. xterm window with login prompt

Log in by typing your name and password at the prompts in the *xterm* window, just as if you were using a standard alphanumeric terminal. Skip to the section "Bringing Up the Window Manager" later in this chapter.

Starting X Manually

If no windows are displayed on the workstation screen (i.e., if your login prompt appears on the full screen), log in, and read on. If another windowing system (such as SunView™) is running, first kill it, and then read on.

To start X manually (using the standard X distribution from MIT), you must run two separate programs to perform the three steps listed at the beginning of the chapter:

`% xinit`	To start the X server and create the first (login) *xterm* window.
`% twm &`	To start the window manager.

In the following discussion, we'll assume that you are bringing up the X Window System manually. In Appendix A, *System Management*, we'll show you how to set things up so that X comes up automatically.

X is very easy to customize. There are countless command options as well as startup files that control the way the screen looks or even what menus a program displays. If you are "trying out" X using someone else's system or login account, things may not work as described here. (See Chapters 8 through 11 for information on customizing the X environment.)

Starting the First xterm Window

First, make sure that the X11 directory containing executable programs is in your search path.* If not, add the pathname */usr/bin/X11* to the path set in your *.profile* or *.login* file. Then at the prompt, type:

```
% xinit
```

xinit starts the X server and creates the first *xterm* window in the upper-left corner of your display.†

---

*For more information on how to set your search path, see Appendix A. Note that the appropriate pathname to add may be different in vendor distributions.

†If *xinit* produces a blank background, with no terminal window, software installation was not completed correctly. Reboot your workstation and try again. Before invoking *xinit*, look in the directory */usr/bin/X11* for a file whose name begins with a capital X but otherwise has a similar name to your workstation (e.g., Xsun). When you find one that seems a likely possibility, try the following command:

```
% xinit -- Xname
```

If that works, link X*name* to X, and *xinit* will thereafter work correctly. For example:

```
% cd /usr/bin/X11
% ln Xsun X
```

Bringing Up the Window Manager

Make sure that the pointer is in the *xterm* window, so that the I-beam cursor is displayed. Start the *twm* window manager by typing:

```
% twm &
```

The screen will momentarily go blank; then the window will be redisplayed, this time with a titlebar. The titlebar provides a quick and easy way to move, resize, and otherwise manipulate windows on the screen. The window manager also allows you to position client windows on the screen, as illustrated by the placement of the *xterm* window described in the next section.

Note that it is important to run *twm* in the background by placing an ampersand (&) at the end of the command line, so that you can continue to enter additional commands into the *xterm* window. If you neglected to do this on a system that supports job control, type Control-Z to suspend *twm*, then use the *bg* command (see *csh*(1)) to place it in the background.

If the system you're on does not support job control, interrupt the process with Delete or Control-C and start over.

Starting a Second xterm Window

If you want to open a second *xterm* window, type the following command at the prompt in the first *xterm* window:

```
% xterm &
```

After a few moments, the pointer becomes an upper-left-corner cursor, as shown in Figure 2-4.

This corner cursor represents the upper-left corner of the window you want to place. The cursor tracks pointer movement as you move the pointer across your screen and allows you to position the *xterm* window.

Move the corner cursor to the desired position on your screen and *click* the left mouse button. (A click is defined as pressing the mouse button down and releasing it.) A new *xterm* window appears on your screen, with a prompt from whatever shell you are using. Figure 2-5 shows how your screen might look now.

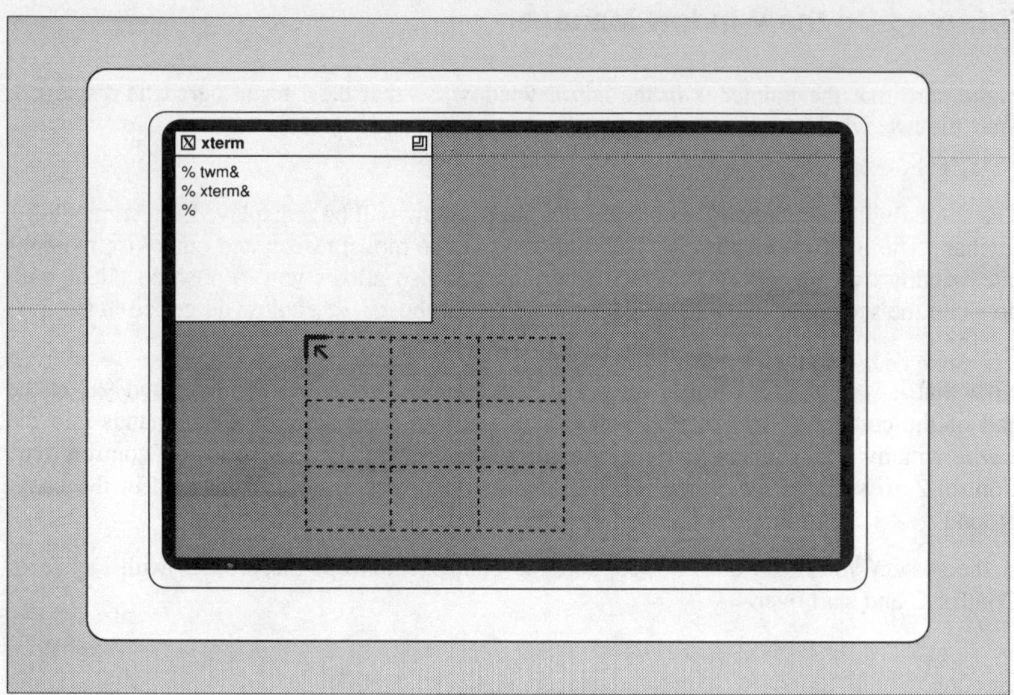

Figure 2-4. Placing a second xterm window

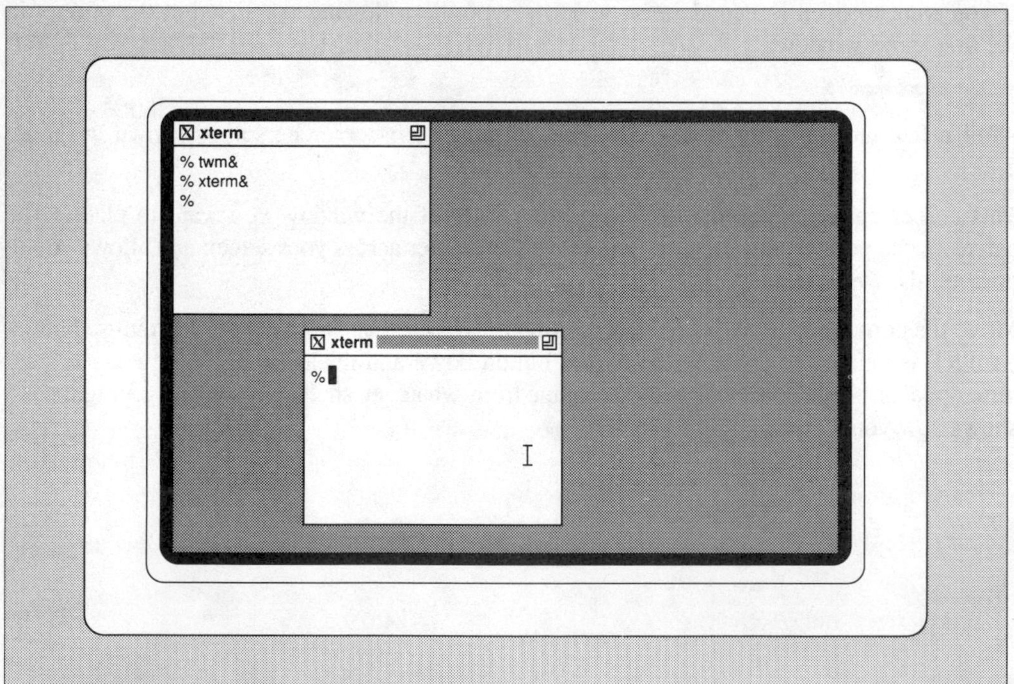

Figure 2-5. Two xterm windows

You can switch back and forth between windows simply by moving the pointer from one to the other.

If you have inadvertently positioned the second *xterm* window in front of the first one, don't be concerned. Just use the front window for now. Chapter 3, *Using the twm Window Manager*, provides information on resizing and moving windows.

Notice how the text cursor, titlebar, and border in each *xterm* window are highlighted when you move the pointer into that window. Whatever you type will appear in the window with the highlighted titlebar. Try starting a command in both windows. For example, start up *vi* or another text editor in the second *xterm* window. Notice how you can switch back to the first window to type a new command, simply by moving the pointer—even if you leave *vi* in insert mode or some other command in the process of sending output to the screen. Whatever process was running in the window you left will continue to run. If it needs input from you to continue, it will wait.

Exiting from an xterm Window

When you are through using an *xterm* window, you can remove it by typing whatever command you usually use to log off your system. Typically, this might be `exit` or Control-D. You can also terminate an *xterm* window by selecting Hangup, Terminate, Kill, or Quit from the xterm menu. (These menu options send different signals to the *xterm* process. Depending on what signals your operating system recognizes, some of the options may not work as intended. See Chapter 4, *The xterm Terminal Emulator*, for more information.)

Be aware that terminating the login *xterm* window (the first *xterm* to appear) kills the X server and all associated clients. (If *xdm* is running X, the server will be reset, but only after all client processes have been killed.) Be sure to terminate all other *xterm* windows before terminating the *xterm* login window. Also, be sure that if you are in an editor such as *vi* that you save your data before you terminate the window

In fact, it may be wise to *iconify* the login window (shrink it into a small symbol, or *icon*, on the screen) and use other *xterm* windows instead, so that you don't inadvertently terminate it. See Chapter 3, *Using the twm Window Manager*, for a discussion of how to do this.

Alternatively, you can enter:

```
% set ignoreeof
```

in the login window. Then typing `exit` becomes the only way you can terminate the window. Note that some C shell implementations have an *autologout* variable, which will automatically terminate the shell if there is no activity for a given period of time.

If your C shell supports this feature, be sure to disable it in the login *xterm* window using the following command:

```
% unset autologout
```

Special Keys

Most workstations have a number of "modifier" keys, so called because they modify the action of other keys.

Three of these modifier keys should be familiar to any user of a standard ASCII terminal or personal computer—Shift, Caps Lock, and Control. However, many workstations have additional modifier keys as well. A PC has an "Alt" key, a Macintosh™ has a "fan" key, a Sony workstation has keys named "Nfer" and "Xfer," and a Sun workstation has no less than three additional modifier keys, labeled "Left," "Right," and "Alternate."

Because X clients are designed to run on many different workstations, with different keyboards, it is difficult to assign functions to special keys on the keyboard. A developer can't count on the same key always being present!

For this reason, many X clients make use of "logical" modifier keynames, which can be mapped by the user to any actual key on the keyboard.

Up to eight separate modifier keys can be defined. The most commonly used (after Shift, Caps Lock, and Control) has the logical keyname "Meta."

We'll talk at length about this subject in Chapter 11, *Setup Clients*, but we wanted to warn you here. When we talk later in this book about pressing the "Meta" key, you should be aware that there is not likely to be a physical key on the keyboard with that name. For example, on one workstation, the Meta key might be labeled "Alt" and, on another, "Funct." And as we'll show in Chapter 11, you can choose any key you want to act as the Meta key.

Unfortunately, X provides no easy way to find out which key on your keyboard has been assigned to be the Meta key. You don't need to know this right away . . . but when you do, please turn to the discussion of key mapping in Chapter 11, *Setup Clients*, for information on how you can find out.

How a Client Looks and Behaves: Application Defaults

The way the *xterm* client looks (and, to some extent, behaves) is partially determined by a system-wide file of *application defaults*. Several clients have application defaults files that determine certain of the client's features. Applications defaults files generally reside in the directory */usr/lib/X11/app-defaults* and are named for the client application. For *xterm*, the application defaults specify such things as the labels for menu items, the fonts used to display menu items, and the shape of the pointer when it's in an *xterm* window.

In describing the appearance and behavior of clients in this guide, we assume all of the standard application defaults file are present on your system and accessible by the client programs. If, by some chance, a client's application defaults file has been edited or removed from your system, the client may not look or behave exactly as we describe it. If a client application appears substantially different than it is depicted in this guide, you may be using a different version of the program or the application defaults may be different. Consult your system administrator.

Within an application defaults file, defaults are set using variables called *resources*. Almost every feature of every client program can be controlled by a resource variable. The resource variables specified in a client's application defaults files are usually just a subset of a greater number of resources that can be set.

As we'll see in Chapter 9, *Setting Resources*, you can override the system-wide defaults *and* control additional features of a client by specifying your own resources in a file in your home directory.

Starting Other Clients

You can start other X clients just like you can start another instance of *xterm*. At the command line prompt in any *xterm* window, type the name of the client followed by an ampersand to make the client run in the background. For example, by typing:

```
% oclock &
```

you can cause a window displaying a clock to be placed on the screen. (The *oclock* client is available as of Release 4. If you are running an earlier release of X, the only clock program available is *xclock*.) First an upper-left corner cursor will appear, just as it did when you created a second *xterm* window. Move the corner cursor to the position you would like the clock to appear, and then click the left mouse button. Figure 2-6 shows the *oclock* display, placed in the upper-right corner of the screen.

Unfortunately, the developers of *oclock* neglected to provide an easy way to remove it. One way to remove the *oclock* display is to identify and kill the process using the standard UNIX process control mechanisms. To find the process ID for *oclock*, go to an *xterm* window and type:

```
% ps -aux | grep oclock
```

at a system prompt. Under System V, type:

```
% ps -e | grep oclock
```

at a system prompt. The resulting display should look something like this:

```
128  p0  0:00  oclock
142  p0  0:00  grep oclock
```

The number in the first column is the process ID. Type:

```
% kill process_id
```

The *oclock* display will be removed, and you will get the message:

```
Terminated    oclock
```

You can also remove the *oclock* display using other methods intended to "kill" the client process. These methods and their liabilities are discussed in Chapter 7, *Other Clients*.

If you are running Release 2 or 3 of X, the *xclock* client must also be removed using the UNIX *kill* command (or another method of killing a client, as described in Chapter 7). As of Release 4, *xclock* can also be removed by a gentler method, namely, the Delete item of the

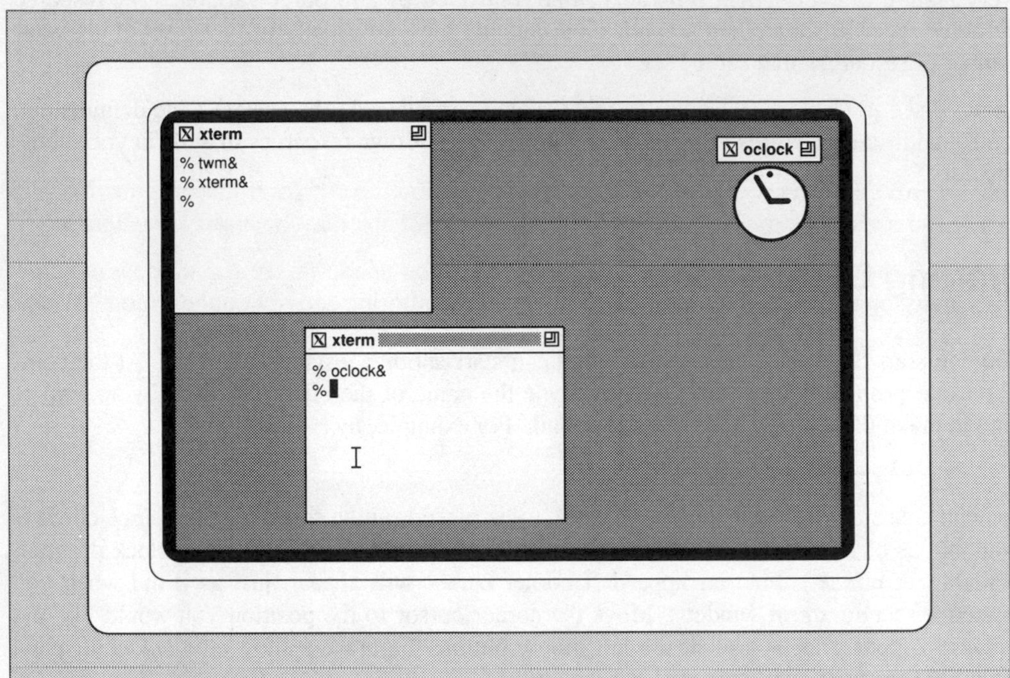

Figure 2-6. The oclock display

Twm menu. See Chapter 3, *Using the twm Window Manager*, for more information about Delete.

Running a Client on Another Machine

Remember that X also allows you to run a client on another machine, while displaying the client's window on the local machine. A client you may wish to run on another machine is *xload*, which is used to keep track of the system load average. By default, *xload* polls the system for the load average at five-second intervals and displays the results in a simple histogram.

If you are running processes on more than one machine, it's useful to gauge the level of activity on the systems in question. This information should help you judge when to start processes and monitor how your processes are impacting system resources.

Say you're running clients both on the local machine (let's call it *host1*) and on another machine (*host2*). On the local display, you can have two *xload* windows, one showing activity on *host1* and one showing activity on *host2*.

To create an *xload* window monitoring activity on *host1*, use the command:

```
% xload &
```

The cursor changes to an upper-left corner cursor, allowing you to place the window.

Then run an *xload* process on *host2* using a remote shell (*rsh*), and display the results in a window on *host1*:

```
% rsh host2 'xload -display host1:0' &
```

Again, you place the window using the pointer.

The `-display` option tells *xload* to create its window on the local display (*host1*). The syntax and use of this option is discussed more fully in Chapter 8, *Command Line Options*.

Figure 2-7 shows the resulting *host1* display: two *xload* windows, the top window monitoring activity on the local system and the bottom one monitoring activity on the remote system.

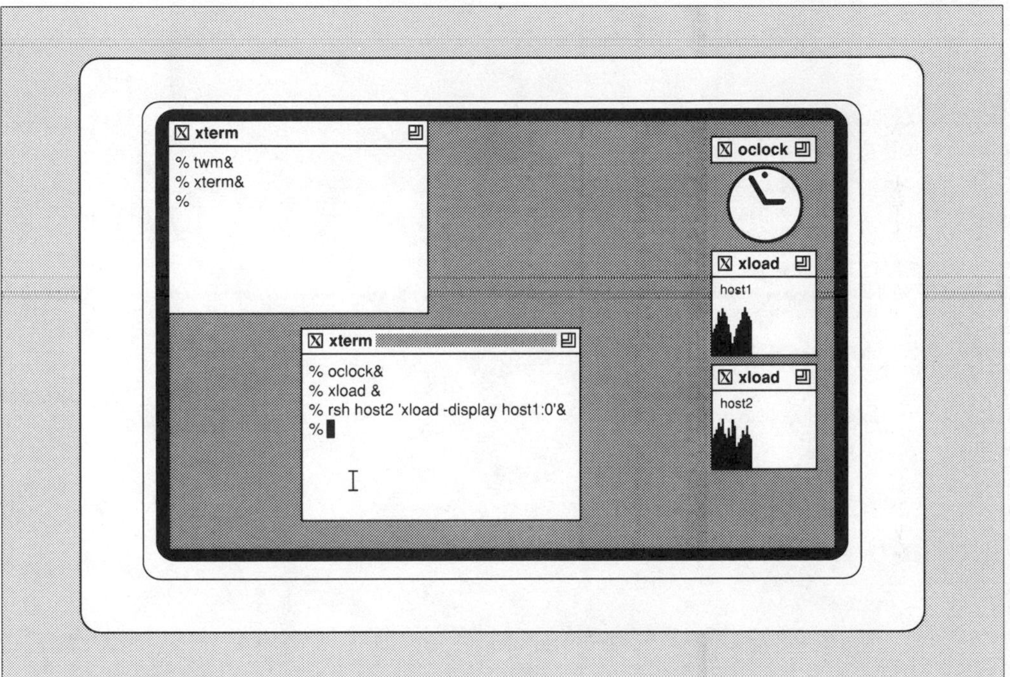

Figure 2-7. Monitoring activity on two systems with xload

If you frequently need to access a remote system, you may want to run an *xterm* on that system using a remote shell and display the window on the local system. For instance, the following command runs an *xterm* on a remote Sony NEWS workstation (with the hostname `sony`) and displays on the local Sun-3 (with the hostname `sun`):

```
% rsh sony 'xterm -display sun:0' &
```

Getting Started

Where to Go From Here

There are many useful client programs supplied with the X Window System. Details of how to use the two most important of these clients, the *twm* window manager and the *xterm* terminal emulator are provided in the next two chapters. Clients to list and display fonts are described in Chapter 5. Chapter 6 describes several graphics utilities available with X. An overview and tutorial for other clients is provided in Chapter 7. All clients are described in detail in a reference page format in Part Three of this guide.

You should read at least the chapter on *twm* before starting up any other clients. You can then go on to read more about *xterm* in Chapter 4 or about other clients in Chapters 5 through 7.

3

Using the twm Window Manager

This chapter describes twm, *the standard window manager distributed with X. Additional information on customizing the operation of* twm *is provided in Chapter 10.*

In This Chapter:

3
Using the twm Window Manager

The *twm* window manager is primarily a window manipulation tool. It allows you to:

- Size and position client windows on the screen interactively.
- Move windows around the screen.
- Change the size of windows.
- Lower windows (send them to the back of others).
- Raise windows (bring them to the front of others).
- Convert windows to icons and icons to windows.
- Remove windows.

The *twm* window manipulation functions can be invoked in four ways:

- Using the titlebar.
- Using the Twm menu.
- By combinations of keyboard keys and pointer buttons.
- Automatically, when a client is started (to allow you to size and place the client window on the screen).

This chapter discusses each of these subjects in detail, but first we'll take a look at starting *twm*.

Starting the Window Manager

As described in Chapter 2, *Getting Started*, you start *twm* from the command line by typing:

```
% twm &
```

in an *xterm* window. If *xdm* (the display manager) is starting X on your system, the *twm* window manager is probably started automatically when you log on. It may also be started automatically from an *.xinitrc* file. (See Appendix A, *System Management*, for details.) When *twm* is started, you will see it add a titlebar to each window. Titlebars are useful; we'll say more about them in the next section.

Note also that you can run *xterm* or other X clients without running a window manager. *twm* allows you to size and place client windows on the screen, but you can also use command line options to do this. However, there is no easy way to change the size or location of windows on the screen without a window manager.

Titlebars

When *twm* starts up, it places a titlebar on every window on the screen. This titlebar contains the name of the window ("xterm," for example), two buttons, and a region that is highlighted when the input focus is in the associated window.

The titlebar provides convenient access to the most commonly used window manager functions: iconify, resize, raise, and lower. Iconify allows you to shrink an unneeded window so that it's out of your way. Resize allows you to change the size of a window. Raise and lower change the window's position with respect to other windows that may be partially or completely covering it. All this without having to bring up a menu or type modifier keys! (See Figure 3-1 for a closer look at the titlebar.)

From the titlebar, you can:

- Iconify the window, by clicking the first pointer button (usually the leftmost) in the left-hand command button in the titlebar (it's marked with an X).
- Resize the window, by pressing the first pointer button in the right-hand command button in the titlebar (which contains a group of nested squares). Then, while holding down the first pointer button, move the pointer across the border you want to move. Drag the pointer to move the border the desired amount and then release the pointer button.
- Raise the window to the top of the stack, by clicking the first pointer button on the titlebar.
- Lower the window to the bottom of the stack, by clicking the middle pointer button on the titlebar.
- Move the window, by pressing and holding down the left pointer button on the titlebar, dragging the window to a new location, and releasing the pointer button.

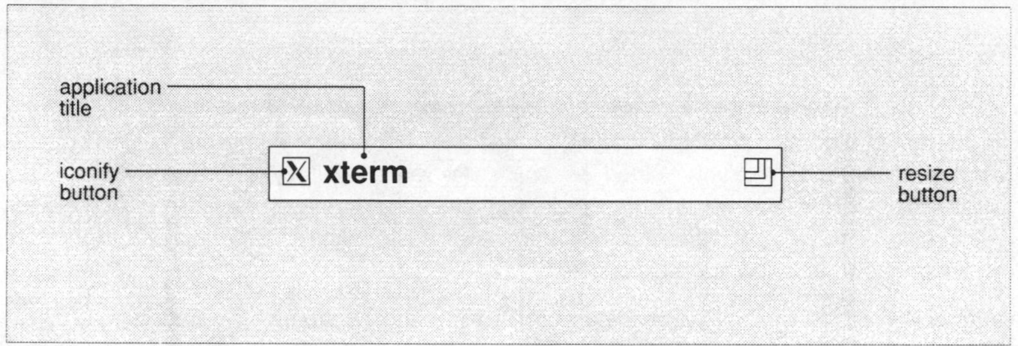

Figure 3-1. Anatomy of a twm titlebar

These functions can also be invoked from a menu and will be discussed more thoroughly in the next section.

The Twm Menu

twm's Twm menu gives you access to many of the most frequently used window manipulation functions. In the standard version of *twm* shipped by MIT, you bring up this menu by moving the pointer to the root window and holding down the left pointer button. The Twm menu and the menu pointer appear as shown in Figure 3-2.

The following pages explain the functions of the Twm menu. Remember that all of the window manager functions are customizable. Items can be added to or deleted from this menu, and new menus can be defined by modifying the *.twmrc* window manager startup file, as described in Chapter 10, *Customizing the twm Window Manager*. The current chapter describes the window manager as it is shipped with the standard release of the X Window System from the MIT X Consortium.

To bring up the Twm menu, move the pointer to the root window and hold down the left button on the pointer. To *select* a menu item, continue to hold down the left button and move the pointer to the desired menu item. A horizontal band, or *highlighting bar*, follows the pointer. When you've highlighted the desired menu item, release the button. The selected function will be executed.

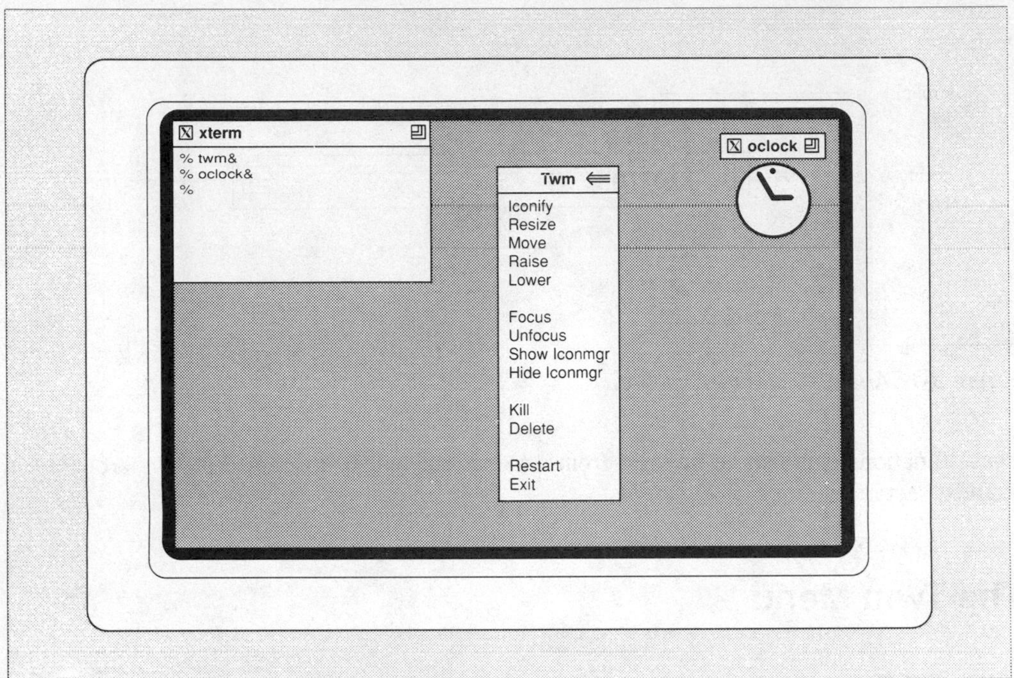

Figure 3-2. Twm menu

Some of the functions on the menus can be invoked simply by pressing a combination of pointer buttons and keyboard keys. We discuss these "keyboard shortcuts" as appropriate when discussing each menu function, and summarize them in Table 3-1 later in this Chapter. Some of these shortcuts make use of the "Meta" modifier key. See Chapter 11, *Setup Clients*, for a discussion of how to determine which key on your keyboard serves as the Meta key. (For the Sun-3 keyboard, for example, Meta is either of the keys labeled "Left" or "Right.")

Displaying Windows as Icons

If you want to make more space available on your screen, you can convert a window into an icon. An *icon* is a small symbol that represents the application window. You can also convert the icon back into a window, as shown in Figure 3-3 and Figure 3-4.

To convert a window to an icon:

1. Bring up the Twm menu.
2. Select Iconify with the menu pointer. The pointer changes to the target pointer.
3. Move the target pointer to the desired window.
4. Click the left button. The window is converted to an icon.

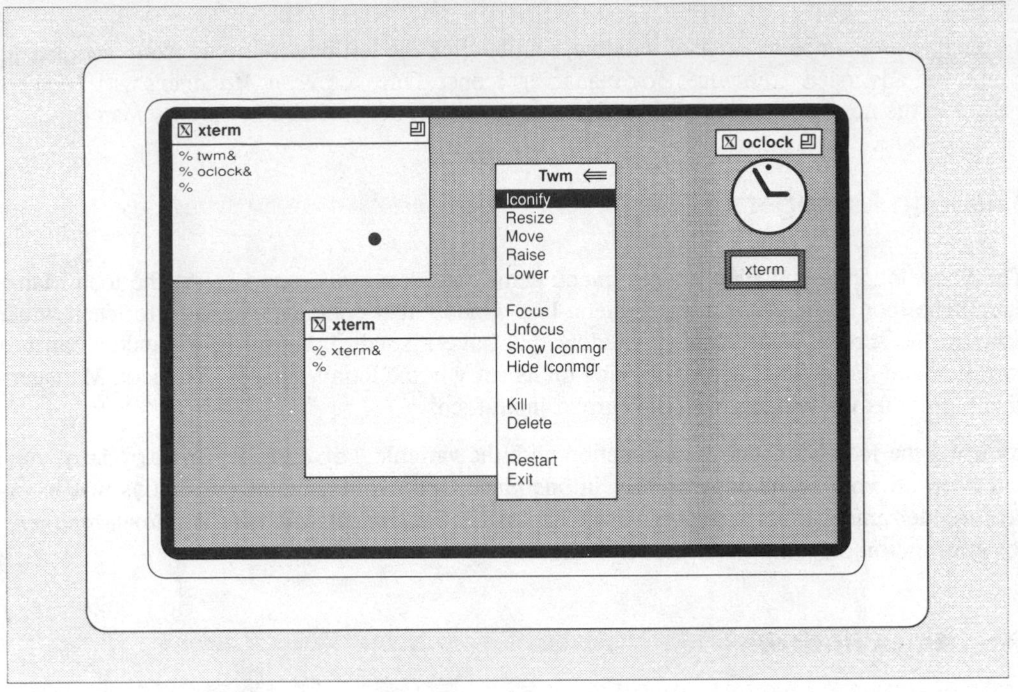

Figure 3-3. The login window is about to become an icon

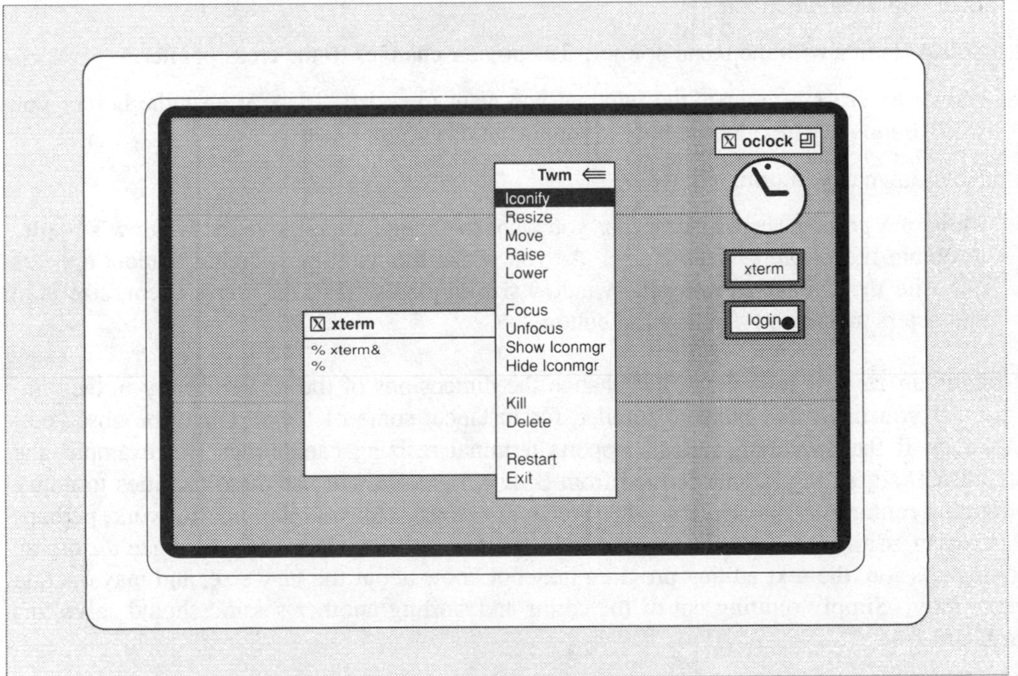

Figure 3-4. The login window is about to be deiconified

To display an icon as its original window, simply click the left button on the icon. *twm* has a couple of advanced techniques for managing icons. One, the *Icon Manager*, will be discussed in the next section. The other, the *Icon Region*, is documented in the *twm* man page.

The Icon Manager

The Show Iconmgr and Hide Iconmgr menu items control a *twm* feature called the Icon Manager. The Icon Manager is a small, menu-like window that contains one entry for each window on the screen. An iconified window will have a small X before it; a window can be iconified and deiconified just by clicking on its entry in the Icon Manager. The Icon Manager also highlights the window with the current input focus.

By using the Icon Manager in conjunction with the variable `IconifyByUnmapping`, you can keep all your icons conveniently in one place, and avoid searching for icons that have been hidden under other windows. See Chapter 10, *Customizing the twm Window Manager*, for information on setting variables in *twm*.

Resizing Windows

The Resize menu item resizes an existing window. See Figure 3-5. To resize a window:

1. Bring up the Twm menu.
2. Select Resize with the menu pointer. The pointer changes to the cross pointer.
3. Move the cross pointer to the window you want to resize. Place it near the border you want to move. The opposite border remains in its current position.
4. Hold down any button.
5. Move the pointer across the border you want to change, then move the window's border to obtain the desired window size. As you resize the window, a digital readout appears opposite the pointer showing the window size in pixels. (For the *xterm* client, size is in characters and lines.) Release the button.

Resizing an *xterm* window will not change the dimensions of the text currently in the window. (If you make the window smaller, for instance, some of the text may be obscured.) However, if the operating system supports terminal resizing capabilities (for example, the SIGWINCH signal in systems derived from BSD 4.3), *xterm* will use these facilities to notify programs running in the window whenever it is resized. As you continue to work, perhaps starting an editing session, the program will use the entire window. If you resize *during* an editing session, the text editing program may not know about the new size, and may operate incorrectly. Simply quitting out of the editor and starting another session should solve this problem.

If your resized *xterm* window does not seem to know its new size, you may be working with an operating system that does not support terminal resizing capabilities. Refer to the discussion of the *resize* client in Chapter 4, *The xterm Terminal Emulator*, (and to the *resize* reference page in Part Three of this guide) for alternative solutions.

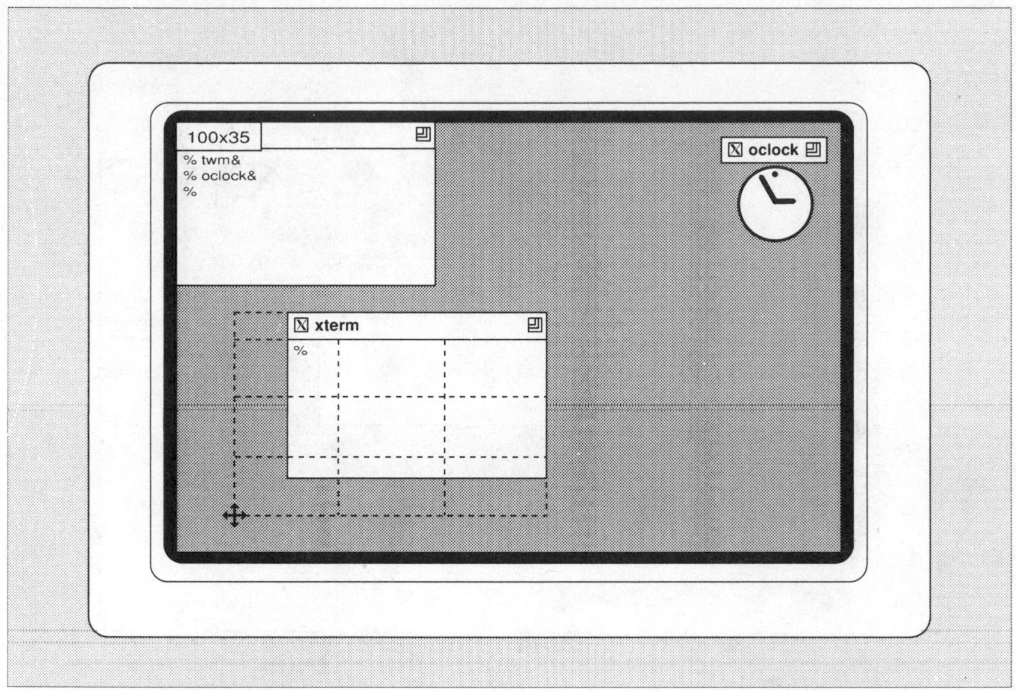

Figure 3-5. Resizing a window

Moving Windows and Icons

The Move menu item moves a window or an icon to a new location. When you use this function, an outline, not the entire window or icon, tracks the pointer movement to the new location. See Figure 3-6. To move a window:

1. Bring up the Twm menu.
2. Select Move with the menu pointer. The pointer changes to the cross pointer.
3. Move the cross pointer to the desired window or icon. Hold down any button. Move the pointer and a window outline appears. This outline tracks the pointer movement.
4. Move the cross pointer with the window outline to the desired location on your screen.
5. Release the button. The window will move to the new location.

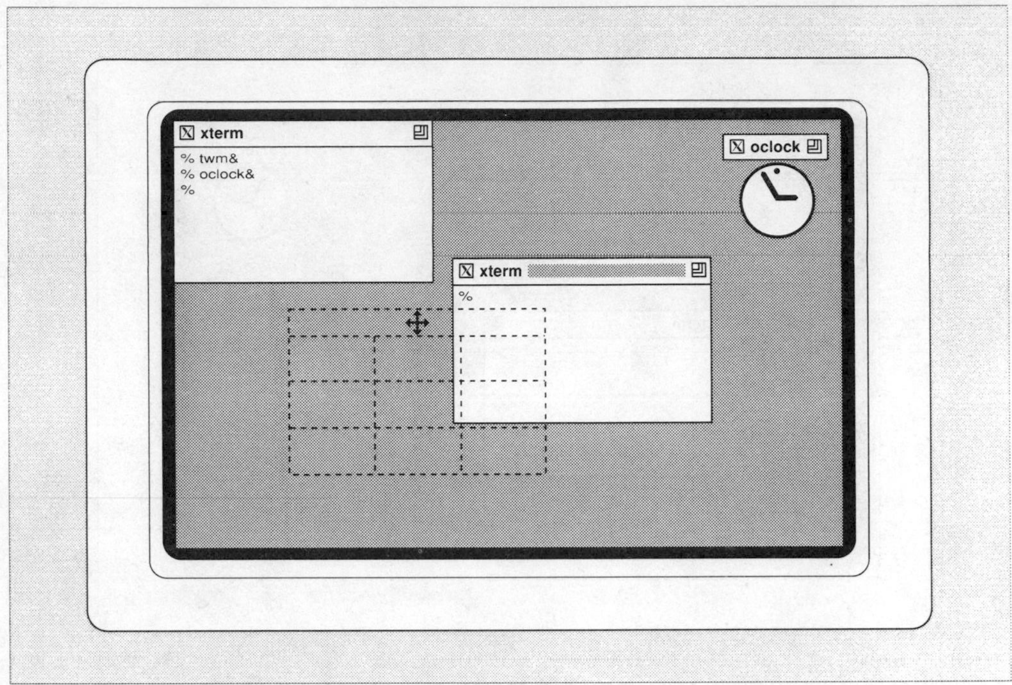

Figure 3-6. Moving windows or icons

You can also move a window or icon simply by moving the pointer to the window or icon you want to move, then pressing the right pointer button while holding down the Meta key. The pointer at first changes to a small image of an icon. You can now let go of the Meta key. Then, as you drag the pointer while holding down the button, the pointer changes to a cross, while the window or icon changes to outline form. Drag the outline to the new location, and let go of the right button. The window will be redrawn in the new location.

Shuffling the Window Stack: Raise and Lower

Under the X Window System, windows can overlap each other. When windows overlap, one or more windows may be fully or partially hidden behind other windows (see Figure 3-7). You can think of these windows as being stacked on top of each other much the way papers are stacked on a desk. *twm* can control the stacking order of the windows by lowering a particular window to the bottom of the stack or raising it to the top.

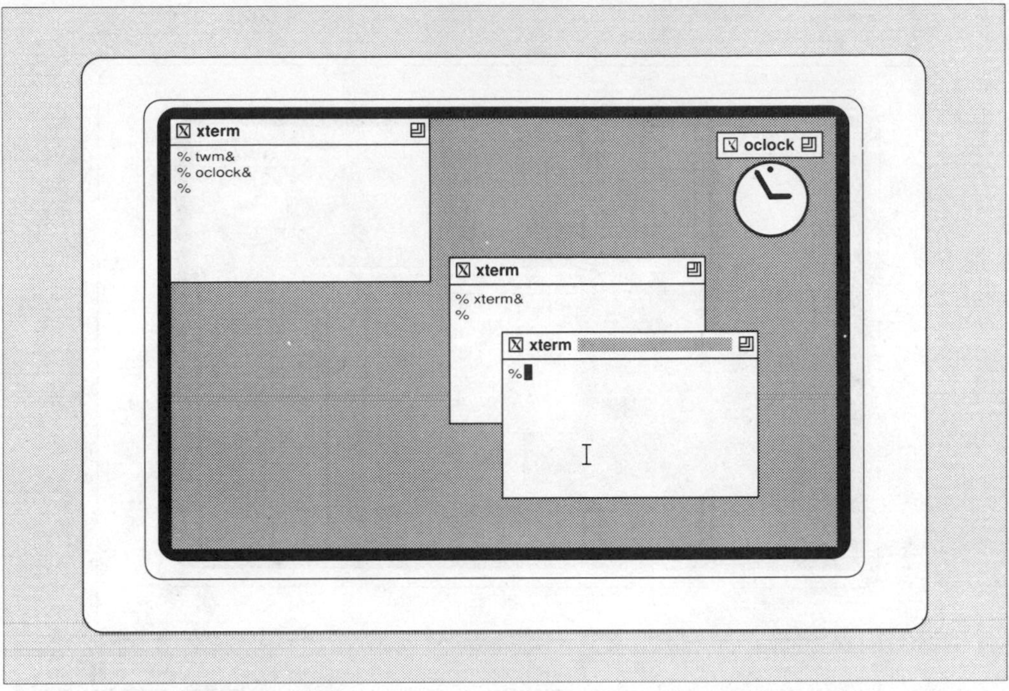

Figure 3-7. One xterm window overlapping another

Raising Windows (bringing in front of others)

The Raise menu item places a window at the top of a window stack. See Figure 3-8. To bring a window to the front:

1. Bring up the Twm menu.
2. Select Raise with the menu pointer. The pointer changes to the target pointer.
3. Move the target pointer to the desired window.
4. Click any button. The window is raised to the top of the stack.

Using the twm Window Manager

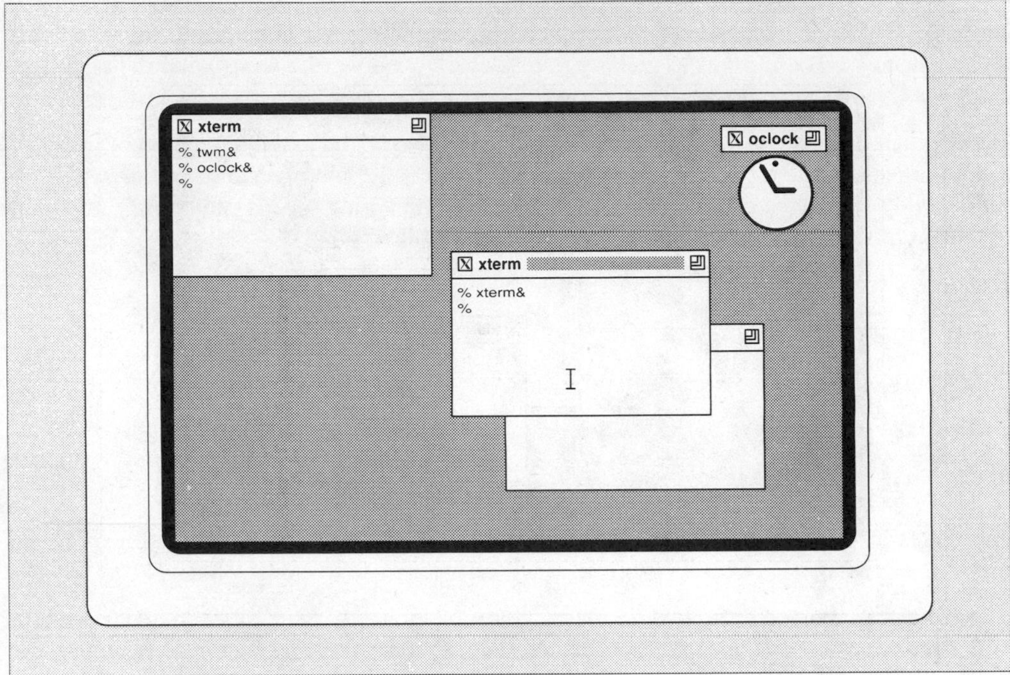

Figure 3-8. Raising a window

Lowering Windows (sending behind others)

The Lower menu item places a window at the bottom of a window stack. To place a window at the bottom:

1. Bring up the Twm menu.
2. Select Lower with the menu pointer. The pointer changes to the target pointer.
3. Move the target pointer to the appropriate window.
4. Click any button. The desired window is placed behind all windows except the root window.

To raise or lower a window without using the menu:

- To raise a window, move the pointer so that the cursor is within the titlebar of the window you want to raise, then click the left pointer button. The window is raised.
- To lower a window, move the pointer so that the cursor is within the titlebar of the window you want to lower, then click the middle pointer button. The window is lowered.

Changing Keyboard Focus

Normally, keyboard input goes to whichever window the pointer is currently in. The Focus option causes keyboard input to go only to a selected window (the *focus* window) regardless of the position of the pointer.

Focusing can be useful if you are working in one window for an extended period of time, and want to move the pointer out of the way. It also prevents the annoying situation in which you inadvertently knock the pointer out of the window while typing. (This can be very important for touch typists who look infrequently at the screen while typing!)

To choose a focus window:

1. Bring up the Twm menu.
2. Select Focus with the menu pointer. The pointer changes to the target pointer.
3. Move the target pointer to the window you want to choose as the focus window.
4. Click any button to choose the window.

The titlebar of the focus window will remain highlighted, no matter where you move the pointer.

In order to take the focus away from the selected window (and reactivate "pointer focus"), select Unfocus. The keyboard focus will once again follow the pointer into any window.

Removing a Window: Delete and Kill

The Delete and Kill menu items provide two different ways of terminating a client window. Most windows can be removed in ways that do not harm relevant processes. Delete is one of these ways. It simply requests that the client close itself down gracefully.

Like other methods of "killing" a program (such as the *xkill* client), the Kill menu item can adversely affect underlying processes. Kill is intended to be used primarily after more conventional methods of removing a window have failed.

To remove a window:

1. Bring up the Twm menu.
2. Select Delete with the menu pointer. The pointer changes to the skull and crossbones pointer.
3. Move the pointer into the window you want to terminate.
4. Click any pointer button.

The window should go away. It may, instead, beep and remain on your screen. You have a stubborn window, which can be killed in the following way:

1. Bring up the Twm menu.
2. Select Kill with the menu pointer. The pointer changes to the skull and crossbones pointer.
3. Move the pointer into the window you want to terminate.
4. Click any pointer button.

The window will go away.

Refer to the section on *xkill* in Chapter 7, *Other Clients*, for a more complete discussion of the hazards of killing a client and a summary of alternatives.

Restarting the Window Manager

The Restart menu item restarts the window manager. This may occasionally become necessary if the window manager functions improperly. To stop and restart the window manager:

1. Bring up the Twm menu.
2. Select Restart with the menu pointer.

You may also want to restart the window manager if you edit your *.twmrc* configuration file to change the functionality of *twm*. See Chapter 10, *Customizing the twm Window Manager*, for more information.

Note that when the window manager is stopped, all icons revert to windows. This happens because the window manager is what allows windows to be iconified. When the window manager is restarted, you can iconify the windows again.

Exiting the Window Manager

The Exit menu item stops the window manager. You may want to stop *twm* in order to start another window manager. To stop *twm*:

1. Bring up the Twm menu.
2. Select Exit with the menu pointer.

The window manager is stopped. All icons revert to windows.

Button Control of Window Manager Functions

Table 3-1 summarizes the keyboard and titlebar shortcuts for window management functions. The first column lists the desired function; the second, the required location for the pointer; and the third, the button-key combination. In this column, "click" means to press and immediately release the specified pointer button; "down" means to press and hold the pointer button, and "drag" means to move the pointer while holding down the pointer button. In all cases, you can let go of the keyboard key as soon as you have pressed the appropriate pointer button.

Note that these key "bindings" can be changed in your *.twmrc* file, as described in Chapter 10. The combinations described in the table work for the *system.twmrc* file.

Table 3-1. Keyboard Shortcuts for Window Manager Functions

Function	Pointer Location	Keyboard Shortcut
move	titlebar	First pointer button down and drag
move	window or icon	Meta key, right pointer button down and drag
resize	"nested squares" titlebutton	Any pointer button down, cross desired border, and drag
raise	titlebar	First pointer button click
raise	window or icon	Meta key, third pointer button click
lower	titlebar	Second (middle) pointer button click
lower	window or icon	Meta key, first pointer button click
iconify	"X" titlebutton	Any pointer button click
iconify	window	Meta key, second pointer button click
deiconify	icon	Second pointer button click
Twm menu	root	First pointer button down

Using the twm Window Manager

Customizing twm

The *twm* window manager is a powerful tool that can perform many more functions than are described in this chapter. You can customize *twm* using the *.twmrc* file in your home directory. Customizing this file, you can:

- Define your own *twm* menus.
- Bind functions to keyboard key/pointer button combinations.
- Issue command strings to the shell.

For details on customizing, and an example of a modified *.twmrc* file, see Chapter 10, *Customizing the twm Manager*.

Some of My Keystrokes are Missing

If you are running Release 4, especially if you are running on a small or slow system, you may notice that the system can't keep up with the movement of the pointer. You may move from one window to another and begin typing, only to find that your first few characters were entered into the original window, or dropped into intervening windows.

This annoying problem is caused by a subtle interaction between the operating system, the X server, and the window manager. It is unlikely to be fixed in the near future, but *twm* provides a workaround: setting the variable `NoTitleFocus` in your *.twmrc* file should keep the bug from popping up. See Chapter 10 for information on creating a *.twmrc* file and setting variables.

4

The xterm Terminal Emulator

This chapter describes how to use xterm, *the terminal emulator. You use this client to create multiple terminal windows, each of which can run any programs available on the underlying operating system.*

In This Chapter:

4
The xterm Terminal Emulator

xterm provides you with a terminal within a window. Anything you can do using a standard terminal, you can do in an *xterm* window. Once you have an *xterm* window on your screen, you can use it to run other clients.

You can bring up more than one *xterm* window at a time. For example, you might want to list the contents of a directory in one window while you edit a file in another window. Although you can display output simultaneously in several windows, you can type into only one window at a time.

Basic operation of *xterm* should be obvious to anyone familiar with a terminal. You should be able to work productively immediately.

Among the less obvious features of *xterm* is a dual functionality. By default, *xterm* emulates a DEC VT102 terminal, a common alphanumeric terminal type. However, *xterm* can also emulate a Tektronix 4014 terminal, which is used to display graphics. For each *xterm* process, you can switch between these two types of terminal windows. You can display both a VT102 and a Tektronix window at the same time, but only one of them can be the "active" window, i.e., the window receiving input and output. Hypothetically, you could be editing in the VT102 window while looking at graphics in the Tektronix window.

You switch between the VT102 window and the Tektronix window using items from certain *xterm* menus. The *xterm* client has four menus that can be used to manipulate the VT102 and Tek windows, to select many terminal settings, and to run other commands that affect the *xterm* process. We'll take a look at some of the more useful items on each menu as well as some alternatives to menu items. For more complete information about menus, see the *xterm* reference page in Part Three of this guide.

We'll also discuss two of *xterm*'s more important features: a scrollbar, which allows you to review text in the window, and a "copy and paste" facility.

Finally, we'll consider problems involved in resizing an *xterm* window and how to run a program in a temporary *xterm* window.

The Release 4 xterm Menus

The Release 4 version of *xterm* has four different menus:

- Main Options menu (formerly called xterm menu).
- VT Options menu (formerly called Modes menu).
- VT Fonts menu (available as of Release 4).
- Tek Options menu (formerly called Tektronix menu).

The VT Fonts menu, which allows you to dynamically change the *xterm* display font, was introduced in Release 4. The other three menus are updated versions of menus available in Release 3. As is indicated above, these three menus have been renamed in Release 4. Most of the *items* available on these menus have not changed in functionality since Release 3, though many have been renamed and some have been reorganized.

For instance, the R3 xterm menu offered an item called Redraw; the R4 Main Options menu offers the same item, renamed Redraw Window. The Visual Bell item available on the R3 xterm menu in R4 has been renamed Enable Visual Bell and moved to the VT Options menu, a more logical location.

A few menu items are entirely new as of Release 4. This chapter describes the R4 *xterm* menus. For those who are still running Release 3, we've tried to point out the differences: the equivalent R3 menu and item names, what items have been moved within a menu or to another menu, and what items are only available in R4.

The xterm Menus at a Glance

As shown in Figure 4-1, three of the four *xterm* menus are divided into sections, separated by horizontal lines. The top portion of each divided menu contains various modes that can be toggled. (The one exception is the Redraw Window item (formerly Redraw) on the Main Options menu, which is a command.) A check mark appears next to a mode that is currently active. Selecting one of these modes toggles its state.

The items on the VT Fonts menu change the font in which text is displayed in the *xterm* window. Only one of these fonts can be active at a time. To toggle one off, you must activate another.

Most mode entries can also be set by command line options when invoking *xterm*, or by entries in a resource startup file (such as *.Xdefaults* or *.Xresources*) as described in Chapter 9, *Setting Resources*. (See the *xterm* reference page in Part Three of this guide for a complete list of command options and resource variables.) The various modes on the menus are very helpful if you've set (or failed to set) a particular mode on the command line and then decide you want the opposite characteristic.

The sections below the modes portion of each menu contain various commands. Selecting one of these commands performs the indicated function. Many of these functions can only be

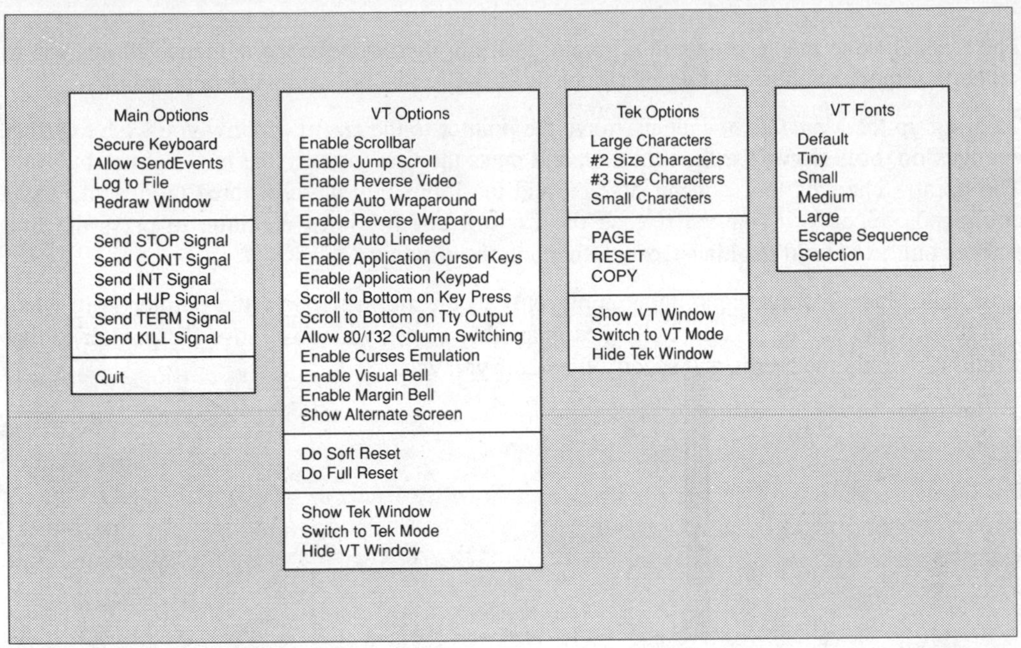

Figure 4-1. The Release 4 xterm menus

invoked from the *xterm* menus. However, some functions can be invoked in other ways: from a *twm* menu, on the command line, by a sequence of keystrokes (such as Control-C). This chapter includes alternatives to some of the menu items, alternatives which in certain cases may be more convenient. Of course, the *xterm* menus can be very helpful when other methods to invoke a function fail.

Menus are displayed by pressing a combination of keyboard keys and pointer buttons. (The exact combination of keys and buttons is described below with each menu.) When you display an *xterm* menu, the pointer becomes the arrow pointer and initially appears in the menu's title. Once the menu appears, you can release any keyboard key. The menu will remain visible so long as you continue to hold down the appropriate pointer button.

If you decide not to select a menu item after the menu has appeared, move the pointer off the menu and release the button. The menu disappears and no action is taken.

In the following discussions of the four *xterm* menus, we'll consider some of the more useful items as well as some alternatives to menu items. For more complete information about each menu, see the *xterm* reference page in Part Three of this guide.

The Main Options Menu

The Main Options menu, shown in Figure 4-2, (formerly called the xterm menu) allows you to set certain modes and to send signals (such as SIGHUP) that affect the *xterm* process.

To bring up the Main Options menu, move the pointer to the *xterm* window you wish to effect changes on, hold down the Control key, and press the first (usually the left) pointer button.* The pointer changes to the menu pointer, and the following menu of three modes and eight commands appears. (You can release the Control key but must continue to press the first pointer button to hold the Main Options menu in the window.)

Note that Main Options menu items apply only to the *xterm* window the pointer is in when you display the menu. To effect changes in another *xterm*, you must move the pointer to that window, display the menu, and specify the items you want.

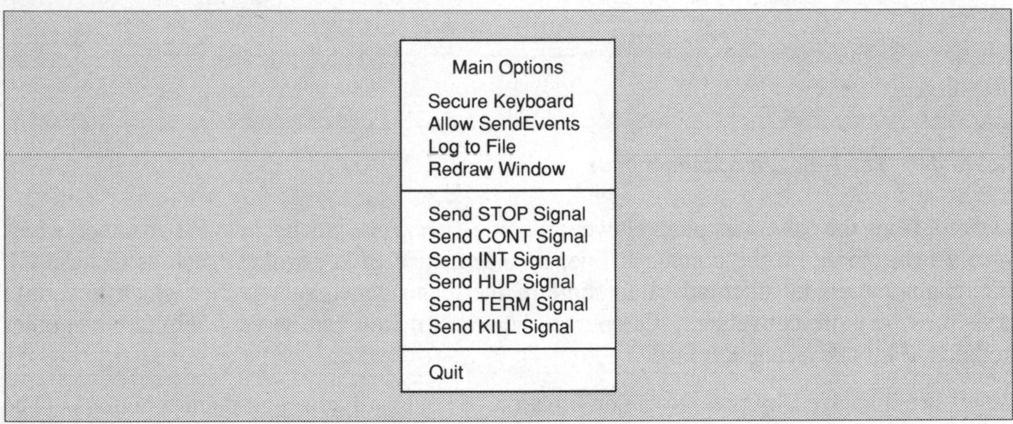

Figure 4-2. The Main Options menu

To select a menu item, move the menu pointer to that item and release the first button. After you have selected a mode (Secure Keyboard, Allow SendEvents, or Log to File), a check mark appears before the item to remind you that it is active.† The Log to File mode on the Main Options menu can also be set by a command line option when invoking *xterm*. In addition, both Log to File and Allow SendEvents can be set by entries in a resource startup file like *.Xresources* (see Chapter 9, *Setting Resources*). The menu selections enable you to change your mind once *xterm* is running. (See the *xterm* reference page in Part Three of this guide for more information on these modes.)

*The right button can be made to function as the "first" button. This is especially useful if you are left-handed. See Chapter 11, *Setup Clients*, for instructions on how to customize the pointer with *xmodmap*.

†The Allow SendEvents mode is available as of Release 4. Log to File is available in Release 3 as Logging. The equivalent Release 3 menu (called xterm) also includes a Visual Bell mode toggle. As of Release 4, this item has been renamed Enable Visual Bell and moved to the VT Options menu.

The Secure Keyboard mode toggle has been added to the menu (in a Release 3 patch) to help counteract one of the security weaknesses of X. This mode is intended to be activated when you want to type a password or other important text in an *xterm* window. Generally, when you press a keyboard key or move the pointer, the X server generates a packet of information that is available for other clients to interpret. These packets of information are known as *events*. Moving the pointer or pressing a keyboard key causes input events to occur.

There is an inherent security problem in the client-server model. Because events such as the keys you type in an *xterm* window are made available via the server to other clients, hypothetically an adept system hacker could access this information. (Naturally, this is not an issue in every environment.) A fairly serious breach of security could easily occur, for instance, if someone were able to find out a user's password or the *root* password. Enabling Secure Keyboard mode causes all user input to be directed *only* to the *xterm* window itself.

Of course, in many environments, this is probably not necessary: if the nature of the work is in no way sensitive, if the system administrator has taken pains to secure the system in other ways, etc. If your environment might be vulnerable, you can enable Secure Keyboard mode before typing passwords and other important information and then disable it again using the menu.

When you enable Secure Keyboard mode, the foreground and background colors of the *xterm* window will be exchanged (as if you had enabled the Reverse Video mode from the VT Options menu), as shown in Figure 4-3. When you disable Secure Keyboard mode, the colors will be switched back.

Be aware that only one X client at a time can secure the keyboard. Thus, if you have enabled Secure Keyboard mode in one *xterm*, you will not be allowed to enable it in another *xterm* until you disable it in the first. If Secure Keyboard mode is not available when you request it, the colors will not be switched and a bell will sound.

If you request Secure Keyboard mode and are not refused, but the colors are *not* exchanged, be careful: you are not in Secure Keyboard mode. If this happens, there's a good chance that someone has tampered with the system. If the application you're running displays a prompt before asking for a password, it's a good idea to enable Secure Keyboard mode before the prompt is displayed and then verify that the prompt is displayed in the proper colors. Before entering the password, you can also display the Main Options menu again and verify that a check mark appears next to Secure Keyboard mode.

Be aware that Secure Keyboard will be disabled automatically if you iconify the *xterm* window, or start *twm* or another window manager that provides a titlebar or other window decoration. This limitation is due to the X protocol. When the mode is disabled, the colors will be switched back and the bell will sound to warn you.

In addition to modes that can be toggled, the Main Options menu includes several commands. All of the commands (except for Redraw Window) send a signal that is intended to affect the *xterm* process: suspend it (Send STOP Signal), terminate it (Send TERM Signal), etc. Given that your operating system may recognize only certain signals, every menu item may not produce the intended function.

Note that most of these commands are equivalent to common keystroke commands, which are generally simpler to invoke. For example, in most terminal setups, Control-C can be used

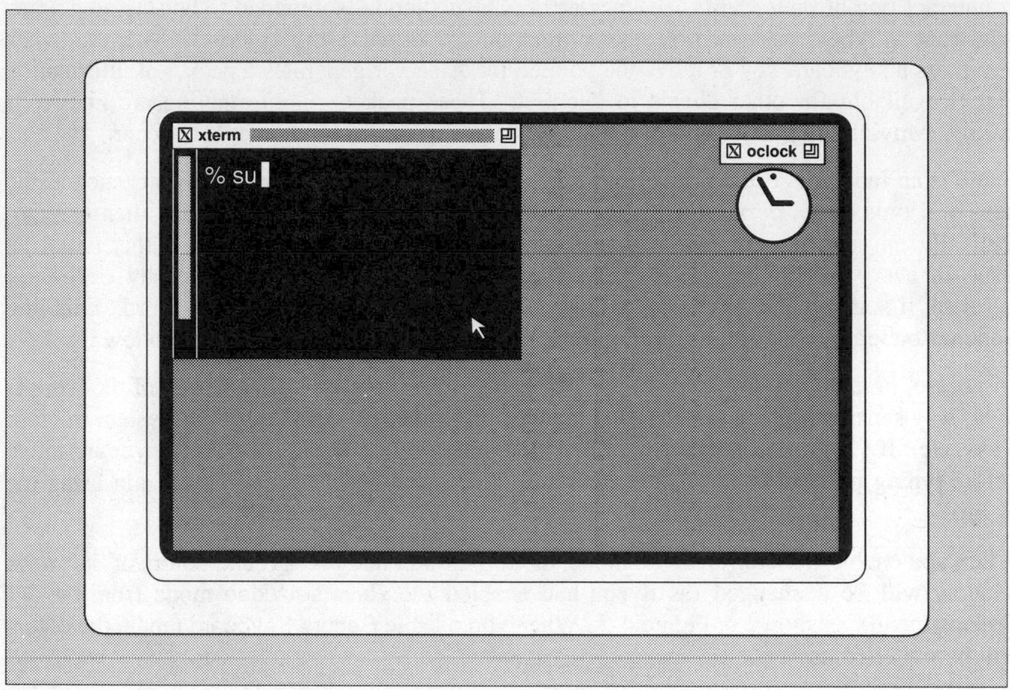

Figure 4-3. Reverse video is enabled when the keyboard is secure

to interrupt a process. This is generally simpler than using the Send INT Signal menu command (Interrupt program in prior releases), which performs the same function.

Similarly, if your system supports job control, you can probably suspend a process by typing Control-Z and start the process again by typing Control-Y, rather than using the Send STOP Signal and Send CONT Signal menu commands. (These commands were called Suspend program and Continue program in Release 3.) If your system does not support job control, neither the menu commands nor the keystrokes will work.

Four of the commands (Send HUP Signal, Send TERM Signal, Send KILL Signal, and Quit*) send signals that are intended to terminate the *xterm* window. Depending on the signals your system recognizes, these commands may or may not work as intended. Be aware that in most cases, you can probably end an *xterm* process simply by typing some sequence (such as Control-D or `exit`) in the window. Of course, the menu items may be very helpful if the more conventional ways of killing the window fail. Also be aware that, in addition to being recognized only by certain systems, some signals are more gentle to systems than others. See the *xterm* reference page in Part Three of this guide for information on the signal sent by each of the menu commands and the *signal*(3C) reference page in the *UNIX Programmer's Manual* for more information on what each signal does.

*The first three of these commands were called Hangup, Terminate, and Kill in Release 3. Quit has not been renamed.

The Quit command sends the SIGHUP signal to the process group of the process running under *xterm*, usually the shell. (The Send HUP Signal command sends the same signal.) This ends up killing the *xterm* process, and the window disappears from the screen.

Quit is separated from the earlier commands by a horizontal line, so it's easier to point at. Sending a SIGHUP signal with Quit is also slightly more gentle to the system than sending a SIGKILL signal with Send KILL Signal.

The Redraw Window command redraws the contents of the window. As an alternative, you can redraw the entire screen using the *xrefresh* client. See the *xrefresh* reference page in Part Three of this guide for more information about this client.

If you are still using the *uwm* window manager, the Redraw and Refresh Screen selections of the WindowOps menu redraw a selected window and the entire screen, respectively. See Appendix B, *The uwm Window Manager*, for more about these *uwm* menu items.

VT Options Menu

The VT Options menu (formerly the Modes menu) provides many VT102 setup functions. Some of these mode settings are analogous to those available in a real VT102's setup mode; others, such as *scrollbar*, are *xterm*-only modes.

The VT Options menu items allow you to reset several modes at once, to select the Tektronix window to accept input, and to hide the VT window.

The Release 4 version of this menu is very similar to the Release 3 version. A majority of the mode toggles have been renamed by adding the first word "Enable." For example, Jump Scroll has been renamed Enable Jump Scroll, making it more apparent when a check mark precedes it that the mode is active. The names of a few of the other items have been changed slightly: Enable Visual Bell has been added from the Main Options menu, and Show Tek Window has been moved from the mode toggles section of the menu below to the commands section.

To bring up the VT Options menu, move the pointer to the *xterm* window, hold down the Control key, and then press and hold down the middle pointer button. (You can release the Control key but must continue to press the middle button to keep the VT Options menu in the window.) The menu shown in Figure 4-4 appears.

Check marks indicate the active modes. For example, Jump Scroll, Auto Wraparound, and Scroll to Bottom on Tty Output are active in the VT Options menu displayed in Figure 4-4. (These are the only modes active by default. In Release 3, Scroll to Bottom on Tty Output was not active by default.*) To turn off one of these modes, move the menu pointer to that mode and release the middle button.

*In Release 3, if you enable the scrollbar for a particular window, the mode Scroll to Bottom on Tty Output is turned on automatically. This mode indicates that if you are using the scrollbar and the window receives output (or a key is pressed, if `stty echo` is enabled), the window scrolls forward so that the cursor is at the current line. (You can use the menu to toggle this mode off, but it is generally desirable to have.)

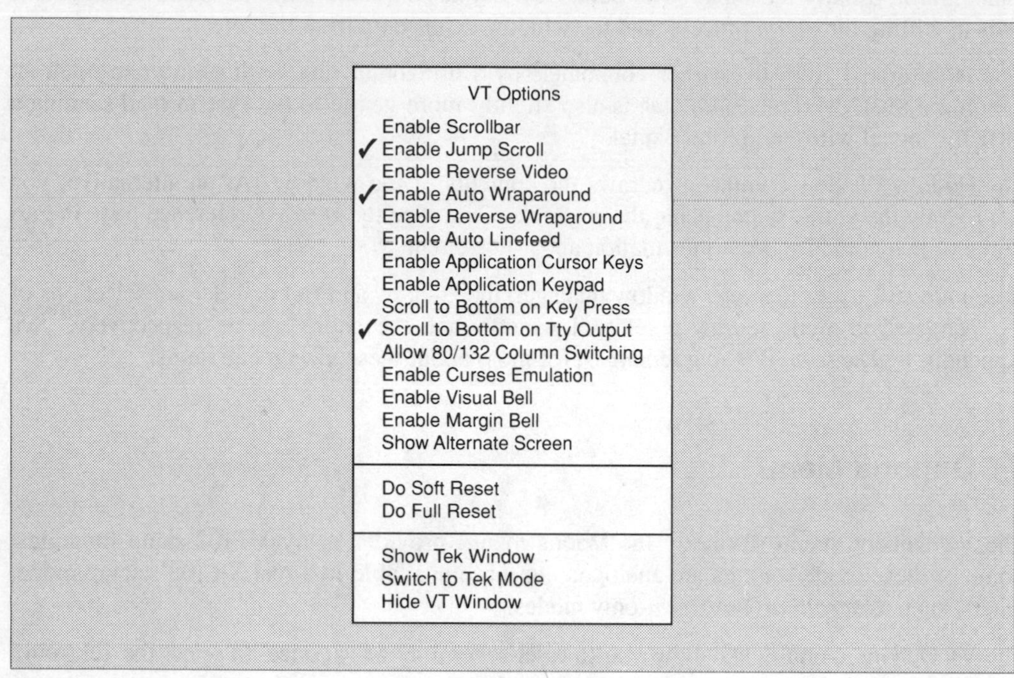

VT Options
Enable Scrollbar
✓ Enable Jump Scroll
Enable Reverse Video
✓ Enable Auto Wraparound
Enable Reverse Wraparound
Enable Auto Linefeed
Enable Application Cursor Keys
Enable Application Keypad
Scroll to Bottom on Key Press
✓ Scroll to Bottom on Tty Output
Allow 80/132 Column Switching
Enable Curses Emulation
Enable Visual Bell
Enable Margin Bell
Show Alternate Screen
Do Soft Reset
Do Full Reset
Show Tek Window
Switch to Tek Mode
Hide VT Window

Figure 4-4. The VT Options menu

Most of these modes can also be set by command line options when invoking *xterm*, or by entries in a resource startup file like *Xresources* (see Chapter 9, *Setting Resources*). The menu selections enable you to change your mind once *xterm* is running.

The toggle Allow 80/132 Column Switching warrants a little more explanation. This mode allows *xterm* to recognize the DECCOLM escape sequence, which switches the terminal between 80- and 132-column mode. The DECCOLM escape sequence can be included in a program (such as a spreadsheet) to allow the program to display in 132-column format. See Appendix F, *xterm Control Sequences*, for more information. This mode is off by default.

The VT Options menu commands (in the second and third partitions of the menu) perform two sets of functions, neither of which can be performed from the command line or a resource definition file. The commands Soft Reset and Full Reset reset some of the modes on the menu to their initial states. See the *xterm* reference page in Part Three of this guide for more information.

The Show Tek Window, Switch to Tek Mode, and Hide VT Window menu items allow you to manipulate the Tektronix and VT102 windows.

The Show Tek Window command displays the Tek window and its contents, without making it the active window (you can't input to it). Use the Switch to Tek Mode command to display a Tektronix window and make it the active window. When you select Switch to Tek Mode, the

Show Tek Window command is enabled automatically, since the Tek window is displayed. (Note that a Tektronix window is not commonly used for general purpose terminal emulation, but for displaying the output of graphics or typesetting programs.)

Both of these commands are toggles. If Show Tek Window is active and you toggle it off, the Tek window becomes hidden. (As we'll see, you can also do this with the Hide Tek Window item on the Tek Options menu.) If both Switch to Tek Mode and Show Tek Window are active (remember, enabling the former automatically enables the latter), toggling either one of them off switches the *xterm* back to VT mode. (This can also be done from the Tek Options menu with the Switch to VT Mode item.)

The Hide VT Window command hides the VT102 window, but does not destroy it or its contents. It can be restored (and made the active window) by choosing Select VT Mode from the Tek Options menu.

VT Fonts Menu

The VT Fonts menu is a welcome Release 4 innovation. It allows you to change the display font of an *xterm* window while the window is running. To bring up the VT Fonts menu, move the pointer inside the *xterm* window. Press the Control key on the keyboard; while holding down the Control key, press the third (right) pointer button. The VT Fonts menu is shown in Figure 4-5.

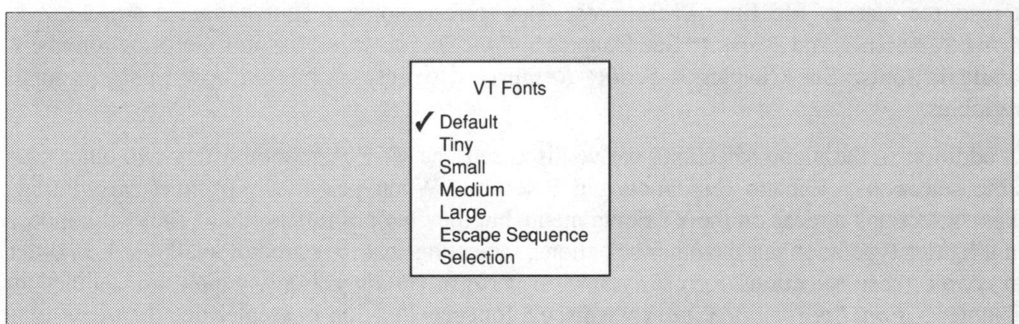

Figure 4-5. VT Fonts menu

If you have not toggled any items on this menu, a check mark will appear before the Default mode setting. The Default is the font that was specified when the *xterm* window was run. This font could have been specified on the *xterm* command line or in a resource file like *.Xresources*. Whatever the case, this font remains the Default for the duration of the current *xterm* process.

The items Default, Tiny, Small, Medium, and Large can be toggled to set the font displayed in the *xterm* window. The font can be changed any number of times, to accommodate a variety of uses. You might choose to use a large font for editing a file (chances are you've chosen a

xterm Terminal Emulator

large enough default font, though). You could then change to a smaller font while a process is running and you don't need to be reading or typing in that *xterm*. Changing the font also changes the size of the window.

There are also default settings for the Tiny, Small, Medium, and Large fonts. They are all constant width fonts from the directory */usr/lib/X11/fonts/misc* and are listed in Table 4-1.

Table 4-1. VT Fonts Menu Defaults

Menu Item	Default Font
Tiny	nil2
Small	6x10
Medium	8x13
Large	9x15

Bring up the VT Fonts menu, and toggle some of these fonts to see what they look like. The default Tiny font, *nil2*, is actually too small to be legible. It is not intended to be read. If you select this font, your *xterm* window becomes tiny, almost the size of some application icons. Though you cannot read the actual text in a window this size, the window is still active and you *can* observe if additional output, albeit minuscule, is displayed. An *xterm* window displaying text in such a small font can serve, in effect, as an *active icon*.

Be aware that you can specify your own Tiny, Small, Medium, and Large fonts using entries in a resource startup file like *.Xresources*. The corresponding resource names are `font1`, `font2`, `font3`, and `font4`. See Chapter 5, *Font Specification*, for more information about available fonts. See Chapter 9, *Setting Resources*, for instructions on how to set resource variables.

In addition to the menu selections we've discussed, the VT Fonts menu offers two other possible selections: Escape Sequence and Selection. When you first run an *xterm* window, these selections appear on the VT Fonts menu, but they are not functional. (They will appear in a lighter typeface than the other selections, indicating that they are not available.) In order to enable these selections for use, you must perform certain actions, which are outlined in Chapter 5, *Font Specification*, after we discuss font specification in greater detail.

Tek Options Menu

The Tek Options menu (formerly Tektronix) controls certain modes and functions of the Tektronix window. The menu can only be displayed from within the Tektronix window. As previously described, you can display the Tek window and make it the active window by using the Switch to Tek Mode command on the VT Options menu.

To display the Tek Options menu, move the pointer inside the Tektronix window. Press the Control key on the keyboard; while holding down the Control key, press the middle pointer button. The Tek Options menu appears. With this menu, you set the size of the text in the Tektronix window and select some commands.

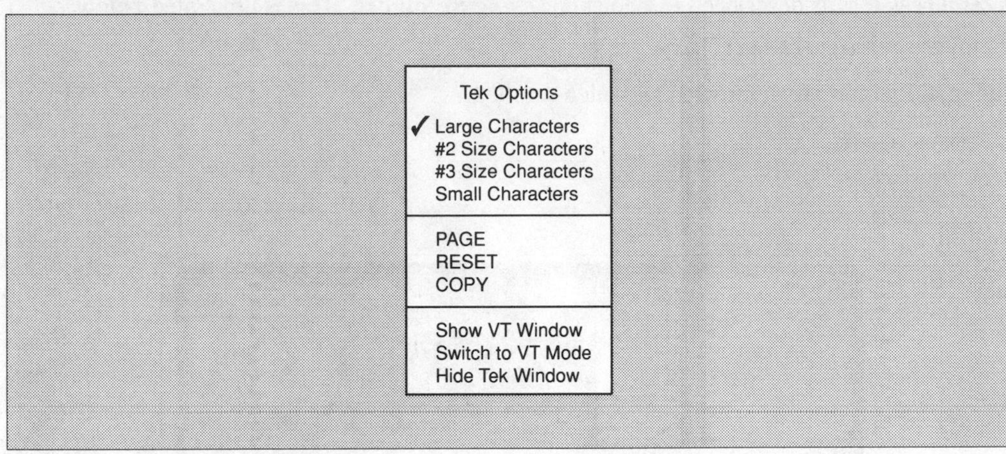

Figure 4-6. The Tek Options menu

Note that these modes (above the first line) can only be set from the Tek Options menu. All of these modes set the point size of the text displaying in the Tektronix window. (Only one of these four modes can be enabled at any time.)

The most important command on the Tek Options menu, shown in Figure 4-6, is Switch to VT Mode (formerly Select VT Mode). If the Tek window has been made the active window (using the Switch to Tek Mode command from the VT Options menu), you can choose Switch to VT Mode to make the VT window the active window again. (If both windows are showing, you can also toggle Switch to Tek Mode on the VT Options menu to *deactivate* it; that is, switch *from* Tek mode and back to VT mode.) Switch to VT Mode is also a toggle; if you deactivate it, *xterm* will switch back to Tek mode.

Selecting Show VT Window (formerly VT Window Showing), displays the VT window if it has been hidden (using the Hide VT Window command from the VT Options menu), or hides it if it is being displayed. (Again, the command is a toggle.) Remember that you cannot input to the VT window until you make it the active window, using Switch to VT Mode.

Using the Scrollbar

When using *xterm*, you are not limited to viewing the 24 lines displayed in the window. By default, *xterm* actually remembers the last 64 lines that have appeared in the window. If the window has a scrollbar, you can scroll up and down through the saved text. If the window was not created with a scrollbar, you can add one using the Enable Scrollbar item on the VT Options menu.

To create a single *xterm* window with a scrollbar, use the `-sb` command line option:

```
% xterm -sb &
```

To display all *xterm* windows with a scrollbar by default, set `scrollBar` in your *.Xresources* file, as described in Chapter 9, *Setting Resources*. This is illustrated below:

```
XTerm*scrollBar: true
```

Figure 4-7 shows an *xterm* window with a scrollbar.

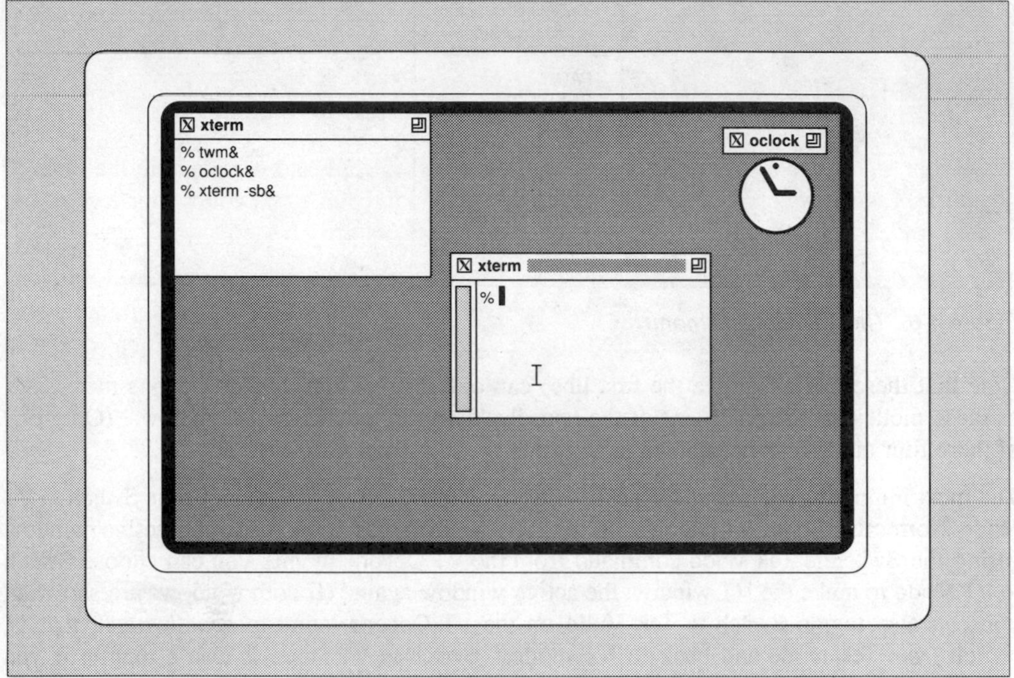

Figure 4-7. An xterm window with a scrollbar

The thumb (the highlighted area within the scrollbar) moves within the scroll region. The thumb displays the position and amount of text currently showing in the window relative to the amount saved. When an *xterm* window with a scrollbar is first created, the thumb fills the entire scrollbar. As more text is saved, the size of the thumb decreases. The number of lines saved is 64 by default, but an alternative can be specified with either the `-sl` command line option or the `saveLines` value in an *.Xresources* file.

When the pointer is positioned in the scrollbar, the cursor changes to a two-headed arrow. Clicking the first (usually the left) pointer button in the scrollbar causes the window to scroll toward the end of information in the window.

Clicking the third (usually the right) pointer button in the scrollbar causes the window to scroll toward the beginning of information in the window.

Clicking the second (usually the middle) pointer button moves the display to a position in the saved text that corresponds to the pointer's position in the scroll region. For example, if you move the pointer to the very top of the scroll region and click the second (middle) button, the display is positioned very near the beginning of the saved area.

If you hold down the second button, you can drag the thumb up and down. Text moves as you move the thumb. If you drag up, the window scrolls back, toward the beginning of information in the window. If you drag down, the window scrolls forward, toward the end of information in the window. When you release the button, the window displays the text at that location. This makes it easy to get to the top of the data by pressing the second button, dragging it off the top of the scrollbar, and releasing it.

Copying and Pasting Text Selections

Once your *xterm* window is created, you can select text to copy and paste within the same or other *xterm* windows using the pointer. You don't need to be in a text editor to use copy and paste. You can also copy or paste text to and from the command line.

Text copied into memory using the pointer is saved in a global cut buffer and also becomes what is known as the PRIMARY text "selection." Both the contents of the cut buffer and the contents of the PRIMARY text selection are globally available to all clients. When you paste text into an *xterm* window, by default the contents of the PRIMARY selection are pasted. If there is no text in the PRIMARY selection, the contents of the cut buffer (called CUT_BUFFER0), are pasted. (Thus, in most cases, these will be the same.)

Copying and pasting is one way in which clients exchange information, in this case, text. Prior to Release 3, many clients exchanged information solely by means of cut buffers. Cut buffers are only useful for transferring information between clients that interpret data in the same format. Thus, cut buffers *could* be used to transfer ASCII text between *xterm* windows. In accordance with the newer interclient communication conventions developed since Release 2, most Release 3 and 4 clients, notably *xterm*, primarily exchange information via selections. The advantage of the selection mechanism is that it allows data from one client to be converted to a different format to be used by another client. Cut buffers do not perform this type of translation.

As we've said, if you are copying text between *xterm* windows, the contents of CUT_BUFFER0 and the PRIMARY selection should be the same. However, as we'll see later, while some applications (notably the current version of *xterm*) copy to both the cut buffer and the selection, other applications (generally prior to Release 3) only copy to the cut buffer. If you are using both types of applications together and trying to transfer text between them, differences between the contents of the cut buffer and the PRIMARY selection may make copying and pasting problematic. If you are only copying text between *xterm* windows (Release 3 or later), problems of this type will never arise.

For our purposes, we are mainly concerned with ASCII text selections from *xterm* windows. First, we'll show you how to copy and paste text between *xterm* windows. Then we'll discuss some of the implications of using selections versus cut buffers, and describe two clients, *xcutsel* and *xclipboard*, which allow you to manipulate text saved in memory. The *xcutsel* client addresses problems that arise when you're copying text between an application that uses selections and one that uses cut buffers. The *xclipboard* allows you to store multiple text selections.

Selecting Text to Copy

To select text, move the pointer to the beginning of the text you want to select. Hold down the first button while moving the pointer to the end of the desired text, then release the button. The text is highlighted, copied into the global cut buffer (called CUT_BUFFER0) and also made the PRIMARY selection.

Note that with the current implementation of the copy and paste feature, tabs are saved as spaces.

You can select a single word or line simply by clicking. To select a single word, place the pointer on the word and double-click the first button.* To select a single line, place the pointer on the line and triple-click the first button.

If you hold the button down after double- or triple-clicking (rather than releasing it) and move the pointer, you will select additional text by words or lines at a time.

The following table describes the button combinations and the resulting selection. Begin by placing the pointer on your desired selection.

Table 4-2. Button Combinations to Select Text for Copying

To select	Do this
Word	Double-click the first button.
Line	Triple-click the first button.
Passage	Hold down the first button, move the pointer, release the button.

Each selection replaces the previous contents of CUT_BUFFER0 and the previous PRIMARY text selection. You can make only one selection at a time.

Once you have made a selection with the first button, you can extend that selection with the third button. The following example shows how this works:

1. Bring up *vi* (or any other text editor with which you are familiar) in an *xterm* window, and type in this sample sentence:

   ```
   The X Window System is a network-based graphics window system that
   was developed at MIT in 1984.
   ```

*To be more precise, double clicking selects all characters of the same class (e.g., alphanumeric characters). By default, punctuation characters and whitespace are in a different class from letters or digits—hence, the observed behavior. However, character classes can be changed. For example, if you wanted to double-click to select e-mail addresses, you'd want to include the punctuation characters !, %, @, and . in the same class as letters and digits. However, redefining the character classes is not something you'd do every day. See the *xterm* reference page in Part Three for details.

2. Place the pointer on the word *graphics* in the sample sentence and select it with two clicks of the first button.
3. Then press and hold the third pointer button. Move the pointer away from the word *graphics*, to the left or right. A new selection now extends from the last selection (*graphics*) to the pointer's location and looks something like the following:

```
The X Window System is a network-based graphics window system that
was developed at MIT in 1984.
```

or:

```
The X Window System is a network-based graphics window system that
was developed at MIT in 1984.
```

Remember that your extension always begins from your last selection. By moving the pointer up or down, right or left of the last selection, you can use this technique to select part of one line or add or subtract several lines of text.

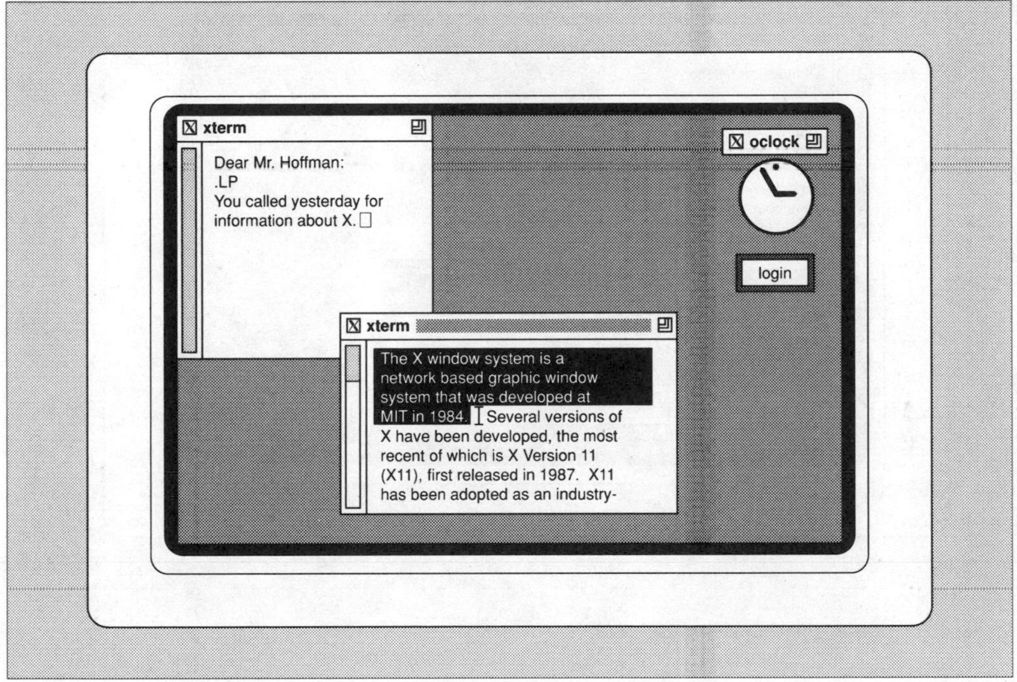

Figure 4-8. Highlighted text saved as the PRIMARY selection

To clear the highlighting, move the pointer off the selection and click anywhere else in the window with the first button. Note, however, that the text still remains in memory until you make another selection.

Pasting Text Selections

The second (middle) button inserts the text from the PRIMARY selection (or CUT_BUFFER0, if the selection is empty) as if it were keyboard input. You can move data from one *xterm* window to another by selecting the data in one window with the first button, moving the pointer to another window, and clicking the second button.

You can paste text either into an open file or at a command line prompt. To paste text into an open file, as illustrated in Figure 4-9, click the second button within the window containing the file. The text from the memory area will be inserted where the text editor cursor is. (Of course, the file must be in a mode where it is expecting text input, such as the insert mode of an editor.) You can paste the same text as often as you like. The contents of the PRIMARY selection remain until you make another selection.

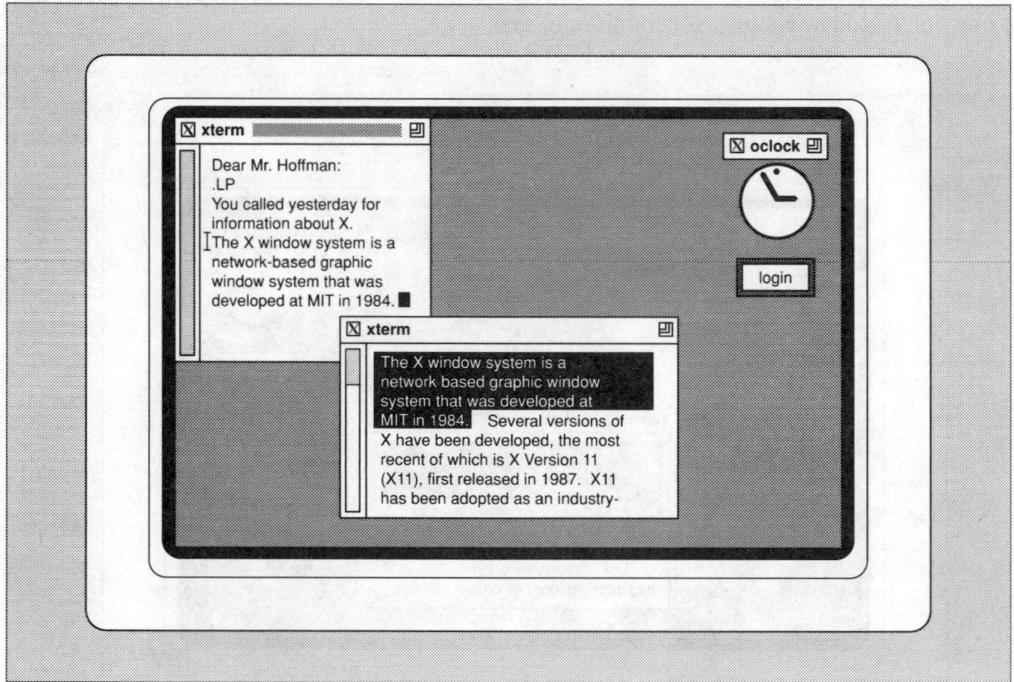

Figure 4-9. Pasting text into an open file

To paste text at a command line prompt, you must first close any open file within the window. Then click the second button anywhere within the window to place the text on the command line at the end of text in the window (note that the window will scroll to the bottom on input).

You can make multiple insertions by repeatedly clicking the second button.

The latest text selected replaces the previous text selected.

You can also paste *over* existing text with the *vi* change text commands (such as cw, for change word). For example, you can paste over five words by specifying the *vi* command 5cw, and then pasting text by clicking the second pointer button. Note that you can paste over existing text in any editor that has an overwrite mode.

Manipulating Text Selections

Prior to Release 3, text copied into memory using the pointer was saved in the global cut buffer, in effect, "owned" by the server, and available to all clients. Cut buffers are only useful for copying and pasting information that does not need to be translated to another format, such as ASCII text between two *xterm* windows.

Since Release 3, text copied into memory from an *xterm* window is saved in the cut buffer *and* as the PRIMARY selection. The PRIMARY selection takes precedence over the contents of the cut buffer. When pasting text between *xterm* windows, if the selection contains text, it is pasted. If not, the contents of the cut buffer are pasted. Selections can be used to transfer data that must be translated to a form the receiving client can interpret.

A selection is globally available, but it is not owned by the server. A selection is owned by a client—initially by the client from which you copy it. Then when the text selection is pasted to another window, that window becomes the owner of the selection.

Because of the rules of precedence governing cut buffers and selections, and the nature of selections (particularly the issue of ownership), certain problems can arise in transferring data:

1. If one client communicates with cut buffers and one with selections, copying and pasting between them is inherently problematic. By default, the selection takes precedence. How do you paste the contents of the cut buffer instead?
2. By default, you can save only one selection at a time.
3. For a selection to be transferred to a client, the selection must be owned by a client. If the client that owns the selection no longer exists, the transfer cannot be made.

The *xcutsel* and *xclipboard* clients address the first two of these problems, respectively.

Most users will probably not encounter the third problem. You are probably doing all your copying and pasting between *xterm* windows. If you've made a selection from an *xterm* window and the window is killed, the *selection* contents are lost. However, the cut buffer contents remain intact and are pasted instead. (Since all *xterm* windows interpret ASCII text, the translation capabilities of the selection mechanism are not needed.)

Problems involving the loss of selections are more likely to happen if you are transferring information between clients that require information to be in different formats. If you are having such problems, you can customize the clients involved to copy information to what is known as the CLIPBOARD selection.

The CLIPBOARD selection is intended to avert problems of selection ownership by providing centralized ownership. Once the CLIPBOARD owns a selection, the selection can be transferred (and translated), even if the client that previously owned the selection goes away.

You can customize a client to send data to the CLIPBOARD selection by using *event translations*, which are discussed in Chapter 9, *Setting Resources*. See the client reference pages for information on the appropriate translations. For more information on selections and translations, see Volume One, *Xlib Programming Manual*.

Copying and Pasting between Release 2 and 3 Clients: xcutsel

The *xcutsel* client is intended to bridge a gap that exists between the ways older and newer clients allow you to copy text. If all the clients you are using are from Release 3 or later, you will probably have no use for *xcutsel* and should skip ahead to the next section.*

Since Release 3, when you select text from an *xterm* window with the pointer, the text is copied into the global cut buffer and made the PRIMARY selection. (Thus, generally, the contents of the cut buffer and the PRIMARY selection are the same.) By default, the PRIMARY selection is what gets pasted into a window. If there is no PRIMARY selection, the contents of the cut buffer are pasted.

Prior to Release 3, clients did not use selections. Text was copied into the cut buffer only (and was not equated with a PRIMARY selection). Problems can arise if you are running clients that use cut buffers only (many Release 2 clients and *uwm*, any release) with clients that primarily use selections (Release 3 and later) and are trying to paste text between them.

For instance, say you copy text in a Release 3 *xterm* window using the pointer. The text is copied into the cut buffer and also becomes the PRIMARY selection. If you paste in any window, the PRIMARY selection is what you get. Then, say you copy text in a R2 *xterm* window. The text is stored in the cut buffer, replacing the text in the cut buffer from the R3 window, but it does *not* replace the PRIMARY selection. You can paste the text from the R2 window in another R2 window because the window only understands cut buffers, but you can't paste it in an R3 window. If you try to, by default you get the PRIMARY selection (from the other R3 window).

xcutsel enables you to switch the text in the cut buffer and the PRIMARY selection so that you can cut and paste between clients that use cut buffers and clients that use selections.

To open an *xcutsel* window, type:

```
% xcutsel &
```

and then place the window on your screen. Figure 4-10 shows an *xcutsel* window.

The window contains three command buttons whose functions are described below:

quit	Exits the *xcutsel* program.
copy PRIMARY to 0	Copies the contents of the PRIMARY selection to CUT_BUFFER0.
copy 0 to PRIMARY	Copies the contents of CUT_BUFFER0 to the PRIMARY selection.

*If you are using *uwm*, you may have use for *xcutsel*. Regardless of the release, *uwm* uses only cut buffers. See Appendix B, *The uwm Window Manager*, of this guide for details.

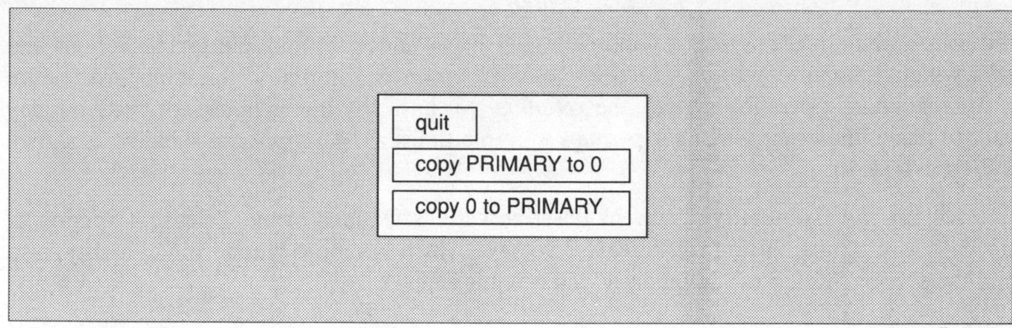

Figure 4-10. An xcutsel window

Now let's go back to the problem we set up earlier in this section. If you copy text from an R2 window and want to paste in an R3 window, you merely click on the copy 0 to PRIMARY button. The contents of the cut buffer (from the R2 client) replace the previous PRIMARY selection (from the R3 client). When you paste, you get the text you want (from the R2 window).

Now say you have the same situation, but the opposite problem. You made a selection from an R3 window, which filled the cut buffer and the PRIMARY selection. Then you copied text from an R2 window, which merely filled the buffer. (The contents of the buffer and the PRIMARY selection are different.) But now say you want to paste the text from the PRIMARY selection (from the R3 window) in an R2 window. If you paste text in an R2 window, you get the contents of the cut buffer (the text from the other R2 window).

To solve this problem, just click on the copy PRIMARY to 0 button in the *xcutsel* window. The contents of the PRIMARY selection (from the R3 window) replace the contents of the cut buffer (from the R2 window). When you paste in an R2 window, you get still get the contents of the cut buffer, but it is now the text you want.

This business of selections versus cut buffers can be pretty confusing. If you have problems pasting the text you want, experiment a little with *xcutsel*.

Saving Multiple Selections: xclipboard (Release 4 Version)

The *xclipboard* client provides a window in which you can paste multiple text selections and from which you can copy text selections to other windows. Similar to the clipboard feature of the Macintosh operating system, the *xclipboard* is basically a storehouse for text you may want to paste into other windows, perhaps multiple times. The *xclipboard* window is shown in Figure 4-11.

This section and the next two sections describe various features of the Release 4 version of *xclipboard*. If you are using the Release 3 version, which has more limited functionality, also read the section "Release 3 xclipboard" later in this chapter.

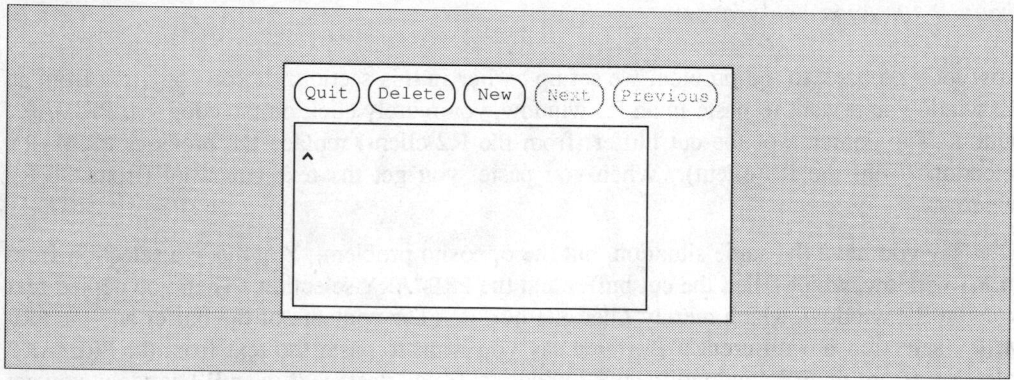

Figure 4-11. The xclipboard window

To open an *xclipboard*, type:

```
% xclipboard &
```

and then place the window interactively with the pointer.

You can paste text into the *xclipboard* window using the pointer in the manner described above and then copy and paste it elsewhere, but this is not its intended usage. To use the *xclipboard* most effectively, you must do some customization involving a resource file, such as *.Xresources*. The necessary steps are described in detail in Chapter 9, *Setting Resources*. For now, suffice it to say that you want to set up the *xclipboard* so that you can select text to be made the CLIPBOARD selection and have that text *automatically pasted* in the *xclipboard* window. This is illustrated in Figure 4-12.

Since the *xclipboard* client is intended to be coordinated with the CLIPBOARD selection, the X server allows you to run only one *xclipboard* at a time.

In order to illustrate how the clipboard works, let's presume it has been set up according to the guidelines in Chapter 9. According to those guidelines, you make text the CLIPBOARD selection by selecting it with the first pointer button (as usual) and then, while continuing to hold the first button, clicking the third button. (You could specify another button combination or a button and key combination, but we've found this one works pretty well. For more information about these specifications, see Chapter 9, *Setting Resources*.) The first pointer action makes the text the PRIMARY selection (and it is available to be pasted in another window using the pointer); the second pointer action additionally makes the text the CLIPBOARD selection (and it is automatically sent to the *xclipboard* window).

These guidelines still allow you to select text with the first pointer button alone, and that text will be made the PRIMARY selection; however, the text will not automatically be sent to the *xclipboard*. This enables you to make many selections, but to direct to the *xclipboard* only those you consider important (perhaps those you might want to paste several times).

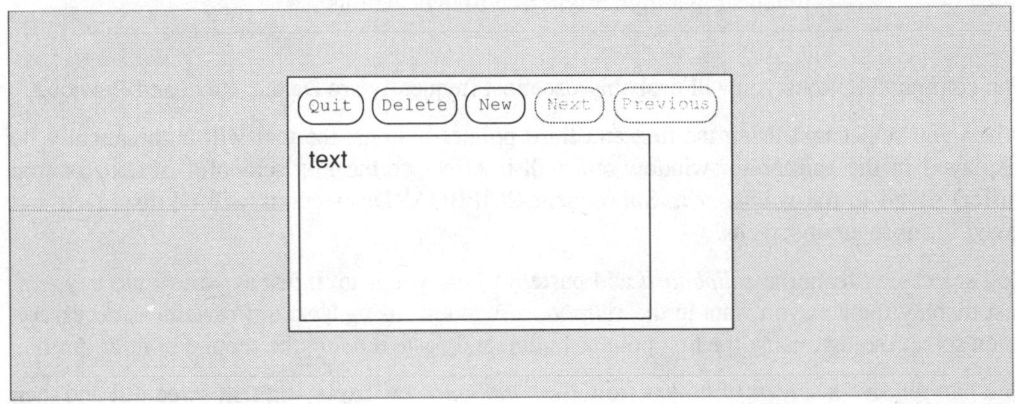

Figure 4-12. Selected text appears automatically in the xclipboard window

In order to allow you to store multiple text selections, the seemingly tiny *xclipboard* actually provides multiple screens, each of which can be thought of as a separate buffer. (However, as we'll see, a single text selection can span more than one screen.) Each time you use the pointer to make text the CLIPBOARD selection, the *xclipboard* advances to a new screen in which it displays and stores the text.

Once you have saved multiple selections, the client's Next and Previous command buttons allow you to move forward and backward among these screens of text. The functionality of the client's command buttons is summarized in Table 4-3. They are all selected by clicking with the first pointer button.

Table 4-3. Command Buttons and Functions

Button	Function
Quit	Causes the application to exit.
Delete	Deletes the current *xclipboard* buffer; the current screenful of text is cleared from the window, and the next screenful (or previous, if there is no next) is displayed.
New	Opens a new buffer into which you can insert text; the window is cleared.

xterm Terminal Emulator

Table 4-3. Command Buttons and Functions (continued)

Button	Function
Next and Previous	Once you have sent multiple selections to the *xclipboard*, Next and Previous allow you to move from one to another (display them sequentially). Before two or more CLIPBOARD selections are made, these buttons are not available for use (their labels will appear in a lighter typeface to indicate this).

The command buttons you will probably use most frequently are Delete, Next, and Previous.

When you select text using the first and third pointer buttons, the text will automatically be displayed in the *xclipboard* window and will in effect be the first screenful of text (or first buffer) saved in the *xclipboard*. Subsequent CLIPBOARD selections will be displayed and saved in subsequent screens.

You select text from the *xclipboard* and paste it where you want it just as you would any text. Just display the text you want in the *xclipboard* window, using Next or Previous as necessary. Then select the text using the first pointer button and paste it using the second pointer button.

You can remove a screenful of text from the *xclipboard* by displaying that screenful and then clicking on the Delete command button. When you delete a screenful of text using this command button, the next screenful (if any) will be displayed in the window. If there is no next screenful, the previous screenful will be displayed.

Certain features (and limitations) of the *xclipboard* become apparent only when you make a very large CLIPBOARD selection. Say you select a full *xterm* window of text with the first and third pointer buttons, as described above. The text extends both horizontally and vertically beyond the bounds of a single *xclipboard* screen. (As we suggested earlier, a CLIPBOARD selection can actually span more than one *xclipboard* screen. Pressing Delete will remove all screenfuls comprising the selection.) When you make a selection that extends beyond the bounds of the *xclipboard* screen (either horizontally, vertically, or both), scrollbars will be activated in the window to allow you to view the entire selection.

If the text extends both horizontally and vertically beyond the bounds of the *xclipboard* screen, as it does in Figure 4-13, the window will display both horizontal and vertical scrollbars. If the text extends beyond the screen in only one of these two ways, the window will display either a horizontal or vertical scrollbar, as needed.* These scrollbars are selection-specific: they are only displayed so long as the current selection cannot be viewed in its entirety without them. If you move to a previous or subsequent selection that *can* be viewed without scrollbars, the scrollbars will be deactivated.

*An application created using the X Toolkit, which provides horizontal and vertical scrollbars, is described as a *viewport*. See Chapter 7, *Other Clients*, for more information about viewports and other X Toolkit features.

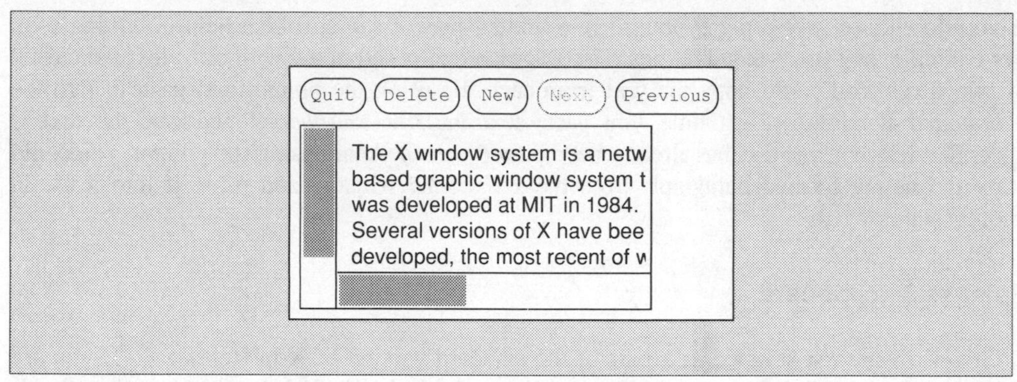

Figure 4-13. xclipboard with scrollbars to view large text selection

Problems with Large Selections

If you experiment making large selections with *xclipboard*, you may discover what seems to be a bug in the program. Though in most circumstances, making a new selection causes the screen to advance and display the new text, this does not happen reliably after a selection vertically spanning more than one screenful. In these cases, the new selection *is* saved in the *xclipboard*; however, the *xclipboard* window does not automatically advance to show you the new current selection. Instead, the previous long selection is still displayed. This is a bit of *xclipboard* sleight-of-hand. The new selection has been successfully made, but the appearance of the window belies this fact. (The Next button will probably add to your confusion; it will not be available for selection, suggesting that the text in the window is the last selection saved. This is not the case.)

In order to get around this and display the actual current selection, press the Previous button. The same long selection (which is, in actuality, the Previous selection) will again be displayed. Then the Next button will be enabled, and you can click on it to display the actual current selection.

Editing Text Saved in the xclipboard

You can edit text you send to the *xclipboard* using the same commands recognized by *xedit*. These commands are described in the section "Text Editing Widget" of Chapter 7, *Other Clients*. A small caret cursor will be visible in each screenful of text. You can move this cursor by clicking the pointer where you'd like it to appear. Then you can backspace to delete letters or type to insert them, or use any of the text editing commands described in Chapter 7. When you edit a screenful of text, the *xclipboard* continues to store the edited version, until you delete it or exit the program.

Be aware that, without performing customization, you can still use *xclipboard* on a very simple level. You can paste text into and copy text from the *xclipboard* window just as you would any other, using the pointer movements described earlier in this chapter. You can also type in the *xclipboard* window, and then copy and paste what you've typed. Just move the pointer into the window and try typing. However, keep in mind that this is not the intended use of the *xclipboard*.

If you do choose to use the clipboard in a limited way, it can still be a helpful editing tool. For example, say you wanted to create a paragraph composed of a few lines of text from each of two files. You could copy the text from each file using the pointer and paste it into the *xclipboard* window. (Each time you paste text into the *xclipboard* window, the text is appended to whatever text has already been pasted there.) Again using the pointer, you could copy the newly formed paragraph from the *xclipboard* window and paste it into a file in another window.

Release 3 xclipboard

xclipboard was first shipped as a part of the standard version of X in Release 3. If you are using the Release 3 *xclipboard*, shown in Figure 4-14, you'll find that it's functionality is considerably more limited than the Release 4 version.

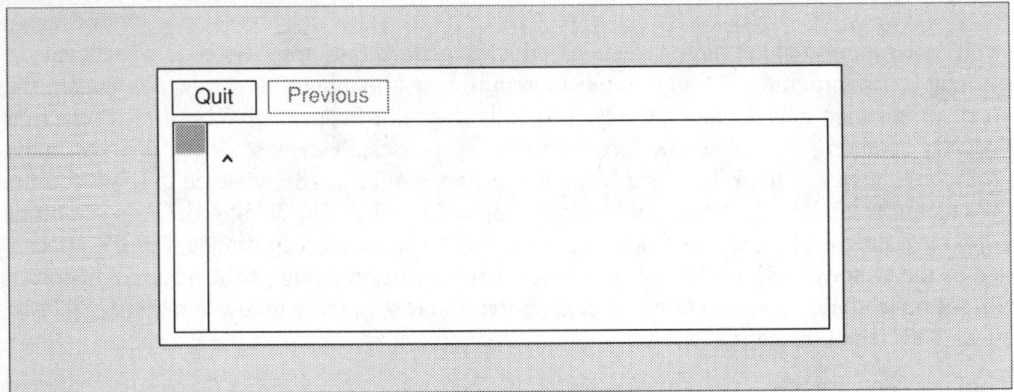

Figure 4-14. The Release 3 xclipboard window

The Release 3 *xclipboard* can also be customized to receive the CLIPBOARD selection automatically. However, this version of the *xclipboard* merely inserts each selection on the line(s) following the previous one. The screen of the *xclipboard* will scroll forward as you add more text, but at line intervals, not at full screen intervals as the Release 4 client does. Thus, while the Release 4 *xclipboard* allows you to save multiple selections that are recognized as such by commands like Delete, the Release 3 *xclipboard* only allows you to save what is, in effect, a single, running selection. This limitation alone makes the Release 3 *xclipboard* far less useful than the Release 4 *xclipboard*.

But the Release 3 *xclipboard* has other serious limitations. It features only one functioning command button, quit. The erase button in the window is not functional, and unfortunately, no other key or combination of keys seems to clear the text from the *xclipboard*.

Unlike the Release 4 version, the Release 3 *xclipboard* does not recognize all of the text editing commands recognized by *xedit*. You can use all of the commands that move the cursor, but none of the commands that delete text. Your only option to remove text is to select the quit button, which closes the window without saving its contents, and open a new *xclipboard* window.

You also cannot change or add to any text once it is placed in the window. You *can* type text in the window, but not within any pre-existing selection. If you type text, the cursor will automatically advance to the line below the last selection, and the new text will be displayed there. If the last text in the window is text you typed in, the cursor will advance to the end of that line and append the new typed text. (Note that since the cursor advances automatically and you cannot edit any text, the *xedit* commands to move the cursor are virtually useless.)

Once you type text in, it is treated just like any other selection—it cannot be deleted or edited in any way. Likewise, if you physically paste text in the window using the pointer (rather than sending it automatically as the CLIPBOARD selection), it will appear after existing text and cannot be edited or deleted.

Despite these limitations, you can still use the Release 3 *xclipboard* on a very simple level as a text editing tool. Whether you customize it to receive CLIPBOARD selections automatically or not, the *xclipboard* can still be used as a storehouse for text. You can paste text into and copy text from the *xclipboard*. You could use it to gather text from several areas, perhaps forming a new paragraph to be pasted into one or more files. If you're a good typist (since you cannot correct your errors), you could also enter text in the window and then copy and paste what you've typed.

Terminal Emulation and the xterm Terminal Type

Anyone who has used a variety of terminals knows that they don't all work the same way. As a terminal emulator, an *xterm* window must be assigned a terminal type, which tells the system how the window should operate, that is, what type of terminal it should emulate. When *xterm* is assigned an invalid terminal type, the window does not display properly at all times, particularly when using a text editor, such as *vi*. If one of your login files (*.login*, *.profile*, *.cshrc*, etc.) currently specifies a default terminal type, you will need to replace this with a type valid for *xterm*. (If none of your login files specifies a terminal type, *xterm* automatically searches the file of TERMCAP entries for the first valid entry.)

xterm can emulate a variety of terminal types, which are listed on the client reference page in Part Three of this guide. An *xterm* window emulates a terminal most successfully when it has been assigned the terminal type xterm. For the xterm terminal type to be recognized on your system, the system administrator will have had to add it to the file containing valid TERMCAP entries. (The xterm TERMCAP entry is supplied with the standard release of X.) If this has not been done, the system will not recognize the xterm terminal type. In these cases, try the vt100 terminal type, which also generally works well, or use one of the other types listed on the client reference page.

See Appendix A, *System Management*, and the *xterm* reference page in Part Three of this guide for information about customizing the *termcap* file.

Resizing an xterm Window

xterm sets the TERMCAP environment variable for the dimensions of the window you create. Clients (including *xterm*) use this TERMCAP information to determine the physical dimensions of input and output to the window.

If you resize an *xterm* window, programs running within the window must be notified so they can adjust the dimensions of input and output to the window. If the underlying operating system supports terminal resizing capabilities (for example, the SIGWINCH signal in systems derived from BSD 4.3), *xterm* will use these facilities to notify programs running in the window whenever it is resized. However, if your operating system does not support terminal resizing capabilities, you may need to request explicitly that TERMCAP be updated to reflect the resized window.

The *resize* client sends a special escape sequence to the *xterm* window and *xterm* sends back the current size of the window. The results of *resize* can be redirected to a file that can then be sourced to update TERMCAP. To update TERMCAP to match a window's changed dimensions, enter:

```
% resize > filename
```

and then execute the resulting shell command file:

```
% source filename                C shell syntax
```

or:

```
$ . filename                     Bourne shell syntax
```

TERMCAP will be updated and the dimensions of the text within the window will be adjusted accordingly.

If your version of UNIX includes the C shell, you can also define the following alias for *resize*:

```
alias rs 'set noglob; eval `resize`; unset noglob'
```

Then use `rs` to update the TERMCAP entry to reflect a window's new dimensions.

Note that even if your operating system supports terminal resizing capabilities, *xterm* may have trouble notifying programs running in the window that the window has been resized. On some older systems (based on BSD 4.2 or earlier), certain programs, notably the *vi* editor, cannot interpret this information. If you resize a window during a *vi* editing session, *vi* will not know the new size of the window. If you quit out of the editing session and start another one, the editor should know the new window size and operate properly. On newer systems (e.g., BSD 4.3 and later), these problems should not occur.

Running a Program in a Temporary xterm Window

Normally, when you start up an *xterm* window, it automatically runs another instance of the UNIX Bourne or C shell (depending on which is set in your *Xresources* file or the SHELL environment variable). If you want to create an *xterm* window that runs some other program, and goes away when that program terminates, you can do so with the *xterm* -e option:

```
% xterm -e command [arguments]
```

For example, if you wanted to look at the file *temp* in a window that would disappear when you quit out of the file, you could use the UNIX *more* program as follows:

```
% xterm -e more temp
```

If you are using other options to *xterm* on the command line, the -e option must appear last. This is because everything after the -e option is read as a command.

Running a Program in a Temporary Xterm Window

Normally, when you start up an xterm window, a command shell runs in it (the UNIX Bourne or C shell (depending on which is set in your [illegible] parameter in the SHELL environment variable). If you want to create an xterm window that runs some other program and goes away when that program terminates, you can do so with the xterm -e option:

```
% xterm -e program [arguments ...] &
```

For example, if you wanted to look at the file temp in a window that would disappear when you quit out of the file, you could use the UNIX more program as follows:

```
% xterm -e more temp &
```

If you are using other options to xterm on the command line, the -e option must appear last, because everything after the -e option is read as a command.

5

Font Specification

This chapter describes what you need to know in order to select display fonts for the various client applications. After acquainting you with some of the basic characteristics of a font, this chapter describes the rather complex font naming conventions and how to simplify font specification. This chapter also describes how to use the xlsfonts, xfd, *and* xfontsel *clients to list, display, and select available screen fonts.*

In This Chapter:

5
Font Specification

Many clients allow you to specify the font used to display text in the window, in menus and labels, or in any other text fields. For example, you can choose the font used for the text in [illegible] menus or in [illegible] windows.

Unfortunately, for the most part, there's no simple "font menu" like there are on systems such as [illegible] has a fairly complex font naming system, which [illegible] [illegible] many applications such as word processors and publishing packages that provide a simple method for selecting fonts. However, for the clients in the X distribution, you are generally limited to selecting fonts via command line [illegible]

This wouldn't be so bad if a typical font name wasn't mind-bending at first glance. The [illegible] command line to create an xterm window with text to be displayed in 14-point [illegible]

[illegible]

[illegible] use the font naming conventions [illegible]

and [illegible] so that you could get by without knowing the [illegible]

In this chapter, we're going to try to take some of the mystery out of font names [illegible] [illegible] the font naming conventions in detail, [illegible] the appearance of some of the [illegible] fonts, [illegible] the variety of utilities, such as [illegible], to help you choose fonts in Windows.

5
Font Specification

Many clients allow you to specify the font used to display text in the window, in menus and labels, or in any other text fields. For example, you can choose the font used for the text in *twm* menus or in *xterm* windows.

Unfortunately, for the most part, there are no simple "font menus" like there are on systems such as the Macintosh.* Instead, X has a fairly complex font naming system (which, like most things about X, is designed for maximum flexibility rather than for simplicity or ease of use). Of course, there will no doubt soon be many applications such as word processors and publishing packages that provide a simple interface for selecting fonts. However, for the clients in the X distribution, you are generally limited to selecting fonts via command line options or resource specifications.

This wouldn't be so bad if a typical font name wasn't mind-bending at first glance. Imagine typing this command line to create an *xterm* window whose text is to be displayed in 14-point Courier bold:

```
% xterm -fn -adobe-courier-bold-r-normal--14-140-75-75-m-90-iso8859-1
```

Fortunately, you can use asterisks as wildcards to simplify this name to a somewhat more reasonable one:

```
% xterm -fn '*courier-bold-r*140*'
```

and you can define even simpler aliases, so that you could end up typing a command line like this:

```
% xterm -fn courierB14
```

In this chapter, we're going to try to make sense out of the sometimes bewildering jungle of information about fonts under X. First, we'll explain the font naming convention in detail. Along the way, we'll acquaint you with the appearance of some of the basic font families (groups of related fonts), and the various permutations (such as weight, slant, and point size) within each family.

*An exception is the VT fonts menu in the R4 *xterm*. But even then, you need to know a lot about font naming to change the fonts on the menu.

Then, we'll talk about how to use font name wildcards to simplify font specification. We'll also talk about the font search path (the directories where the font files are stored), and how to define aliases for font names.

Finally, we'll talk about some of the utilities X provides for dealing with fonts:

- *xlsfonts*, which lists the names of the fonts available on your server, as well as any aliases.
- *xfd* (font displayer), which allows you to display the character set for any individual font you specify on the command line.
- *xfontsel* (font selector), which allows you to preview fonts and select the name of the one you want. (This name can then be pasted onto a command line, into a resource file, etc.)

Font Naming Conventions

In Release 2 and earlier, fonts were simply identified by the name of the file in which they were stored, minus the *.snf* ("server natural format") extension. For example, the file *8x13.snf* contained a font named *8x13*.

However, starting with Release 3, a new logical font naming convention was adopted. As we'll see in a moment, these logical font names allow for complete specification of all of the characteristics of each font. Unfortunately, this completeness makes them somewhat difficult to work with, at least until you learn what all the parts of the names mean, and get a handle on which parts you need to remember, and which you can safely ignore. (By the end of this chapter, you should have that knowledge.)

The *xlsfonts* client can be used to display the names of all the fonts available on your server. When you run *xlsfonts*, you'll get an intimidating list of names similar to the name in Figure 5-1.

Upon close examination, this rather verbose name contains a great deal of useful information: the font's developer, or foundry (Adobe), the font family (Courier), weight (bold), slant (oblique), set width (normal), size of the font in pixels (10), size of the font in tenths of a point (100 tenths of a point, thus 10 points), horizontal resolution (75-dpi), vertical resolution (75-dpi), spacing (m, for monospace), average width (60—measured in tenths of a pixel, thus 6 pixels), and character set (iso8859-1).

As mentioned earlier, font name wildcarding can eliminate a lot of the unnecessary detail. If you are already familiar with font characteristics, skip ahead to the section "Font Name Wildcarding" later in this Chapter for some tips and tricks. If you need a refresher on fonts, read on, as we illustrate and explain each of the elements that make up the font name.

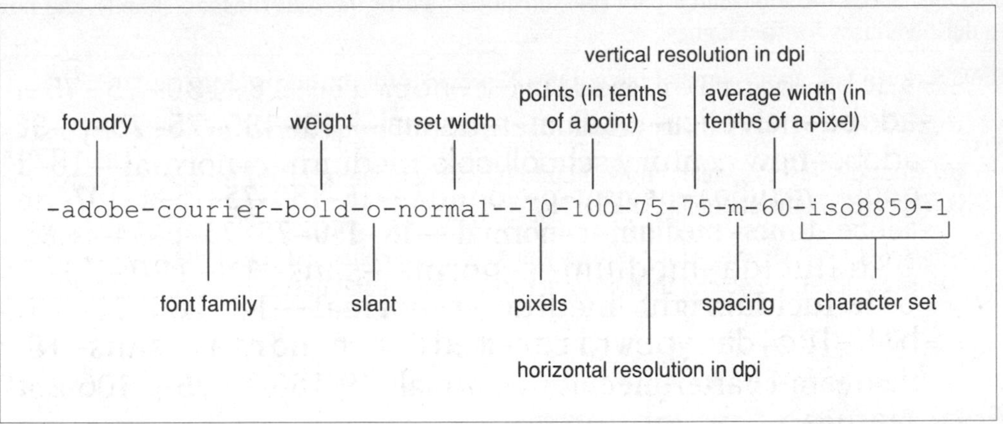

Figure 5-1. Font name, Releases 3 and 4

Font Families

It has been several years since the advent of desktop publishing, and by now, it is unlikely that anyone in the computer industry is unaware that text can be displayed on the screen and printed on the page using different fonts.

However, the term *font* is used somewhat ambiguously. Does it refer to a family of typefaces (such as Times® Roman or Helvetica®), which comes in different sizes, weights, and orientations? Or should each distinct set of character glyphs be considered a separate font?

X takes the latter approach. When the documentation says that Release 3 includes 157 fonts, and Release 4 more than 400, this sounds either intimidating or impressive, depending on your mood. But, in fact, the R3 X distribution includes only six font families (Courier, Helvetica, New Century Schoolbook®, Symbol, and Times), plus several miscellaneous fonts that are found only in individual sizes and orientations.* R4 includes two more font families, Lucida® and the Clean family of fixed width fonts, plus many more special purpose fonts.

When you think about it this way, you can quickly reduce the clutter. Figure 5-2 shows the major families of commercial fonts that are available under X. To illustrate the fonts, we've used the simple expedient of printing each font name in the font itself. Font names are truncated to fit on the page.† (For those of you who don't read the Greek alphabet, the fourth line down reads "-adobe-symbol-medium-r-normal--18 ..." This font is used for mathematical equations and so forth, rather than for normal display purposes.)

*By contrast, the Macintosh supports dozens of font families, and commercial typesetters support hundreds, and in some cases, even thousands of families. Many of these fonts will doubtless be made commercially available for X.

†To generate the figures in this section and in Appendix E, *Release 3 and 4 Standard Fonts*, we wrote a short program called *xshowfonts*, which displays a series of fonts in a scrollable window. In each case, we used wildcards (discussed later in this chapter) to select the fonts we wanted, and then did screendumps of the resulting images. Note that the fonts look better on the screen than they do in the illustration, since the scaling factor used to make the screen dumps exacerbates the "jaggies" endemic to bitmap fonts.

Source code for *xshowfonts* is listed in Appendix E, along with the name of every font, printed in the font itself. Appendix E also includes complete character-set dumps of some of the more unusual fonts.

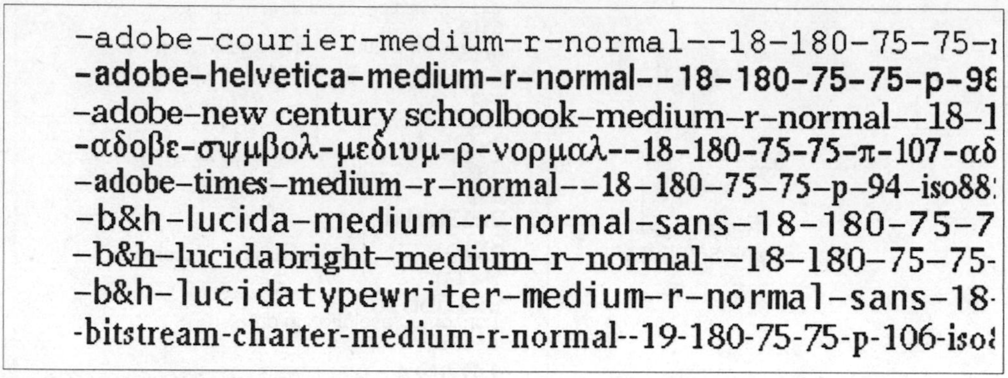

-adobe-courier-medium-r-normal--18-180-75-75-ı
-adobe-helvetica-medium-r-normal--18-180-75-75-p-98
-adobe-new century schoolbook-medium-r-normal--18-1
-αδοβε-σψμβολ-μεδιυμ-ρ-νορμαλ--18-180-75-75-π-107-αδ
-adobe-times-medium-r-normal--18-180-75-75-p-94-iso88:
-b&h-lucida-medium-r-normal-sans-18-180-75-7
-b&h-lucidabright-medium-r-normal--18-180-75-75-
-b&h-lucidatypewriter-medium-r-normal-sans-18-
-bitstream-charter-medium-r-normal--19-180-75-75-p-106-iso8

Figure 5-2. The major commercial font families available in the standard X distribution

You'll notice that with the exception of Courier and Lucidatypewriter, all of the fonts in the figure are *proportionally-spaced*. That is, each character has a separate width. This makes them look good on a printed page, but makes them less appropriate for screen display in terminal windows (especially for program editing), since text will not line up properly unless all characters are the same width.

You will most likely use these proportional fonts for labels or menu items, rather than for running text. (Word processing or publishing programs will, of course, use them to represent proportional type destined for the printed page.)

Courier and Lucidatyperwriter are *monospaced* fonts. Every character has the same width. Monospaced fonts can be used effectively for the text font in *xterm* windows. There are also some special monospaced fonts originally designed for computer displays. You can think of these as *character cell fonts*. They too are monospaced, but the spacing relates to the size of a cell that contains each character, rather than (necessarily) to the character itself. Some of these fonts were originally available in Release 2, and even in R3 they don't have the same complex names as the proportional fonts. Instead, they have simple names expressing their size in pixels. For example, in the font named 8x13, each character occupies a box 8 pixels wide by 13 pixels high.

In R4, they were renamed to use the logical font naming conventions, with a foundry name of "misc", and a font-family of "fixed." There are also one or two larger fixed fonts donated by Sony for use with their extra-high resolution monitor, with a foundry name of "sony." Figure 5-3 shows the character cell fonts, using their R3 names, which still exist as aliases in R4. (Not all of these fonts were available in R3.)

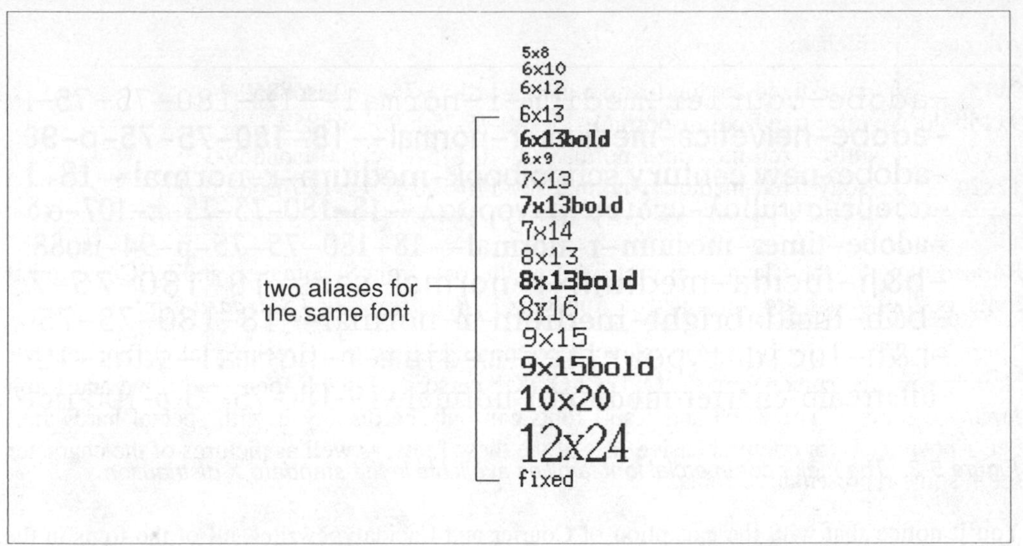

Figure 5-3. Miscellaneous fonts for xterm text

Table 5-1 shows the correspondence between these aliases and full font names. Note that the 6x13 font also has an alias called "fixed" defined for it. The "fixed" alias is used as the default font for *xterm* windows. (Twelve-point Helvetica bold roman has the alias "variable" and is used by default for labels such as those in the titlebar *twm* puts on windows.)

Table 5-1. Fixed Font Aliases and Font Names

Alias	Filename
fixed	-misc-fixed-medium-r-semicondensed--13-120-75-75-c-60-iso8859-1
5x8	-misc-fixed-medium-r-normal--8-80-75-75-c-50-iso8859-1
6x9	-misc-fixed-medium-r-normal--9-90-75-75-c-60-iso8859-1
6x10	-misc-fixed-medium-r-normal--10-100-75-75-c-60-iso8859-1
6x12	-misc-fixed-medium-r-semicondensed--12-110-75-75-c-60-iso8859-1
6x13	-misc-fixed-medium-r-semicondensed--13-120-75-75-c-60-iso8859-1
6x13bold	-misc-fixed-bold-r-semicondensed--13-120-75-75-c-60-iso8859-1
7x13	-misc-fixed-medium-r-normal--13-120-75-75-c-70-iso8859-1
7x13bold	-misc-fixed-bold-r-normal--13-120-75-75-c-70-iso8859-1
7x14	-misc-fixed-medium-r-normal--14-130-75-75-c-70-iso8859-1
8x13	-misc-fixed-medium-r-normal--13-120-75-75-c-80-iso8859-1
8x13bold	-misc-fixed-bold-r-normal--13-120-75-75-c-80-iso8859-1
8x16	-sony-fixed-medium-r-normal--16-120-100-100-c-80-iso8859-1

Table 5-1. Fixed Font Aliases and Font Names (continued)

Alias	Filename
9x15	-misc-fixed-medium-r-normal--15-140-75-75-c-90-iso8859-1
9x15bold	-misc-fixed-bold-r-normal--15-140-75-75-c-90-iso8859-1
10x20	-misc-fixed-medium-r-normal--20-200-75-75-c-100-iso8859-1
12x24	-sony-fixed-medium-r-normal--24-170-100-100-c-120-iso8859-1

R4 also includes the Clean family of fixed-width fonts from Schumaker, and DEC's terminal fonts, both of which are illustrated in Appendix E, *Release 3 and 4 Standard Fonts*.

There are also many other special purpose fonts, such as the Greek Symbol font that we already saw, the cursor font, the OPEN LOOK™ cursor and glyph fonts, and Kana and Kanji Japanese fonts. (The Kana and Kanji fonts can only be displayed with special hardware.) See Appendix E for comprehensive lists of the these fonts, as well as pictures of the character set in some representative fonts.

Stroke Weight and Slant

The characters in a given font family can be given a radically different appearance by changing the *stroke weight* or the *slant*, or both.

The most common weights are medium and bold. The most common slants are roman (upright), italic, or oblique. (Both italic and oblique are slanted; however, italic versions of a font generally have had the character shape changed to make a more pleasing effect when slanted, while oblique fonts are simply a slanted version of the upright font. In general, *serif* fonts (those with little decorations on the ends and corners of the characters) are slanted via italics, while *sans-serif* fonts are made oblique.)

Figure 5-4 compares the medium and bold weights, and the roman and italic or oblique slants in the Charter® and Helvetica font families.

Release 4 also includes one font that has an in-between weight called *demibold*. Weight names are somewhat arbitrary, since a demibold weight in one family may be almost as dark as a bold weight in another.

The font naming convention also defines two counter-clockwise slants, called *reverse italic* (ri) and *reverse oblique* (ro), as well as a catch-all called *other* (ot).

Font Sizes

Font sizes are often given in a traditional printer's measure known as a *point*. A point is approximately one seventy-second of an inch.

Most of the font families are provided in the six point sizes shown in Figure 5-5.

-adobe-helvetica-medium-o-normal--18-180-75-75-p-98-
-adobe-helvetica-medium-r-normal--18-180-75-75-p-98-
-adobe-helvetica-bold-o-normal--18-180-75-75-p-104-
-adobe-helvetica-bold-r-normal--18-180-75-75-p-103
-bitstream-charter-medium-i-normal--19-180-75-75-p-103-iso885
-bitstream-charter-medium-r-normal--19-180-75-75-p-106-iso8
-bitstream-charter-bold-i-normal--19-180-75-75-p-11
-bitstream-charter-bold-r-normal--19-180-75-75-p-11

Figure 5-4. The same fonts in different weights and slants

8 point	-bitstream-charter-medium-r-normal--8-80-75-75-p-45-iso8859-1
10 point	-bitstream-charter-medium-r-normal--10-100-75-75-p-56-iso8859-1
12 point	-bitstream-charter-medium-r-normal--12-120-75-75-p-67-iso8859-1
14 point	-bitstream-charter-medium-r-normal--15-140-75-75-p-84-iso8859-1
18 point	-bitstream-charter-medium-r-normal--19-180-75-75-p-106
24 point	-bitstream-charter-medium-r-normal--25-2

Figure 5-5. The same font in six different point sizes

However, the size story doesn't end there. Note that some servers (such as Sun's combined X11/NeWS™ server) support scalable outline fonts, which are device-independent, and thus true to size regardless of the output device. But the standard X fonts are simply bitmaps. Because of the different resolution of computer monitors, a font with a given nominal point size might actually appear larger or smaller on the screen.

Most monitors on the market today have a resolution between 75 dots per inch and 100 dots per inch (dpi). Accordingly, there are both 75-dpi and 100-dpi versions of a few of the fonts in R3, and of most of them in R4. These separate versions of each font are stored in different directories. By setting the font search path so that the appropriate directory comes first, you can arrange to get the correct versions without having to specify them in the font name.* But how do you tell which kind of monitor you have?

If you have the manufacturer's specs on your monitor, they might give you this figure. But more likely, they'll give you the overall resolution in rows and columns. After measuring the physical screen, you can do some rough calculations to arrive at the equivalent in dots per

*We'll talk about how to set the font search path later in this chapter.

inch. For example, the 16-inch monitor on the Sony NEWS workstation has an advertised resolution of 1280 x 1024 pixels. The actual viewing area is approximately 13 inches wide by 10 inches high. Dividing the resolution by the size, you come up with a vertical resolution of 102.4 dpi and a horizontal resolution of 98.5 dpi.

The Sun 19-inch monitor, by contrast, has an advertised resolution of 1152 x 900. The horizontal and vertical dimensions of the viewing area are approximately 13.75 x 10.75 inches. This yields a resolution of about 84 dpi.

What happens if you select the wrong resolution for your monitor? Given the difference in the pixel size, the same size font will appear larger or smaller than the nominal point size.

For example, consider the 75- and 100-dpi versions of the 24-point charter medium italic font:

```
-bitstream-charter-medium-i-normal--25-240-75-75-p-136-iso8859-1
-bitstream-charter-medium-i-normal--33-240-100-100-p-179-iso8859-1
```

If you look at the pixel size field, you will notice that the height of the 75-dpi version is 25 pixels, while the height of the 100-dpi version is 33 pixels. If you use the 75-dpi version on the Sun, you actually get something closer to 21.5 points (75/84*24); on a 100-dpi monitor, you will actually get something closer to 18 points (75/100*24). We noticed this right away when we first began using the Sony workstation. Because of its higher resolution, the font size we had been using on the Sun appeared much smaller.

If you are working on a lower-resolution monitor, you can take advantage of this artifact to display type as large as 32 points (the size that a 24-point 100-dpi font will appear on a 75-dpi monitor.) Figure 5-6 shows the 75- and 100-dpi versions of the same 24-point font, as displayed on a Sun workstation with a 19-inch monochrome monitor. As shown, neither is actually 24 points. The 75-dpi version is actually 21.5 points, as discussed above; the 100-dpi version is about 28.5 points.*

```
-adobe-new century schoolbook-medium-r-n
-adobe-new century schoolbook-m
```

Figure 5-6. The 100-dpi version of a 24-point font appears larger on a 75-dpi monitor

Note that the logical font naming convention allows for different horizontal and vertical resolution values. This would allow server manufacturers to support fonts that were "tuned" for their precise screen resolution. However, the fonts that are shipped with the generic X11 distribution all use the same horizontal and vertical resolution.

*Note that the differences are exaggerated further in printing the screen dump of this display. *xpr* lets you select a scale factor, such that each pixel on the screen appears as *scale* pixels in the printout. Since the laser printer has a 300-dpi resolution, a scale factor of 4 would produce a true scale screen dump if the resolution on the Sun monitor were truly 75 dpi by 75 dpi. Since it is actually 84 by 84, the printed image is enlarged by about 10%.

As suggested above, this resolution may not exactly match the actual resolution of any particular screen, resulting in characters that are not true to their nominal point size. In the case of the Sony monitors, the actual resolution is quite close to the design of the 100-dpi fonts. However, on the Sun monitor, neither the 75- nor 100-dpi fonts will be right. (Of course, if you are using the X11/NeWS server rather than the MIT sample server, you won't be using bitmapped fonts at all, but scalable outline fonts, so this isn't a problem.)

Other Information in the Font Name

What we've already shown summarizes the most important information in the font name. The remaining fields are explained below:

Foundry — Font manufacturers are still referred to as foundries, from the days when type was cast from lead. The X font naming convention specifies that the foundry is the company that digitized or last modified the font, rather than its original creator.

For the fonts contained in the standard X distribution, the foundry is not terribly significant, since there are no cases where the same font family is available from different foundries. However, there are numerous commercial font families available from more than one foundry. In general, the appearance of the fonts should be quite similar, since the font family defines the design of the typeface. However, there may be some small differences in the quality of some of the characters, and there may be more significant differences in the font metrics (the vertical or horizontal measurements of the characters). This might be significant for a publishing application that was using the bitmapped font for a *wysiwyg* screen display that needed to match the fonts in a particular laser printer or typesetter.

Set width — A value describing a font's proportionate width, according to the foundry. Typical set widths include: normal, condensed, semicondensed, narrow, double width. All of the Release 3 fonts and most of the Release 4 fonts have the set width *normal*. A few of the Release 4 fonts have the set width *semicondensed*.

Spacing — All standard Release 3 fonts are either m (monospace, i.e., fixed-width) or *p* (proportional, i.e., variable-width). In Release 4, fonts may also have the spacing characteristic c (character cell, a fixed-width font based on the traditional typewriter model, in which each character can be thought to take up the space of a "box" of the same height and width). As mentioned earlier, the original R2 fonts were of this type.

Average width — Mean width of all characters in the font, measured in tenths of a pixel. You'll notice, if you look back at Figure 5-2, that two fonts with the same point size (such as New Century Schoolbook and Times) can have a very different average character width. This field can sometimes be useful if you are looking for a font that is especially wide or especially narrow.

The Clean family of fonts from Schumacher offers several fonts in the same point size, but with different average widths.*

Character set — In the initial illustration of the font naming convention (Figure 5-1), we identified the character set as a single field. If you look more closely, you'll realize it is actually two fields, the first of which identifies the organization or standard registering the character set, the second of which identifies the actual character set.

Most fonts in the standard X distribution contain the string "iso8859-1" in their names, which represents the ISO Latin-1 character set. The ISO Latin-1 character set is a superset of the standard ASCII character set, which includes various special characters used in European languages other than English. See Appendix H of Volume Two, *Xlib Reference Manual*, for a complete listing of the characters in the ISO Latin-1 character set.

Note, however, that the symbol font contains the strings "adobe-fontspecific" in this position. This means that Adobe Systems defined the character set in this font, and that it is font-specific. You can see from this example that the usage of these fields is somewhat arbitrary.

Style — Not represented in the example or in most R3 or R4 font names. However, according to the logical font convention, the style of a font may be specified in the field between set width and pixels. Some of the possible styles are *i* (informal), *r* (roman), *serif* and *sans* (serif). Note that the *r* for roman may also be used in the slant field.

For a complete technical description of the font naming conventions, see the X Consortium Standard, *X Logical Font Description Conventions*. This document is available as part of the standard MIT X distribution, and is reprinted as Appendix M in the second edition of Volume 0, *X Protocol Reference Manual*.

Font Name Wildcarding

Prior to Release 3, the use of wildcards within font names was restricted to specifying fonts to list with *xlsfonts*. If you are running Release 3 or Release 4, wildcarded font names can also be used to specify the display font for a client, either on the command line or in a resource specification.

An asterisk (*) can be used to represent any part of the font name string; a question mark (?) can be used to represent any single character. You can usually get the font you want by specifying only the font family, the weight, the slant, and the point size, and wildcarding the rest. For example, to get Courier bold at 14 points, you could use the command line option:

```
-fn '*courier-bold-r*140*'
```

*These fonts all (incorrectly to our minds) have a set width of "normal." They should be distinguished by set widths such as condensed, semi-condensed, etc. Since they do not, they can be distinguished by the difference in their average width.

That's starting to seem a little more intuitive!

However, there are a number of "gotchas."

- First, since the UNIX shell also has a special meaning for the * and ? wildcard characters, wildcarded font names must be quoted. This can be done by enclosing the entire font name in quotes (as in the previous example), or by "quoting" each wildcard character by typing a backslash before it. (If you don't do this, the shell will try to expand the * to match any filenames in the current directory, and will give the message "No match.") Wildcards need not be quoted in resource files.

- Second, if the wildcarded font name matches more than one font, the server will use the first one that matches. And unfortunately, because the names are sorted in simple alphabetical order, the bold weight comes before medium, and italic and oblique slants before roman. As a result, a specification like:

  ```
  -fn '*courier*'
  ```

  will give you Courier bold oblique, rather than the Courier medium roman you might intuitively expect.

  If you aren't sure whether your wildcarded name is specific enough, try using it as an argument to *xlsfonts*. If you get more than one font name as output, you may not get what you want. Try again with a more specific name string.

  The exception to this rule has to do with the *75dpi* and *100dpi* directories. If a wildcard matches otherwise identical fonts in these two directories, the server will actually use the one in the directory that comes first in the font path. This means that you should put the appropriate directory first in the font path. (We'll tell you how to do this in the next section.) Thereafter, you can generally wildcard the resolution fields (unless you specifically want a font from the directory later in the path).*

- Third, the * wildcard expansion is resolved by a simple string comparison. So, for example, if you were to type:

  ```
  -fn '*courier-bold*r*140*'
  ```

  instead of:

  ```
  -fn '*courier-bold-r*140*'
  ```

  (the difference being the asterisk instead of the hyphen before the "r" in the slant field), the "r" would also match the "r" in the string "normal" in the set width field. The result is that you would select all slants. Since o (oblique) comes before r (roman), and you always get the first font that matches, you'd end up with Courier oblique.

---

*Unlike *xfontsel*, which displays fonts in the order of wildcard matches, *xlsfonts* will always list fonts in straight sort order, with the sort done character-by-character across the line. Since size in pixels comes before point size in the name, and the size in pixels of the 100-dpi fonts is larger than that of the equivalent 75-dpi font, the 75-dpi font will always be listed first for a given point size. But when listing more than one point size, the fonts will be jumbled. For example, the size in pixels of the 8-point charter font at 100-dpi is 11, so it will come after the 10-point charter font at 75-dpi, with a size in pixels of 10. The 8-point charter font at 75-dpi gets sorted to the very end of the list, since to a character-by-character sort, its size in pixels (8) looks larger to the size in pixels of even the largest 100-dpi font (the 24-point, with a height of 33 pixels).

The trick is to be sure to include at least one of the hyphens to set the -r- off as a separate field rather than as part of another string.

Even though a wildcarded name such as:

```
*cour*b*r-*140*
```

should get you 14-point Courier bold roman, we think it is good practice to spell out the font family and the weight, and to use hyphens between adjacent fields. As usual, there are exceptions: the Lucida family really has three subfamilies; you can get all three by specifying the family as "Lucida*" rather than "Lucida-"; and you might certainly want to abbreviate "New Century Schoolbook" to "New Century*" or "*Schoolbook."

- Font names are case-insensitive. "Courier" is the same as "courier."

Table 5-2 summarizes the values you can use to specify a unique font name (assuming only the standard fonts are loaded). Choose one element from each column. Don't forget to include the leading and trailing asterisks, and the hyphen before the slant.

Table 5-2. Essential Elements of a Font Name

*	Family	–	Weight	–	Slant	*	Point Size	*
	Charter		Medium		r (roman)		80 (8 pt.)	
	Courier		Bold		i (italic)		100 (10 pt.)	
	Helvetica		Demibold		o (oblique)		120 (12 pt.)	
	New century schoolbook				ri (reverse italic)		140 (14 pt.)	
	Symbol				ro (reverse oblique)		180 (18 pt.)	
	Times				ot (other)		240 (24 pt.)	
	Fixed (R4)							
	Clean (R4)							
	OPEN LOOK (R4)							
	Lucida (R4)							
	Terminal (R4)							

The Font Search Path

In both Release 3 and Release 4, fonts are stored in three directories, as shown in Table 5-3.

Table 5-3. Standard Font Directories, Releases 3 and 4

Directory	Contents
/usr/lib/X11/fonts/misc	Release 3: Six fixed-width fonts (also available in Release 2), plus the cursor font. Release 4: Sixty fixed-width fonts, including the six available in Release 3, the cursor font, several Clean family fonts provided by Schumacher, a Kanji font, Kana fonts, and OPEN LOOK cursor and glyph fonts.
/usr/lib/X11/fonts/75dpi	Fixed- and variable-width fonts, 75 dots per inch.
/usr/lib/X11/fonts/100dpi	Release 3: The Adobe Charter font family, 100 dots per inch. Release 4: Fixed- and variable-width fonts, 100 dots per inch (all font families).

These three directories (in this order) comprise X's default font path.

Other directories can be added to the font search path, or its order can be rearranged, using *xset* with the `fp` option. To completely replace the font path, simply specify a comma-separated list of directories. For example, to put the *100dpi* directory before the *75dpi* directory, you might enter:

```
% xset fp= /usr/lib/X11/fonts/misc,/usr/lib/X11/fonts/100dpi,\
           /usr/lib/X11/fonts/75dpi
```

(Note that a space must follow the equal sign, and that the example above is broken onto two lines escaped with a backslash only so that it can be printed within the page margins.) To restore the default font path, type:

```
% xset fp default
```

Use the `fp+` option to add a directory or list of directories to the end of the font path, or `+fp` to add them at the start. Use `-fp` and `fp-` to delete directories from the beginning or end of the font path.

For a complete listing of the fonts in each directory and samples of each font, refer to Appendix E, *Release 3 and 4 Standard Fonts*.

The fonts.dir Files

In addition to font files, each font directory contains a file called *fonts.dir*. The *fonts.dir* files serve, in effect, as databases for the X server. When the X server searches the directories in the default font path, it uses the *fonts.dir* files to locate the font(s) it needs.

Each *fonts.dir* file contains a list of all the font files in the directory with their associated font names, in two-column form. (The first column lists the font file name and the second column lists the actual font name associated with the file.) The first line in *fonts.dir* lists the number of entries in the file (i.e., the number of fonts in the directory).

Example 5-1 shows a portion of the *fonts.dir* file from the Release 4 */usr/lib/X11/fonts/100dpi* directory. As the first line indicates, the directory contains 200 fonts. The first group of fonts listed below (up to the second ellipse) are available as of Release 4. They are all Courier family fonts. (These fonts are 100-dpi equivalents of fonts that in Release 3 were only available in 75-dpi.) The second group of fonts shown in the list below (a few sizes from the Charter family) are also available in the Release 3 *100dpi* directory.

Example 5-1. Subsection of the Release 4 fonts.dir file in /usr/lib/X11/fonts/100dpi

```
200
 .
 .
 .
courBO08.snf -adobe-courier-bold-o-normal--11-80-100-100-m-60-iso8859-1
courBO10.snf -adobe-courier-bold-o-normal--14-100-100-100-m-90-iso8859-1
courBO12.snf -adobe-courier-bold-o-normal--17-120-100-100-m-100-iso8859-1
courBO14.snf -adobe-courier-bold-o-normal--20-140-100-100-m-110-iso8859-1
courBO18.snf -adobe-courier-bold-o-normal--25-180-100-100-m-150-iso8859-1
courBO24.snf -adobe-courier-bold-o-normal--34-240-100-100-m-200-iso8859-1
courB08.snf -adobe-courier-bold-r-normal--11-80-100-100-m-60-iso8859-1
courB10.snf -adobe-courier-bold-r-normal--14-100-100-100-m-90-iso8859-1
courB12.snf -adobe-courier-bold-r-normal--17-120-100-100-m-100-iso8859-1
courB14.snf -adobe-courier-bold-r-normal--20-140-100-100-m-110-iso8859-1
courB18.snf -adobe-courier-bold-r-normal--25-180-100-100-m-150-iso8859-1
courB24.snf -adobe-courier-bold-r-normal--34-240-100-100-m-200-iso8859-1
courO08.snf -adobe-courier-medium-o-normal--11-80-100-100-m-60-iso8859-1
courO10.snf -adobe-courier-medium-o-normal--14-100-100-100-m-90-iso8859-1
courO12.snf -adobe-courier-medium-o-normal--17-120-100-100-m-100-iso8859-1
courO14.snf -adobe-courier-medium-o-normal--20-140-100-100-m-110-iso8859-1
courO18.snf -adobe-courier-medium-o-normal--25-180-100-100-m-150-iso8859-1
courO24.snf -adobe-courier-medium-o-normal--34-240-100-100-m-200-iso8859-1
courR08.snf -adobe-courier-medium-r-normal--11-80-100-100-m-60-iso8859-1
courR10.snf -adobe-courier-medium-r-normal--14-100-100-100-m-90-iso8859-1
courR12.snf -adobe-courier-medium-r-normal--17-120-100-100-m-100-iso8859-1
courR14.snf -adobe-courier-medium-r-normal--20-140-100-100-m-110-iso8859-1
courR18.snf -adobe-courier-medium-r-normal--25-180-100-100-m-150-iso8859-1
courR24.snf -adobe-courier-medium-r-normal--34-240-100-100-m-200-iso8859-1
 .
 .
 .
charBI08.snf -bitstream-charter-bold-i-normal--11-80-100-100-p-68-iso8859-1
charBI10.snf -bitstream-charter-bold-i-normal--14-100-100-100-p-86-iso8859-1
charBI12.snf -bitstream-charter-bold-i-normal--17-120-100-100-p-105-iso8859-1
charBI14.snf -bitstream-charter-bold-i-normal--19-140-100-100-p-117-iso8859-1
charBI18.snf -bitstream-charter-bold-i-normal--25-180-100-100-p-154-iso8859-1
charBI24.snf -bitstream-charter-bold-i-normal--33-240-100-100-p-203-iso8859-1
 .
 .
 .
```

The *fonts.dir* files are created by the *mkfontdir* client when X is installed. *mkfontdir* reads the font files in directories in the font path, extracts the font names, and creates a *fonts.dir* file in each directory. If *fonts.dir* files are present on your system, you probably won't have to deal with them, or with *mkfontdir* at all. If the files are not present, or if you have to load new fonts or remove existing ones, you will have to create files with *mkfontdir*. Refer to Appendix A, *System Management*, for details.

Font Name Aliasing

Another way to abbreviate font names is by aliasing (that is, by associating fonts with alternative names of your own choosing). You can edit or create a file called *fonts.alias*, in any directory (or multiple directories) in the font search path, to set aliases for existing fonts. The X server uses both *fonts.dir* files and *fonts.alias* files to locate fonts in the font path.

If you are running Release 3, there should already be an alias file in the *misc* directory. Release 4 provides a default *fonts.alias* file for each of the three font directories. Take the time to look at the contents of each of these files, since many of the existing aliases may be easier to type than even wildcarded font names. You can also add aliases to the file, change existing aliases, or even replace the entire file. However, this should be done with caution. To play it safe, it's probably a good idea merely to *add* to existing *fonts.alias* files. If you're working in a multi-user environment, the system administrator should definitely be consulted before aliases are added or changed. Note that when you create or edit a *fonts.alias* file, the server does not *automatically* recognize the aliases in question. You must make the server aware of newly created or edited alias files by resetting the font path with *xset*.

The *fonts.alias* file has a two-column format similar to the *fonts.dir* file: the first column contains aliases, the second contains the actual font names. If you want to specify an alias that contains spaces, enclose the alias in double quotes. If you want to include double quotes or other special characters as part of an alias, precede each special symbol with a backslash.

When you use an alias to specify a font in a command line, the server searches for the font associated with that alias in every directory in the font path. Therefore, a *fonts.alias* file in one directory can set aliases for fonts in other directories as well. You might choose to create a single aliases file in one directory of the font path to set aliases for the most commonly used fonts in all the directories. Example 5-2 shows three sample entries that could be added to an existing *fonts.alias* file (or comprise a new one).

Example 5-2. Sample fonts.alias file entries

```
xterm12    -adobe-courier-medium-r-normal--12-120-75-75-m-70-iso8859-1
xterm14    -adobe-courier-medium-r-normal--14-140-75-75-m-90-iso8859-1
xterm18    -adobe-courier-medium-r-normal--18-180-75-75-m-110-iso8859-1
```

As the names of the aliases suggest, these sample entries provide aliases for three fonts (of different point sizes) that are easily readable in *xterm* windows. (We also recommend the fixed-width font stored in the file *9x15.snf*,* in the *misc* directory.) You can also use

*In Release 3, the actual name of this font is *9x15*. The Release 4 name is:

```
-misc-fixed-medium-r-normal--15-140-75-75-c-90-iso8859-1
```

but is aliased to *9x15* in the default *fonts.alias* file in the *misc* directory.

wildcards within the font names in the right-hand column of an alias file. For instance, the alias file entries above might also be written:

```
xterm12    *courier-medium-r-*-120*
xterm14    *courier-medium-r-*-140*
xterm18    *courier-medium-r-*-180*
```

In Release 2 of X, a font name is equivalent to the name of the file in which it is stored, without the *.snf* extension. In the previous edition of this book (which dealt primarily with Release 3 of X), we recommended a method for emulating this convention. This involved creating a *fonts.alias* file containing the following line in every directory in the font path:

```
FILE_NAMES_ALIASES
```

You could then use a filename (without the *.snf* extension) to specify a font. Due to changes implemented in the Release 4 server, **X Window System developers are now discouraging this practice.**

If you would still like to emulate Release 2 conventions in Release 3 or Release 4, you must explicitly assign every font name an alias corresponding to the name of the file in which it is stored, without the *.snf* extension. This could actually be done rather easily by editing a copy of each *fonts.dir* file and appending the copy to the *fonts.alias* file in the same directory. (If you are running Release 3, remember that neither the *75dpi* nor the *100dpi* directory has a default *fonts.alias* file. You may need to create one, rather than append to an existing one. These aliases could also be appended to the *fonts.alias* file in the *misc* directory, since the server searches all directories in the font path.)

Once the server is made aware of aliases, you can specify an alias on the command line. For example, you can use a font name alias as an argument to *xfd*. If you've used an alias file or files to emulate the Release 2 font naming conventions, you can display the font stored in the file *courR12.snf* using the command:

```
% xfd -fn courR12
```

A special note about the *misc* directory: when X was configured for your system, a *fonts.alias* file should have been created in this directory. The first two entries in this file are shown below.

```
fixed     -misc-fixed-medium-r-semicondensed--13-120-75-75-c-60-iso8859-1
variable -*-helvetica-bold-r-normal-*-*-120-*-*-*-*-*-*
```

The default file contains an additional 56 entries, but the entries pictured above are particularly important. The aliases called "fixed" and "variable" are invoked as the default fonts for many clients. The "fixed" font can be thought of as a system-wide default. The "variable" font, described in the right-hand column as a 12-point bold Helvetica font, is used as the default font by *bitmap*, as well as by other clients. If this file is removed or replaced, when you run *bitmap*, you'll get an error message that the server cannot open the variable font, and text in the *bitmap* window will display in the smaller, somewhat less readable "fixed" font.

If you do choose to edit the *fonts.alias* file in the *misc* directory, it is important to preserve at least these two aliases. (As we've said, it's probably a better idea to keep all the default entries and merely append any new ones.)

If you're running Release 3, the *fonts.alias* file in the *misc* directory will be somewhat different. The Release 3 version of the *fonts.alias* file in the *misc* directory is comprised of only the following two lines:

```
fixed          6x13
variable       *-helvetica-bold-r-normal-*-*-140-*
```

Regardless of what edits you make to the file, the line specifying the variable alias must not be changed.

The variable font is slightly larger in Release 3 (14-point) than in Release 4 (12-point). If you examine the Release 3 alias file a little more closely, you may notice that the first line contains an *incorrect* alias specification. Remember, in Release 3, *fixed* is actually the name of the default system font—it is not an alias. The first column should contain aliases and the second column should contain proper font names. However, 6x13 is not a proper font name. It is actually the name of the file that contains the font named "fixed." You can specify fixed as a font on the command line and it will work—but as a font name, not an alias.

Making the Server Aware of Aliases

After you create (or update) an alias file, the server does not automatically recognize the aliases in question. You must make the server aware of newly created or edited alias files by "rehashing" the font path with *xset*. Enter:

```
% xset fp rehash
```

on the command line. The *xset* option `fp` (font path) with the `rehash` argument causes the server to reread the *fonts.dir* and *fonts.alias* files in the current font path. You need to do this every time you edit an alias file. (You also need to use *xset* if you add or remove fonts. See Appendix A, *System Management*, for details.)

Utilities for Displaying Information about Fonts

We've already mentioned *xlsfonts*, which simply displays the names and aliases of available fonts. In addition, *xfd* can be used to display the full character set of a particular font, and *xfontsel* can be used to interactively preview and select a font for use in another window.

The Font Displayer: xfd

If you're unfamiliar with general appearance of a particular font, we've included pictures of some representative fonts in Appendix E, *Release 3 and 4 Standard Fonts.*

You can also display the characters in a font using the *xfd* (font displayer) client. Note that since Release 3, *xfd* has taken an option, `-fn`, before the font name. For example, to display the default system font, a 6x13 pixel fixed-width font known as *fixed**, enter:

*In Release 3, *fixed* is a legitimate font name. In Release 4, it is an *alias* for a longer font name that follows the conventions outlined above.

```
% xfd -fn fixed &
```

The *xfd* window will display the specified font as shown in Figure 5-7.

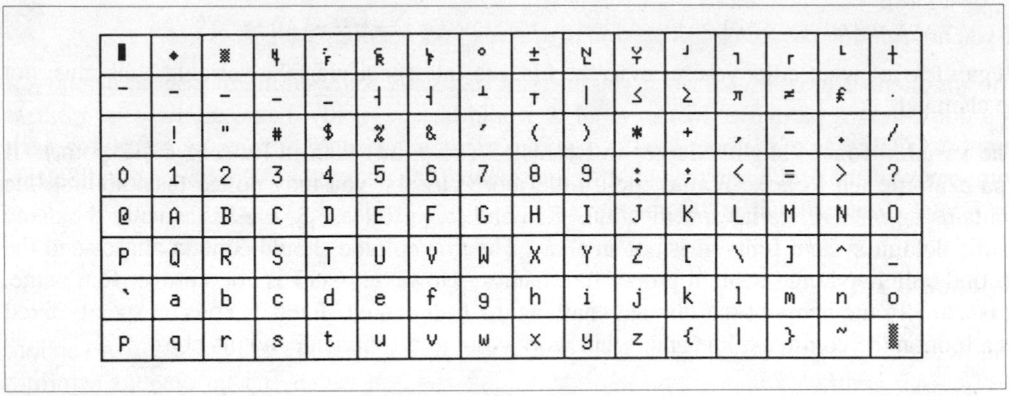

Figure 5-7. Fixed font, 6x13 pixels

This figure depicts the Release 4 version of *xfd*, which has been greatly enhanced since Release 3. The font name is now displayed across the top of the window. (This is the actual font name, which we specified on the command line by the alias *fixed*.) Three command buttons have also been added to the application in Release 4. They appear in the upper-left of the window, below the font name. If the font being displayed doesn't fit within a single *xfd* screen, Prev Page and Next Page allow you to scroll through multiple screens. (The horizontal and vertical dimensions of the window can vary slightly to accommodate different fonts, but certain fonts will still require multiple screens.) The Quit button causes the application to exit, though this can also be done by typing q or Q anywhere within the window.

In addition to displaying a font, *xfd* also allows you to display certain information about the individual characters. But before we examine these capabilities, let's take a closer look at the way the characters in a font are identified and how the *xfd* window makes use of this information.

Within a font, each character is considered to be numbered. The *xfd* client displays a font's characters in a grid. By default, the first character of the font appears in the upper-left position; this is character number 0. The two text lines above the grid identify the upper-left character and the range of characters in the window, by character number(s) both in hexadecimal and in decimal notation (in parentheses following the hex character number).

You can specify a character other than character number 0 to be in the first position in the window using the `-start` option. For example, if you enter the following command line:

```
% xfd -start 15 -fn fixed &
```

the *xfd* window begins with character number 15.

Notice the instruction `Select a character` below the command buttons. To display information about a particular character, click any pointer button within its grid square. Statistics about the character's width, left bearing, right bearing, ascent, and descent are displayed where the line `Select a character` previously appeared.

If you are running the Release 3 version of *xfd*, read the section "Release 3 xfd."

The *xfd* client is most useful when you have an idea what font you might want to display. If you don't have a particular font in mind or would like to survey the possibities, the *xfontsel* client (available as of Release 4) allows you to preview a variety of fonts by specifying each component of the font name using a different menu. See the section "Previewing and Selecting Fonts: xfontsel" later in this chapter.

Release 3 xfd

The Release 3 version of *xfd* is not as flexible or as self-explanatory as the Release 4 version. It offers no command buttons, no line identifying the font name, and no obvious scrolling capabilities. However, it is still very useful for looking at a particular font.

Like the Release 4 version, by default the Release 3 *xfd* displays character number 0 of the font at the upper left of the window. To see a character's number, move the pointer to the desired character and click the middle button. That character's number is displayed both in decimal and in hexadecimal notation at the bottom of the window, as in the following:

```
85.(0x55):
```

This version of *xfd* also accepts the `-start` option, which lets you specify the first character of the font that appears at the upper left of the window.

Every character in the font may not fit in the window at once. Though this version of the application does not feature the handy command buttons introduced at Release 4, you can still view the obscured characters. To see additional characters, move the pointer to the *xfd* window and click the third (usually the right) mouse button. The next window full of characters is displayed. To see the previous window of characters, click the first (usually the left) mouse button. *xfd* beeps if an attempt is made to go back past the first (0) character.

The Release 3 *xfd* also provides statistics about the individual characters in a font, but you must run the client with the `-verbose` option to access this information. Then, to see information about a character's width, left bearing, right bearing, ascent, and descent, move the pointer to the desired character and click the second (usually the middle) button. The information is displayed in a portion of the window below the character grid.

To display the minimum or maximum values taken by each of these fields over the entire font, move the pointer to the desired character and type a less than symbol (<) to display the minimum values or a greater than symbol (>) to display the maximum. Information similar to the following is displayed below the grid:

```
maximum bounds:
left bearing = 2, right bearing = 6
ascent= 10 , descent = 3
width = 6
```

To delete an *xfd* window that is running in the background, you can move the pointer to the window and type either q, Q, or Control-C.

Previewing and Selecting Fonts: xfontsel

The *xfontsel* client, available as of Release 4, provides a font previewer window in which you select the font to view using 14 menus corresponding to the 14 components of a font name. By specifying various font name components, you can take a look at a variety of fonts. This is particularly useful if you are trying to pick good display fonts and you don't have a very clear idea what type of font would be best. Rather than running several instances of *xfd*, you can dynamically change the font displayed in the *xfontsel* window by changing the font name components. (Despite the flexibility of *xfontsel*, it's certainly not practical to preview *all* of the available fonts. If you have no idea what particular font families look like, see the discussion earlier in this chapter, or refer to Appendix E, *Release 3 and 4 Standard Fonts*, for complete listings.)*

Once you've displayed the desired font using the menus, you can make the name of that font the PRIMARY text selection by clicking on the window's select button. (Selecting text is described in Chapter 4, *The xterm Terminal Emulator*.) You can then paste the font name into another window using the pointer: onto a command line, into a resource file, etc. Making a font name the PRIMARY selection also enables you to choose that font from the *xterm* VT Fonts menu, described in Chapter 4.

Previewing Fonts with the xfontsel Menus

To run *xfontsel*, enter the following command in an *xterm* window:

```
% xfontsel &
```

If your system is using the standard Release 4 fonts, the *xfontsel* window initially displays a bold, constant-width, 7x13 pixel font, from the *misc* font directory, as shown in Figure 5-8. This is the first font in the default font search path.

The upper-left corner of the *xfontsel* window features two command buttons: quit and select. As we've explained, clicking on select (with the first pointer button) makes the font displayed in the window the PRIMARY text selection. Obviously, quit causes the application to exit.

Below the command buttons is, in effect, a generic font name or font name template. It is divided into 14 fields corresponding to the 14 parts of a standard font name. Each field is an abbreviation for one part of a font name. Take a look again at the sample font name in Figure

*To our minds, the major drawback of *xfontsel* is that it shows you only the first font that matches a given wildcarded font name. A far better interface would list all of the matching fonts, so that you could compare and choose the one that most suited your needs. There is no way in the standard X distribution to display the appearance of a group of fonts. To produce the figures in this book, we had to write such a program, which we called *xshowfonts*. The program has since been posted to *comp.sources.x*, and a listing appears in Appendix E.

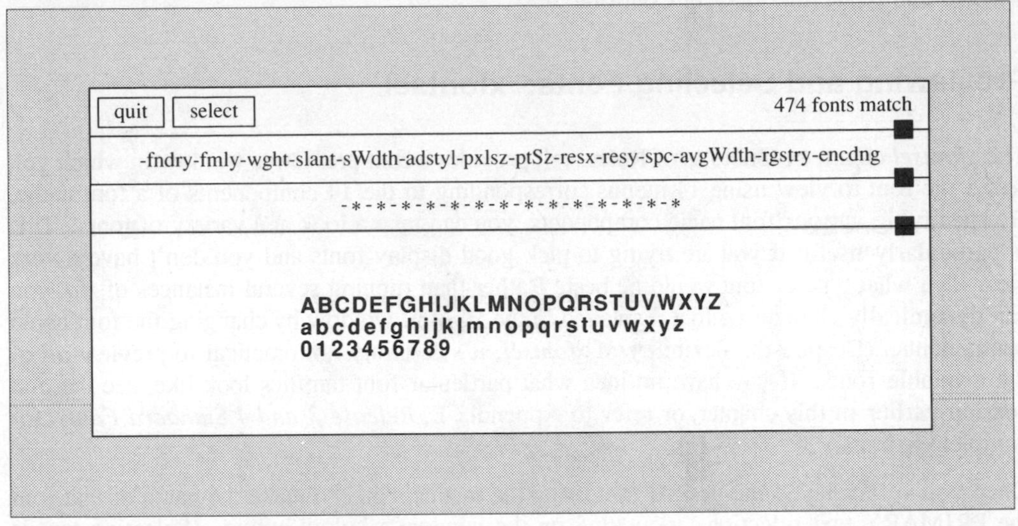

Figure 5-8. xfontsel window displaying 7x13 bold font

5-1 to refresh your memory as to the components. Each of the fields in the *xfontsel* window is actually the handle to a menu, which lets you specify this part of the font name.

To get a clearer idea of how this works, move the pointer onto the generic font name, specifically onto the first field, fndry. (This is an abbreviation for the first part of a font name, the foundry.) When you place the pointer on fndry, the field title should be highlighted by a box. You can then display a menu of foundry names by pressing and holding down the first pointer button, as in Figure 5-9.

Notice that the first choice is the asterisk (*) wildcard character. This is the first choice on all of the menus and thus allows you to include wildcards in the font name you specify, rather than explicitly selecting something from all 14 menus.

To specify a font name component (i.e., make a selection from the menu), continue to hold down the first pointer button and move the pointer down the menu. As the pointer rests on each menu item, it is highlighted by reverse video. To select a highlighted menu item, release the first pointer button.

The line below the font name menus represents the actual font name. When you first run *xfontsel*, all of these fields contain wildcard characters because no menu selections have been made. The number of fonts matched by the font name is displayed in the upper-right corner of the window. The number of fonts matched initially depends on the number of fonts with this naming convention available on your system. In this example, 474 fonts match. (Since this line of wildcards can match *any* 14 part font name, the server chooses the first font in the font path that reflects this naming convention.)

Figure 5-9. xfontsel window with foundry menu displayed

When you select a font name component from one of the 14 menus, the component appears in the actual font name, and the *xfontsel* window displays the first font that matches this name. For example, say we select adobe from the fndry menu, the *xfontsel* window would look like Figure 5-10.

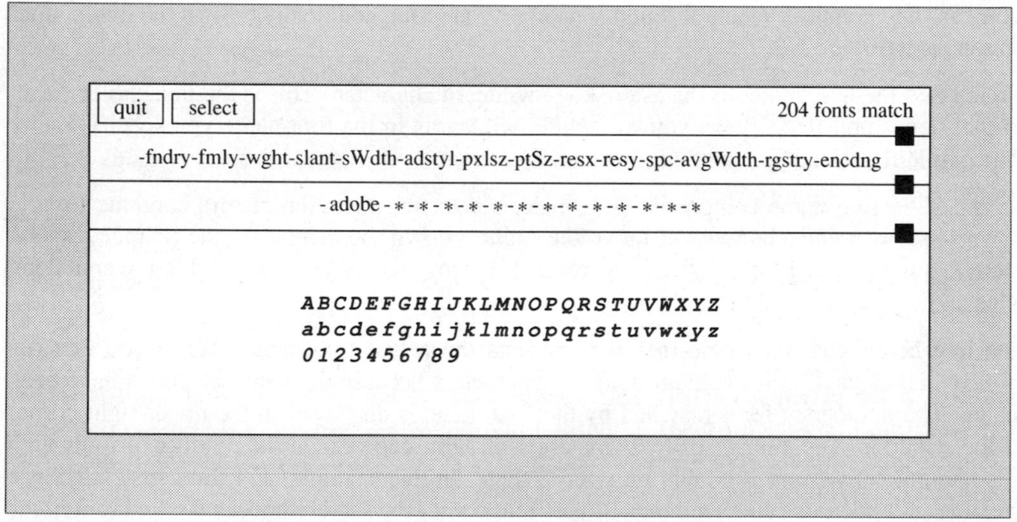

Figure 5-10. xfontsel after choosing Adobe from the foundry menu

The font name is now:

```
-adobe-*-*-*-*-*-*-*-*-*-*-*-*-*
```

and the window displays the first font in the font path to match this wildcarded name. In this case, the first font to match is a 12-point bold Oblique Courier font, which is stored in the file *courBO10.snf* and has the actual font name:

```
-adobe-courier-bold-o-normal-*-10-100-75-75-m-60-iso8859-1
```

Once you make a selection from one menu, the number of possible fonts matched by the name changes. (Notice the line `204 fonts match` in the upper-right corner of the window.) Choosing one font name component also eliminates certain choices on other menus. For example, after you select Abobe as the foundry, the possible choices for font family (the second menu, fmly) are narrowed from 14 to 5 (not counting the asterisk). Again display the fmly menu using the first pointer button. The available choices for font family appear in a regular typeface; the items that cannot be selected appear in a lighter typeface. Families such as Clean, Lucida, and Charter are in a lighter typeface because none of the standard X fonts provided by Adobe are from these families. Adobe fonts in the standard X distribution are limited to the five families Courier, Helvetica, New Century Schoolbook, Symbol, and Times, and these are the items available on the fmly menu.

In order to display a particular font, you'll probably have to make selections from several of the menus. As described earlier in the section "Font Name Wildcarding," we suggest you explicitly select at least the following parts of the font name:

- Font family
- Weight
- Slant
- Point size

Thus, you would make selections from the fmly, wght, slant, and ptSz menus.

You can also use the *-pattern* option with a wildcarded font name to start out with a more limited range of options. For example, if you typed:

```
% xfontsel -pattern '*courier-bold-o-*'
```

you'd start out with the pattern you specified in the filename template part of the *xfontsel* display. You could then simply select from the ptSz menu to compare the various point sizes of Courier bold oblique until you found the one you wanted.

Note that if the pattern you specify to *xfontsel* matches more than one font, the one that is displayed (the first match found) is the one that the server will use. This is in contrast to *xlsfonts*, which sorts the font names. You can always rely on *xfontsel* to show you the actual font that will be chosen given any wildcard specification.

Selecting a Font Name

Once you compose the name of the font you want by making selections from the menus, the corresponding font is displayed in the *xfontsel* window. Then you can select that font name by clicking on the select command button with the first pointer button. The font name becomes the PRIMARY text selection and thus can be pasted in another window using the second (usually the middle) pointer button, as described in Chapter 4, *The xterm Terminal Emulator*.

You might paste the font name on a client command line in an *xterm* window, in order to specify it as the client's display font. (See Chapter 8, *Command Line Options*.) You might paste it into a resource file such as *Xresources* to specify it as the default font for a client or some feature of a client (such as a menu). (See Chapter 9, *Setting Resources*, for more information.)

Less obviously, once a font name is made the PRIMARY text selection, it can be toggled as the *xterm* display font using the Selection item of the *xterm* VT Fonts menu. The Selection menu item can only be chosen from the VT Fonts menu when there is a PRIMARY text selection. (Otherwise, the menu item appears in a lighter typeface, indicating that it is not available.) If the PRIMARY text selection is a valid font name (as it is when you've pressed the select button in the *xfontsel* window), the *xterm* window displays in that font. (In cases where the PRIMARY selection is not a valid font name, the *xterm* display font does not change.)

By default, *xfontsel* displays the lower and uppercase letters a through z and the digits 0 through 9. You can specify alternative sample text using the `-sample` option. For more information about this and other options, see the *xfontsel* reference page in Part Three of this guide.

Changing Fonts in xterm Windows

As discussed in Chapter 4, *The xterm Terminal Emulator*, *xterm* includes a VT Fonts menu that allows you to change fonts on the fly. We discussed most of the menu entries in Chapter 4. However, two of the many items require a greater understanding of font naming than we'd covered by that point. So we've saved them until now.

The Great Escape

Though it is by no means obvious, *xterm* allows you to change the display font by sending an escape sequence, along with the new font name, to the terminal window. Once you change the font in this way, the Escape Sequence item on the *xterm* VT Fonts menu becomes available and choosing it toggles the font you first specified with the escape sequence. (In effect, whatever font you specify using the escape sequence is stored in memory as the menu's Escape Sequence font selection.)

You send an escape sequence to the terminal window by using the UNIX *echo*(1) command. The escape sequence to change the *xterm* display font is comprised of the following keystrokes:

```
Esc ] 50 ; fontname Control-G
```

To clarify, these keystrokes are: the Escape key, the right bracket (]), the number 50, a semicolon (;), a *fontname*, and the Control-G key combination. We've shown the keystrokes with spaces between them for readability, but when you type the sequence on the command line, there should be no spaces. Note also that to supply this sequence as an argument to *echo*, you must enclose it in quotes:

```
% echo "Esc]50;fontnameControl-G"
```

These are the literal keys you type. However, be aware that when you type these keys as specified, the command line will not look exactly like this. Certain keys, like Escape, and key combinations, like Control-G, are represented by other symbols on the command line. When you type the key sequence above, the command line will actually look like this:

```
% echo "^[]50;fontname^G"
```

Typing the Escape key generates the ^[symbol and typing the Control-G key combination generates ^G. You can use a full fontname, an alias, or a wildcarded font specification as the fontname. You should be aware that if the wildcarded specification matches more than one font, you will get the first font in the search path that matches. For example:

```
% echo "^[]50;*courier*^G"
```

will get you a 10-point courier bold oblique. The advantage of being able to change the display font with an escape sequence is that it allows you to add another font to your choices on the fly.* Changing the fonts associated with the Tiny, Small, Medium, and Large menu items is a more laborious process. It involves specifying other fonts in a resource file, making those resources available to the server, and then running another *xterm* process. (See Chapter 9, *Setting Resources*, for more information.) However, you can change the font specified by the Escape Sequence menu item as often as you want during the current *xterm* process, simply by typing the escape sequence described above.

Now that we've looked at the mechanics of the escape sequence, let's consider its practical use. Say you want to run a program in an *xterm* window and you want to be able to read the output easily, but you would like the window to be moderately small. You discover that toggling the Medium font, the `8x13` font by default, makes the window a good size, but the typeface is too light to be read easily. (We presume you are using the default menu fonts and have not customized them using a resource file.) You could dynamically change the display font to a bold font of the same size by entering the following command line:

```
% echo "Esc]50;8x13boldControl-G"
```

The *xterm* font becomes the desired `8x13bold`, a good choice; in addition, the Escape Sequence item of the VT Fonts menu becomes available for selection. This menu item allows you to toggle the `8x13bold` font at any time during the *xterm* process. Thus, you could switch back to any of the other fonts available on the menu (Small, Large, etc.) and then use Escape Sequence to again select `8x13bold`.

---

*Specifying a font with an escape sequence affects only the current *xterm* window and enables only that window's Escape Sequence menu selection.

This font will remain the Escape Sequence font for the duration of the *xterm* process, unless you again change the display font with an escape sequence. If you enter another font name using the escape sequence described above, the window will display in that new font and the Escape Sequence menu item will toggle it.

The Selection Menu Item

The Selection menu item allows you to toggle a font whose name you've previously "selected." The font name could be selected with the pointer, for example, from *xlsfonts* output, using the "cut-and-paste" techniques described in Chapter 4, *The xterm Terminal Emulator*. It is far more likely, though, that you would use this menu item after selecting a font with *xfontsel*. This menu item was clearly designed with *xfontsel* in mind. (If no text is currently selected, this menu item is "grayed out," indicating that it is unavailable.)

The main limitation of this menu item is that it uses the *last text selected* as the font name, regardless of what that text is. If you select a font name, that name is only available through Selection until you use the pointer to select other text. Since cutting and pasting text is one of the most useful features of *xterm*, you will probably be making frequent selections. If the last selected text was not a valid font name, toggling Selection will not change the display font, and a beep will inform you that the toggle failed.

Release 2 versus Subsequent Release Fonts

The primary intent of this guide is to describe the features of Release 4 of the standard X Window System shipped by MIT. However, we assume that many people are still using Release 3 and that some are still using Release 2. The available display fonts, font naming conventions, and possible system administration tasks supporting fonts changed radically from Release 2 to Release 3. For those who have been using Release 2 display fonts, switching to Release 3 or 4 may take some adjustment. The following two sections will acquaint you with the differences between Release 2 fonts and the fonts provided in later releases and show you how to work effectively with the fonts you have.

Font Specification in Release 2

All Release 2 screen fonts are stored in a single directory called */usr/lib/X11/fonts*.* If you do a listing of that directory, you'll see a list of filenames with *.snf* extensions. These are the font files. In Release 2, the name of a font is equivalent to the name of the file in which it is stored, *without* the *.snf* extension.

Thus, the file *fg-16.snf* contains the font fg-16. To create an *xterm* window in which text will be displayed with the font named *fg-16*, type the command line:

*At Release 3, most Release 2 fonts were moved from the standard distribution of X to the user-contributed distribution.

```
% xterm -fn fg-16 &
```

You can find out which fonts are available by using the *xlsfonts* client. If you type `xlsfonts` in an *xterm* window, you should get a list of the available fonts, which are summarized in Table 5-4.

Table 5-4. Fonts in the Standard Distribution, Release 2

Fixed-width Fonts			Variable-width Fonts			
6x10	fgb1-25	oldera	apl-s25	hbr-s40	vg-25	vr-30
6x12	fgb1-30	rot-s16	arrow3	krivo	vg-31	vr-31
6x13	fgi-20	sans12	chp-s25	met25	vg-40	vr-40
8x13	fgi1-25	sansb12	chs-s50	mit	vgb-25	vrb-25
8x13bold	fgs-22	sansi12	cursor	plunk	vgb-31	vrb-30
9x15	fixed	serif10	cyr-s25	runlen	vgbc-25	vrb-31
crturz	fqxb-25	serif12	cyr-s30	stan	vgh-25	vrb-35
dancer	fr-25	serifb10	cyr-s38	sub	vgi-20	vrb-37
fg-13	fr-33	serifb12	ent	subsub	vgi-25	vri-25
fg-16	fr1-25	serifi10	fcor-20	sup	vgi-31	vri-30
fg-18	fr2-25	serifi12	fgb-13	supsup	vgl-40	vri-31
fg-20	fr3-25	stempl	fgb-25	sym-s25	vgvb-31	vri-40
fg-22	frb-32	swd-s30	fri-33	sym-s53	vmic-25	vsg-114
fg-25	ipa-s25	vtbold	fri1-25	variable	vply-36	vsgn-57
fg-30	lat-s30	vtsingle	ger-s35	vbee-36	vr-20	vshd-40
fg-40	micro	xif-s25	grk-s25	vctl-25	vr-25	vxms-37
fg1-25			grk-s30	vg-13	vr-27	vxms-43
			hbr-s25	vg-20		

These fonts are divided into fixed-width fonts (`typewriter style`) and variable-width fonts (proportional). Use only fixed-width fonts for text in an *xterm* window. (Variable-width fonts would be treated as fixed-width, and would be spaced unevenly.) Use variable-width fonts only with programs designed to use them, such as a PostScript previewer or *wysiwyg** editor.

The characters in each font can be displayed using the *xfd* client. To display the default font, a 6x13 pixel fixed-width font named *fixed*, type:

```
% xfd fixed
```

The resulting *xfd* window is shown in Figure 5-11.

When a font is referenced by an X client, the font is taken from the directory */usr/lib/X11/fonts* unless an explicit path name to another font directory is provided. You can specify an alternative font path using the `fp` option to *xset*, as described in Chapter 11, *Setup Clients*.

*This is an acronym for "what you see is what you get" and describes a type of text editor or word processor that displays the page exactly as it would appear in print. MacWrite® is a *wysiwyg* program.

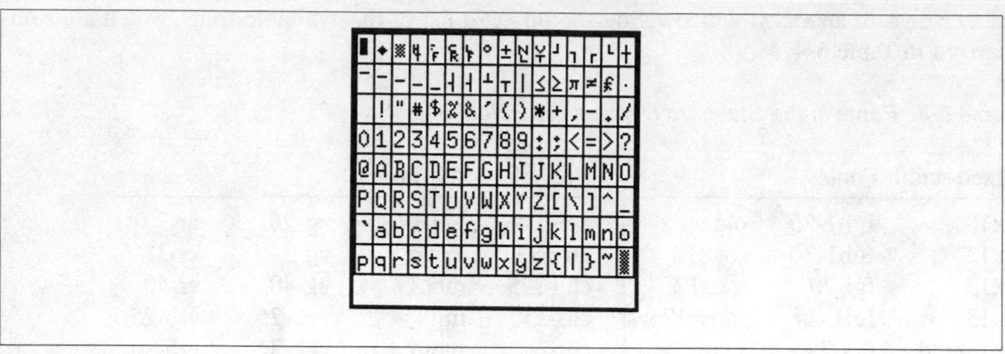

Figure 5-11. Default font, fixed

When a font is referenced by an X client, the font is taken from the directory */usr/lib/X11/fonts* unless an explicit path name to another font directory is provided. You can specify an alternative font path using the `fp` option to *xset*, as described in Chapter 11, *Setup Clients*.

6

Graphics Utilities

This chapter describes how to use the major graphics clients included with X, notably the bitmap *editor.*

In This Chapter:

6
Graphics Utilities

The standard release of X includes four utilities to help you create bitmap images: *bitmap*, *bmtoa*, *atobm*, and *xmag*. The most powerful and useful of these clients is *bitmap*, a program that lets you create and edit bitmap files. The following sections include detailed instructions for using the *bitmap* client.

The *bmtoa* and *atobm* clients are programs that convert bitmaps to arrays (of ASCII characters) and arrays to bitmaps. They are used to facilitate printing and file manipulation and can help you convert a font character to a bitmap.

In a sense, the *xmag* client is a desk accessory for graphics programs. This client is used to magnify a portion of the screen, assisting you in creating images with a graphics editor, such as *bitmap*.

Creating Icons and Other Bitmaps

The *bitmap* program allows you to create and edit small bitmaps. A bitmap is a grid of pixels, or picture elements, each of which is white, black, or, in the case of color displays, a color. You can use *bitmap* to create backgrounds, icons, and pointers.

At this point in X Window System development, *bitmap* is primarily a programming tool for application developers. However, several applications allow you to design your own icon or background pattern with *bitmap*, save it in a bitmap file, and specify that filename on the command line.* For example, *xsetroot* (described in Chapter 11, *Setup Clients*) allows you to specify a bitmap that will be used as the background pattern for the root window.

To invoke *bitmap*, type:

```
% bitmap filename &
```

An upper-left corner cursor appears on the screen for you to interactively place the *bitmap* window, shown in Figure 6-1.

*There are many bitmaps included in the X distribution. These can be found in the directory */usr/include/X11/bitmaps*. Samples are shown in Appendix G, *Standard Bitmaps*.

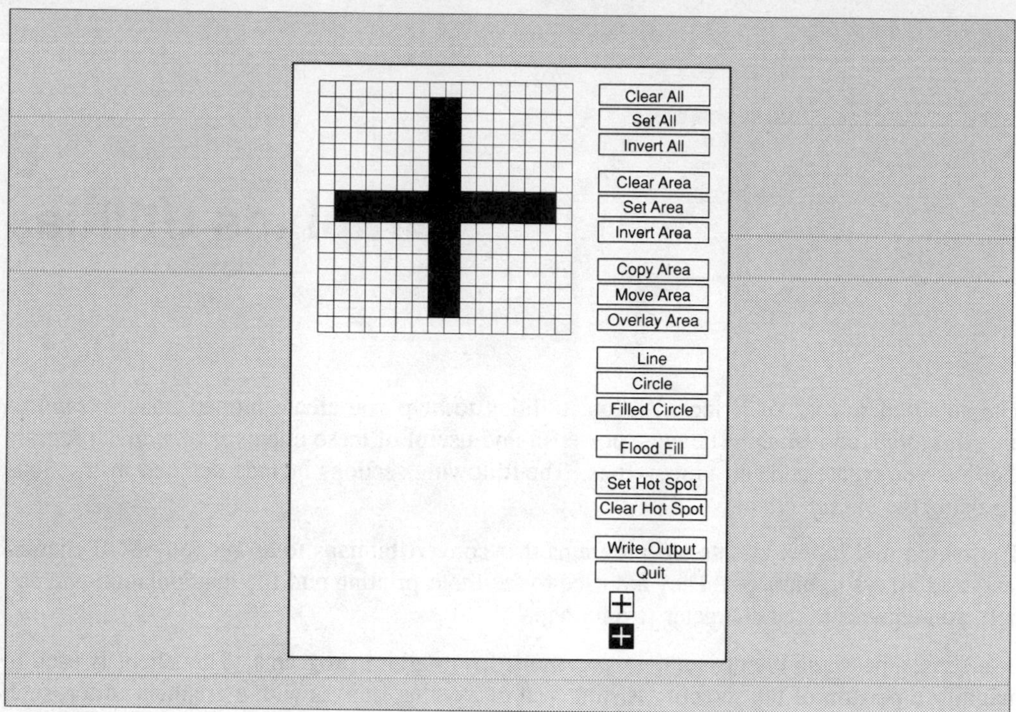

Figure 6-1. Bitmap window

The window that *bitmap* creates has three sections:

1. The largest section is the checkerboard grid, which is a magnified version of the bitmap you are editing. The default-size grid is 16x16. If this grid isn't large enough for comfortable editing, resize the window. Each square on the grid will be enlarged proportionally.
2. On the right-hand side of the window is a list of commands in command boxes that you can invoke with any mouse button.
3. Beneath the commands is an actual-size picture of the bitmap you are editing; below this is an inverted version of the same bitmap. Each time the grid changes, the same change occurs in the actual-size bitmap and its inverse.

If you want to edit in a grid of different proportions than the default-size 16x16 grid, you can specify *WIDTH*x*HEIGHT* on the command line, after *filename*. For example, to create a grid double the size of the default, enter:

```
% bitmap filename 32x32 &
```

Figure 6-2 shows a 40x40 grid with a bitmap we created of Gumby©. We think it makes a fun root window pattern. (See the discussion of *xsetroot* in Chapter 11, *Setup Clients*, for instructions on specifying a bitmap as your root window pattern.)

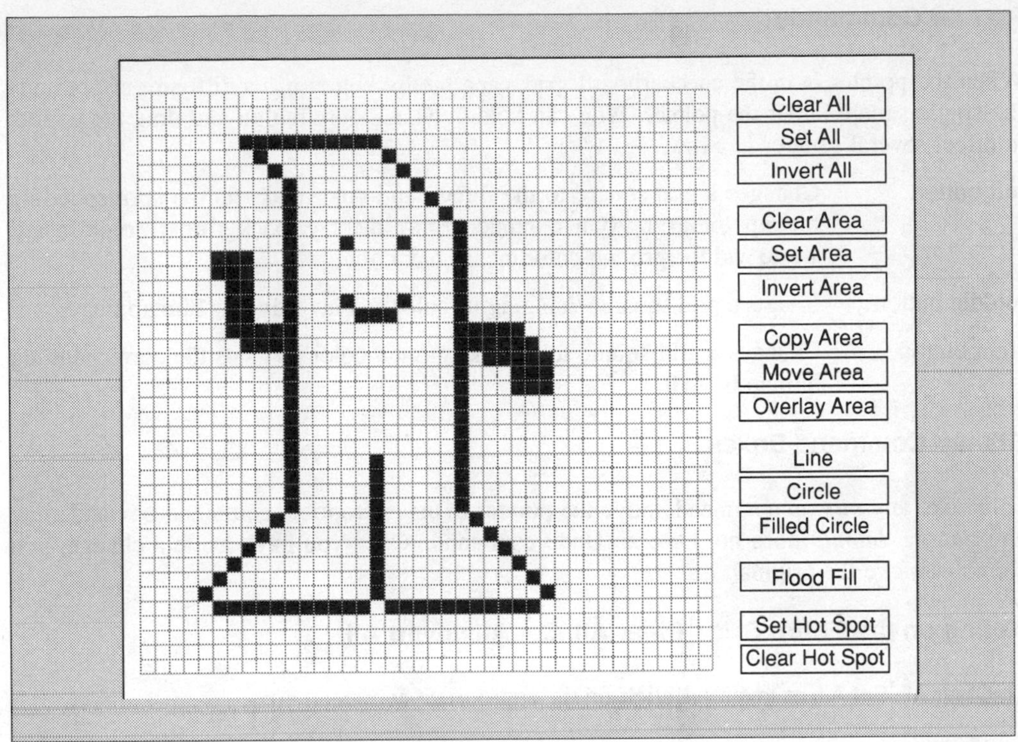

Figure 6-2. Gumby bitmap

Figure 6-2 shows our own rendition of Gumby, created using various *bitmap* editing commands. The standard cursor font also contains a Gumby character. (You can specify the Gumby cursor as the *xterm* window pointer, as described in Chapter 9, *Setting Resources*, or as the root window pointer using the *xsetroot* client, as described in Chapter 11, *Setup Clients*.) Later in this chapter, we'll show you how to convert the Gumby character of the cursor font to a bitmap file, using the *atobm* client.

Bitmap Editing Commands

You can create and edit a bitmap using a combination of pointer commands and commands that appear in boxes on the right-hand side of the window. The pointer commands work on one square of the grid at a time, while the command boxes can work on the entire grid or a specified area.

Pointer Commands

When the pointer is in the checkerboard grid, each mouse button has a different effect upon the single square under the pointer. You can hold down a mouse button and drag the pointer to effect several squares in a row.

left button — Changes a grid square to the foreground color and sets the corresponding bitmap bit to 1. (On a monochrome display, background color means white and foreground color means black.)

middle button — Inverts a grid square, changing its color and inverting its bitmap bit.

right button — Changes a grid square to the background color and sets the corresponding bitmap bit to 0.

Bitmap Command Boxes

To invoke any *bitmap* command, move the pointer to the appropriate command box and click any button. *bitmap* does not have an Undo command. Once you have made a change, you cannot retrieve the original.

Acting on the Entire Grid: Clear All, Set All, Invert All

To Clear All, Set All, or Invert All, click on the appropriate command box.

Clear All — Changes all the grid squares to the background color and sets all bitmap bits to 0.

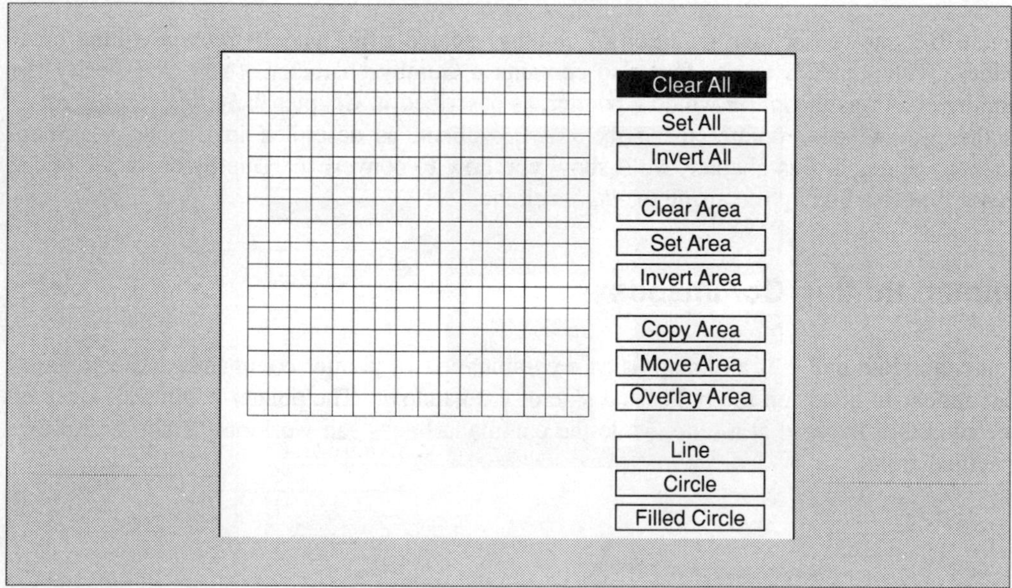

Figure 6-3. Clearing all

Set All — Changes all the grid squares to the foreground color and sets all bitmap bits to 1.

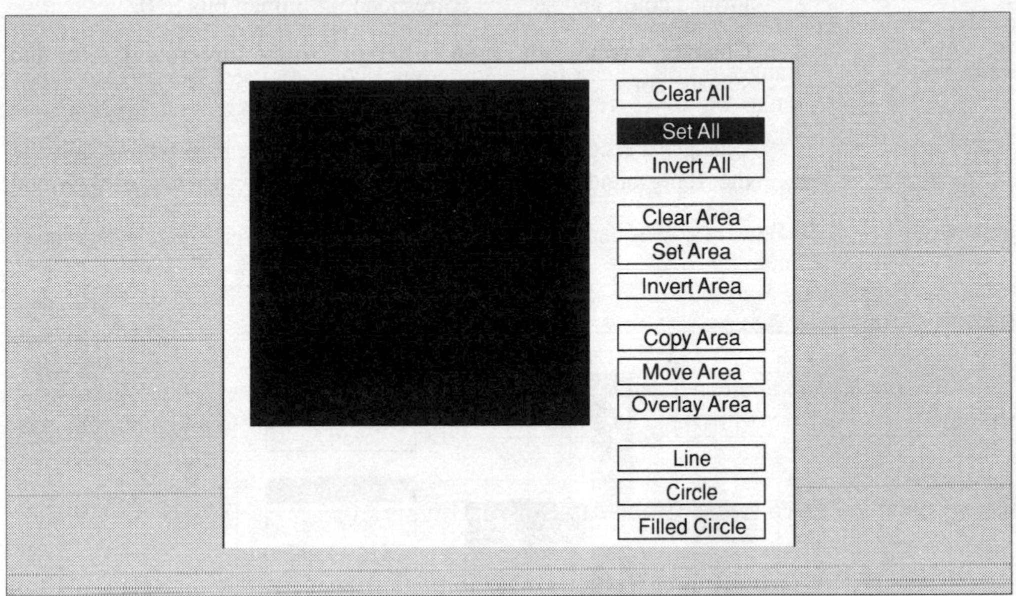

Figure 6-4. Setting all

Invert All — Inverts all the grid squares and bitmap bits, as if you had pressed the middle button over each square.

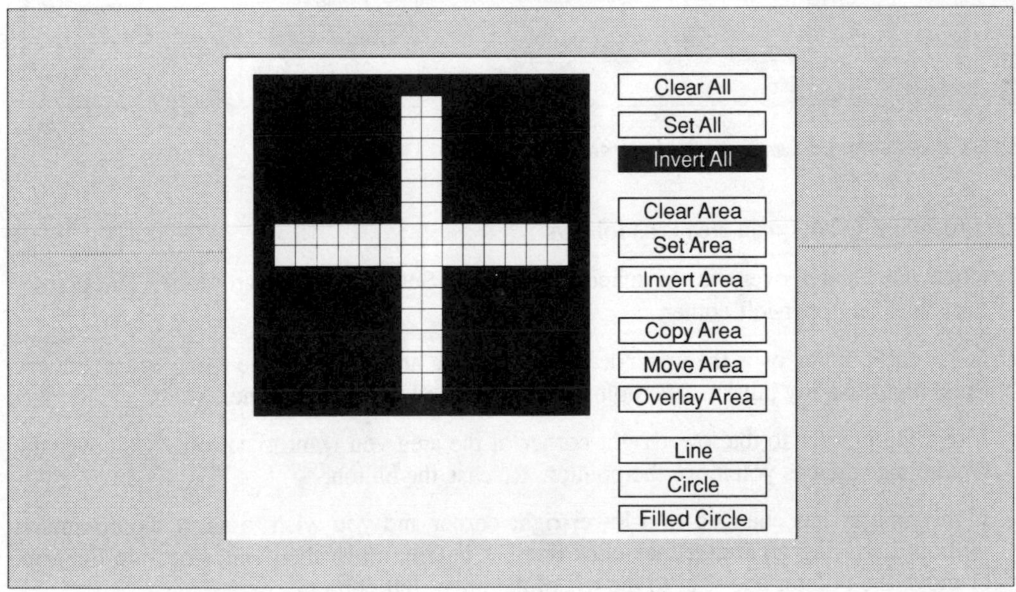

Figure 6-5. Inverting all

Acting on an Area: Clear Area, Set Area, Invert Area

Clear Area — Clears a rectangular area of the grid, i.e., changes it to the background color, and sets the corresponding bitmap bits to 0.

Set Area — Changes a rectangular area of the grid to the foreground color and sets the corresponding bitmap bits to 1.

Invert Area — Changes a rectangular area of the grid from the background color to the foreground color or the foreground color to the background color.

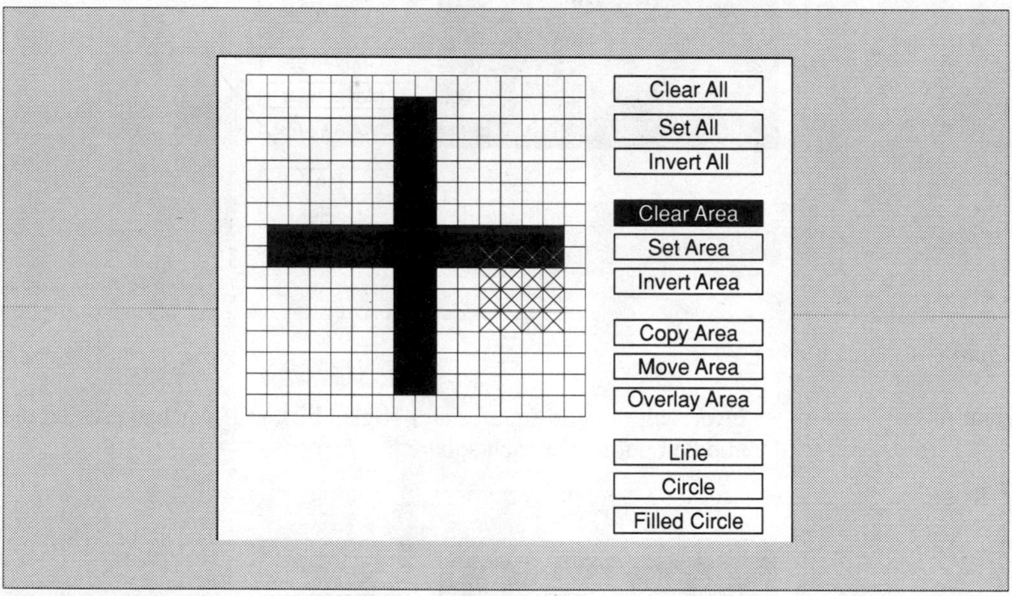

Figure 6-6. Selecting an area to clear, set, or invert

The procedure to act on an area is as follows:

1. Click the pointer over the command (Clear Area, Set Area, or Invert Area). The pointer turns into an upper-left corner.
2. Move the pointer over the upper-left corner of the area you want to clear, set, or invert. Press and hold any button. The pointer changes to a lower-right corner.
3. Move the pointer to the lower-right corner of the area you want to act on. X's cover the rectangular area as you move the pointer. Release the button.

   If the pointer has changed to a lower-right corner and you wish to abort the command without inverting an area, either click another button, move the pointer outside the grid, or move the pointer above or to the left of the upper-left corner.

Copy Area, Move Area, Overlay Area

Copy Area — Copies a rectangular area from one part of the grid to another.

Move Area — Moves a rectangular area from one part of the grid to another.

Overlay Area — Lays a rectangular area from one part of the grid over a rectangular area in another part of the grid. Overlay is not a pixel-for-pixel replacement, but those pixels that are clear (bitmap bits set to 0) allow those pixels that are set (bitmap bits set to 1) to show through the overlay.

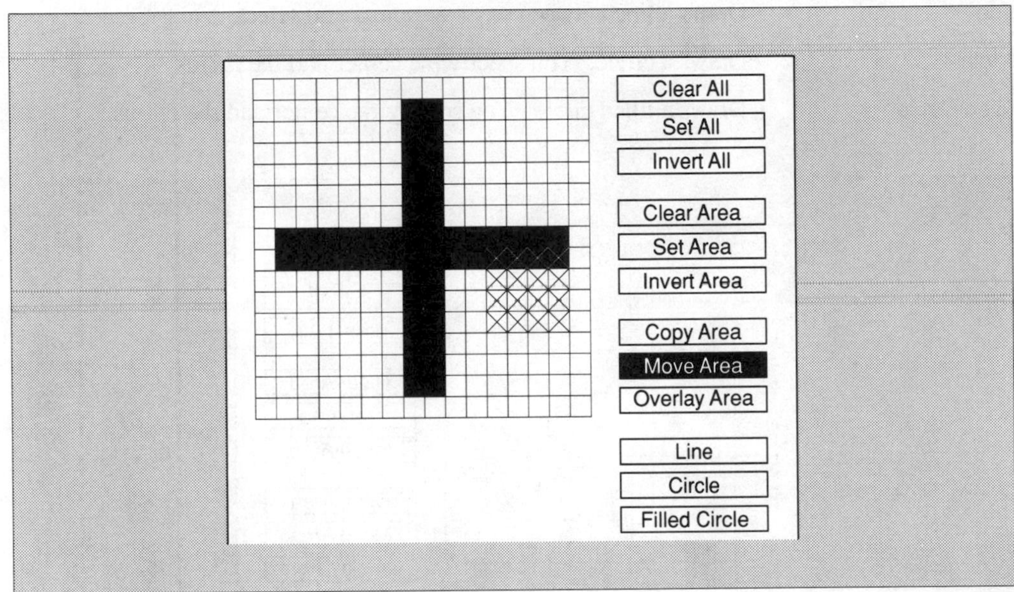

Figure 6-7. Selecting an area to copy, move, or overlay

The procedure to Copy Area, Move Area, or Overlay Area is as follows:

1. Click the pointer over the command (Copy Area, Move Area, or Overlay Area). The pointer turns into an upper-left corner.
2. Move the pointer over the upper-left corner of the area you want to copy, move, or overlay. Press and hold any button. The pointer changes to a lower-right corner.
3. Move the pointer to the lower-right corner of the area you want to act on. X's cover the rectangular area as you move the pointer. Release the button. The pointer changes to an upper-left corner.

4. Move the pointer to the desired location and click any button.

   OR:

   Press and hold any button to see the outline of the destination rectangle, move the pointer to the desired location, then release the button.

5. To cancel an overlay, copy, or move command, move the pointer outside the grid and release the button.

Drawing: Line, Circle, Filled Circle

When you use a drawing command, the drawing is always done in the foreground color.

Line	Draws a line between any two points you select.
Circle	Draws a circle. You specify the center and the radius.
Filled Circle	Draws a filled circle. You specify the center and the radius.

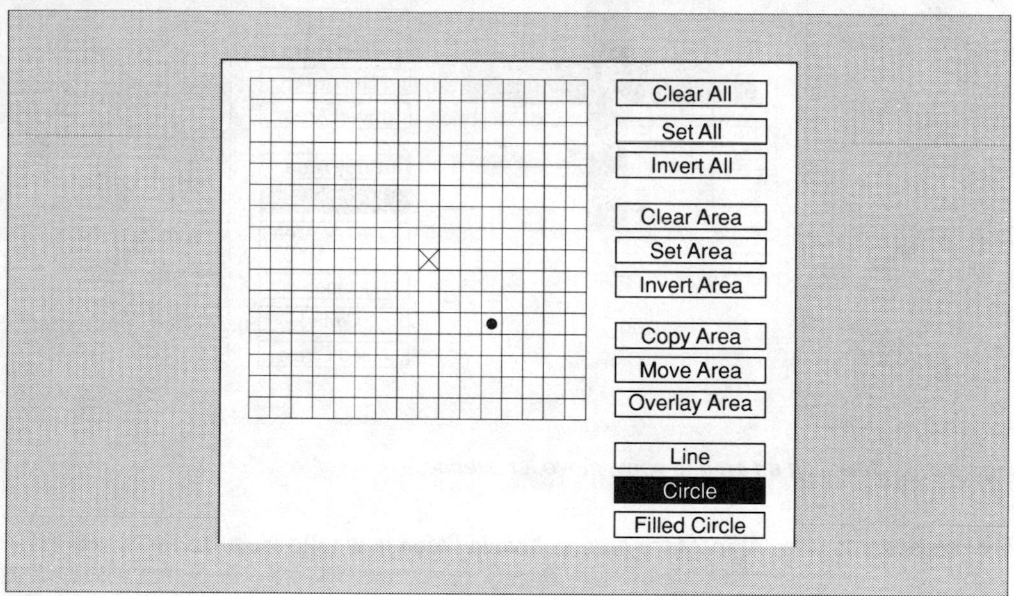

Figure 6-8. Selecting center and radius of circle

To draw a line or circle:

1. Click the pointer over the command Line, Circle, or Filled Circle. The pointer changes to the dot cursor shape (•).
2. Move the pointer to the first point of the line or to the center of the circle. Click any button. An X fills the square which is the starting point of the line or center of the circle.
3. Move the pointer to the end point of the line or to the outside circumference of the circle. Click any button. The graphic is drawn.

Filling in a Shape: Flood Fill

Flood Fill — Fills all clear squares in a closed shape.

To fill a shape:

1. Click the pointer over the command Flood Fill. The pointer changes to the dot cursor shape (•).
2. Move the pointer into the shape you want to fill.
3. Click on any clear square inside the closed shape and all clear squares are filled out to the shape's border. If the shape is not closed, the entire grid will be filled.

Graphics Utilities

Hot Spots: Set Hot Spot, Clear Hot Spot

Set Hot Spot — Designates a point on the bitmap as the hot spot. If a program is using your bitmap as a pointer, the hot spot indicates which point on the bitmap will track the actual location of the pointer. For instance, if your pointer is an arrow, the hot spot should be the tip of the arrow; if your pointer is a cross, the hot spot should be that point at which the perpendicular lines intersect.

Clear Hot Spot — Removes a hot spot defined on this bitmap.

To set or clear a hot spot:

1. Click the pointer over Set Hot Spot or Clear Hot Spot.
2. Move the pointer to the location of the hot spot. Click any button. When a hot spot is active a diamond (◊) appears in the square.

Saving and Quitting: Write Output, Quit

Write Output — Writes the current bitmap value to the file specified in the command line. If the file already exists, the original file is first renamed to *filename~*.

If either the renaming or the writing causes an error (e.g., permission denied), a dialog box appears, asking if you want to write the file */tmp/filename* instead. If you click Yes, all future Write Output commands in the current *bitmap* editing session write to */tmp/filename*. See the *bitmap* reference page in Part Three of this guide for information on the format of the output file.

Quit — Terminates *bitmap*. If you have edited the bitmap and have not invoked Write Output, or you have edited it since the last time you invoked Write Output, a dialog box appears, asking if you want to save changes before quitting. Yes does a Write Output before terminating; No just terminates, losing the edits; Cancel means you decided not to terminate after all.

You can also terminate *bitmap* by typing Control-C or q anywhere in the window. If you have edited the bitmap and have not invoked Write Output, a dialog window appears, asking if you want to save changes before quitting.

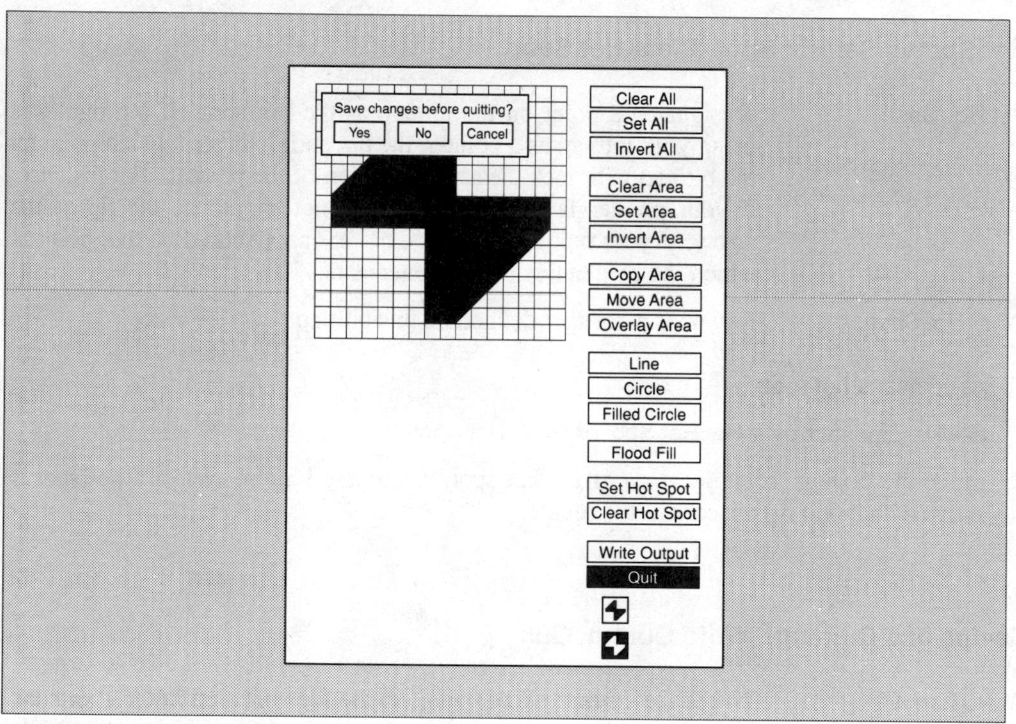

Figure 6-9. Bitmap window with quit dialog box

Creating a Bitmap from a Cursor

The *atobm* and *bmtoa* clients allow you to convert *a*rrays (of ASCII characters) *to bitm*ap files and to convert *bitm*ap files *to a*rrays. These clients are commonly used to facilitate printing: a bitmap file that is converted to ASCII text can be printed more readily and can also be included in standard ASCII text files. Once converted to ASCII, bitmap files can also be more quickly copied or mailed to other directories or systems, where they can be used in ASCII format or converted back to bitmap format.

Among their uses, the *bmtoa* and *atobm* utilities make it possible to convert a character from a font, such as the cursor font, to the *bitmap* file format. Once converted, the file can be edited using the *bitmap* client, and used as you would any other bitmap file: specified as the root window pattern (with *xsetroot*), etc.

When a bitmap file is converted to ASCII text, it is in the form of an array consisting of two types of characters. (An array is a number of elements arranged in rows and columns; it is sometimes called a matrix.) One character represents set or filled squares of the bitmap (bitmap bit 1) and the other character represents empty squares (bitmap bit 0). By default, the number sign character (#) represents filled squares and the hyphen (–) represents empty squares. Figure 6-10 shows the British pound sign character of the 9x15 font (in the *misc* directory) as an array of these ASCII symbols.

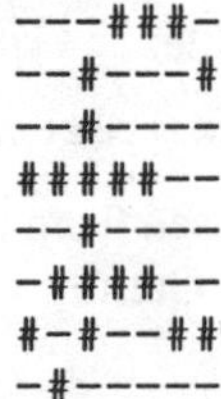

Figure 6-10. ASCII array representing the pound sign

As you can see, the array is a perfect rectangle. In a sense, the array is very similar to the *bitmap* grid. (You can edit or create the array using an ASCII text editor, so long as you use the standard two characters and keep the array rectangular.)

To convert the Gumby character of the cursor font to a bitmap, the first thing you must do is display the cursor font as ASCII text. This can be done with the *showsnf* client, which allows you to display the contents of a font file (with a *.snf* extension). The `-g` option specifies that arrays of all the characters in the font be displayed as well.

To display the cursor font with each character represented as an array, use *showsnf*, with the font filename as an argument, and redirect output to a file called */tmp/cursor.array*:

```
% showsnf -g /usr/lib/X11/fonts/misc/cursor.snf > /tmp/cursor.array
```

The *cursor.array* file contains information about the font and an array for each character. Using your ASCII text editing program, edit the file, writing the Gumby array to another file called */tmp/gumby.array*. The Gumby array is pictured in Figure 6-11.

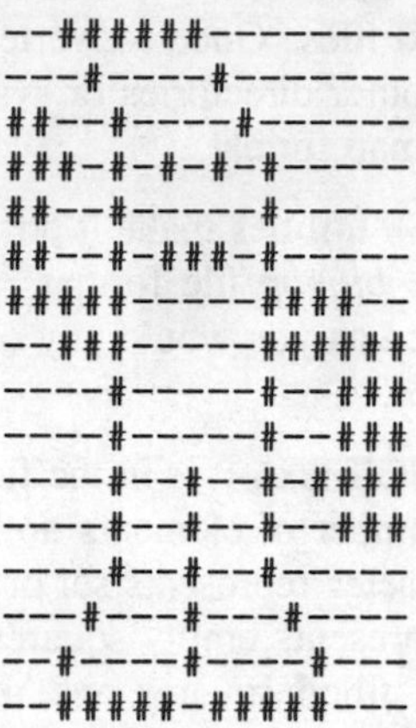

```
--######--------
---#----#-------
##--#----#------
###-#-#-#-#-----
##--#-----#-----
##--#-###-#-----
#####-----####--
--###-----######
----#-----#--###
----#-----#--###
----#--#--#-####
----#--#--#--###
----#--#--#-----
---#---#---#----
--#----#----#---
--#####-#####---
```

Figure 6-11. /tmp/gumby.array

You can then use the *atobm* client to convert this array to a bitmap. Use the *gumby.array* file as an argument and redirect the output to a bitmap file:

```
% atobm /tmp/gumby.array > /tmp/gumby.bitmap
```

Figure 6-12 shows the Gumby bitmap. As you can see from the bitmap, the Gumby character of the cursor font is considerably smaller than the Gumby we created (Figure 6-2) with *bitmap*.

If you want, you can then edit the *gumby.bitmap* file using the *bitmap* client.

If you specify the bitmap as the root window pattern, you'll notice that there is virtually no space between the Gumby figures. This is because the array file had no extra hyphens (representing empty *bitmap* squares) padding it. If you want, you can add some hyphens to the *gumby.array* file (keeping the image symmetrical) and then use *atobm* to create a more padded version of the bitmap. Figure 6-13 shows the *gumby.array* file after being padded with hyphens.

See the *bitmap* reference page in Part Three of this guide for more information on the *atobm* and *bmtoa* conversion clients.

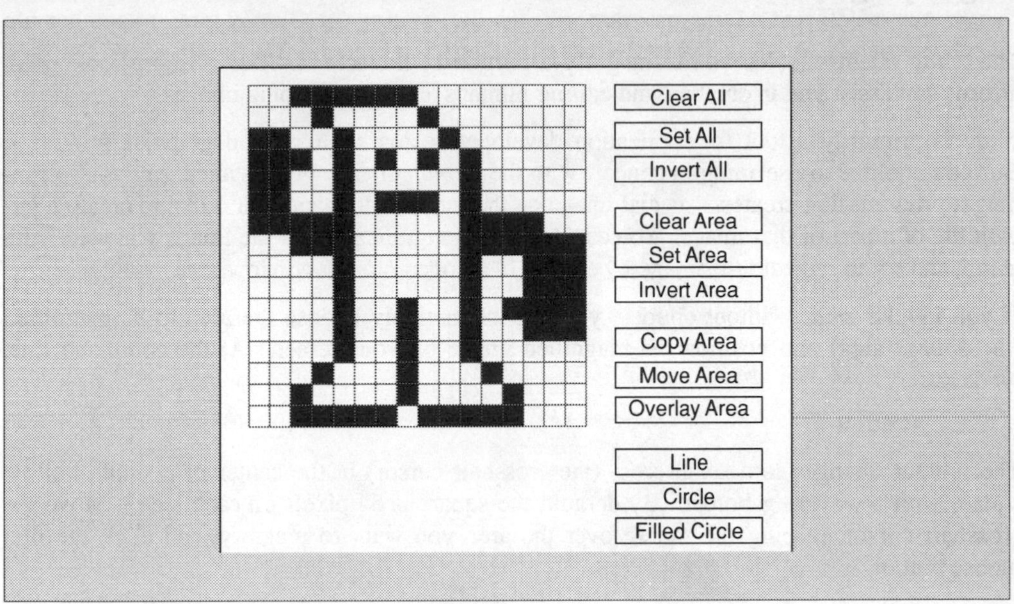

Figure 6-12. Bitmap of the Gumby cursor

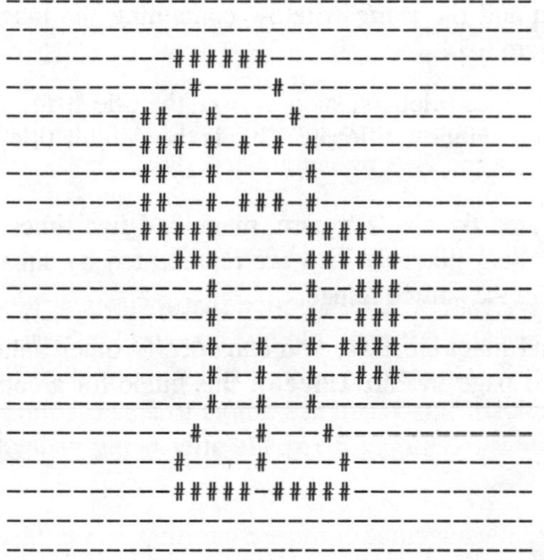

```
--------------------------------
--------------------------------
----------######----------------
-----------#----#---------------
--------##--#----#--------------
--------###-#-#-#-#-------------
--------##--#-----#-------------
--------##--#-###-#-------------
--------#####-----####----------
----------###-----######--------
------------#-----#--###--------
------------#-----#--###--------
------------#--#--#-####--------
------------#--#--#--###--------
------------#--#--#-------------
-----------#---#---#------------
----------#----#----#-----------
----------#####-#####-----------
--------------------------------
--------------------------------
```

Figure 6-13. gumby.array padded by hyphens

Magnifying Portions of the Screen: xmag

The *xmag* client enables you to magnify a portion of the screen. The close-up look *xmag* affords can assist you in creating and editing bitmaps and other graphic images.

xmag is primarily a tool for application developers using sophisticated graphics programs. But you could also use *xmag* in concert with the *bitmap* client. For instance, say you're running a program that creates a special image on the root window and you'd like to create a *bitmap* file of a part of that image. You can display a magnification of the image you want with *xmag*, and try to recreate the image by editing in an open *bitmap* window.

If you invoke *xmag* without options, you can interactively choose the area to be magnified (the *source* area) and position the magnified image on your screen. At the command line, type:

```
% xmag &
```

The pointer changes to a small cross (the crosshair cursor) in the center of a small, hollow square with a wavering border. (By default, the square is 64 pixels on each side.) Move the crosshair cursor, placing the square over the area you want to magnify, and click the first mouse button.

The crosshair changes to an upper-left corner cursor, and the hollow square becomes enlarged to the size of the magnified image. (By default, the image is magnified five times.) Move the upper-left corner cursor, positioning the square where you want the magnified image. Again click the first mouse button and the *xmag* window containing the magnified bitmap image is displayed, as shown in Figure 6-14.

If you are using a window manager that provides titlebars, such as *twm*, the title string "Magnifying Glass" will be displayed in the *xmag* window titlebar. This is the default title string of the application.*

The default-size *xmag* window shows an area 64 pixels square, magnified five times. This magnification enables you to see the individual pixels, which are represented by squares of the same color as the corresponding pixels in the source image.

Rather than use the default source area and magnification, you can specify other values on the command line. See the *xmag* reference page in Part Three of this guide for a complete list of options.

*Applications written using the X Toolkit allow you to change the title string. See the section "Title and Name" in Chapter 8, *Command Line Options*, for details. The *xmag* client was not written using the X Toolkit and provides no method for changing the title string.

Figure 6-14. xmag window displaying magnified screen area

Quitting xmag

To exit the program, type q, Q, or Control-C in the *xmag* window.

What xmag Shows You

xmag enables you to determine the x and y coordinates, bitmap bit setting, and RGB color value of every pixel in the *xmag* window. (See Chapter 8, *Command Line Options*, for a discussion of the RGB color model.) If you move the pointer into the *xmag* window, the cursor becomes an arrow. Point the arrow at one of the magnified pixels and press and hold down the first mouse button. Across the top edge of the window, a banner displays information about the pixel, as shown in Figure 6-15.

Graphics Utilities

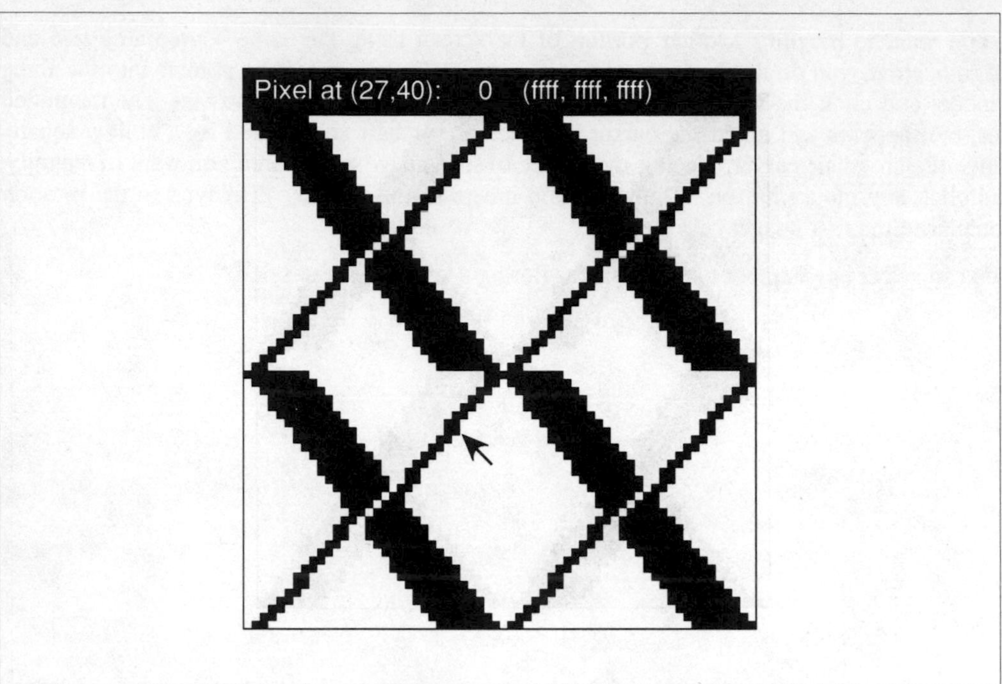

Figure 6-15. Displaying pixel statistics with xmag

The banner displays the following information about the specified pixel:

- The x and y coordinates *relative to the window*. The default *xmag* window is, in effect, a grid of 64 squares on each side. Therefore, each pixel has x,y coordinates between 0,0 and 63,63.
- The bitmap bit setting. This is either 0, if the pixel is in the background color, or 1, if the pixel is in the foreground color.
- The RGB value. This is a 16-bit value. The RGB specification is in three parts (of four hexadecimal digits each), corresponding to the three primaries in the RGB color model.

If you are trying to create a graphic image on a grid (such as the *bitmap* client provides), the x and y coordinates of each pixel can be especially useful. Also, the 16-bit RGB value specifies the color of each pixel with incredible precision. Depending on the number of colors available on your display, you can learn to use RGB values to specify an enormous range of colors.

xmag provides these pixel statistics dynamically. If you continue to hold down the first mouse button and drag the pointer across the window, the banner will display values for each pixel as the pointer indicates it.

Note that if you select a pixel near the top edge of the window, the banner will appear across the bottom edge. Otherwise, the banner would obscure the pixel you are pointing at.

Dynamically Choosing a Different Source Area

If you want to magnify another portion of the screen using the same source area size and magnification, you do not have to start *xmag* again. Simply move the pointer into the *xmag* window and click the second or third mouse button, or press the space bar. The magnified image disappears and again the cursor becomes a crosshair surrounded by a hollow square. Move the crosshair cursor, placing the square over the new source area you want to magnify, and click any mouse button. The magnified image is immediately displayed in the location you placed the first image.

You can select any number of source areas during a single *xmag* session.

7

Other Clients

This chapter gives an overview of other clients available with X, including window and display information clients, printing utilities, the xkill *program, and several "desk accessories."*

In This Chapter:

7
Other Clients

In addition to *twm* and *xterm*, the MIT distribution includes many other clients. As X becomes more widely available, there will doubtless be many applications available from third parties, just as there are in the PC world.

The clients discussed in this chapter are grouped according to basic functionality, as follows:

- Desk accessories: *xclock*, *oclock*, *xcalc*, *xbiff*, *xload*, and *xman*.
- Printing utilities: *xwd*, *xpr*, and *xdpr*.
- Program to remove a client window: *xkill*.
- Window and display information programs: *xwininfo*, *xlswins*, *xlsclients*, and *xdpyinfo*.
- Alternative window managers and other user-contributed clients.

In addition, we've included a brief discussion of X Toolkit applications.

Most sections in this chapter are intended to acquaint you with the major features of some of the available clients. Additional detailed information is provided on the reference pages for each client in Part Three of this guide.

Desk Accessories

The clients *xclock*, *oclock*, *xcalc*, *xload*, *xbiff*, and *xman* can be thought of as *desk accessories*. (Desk accessories is a term we've borrowed from the Macintosh environment, meaning small applications available—and useful—at any time.)

You can start these clients from the command line in any *xterm* window, or, if you like, you can add them to a *twm* menu (see Chapter 10, *Customizing the twm Window Manager*).

Clock Programs: xclock and oclock

The standard release of X includes two clients that display the time: *xclock* and *oclock*. The *oclock* client has been added to the standard distribution of X in Release 4.

xclock continuously displays the time, either in analog or digital form, in a standard window. The analog *xclock* shows a round 12-hour clock face, with tick marks representing the minutes. The digital *xclock* shows the 24-hour time (14:30 would be 2:30 PM) as well as the day, month, and year. You can run more than one clock at a time. The analog clock is the default. Figure 7-1 shows two *xclock* applications being run (an analog clock above a digital clock).

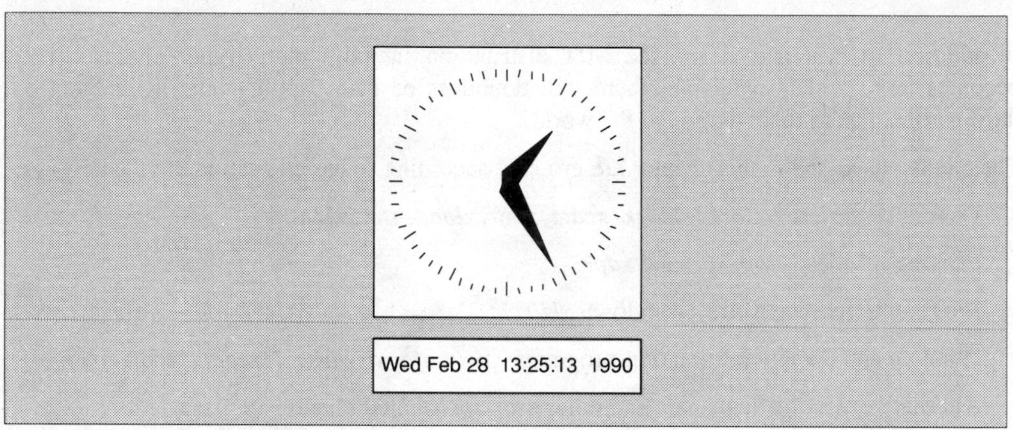

Figure 7-1. Two xclock displays: analog clock above digital clock

Usually when you invoke *xclock* you will leave the clock running. However, if you experiment with *xclock* to test size, location, or color, you will notice that there is no obvious way to delete an unwanted clock. (Moving the cursor to the clock and pressing Control-C, Control-D, q, or Q doesn't work with *xclock*.) Actually, if you are running Release 2 or 3 of X, the only way to kill the *xclock* process is as follows. First, display the current X processes with the command:

```
% ps -aux | grep xclock
```

For System V, use the command:

```
% ps -e  | grep xclock
```

and then kill the process number for the clock as described in Chapter 2, *Getting Started*.

If you are running Release 4 of X, and thus are using the *twm* window manager, you can remove an *xclock* by using the Delete command of the Twm menu. (See Chapter 3, *Using the twm Window Manager*, for more details.)

The *oclock* client (available as of Release 4) displays the time in analog form, on a round 12-hour clock face without tick marks. The only features of an *oclock* display are the round clock outline, hour and minute hands, and the "jewel" marking 12 o'clock.

Figure 7-2. oclock display

Though it is somewhat more difficult to read the precise time on the simple *oclock* display, the *oclock* is perhaps a little more aesthetic than the analog *xclock*. If you try to resize the *oclock*, you'll discover that it's possible to "stretch" it into various oblong shapes.

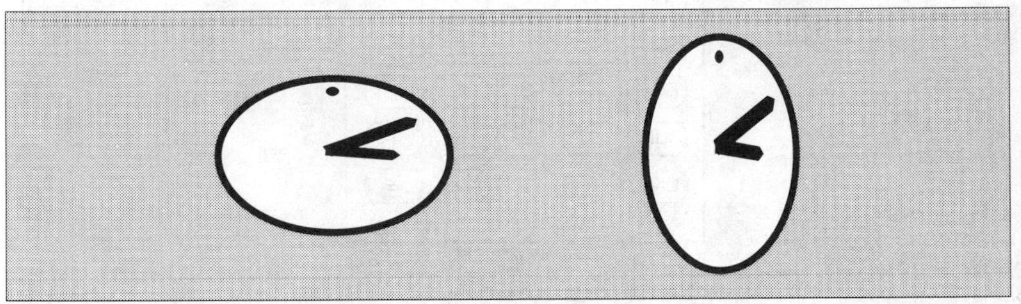

Figure 7-3. Oblong oclock displays

Though the default colors for *oclock* are black and white, it was designed to be run in color. The minute hand, hour hand, jewel, clock border, and background can all be set to a color, using either command line options (as described in Chapter 8, *Command Line Options*) or by specifying client resources (as described in Chapter 9, *Setting Resources*). See the *oclock* reference page in Part Three of this guide for the necessary command line options and color suggestions.

As is the case with *xclock*, there is no simple way to remove an *oclock* window. Use the UNIX commands *ps*, *grep*, and *kill* in the sequence described above.

The time displayed by both *xclock* and *oclock* is the system time set and displayed with the UNIX *date*(1) command.

A Scientific Calculator: xcalc

xcalc is a scientific calculator that can emulate a TI-30 or an HP-10C. Once you place the pointer within the *xcalc* window, the calculator can be operated in two ways: with the pointer, by clicking the first pointer button on the buttons in the calculator window, or with the keyboard, by typing the same numbers and symbols that are displayed in the calculator window. When using the first method, notice that the pointer appears as a small hand, enabling you to "press" the buttons. Figure 7-4 shows *xcalc* on the screen.

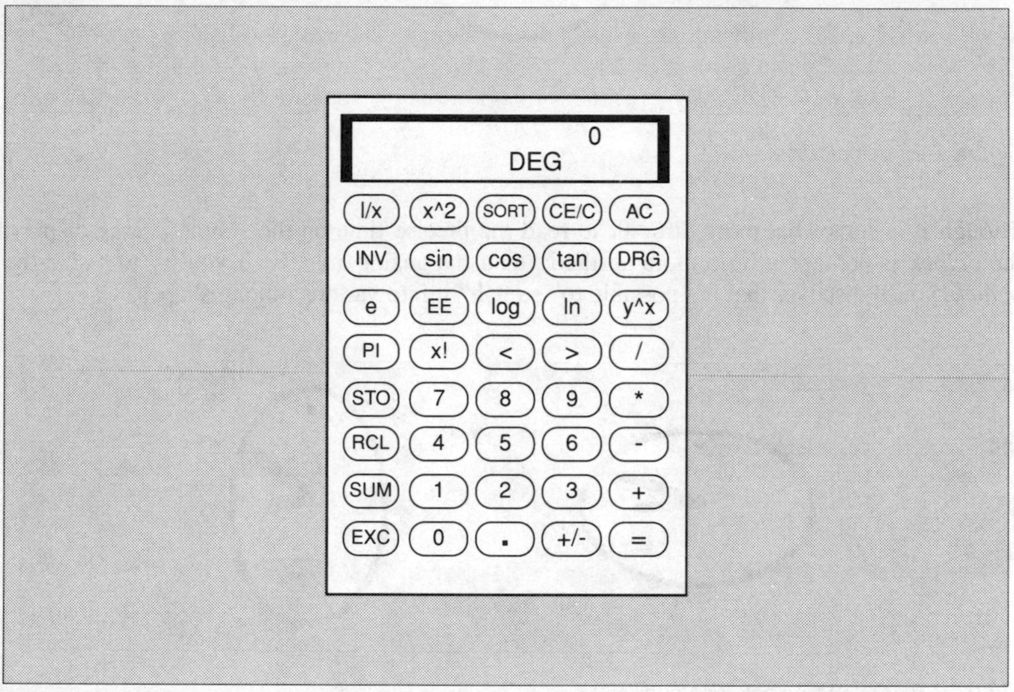

Figure 7-4. The default xcalc (TI-30 mode) on the screen

This is the version of the calculator provided with Release 4 of X. As you can see, it features oval buttons. If you are running an earlier release, the calculator will have rectangular buttons and may also have darker background coloring. These differences do not affect functionality. However, the Release 3 and Release 4 versions of *xcalc* do work somewhat differently. We've described some of those differences below. For additional information, see the *xcalc* reference page in Part Three of this guide.

The long horizontal window along the top of the calculator is the display in which the values are punched on the calculator and their results are displayed. You can enter values either by clicking on the calculator keys with the pointer, or by pressing equivalent keys on the keyboard. Most of the calculator keys have keyboard equivalents. The non-obvious equivalents are described on the *xcalc* reference page in Part Three.

By default, *xcalc* works like a Texas Instruments *TI-30* calculator. To interactively place *xcalc* in this mode, type:

```
% xcalc &
```

You can also operate the calculator in Reverse Polish Notation (like a Hewlett-Packard *HP-10C* calculator), by typing:

```
% xcalc -rpn &
```

In Reverse Polish Notation the operands are entered first, then the operator. For example, 5 `* 4 =` would be entered as 5 `Enter 4 *`. This entry sequence is designed to minimize keystrokes for complex calculations.

As of Release 4, *xcalc* allows you to select the number in the calculator display using the first (left) pointer button and paste it in another window using the second (middle) button. See Chapter 4, *The xterm Terminal Emulator*, for information about copying and pasting text selections.

The Release 4 *xcalc* can also be resized. In prior releases, this was not possible.

Also as of Release 4, *xcalc* no longer emulates a slide rule.*

For more information on the function of each of the calculator keys, see the *xcalc* reference page in Part Three of this guide.

Terminating the calculator

Terminate the calculator by either:

- Clicking the third pointer button (usually the rightmost button) on the TI calculator's AC key or the HP calculator's ON key, or:
- Positioning the pointer on the calculator and typing q, Q, or Control-C.

Mail Notification Client: xbiff

xbiff is a simple program that notifies you when you have mail. It puts up a window showing a picture of a mailbox. When you receive new mail, a beep is emitted from the keyboard, the flag on the mailbox goes up, and the image changes to reverse video. Figure 7-5 shows the *xbiff* mailbox before and after mail is received.

After you read your mail, the image changes back to its original state. Or you can click on the full mailbox icon with any pointer button to change it back to empty. (Regardless of the number of mail messages when you do this, *xbiff* remembers the current size of your mail file to be the *empty* size.)

*If you are running an earlier release of X, you can operate *xcalc* as a slide rule by using the `-analog` option. You drag the slide using the first pointer button. Be aware that the slide rule mode doesn't work very well. To terminate the slide rule, use *kill*(1), as described above for *xclock*. The slide rule emulation has been eliminated in Release 4.

Figure 7-5. xbiff before and after mail is received

Monitoring System Load Average: xload

xload periodically polls the system for the load average, and graphically displays that load using a simple histogram. By default, *xload* polls the system every 5 seconds. You can change this frequency with the `-update` option. For example, if you type the following command at an *xterm* window:

```
% xload -update 3 &
```

you can interactively place an *xload* window polling every 3 seconds.

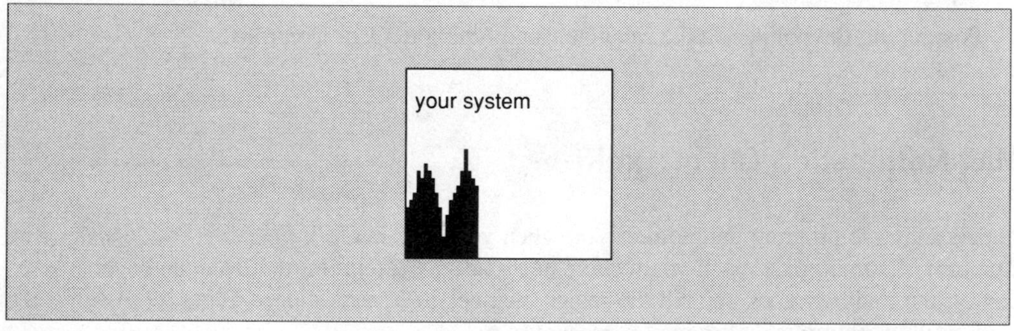

Figure 7-6. A sample xload window

If you are using both the local machine and remote machines, you can display loads for all systems and do your processing on the system that is fastest at the time.

Browsing Reference Pages: xman

The *xman* client allows you to display and browse through formatted versions of *man*ual pages (reference pages). By default, *xman* lets you look at the standard UNIX manpages found in subdirectories of the directory */usr/man*. The standard version of X assumes there are ten subdirectories: *man1* through *man8*, corresponding to the eight sections of manpages in the UNIX documentation set; *manl* (man local) and *mann* (man new). You can specify other directories by setting the MANPATH system variable. (The individual directory names should be separated by colons.)

This section describes the version of *xman* provided with Release 4 of X. From a user's viewpoint, the general operation of the client has not changed much since prior releases, but the organization of menus and options has changed. If you are running Release 3 of X, read this section for an idea of how the client works and then take a look at the next section, "Release 3 xman," for a summary of the differences.

Regardless of the version of X, you run *xman* by typing:

```
% xman &
```

in an *xterm* window.

The initial *xman* window, shown in Figure 7-7, is a small window containing only a few commands.

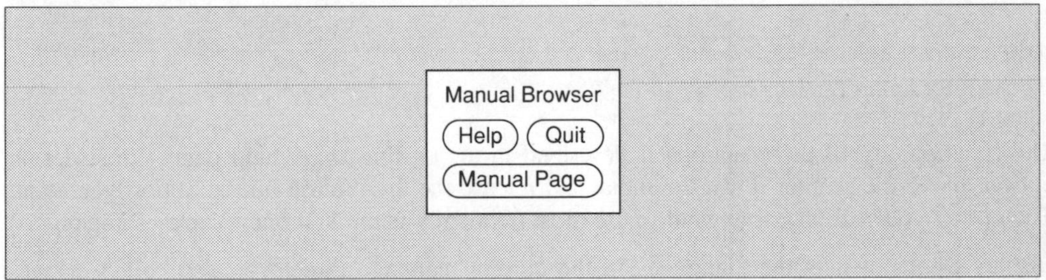

Figure 7-7. Initial xman window

This window is small enough to be displayed for prolonged periods during which you might have need to examine UNIX manual pages. You select a command by clicking on it with the first pointer button.

The Manual Page command brings up a larger window in which you can display a formatted version of any manual page in the MANPATH. By default, the first page displayed contains general help information about *xman*. Use this information to acquaint yourself with the client's features. (The actual *xman* reference page in Part Three of this guide primarily describes how to customize the client.)

Once you've opened this larger window, you can display formatted manual pages in it.* Notice the horizontal bar spanning the top edge of the window. (If you're running *twm* or a similar window manager, this bar appears beneath the titlebar provided by the window manager.) The bar is divided into three parts, labeled Options, Sections, and Xman Help. The part currently labeled Xman Help is merely informational and the text displayed in it will change depending on the contents of the window. The parts labeled Options and Sections are actually handles to two *xman* menus.

If you place the pointer on the Options box and press and hold down the first button, a menu called Xman Options will be displayed below. The menu is pictured in Figure 7-8.

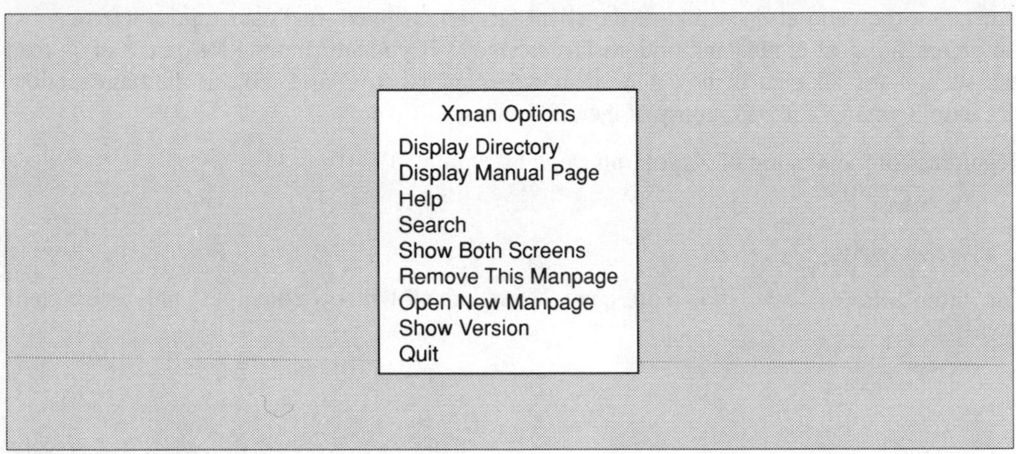

Figure 7-8. Xman Options menu

The functionality of these options is described in the on-line *xman* help page. To select an option, move the pointer down the menu and release the first button on the option you want. The option you will probably want to use most frequently is the first one, Display Directory.

Display Directory lists the manpages in the current manpage directory (also called a "section"). By default, this is *man1*, the user commands. When you list the contents of *man1* in this way, the informational section of the horizontal bar reads Directory of: (1) User Commands. You can then display a formatted version of any command reference page in the list by clicking on the command's name with the first pointer button. Figure 7-9 shows the formatted reference page for the UNIX *cd*(1) command.

*Selecting the Help command also opens a large window in which the same help information is displayed. The Help command is something of a dead end, however. You cannot display any other text in this window.

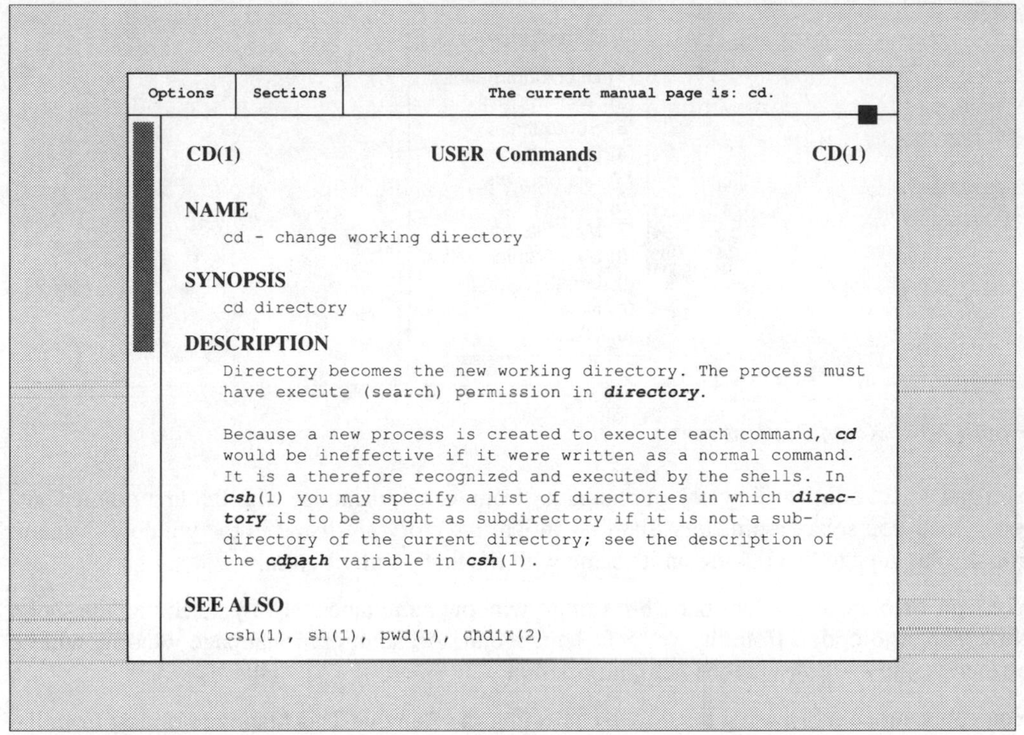
Options | Sections | The current manual page is: cd.

CD(1) USER Commands CD(1)

NAME

cd - change working directory

SYNOPSIS

cd directory

DESCRIPTION

Directory becomes the new working directory. The process must have execute (search) permission in ***directory***.

Because a new process is created to execute each command, ***cd*** would be ineffective if it were written as a normal command. It is a therefore recognized and executed by the shells. In ***csh***(1) you may specify a list of directories in which ***directory*** is to be sought as subdirectory if it is not a subdirectory of the current directory; see the description of the ***cdpath*** variable in ***csh***(1).

SEE ALSO

csh(1), sh(1), pwd(1), chdir(2)

To display another manual page from the same directory, display the Xman Options menu again. Select Display Directory, and the directory listing is again displayed in the window. Then click on another command name to display its manual page in the window. (If you decide not to display another manpage, you can remove the directory listing and go back to the manpage previously displayed by using the second Xman Options menu selection, Display Manual Page. Display Directory and Display Manual Page are toggles of one another.)

To display a manual page from another directory in the MANPATH, you must first change to that directory using the second *xman* menu, Xman Sections. You bring up the menu by placing the pointer in the Sections box in the application's titlebar and holding down the first button. The Xman Sections menu lists the default directories of UNIX manual pages, as in Figure 7-10.

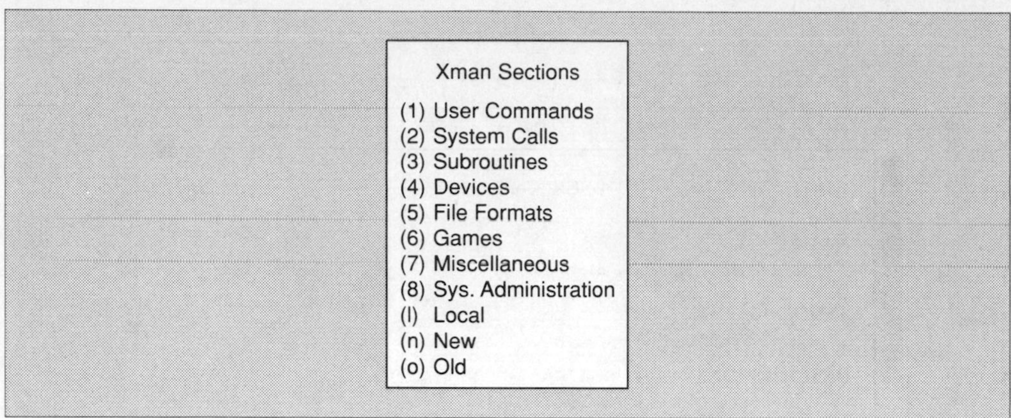

Figure 7-10. Xman Sections menu

You can select another directory of manpages from which to choose with the first pointer button. Once you select a directory, the files in that directory are listed in the window. Again, you display a page by clicking on its name with the first pointer button.

You can display more than one "browsing" window simultaneously by selecting the Open New Manpage option from the Xman Options menu. An additional manpage window will be opened, again starting with the help information.

You can remove a browsing window by selecting the Remove This Manpage option from the Xman Options menu. (Prior to Release 4, selecting this option resulted in an error and caused the *xman* program to exit.)

Selecting Quit from the Xman Options menu or from the initial *xman* window causes the client to exit.

Release 3 xman

In the Release 3 version of *xman*, the horizontal bar spanning the top of the browsing window merely contains information about the contents of the window. It is not divided and it does not contain obvious text handles to any menus.

Though it may not be readily apparent, you can access the Xman Options menu simply by placing the pointer in the horizontal bar. You can then display manpages from the default directory by following the steps outlined in the previous section. Xman Options is the only menu directly accessible from the horizontal bar.

The Release 3 Xman Options menu differs slightly in options and organization from the Release 4 menu. The Release 3 menu is pictured in Figure 7-11.

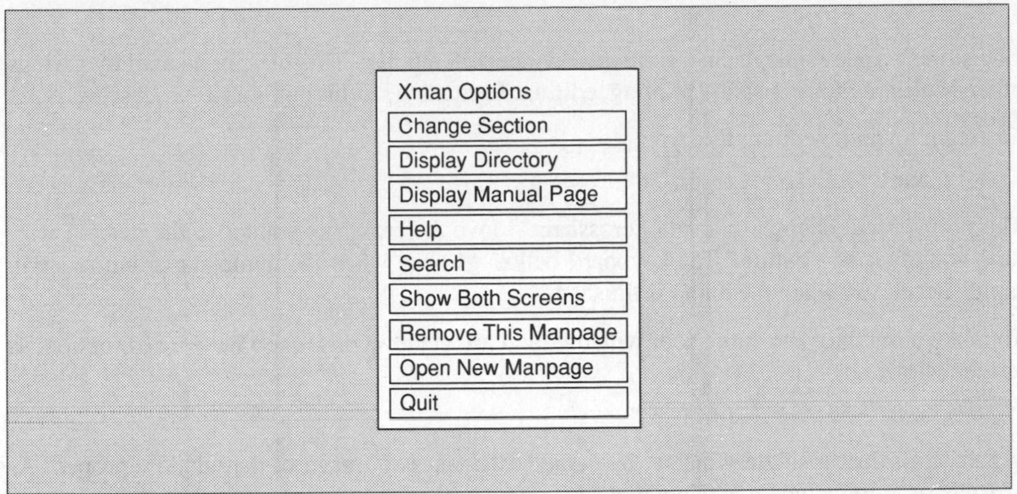

Figure 7-11. Release 3 Xman Options menu

Again, you can acquaint yourself with the various options by reading the help information displayed on the initial manual page. Most of the options and functionality are the same as described above for Release 4.

The most significant difference is the method of changing directories within the MANPATH. As we've seen in the Release 4 version of *xman*, this is accomplished through the Xman Sections menu, which is accessible directly from the horizontal bar. In the Release 3 version, in order to change directories you must first bring up the Xman Options menu. Then select the first option, Change Section (which has been removed from the Release 4 menu). A *sub-menu* of Xman Options, called Manual Sections, will be displayed. This sub-menu is the R3 equivalent of the R4 Xman Sections menu.

Like Xman Sections, the Manual Sections menu lists the default directories of UNIX manual pages. You can select an alternate directory by the method described in the previous section.

The Release 3 version of *xman* has one serious limitation. Selecting the option Remove This Manpage from the Xman Options menu results in an error and causes the *xman* program to exit. (This error has been corrected in Release 4.)

Printing Utilities: xwd, xpr, xdpr

xwd stores window images in a formatted window dump file. This file can be read by various other X utilities for redisplay, printing, editing, formatting, archiving, image processing, etc.

To create a window dump file, type:

```
% xwd > file
```

The pointer will change to a small crosshair. Move the crosshair pointer to the desired window and click any button. The keyboard bell rings once when the dump starts and twice in rapid succession when the dump is finished.

To make a dump of the entire root window (and all windows on it), use the `-root` option, as in the following:

```
% xwd -root > file
```

When you select a single window, by default *xwd* takes an image of the window proper. As of Release 4, to include a window manager frame or titlebar, use the `-frame` option.

To redisplay a file created with *xwd* in a window on the screen, use the *xwud* client, an *u*ndumping utility. Specify the dump file to display as an argument to the `-in` option, as in the following:

```
% xwud -in file
```

Then remove the image be typing Control-C in the *xterm* from which you started *xwud.*

xpr takes as input an X Window System dump file produced by *xwd* and converts it to a printer-specific format that can be printed on the DEC LN03 or LA100 printer, a PostScript printer such as the Apple LaserWriter, the IBM PP3812 page printer, and as of Release 4, the HP LaserJet (or other PCL printers) or the HP PaintJet. By default, output is formatted for the DEC LN03 printer. Use the `-device` option to format for another printer. For example, to format a window dump file for a PostScript printer, type:

```
% xpr -device ps file > file.ps
```

Other options allow you to change the size, add headers or footers, and so on. See the *xpr* reference page in Part Three of this guide for details.

You can use *xwd* and *xpr* together, using the standard UNIX pipe mechanism. For example:

```
% xwd | xpr -device ps | lpr
```

The *xdpr* command rolls these three separate commands into one. See the *xdpr* reference page in Part Three of this guide for details.

Note that when you start piping together the output of X clients, you run into some ambiguities. For example, if you pipe the output of *xwd* to *xpr*, and for some reason, the *xpr* command fails, *xwd* will still be there waiting for pointer input. The original UNIX pipe mechanism doesn't have the concept of data dependent on pointer input! The integration of the UNIX model of computing (in which standard input and output are always recognized), and the window model, is not always complete, leading sometimes to unexpected behavior.

As an even more flagrant example, you can create a pipe between two programs the first of which doesn't produce standard output, and the second of which doesn't recognize standard input. The shell doesn't know any better, and the programs themselves go on their merry way with pointer and windows.

However, it is nice to know that you can pipe together output of programs, even when some of those programs may not produce output until you intervene with the pointer.

Even without pipes, you should start thinking about how these programs could work together. For example, the pictures of fonts in Appendix E, *Release 3 and 4 Standard Fonts*, were created by these steps:

1. Display a font with *xfd*. (See Chapter 5, *Font Specification*, for instructions on how to use *xfd*.)
2. Resize the window to improve readability, using the *twm* resize box on the titlebar.
3. Create a window dump file with the command `xwd >` *`file`*.
4. Create a PostScript file from the dump with the command:

   ```
   xpr -device ps file> file.ps
   ```

5. Print the PostScript file on an Apple LaserWriter with the standard print command *lpr*(1).

Even though the UNIX shell will accept a pipe between *xfd*, *xwd*, and *xpr*, what actually happens is that *xwd* starts up faster than *xfd*, and is ready to dump a window before the *xfd* window appears.

Killing a Client Window with xkill

The *xkill* program allows you to kill a client window, or more specifically, to force the server to end the connection to the client. The process exits and the associated window is removed.

xkill is a fairly drastic method of terminating a client and should *not* be used as the method of preference. In most cases, clients can be terminated in other ways. The possible repercussions of using *xkill* and some of the alternatives are discussed in the next section.

xkill is intended primarily to be used in cases where more conventional methods of removing a client window do not work. It is especially useful when programs have displayed undesired windows on the screen. To remove a stubborn client window, type:

```
% xkill
```

on the command line of an *xterm* window. The pointer changes to a "draped box" pointer and you are instructed to:

```
Select the window whose client you wish to kill with button 1 . . .
```

Move the draped box pointer to the window you want to remove, as in Figure 7-12, and click the first pointer button. The window is removed. (*xkill* does not allow you to select the root window.)

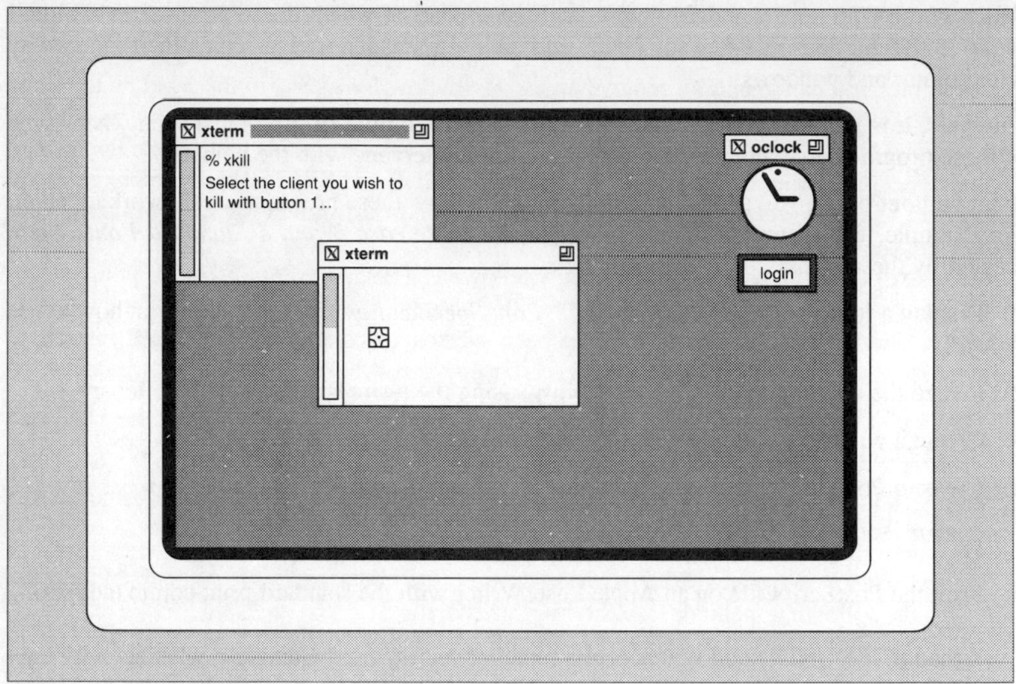

Figure 7-12. Selecting the window to be removed

You can also specify the window to be killed by its *resource ID*. Every window has an identification number associated with it. The *xwininfo* client can be used to display a window's resource ID (see the section "Window and Display Information" later in this chapter).

To remove a window using its ID number, type:

```
% xkill -id number
```

The window with the ID `number` is removed. Killing a window by its ID number is more cumbersome, but it's somewhat safer than choosing the window to be killed with the pointer. It's too easy to click in the wrong place. (Of course, it's less treacherous to use the pointer on an isolated window than a window in a stack.)

Problems with Killing a Client

The most obvious problem with *xkill* is that it's possible to kill the wrong window inadvertently. Perhaps less obvious is a problem inherent in 'killing' a program. As a general rule, a command that 'kills' a program does not give the program time to save or complete processes that are still running—in effect, to clean up after itself. The processes that can be adversely affected may be visible to the user, like an editing session, or they may be underlying system processes, like writing to or reading from a socket.

Most clients can be terminated in ways that allow them to finish all relevant processes and then exit cleanly. These methods should be attempted *before* you use *xkill*, or some other program that kills the client.

For example, you can generally remove an *xterm* window by typing in the window the same command you use to log off the system. You should also be able to remove an *xterm* window with various Main Options menu commands, depending on the signals that can be interpreted by your system. (Some of these signals, such as SIGHUP and SIGTERM, are more gentle to the system. See the *xterm* reference page in Part Three of this guide for a list of menu commands and the signals they send.) An *xcalc* window can generally be removed by typing q, Q, or Control-C in the window. A *bitmap* window has a Quit button box, etc. If you are running Release 4 of X, the Twm menu also provides an item, Delete, which allows you to safely remove a client window if the client has been written to comply with standard interclient communication conventions. (See Chapter 3, *Using the twm Window Manager*, for details.)

A few clients, such as *oclock*, cannot be removed *except* by killing. You must use *xkill*, or a similar method, to remove an *oclock* window.

Generally, however, you should exhaust the safer alternatives before you use *xkill* and other commands that kill a client.

When you want to remove a window, depending on the client and what commands it recognizes, try the following methods (roughly) in this order:

1. Methods that cause the client to exit after finishing relevant processes:

   a. Special commands (e.g., `logout`, `exit`) or key sequences (e.g., Control-D, Control-C, q, Q) recommended to stop a client.

   b. Certain application-specific menu items (e.g., for *xterm*, the Main Options menu commands Send HUP Signal, Send TERM Signal, and Quit; the *bitmap* Quit box).

   c. The Delete item on the Twm menu. (Whether this works depends on whether the client to be removed has been written to comply with the interclient communication conventions. If other safe methods have failed and Delete doesn't work, you may need to take more drastic measures.)

2. When these methods don't work, or don't apply (as in the case of *oclock*), *then* use commands or menu items that kill the client:

   a. The Send KILL Signal item on the *xterm* Main Options menu, for removing *xterm* windows only (see Chapter 4, *The xterm Terminal Emulator*).

   b. The Kill item on the Twm menu (see Chapter 3, *Using the twm Window Manager*). (If you are running Release 3 of X, you can use the KillWindow item on the *uwm* WindowOps menu. See Appendix B, *The uwm Window Manager*, for details.)

c. The UNIX *kill* command with the client's process id number, which is determined using *ps*. (This method of removing a window is described for *xclock* in Chapter 2, *Getting Started*.*)

d. The *xkill* client.

Be warned that older versions of *xkill* can have surprising complications. For example, some older versions of *xkill* do not seem to work properly with the window manager *twm*. *twm* automatically becomes the parent process of all the top level windows in the window hierarchy. (See the discussion of *xlswins* later in this chapter for more information about the window hierarchy.) If you use *xkill* to kill a top level window, *twm* is killed instead, and the window remains. Most problems such as these should have been solved as of Release 3.

Window and Display Information Clients

The standard release of X includes four clients that provide information about windows on the display and about the display itself. Much of the information is probably more relevant to a programmer than to the typical user. However, these clients also provide certain pieces of information, such as window geometry, window ID numbers, and the number and nature of screens on the display, that can assist you in using other clients.

Displaying Information about a Window: xwininfo

The *xwininfo* client displays information about a particular window. As described in Chapter 8, *Command Line Options*, much of this information is useful in determining or setting window geometry. *xwininfo* also provides you with the *window ID* (also called the resource ID). Each window has a unique identification number associated with it. This number can be used as a command line argument with several clients. Most notably, the window ID can be supplied to the *xkill* client to specify the window be killed.†

To display information about a window, type the following command in an *xterm* window:

```
% xwininfo
```

The pointer changes to the crosshair pointer, and you are directed to select the window about which you want information:

---

*This method is powerful, but in practice has limitations. Many versions of UNIX only allow you to kill a process if you are the owner of the process or if you are root. Thus, if a client has been started on your display from a remote system, and you don't know the root password, you may not be in a position to use the UNIX *kill* command.

†You can also use the window ID as an argument to the *xprop* client, which displays various window "properties." A property is a piece of information associated with a window or a font. Properties facilitate communication between clients via the server. They are used by clients to store information that other clients might need to know, and to read that information when it is provided by other clients. See the *xprop* reference page in Part Three of this guide, and Volume One, *Xlib Programming Manual* for more information about properties and the *xprop* client.

```
xwininfo ==> Please select the window about which you
         ==> would like information by clicking the
         ==> mouse in that window.
```

You can select any window on the display, including the window in which you've typed the command and the root window. (Rather than using the pointer, you can specify a window on the command line by supplying its title, or name, if it has no title, as an argument to *xwininfo*'s own `-name` option. See Chapter 8, *Command Line Options*, for information about setting a client's title and name. See the *xwininfo* reference page in Part Three of this guide for a list of its options.)

Figure 7-13 shows the statistics the Release 4 version of *xwininfo* supplies, with some typical readings.

```
xwininfo ==> Window id: 0x40000f (xterm)

         ==> Absolute upper-left X: 0
         ==> Absolute upper-left Y: 0
         ==> Relative upper-left X: 0
         ==> Relative upper-left Y: 21
         ==> Width: 578
         ==> Height: 316
         ==> Depth: 1
         ==> Border width: 1
         ==> Window class: InputOutput
         ==> Colormap: 0x80065
         ==> Window Bit Gravity State: NorthWestGravity
         ==> Window Window Gravity State: NorthWestGravity
         ==> Window Backing Store State: NotUseful
         ==> Window Save Under State: no
         ==> Window Map State: IsViewable
         ==> Window Override Redirect State: no
         ==> Corners:  +0+0  -572+0  -572-582  +0-582
```

Figure 7-13. Window information displayed by xwininfo

These readings are for a login *xterm* window displayed using a 12 point Roman Courier font. All numerical information is in pixels, except depth, which is in bits per pixel. The *twm* window manager is also running. The statistics that are most significant for the average user are listed below:

```
xwininfo ==> Window id: 0x40000f (xterm)

         ==> Absolute upper-left X: 0
         ==> Absolute upper-left Y: 0
         ==> Relative upper-left X: 0
         ==> Relative upper-left Y: 21
         ==> Width: 578
         ==> Height: 316
         ==> Depth: 1
         ==> Border width: 1
         ==> Colormap: 0x80065
         ==> Corners:  +0+0  -572+0  -572-582  +0-582
```

The first piece of information is the window ID, which can be used as an argument to *xkill*. Specifying the window to be killed by its ID number is somewhat less risky than choosing it with the pointer.

The other statistics (with the exception of depth) can be used to gauge the window's geometry (size and position). The absolute upper-left X and Y correspond to the positive x and y offsets of the window from the root window. These figures can be used on the command line to specify window placement, as described in Chapter 8, *Command Line Options*.

The relative upper-left X and Y are significant only if you're running a window manager, such as *twm*, that provides some sort of frame. The relative upper-left X and Y are the window's x and y offsets relative to its frame. In this example, the relative upper-left Y of 21 pixels refers to the height of the window's titlebar.

The four corners are listed with the upper left corner first and the other three clockwise around the window (i.e., upper right, lower right, lower left). The upper left corner always gives the positive x and y offsets for the window. The width and height in pixels are somewhat less useful, since the geometry option to *xterm* requires that these figures be specified in characters and lines. See Chapter 8, *Command Line Options*, for more information about window geometry and how to set it based on the results of *xwininfo*.

The values for window depth and colormap relate to how color is specified. See the discussion of color in Chapter 8 for more information.

Be aware that the Release 3 version of *xwininfo* does not provide relative x and y offsets. It does provide absolute x and y offsets, though they are labeled simply as:

```
==> Upper left X: 0
==> Upper left Y: 0
```

The other statistics provided by *xwininfo* are listed below:

```
==> Window class: InputOutput
==> Window Bit Gravity State: NorthWestGravity
==> Window Window Gravity State: NorthWestGravity
==> Window Backing Store State: NotUseful
==> Window Save Under State: no
==> Window Map State: IsViewable
==> Window Override Redirect State: no
```

These statistics have to do with the underlying mechanics of how a window is resized, moved, obscured, unobscured, and otherwise manipulated. They are inherent in the client program and you cannot specify alternatives. For more information on these and other window attributes, see Chapter 4 in Volume One, *Xlib Programming Manual*.

You can also use *xwininfo* with various options to display other window attributes. See the reference page in Part Three of this guide for details.

Listing the Window Tree: xlswins

Windows are arranged in a hierarchy, much like a family tree, with the root window at the top. The *xlswins* client displays the window tree starting with the root window, listing each window by its resource ID and title (or name), if it has one. (See Chapter 8, *Command Line Options*, for a discussion of setting a client's title and name with command line options.)

A resource ID can be supplied to *xkill* to specify the window to kill. You can also supply a resource ID to *xwininfo* to specify the window you want information about, or to *xprop* to get the window's properties. Being able to display the ID numbers of all windows on the screen at once is especially helpful if one or more windows is obscured in the stack. The *xwininfo* client is virtually useless in situations in which one window is hidden behind another. *xlswins* allows you to determine, by process of elimination, which window is hidden—without having to circulate all the windows on your screen. You can then use *xwininfo* with the ID number (displayed by *xlswins*) to get information about the obscured window.

Figure 7-14 shows the results of *xlswins* for a simple window arrangement: a single *xterm* (login) window on a root window.

```
0x8006e  ()
  0x30000e   (xterm)
    0x300015   ()
      0x300016   ()
```

Figure 7-14. Window tree displayed by xlswins

The *xterm* window is easily identified. Any client that displays a window, such as *xterm*, *xclock*, *xfd*, *bitmap*, etc., will be listed by name (in parentheses) following the ID number.* The root window is listed above the *xterm* in the window hierarchy. Client (and other) windows displayed on the root window are called *children* of the root window, in keeping with the family tree analogy. Thus, the root window is the parent of the *xterm* window. In the *xlswins* listing, a child window is indented once under its parent.

But what are the other windows listed in Figure 7-14? A superficial examination of these other windows provides a brief introduction to the inner workings of X. An underlying feature of X is that menus, boxes, icons, and even *features* of client windows, such as scrollbars, are actually windows in their own right. What's more, these windows (and client window icons) may still be considered to exist, even when they are not displayed.

The two remaining windows are unnamed. From the relative indents of the windows, we can tell certain information. The first unnamed window is a child of the *xterm*, the second is a child of the child.

If we again run *xlswins*, this time requesting a long listing (with the `-l` option), we get geometry information that helps identify each window, as shown in Figure 7-15.

```
0:  0x8006e  ()     1152x900+0+0  +0+0
1:    0x30000e  (xterm)    818x484+0+0  +0+0
2:      0x300015  ()     818x484+0+0  +1+1
3:        0x300016  ()     14x484+-1+-1   +0+0
```

Figure 7-15. Window tree with geometry specifications

The first number on each line refers to the level of the window in the hierarchy, the root window being at level 0, client windows at 1, etc. The first geometry string is the complete

***Most likely, you will not have to deal with the ID numbers for windows other than the explicitly named client windows. You can use the IDs of the client windows in all of the ways we've discussed: with *xkill*, *xwininfo*, *xprop*, etc.**

specification relative to the *parent* window. The second geometry string is the current position relative to the *root* window. A window at coordinates 0,0 would have the position +0+0 relative to the root. The two unnamed windows under *xterm* are the VT102 window and the window's scrollbar, respectively. (The first *xterm* listing is the application shell window, which can be displayed both as a VT102 and a Tektronix window.)

The listing in Figure 7-15 was generated when the *twm* window manager was not running. Many of the features provided by *twm*, such as the window "frame" and its command buttons, the icon manager, and menus, are actually all windows. This *greatly* complicates the window hierarchy. If you run *xlswins* while *twm* is running, you can assume that most of the mysterious windows in the hierarchy are features provided by the window manager.

For more information on the window hierarchy, see Volume One, *Xlib Programming Manual*.

Listing the Currently Running Clients: xlsclients

You can get a listing of the client applications running on a particular display by using *xlsclients*. Without any options, *xlsclients* displays a two-column list, similar to the following:

```
colorful  xterm -geometry 80x24+10+10 -ls
colorful  xclock -geometry -0-0
```

The first column shows the name of the display (machine) and the second the client running on it. The client is represented by the command line used to initiate the process.

This sample listing indicates that there is one *xterm* window and one *xclock* window running on the display `colorful`. (The option `-ls` following the *xterm* command reveals that the shell running in this window is a login shell.) The list is alphabetical.

You can use *xlsclients* to create an *.xsession* file, which specifies the clients you want to be run automatically when you log in. In order to do this, you must have set up client windows in an arrangement you like using command line options alone (that is, without having moved or resized windows via the window manager). You can then run *xlsclients* to print a summary of the command lines you used to set up the display and include those command lines in your *.xsession* file. See Appendix A, *System Management*, for information on setting up a user session.

By default, *xlsclients* lists the clients running on the display corresponding to the DISPLAY environment variable, almost always the local display. You can list the clients running on another display by using the `-display` command line option. See Chapter 8, *Command Line Options*, for details.

With the option `-l` (indicating long), *xlsclients* generates a more detailed listing. Figure 7-16 shows the long version of the listing above.

For each client, *xlsclients* displays six items of information: the window ID number, machine name, client name, icon name, command line used to run the client, and what are known as the instance and class resource names associated with the client.

```
Window 0x30000e:
  Machine:  colorful
  Name:  xterm
  Icon Name:  xterm
  Command:  xterm -geometry 80x24+10+10 -ls
  Instance/Class:  xterm/XTerm
Window 0x40000b:
  Machine:  colorful
  Name:  xclock
  Icon Name:  xclock
  Command:  xclock -geometry -0-0
  Instance/Class:  xclock/XClock
```

Figure 7-16. Long xlsclients listing

As we'll see in Chapter 8, *Command Line Options*, many clients, including *xterm*, allow you to specify an alternate name for a client and a title for the client's window. If you've specified a title, it will appear in the *xlsclients* `Name` field. If you haven't specified a title, but have specified a name for the application, the name will appear in this field. Neither of the clients in the sample display has been given an alternate name or title.

You use the instance and class resource names to specify default window characteristics, generally by placing them in a file in your home directory. This is described in detail in Chapter 9, *Setting Resources*.

Generating Information about the Display: xdpyinfo

The *xdpyinfo* client gives information about the X display, including the name of the display (contents of the DISPLAY variable), version and release of X, number of screens, current screen, and statistics relating to the color, resolution, input, and storage capabilities of each screen. The *xdpyinfo* reference page in Part Three of this guide shows a listing for a display that supports both a color and monochrome screen.

Much of the information provided by *xdpyinfo* has to do with how clients communicate information to one another and is more relevant to a programmer than to the typical user. However, the basic statistics about the name of the display, the version and release of X, and the number and nature of screens might be very helpful to a user, particularly one who is using a display for the first time.

In addition, the detailed information about each screen's color capabilities can also be very valuable in learning how to use color more effectively. This information includes the default number of colormap cells: the number of colors you can use on the display at any one time. See Chapter 8, *Command Line Options*, for more information on the use of color and how to specify colors for many clients.

See Volume One, *Xlib Programming Manual*, for insights into some of the other information provided by *xdpyinfo*.

User-contributed Clients

In addition to the clients in the standard MIT X distribution, there are many user-contributed clients available in the X source tree, distributed over Usenet, and perhaps included with various commercial distributions. If you have access to Usenet, the newsgroup *comp.windows.x* contains voluminous discussions of X programming and the newsgroup *comp.sources.x* contains sources.

Prior to Release 4, *uwm* (the *u*niversal *w*indow *m*anager) was the official window manager shipped with the standard X Window System. As of Release 4, *uwm* is no longer supported, but is still available as a user-contributed client. However, be aware that *uwm* does not comply with accepted interclient communication conventions and thus, should probably not be the window manager of choice.

Several other window managers are widely used and have been tailored to reflect the interclient communication conventions proposed in Release 3. Some of the more popular window managers that reflect these conventions are:

awm — Ardent window manager (written by Jordan Hubbard of Ardent Computer Corporation).

rtl — Tiled window manager (written by Ellis Cohen at Siemens Research & Technology Laboratories, RTL).

olwm — OPEN LOOK window manager (developed by AT&T).

mwm — Motif window manager (written by Ellis Cohen at the Open Software Foundation).

Appendix C, *The OSF/Motif Window Manager*, discusses *mwm* in greater detail.

Commercial products (such as spreadsheets, word processors, and graphics or publishing applications) based on the X Window System are also becoming available.

X Toolkit Applications

Many clients have been written (or rewritten) with a programming library called the X Toolkit. The X Toolkit provides a number of predefined components called *widgets*. Widgets make it easier to create complex applications; they also ensure a consistent user interface between applications.

Most of the clients described in this guide were written before the X Toolkit was fully developed. Although they have since been rewritten to use the X Toolkit, they don't necessarily make full use of all its features.

However, most of the standard clients use enough of these features that you can see what to expect from future applications that are based more fully on the X Toolkit.

This section briefly reviews some features of X Toolkit applications, with reference to where they are implemented in the current crop of clients. For a comprehensive treatment of the X Toolkit, see Volumes Four and Five, *X Toolkit Intrinsics Programming Manual* and *X Toolkit Intrinsics Reference Manual*.

Dialog Boxes and Command Buttons

A *dialog box* is used when an application requires a small piece of information from the user, such as a filename. A dialog box typically has three elements: it always has the first element, and may or may not have the second and/or third elements in the following list:

- A prompt that identifies the purpose of the widget. This might be as simple as the string "Filename:".
- An area in which you can type your response.
- Command buttons that allow you to confirm or cancel the dialog input.

A dialog box is usually a pop-up window, which goes away after the required information is provided.

The X client *bitmap* is one of the few current applications that use a dialog box. It displays the dialog displayed in Figure 7-17 when you quit the application. Future X applications can be expected to make far more extensive use of dialogs like this.

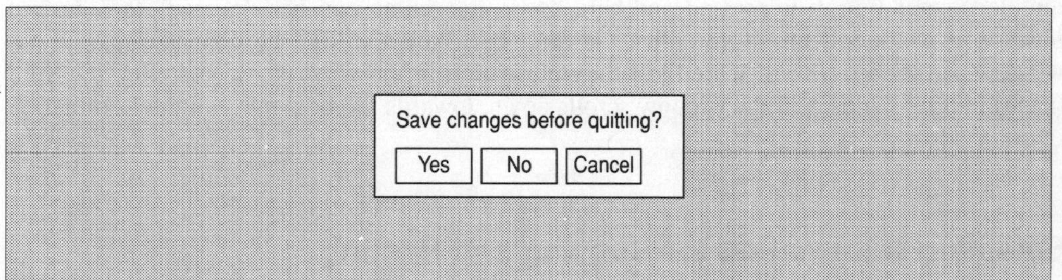

Figure 7-17. A dialog box with Yes, No, and Cancel command buttons

Each *command button* in the box is itself a widget. A command button is a rectangle that contains a text label. When the pointer is on the button, its border is highlighted to indicate that the button is available for selection. When a pointer button is clicked, some action (presumably indicated by the label) is performed by the program.

Some applications use the following convention for command buttons. Whenever you press a button that may cause you to lose some work or is otherwise dangerous, a second dialog box will appear asking you to confirm the action. This dialog box will contain an Abort button and a Confirm button. Pressing the Abort button cancels the operation, and pressing the Confirm button will proceed with the operation.

(A very handy shortcut exists in some applications: if you press the original button again, it will be interpreted as a Confirm. If you press any other command button, it will be interpreted as an Abort.)

Scrollbars

As described in the discussion of *xterm* in Chapter 4, *The xterm Terminal Emulator*, applications can use a scrollbar to move up and down through data that is too large to fit in a window. A *scrollbar* is an X Toolkit widget.

The scrollbar consists of a sliding bar (often called the *thumb*) within a columnar slide region. The size of the thumb within the scrollbar corresponds to the amount of the data displayed within the visible portion of the window with respect to the entire body of data. If no data has yet been displayed in the window, the thumb fills the entire scrolling region, as shown in Figure 7-18.

xterm uses a vertical scrollbar; other applications may use a horizontal scrollbar, or both. One type of widget that can have both horizontal and vertical scrollbars is called a *viewport*.

When the pointer is moved into the scrollbar, the cursor appears as an arrow that points in the direction that scrolling can occur. If scrolling can occur in either direction, the cursor appears as a two-headed arrow.

When the middle pointer button is clicked at any point in the scrollbar, the thumb moves to that point, and the data in the window scrolls to the corresponding position. When the middle pointer button is pressed and held down, the thumb can be "dragged" to a desired position in the scrollbar. If you click the first (left) button in the scrollbar, the data in the window scrolls up, toward the end of the information in the window. If you click the third (right) button, the data in the window scrolls down, towards the beginning of the information in the window.

Selecting Information for Copying and Pasting

As described in the discussion of *xterm* in Chapter 4, when you select contents from one file, those contents become the PRIMARY selection, which is available to other clients. For example, you can select text in one *xterm* window and paste the text into any other *xterm* window. See Chapter 4, *The xterm Terminal Emulator*, for a complete discussion of copying and pasting. In applications written with the X Toolkit, selections are a method of widget-to-widget communication.

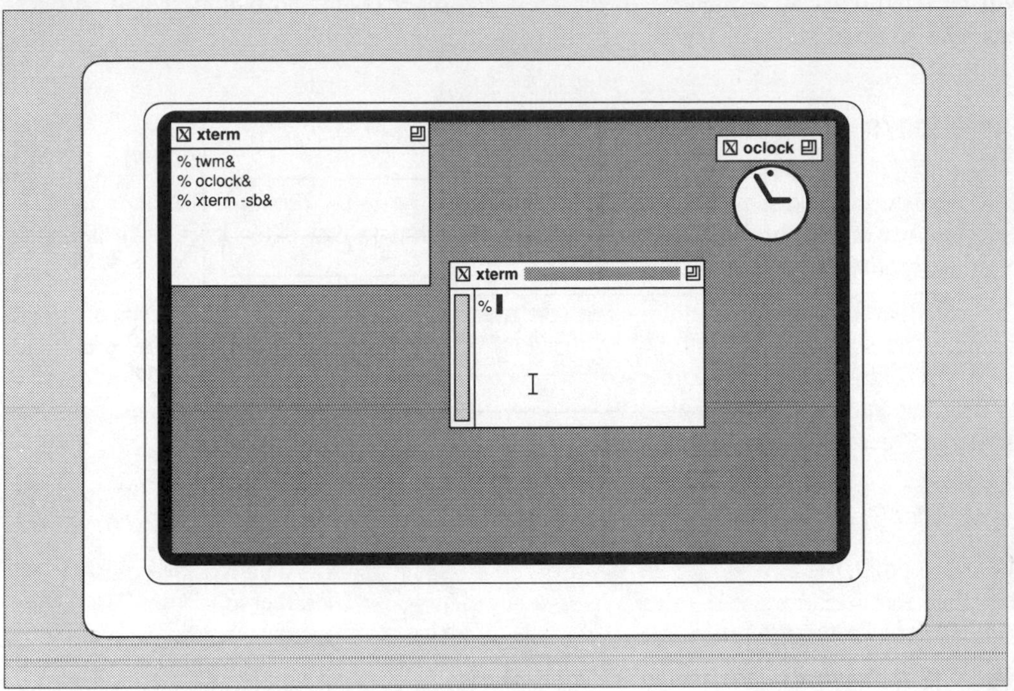

Figure 7-18. An xterm window with scrollbar

Vertical Panes

A *VPaned* widget arranges a series of windows one above the other without overlapping (i.e., they are *vertically tiled*).

A small region, called a *grip*, appears on the border between each subwindow. When the pointer is positioned on the grip and a button pressed, an arrow is displayed that indicates the direction in which the border between the two windows can be moved. If you move the pointer in the direction of the arrow (while keeping the button depressed), one subwindow will grow, while the other will shrink.

The individual panes can be any other type of widget. For example, the *xmh* mail handler includes dialog boxes with buttons, viewports containing text widgets and so on, as shown in Figure 7-19. (We refer to the *xmh* client solely to illustrate vertical panes that can be used by other X clients. The current *xmh* client is not discussed in this guide.)

Other Clients

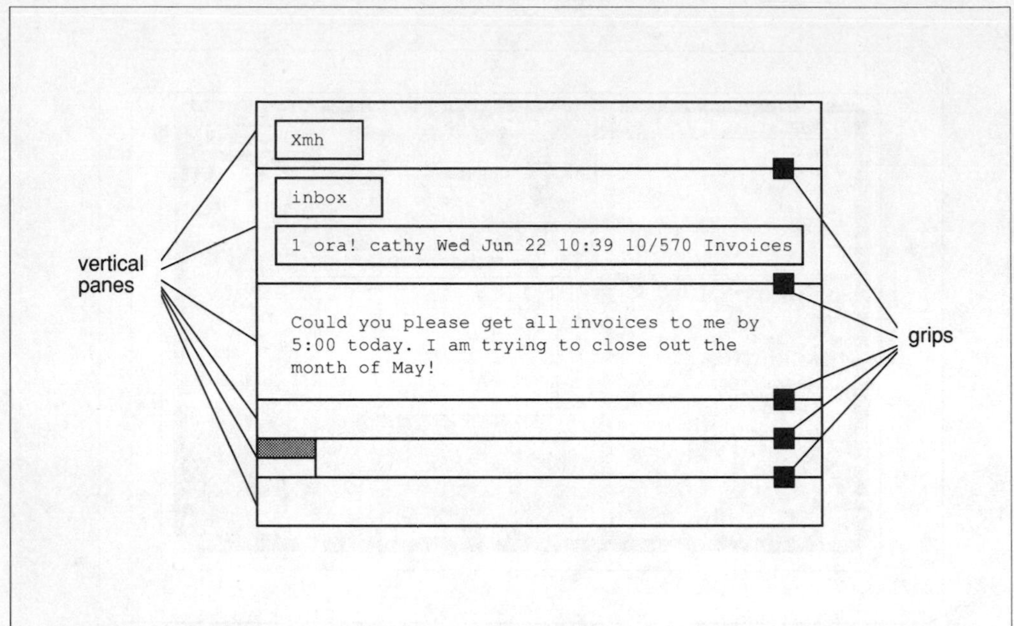

Figure 7-19. Vertical panes and grips in the xmh client

Viewports

A *viewport* is a composite widget that provides a main window and horizontal and/or vertical scrollbars. *xman* is an application that uses a viewport widget, as illustrated by Figure 7-20.

Text Editing Widget

Many applications include one or more areas in which you can enter text. All such text entry areas support the same set of editing commands. At this point, *xedit*, *xmh*, and several user-contributed clients use the *text* widget.

In applications (such as *xedit*) that use the text widget, various Control and Meta keystroke combinations are bound to a set of commands similar to those provided by the *emacs* text editor.* In addition, the pointer buttons may be used to select a portion of text or to move the insertion point in the text. Pressing the first pointer button (usually the left button) causes the insertion point to move to the pointer. Double-clicking the first button selects a word, triple-clicking selects a paragraph, and quadruple-clicking selects everything. Any selection may be extended in either direction by using the third pointer button (usually the right).

*The commands may be bound to keys different from the defaults described below through the standard X Toolkit key rebinding mechanisms.

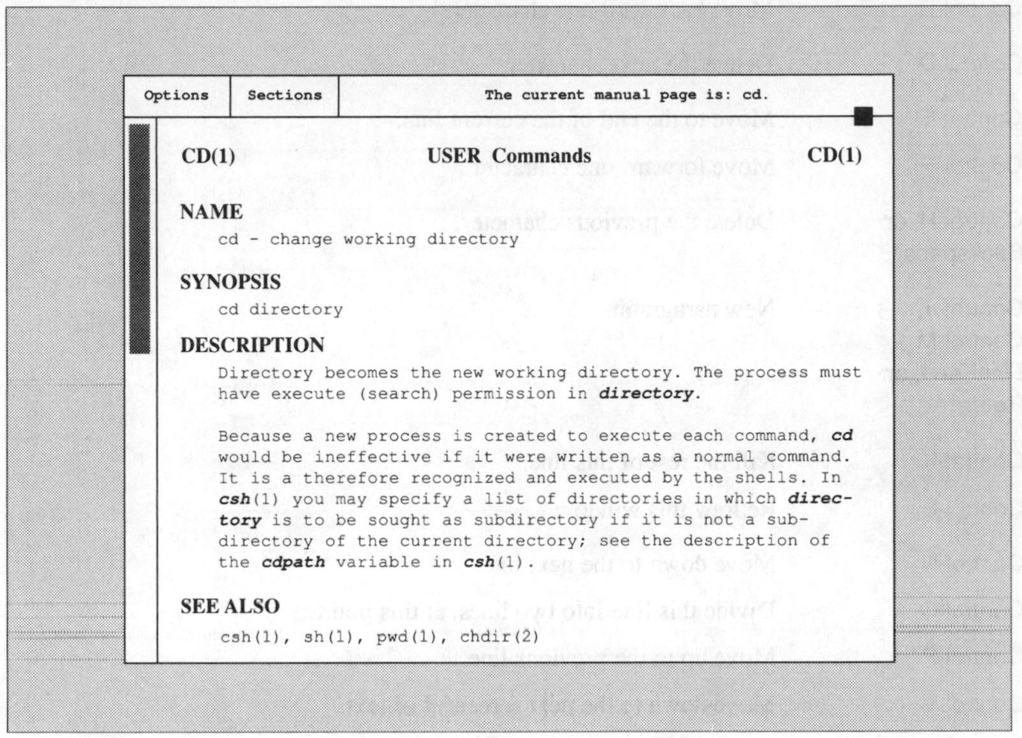

Options
Sections
The current manual page is: cd.
CD(1)
USER Commands
CD(1)
NAME
cd - change working directory
SYNOPSIS
cd directory
DESCRIPTION
Directory becomes the new working directory. The process must have execute (search) permission in directory.
Because a new process is created to execute each command, cd would be ineffective if it were written as a normal command. It is a therefore recognized and executed by the shells. In csh(1) you may specify a list of directories in which directory is to be sought as subdirectory if it is not a subdirectory of the current directory; see the description of the cdpath variable in csh(1).
SEE ALSO
csh(1), sh(1), pwd(1), chdir(2)

Figure 7-20. xman uses a viewport widget

In the following list of commands, a *line* refers to one displayed row of characters in the window. A *paragraph* refers to the text between manually inserted carriage returns or blank lines. Text within a paragraph is automatically broken into lines based on the current width of the window.

In Release 4 of X, the following keystroke combinations are defined as indicated. (Note that "Control" and "Meta" are two of the "soft" key names X recognizes. They are mapped to particular physical keys which may vary from keyboard to keyboard. See the "xmodmap" section in Chapter 11, *Setup Clients*, for a discussion of modifier key mapping.) If you are using an earlier release of X, a few of the following keystroke combinations may produce slightly different results.

Key	Action
Control-A	Move to the beginning of the current line.
Control-B	Move backward one character.
Control-D	Delete the next character.
Control-E	Move to the end of the current line.
Control-F	Move forward one character.
Control-H, or Backspace	Delete the previous character.
Control-J, Control-M, LineFeed, or Return	New paragraph.
Control-K	Kill the rest of this line.
Control-L	Redraw this window.
Control-N	Move down to the next line.
Control-O	Divide this line into two lines, at this point.
Control-P	Move up to the previous line.
Control-V	Move down to the next screenful of text.
Control-W	Kill the selected text.
Control-Y	Insert the last killed text.
Control-Z	Scroll the text one line up.
Meta-<	Move to the beginning of the file.
Meta->	Move to the end of the file.
Meta-[	Move backward one paragraph.
Meta-]	Move forward one paragraph.
Meta-B	Move backward one word.
Meta-D	Kill the next word.
Meta-F	Move forward one word.
Meta-H, or Meta-Delete	Kill the previous word.
Meta-I	Insert a file. If any text is selected, use the selected text as the filename. Otherwise, a dialog box will appear in which you can type the desired filename.
Meta-V	Move up to the previous screenful of text.

Meta-Y	Insert the last selected text here. Note that this can be text selected in some other text subwindow. Also, if you select some text in an *xterm* window, it may be inserted in an *xmh* window with this command. Pressing pointer button 2 is equivalent to this command.
Meta-Z	Scroll the text one line down.
Delete	Delete the previous character.

Part Two:

Customizing X

X has been designed to put the user in the driver's seat. Everything from the colors and sizes of windows to the contents of twm *menus can be customized by the user. This part of the book tells you how to reshape X to your liking.*

Part Two

Customizing X

8

Command Line Options

This chapter describes command-line options that are common to most clients. Some arguments to command-line options can also be specified as the values of resource variables, described in Chapter 9. For example, the format of a geometry string or a color specification is the same whether it is specified as an argument to an option or as the value of a resource definition.

In This Chapter:

8
Command Line Options

X allows the user to specify numerous (very numerous!) command line options when starting most clients. The command line options for each client are detailed on the reference pages in Part Three of this guide.

As a general rule, all options can be shortened to the shortest unique abbreviation. For example, `-display` can be shortened to `-d` if there is no other option beginning with "d." (Note that while this is true for all the standard MIT clients, it may not be true of any random client taken off the net.)

In addition to certain client-specific options, all applications built with the X Toolkit accept certain standard options, which are listed in Table 8-1. (Some non-Toolkit applications may also recognize these options.) The first column gives the name of the option, the second the name of the resource to which it corresponds (see Chapter 9, *Setting Resources*), and the third a brief description of what the option does. This chapter discusses some of the more commonly used Toolkit options and demonstrates how to use them. (For the syntax of the other Toolkit options, see the *X* reference page in Part Three of this guide.)

The options `-selectionTimeout` and `-xnllanguage` are available as of Release 4.

Table 8-1. Standard Options

Option	Resource	Description
`-bg`	`background`	Background color of window.
`-background`	`background`	Background color of window.
`-bd`	`borderColor`	Color of window border.
`-bordercolor`	`borderColor`	Color of window border.
`-bw`	`borderWidth`	Border width of window in pixels.
`-borderwidth`	`borderWidth`	Border width of window in pixels.
`-display`	`display`	Display for client to run on.
`-fn`	`font`	Font for text display.
`-font`	`font`	Font for text display.

Command Line Options

Table 8-1. Standard Options (continued)

Option	Resource	Description
-fg	foreground	Foreground (drawing or text) color of window.
-foreground	foreground	Foreground (drawing or text) color of window.
-geometry	geometry	Geometry string for window size and placement.
-iconic		Start the application in iconified form.
-name	name	Specify a name for the application being run.
-rv	reverseVideo	Reverse foreground and background colors.
-reverse	reverseVideo	Reverse foreground and background colors.
+rv	reverseVideo	Don't reverse foreground and background.
-selectionTimeout	selectionTimeout	Timeout in milliseconds within which two communicating applications must respond to one another for a selection request.
-synchronous	synchronous	Enable synchronous debug mode.
+synchronous	synchronous	Disable synchronous debug mode.
-title	title	Specify a window title (e.g., to be displayed in a titlebar).
-xnllanguage	xnlLanguage	The language, territory, and codeset for National Language Support; this information helps resolve resource and other filenames.
-xrm	value of next arg	Next argument is a quoted string containing a resource manager specification as described in Chapter 9.

Though all Toolkit options are preceded by a minus sign, client-specific options may or may not require it. See the reference page for each client in Part Three of this guide for the syntax of all options.

Which Display to Run On

Generally, the results of a client program are displayed on the system where the client is running. However, if you are running a client on a remote system, you probably want to display the results on your local server.

An option of the form:

```
-display [host]:server[.screen]
```

can be used to tell a client which server to display results on.

The *host* specifies on which machine to create the window, the *server* specifies the server number, and the *screen* specifies the screen number. Note that the *server* parameter always begins with a colon (a double colon after a DECnet node*), and that the *screen* parameter always begins with a period. If the host is omitted or is specified as `unix`, the local node is assumed. If the screen is omitted, screen 0 is assumed.

xterm and other X clients normally get the host, server, and screen from the DISPLAY environment variable. (In most configurations, DISPLAY will be set to the local host, server 0 and screen 0.)

However, you may want to specify the host, server, and screen explicitly. You can do this for all clients by resetting the value of the DISPLAY variable, or for a single invocation of a client by using the `-display` option.

For example:

```
% xterm -display other_node:0.0 &
```

creates an *xterm* window on screen 0 of server 0 on the machine named `other_node`.

Although much of the current X Window System documentation suggests that any of the parameters to the `-display` option can be omitted and will default to the local node, server and screen 0, respectively, we have not found this to be true. In our experience, only the *host* and *screen* parameters (and the period preceding *screen*) can be omitted. The colon and *server* are necessary in all circumstances.

The `-display` option can be abbreviated as `-d`.

Title and Name

The name of the program (as known to the server) and the title of the window can be specified on the command line. The `-title` option allows you to specify a text string as the title of the application's window. If your application has a titlebar, or if the window manager you are using puts titlebars on windows, this string will appear in the titlebar. Window titles can be useful in distinguishing multiple instances of the same application.

The `-name` option actually changes the name by which the server identifies the program. Changing the name of the application itself (with the `-name` option) affects the way the application interprets resource files. This option is discussed further in Chapter 9, *Setting Resources*. If a name string is defined for an application, that string will appear as the application name in its icon.

If you display information about currently running windows using the *xwininfo* or *xlswins* client, title strings will appear in parentheses after the associated window ID numbers. (If there is no title string, but there is a name string, the name string will be displayed.)

*By convention, DECnet node names end with a colon.

You can also use the *xwininfo* client to request information about a particular window by title, or name, if no title string is defined, using that application's own `-name` option. See the *xlswins* and *xwininfo* reference pages in Part Three and the section "Window and Display Information Clients" in Chapter 7, *Other Clients*, to learn more about these clients.

Window Geometry

All clients that display in a window take a geometry option that specifies the size and location of the client window. The syntax of the geometry option is:

```
-geometry geometry
```

The `-geometry` option can be (and often is) abbreviated to `-g`, unless there is a conflicting option that begins with "g."

The parameter to the geometry option (`geometry`), referred to as a "standard geometry string," has the form:

```
widthxheight±xoff±yoff
```

The variables, `width`, `height`, `xoff` (x offset), and `yoff` (y offset) are values in pixels for many clients. However, application developers are encouraged to use units that are meaningful to the application. For example, *xterm* uses columns and rows of text as width and height values in the *xterm* window.

You can specify any or all elements of the geometry string. Incomplete geometry specifications are compared to the resource manager defaults and missing elements are supplied by the values specified there. If no default is specified there, and *twm* is running, the window manager will require you to place the window interactively.

The values for the x and y offsets and their effects are shown in Table 8-2.

Table 8-2. Geometry specification x and y offsets

Offset Variables	Description
`+xoff`	A positive x offset specifies the distance the left edge of the window is offset from the left side of the display.
`+yoff`	A positive y offset specifies the distance the top edge of the window is offset from the top of the display.
`-xoff`	A negative x offset specifies the distance the right edge of the window is offset from the right side of the display.
`-yoff`	A negative y offset specifies the distance the bottom edge of the window is offset from the bottom of the display.

For example, the command line:

```
% xclock -geometry 125x125-10+10 &
```

places a clock 125x125 pixels in the upper-right corner of the display, 10 pixels from both the top and right edge of the screen.

For *xterm*, the size of the window is measured in characters and lines. (The default size is 80 characters wide by 24 lines long.) If you wanted to use a large VT100 window, 120 characters wide by 40 lines long, you could use the following geometry specification:

```
% xterm -geometry 120x40-10+350 &
```

This command places the large *xterm* window in the lower-right corner, 10 pixels from the right edge of the screen and 350 pixels from the top of the screen. Figure 8-1 illustrates window offsets.

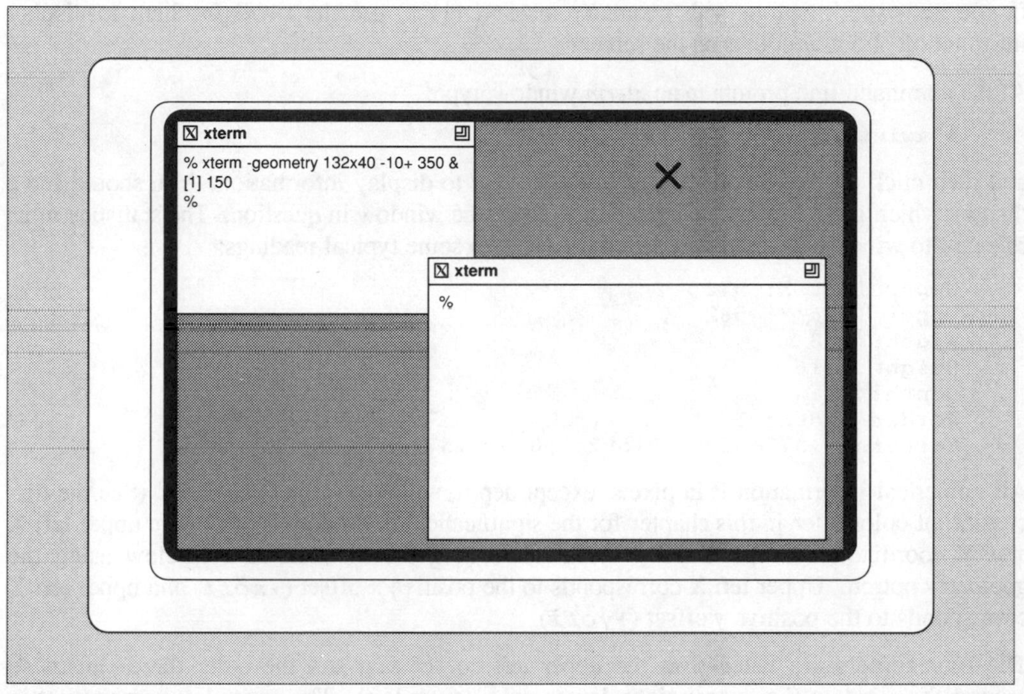

Figure 8-1. Window offsets

Several clients, including *xterm*, allow you to set the size and position of the icon or alternative window using resource variables (in an *Xdefaults* or other resource file). See the appropriate client reference pages in Part Three of this guide for a complete list of available resources. Refer to Chapter 9, *Setting Resources*, for instructions on how to set resources.

You should be aware that, as with all user preferences, you may not always get exactly what you ask for. Clients are designed to work with a window manager, which may have its own rules for window or icon size and placement. However, priority is always given to specific user requests, so you won't often be surprised.

Border Width

Many clients also allow you to specify the width of the border to be placed around the window. The border width is specified in pixels. For example:

```
% xterm -bw 10 &
```

sets a border of 10 pixels around the *xterm* window.

You will have to experiment to get a feeling for the translation between the number of pixels and actual sizes and distances. It will vary, depending on the type of workstation you are using.

If you are experimenting with geometry measurements, use the *xwininfo* client to display information about windows on the screen.

At the command line prompt in an *xterm* window, type:

```
% xwininfo
```

and then click on the window for which you want to display information. You should see a display which gives various characteristics about the window in question. The statistics most relevant to window geometry are listed below, with some typical readings:

```
Upper left X: 572
Upper left Y: 582
Width: 578
Height: 316
Depth: 1
Border width: 1
Corners: +572+582   -0+582   -0-0   +572-0
```

All numerical information is in pixels, except depth, which is in bits per pixel. (See the discussion of color later in this chapter for the significance of window depth.) The upper left X and Y coordinates are particularly useful for setting the location of a window using the geometry option. Upper left X corresponds to the positive x offset (+`xoff`) and upper left Y corresponds to the positive y offset (+`yoff`).

The four corners are listed with the upper left corner first and the other three clockwise around the window (i.e., upper right, lower right, lower left). The upper left corner (first in the list) always gives the positive x and y offsets for the window. In other words, the upper left corner specification *is* the `+xoff+yoff` part of the geometry string.

The width and height in pixels are somewhat less useful, since the geometry option to *xterm* requires that these figures be specified in characters and lines. The readings above are for a standard size *xterm* window using a 12 point Roman Courier font. However, you will undoubtedly become accustomed to thinking in terms of pixels by specifying the geometry of other clients.

See the *xwininfo* reference page in Part Three and the section "Window and Display Information Clients" in Chapter 7, *Other Clients*, for more details.

Color Specification

Many clients have options that allow you to specify the color of the window border, background, and foreground (the color text or graphic elements will be displayed in). These options generally have the form:

`-bg` *`color`* Sets the background color.

`-fg` *`color`* Sets the foreground color.

`-bd` *`color`* Sets the border color.

By default, the background of an application window is usually white and the foreground black, even on color workstations. You can specify a new color using either the color names listed in a system file called *rgb.txt* or hexadecimal values representing colors.

In the next section, we'll take a look at some of the colors available in the *rgb.txt* file. For now, let's consider the syntax of a command line specifying an *xterm* to be displayed in three colors:

```
% xterm -bg lightblue -fg darkslategrey -bd plum &
```

This command creates an *xterm* window with a background of light blue, foreground of dark slate grey, and window border of plum (all colors are available in both Releases 3 and 4).

At the command line, a color name should be typed as a single word (for example, `darkslategrey`). However, you can type the words comprising a color name separately if you enclose them in quotes, as in the following command line:

```
% xterm -bg "light blue" -fg "dark slate grey" -bd plum &
```

As we'll see, the *rgb.txt* file contains variants of the same color name (for example, "navy blue" and "NavyBlue," or "grey" and "gray") to allow a range of spelling, spacing, and capitalization on the command line.

Some clients allow additional options to specify color for other elements, such as the cursor, highlighting, and so on. See the appropriate client reference pages in Part Three of this guide for details.

The rgb.txt File

The *rgb.txt* file, usually located in */usr/lib/X11*, is supplied with the standard distribution of X and consists of predefined colors assigned to specific text names.

A corresponding compiled file called *rgb.dir* contains the definitions used by the server; this machine-readable file serves as a color name database, and is discussed more fully in Appendix A, *System Management*. The *rgb.txt* file is the human-readable equivalent.

Release 4 Color Names

The default *rgb.txt* file shipped with Release 4 of X contains 738 color name definitions. This number is slightly deceptive, since as we've said, a number of the color names are merely variants of another color name (differing only in spelling, spacing and capitalization).

Still, the number of colors available in Release 4 is more than double the number available in Release 3. Some of the Release 4 colors are entirely new (like snow and misty rose), but many are just slightly different shades of colors available in prior releases.

For example, the Release 3 *rgb.txt* file includes the color sea green. The Release 4 *rgb.txt* file offers the following shades of that color:

```
light sea green
sea green
medium sea green
dark sea green
SeaGreen1
SeaGreen2
SeaGreen3
SeaGreen4
DarkSeaGreen1
DarkSeaGreen2
DarkSeaGreen3
DarkSeaGreen4
```

Each of these names corresponds to a color definition. (This list does not include the variants SeaGreen, LightSeaGreen, MediumSeaGreen, and DarkSeaGreen, which also appear in the file.) As you can see, some of these shades are distinguished in the fairly traditional way of being called "light," "medium," and "dark." The light, medium, and dark shades of a color can probably be distinguished from one another on virtually any monitor.

Beyond this distinction, there are what might be termed "sub-shades;" gradations of a particular shade identified by number (SeaGreen1, SeaGreen2, etc.). Numerically adjacent sub-shades of a color may not be clearly distinguishable on all monitors. For example, SeaGreen1 and 2 may look very much the same. (You certainly would not choose to create a window with a SeaGreen1 background and SeaGreen2 foreground! On the other hand, sub-shades a couple of numbers apart are probably sufficiently different to be used on the same window.)

By supplying many different shades of a single, already fairly precise color like sea green, X developers have tried to provide definitions that work well on a variety of commonly-used monitors.* You may have to experiment to determine which colors (or shades) display best on your monitor.

The color names in the Release 4 *rgb.txt* file are too numerous to list here. Although there are no literal dividers within the file, it can roughly be considered to fall into three sections:

*The color database shipped with prior releases of X was originally designed to display optimally on the vt240 series terminals manufactured by Digital Equipment Corporation.

Section 1: A standard spectrum of colors, many available in or similar to colors in Release 3 (such as sea green). These colors seem to be ordered roughly as follows: off-whites and other pale colors, greys, blues, greens, yellows, browns, oranges, pinks, reds, and purples.

Section 2: Sub-shades of Section 1 colors (such as SeaGreen 1 through 4). These sub-shades comprise the largest part of the file.

Section 3: One hundred and one additional shades of grey, numbered 0 through 100 (also available in Release 3). This large number of precisely graduated greys provides a wide variety of shading for monochrome screens.

Rather than list every color in the *rgb.txt* file, we've compiled the following table of representative colors. We've chosen some of the more esoteric color names. Naturally, all of the primary and secondary colors are available also.

Section 1:

ghost white	peach puff	lavendar blush	lemon chiffon
slate grey	midnight blue	cornflower blue	medium slate blue
dodger blue	powder blue	turquoise	pale green
lawn green	chartreuse	olive drab	lime green
khaki	light yellow	goldenrod	indian red
sienna	sandy brown	salmon	coral
tomato	hot pink	maroon	violet red
magenta	medium orchid	blue violet	purple

Section 2:

snow1 - 4	bisque1 - 4	cornsilk1 - 4	honeydew1 -4
azure1 - 4	SteelBlue1 - 4	DeepSkyBlue1 - 4	LightCyan1 - 4
PaleTurquoise1 - 4	aquamarine1 - 4	PaleGreen1 - 4	DarkOliveGreen1 - 4
SpringGreen1 -4	gold1 - 4	RosyBrown1 - 4	burlywood1 - 4
chocolate1 - 4	firebrick1 - 4	DarkOrange1 - 4	OrangeRed1 - 4
DeepPink1 - 4	PaleVioletRed1 - 4	plum1 - 4	DarkOrchid1 - 4

Section 3:

`grey0 (gray0)` through `grey100 (gray100)`

If you want to look more closely at the *rgb.txt* file, you can open it with any text editor. As an alternative, you can also display the contents of the file using the *showrgb* client. *showrgb* seems to do nothing more than *cat*(1) the file to your terminal window. Given the size of the file, it's necessary to pipe the command's output to a paging program, such as *pg*(1) or *more*(1).

```
% showrgb | more
```

See Appendix A, *System Management*, for information on customizing color name definitions.

Command Line Options

Release 3 Color Names

The following are the default color names shipped with Release 3 of the X Window System. Again, this list does not include the many variants of these names.

aquamarine	medium aquamarine	black	blue
cadet blue	corn flowerblue	dark slate blue	light blue
light steel blue	medium blue	medium slate blue	midnight blue
navy blue	navy	sky blue	slate blue
steel blue	coral	cyan	firebrick
brown	sandy brown	gold	goldenrod
medium goldenrod	green	dark green	dark olive green
forest green	lime green	medium forest green	medium sea green
medium spring green	pale green	sea green	spring green
yellow green	dark slate grey	grey	dim grey
light grey	khaki	magenta	maroon
orange	orchid	dark orchid	medium orchid
pink	plum	red	indian red
medium violet red	orange red	violet red	salmon
sienna	tan	thistle	turquoise
dark turquoise	medium turquoise	violet	blue violet
wheat	white	yellow	green yellow

`grey0 (gray0)` through `grey100 (gray100)`

Alternative Release 4 Color Databases

In addition to the standard color database described above, Release 4 also includes three other databases that can be compiled by your system administrator. These files can be found in the general release in the directory *./rgb/others*.

raveling.txt — Designed by Paul Raveling, this database rivals the default database in size and scope, but has been tuned to display optimally on Hewlett-Packard monitors.

thomas.txt — Based on the Release 3 database, this file has been modified by John Thomas of Tektronix to approximate the colors in a box of Crayola Crayons.

old-rgb.txt — This is nothing more than the Release 3 database.

Hexadecimal Color Specification

You can also specify colors more exactly using a hexadecimal color string. You probably won't use this method unless you require a color not available by using a color name. In order to understand how this works, you may need a little background on how color is implemented on most workstations.

The RGB Color Model

Most color displays on the market today are based on the RGB color model. Each pixel on the screen is actually made up of three phosphors: one red, one green, and one blue. Each of these three phosphors is excited by a separate electron beam. When all three phosphors are fully illuminated, the pixel appears white to the human eye. When all three are dark, the pixel appears black. When the illumination of each primary color varies, the three phosphors generate a subtractive color. For example, equal portions of red and green, with no admixture of blue, makes yellow.

As you might guess, the intensity of each primary color is controlled by a three-part digital value—and it is the exact makeup of this value that the hexadecimal specification allows you to set.

Depending on the underlying hardware, different servers may use a larger or smaller number of bits (from 4 to 16 bits) to describe the intensity of each primary. To insulate you from this variation, most clients are designed to take color values containing anywhere from 4 to 16 bits (1 to 4 hex digits), and the server then scales them to the hardware. As a result, you can specify hexadecimal values in any one of the following formats:

```
#RGB
#RRGGBB
#RRRGGGBBB
#RRRRGGGGBBBB
```

where R, G, and B represent single hexadecimal digits and determine the intensity of the red, green, and blue primaries that make up each color.

When fewer than four digits are used, they represent the most significant bits of the value. For example, `#3a6` is the same as `#3000a0006000`.*

What this means concretely is perhaps best illustrated by looking at the values that correspond to some colors in the color name database. We'll use 8-bit values—two hexadecimal digits for each primary. The following definitions are the hexadecimal equivalents of the decimal values for some of the colors found in the *rgb.txt* file:

```
#000000     black
#FFFFFF     white
#FF0000     red
#00FF00     green
#0000FF     blue
#FFFF00     yellow
#00FFFF     cyan
#FF00FF     magenta
#5F9EA0     cadet blue
#6495ED     cornflower blue
#ADD8E6     light blue
#B0C4DE     light steel blue
#0000CD     medium blue
#000080     navy blue
```

*If you are unfamiliar with hexadecimal numbering, see the Glossary for a brief explanation, or a basic computer textbook for a more extended discussion.

```
#87CEED        sky blue
#6A5ACE        slate blue
#4682B4        steel blue
```

As you can see from the colors given above, pure red, green, and blue result from the corresponding bits being turned full on. All primaries off yields black, while all nearly full on gives white. Yellow, cyan, and magenta can be created by pairing two of the other primaries at full intensity. The various shades of blue shown above are created by varying the intensity of each primary—sometimes in unexpected ways.

The bottom line here is that if you don't intimately know the physics of color, the best you can do is to look up existing colors from the color name database and experiment with them by varying one or more of the primaries till you find a color you like. Unless you need precise colors, you are probably better off using color names.

How Many Colors are Available?

The number of distinct colors available on the screen at any one time depends on the amount of memory available for color specification. (The *xdpyinfo* client provides information about a display, including the number of colors available at one time. See Chapter 7, *Other Clients*, and the *xdpyinfo* reference page in Part Three for details.)

A color display uses multiple bits per pixel (also referred to as multiple planes or the *depth* of the display) to select colors. Programs that draw in color use the value of these bits as a pointer to a lookup table called a *colormap*, in which each entry (or *colorcell*) contains the RGB values for a particular color.* As shown in Figure 8-2, any given pixel value is used as an index into this table—for example, a pixel value of 16 will select the sixteenth colorcell.

Why is this technical detail important? Because it explains several issues that you might encounter in working with color displays.

First, the range of colors possible on the display is a function of the number of bits available in the colormap for RGB specification. If eight bits is available for each primary, then the range of possible colors is 256^3 (somewhere over 16 million colors). This means that you can create incredibly precise differences between colors.

However, the number of different colors that can be displayed on the screen at any one time is a function of the number of planes. A four-plane system can index 2^4 colorcells (16 distinct colors); an eight-plane system can index 2^8 colorcells (256 distinct colors); and a 24-plane system can index 2^{24} colorcells (over 16 million distinct colors).

If you are using a four-plane workstation, the fact that you can precisely define hundreds of different shades of blue is far less significant than the fact that you can't use them all at the same time. There isn't space for all of them to be stored in the colormap at one time, or any mechanism for them to be selected even if they could be stored.

---

*There is a type of high-end display in which pixel values are used directly to control the illumination of the red, green, and blue phosphors, but far more commonly, the bits per pixel are used indirectly, with the actual color values specified independently, as described here.

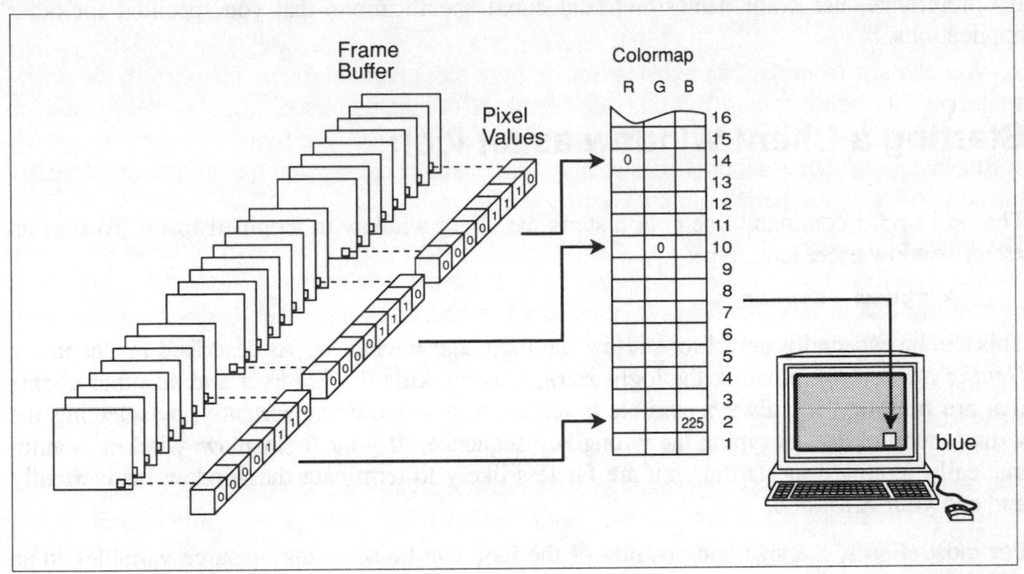

Figure 8-2. Multiple planes used to index a colormap

This limitation is made more significant by the fact that X is a multi-client environment. When X starts up, usually no colors are loaded into the colormap. As clients are invoked, certain of these cells are allocated. But when all of the free colorcells are used up, it is no longer possible to request new colors. When this happens, you will usually be given the closest possible color from those that have already been allocated. However, you may instead be given an error message and told that there are no free colorcells.

In order to minimize the chance of running out of colorcells, many programs use "shared" colorcells. Shared colorcells can be used by any number of applications, but they can't be changed by any of them. They can only be deallocated by each application that uses them, and when all applications have deallocated the cell, it is available for setting one again. Shared cells are most often used for background, border, and cursor colors.

Alternately, some clients have to be able to change the color of graphics they have already drawn. This requires another kind of cell, called private, which can't be shared. A typical use of a private cell would be for the pallete of a color mixing application. Such a program might have three bars of each primary color, and a box which shows the mixed color. The primary bars would use shared cells, while the mixed color box would use a private cell.

In summary, some programs define colorcells to be read-only and shareable, while others define colorcells to be read/write and private.

To top it off, there are even clients that may temporarily swap in a whole private colormap of their own. Because of the way color is implemented, if this happens, all other applications will be displayed in unexpected colors.

In order to minimize such conflicts, you should request precise colors only when necessary. By preference, use color names or hexadecimal specifications that you specified for other applications.

Starting a Client Window as an Icon

The `-iconic` command line option starts the client window in iconified form. To start an *xterm* window as an icon, type:

```
% xterm -iconic &
```

This can be especially useful for starting the login *xterm* window. As described in Chapter 2, *Getting Started*, terminating the login *xterm* window kills the X server and all other clients that are running. It's always possible to terminate a window inadvertently, by selecting the wrong menu option or typing the wrong key sequence. If your login *xterm* window is automatically iconified at startup, you are far less likely to terminate the window inadvertently and end your X session.

For most clients, the size and position of the icon can be set using resource variables in an *.Xdefaults* or other resource file. (This is highly recommended if you are starting the login *xterm* window as an icon.) See the appropriate client reference pages in Part Three for a complete list of available resources. Refer to Chapter 9, *Setting Resources*, for instructions on how to set resources.

Specifying Fonts on the Command Line

Many clients allow you to specify the font to be used when displaying text in the window. (These are known as *screen fonts* and are not to be confused with *printer fonts*.) For clients written with the X Toolkit, the option to set the display font is `-fn`. For example, the command line:

```
% xterm -fn fontname &
```

creates an *xterm* window in which text will be displayed with the font named `fontname`.

Chapter 5, *Font Specification*, describes the available screen fonts and font naming conventions.

Reverse Video

There are three options to control whether or not the application will display in reverse video—that is, with the foreground and background colors reversed. The `-rv` or `-reverse` option is used to request reverse video.

The `+rv` option is used to override any reverse video request that might be specified in a resource file (see Chapter 9, *Setting Resources*). This is important, because not all clients handle reverse video correctly, and even those that do usually do so only on black and white displays.

Reverse Video

There are three options to control whether or not the application will display in reverse video—that is, with the foreground and background colors reversed. The -rv or -reverse option is used to request reverse video.

The +rv option is used to override any reverse video requests that might be specified in a resource file (see Chapter 9, Setting Resources). This is important, because not all clients handle reverse video correctly, and even those that do usually do so only on black and white displays.

9

Setting Resources

This chapter describes how to set resource variables that determine application features such as color, geometry, fonts, and so on. It describes the syntax of resource definition files such as .Xresources, as well as the operation of xrdb*, a client that can be used to change resource definitions dynamically, and make resources available to clients running on other machines.*

In This Chapter:

Setting Resources

9
Setting Resources

Virtually all X clients are customizable. You can specify how a client looks on the screen—its size and placement, its border and background color or pattern, whether or not the window has a scrollbar, and so on. Some applications even allow you to redefine the keystrokes or pointer actions used to control the application.

Traditional UNIX applications rely on command line options to allow users to customize the way they work. As we've already discussed in Chapter 8, *Command Line Options*, X applications support command line options too, but often not for all of their features. Also, there can be so many customizable features in an application that a command line to set them all would be completely impractical. (Imagine the aggravation of misspelling an option in a command that was three lines long.)

X offers an alternative to customizing an application on the command line. Almost every feature of a program can be controlled by a variable called a *resource*; you can change the behavior or appearance of a program by changing the *value* associated with a resource variable. (All of the standard X Toolkit *Command Line Options* described in Chapter 8 have corresponding resource variable names. See Table 8-1 for more information.)

Resource variables may be Boolean (such as `scrollBar: True`) or take a numeric or string value (`borderWidth: 2` or `foreground: blue`). What's more, in applications written with the X Toolkit (or other object-oriented systems), resources may be associated with separate *objects* (or "widgets") within an application. There is a syntax that allows for separate control over both a *class* of objects in the application and an individual *instance* of an object. This is illustrated by the following resource specifications for a hypothetical application called *xclient*:

```
xclient*Buttons.foreground:   blue
xclient*help.foreground:      red
```

The first resource specification makes the foreground color of all buttons in the *xclient* application (in the class `Buttons`) blue; the second resource specification makes the foreground color of the `help` button in this application (an instance of the class `Buttons`) red.

The values of resources can be set as application defaults using a number of different mechanisms, including resource files in your home directory and a program called *xrdb* (X resource database manager). As we'll see, the *xrdb* program stores resources directly in the server, thus making them available to all clients, regardless of the machine the clients are running on.

Placing resources in files allows you to set many resources at once, without the restrictions encountered when using command line options. In addition to a primary resource file (often called *Xdefaults* or *Xresources*) in your home directory, which determines defaults for applications you run, you can create system-wide resource files to set application defaults. You can also create resource files to set some resources only for the local machine, some for all machines in a network, and some for one or more specific machines.

The various resource files are automatically read in and processed in a certain order within an application by a set of routines called the *resource manager*. The syntax for resource specifications and the rules of precedence by which the resource manager processes them are intended to give you the maximum flexibility in setting resources, with the minimum amount of text. You can specify a resource that controls only one feature of a single application, such as the red `help` button in the hypothetical *xclient* settings above. You can also specify a resource that controls one feature of multiple objects within multiple applications with a single line.

It is important to note that command line options normally take precedence over any prior resource settings, so you can set up the files to control the way you *normally* want your application to work, and then use command line options to specify changes you need for only one or two instances of the application.

In this chapter, we'll first look at the syntax of resource specifications. Then we'll consider some methods of setting resources, primarily some special command line options and the *xrdb* program. Finally, we'll take a brief look at the section "Other Sources of Resource Definition," additional files that can be created or edited to set application resources.

Resource Naming Syntax

The basic syntax of a resource definition file is fairly simple. Each client recognizes certain resource variables that can be assigned a value. The variables for each client are documented on its reference page in Part Three of this guide.

Most of the common clients are written to use the X Toolkit. As described in Chapter 7, *Other Clients*, toolkits are a mechanism for simplifying the design and coding of applications, and making them operate in a consistent way. Toolkits provide a standard set of objects, or "widgets," such as menus, command buttons, dialog boxes, scrollbars, and so on. As we'll see, the naming syntax for certain resources parallels the object hierarchy that is built into X Toolkit programs.*

The most basic line you can have in a resource definition file consists of the name of a client, followed by a period or an asterisk and the name of a variable. A colon and whitespace sepa-

*If a client was built with the X Toolkit, this should be noted on the reference page. In addition to certain application-specific resource variables, clients that use the X Toolkit have a common set of resource variables. These common variables may not be shown on each reference page, but all of the Toolkit variables are listed in Table 8-1, in Chapter 8, *Command Line Options* and are described in slightly greater detail on the *X* reference page in Part Three of this guide. A few of the more common variables also appear in Table 9-1 later in this chapter.

rate the client and variable names from the actual value of the resource variable. The following line specifies that all instances of the *xterm* application have a scrollbar:

```
xterm*scrollBar:   True
```

If the name of the client is omitted, the variable applies to all instances of all clients (in this case, all clients that can have a scrollbar). If the same variable is specified as a global variable and a client-specific variable, the value of the client-specific variable takes precedence for that client. Note, however, that if the name of the client is omitted, the line should generally begin with an asterisk.

Be sure that you don't inadvertently omit the colon at the end of a resource specification. This is an easy mistake to make and the resource manager provides no error messages. If there is an error in a resource specification (including a syntax error like the omission of the colon or a misspelling), the specification is ignored. The value you set will simply not take effect. To include a comment in a resource file or comment out one of the resource specifications, begin the line in question with an exclamation point (!). If the last character on a line is a backslash (\), the resource definition on that line is assumed to continue on the next line.

Syntax of Toolkit Client Resources

As mentioned above, X Toolkit applications are made up of predefined components called *widgets*. There can be widgets within widgets (e.g., a command button within a dialog box). The syntax of resource specifications for Toolkit clients parallels the levels of the widget hierarchy. Accordingly, you should think of a resource specification as having the following format:

object.subobject[.subobject...].attribute: value

where:

object is the client program, or a specific instance of the program. (See *The –name Option* later in this chapter.)

subobjects correspond to levels of the widget hierarchy (usually the major structures within an application, such as windows, menus, scrollbars, etc.).

attribute is a feature of the last *subobject* (perhaps, a command button), such as background color or a label that appears on it.

value is the actual setting of the resource *attribute*, i.e., the label text, color, or other feature.

The type of *value* to supply should usually be evident from the name of the resource or from the description of the resource variable on the reference page. Most of these values are similar to those used with the command line options described in Chapter 8, *Command Line Options*.

For example, various resources, such as `borderColor` or `background`, take color specifications; `geometry` takes a geometry string, `font` takes a font name, and so on. Logical values, such as the values taken by `scrollBar`, can be generally specified as `on` or `off`, as `yes` or `no`, or as `True` or `False`.

Setting Resources

Tight Bindings and Loose Bindings

Binding refers to the way in which components of a resource specification are linked together. Resource components can be linked in two ways:

- By a *tight* binding, represented by a dot (.).
- By a *loose* binding, represented by an asterisk (*).

A tight binding means that the components on either side of the dot must be next to one another in the widget hierarchy. A loose binding is signalled by an asterisk, a wildcard character, which means there can be any number of levels in the hierarchy between the two surrounding components.

If you want to specify tight bindings, you must be very familiar with the widget hierarchy. It's easy to use tight bindings incorrectly.

For example, the following resource specification to request that *xterm* windows be created with a scrollbar doesn't work:

```
xterm.scrollBar:   True
```

This specification ignores the widget hierarchy of *xterm*, in which the VT102 window is considered to be one widget, the Tektronix window another, and the menus a third. This means that if you want to use tight bindings to request that *xterm* windows be created with a scrollbar, you should specify:

```
xterm.vt100.scrollBar: True
```

Of course, rather than decipher the widget hierarchy (which may even change with subsequent versions of an application), it is far simpler just to use the asterisk connector in the first place:

```
xterm*scrollBar:   True
```

In an application that supports multiple levels of widgets, you can mix asterisks and periods. In general, though, the developers of X recommend always using the asterisk rather than the dot as the connector even with simple applications, since this gives application developers the freedom to insert new levels in the hierarchy as they produce new releases of an application.

Instances and Classes

Each component of a resource specification has an associated *class*. Several different widgets, or widget attributes, may have the same class. For example, in the case of *xterm*, the color of text (`foreground`), the pointer color, and the text cursor color are all defined as *instances* of the class `Foreground`. This makes it possible to set the value of all three with a single resource specification. That is, if you wanted to make the text, the pointer, and the cursor dark blue, you could specify either:

```
xterm*foreground:     darkblue
xterm*cursorColor:    darkblue
xterm*pointerColor:   darkblue
```

or:

```
xterm*Foreground:     darkblue
```

Initial capitalization is used to distinguish class names from instance names. Class names always begin with an uppercase letter, while instance names always begin with a lowercase letter. Note however that if an instance name is a compound word (such as `cursorColor`), the second word is usually capitalized.

The real power of class and instance naming is not apparent in applications like *xterm* that have a simple widget hierarchy. In complex applications written with the X Toolkit, class and instance naming allows you to do such things as specify that all buttons in dialog box be blue, but that one particular button be red. For example, in the hypothetical *xclient* application, you might have a resource file that reads:

```
xclient*buttonbox*Buttons*foreground:   blue
xclient*buttonbox*delete*foreground:    red
```

where `Buttons` is a class name and the `delete` button is an instance of the `Buttons` class. This type of specification works because an instance name always overrides the corresponding class name, for that instance. Class names thus allow default values to be specified for all instances of a given type of object. Instance names can be used to specify exceptions to the rules outlined by the class names. Note that a class name can be used with a loose binding to specify a resource for all clients. For example, the following specification would say that the foreground colors for all clients should be blue:

```
*Foreground:     blue
```

The reference page for a given program should always give you both instance and class names for every resource variable you can set. You'll notice that in many cases, the class name is identical to the instance name, with the exception of the initial capital letter. Often (but not always) this means that there is only one instance of that class. In other cases, the instance with the same name is simply the primary or most obvious instance of the class.

Precedence Rules for Resource Specification

Even within a single resource file, such as *.Xresources*, resource specifications often conflict. For instance, recall the example from the first page of the chapter, involving the hypothetical *xclient* application:

```
xclient*Buttons.foreground:   blue
xclient*help.foreground:      red
```

The first resource specification makes the foreground color of all buttons (in the class `Buttons`) blue. The second resource specification overrides the first in one instance: it makes the foreground color of the `help` button (an instance of the class `Buttons`) red. In the event of conflicting specifications, there are a number of rules that the resource manager follows in deciding which resource specification should take effect.

We've already seen two of these rules, which are observable in the way the resource manager interprets definitions in a user-created resource file. (The first rule applies in the *xclient* example above.)

- Instance names take precedence over class names.
- Tight bindings take precedence over loose bindings.

From just these two rules, we can deduce a general principle: the more specific a resource definition is, the more likely it is to be honored in the case of a conflict.

However, for cases in which you want to set things up very carefully, you should know a bit about how programs interpret resource specifications.

For each resource, the program has both a complete, fully-specified, tightly-bound instance name and class name. In evaluating ambiguous specifications, the program compares the specification against both the full instance name and the full class name. If a component in the resource specification matches either name, it is accepted. If it matches more than one element in either name, it is evaluated according to the following precedence rules:

1. The levels in the hierarchy specified by the user must match the program's expectations, or the entry will be ignored. For example, if the program expects either of the following:

   ```
   xterm.vt100.scrollBar:        value      instance name
   XTerm.VT100.ScrollBar:        value      class name
   ```

   the resource specification:

   ```
   xterm.scrollBar:    True
   ```

   won't work, because the tight binding is incorrect. The objects `xterm` and `scrollBar` are not adjacent in the widget hierarchy. There is another widget, `vt100`, between them. The specification would work if you used a loose binding, however:

   ```
   xterm*scrollBar:    True
   ```

   (Note that the class name of *xterm* is `XTerm`, not `Xterm` as you might expect.)

2. Tight bindings take precedence over loose bindings. That is, entries with instance or class names prefixed by a dot are more specific than entries with names prefixed by an asterisk, and more specific entries take precedence. For example, the entry `xterm.vt100.geometry` will take precedence over the entry `xterm*geometry`.

3. Similarly, instances take precedence over classes. For example, the entry `*scrollBar` will take precedence over the entry `*Scrollbar`.

4. An instance or class name that is explicitly stated takes precedence over one that is omitted. For example, the entry `xterm*scrollbar` is more specific than the entry `*scrollBar`.

5. Left components carry more weight than right components. For example, the entry `xterm*background` will take precedence over `*background`.

To illustrate these rules, let's consider the following resource specifications for the hypothetical Toolkit application *xclient*, as shown in Example 9-1.

Example 9-1. Sample resources

```
xclient.toc*Command.activeForeground:        black
*Command.Foreground:    green
```

The program would try to match these specifications against the complete tightly-bound instance and class specifications following:

`xclient.toc.messageFunctions.include.activeForeground`	***instance name***
`Xclient.Box.SubBox.Command.Foreground`	***class name***

Note that these specifications are the instance and class names for the same resource. Each component of the instance name belongs to the class in the corresponding component of the class name. Thus, the instance `toc` occurs in the class `Box`, the `messageFunctions` instance name is from the class `SubBox`, etc.

Both resource specifications in Example 9-1 match these instance and class names. However, with its tight bindings and instance names, `xclient.toc*Command.activeForeground` matches more explicitly; i.e., with higher precedence. That resource is set: the `foreground` color of the `include` button in its `active` state is set to `black`.

The specification `*Command.Foreground` also matches the instance and class names, but is composed entirely of class names which are less specific. Thus, it takes lower precedence than the first line in Example 9-1 (which sets the `include` button to `black`).

However, since the second line is an acceptable specification, hypothetically it would set the foreground color of other objects in the `Command` class. This would be true for *xclient*, as well as any other application, since the line begins with the asterisk wildcard. So if there were other *xclient* command buttons comparable to the `include` button in the hierarchy, this second line would set the foreground color of these buttons to `green`. If you want a more detailed description of how resource precedence works, see Section 9.2.3 of Volume Four, *X Toolkit Intrinsics Programming Manual*.

Some Common Resources

Most applications written using the X Toolkit have a set of class and instance names in common. These Toolkit resources correspond to the Toolkit options described in Chapter 8, *Command Line Options*. Among those Toolkit resource variables you might want to set are:

Table 9-1. Core Toolkit Resources

Instance Name	Class Name	Default	Description
`background`	`Background`	White	Background color.
`foreground`	`Foreground`	Black	Foreground color.
`borderColor`	`BorderColor`	Black	Border color.

Note that in a complex Toolkit application, these values can occur at every level in a widget hierarchy. For example, our hypothetical *xclient* application might support the following complete instance names:

```
xclient.background
xclient.buttonBox.background
xclient.buttonBox.commandButton.background
xclient.buttonBox.quit.background
```

These resources would specify the background color for the application window, the button box area, any command buttons, and the quit command button, respectively.

Of course, the specification:

```
xclient*background
```

would match any and all of them. See Table 8-1 for a comprehensive list of the common X Toolkit resources.

Event Translations

We've discussed the basics of resource naming syntax. From the sample resource settings, it appears that what many resource variables do is self-evident, or nearly so. Among the less obvious resource variables, there is one type of specification, an event translation, that can be used with many clients and warrants somewhat closer examination.

User input and several other types of information pass from the server to a client in the form of *events*. An event is a packet of information that tells the client something it needs to act on, such as keyboard input. As mentioned in Chapter 4, *The xterm Terminal Emulator*, moving the pointer or pressing a key, etc., causes *input* events to occur. When a program receives a meaningful event, it responds with some sort of action.

For many clients, the resource manager recognizes mappings between certain input events (like a pointer button click) and some sort of action by the client program (like selecting text). A mapping between one or more events and an action is called a *translation*. A resource containing a list of translations is called a *translation table*.

Many event translations are programmed into an application and are invisible to the user.* For our purposes, we are only concerned with very visible translations of certain input events, primarily the translation of keystrokes and pointer button clicks to particular actions by a client program.

*For more information on events and translations, see Volume Four, *X Toolkit Programming Manual*.

The Syntax of Event Translations

The operation of many clients, notably *xterm*, is partly determined by default input event translations. For example, as explained in Chapter 4, *The xterm Terminal Emulator*, selecting text with the first pointer button (an event) saves that text into memory (an action).

In this case, the input "event" is actually three separate X events:

1. Pushing the first pointer button down.
2. Moving the pointer while holding the first button down.
3. Releasing the button.

Each of these input events performs part of the action of selecting text:

1. Unselects any previously selected text and begins selecting new text.
2. Extends the selection.
3. Ends the selection, saving the text into memory (both as the PRIMARY selection and CUT_BUFFER0).

The event and action mappings would be expressed in a translation table as follows:

```
<Btn1Down>: select-start()\n\
<Btn1Motion>: select-extend()\n\
<Btn1Up>: select-end(PRIMARY,CUT_BUFFER0)
```

where each event is enclosed in angle brackets (<>) and produces the action that follows the colon. A space or tab generally precedes the action, though this is not mandatory:

```
<event>: action
```

A translation table must be a continuous string. In order to link multiple mappings as a continuous string, each event-action line should be terminated by a newline character (\n), which is in turn followed by a backslash (\) to escape the actual newline.

These are default translations for *xterm*.* All of the events are simple, comprised of a single button motion. As we'll see, events can also have modifiers, i.e., additional button motions or keystrokes (often Control or Meta) that must be performed with the primary event to produce the action. (Events can also have modifiers that *must not* accompany the primary event if the action is to take place.)

As you can see, the default actions listed in the table are hardly intuitive. The event-action mappings that can be modified using translation resources are usually described on the reference page for the particular client.

---

*They are actually slightly simplified versions of default translations. Before you can understand the actual translations listed on the *xterm* reference page in Part Three of this guide, you must learn more about the syntax of translations. In addition to the current chapter, read Appendix H, *Translation Table Syntax*.

You can specify non-default translations using a translation table (a resource containing a list of translations). Since actions are part of the client application and cannot be modified, what you are actually doing is specifying alternative events to perform an action.*

The basic syntax for specifying a translation table as a resource is as follows:

```
[object*[subobject...]]*translations:    #override\
        [modifier]<event>:    action
```

The first line is basically like any other resource specification, with a few exceptions. First, the final *argument* is always `translations`, indicating that one (or more) of the event-action bindings associated with the `[object*[subobject...]]` are being modified.

Second, note that `#override` is not the *value* of the resource; it is literal and indicates that what follows should override any default translations. In effect, `#override` is no more than a pointer to the true *value* of the resource: a new event-action mapping (on the following line), where the event may take a modifier.†

A non-obvious principle behind overriding translations is that you only literally "override" a default translation when the event(s) of the new translation match the event(s) of a default translation *exactly*. If the new translation does not conflict with any existing translation, it is merely appended to the defaults.

In order to be specified as a resource, a translation table must be a single string. The `#override` is followed by a backslash (\) to indicate that the subsequent line should be a continuation of the first.

In the basic syntax example above, the *value* is a single event-action mapping. The *value* could also be a list of several mappings, linked by the characters \n\ to make the resource a continuous string.

The following *xterm* translation table shows multiple event-action mappings linked in this manner:

```
*VT100.Translations:    #override\
     <Btn1Down>:        select-start()\n\
     <Btn1Motion>:      select-extend()\n\
     <Btn1Up>:          select-end(PRIMARY,CUT_BUFFER0)
```

*As we'll see, in certain cases you may be able to supply an alternative *argument* (such as a selection name) to an action. These changes *are* interpreted by the resource manager.

†The use of modifiers can actually become quite complicated, sometimes involving multiple modifiers. For our purposes, we'll deal only with simple modifiers. For more information on modifiers, see Appendix H, *Translation Table Syntax*, in this guide, and Volume Four, *X Toolkit Programming Manual*.

xterm Translations to Use xclipboard

As stated in Chapter 4, *The xterm Terminal Emulator*, you can specify *xterm* translations to have copied text made the CLIPBOARD selection. The CLIPBOARD selection is the property of the *xclipboard* client. If you are running *xclipboard* and you copy text to be made the CLIPBOARD selection, this text automatically appears in the *xclipboard* window. The *xclipboard* window allows you to store text that can then be copied to other windows.

Some sample translations that would allow you to use the *xclipboard* in this way follow:

```
*VT100.Translations:    #override\
        Button1 <Btn3Down>:     select-end(CLIPBOARD)\n\
        ~Ctrl ~Meta <Btn2Up>: insert-selection(PRIMARY,CLIPBOARD)
```

According to this table, while selecting text with `Button1` (the modifier), the event of pressing the third pointer button (`Btn3Down`) (while continuing to hold down the first button), produces the action of making the text the CLIPBOARD selection. (Notice that we've taken the `select-end` action and combined it with the argument `CLIPBOARD`. The default translation uses the arguments `PRIMARY,CUT_BUFFER0`.)

The second line modifies the way selected text is pasted into a window so that the `CLIPBOARD` selection can be pasted. As described in Chapter 4, *The xterm Terminal Emulator*, pressing the second pointer button pasted the contents of the PRIMARY selection, by default. If there is no PRIMARY selection, the contents of the cut buffer are pasted. The default translation that sets this behavior is as follows:

```
~Ctrl ~Meta <Btn2Up>:       insert-selection(PRIMARY,CUT_BUFFER0)
```

This translation specifies that releasing pointer button 2, while pressing any modifier button or key other than Control or Meta, inserts text from the PRIMARY selection, or if the selection is empty, from cut buffer 0. In the second line of our translation table, we've replaced `CUT_BUFFER0` with the `CLIPBOARD` selection. The new behavior is that releasing the second pointer button pastes the PRIMARY selection, or if there is none, the CLIPBOARD selection.

Thus, according to the translations in the example, if you select text as usual with the first pointer button, and then additionally push the third button down (while continuing to hold the first button), the text becomes the CLIPBOARD selection and appears automatically in the *xclipboard* window, as in Figure 9-1.

Since our first translation specifies a different event/action mapping than the default translation for selecting text (discussed in the previous section), the default translation still applies. If you select text with the first pointer button alone, that text is still made the PRIMARY selection and fills CUT_BUFFER0. To send text to the *xclipboard*, you would need to use the third pointer button as well. Thus, not all selected text need be made the CLIPBOARD selection (and sent automatically to the *xclipboard*).

There are advantages to making only certain selections CLIPBOARD selections. You can keep *xclipboard* running and make many text selections by the default method (first pointer button), without filling up the *xclipboard* window. And chances are you don't want to save every piece of text you copy for an extended period of time, anyway.

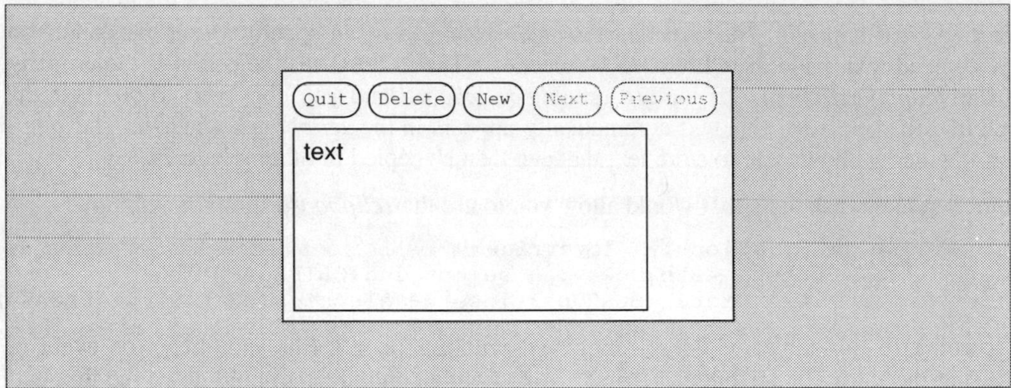

Figure 9-1. Selected text appears automatically in the xclipboard window

The CLIPBOARD selection and the *xclipboard* client also get around the potential problems of selection ownership discussed in Chapter 4. Once text becomes the CLIPBOARD selection, it is owned by the *xclipboard* client. Thus, if the client from which text was copied (the original owner) goes away, the selection is still available, owned by the *xclipboard*, and can be transferred to another window (and translated to another format if necessary).

The operation of many clients can be modified by specifying event translations as resources. See the relevant client reference pages in Part Three of this guide.

For information about events, actions, and translation table syntax, see Appendix H, *Translation Table Syntax*, in this guide, and Volume Four, *X Toolkit Programming Manual*.

How to Set Resources

Learning to write resource specifications is a fairly manageable task, once you understand the basic rules of syntax and precedence. In contrast, the multiple ways you can set resources—for a single system, for multiple systems, for a single user, for all users—can be confusing. For our purposes, we are primarily concerned with specifying resources for a single user running applications both on the local system and on remote systems in a network.

As we've said, resources are generally specified in files. A resource file can have any name you like. Resources are generally "loaded" into the X server by the *xrdb* client, which is normally run from your startup file or run automatically by *xdm* when you log in. (See Appendix A, *System Management*, for information about startup files and *xdm*.) Prior to Release 2 of X, there was only one resource file called *.Xdefaults*, placed in the user's home directory. If no resource file is loaded into the server by *xrdb*, the *.Xdefaults* file will still be read.

Remember that X allows clients to run on different machines across a network, not just on the machine that supports the X server. The problem with the older *.Xdefaults* mechanism was that users who were running clients on multiple machines had to maintain multiple

Xdefaults files, one on each machine. By contrast, *xrdb* stores the application resources directly in the server, thus making them available to all clients, regardless of the machine the clients are running on. As we'll see, *xrdb* also allows you to change resources without editing files.

Of course, you may want certain resources to be set on all machines and others to be set only on particular machines. See the section "Other Sources of Resource Definition" later in this chapter for information on setting machine-specific resources. This section gives an overview of additional ways to specify resources, using a variety of system files.

In addition to loading resource files, you can specify defaults for a particular instance of an application from the command line using two options: `-xrm` and `-name`.

First we'll consider a sample resources file. Then we'll take a look at the use of the `-xrm` and `-name` command line options. Finally, we'll discuss various ways you can load resources using the *xrdb* program and consider "Other Sources of Resource Definition."

A Sample Resources File

Figure 9-2 shows a sample resources file. This file sets the border width for all clients to a default value of 2 pixels, and sets other specific variables for *xclock* and *xterm*. The meaning of each variable is fairly obvious from its name (for example, `xterm*scrollBar: True` means that *xterm* windows should be created with a scrollbar.

Note that comments are preceded by an exclamation point (!).

For a detailed description of each possible variable, see the appropriate client reference pages in Part Three of this guide.

```
*borderWidth:          2
!
! xclock resources
!
xclock*borderWidth:    5
xclock*geometry:       64x64
!
! xterm resources
!
xterm*curses:          on
xterm*cursorColor:     skyblue
xterm*pointerShape:    pirate
xterm*jumpScroll:      on
xterm*saveLines:       300
xterm*scrollBar:       True
xterm*scrollKey:       on
xterm*background:      black
xterm*borderColor:     blue
xterm*borderWidth:     3
xterm*foreground:      white
xterm*font:            8x13
```

Figure 9-2. A sample resources file

Specifying Resources from the Command Line

Two command line options that are supported by all clients written with the X Toolkit can be useful in specifying resources.

The -xrm Option

The `-xrm` option allows you to set on the command line any specification that you would otherwise put into a resources file. For example:

```
% xterm -xrm 'xterm*Foreground: blue' &
```

Note that a resource specification on the command line must be quoted using the single quotes in the line above.

The `-xrm` option only specifies the resource(s) for the current instance of the application. Resources specified in this way do not become part of the resource database.

The `-xrm` option is most useful for setting classes, since most clients have command line options that correspond to instance variable names. For example, the `-fg` command line option sets the `foreground` attribute of a window, but `-xrm` must be used to set `Foreground`.

Note also that a resource specified with the `-xrm` option will not take effect if a resource that takes precedence has already been loaded with *xrdb*. For example, say you've loaded a resource file that includes the specification:

```
xterm*pointerShape:    pirate
```

The following command line specification of another cursor will fail:

```
% xterm -xrm '*pointerShape:    gumby' &
```

because the resource `xterm*pointerShape` is more specific than the resource `*pointerShape`. Instead, you'll get an *xterm* with the previously specified pirate cursor.

To override the resource database (and get the Gumby cursor), you'd need to use a resource as or more specific, such as the following:

```
% xterm -xrm 'xterm*pointerShape:    gumby' &
```

The -name Option

The `-name` option, which lets you name one instance of a client using an arbitrary alias, can also be used to set resources. If a client supports the `-name` option, you can create instance resources using the arbitrary alias as the `object`. You can then run the client using the alias as the `-name` argument. The client automatically uses the resources that begin with that alias.

For example, you could put the following entries into a resource file such as *.Xresources*:

```
XTerm*Font:            8x13
smallxterm*Font:       6x10
```

```
smallxterm*Geometry:  80x10
bigxterm*Font:        9x15
bigxterm*Geometry:    80x55
```

You could then use the following commands to create *xterms* of different sizes:

```
% xterm &
```

would create an *xterm* with the default specifications, while:

```
% xterm -name smallxterm &
```

would create a small *xterm*, 80 characters across by 10 lines down, displaying in the font 6x10. In addition:

```
% xterm -name bigxterm &
```

would create a big *xterm*, 80 characters across by 55 lines down, displaying in the font 9x15.

Setting Resources with xrdb

The *xrdb* program saves you from the difficulty of maintaining multiple resource files if you run clients on multiple machines. It stores resources in the X server, where they are accessible to all clients using that server. (Technically speaking, the values of variables are stored in a data structure referred to as the RESOURCE_MANAGER property of the root window of screen 0 for that server. From time to time, we may refer to this property colloquially simply as the resource database.)

The appropriate *xrdb* command line should normally be placed in your *.xinitrc* file or *.xsession* file to initialize resources at login, although it can also be invoked interactively. It has the following syntax:

xrdb [*options*] [*filename*]

The *xrdb* client takes several options, all of which are documented on the reference page in Part Three of this guide. Several of the most useful options are discussed in subsequent sections. (Those that are not discussed here have to do with *xrdb*'s ability to interpret C preprocessor-style defined symbols; this is an advanced topic. For more information, see the *xrdb* reference page in Part Three of this guide, and the *cpp*(1) reference page in your *UNIX Reference Manual*.)

The optional *filename* argument specifies the name of a file from which the values of client variables (resources) will be read. If no filename is specified, *xrdb* will expect to read its data from standard input. That is, the program will appear to hang, until you type some data, followed by an end-of-file (Control-D). Note that whatever you type will override the previous contents of the RESOURCE_MANAGER property, so if you inadvertently type *xrdb* without a filename argument, and then quit with Control-D, you will delete any previous values. (You can append new settings to current ones using the `-merge` option discussed later in this chapter.)

The resource *`filename`* can be anything you want. Two commonly used names are *.Xdefaults* and *.Xresources*.

You should load a resource file with the *xrdb* `-load` option. For example, to load the contents of your *.Xresources* file into the RESOURCE_MANAGER, you would type:

```
% xrdb -load .Xresources
```

Querying the Resource Database

You can find out what options are currently set by using the `-query` option. For example:

```
% xrdb -query
XTerm*ScrollBar:        True
bigxterm*font:          9x15
bigxterm*Geometry:      80x55
smallxterm*Font:        6x10
smallxterm*Geometry:    80x10
xterm*borderWidth:      3
```

If *xrdb* has not been run, this command will produce no output.

Loading New Values into the Resource Database

By default, *xrdb* reads its input (either a file or standard input) and stores the results into the resource database, replacing the previous values. If you simply want to merge new values with the currently active ones (perhaps by specifying a single value from standard input), you can use the `-merge` option. Only the new values will be changed; variables that were already set will be preserved rather than overwritten with empty values.

For example, let's say you wanted to add new resources listed in the file *new.values*. You could say:

```
% xrdb -merge new.values
```

As another example, if you wanted all subsequently run *xterm* windows to have scrollbars, you could use standard input, and enter:

```
% xrdb -merge
xterm*scrollBar:    True
```

and then press Control-D to end the standard input. Note that because of precedence rules for resource naming, you may not automatically get what you want. For example, if you specify:

```
xterm*scrollBar:  True
```

and the more specific value:

```
xterm*vt100.scrollBar: False
```

has already been set, your new, less specific setting will be ignored. The problem isn't that you used the `-merge` option incorrectly—you just got caught by the rules of precedence.

If your specifications don't seem to work, use the `-query` option to list the values in the RESOURCE_MANAGER property, and look for conflicting specifications.

Note also that when you add new specifications, they won't affect any programs already running, but only programs started after the new resource specifications are in effect. (This is also true even if you overwrite the existing specifications by loading a new resource file. Only programs run after this point will reflect the new specifications.)

Saving Active Resource Definitions in a File

Assume that you've loaded the RESOURCE_MANAGER property from an *.Xresources* or other file. However, you've dynamically loaded a different value using the `-merge` option, and you'd like to make the new value your default.

You don't need to edit the file manually (although you certainly could.) The `-edit` option allows you to write out the current value of the RESOURCE_MANAGER property into a file. If the file already exists, it is overwritten with the new values. However, *xrdb* is smart enough to preserve any comments and preprocessor declarations in the file being overwritten, replacing only the resource definitions.

For example:

```
% xrdb -edit ~/.Xresources
```

will save the current contents of the RESOURCE_MANAGER property in the file *.Xresources* in your home directory.

If you want to save a backup copy of an existing file, use the `-backup` option as follows:

```
% xrdb -edit .mydefaults -backup old
```

The string following the `-backup` option is used as an extension to be appended to the old filename. In the example shown above, the previous copy of *.mydefaults* would be saved as *.mydefaults.old*.

Removing Resource Definitions

You can delete the definition of the RESOURCE_MANAGER property from the server by calling *xrdb* with the `-remove` option.

There is no way to delete a single resource definition, other than to read the current *xrdb* values to a file. For example:

```
% xrdb -query > filename
```

Use an editor to edit and save the file, deleting the resource definitions you no longer want:

```
% vi filename
```

Then read the edited values back into the RESOURCE_MANAGER with *xrdb*:

```
% xrdb -load filename
```

Listing the Current Resources for a Client: appres

The *appres* (*app*lication *res*ource) program, available as of Release 4, lists the resources that currently might apply to a client. These resources may be derived from several sources, including the user's *Xresources* file and a system-wide application defaults file. The directory */usr/lib/X11/app-defaults* contains application default files for several clients. The function of these files is discussed in the next section. For now, be aware that all of the resources contained in these files begin with the class name of the application.

Also be aware that *appres* has one serious limitation: it cannot distinguish between valid and invalid resource specifications. It lists all resources that *might* apply to a client, whether the resources are correctly specified or not.

appres lists the resources that apply to a client having the `class_name` and/or `instance_name` you specify. Typically, you would use *appres* before running a client program to find out what resources the client program will access.

For example, say you want to run *xterm*, but you can't remember the latest resources you've specified for it, whether you've loaded them, or perhaps what some of the application defaults are, etc. You can use the *appres* client to check the current *xterm* resources. If you specify only a class name, as in the following command line:

```
% appres XTerm
```

appres lists the resources that any *xterm* would load. In the case of *xterm*, this is an extensive list, encompassing all of the system-wide application defaults, as well as any other defaults you have specified in a resource file.

You can additionally specify an instance name to list the resources applying to a particular instance of the client, as in the following:

```
% appres XTerm bigxterm
```

If you omit the class name, *xappres* assumes the class `-NoSuchClass-`, which has no defaults, and returns only the resources that would be loaded by the particular instance of the client.

Note that the instance can simply be the client name, for example, `xterm`. In that case, none of the system-wide application defaults would be listed, since all begin with the class name `XTerm`. For example, the command:

```
% appres xterm
```

might return resources settings similar to the following:

```
xterm.vt100.scrollBar:   True
xterm*PhonyResource:     youbet
xterm*pointerShape:      gumby
xterm*iconGeometry:      +50+50
*VT100.Translations:     #override\
     Button1 <Btn3Down>:   select-end(CLIPBOARD)\n\
     ~Ctrl ~Meta <Btn2Up>: insert-selection(PRIMARY,CLIPBOARD)
```

Most of these resources set obvious features of *xterm*. The translation table sets up *xterm* to use the *xclipboard*. Notice also that *appres* has returned an invalid resource called

`PhonyResource` that we created for demonstration purposes. You can't rely on *appres* to tell you what resources a client will actually load, because the *appres* program cannot distinguish a valid resource specification from an invalid one. Still it can be fairly useful to jog your memory as to the defaults you've specified in your *Xresources* file, as well as the system-wide application defaults.

Other Sources of Resource Definition

If *xrdb* has not been run, the RESOURCE_MANAGER property will not be set. Instead, the resource manager looks for a file called *Xdefaults* in the user's home directory. As we discussed earlier, resources found in this way are only available to clients running on the local machine.

Whether or not resources have been loaded with *xrdb*, when a client is run the following sources of resource definition are consulted in this order:

1. A file with the same name as the client application, in the directory */usr/lib/X11/app-defaults* will be loaded into the resource manager.
2. Files in the directory named by the environment variable XAPPLRESDIR, or if the variable is not set, in the user's home directory, with the name *Class* where *Class* is the class name of a client program.
3. Resources loaded into the RESOURCE_MANAGER property of the root window with *xrdb*; these resources are accessible regardless of the machine on which the client is running.

   If no resources are loaded in this way, the resource manager looks for a *Xdefaults* file in the user's home directory; these resources are only available on the local machine.
4. Next, the contents of any file specified by the shell environment variable XENVIRONMENT will be loaded.

   If this variable is not defined, the resource manager looks for a file named *Xdefaults-**hostname*** in the user's home directory, where ***hostname*** is the name of the host where the client is running. These methods are used to set machine-specific resources.
5. Any values specified on the command line with the `-xrm` option will be loaded for that instance of the program.

All of these various sources of defaults will be loaded and merged, according to the precedence rules described above in the section "Precedence Rules for Resource Specification."

The client will then merge these various defaults specified by the user with its own internal defaults, if any.

Finally, if the user has specified any options on the command line (other than with the `-xrm` option), these values will override those specified by resource defaults, regardless of their source.

10

Customizing the twm Window Manager

This chapter describes the syntax of the .twmrc startup file that can be used to customize the operation of the twm *window manager. It describes how to bind functions to keys, and how to define your own* twm *menus. An alternative* .twmrc *file is included.*

In This Chapter:

10
Customizing the twm Window Manager

Difficult as it may be to believe, every function of the window manager described in Chapter 2 and Chapter 3 of this guide can be modified by the user. The function itself will remain the same (for example, you will still resize a window by moving the pointer over the border you want to change, and stretching or shrinking the window to the size you want), but the keys and/or menu items used to invoke the function may be completely different. The flexibility of *twm* allows you to redesign the Twm menu by reordering, adding and removing items, and changing key/button combinations; and to create entirely new menus. The operation of the window manager, as distributed, is controlled by a text file called *system.twmrc* in the directory */usr/lib/X11/twm*. This file has three parts:

- A variables section, which contains various settings, such as the font with which menus should be displayed, the volume of the keyboard bell, and so on.
- A key bindings section, which defines the keys, pointer buttons, and key and pointer button combinations that will be used to invoke each window manager function (including the display of menus).
- A menus section, which defines the contents of the menus.

As users gain experience with the window manager, each can create a file called *.twmrc* in his or her home directory. This file can simply extend *system.twmrc*, resetting a variable or two, perhaps changing a key binding or adding a menu item—or it can replace it completely, changing every aspect of the way the window manager operates.

Rather than abstractly explaining the syntax of these various sections in a *.twmrc* file, let's plunge right in, by looking at the *system.twmrc* file from the MIT X11 distribution, as shown in Example 10-1. (Note that if you are using a commercial version of X, this file may be significantly different. However, in that case, you most likely have a user's guide specific to your system—perhaps even a customized version of this one!)

Example 10-1. The system.twmrc file from the MIT distribution

```
#
# $XConsortium: system.twmrc,v 1.7 89/12/01 11:23:47 jim Exp $
#
# Default twm configuration file; needs to be kept small to conserve
# string space in systems whose compilers don't handle medium-sized
# strings.
```

Example 10-1. The system.twmrc file from the MIT distribution (continued)

```
#
# Sites should tailor this file, providing any extra title buttons,
# menus, etc., that may be appropriate for their environment.  For
# example, if most of the users were accustomed to uwm, the defaults
# could be set up not to decorate any windows and to use meta-keys.
#

NoGrabServer
DecorateTransients
TitleFont "-adobe-helvetica-bold-r-normal--*-120-*-*-*-*-*-*"
ResizeFont "-adobe-helvetica-bold-r-normal--*-120-*-*-*-*-*-*"
MenuFont "-adobe-helvetica-bold-r-normal--*-120-*-*-*-*-*-*"
IconFont "-adobe-helvetica-bold-r-normal--*-100-*-*-*-*-*-*"
IconManagerFont "-adobe-helvetica-bold-r-normal--*-100-*-*-*"
#ClientBorderWidth

Color
{
    BorderColor "slategrey"
    DefaultBackground "maroon"
    DefaultForeground "gray85"
    TitleBackground "maroon"
    TitleForeground "gray85"
    MenuBackground "maroon"
    MenuForeground "gray85"
    MenuTitleBackground "gray70"
    MenuTitleForeground "maroon"
    IconBackground "maroon"
    IconForeground "gray85"
    IconBorderColor "gray85"
    IconManagerBackground "maroon"
    IconManagerForeground "gray85"
}

#
# Define some useful functions for motion-based actions.
#
MoveDelta 3
Function "move-or-lower" { f.move f.deltastop f.lower }
Function "move-or-raise" { f.move f.deltastop f.raise }
Function "move-or-iconify" { f.move f.deltastop f.iconify }

#
# Set some useful bindings.  Sort of uwm-ish, sort of simple-button-ish
#
Button1 =       : root :        f.menu          "defops"

Button1 =    m  : window|icon : f.function      "move-or-lower"
Button2 =    m  : window|icon : f.iconify
Button3 =    m  : window|icon : f.function      "move-or-raise"

Button1 =       : title :       f.function      "move-or-raise"
Button2 =       : title :       f.raiselower

Button1 =       : icon :        f.function      "move-or-iconify"
Button2 =       : icon :        f.iconify

Button1 =       : iconmgr :     f.iconify
Button2 =       : iconmgr :     f.iconify
```

Example 10-1. The system.twmrc file from the MIT distribution (continued)

```
#
# And a menu with the usual things
#
menu "defops"
{
"Twm"                   f.title
"Iconify"               f.iconify
"Resize"                f.resize
"Move"                  f.move
"Raise"                 f.raise
"Lower"                 f.lower
""                      f.nop
"Focus"                 f.focus
"Unfocus"               f.unfocus
"Show Iconmgr"          f.showiconmgr
"Hide Iconmgr"          f.hideiconmgr
""                      f.nop
"Kill"                  f.destroy
"Delete"                f.delete
""                      f.nop
"Restart"               f.restart
"Exit"                  f.quit
}
```

If you wish to change the operation of the window manager, you shouldn't change the *system.twmrc* file. Instead, copy it to your home directory, under the name *.twmrc*, and make changes to that copy. Note that settings in *system.twmrc* and your own local *.twmrc* file are *not* cumulative; even if you only want to make a small change, you will need to copy the whole file.

Setting .twmrc Variables

The first section of the file sets global variables. Some variables are Boolean—that is, their presence or absence "toggles" some attribute of the window manager—while others have the form:

```
variable value
```

where *value* is a number, a text string, keyword, or list of any of these. Variable names and keywords are case insensitive.

An example of a Boolean variable is `DecorateTransients`, which, if present, causes all windows to have titlebars, even if they are only intended to appear for a short time.

An example of a text string variable is:

```
MenuFont "-adobe-helvetica-bold-r-normal--*-120-*-*-*-*-*-*"
```

which names the font that should be used in all menus. Text string variables are case sensitive, and must always be surrounded by double quotes. (See Appendix E, *Release 3 and 4 Standard Fonts*, for lists and illustrations of fonts in the standard X11 distribution.)

An example of a numeric variable is:

```
IconBorderWidth 5
```

which sets the width of an icon's window border in pixels.

In the following example, *TitleHighlight* is a keyword:

```
Pixmaps
{
TitleHighlight "gray1"
}
```

An example of a list variable is:

```
NoTitle { "oclock" "xclock" "xscreensaver" "zwgc" }
```

The available variables are described in detail on the *twm* reference page in Part Three of this guide, so we won't go into detail on each of them here.

Button/Key Bindings

The second section of the *.twmrc* file specifies which combination of keys, pointer buttons, and title buttons (and in which context) will be used to invoke each predefined *twm* function. Let's see how this works, by looking at the first few lines of the function binding section of *system.twmrc*.

```
# BUTTON/KEY =  KEYS   : CONTEXT :       FUNCTION        ACTION
Button1 =              : root :          f.menu          "defops"

Button1 =       m      : window|icon :   f.function      "move-or-lower"
Button2 =       m      : window|icon :   f.iconify
```

The first line we've shown is just a comment line, which is not present in the original file. It labels each of the fields in the line below. The first field is separated from the others by an equals sign; subsequent fields are separated by colons. In *system.twmrc*, fields are separated by tabs for clarity, making the colons (falsely) appear to be delimiters only for the context field; they could instead follow each other without intervening whitespace.

Let's talk about each of the fields in turn.

Pointer Buttons

The first field defines which keys or pointer buttons are used to invoke the function.

twm can handle a pointer with up to five buttons, which would be named Button1, Button2, Button3, Button4, and Button5. To bind a key to a *twm* function, just use that key's *keysym*—the name that represents the label on a key. For example, the keysym for the F1 key on a DECstation 3100 is "F1". For more information about keysyms, see Chapter 11, *Setup Clients*.

Keys

The second field lists modifier keys, if any, which must be held down while invoking the specified function. *twm* recognizes the Shift, Control and Meta keys. (See Chapter 11, *Setup Clients*, for more discussion.) These names must be entered in the *.twmrc* file in lower case, and can be abbreviated s, c, and m.

If two keys must be held down at once, the names should be separated by a vertical bar (|). For example, `c|s` would mean that the Control and Shift keys should be pressed simultaneously. It is not permissible to bind a function to three keys at once. If the field is left blank, no key needs to be pressed while invoking the function.

Control and Shift should be familiar to most users. But what is a "Meta" key? There isn't a key by that name on many keyboards—instead, Meta is a user-definable Control key that can be mapped to an actual key on the physical keyboard using the *xmodmap* client as described in Chapter 11. Most implementations of X will include a mapped Meta key. Type *xmodmap* without any arguments to display the map. The *system.twmrc* specifies the Meta key in many keyboard bindings. On workstations without a special key corresponding to Meta, you will have to use *xmodmap* to find out or change the definition of Meta to something reasonable.

Meta could be mapped to the Control key, although this could potentially lead to conflicts with applications that want to use the Control key. In particular, certain functions of *xedit* will operate strangely or not at all if Meta is mapped to Control.

If you want to map the Meta key, it is best to choose a keyboard key that's within easy reach and is not used frequently for other applications (perhaps an Alt or Funct key). Left- or right-handedness could also be a factor in choosing a Meta key.

Some X developers warn against binding functions to the Shift key alone, since they say certain applications use it as a Control key. If you use it in *twm*, it will perform both functions simultaneously, which is likely to be confusing. For the same reason, you should not bind functions to buttons without modifier keys in the context of a window, as an application may want to use the pointer buttons for its own purposes.

Context

The third field defines the context—the location the pointer must be in before the function can be invoked. This field may be blank, or may contain one or more of: window, title, icon, root, frame, iconmgr, their first letters (icon is i, iconmgr is m), or all. Multiple context specifications should be separated by vertical bars.

If root is specified, it means that the pointer must be in the root (background) window, and not in any other window or icon. If the context is window, icon, title, frame, or iconmgr, the pointer must be in the specified place(s) for the function to be invoked.

The context field makes perfect sense if you consider the sample function binding:

```
Button2 =   m   : window|icon : f.iconify
```

`f.iconify` turns a window into an icon, or an icon into a window. The pointer must be in a window or an icon for the function to be used.

Function Names

The first field in a key binding contains the name of a function, followed by an equals sign. *twm* has a number of predefined functions. Each of these functions has a name beginning with "`f.`". The meaning of most of these functions should be fairly obvious to you from the name, if not from your experience using the window manager. For example, `f.resize` is used to resize a window, `f.move` to move a window, or `f.iconify` to change a window to an icon.

Others are less obvious. For example, `f.identify` provides a summary of the name and geometry of the window it's invoked on. Notice the function `f.nop`, which appears coupled with a set of empty quotes rather than a menu selection. This line in the *.twmrc* creates a blank line on the Twm menu, to isolate the KillWindow and Exit selections from the others. If you select the blank line, nothing happens. If you substituted `f.beep` for `f.nop`, the keyboard would beep when the blank line was selected.

Each of the functions is described in detail on the reference page for *twm* in Part Three of this guide.

Action

The fifth field, labeled "Action," is typically used only for the `f.menu` and `f.function` functions, which allow you to invoke user-defined menus and functions. The fifth field specifies the name of a menu or function, whose contents are defined in the third section of the *.twmrc* file. If the menu or function name contains quotes, special characters, parentheses, tabs or blanks, it must be enclosed in double quotes. For consistency, you may want to always quote menu and function names. For example:

```
Button1 =       : root :          f.menu    "defops"
Button1 = m|s   : w|t|i|f|m :     f.menu    "defops"
Button3 =       : root :          f.menu    "utilities"
```

Going back to our sample function binding:

```
Button1 =       : root :          f.menu    "defops"
```

you can now understand that the `f.menu` function is invoked (bringing up the menu named "defops") by moving the pointer to the root window and pressing the left pointer button.

All of the other function definitions should be equally readable to you. Go back for a moment and review the bindings shown in the *system.twmrc* file in Example 10-1.

You'll notice that it is possible to bind the same function to more than one set of keys, buttons, and/or contexts. For example, the `f.iconify` function can be invoked while on a window by pressing the Meta key together with the middle button on the pointer. But when the pointer is in the icon, you can invoke this function by pressing only the middle button on the pointer. The reason for this becomes obvious if you realize that when the pointer is on a window, the middle pointer button alone might have some other meaning to the application running in that window. In order to avoid conflict with other applications, *twm* uses the more complex key/button combination. But when the pointer is in an icon or in the root window, there is no possibility of conflict, and it can take a more forgiving approach.

Customizing twm

Defining Menus

The third section of a *.twmrc* file contains menu definitions. These definitions have the format:

```
menu  "menu_name" {
"item_name"  action
                .
                .
                .
}
```

The menu name must exactly match a name specified with the `f.menu` function.

Each item on the menu is given a label (*item_name*), which will appear on the menu. This is followed by the action to be performed. The action may be one of *twm*'s functions, or if prefixed by a ! character, it can be a system command to be executed, as if in an *xterm* window. The Utilities menu shown in Example 10-2 demonstrates both types of action.

Example 10-2. The Utilities menu

```
menu = "Utilities" {
"Identify"          f.identify
"Source .twmrc"     f.twmrc
""                  f.beep
"Check Mail"        !"/usr/bin/X11/xbiff -display $DISPLAY&"
"Clock"             !"/usr/bin/X11/oclock -display $DISPLAY &"
"New Window"        !"/usr/bin/X11/xterm -ls -display $DISPLAY &"
"Phase of Moon"     !"/usr/bin/X11/xphoon &"
""                  f.beep
"news"              !"/usr/bin/X11/xhost news.mit.edu;
                       /usr/bin/X11/xterm -title news.mit.edu
                       -e rlogin news.mit.edu &"
"mintaka"           !"/usr/bin/X11/xhost mintaka.lcs.mit.edu;
                       /usr/bin/X11/xterm -title mintaka.lcs.mit.edu
                       -e rlogin mintaka.lcs.mit.edu &"
}
```

New Window is accomplished by running another instance of *xterm*. CheckMail, Clock, PhaseofMoon, news, and mintaka are also implemented by running a system function. The other functions are accomplished simply by invoking one of *twm*'s predefined functions.

The Preferences menu shown in Example 10-3 simply invokes *xset* with a number of different options:

Example 10-3. The Preferences menu

```
menu  "Preferences" {
"Bell Loud"             !"xset b 80&"
"Bell Normal"           !"xset b on&"
"Bell Off"              !"xset b off&"
"Click Loud"            !"xset c 80&"
"Click Soft"            !"xset c on&"
"Click Off"             !"xset c off&"
"Lock On"               !"xset led on&"
"Lock Off"              !"xset led off&"
"Mouse Fast"            !"xset m 4 2&"
"Mouse Normal"          !"xset m 2 5&"
"Mouse Slow"            !"xset m 1 1&"
}
```

Submenus

While the menu defined by the *system.twmrc* file is a drastic improvement over the cluttered menus provided by *uwm* in previous releases of X11, it is still far from complete. We'd like to modify it to add a couple of menus which contain commands that, while still worth putting in a menu, aren't used as frequently as the commands in the Twm menu.

For the moment, let's assume that we want to leave the variable definitions and function key bindings alone, but want to add two submenus to the Twm menu. For example, we might copy *system.twmrc* to a local *.twmrc* file, and modify the menus section to be like the one shown in Example 10-4.

Example 10-4. Window operations divided into three menus

```
menu "defops"
{
"Twm"                  f.title
"Iconify"              f.iconify
"Resize"               f.resize
"Move"                 f.move
"Raise"                f.raise
"Lower"                f.lower
""                     f.nop
"..Utilities"          f.menu "Utilities"
"..Preferences"        f.menu "Preferences"
""                     f.nop
"Focus"                f.focus
"Unfocus"              f.unfocus
"Show Iconmgr"         f.showiconmgr
"Hide Iconmgr"         f.hideiconmgr
""                     f.nop
"Kill"                 f.destroy
"Delete"               f.delete
""                     f.nop
"Restart"              f.restart
"Exit"                 f.quit
}

menu "Utilities" {
```

Example 10-4. Window operations divided into three menus (continued)

```
"Utilities"      f.title
""               f.beep
"Identify"       f.identify
"Source .twmrc" f.twmrc
""               f.beep
"Mail Box"       !"/usr/bin/X11/xbiff -display $DISPLAY&"
"Clock"          !"/usr/bin/X11/oclock -display $DISPLAY &"
"New Window"     !"/usr/bin/X11/xterm -ls -display $DISPLAY &"
"Phase of Moon" !"/usr/bin/X11/xphoon &"
""               f.beep
"news"           !"/usr/bin/X11/xhost news.mit.edu;
                    /usr/bin/X11/xterm -title news.mit.edu
                    -e rlogin news.mit.edu &"
"mintaka"        !"/usr/bin/X11/xhost mintaka.lcs.mit.edu;
                    /usr/bin/X11/xterm -title mintaka.lcs.mit.edu
                    -e rlogin mintaka.lcs.mit.edu &"
}

menu  "Preferences" {
"Preferences"    f.title
"Bell Loud"      !"xset b 80&"
"Bell Normal"    !"xset b on&"
"Bell Off"       !"xset b off&"
"Click Loud"     !"xset c 80&"
"Click Soft"     !"xset c on&"
"Click Off"      !"xset c off&"
"Lock On"        !"xset led on&"
"Lock Off"       !"xset led off&"
"Mouse Fast"     !"xset m 4 2&"
"Mouse Normal"   !"xset m 2 5&"
"Mouse Slow"     !"xset m 1 1&"
}
```

To get from one menu to another, we simply define `f.menu` as the action for one item on the menu. No key, button, or context is defined, so we go right to the next menu when selecting that item.

Executing System Commands from a Menu

We mentioned above that it is possible to specify a system command as a menu action simply by placing an exclamation point in front of the string to be executed.

It is easy to cook up a menu that contains a miscellany of useful commands, as shown in Example 10-5.

Example 10-5. A Useful Commands menu

```
Button1 = : root : f.menu "Useful Commands"
          .
          .
          .
menu "Useful Commands" {
Analog clock              !"xclock -geometry 162x162-10+10&"
```

Example 10-5. A Useful Commands menu (continued)

```
Digital clock                !"xclock -digital -geometry 162x37-10+174&"
Edit File                    !"xterm -e vi"
Calculator                   !"xcalc -geometry 126x230-180+10&"
Mailbox                      !"xbiff -geometry 65x65-353+10&"
Display keyboard mappings !"xmodmap&"
}
```

As you can quickly see, you can run any window-based programs directly, but you need to run other programs using *xterm*'s `-e` option (discussed in Chapter 4, *The xterm Terminal Emulator*). You are limited only by your imagination in what commands you might want to put on a menu. Each command runs in its own window, but that isn't necessarily the case, as we'll see in a moment.

Color Menus

So far, we've assumed that all menus are black and white. But you can also create color menus. You can even assign different colors to the menu title, the highlighting bar (the horizontal band that follows the pointer within the menu and shows which item is selected) and the individual selections on the menu.

Colors are added to menus when they're defined, using optional arguments. In Example 10-6, we show a "colorized" version of the Preferences menu that we defined earlier.

Example 10-6. A menu with color definitions

```
menu  "Preferences"  ("WhiteSmoke" : "HotPink") {
"Preferences"      ("DarkSlateGray" : "thistle") f.title
"Bell Loud"        ("DarkSlateGray" : "bisque1") !"xset b 80&"
"Bell Normal"      ("DarkSlateGray" : "bisque1") !"xset b on&"
"Bell Off"         ("DarkSlateGray" : "bisque1") !"xset b off&"
"Click Loud"       ("DarkSlateGray" : "azure1") !"xset c 80&"
"Click Soft"       ("DarkSlateGray" : "azure1")  !"xset c on&"
"Click Off"        ("DarkSlateGray" : "azure1")  !"xset c off&"
"Lock On"                                        !"xset led on&"
"Lock Off"                                       !"xset led off&"
"Mouse Fast"       ("DarkSlateGray" : "gold1")   !"xset m 4 2&"
"Mouse Normal"     ("DarkSlateGray" : "gold1")   !"xset m 2 5&"
"Mouse Slow"       ("DarkSlateGray" : "gold1")   !"xset m 1 1&"
}
```

In this example, WhiteSmoke and HotPink are the foreground and background (respectively) of a highlighted menu item. The colors defined for each menu item are the foreground and background colors (in that order) for that item when it is not highlighted. The default foreground and background colors for menu items are controlled by the variables `MenuForeground` and `MenuBackground`.

twm has eighteen variables controlling different aspects of its color:

`BorderColor` The default color of a window's border.

`BorderTileBackground`	The default background color of the gray pattern used in an unhighlighted window border.
`BorderTileForeground`	The default foreground color of the gray pattern used in an unhighlighted window border.
`DefaultBackground`	The background color to be used for sizing and information windows.
`DefaultForeground`	The foreground color to be used for sizing and information windows.
`IconBackground`	The background color of icons.
`IconForeground`	The foreground color of icons.
`IconBorderColor`	The default color of an icon's border.
`IconManagerBackground`	The background color to use for icon manager entries.
`IconManagerForeground`	The foreground color to use for icon manager entries.
`IconManagerHighlight`	The border color used when highlighting the icon manager entry which has the focus.
`MenuBackground`	The background color used for menus.
`MenuForeground`	The foreground color used for menus.
`MenuShadowColor`	The color used for the shadow behind pull-down menus.
`MenuTitleBackground`	The background color of the highlighting bar.
`MenuTitleForeground`	The background color of the highlighting bar.
`TitleBackground`	The background color of the highlighting bar.
`TitleForeground`	The background color of the highlighting bar.

These variables are most commonly used as arguments to the `Color` and `Monochrome` variables, as seen in Example 10-1.

Colors can be specified either with color names or hex strings, as described in Chapter 8, *Command Line Options*.

A Complete Revamp of twm

Using the various techniques described in this chapter, we've modified the *system.twmrc* file to create an interface we think is more helpful to the average user.

Our modified *.twmrc* file sets up three pull-right menus, each with a slightly different focus. The second menu offers some utilities, including *oclock* and *xcalc*, and some system commands, such as *rlogin*. The final menu is a Preferences menu, which sets different keyclick volumes, leds, and pointer speeds than the default.

You can test our *.twmrc*, shown in Example 10-7, or just use it as a touchstone to create your own.

Example 10-7. Modified .twmrc file

```
#
# O'Reilly custom .twmrc, modified from the X11R4 system.twmrc
NoGrabServer
AutoRelativeResize
DecorateTransients
UsePPosition "on"
RestartPreviousState
SortIconManager
ShowIconManager
IconifyByUnmapping
NoTitle
{
"oclock"
"xclock"
"xscreensaver"
"zwgc"
}
TitleFont "-adobe-helvetica-bold-r-normal--*-120-*-*-*-*-*-*"
ResizeFont "-adobe-helvetica-bold-r-normal--*-120-*-*-*-*-*-*"
MenuFont "-adobe-helvetica-bold-r-normal--*-120-*-*-*-*-*-*"
IconFont "-adobe-helvetica-bold-r-normal--*-100-*-*-*-*-*-*"
IconManagerFont "-adobe-helvetica-bold-r-normal--*-100-*-*-*"
Color
{
    BorderColor "slategrey"
    DefaultBackground "maroon"
    DefaultForeground "gray85"
    TitleBackground "maroon"
    TitleForeground "gray85"
    MenuBackground "maroon"
    MenuForeground "gray85"
    MenuTitleBackground "gray70"
    MenuTitleForeground "maroon"
    IconBackground "maroon"
    IconForeground "gray85"
    IconBorderColor "gray85"
    IconManagerBackground "maroon"
    IconManagerForeground "gray85"
}
#
# Define some useful functions for motion-based actions.
#
MoveDelta 3
Function "move-or-lower" { f.move f.deltastop f.lower }
Function "move-or-raise" { f.move f.deltastop f.raise }
Function "move-or-iconify" { f.move f.deltastop f.iconify }
#
# Set some useful bindings.  Sort of uwm-ish, sort of simple-button-ish
#
Button1 =        : root :          f.menu         "defops"
Button2 =        : root :          f.menu         "Preferences"
Button3 =        : root :          f.menu         "Utilities"

Button1 =    m   : window|icon :   f.function     "move-or-lower"
```

Example 10-7. Modified .twmrc file (continued)

```
Button2 =   m   : window|icon : f.iconify
Button3 =   m   : window|icon : f.function    "move-or-raise"

Button1 =       : title :       f.function    "move-or-raise"
Button2 =       : title :       f.raiselower

Button1 =       : icon :        f.function    "move-or-iconify"
Button2 =       : icon :        f.iconify

Button1 =       : iconmgr :     f.iconify
Button2 =       : iconmgr :     f.iconify

#
# And a menu with the usual things
#
menu "defops"
{
"Twm"                   f.title
"Iconify"               f.iconify
"Resize"                f.resize
"Move"                  f.move
"Raise"                 f.raise
"Lower"                 f.lower
""                      f.nop
"..Utilities"           f.menu    "Utilities"
"..Preferences"         f.menu    "Preferences"
""                      f.nop
"Focus"                 f.focus
"Unfocus"               f.unfocus
"Show Iconmgr"          f.showiconmgr
"Hide Iconmgr"          f.hideiconmgr
""                      f.nop
"Kill"                  f.destroy
"Delete"                f.delete
""                      f.nop
"Restart"               f.restart
"Exit"                  f.quit
}

menu "Utilities" {
"Utilities"     f.title
""              f.beep
"identify"      f.identify
"source .twmrc" f.twmrc
""              f.beep
"mail box"      !"/usr/bin/X11/xbiff -display $DISPLAY&"
"clock"         !"/usr/bin/X11/oclock -display $DISPLAY &"
"xterm"         !"/usr/bin/X11/xterm -ls -display $DISPLAY &"
"xphoon"        !"/usr/bin/X11/xphoon &"
""              f.beep
"news"          !"/usr/bin/X11/xhost news.mit.edu;
                        /usr/bin/X11/xterm -title news.mit.edu
                        -e rlogin news.mit.edu &"
"mintaka"       !"/usr/bin/X11/xhost mintaka.lcs.mit.edu;
                        /usr/bin/X11/xterm -title mintaka.lcs.mit.edu
                        -e rlogin mintaka.lcs.mit.edu &"
}
```

Example 10-7. Modified .twmrc file (continued)

```
menu  "Preferences" {
"Preferences"      ("DarkSlateGray" : "thistle") f.title
"Bell Loud"        ("HotPink" : "bisque1")        !"xset b 80&"
"Bell Normal"      ("HotPink" : "bisque1")        !"xset b on&"
"Bell Off"         ("HotPink" : "bisque1")        !"xset b off&"
"Click Loud"       ("HotPink" : "azure1")         !"xset c 80&"
"Click Soft"       ("HotPink" : "azure1")         !"xset c on&"
"Click Off"        ("HotPink" : "azure1")         !"xset c off&"
"Lock On"          !"xset led on&"
"Lock Off"         !"xset led off&"
"Mouse Fast"       ("HotPink" : "gold1")          !"xset m 4 2&"
"Mouse Normal"     ("HotPink" : "gold1")          !"xset m 2 5&"
"Mouse Slow"       ("HotPink" : "gold1")          !"xset m 1 1&"
}
```

11

Setup Clients

This chapter describes three useful setup clients that can be used to customize the appearance of your display, and the operation of your keyboard and pointer.

In This Chapter:

11
Setup Clients

Setup Clients

This chapter discusses how to set up certain features of your working environment, using the following clients:

xset	To set certain characteristics of the keyboard, pointer and display.
xsetroot	To set root window characteristics.
xmodmap	To change pointer and modifier key mappings.

xset: Setting Display and Keyboard Preferences

The *xset* client allows you to set an assortment of user preference options for the display and keyboard. Some of these are followed by *on* or *off* to set or unset the option. Note that *xset* is inconsistent in its use of a dash (–) as an option flag. Some options use a preceding "–" to indicate that a feature be disabled; this can be confusing at first to users accustomed to seeing "–" as an introductory symbol on all options.

Although *xset* can be run any time, it is suggested that you run it at startup. These settings reset to the default values when you log out. Not all X implementations are guaranteed to honor all of these options.

Keyboard Bell

The b option controls bell volume (as a percentage of its maximum), pitch (in hertz), and duration (in milliseconds). It accepts up to three numerical parameters:

```
b volume pitch duration
```

If no parameters are given, the system defaults are used. If only one parameter is given, the bell volume is set to that value. If two values are listed, the second parameter specifies the bell pitch. If three values are listed, the third one specifies the duration.

For example, the command:

```
% xset b 70 1000 100
```

sets the volume of the keyboard bell to 70 percent of the maximum, the pitch to 1000 hertz, and the duration to 100 milliseconds.

Note that bell characteristics vary with different hardware. The X server sets the characteristics of the bell as closely as it can to the user's specifications.

The b option also accepts the parameters on or off. If you specify xset b on, system defaults for volume, pitch and duration are used.

The bell can also be turned off with the option -b, or by setting the volume parameter to 0 (xset b 0).

Bug Compatibility Mode

Some Release 3 clients were written to work with "features" of the Release 3 server, which could more accurately be called bugs. Many of these bugs have been eliminated in Release 4. In order to allow certain Release 3 clients to work under the Release 4 server, the Release 4 server has a bug compatibility mode that can be enabled using *xset*. In this mode, the Release 4 server is compatible with Release 3 clients that depended on bugs in the Release 3 server to work properly (most notably the Release 3 version of *xterm*).

To enable bug compatibility mode, use the command xset bc; to disable it, use the command xset -bc.

Keyclick Volume

The c option sets the volume of the keyboard's keyclick and takes the form:

```
c volume
```

volume can be a value from 0 to 100, indicating a percentage of the maximum volume. For example:

```
% xset c 75
```

sets a moderately loud keyclick. The X server sets the volume to the nearest value that the hardware can support.

The c option also accepts the parameters on or off. If you specify xset c on, the system default for volume is used.

The keyclick can also be turned off with the option -c, or by setting the volume parameter to 0 (xset c 0).

On some hardware, a volume of 0 to 50 turns the keyclick off, and a volume of 51 to 100 turns the keyclick on.

Enabling or Disabling Auto-repeat

The `r` option controls the keyboard's auto-repeat feature. (Auto-repeat causes a keystroke to be repeated over and over when the key is held down.) Use `xset r` or `xset r on` to enable key repeat. Use `xset -r` or `xset r off` to disable key repeat. On some keyboards (notably Apollo), only some keys repeat, regardless of the state of this option.

Changing or Rehashing the Font Path

As discussed in Chapter 8, *Command Line Options*, when a client is to be displayed in a particular font, the server by default looks for the font in three subdirectories of */usr/lib/X11/fonts*: *misc*, *75dpi*, and *100dpi*.

The `fp` (font path) option of *xset* can be used to change the font path, i.e., to direct the X server to search other directories for fonts called by a client. The option must be followed by a directory or a comma-separated list of directories, as in the following example:

```
% xset fp /work/andy/fonts,/usr/lib/X11/newfonts
```

To restore the default font path, type:

```
% xset fp default
```

As discussed in Chapter 8, the `fp` option with the `rehash` parameter causes the server to reread the *fonts.dir* and *fonts.alias* files in the current font path. You need to do this every time you edit an alias file to make the server aware of the changes.

To make the server aware of aliases, type:

```
% xset fp rehash
```

You also have to do this if you add or remove fonts. See Appendix A, *System Management*, for more information.

Keyboard LEDs

The `led` option controls the turning on or off of one or all of the keyboard's LEDs. It accepts the parameters `on` or `off` to turn all of the LEDs on or off. A preceding dash also turns all of the LEDs off (`-led`).

You can also turn individual LEDs on or off by supplying a numerical parameter (a value between 1 and 32) that corresponds to a particular LED. The `led` option followed by a numerical parameter turns that LED on. The `led` option preceded by a dash and followed by a numerical parameter turns that LED off. For example:

```
% xset led 3
```

would turn LED #3 on, while:

```
% xset -led 3
```

would turn LED #3 off.

Note that the particular LED values may refer to different LEDs on different hardware.

Pointer Acceleration

The `m` (mouse) option controls the rate at which the mouse or pointer moves across the screen. This option takes two parameters: *`acceleration`* and *`threshold`*. They must be positive integers. (The acceleration can also be written as a numerator/denominator combination separated by a '/', for example, 5/4.)

The mouse or pointer moves *`acceleration`* times as fast when it travels more than the *`threshold`* number of pixels in a short time. This way, the mouse can be used for precise alignment when it is moved slowly, yet it can be set to travel across the screen by a flick of the wrist when desired. If only one parameter is given, it is interpreted as the acceleration.

For example, the command:

```
% xset m 5 10
```

sets the mouse movement so that if you move the mouse more than ten pixels, the mouse cursor moves five times as many pixels on the screen as you moved the mouse on the pad.

If no parameter or the value `default` is used, the system defaults will be set.

If you want to change the threshold and leave the acceleration unchanged, enter the value `default` for acceleration.

Screen Saver

X supports a screen saver to blank or randomly change the screen when the system is left unattended for an extended period. This avoids the "burn in" that can occur when the same image is displayed on the screen for a long time. The `s` (screen saver) option to *xset* determines how long the server must be inactive before the screen saver is started.

The `s` option takes two parameters: *`time`* and *`cycle`*. The screen goes blank if the server has not received any input for the time interval specified by the *`time`* parameter. The contents of the screen reappear upon receipt of any input. If the display is not capable of blanking the screen, then the screen is shifted a pixel in a random direction at time intervals set by the *`cycle`* parameter. The parameters are specified in seconds.

For example, the command:

```
% xset s 600
```

sets the length of time before the screen saver is invoked to 600 seconds (ten minutes).

For a display not capable of blanking the screen, the command:

```
% xset s 600 10
```

sets the length of time before the screen saver is invoked to ten minutes and shifts the screen every ten seconds thereafter, until input is received.

The `s` option also takes the parameters:

`default`	Resets the screen save option to the default.
`blank`	Turns on blanking and overrides any previous settings.
`noblank`	Displays a background pattern rather than blanking the screen; overrides any previous settings.
`off`	Turns off the screen saver option and overrides any previous settings.
`expose`	Allows window exposures (the server can discard window contents).
`noexpose`	Disables screen saver unless the server can regenerate the screens without causing exposure events (i.e., without forcing the applications to regenerate their own windows).

Color Definition

On color displays, every time a client requests a private read/write colorcell, a new color definition is entered in the display's colormap. The `p` option sets one of these colormap entries even though they are supposed to be private. The parameters are a positive integer identifying a cell in the colormap to be changed, and a color name:

```
p entry_number color_name
```

The root window colors can be changed on some servers using *xsetroot*. An error results if the map entry is a read-only color.

For example, the command:

```
% xset p 3 blue
```

sets the third cell in the colormap to the color blue, but only if some client has allocated this cell read/write.

The client that allocated the cell is likely to change it again sometime after you try to set it, since this is the usual procedure for allocating a read/write cell.

Help with xset Options

The `q` option lists the current values of all *xset* preferences.

Setup Clients

xsetroot: Setting Root Window Characteristics

You can use the *xsetroot* client to tailor the appearance of the background (root) window on a display running X.

The *xsetroot* client is primarily used to specify the root window pattern: as a plaid-like grid, tiled grey pattern, solid color, or a bitmap. You can also specify foreground and background colors (defaults are black and white), reverse video, and set the shape of the pointer when it's in the root window.

If no options are specified, or the `-def` option is specified, *xsetroot* resets the root window to its default state, a grey mesh pattern, and resets the pointer to the hollow X pointer. The `-def` option can also be specified with other options; those characteristics that are not set by other options are reset to the defaults.

Although *xsetroot* can be run any time, it is suggested that you run it from a startup shell script, as described at the end of this chapter. All settings reset to the default values when you log out.

For a complete list of options, see the *xsetroot* reference page in Part Three of this guide. Not all X implementations are guaranteed to support all of these options. Some of the options may not work on certain hardware devices.

The `-help` option prints all the *xsetroot* options to standard output. The options you'll probably use most frequently are explained in the next section. Since only one type of background pattern can be specified at a time, the `-solid`, `-gray`, `-grey`, `-bitmap` and `-mod` options are mutually exclusive.

Setting Root Window Patterns

The default root window pattern is called a "grey mesh." On most displays, it is fairly dark.

The *xsetroot* client allows you to specify an alternative grey background with the `-grey` (or `-gray`) option. This tiled grey pattern is slightly lighter than the default grey mesh pattern.

The *xsetroot* client also allows you to create a root window made up of repeated "tiles" of a particular bitmap, using the option:

```
-bitmap filename
```

where *`filename`* is the bitmap file to be used as the window pattern.

You can choose any of the bitmaps in the directory */usr/include/X11/bitmaps* or make your own bitmap files using the *bitmap* client (see Chapter 7, *Other Clients*).

For example, the command:

```
% xsetroot -bitmap /usr/andy/gumby -fg red -bg blue
```

fills the root window with a tiling of the bitmap */usr/andy/gumby* (a virtual army of Gumbys!), using the colors red and blue.

The -mod option sets a plaid-like grid pattern on the root window. You specify the horizontal (x) and vertical (y) dimensions in pixels of each square in the grid. The syntax of the option is:

```
-mod x y
```

where the parameters *x* and *y* are integers ranging from 1 to 16 (pixels). (Zero and negative numbers are taken as 1.)

The larger the x and y values you specify, the larger (and more visible) each square on the root window grid pattern. Try the command:

```
% xsetroot -mod 16 16
```

for the largest possible grid squares. Then test different x and y specifications.

The *xsetroot* option:

```
-solid color
```

sets the color of the root window to a solid color. This can be a color from the color name database or a more exact color name specified by its RGB value.

The command:

```
% xsetroot -solid lightblue
```

sets the color of the root window to light blue.* See Chapter 8, ***Command Line Options***, for more information on how to specify colors.

Foreground, Background Color and Reverse Video

In addition to specifying a solid color for the root window pattern, *xsetroot* allows you to specify foreground and background colors if you set the pattern with -bitmap or -mod. The standard Toolkit options are used to set foreground and background colors: -fg and -bg. The defaults are black and white.

Colors can be specified as names from the color name database, or as RGB values. See Chapter 8 for more instructions on how to specify color.

If you specify reverse video (-rv), the foreground and background colors are reversed.

---

*For technical reasons, colors set with xsetroot -solid may change on you unexpectedly. When you set a color with the -solid option to *xsetroot*, the client allocates a colorcell, sets the color, and deallocates the colorcell. The root window changes to that color. If another client is started that sets a new color, it allocates the next available colorcell—which may be the same one *xsetroot* just deallocated. This results in that color changing to the new color. The root window also changes to the new color. If this happens, you can run *xsetroot* again and if there are other colorcells available, the root window changes to the new color. If all colorcells are allocated, any call to change a colorcell results in an error message.

While this behavior may seem to be a vicious bug, it is actually an optimization designed to make sure applications don't run out of colors unnecessarily. Free colormap cells can be a scarce resource. See Volume One, ***Xlib Programming Manual***, for more information.

Foreground and background colors also take effect when you set the root window pointer, as described in the following section.

Changing the Root Window Pointer

By default, the pointer is an X when it's in the root window. You can change the shape of the root window pointer to one of the standard X cursor shapes or to any bitmap, using the following options:

```
-cursor_name standard_cursor_name
-cursor cursorfile maskfile
```

Available as of Release 4, the first option allows you to set the root window pointer to one of the standard cursor symbols, which are generally listed in the file */usr/include/X11/cursorfont.h*. We've provided a list of the standard cursors in Appendix D. To specify a standard cursor on a command line or in a resource file, strip the `XC_` prefix from the name. Thus, to set the root window pointer to the pirate cursor symbol, you would enter:

```
% xsetroot -cursor_name pirate
```

If you are running the Release 3 version of *xsetroot*, you have to use a more roundabout method to set the root window pointer to one of the standard cursor shapes. You must first convert the cursor character you want to a bitmap, using the *atobm* client, described in Chapter 6, *Graphics Utilities*. Then you can specify the bitmap as the root window cursor shape using the *xsetroot* option described in the following paragraphs.

This second option is intended to allow you to set the root window pointer to a bitmap, perhaps one you create. The parameters *cursorfile* and *maskfile* are bitmaps. The *cursorfile* sets the bitmap for the pointer shape. In effect, the *maskfile* is placed behind the *cursorfile* bitmap to set it off from the root window. The *maskfile* should be the same shape as the *cursorfile*, but should generally be at least one pixel wider in all directions.*

For the *cursorfile*, you can use any of the standard bitmaps in */usr/include/X11/bitmaps* or you can make your own with the *bitmap* client (see Chapter 6, *Graphics Utilities*).

Every standard cursor has an associated mask. Pictures of the cursors appear in Appendix D, *Standard Cursors*. To get an idea of what masks look like, display the cursor font using the command:

```
% xfd -fn cursor.
```

If you are using your own bitmap as the *cursorfile*, until you get used to the way masks work, create a *maskfile* that is a copy of the *cursorfile* with all bits set, i.e., the

*Technically speaking, the mask determines the pixels on the screen that are disturbed by the cursor. It functions as a sort of outliner or highlighter for the cursor shape. The mask appears as a white (or background color) border around the cursor (black or another foreground color), making it visible over any root window pattern. This is especially important when a black cursor appears on a black root window.

With the *xsetroot* defaults, you can observe the effect of a mask. When you move the X pointer onto the dark grey root window, the X should have a very thin white border, which enables you to see it more clearly.

`maskfile` should be all black* (or the foreground color). Then edit the `maskfile` to make it wider than the `cursorfile` by at least one pixel in all directions.

To specify a root window pointer made from the smiling Gumby bitmap we created for Figure 6-2, first copy the bitmap to make a mask file:

```
% cp gumby gumby.mask
```

Then edit the *gumby.mask* file using the *bitmap* client, setting all squares inside the Gumby. (You can use the *bitmap* command box Flood Fill to set all the empty squares at once.) Continue to edit the bitmap, making it one pixel wider in all directions.

Then specify the new pointer with *xsetroot*:

```
% xsetroot -cursor gumby gumby.mask
```

See Chapter 6, *Graphics Utilities*, for more information on using *bitmap*.

xmodmap: Modifier Key and Pointer Customization

The *xmodmap* client is used to assign (or map) key functions to physical keys on the keyboard. Primarily, *xmodmap* is used to assign so-called "modifier" key functions to physical keys, but it can also change the way other keys (and even pointer buttons) function.

As described in Chapter 2, *Getting Started*, keys with labels such as Shift, Control, Caps Lock, etc. are called "modifier" keys because they modify the action of other keys. The number and names of modifier keys differ from workstation to workstation. Every keyboard is likely to have a Shift, Caps Lock, and Control key, but after that, the babble begins. One workstation might have an Alt key, another might have a Funct key, and yet another a "Gold" key. On the Sun-3 keyboard, there are no less than three additional modifier keys, labeled Alternate, Right, and Left.

Because of the differences between keyboards, X programs are designed to work with "logical" modifier keynames. The logical keynames represent functions recognized by X programs. These modifier keynames can be mapped by the user to any physical key on the keyboard with the *xmodmap* client.

The logical keynames that X recognizes are:

- Shift
- Lock
- Ctrl
- Mod1 (also meta or 1 in *uwm*)
- Mod2 (also 2 in *uwm*)

*Don't be confused by the idea of a black cursor with a black mask on a black root window. Remember, the mask determines the pixels that are disturbed by the cursor—in effect creating an outline around the cursor. The outline appears in white (or specified background color), regardless of the color of the `maskfile`.

Setup Clients

- Mod3 (also 3 in *uwm*)
- Mod4 (also 4 in *uwm*)
- Mod5 (also 5 in *uwm*)

These keynames are case insensitive.

Of these X modifier keys, only Shift, Caps Lock, Control, and Meta are in common use. Note that *uwm* also recognizes the mod keys simply by number alone (1-5) and recognizes mod1 as meta (i.e., mod1, meta and 1 are equivalent).

The primary function of *xmodmap* is to allow you to assign these important modifier keyname functions (Shift, Control, Meta, etc.) to convenient keys on the keyboard. For example, you could choose to map the Shift function to a single key called "Shift," to two "Shift" keys (one on either side of the keypad), to an "Alt" key, or to any other convenient key or keys on the physical keyboard. A left-handed person might choose to map modifier keys on the right side of the keyboard that more often are found on the left side, such as Control.

In practical terms, each server will have a default keyboard configuration. The Shift, Caps Lock, and Control modifier keynames will be mapped to obvious keys. The assignment of the Meta key might be less obvious.

The *xmodmap* client allows you to print out the current assignments of modifier keyname functions to physical keys and/or to change the assignments.

xmodmap also has two other functions, which you will probably use less frequently. In addition to mapping modifier keyname functions to physical keys, *xmodmap* also allows you to assign the function of *any* key on the keyboard to any other key. For instance, you can make the Backspace key and the Delete key both function as Delete keys. (This may be helpful if the Backspace key is easier to reach.)

Also, in addition to keyboard mappings, *xmodmap* can be used to display or change the pointer button assignments. Many X clients recognize logical pointer button commands. For example, holding down and dragging the first logical pointer button in an *xterm* window copies the text into memory. (In many default pointer maps, the first logical button is the leftmost button, designed to be pressed by the right index finger.) Each logical button is associated with a *button code*. The first logical button generates button code 1, the second logical button generates button code 2, etc. *xmodmap* allows you to reassign logical buttons to different physical buttons on the pointer.

Thus, basically, *xmodmap* can perform three types of mappings:

1. Assign modifier keyname functions (such as Shift, Control, Meta) recognized by X to physical keys.

2. Make any key on the keyboard function as any other key (for example, making Backspace function like Delete).

3. Reassign logical pointer button functions to other physical buttons (for example, making the third physical button function as the first logical button).

In the following sections, we discuss key mapping, with an emphasis on the first type of mapping, of modifier keyname functions. Chances are, you'll have relatively little call to map other key functions (such as Backspace), though we have included an example of one such mapping, just in case.

After considering key mapping, we'll take a look at the much simpler issues involved in mapping pointer button functions. As you might expect, when you're changing the functionality of (up to) three pointer buttons, it's fairly simple to keep track of what you're doing.

On the other hand, mapping modifier key functions to physical keys can be more than a little confusing. In order to understand the mechanics of mapping keys, we first need to take a look at some terms used to describe keyboard keys.

Keycodes and Keysyms

Each key on a physical keyboard can be identified by a number known as a *keycode*. (Technically speaking, a keycode is the actual value that the key generates.) Keycodes cannot be mapped to other keys. No matter what functions you assign to various keys with *xmodmap*, the keycode associated with each physical key remains the same.

In addition to a keycode, each physical key is associated with a name known as a *keysym*. A keysym ("key symbol" name) is a name that represents the label on a key (theoretically) and corresponds to its function.

Alphanumeric keys generally have obvious keysyms, corresponding to the label on the key: for example, the keysym for the key labeled "H" is *h*. Unfortunately, a keysym does not always correspond to the key label. For example, on a Sun-3 workstation, though the keysym for the key labeled "Return" is *Return*, the keysym for the key labeled "Alternate" is *Break*, and the keysym for the key labeled "Right" is *Meta_R*.

While each keycode is tied to a physical key, each keysym corresponds to a *function*—and the keysym/function is mapped to a particular physical key (keycode). Every keyboard has a default assignment of keysyms to keycodes. In most cases, each physical key on the keyboard will be associated with a different keysym. As we'll see, however, the keysym (function) associated with a particular physical key (keycode) can be changed. This is done by assigning the keysym of one key to the keycode of another.

The modifier keynames recognized by X are not to be confused with keysyms. The X modifier keys are limited to the eight keynames discussed previously and are assigned *in addition* to the regular keysym/keycode pairings. In other words, when a physical key is mapped to function as the X Control key, it already has a default functionality (keysym) and keycode.

By default, most modifier keyname functions are mapped to keys having keysyms representing the same function. For example, the X Control keyname is probably mapped to the key labeled Control, and having the keysym Control.

The Meta modifier keyname is probably also assigned to a key having the keysym Meta. However, determining which physical key has the keysym Meta can be something of a puzzle. Later in this chapter, we'll consider a program called *xev*, which can be used to determine the keysym and keycode of any physical key.

With this background information in mind, we can now tackle a procedure to map modifier keynames.

Procedure to Map Modifier Keys

In order to change modifier key mappings with a minimum of confusion, you should perform the following steps:

1. Display the current *modifier* key mappings using *xmodmap*.
2. Then print out the default assignments of keysyms to keycodes for *all* keys, using *xmodmap* with the `-pk` option. Save this list of the default key assignments as a reference.
3. Experiment with the *xev* client to determine the keysyms associated with certain physical keys. This will help you find the key(s) assigned as the Meta modifier key (which probably also has the keysym Meta).
4. Once you're familiar with the current assignments, you can remap modifier keys using *xmodmap*.

Displaying the Current Modifier Key Map

Before mapping any modifier keynames, you should take a look at the current assignments. With no options, *xmodmap* displays the current map of X modifier keynames to actual keys. Type *xmodmap* and you get a display similar to this:

```
xmodmap: up to 2 keys per modifier, (keycodes in parentheses):

shift       Shift_L (0x6a), Shift_R (0x75)
lock        Caps_Lock (0x7e)
control     Control_L (0x53)
mod1        Meta_L (0x7f),  Meta_R (0x81)
mod2
mod3
mod4
mod5
```

For each logical keyname (on the left), *xmodmap* lists one or more keysyms, each followed in parentheses by an actual hardware keycode. The keycodes displayed by *xmodmap* are represented in hex. As we'll see, the equivalent decimal and octal keycodes are also accepted as arguments to *xmodmap*.

"Logical" modifier keyname recognized by X	Keysym	Keycode (hex version)
Shift	Shift_L	(0x6a)
	Shift_R	(0x75)
Lock	Caps_Lock	(0x7e)
Control	Control_L	(0x53)
Mod1	Meta_L	(0x7f)
	Meta_R	(0x81)

In this mapping, two keys are assigned as Meta (mod1) keys: keys having the keysyms Meta_L and Meta_R (for left and right, apparently one on each side of the keyboard). Unfortunately, as you can see, this doesn't really tell you which keys these are on the physical keyboard. You still need to know which physical keys (keycodes) have the keysyms Meta_L and Meta_R. You can determine this using the *xev* client, described later in this chapter.

Determining the Default Key Mappings

Before you start mapping keys, you should display and save a map of the default assignments of keysyms to keycodes. Running *xmodmap* with the `-pk` option prints a current map of all keyboard keys to standard output. This map, called a keymap table, lists the decimal keycode on the left and the associated keysym(s) on the right. Figure 11-1 shows a portion of a typical keymap table, for a Sun-3 keyboard.

Notice that each keysym is listed by a keysym name (comma, Caps_Lock, etc.) and a keysym value (0x002c, 0xffe5, etc). For our purposes, this value is irrelevant. It cannot be supplied as a keysym argument to *xmodmap*.

As you can see, the keymap table lists regular keyboard keys (C, V, comma, slash, space, etc.), and function/numeric keypad keys (R13, F35, etc.) as well as modifier keys (Caps_Lock, Meta_L and Meta_R). If you map several keys, you may get confused as to the original assignments. Before you map any keys, we suggest you redirect the keymap table to a file to save and use as a reference:

```
% xmodmap -pk > keytable
```

The keysyms recognized by your server are a subset of a far greater number of keysyms recognized internationally. The file */usr/include/X11/keysym.h* lists the keysym *families* that are enabled for your server. The file */usr/include/X11/keysymdef.h* lists the keysyms in each of the families enabled for your server, as well as the keysyms in several other families. See Appendix H, *Keysyms*, of Volume Two, *Xlib Reference Manual*, for more information on keysyms and tables of the most common ones.

```
Keycode        Keysym
               value  (name)

109            0x0043  (C)
110            0x0056  (V)
111            0x0042  (B)
112            0x004e  (N)
113            0x004d  (M)
114            0x002c  (comma)   0x003c  (less)
115            0x002e  (period)  0x003e  (greater)
116            0x002f  (slash)   0x003f  (question)
117            0xffe2  (Shift_R)
118            0xff0a  (Linefeed)
119            0xffde  (R13)
120            0xff54  (Down)    0xffdf  (F34)
121            0xffe0  (F35)
         .
         .
         .
126            0xffe5  (Caps_Lock)
127            0xffe7  (Meta_L)
128            0x0020  (space)
129            0xffe8  (Meta_R)
```

Figure 11-1. Partial keymap table

Matching Keysyms with Physical Keys Using xev

The keysym and keycode for any key can be determined with the *xev* client.* This is particularly useful for finding the Meta key(s). The *xev* client is used to keep track of *events*, packets of information that are generated by the server when actions occur and are interpreted by other clients. Moving the pointer or pressing a keyboard key cause input events to occur. (For more information about events, see Volume One, *Xlib Programming Manual*.)

To use *xev*, enter the command:

```
% xev
```

in an *xterm* window, and then use the pointer to place the *xev* window, as in Figure 11-2.

Within the *xev* window is a small box. Move the pointer inside this box. When you type a key inside the box, information about the key, including its keysym and keycode, will be displayed in the *xterm* window from which you started *xev*. The relevant information will look like this:

**xev* is a Release 3 standard client. In Release 4, it has been moved to the *demos* directory. If an executable version does not exist on your system, ask your system administrator.

If you cannot use *xev*, you must rely on the keymap table and a little deductive reasoning. Since certain *twm* functions have keyboard shortcuts involving the Meta key, testing these shortcuts should help you locate this key. See Chapter 3, *Using the twm Window Manager*, for more information.

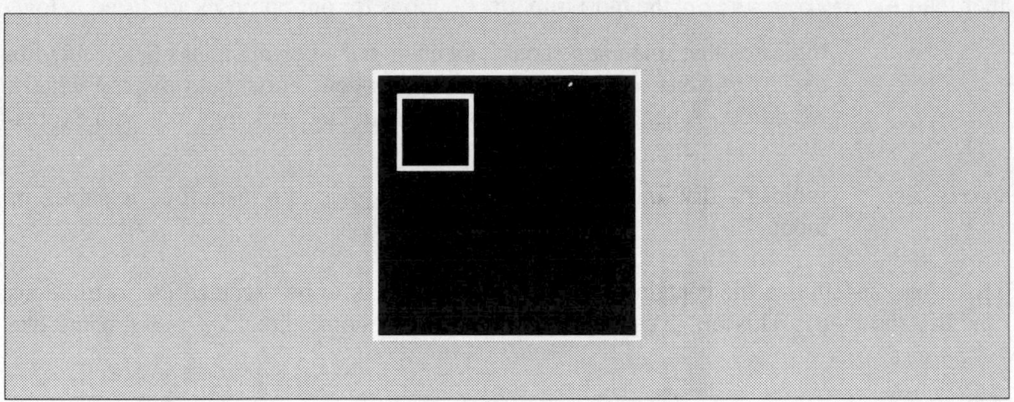

Figure 11-2. xev window

```
. . . keycode 127 (keysym 0xffe7, Meta_L) . . .
```

Notice that the keycode is given as a decimal number. You can use the decimal keycode as an argument to *xmodmap*. The keysym is listed by name, Meta_L, and value, 0xffe7. Again, this value cannot be supplied as a keysym argument to *xmodmap*. (See the *xev* reference page in Part Three for more information.)

To find the Meta key, type a few likely keys in the *xev* window. Type Control-C in the window from which you invoked *xev* to terminate the program. (If you ran *xev* in the background, you'll have to kill the *xev* window. See Chapter 7, *Other Clients*, for ways to do this.)

Changing the Map with xmodmap

xmodmap executes an expression or list of expressions that are interpreted as instructions to modify the key (or pointer) map. The expressions that can be interpreted by *xmodmap* are described in the next section.

xmodmap has the following syntax:

xmodmap [*options*] [*filename*]

An expression can be executed in either one of two ways:

- From the command line, using the `-e` *`expression`* option. This option specifies an expression to be executed (as an instruction to modify the map). Any number of expressions may be specified from the command line. An *`expression`* should be enclosed in quotes.
- Entered in a file that is used as an argument to *xmodmap*. Several expressions can be entered in one file.

Setup Clients

See the *xmodmap* reference page in Part Three of this guide for a complete list of options. Other than `-e expression`, the most important options for our purposes are listed below.

`-n` Indicates that *xmodmap* should not change the key mappings as specified in the `filename` or command line expression, but should display what it would do. A handy test. (Only works with key mappings, not with expressions that change the pointer map.)

`-verbose` Indicates that *xmodmap* should print logging information as it parses its input.

`filename` specifies a file containing *xmodmap* expressions to be executed (as instructions to modify the map). This file is usually kept in the user's home directory with a name like *.xmodmaprc*.

Expressions to Change the Key Map

The expressions interpreted by *xmodmap* can be used to perform the following types of key mappings:*

1. Assign and remove keysyms as modifier keynames recognized by X.
2. Map any keysym (function) to any physical key (keycode).

The following list shows allowable expressions, divided by function. (Using *xmodmap* with the `-grammar` option returns a help message with much of this information.) Those expressions that include an equal sign require a space before and after the sign.

1. To assign and remove keysyms as modifier keynames:

`clear` *MODIFIERNAME*

Removes all entries in the modifier map for the given modifier, where valid modifier names are: shift, lock, control, mod1, mod2, mod3, mod4, and mod5 (case does not matter in modifier names, although it does matter for all other names). For example, the expression `clear Lock` will remove all keys that were bound to the lock modifier.

`add` *MODIFIERNAME* `=` *KEYSYMNAME*

Adds the given keysym to the indicated modifier map. For example, you could make the Alt key an additional shift modifier key. The keysym name is evaluated after all input expressions are read to make it easy to write expressions to swap keys.

`remove` *MODIFIERNAME* `=` *KEYSYMNAME*

Removes the given keysym from the indicated modifier map (unmaps it). For example, remove Caps_Lock as the lock modifier key. Unlike with the `add`

*Expressions to change the pointer map are discussed in the section *Displaying and Changing the Pointer Map*, later in this chapter.

expression, the keysym names are evaluated as the line is read in. This allows you to remove keys from a modifier without having to worry about whether or not they have been reassigned.

2. To map any keysym(s) to any physical key (keycode):

`keycode` *NUMBER* = *KEYSYMNAME*

Assigns the keysym to the indicated keycode (which may be specified in decimal, hex or octal). Usually only one keysym is assigned to a given code.

`keysym` *KEYSYMNAME* = *KEYSYMNAME*

Assigns the keysym on the right to the keycode of the keysym on the left. Note that if you have the same keysym bound to multiple keys, this might not work.

Setup Clients

Key Mapping Examples

Expressions can be used on the *xmodmap* command line or entered in a file that is then used as an argument to *xmodmap*. Note that *xmodmap* should be run from your startup script (discussed later in this chapter) to take effect for all clients in the login session. This section includes three examples, corresponding to the three types of mappings you can perform.

Remember that including the `-n` option on the *xmodmap* command line allows you to see what the new mappings *would* be, without actually performing them. This can be very useful, particularly while you're learning to use *xmodmap* and getting used to the syntax of expressions. (Note, however, that `-n` cannot be used with expressions to change the pointer mapping.)

First, the *xmodmap* client also allows you to assign logical modifier keynames to physical keys. A not so obvious feature of *xmodmap* is that to change the mapping of a modifier key, you must first remove that key from the current modifier map. For example, to swap the left Control and (Caps) Lock keys, you would first need to unmap both physical keys (Caps_Lock, Control_L) from their respective modifier keynames (lock, control):

```
remove lock = Caps_Lock
remove control = Control_L
```

And then reverse the mappings:

```
add lock = Control_L
add control = Caps_Lock
```

If you then type *xmodmap* without options, you see the new map:

```
xmodmap: up to 2 keys per modifier, (keycodes in parentheses):
shift       Shift_L (0x6a), Shift_R (0x75)
lock        Control_L (0x53)
control     Caps_Lock (0x7e)
mod1        Meta_L (0x7f), Meta_R (0x81)
mod2
mod3
mod4
mod5
```

The key with the keysym Control_L functions as a Lock key and the key with the keysym Caps_Lock functions as a Control key.

Second, *xmodmap* allows you to assign any keysym to any other key. For example, you might make the Backspace key function as a Delete key:

```
% xmodmap -e 'keysym BackSpace = Delete'
```

Then when you display the keymap table and grep for the Delete keysym, you'll see that it is assigned twice. On the command line of an *xterm* window, type:

```
% xmodmap -pk | grep Delete
```

and you'll get two lines from the current keymap table, similar to these:

```
50          0xffff (Delete)
73          0xffff (Delete)
```

The 50 and 73 are keycodes representing two physical keys. As you can see, both of these keys now function as Delete keys.

This example suggests some of the confusion you can experience using *xmodmap*. We know that one of these keys previously functioned as the Backspace key. But how can we tell which one? Here is an instance when our default keymap table comes in handy. If you've run `xmodmap -pk` and redirected it to a file before changing any mappings, you can check the file for the keysyms originally associated with the keycodes 50 and 73. In this case, the file tells us 50 was originally Backspace and 73 was Delete.

Of course, you could also figure out the original assignments by remapping one of the keycodes to Backspace. Then, if the key marked Backspace functions as marked, you know you've mapped the keysym to the original keycode. But, as you can see, the default keymap table can greatly simplify matters.

This example also implies that there are advantages to using expressions of the form:

```
keycode number = keysymname
```

This expression syntax requires you to be aware of default keycode/keysym assignments. Also, if you explicitly assign a keysym to a particular keycode, it's much easier to keep track of what you're doing and retrace your steps if necessary. On the down side, though keysyms are portable, keycodes may vary from server to server. Thus, expressions using this syntax cannot be ported to other systems.

Displaying and Changing the Pointer Map

If you want to change the assignment of logical pointer buttons to physical buttons, you should first display the current pointer map with the `-pp` option to *xmodmap*. A typical pointer map appears in Figure 11-3.

This is a fairly simple map: the physical buttons are listed on the left and the corresponding logical functions (button codes) are listed on the right.

```
There are 3 pointer buttons defined.

    Physical        Button
     Button          Code
        1              1
        2              2
        3              3
```

Figure 11-3. Pointer map

These are typical assignments for a right-handed person: the first logical button is the left-most button, designed to be pressed by the right index finger. The *xmodmap* client allows you to reassign logical buttons so that the pointer can be more easily used with the left hand.

The *xmodmap* client allows you to change the pointer map.* There are two *xmodmap* expressions: one to assign logical pointer buttons (button codes) to physical buttons; and another to restore the default assignments. The syntax of the expressions is as follows:

`pointer = x y z`

Sets the first, second, and third physical buttons to the button codes *x*, *y*, and *z*.

`pointer = default`

Sets the pointer map back to its default settings (button 1 generates a code of 1, button 2 generates a code of 2, etc.).

Being able to change the pointer button assignments is very useful if you happen to be left-handed and would like the rightmost physical button to function as the first logical button (i.e., generate button code 1). To configure the pointer for a southpaw:

```
% xmodmap -e 'pointer = 3 2 1'
```

Then if you display the pointer mappings with `xmodmap -pp`, you get the following:

```
There are 3 pointer buttons defined.

    Physical        Button
     Button          Code
        1              3
        2              2
        3              1
```

You can then push the first logical button (button code 1) with the index finger of your left hand.

You can return to the default pointer button assignments by entering:

```
% xmodmap -e 'pointer = default'
```

*Remember that the `-n` option, which allows you to see what *xmodmap would* do, without performing the changes, cannot be used with expressions to change the pointer mapping.

Part Three

The Reference Pages

Part Three:

Client Reference Pages

This part of the guide provides UNIX-style "man-pages" for each of the X programs. These pages are arranged alphabetically for ease of reference, and they contain detailed information (such as all options to a program) that is not covered in other parts of this guide.

The following reference pages appear in this section:

Name

Intro – overview of reference page format.

Syntax

This section describes the command line syntax for invoking the client.

Description

This section explains the operation of the client.

Options

This section lists available command line options. In some cases, reference is made to "all of the standard X Toolkit command line options." These X Toolkit options are listed in Chapter 8 of this guide.

Resources

This section lists the resource variable names that can be specified in an *.Xresources* or other resource file. In some cases, reference is made to "all the core resource names and classes." A list of the core names and classes appears on the reference page for *X* and in Table 8-1 in Chapter 8, *Command Line Options*. See Chapter 9, *Setting Resources*, for syntax rules and examples. For complete information, see Volume Four, *X Toolkit Intrinsics Programming Manual*.

Environment

If present, this section lists shell environment variables used by the client. This section does not list the DISPLAY and XENVIRONMENT variables, which are used by all clients. They are used as follows:

DISPLAY	To get the default host and display number.
XENVIRONMENT	To get the name of a resource file that overrides the global resources stored in the RESOURCE_MANAGER property.

See Also

This section lists other pages in Part Three of this guide that may also be of interest. Note that versions of these pages may have been installed in the usual on-line manual hierarchy, and may be available via the UNIX *man*(1) command. References such as *stat*(2) can be found in the standard UNIX documentation. This section may also include references to documentation on Xlib, the X Toolkit, various widgets, etc.

Bugs

If present, this section lists areas in which the author of the program thinks it could be improved. In a few cases, we've added additional bugs we've noted.

Author

The authors of the program and (generally) the reference page as well. Most of the reference pages are subject to the copyright provisions in the "Copyright" section of the X reference page. Where appropriate, additional copyrights are noted on individual pages.

Note, however, that those portions of this document that are based on the original X11 documentation and other source materials have been revised and that all such revisions are copyright © 1987, 1988, 1989 O'Reilly & Associates, Inc. Inasmuch as the proprietary revisions can't be separated from the freely copyable MIT source material, the net result is that copying of this document is not allowed. Sorry for the doublespeak!

Name

X – a portable, network transparent window system.

Description

X is a network transparent window system developed at MIT that runs on a wide range of computing and graphics machines. The Release 4 core distribution from MIT has support for the following operating systems:

Ultrix 3.1 (Digital)
SunOS 4.0.3 (Sun)
HP-UX 6.5 (Hewlett-Packard)
Domain/OS 10.1 (HP/Apollo)
A/UX 1.1 (Apple)
AIX RT-2.2 and PS/2-1.1 (IBM)
AOS-4.3 (IBM)
UTEK 4.0 (Tektronix)
NEWS-OS 3.2 (Sony; client only)
UNICOS 5.0.1 (Cray; client only)
UNIX(tm) System V, Release 3.2 (AT&T 6386 WGS; client only)

It should be relatively easy to build the client-side software on a variety of other systems. Commercial implementations are also available for a much wider range of platforms.

The X Consortium requests that the following names be used when referring to this software:

X
X Window System
X Version 11
X Window System, Version 11
X11

X Window System is a trademark of the Massachusetts Institute of Technology.

X window system servers run on computers with bitmap displays. The server distributes user input to and accepts output requests from various client programs through a variety of different interprocess communication channels. Although the most common case is for the client programs to be running on the same machine as the server, clients can be run transparently from other machines (including machines with different architectures and operating systems) as well.

X supports overlapping hierarchical subwindows and text and graphics operations, on both monochrome and color displays. For a full explanation of the functions that are available, see Volume Four, *X Toolkit Intrinsics Programming Manual* and Volume Five, *X Toolkit Intrinsics Reference Manual*.

The number of programs that use X is growing rapidly. Of particular interest are: a terminal emulator (*xterm*), a window manager (*twm*), a display manager (*xdm*), mail managing utilities (*xmh* and *xbiff*), a manual page browser (*xman*), a bitmap editor (*bitmap*), access control programs (*xauth* and *xhost*), user preference setting programs (*xrdb*, *xset*, *xsetroot*, and *xmodmap*), a load monitor (*xload*), clocks (*oclock* and *xclock*), a font displayer (*xfd*), utilities for listing information about fonts, windows, and displays (*xlsfonts*, *xfontsel*, *xlswins*, *xwininfo*, *xdpyinfo*, *xlsclients*, and *xprop*), a diagnostic for seeing what events are generated and when (*xev*), screen image manipulation utilities (*xwd*, *xwud*, *xpr*, and *xmag*), and various demos (*xeyes*, *ico*, *muncher*, *puzzle*, *xgc*, etc.).

Many other utilities, window managers, games, toolkits, etc. are available from the user-contributed distribution. See your site administrator for details.

Starting Up

There are currently three ways of starting the X server and an initial set of client applications. The particular method used depends on what operating system you are running and on whether or not you use other window systems in addition to X.

xdm (the X Display Manager)

If you want to always have X running on your display, your site administrator can set your machine up to use the X Display Manager *xdm*. This program is typically started by the system at boot time and takes care of keeping the server running and getting users logged in. If you are running *xdm*, you will see a window on the screen welcoming you to the system and asking for your username and password. Simply type them in as you would at a normal terminal, pressing the Return key after each. If you make a mistake, *xdm* will display an error message and ask you to try again. After you have successfully logged in, *xdm* will start up your X environment. By default, if you have an executable file named *.xsession* in your home directory, *xdm* will treat it as a program (or shell script) to run to start up your initial clients (such as terminal emulators, clocks, a window manager, user settings for things like the background, the speed of the pointer, etc.). Your site administrator can provide details.

xinit (run manually from the shell)

Sites that support more than one window system might choose to use the *xinit* program for starting X manually. If this is true for your machine, your site administrator will probably have provided a program named "x11", "startx", or "xstart" that will do site-specific initialization (such as loading convenient default resources, running a window manager, displaying a clock, and starting several terminal emulators) in a nice way. If not, you can build such a script using the *xinit* program. This utility simply runs one user-specified program to start the server, runs another to start up any desired clients, and then waits for either to finish. Since either or both of the user-specified programs may be a shell script, this gives substantial flexibility at the expense of a nice interface. For this reason, *xinit* is not intended for end users.

xterm –L (started from */etc/init*)

This method can be used only with Release 3 (or an earlier release) of X. Some versions of UNIX that are derived from BSD 4.3 support starting the window system and an initial *xterm* window from the system terminal line configuration file */etc/ttys*. As with *xdm*, there will be a window requesting your username and password. However, this window will become your primary window and is not configurable on a per-user basis. Sites using this method should switch to *xdm* as *xterm -L* is not be supported as of Release 4.

Display Names

From the user's perspective, every X server has a `displayname` of the form:

`host:display.screen`

This information is used by the application to determine how it should connect to the server and which screen it should use by default (on displays with multiple monitors):

`host` The name of the machine to which the display is physically connected. If the `host` name is not given, the most efficient way of communicating to a server on the same machine will be used.

`display` The `display` number. The phrase "display" is usually used to refer to a collection of monitors that share a common keyboard and pointer (mouse, tablet, etc.). Most workstations tend to only have one keyboard, and therefore, only one display. Larger, multi-user systems, however, will frequently have several displays so that more than one person can be doing graphics work at once. To avoid confusion, each display on a machine is assigned a display number (beginning at 0) when the X server for that display is started. The `display` number must always be given in a display name. In this guide, the `display` number is also referred to as the `server` number (referring to the phrase *display server*).

`screen` The `screen` number. Some displays share a single keyboard and pointer among two or more monitors. Since each monitor has its own set of windows, each screen is assigned a `screen` number (beginning at 0) when the X server for that display is started. If the screen number is not given, then screen 0 will be used.

On POSIX systems, the default display name is stored in your DISPLAY environment variable. This variable is set automatically by the *xterm* terminal emulator. However, when you log into another machine on a network, you'll need to set DISPLAY by hand to point to your display. For example,

```
% setenv DISPLAY myws:0
$ DISPLAY=myws:0; export DISPLAY
```

Finally, most X programs accept a command line option of `-display displayname` to temporarily override the contents of DISPLAY. This is most commonly used to pop windows on another person's screen or as part of a "remote shell" command to start an xterm pointing back to your display. For example,

```
% xeyes -display joesws:0 -geometry 1000x1000+0+0
% rsh big xterm -display myws:0 -ls </dev/null &
```

X servers listen for connections on a variety of different communications channels (network byte streams, shared memory, etc.). Since there can be more than one way of contacting a given server, the `host` name part of the display name is used to determine the type of channel (also called a transport layer) to be used. The sample servers from MIT support the following types of connections:

local The host part of the display name should be the empty string. For example: `:0`, `:1`, and `:0.1`.

TCP/IP The host part of the display name should be the server machine's IP address name. Full Internet names, abbreviated names, and IP addresses are all allowed. For example: `expo.lcs.mit.edu:0`, `expo:0`, `18.30.0.212:0`, `bigmachine:1`, and `hydra:0.1`.

DECnet The host part of the display name should be the server machine's nodename followed by two colons instead of one. For example: `myws::0`, `big::1`, and `hydra::0.1`.

Access Control

The sample server provides two types of access control: an authorization protocol that provides a list of "magic cookies" clients can send to request access (available as of Release 4); and a list of hosts from which connections are always accepted. *xdm* initializes magic cookies in the server, and also places them in a file accessible to the user. Normally, the list of hosts from which connections are always accepted should be empty, so that only clients that are explicitly authorized can connect to the display. When you add entries to the host list (with *xhost*), the server no longer performs any authorization on connections from those machines. Be careful with this.

The file for authorization used by both *xdm* and Xlib can be specified with the environment variable XAUTHORITY, and defaults to the file *Xauthority* in the home directory. *xdm* uses *$HOME/Xauthority* and will create it or merge in authorization records if it already exists when a user logs in.

To manage a collection of authorization files containing a collection of authorization records, use *xauth*. This program allows you to extract records and insert them into other files. Using this, you can send authorization to remote machines when you login. As the files are machine-independent, you can also simply copy the files or use NFS to share them. If you use several machines, and share a common home directory with NFS, then you never really have to worry about authorization files, the system should work correctly by default. Note that magic cookies transmitted "in the clear" over NFS or using *ftp* or *rcp* can be "stolen" by a network eavesdropper, and as such may enable unauthorized access. In many environments this level of security is not a concern, but if it is, you need to know the exact semantics of the particular magic cookie to know if this is actually a problem.

Geometry Specifications

One of the advantages of using window systems instead of hardwired terminals is that applications don't have to be restricted to a particular size or location on the screen. Although the layout of windows on a display is controlled by the window manager that the user is running (described below), most X programs accept a command line argument of the form `-geometry widthxheight+xoff+yoff` (where *width*, *height*, *xoff*, and *yoff* are numbers) for specifying a preferred size and location for this application's main window.

The *width* and *height* parts of the geometry specification are usually measured in either pixels or characters, depending on the application. The *xoff* and *yoff* parts are measured in pixels and are used to specify the distance of the window from the left or right and top and bottom edges of the screen, respectively. Both types of offsets are measured from the indicated edge of the screen to the corresponding edge of the window. The x offset may be specified in the following ways:

+xoff The left edge of the window is to be placed *xoff* pixels in from the left edge of the screen (i.e., the x coordinate of the window's origin will be *xoff*). *xoff* may be negative, in which case the window's left edge will be off the screen.

-xoff The right edge of the window is to be placed *xoff* pixels in from the right edge of the screen. *xoff* may be negative, in which case the window's right edge will be off the screen.

The y offset has similar meanings:

+yoff The top edge of the window is to be *yoff* pixels below the top edge of the screen (i.e., the y coordinate of the window's origin will be *yoff*). *yoff* may be negative, in which case the window's top edge will be off the screen.

-yoff The bottom edge of the window is to be *yoff* pixels above the bottom edge of the screen. *yoff* may be negative, in which case the window's bottom edge will be off the screen.

Offsets must be given as pairs; in other words, in order to specify either *xoff* or *yoff* both must be present. Windows can be placed in the four corners of the screen using the following specifications:

`+0+0` The upper left hand corner.

`-0+0` The upper right hand corner.

`-0-0` The lower right hand corner.

`+0-0` The lower left hand corner.

In the following examples, a terminal emulator will be placed in roughly the center of the screen and a load average monitor, mailbox, and clock will be placed in the upper right hand corner:

Reference Pages

```
% xterm -fn 6x10 -geometry 80x24+30+200 &
% xclock -geometry 48x48-0+0 &
% xload -geometry 48x48-96+0 &
% xbiff -geometry 48x48-48+0 &
```

Window Managers

The layout of windows on the screen is controlled by special programs called *window managers*. Although many window managers will honor geometry specifications as given, others may choose to ignore them (requiring the user to explicitly draw the window's region on the screen with the pointer, for example).

Since window managers are regular (albeit complex) client programs, a variety of different user interfaces can be built. In Release 4, the core distribution comes with a window manager named *twm*, which supports overlapping windows, popup menus, point-and-click or click-to-type input models, titlebars, nice icons (and an icon manager for those who don't like separate icon windows).

Several other window managers are available in the Release 4 user-contributed distribution: *uwm*, *gwm*, *m_swm*, *olwm*, and *tekwm*.

Font Names

Collections of characters for displaying text and symbols in X are known as *fonts*. A font typically contains images that share a common appearance and look nice together (for example, a single size, boldness, slant, and character set). Similarly, collections of fonts that are based on a common type face (the variations are usually called roman, bold, italic, bold italic, oblique, and bold oblique) are called *families*.

Sets of font families of the same resolution (usually measured in dots per inch) are further grouped into *directories* (so named because they were initially stored in file system directories). Each directory contains a database that lists the name of the font and information on how to find the font. The server uses these databases to translate *font names* (which have nothing to do with filenames) into font data.

The list of font directories in which the server looks when trying to find a font is controlled by the *font path*. Although most installations will choose to have the server start up with all of the commonly used font directories, the font path can be changed at any time with the *xset* program. However, it is important to remember that the directory names are on the *server's* machine, not on the application's.

The default font path for the sample server contains three directories:

/usr/lib/X11/fonts/misc

This directory contains several miscellaneous fonts that are useful on all systems. It contains a small family of fixed-width fonts in pixel heights 5 through 10, a family of fixed-width fonts from Dale Schumacher in similar pixel heights, several Kana fonts from Sony Corporation, a Kanji font, the standard cursor font, two cursor fonts from Digital Equipment Corporation, and OPEN LOOK cursor and glyph fonts from Sun Microsystems. It also has font name aliases for the fonts fixed and variable.

/usr/lib/X11/fonts/75dpi
: This directory contains fonts contributed by Adobe Systems, Inc., Digital Equipment Corporation, Bitstream, Inc., Bigelow and Holmes, and Sun Microsystems, Inc. for 75 dots per inch displays. An integrated selection of sizes, styles, and weights is provided for each family.

/usr/lib/X11/fonts/100dpi
: This directory contains 100 dots per inch versions of the fonts in the *75dpi* directory.

Font databases are created by running the *mkfontdir* program in the directory containing the source or compiled versions of the fonts (in both compressed and uncompressed formats). Whenever fonts are added to a directory, *mkfontdir* should be rerun so that the server can find the new fonts. To make the server reread the font database, reset the font path with the *xset* program. For example, to add a font to a private directory, the following commands could be used:

```
% cp newfont.snf ~/myfonts
% mkfontdir ~/myfonts
% xset fp rehash
```

The *xlsfonts* program can be used to list all of the fonts that are found in font databases in the current font path. Font names tend to be fairly long as they contain all of the information needed to uniquely identify individual fonts. However, the sample server supports wildcarding of font names, so the full specification:

```
-adobe-courier-medium-r-normal--10-100-75-75-m-60-iso8859-1
```

could be abbreviated as:

```
*-courier-medium-r-normal--*-100-*
```

Because the shell also has special meanings for * and ?, wildcarded font names should be quoted:

```
% xlsfonts -fn '*-courier-medium-r-normal--*-100-*'
```

If more than one font in a given directory in the font path matches a wildcarded font name, the choice of which particular font to return is left to the server. However, if fonts from more than one directory match a name, the returned font will always be from the first such directory in the font path. The example given above will match fonts in both the *75dpi* and *100dpi* directories; if the *75dpi* directory is ahead of the *100dpi* directory in the font path, the smaller version of the font will be used.

Color Names

Most applications provide ways of tailoring (usually through resources or command line arguments) the colors of various elements in the text and graphics they display. Although black and white displays don't provide much of a choice, color displays frequently allow anywhere between 16 and 16 million different colors.

Colors are usually specified by their commonly-used names (for example, *red*, *white*, or *medium slate blue*). The server translates these names into appropriate screen colors using a color database that can usually be found in */usr/lib/X11/rgb.txt*. Color names are case-insensitive, meaning that *red*, *Red*, and *RED* all refer to the same color.

Many applications also accept color specifications of the following form:

```
#rgb
#rrggbb
#rrrgggbbb
#rrrrggggbbbb
```

where *r*, *g*, and *b* are hexidecimal numbers indicating how much *red*, *green*, and *blue* should be displayed (zero being none and ffff being on full). Each field in the specification must have the same number of digits (e.g., #rrgb or #gbb are not allowed). Fields that have fewer than four digits (e.g., #rgb) are padded out with zero's following each digit (e.g., #r000g000b000). The eight primary colors can be represented as:

black	#000000000000 (no color at all)
red	#ffff00000000
green	#0000ffff0000
blue	#00000000ffff
yellow	#ffffffff0000 (full red and green, no blue)
magenta	#ffff0000ffff
cyan	#0000ffffffff
white	#ffffffffffff (full red, green, and blue)

Unfortunately, RGB color specifications are highly unportable since different monitors produce different shades when given the same inputs. Similarly, color names aren't portable because there is no standard naming scheme and because the color database needs to be tuned for each monitor. Application developers should take care to make their colors tailorable.

Keys

The X keyboard model is broken into two layers: server-specific codes (called *keycodes*) which represent the physical keys, and server-independent symbols (called *keysyms*) which represent the letters or words that appear on the keys. Two tables are kept in the server for converting keycodes to keysyms:

modifier list Some keys (such as Shift, Control, and Caps Lock) are known as *modifier* and are used to select different symbols that are attached to a single key (such as Shift-a generates a capital A, and Control-L generates a formfeed character ^L). The server keeps a list of keycodes corresponding to the various modifier keys. Whenever a key is pressed or released, the server generates an *event* that contains the keycode of the indicated key as well as a mask that specifies which of the modifer keys are currently pressed. Most servers set up this list to initially contain the various shift, control, and shift lock keys on the keyboard.

keymap table Applications translate event keycodes and modifier masks into keysyms using a *keysym table* which contains one row for each keycode and one column for each of the modifiers. This table is initialized by the server to correspond to normal typewriter conventions, but is only used by client programs.

Although most programs deal with keysyms directly (such as those written with the X Toolkit Intrinsics), most programming libraries provide routines for converting keysyms into the appropriate type of string (such as ISO Latin-1).

Options

Most X programs attempt to use the same names for command line options and arguments. All applications written with the X Toolkit Intrinsics automatically accept the following options:

`-display [`*host*`]:`*server*`[.`*screen*`]`
: Specifies the name of the X server to use. `host` specifies the machine, `server` specifies the display server number, and `screen` specifies the screen number. Either or both the `host` and `screen` elements to the display specification can be omitted. If `host` is omitted, the local machine is assumed. If `screen` is omitted, screen 0 is assumed (and the period is unnecessary). The colon and (display) `server` are necessary in all cases.

`-geometry` *geometry*
: Specifies the initial size and location of the application window. The `-geometry` option can be (and often is) abbreviated to `-g`, unless there is a conflicting option that begins with "g." The argument (*geometry*) is referred to as a "standard geometry string," and has the form *widthxheight±xoff±yoff*.

`-bg` *color*, `-background` *color*
: Either option specifies the color to use for the window background.

`-bd` *color*, `-bordercolor` *color*
: Either option specifies the color to use for the window border.

`-bw` *pixels*, `-borderwidth` *pixels*
: Either option specifies the width in pixels of the window border.

`-fg` *color*, `-foreground` *color*
: Either option specifies the color to use for text or graphics.

`-fn` *font*, `-font` *font*
: Either option specifies the font to use for displaying text.

`-iconic` Indicates that the user would prefer that the application's windows initially not be visible as if the windows had been immediately iconified by the user. Window managers may choose not to honor the application's request.

`-name` Specifies the name under which resources for the application should be found. This option is useful in shell aliases to distinguish between invocations of an application, without resorting to creating links to alter the executable filename.

Reference Pages

`-rv, -reverse`
: Either option indicates that the program should simulate reverse video if possible, often by swapping the foreground and background colors. Not all programs honor this or implement it correctly. It is usually only used on monochrome displays.

`+rv`
: Indicates that the program should not simulate reverse video. This is used to override any defaults since reverse video doesn't always work properly.

`-selectionTimeout`
: Specifies the timeout in milliseconds within which two communicating applications must respond to one another for a selection request.

`-synchronous`
: Indicates that requests to the X server should be sent synchronously, instead of asynchronously. Since Xlib normally buffers requests to the server, errors do not necessarily get reported immediately after they occur. This option turns off the buffering so that the application can be debugged. It should never be used with a working program.

`-title` *`string`*
: Specifies the title to be used for this window. This information is sometimes used by a window manager to provide some sort of header identifying the window.

`-xnllanguage` *`language[_territory][.codeset]`*
: Specifies the language, territory, and codeset for use in resolving resource and other filenames.

`-xrm` *`resourcestring`*
: Specifies a resource name and value to override any defaults. It is very useful for setting resources that don't have explicit command line arguments.

Resources

To make the tailoring of applications to personal preferences easier, X supports several mechanisms for storing default values for program resources (e.g., background color, window title, etc.) Resources are specified as strings of the form:

```
appname*subname*subsubname...: value
```

that are read in from various places when an application is run.

By convention, the application class name is the same as the program name, but with the first letter capitalized (e.g., *Bitmap* or *Emacs*) although some programs that begin with the letter "x" also capitalize the second letter for historical reasons. The precise syntax for resources is:

```
ResourceLine    =   Comment | ResourceSpec
Comment         =   "!" string | <empty line>
ResourceSpec    =   WhiteSpace ResourceName WhiteSpace ":" WhiteSpace value
ResourceName    =   [Binding] ComponentName {Binding ComponentName}
Binding         =   "." | "*"
WhiteSpace      =   {" " | "\t"}
```

```
ComponentName =  {"a"-"z" | "A"-"Z" | "0"-"9" | "_" | "-" "}
value         =  string
string        =  {<any character not including "\n">}
```

Note that elements enclosed in curly braces ({...}) indicate zero or more occurrences of the enclosed elements.

To allow values to contain arbitrary octets, the 4-character sequence \nnn, where *n* is a digit in the range of "0"–"7", is recognized and replaced with a single byte that contains this sequence interpreted as an octal number. For example, a value containing a NULL byte can be stored by specifying "\000".

The Xlib routine *XGetDefault*(3X) and the resource utilities within the X Toolkit obtain resources from the following sources:

RESOURCE_MANAGER root window property

Any global resources that should be available to clients on all machines should be stored in the RESOURCE_MANAGER property on the root window using the *xrdb* program. This is frequently taken care of when the user starts up X through the display manager or *xinit*.

application-specific files

Any application- or machine-specific resources can be stored in the class resource files located in the XAPPLOADDIR directory (this is a configuration parameter that is */usr/lib/X11/app-defaults* in the standard distribution). Programs that use the X Toolkit will also look in the directory named by the environment variable XAPPLRESDIR (default value is user's home directory) for files named *Class* where *Class* is the class name of the particular application. XAPPLOADDIR and XAPPLRESDIR configuration files are actually loaded *before* the RESOURCE_MANAGER property, so that the property can override the values.

XENVIRONMENT

Any user- and machine-specific resources may be specified by setting the XENVIRONMENT environment variable to the name of a resource file to be loaded by all applications. If this variable is not defined, the X Toolkit looks for a file named *.Xdefaults-**hostname***, where ***hostname*** is the name of the host where the application is executing.

`-xrm` *`resourcestring`*

Applications that use the X Toolkit can have resources specified from the command line. The *`resourcestring`* is a single resource name and value as shown above. Note that if the string contains characters interpreted by the shell (e.g., asterisk), they must be quoted. Any number of `-xrm` arguments may be given on the command line.

Program resources are organized into groups called *classes*, so that collections of individual resources (each of which are called *instances*) can be set all at once. By convention, the instance name of a resource begins with a lowercase letter and class name with an upper case letter. Multiple word resources are concatentated with the first letter of the succeeding words capitalized. Applications written with the X Toolkit Intrinsics will have at least the following resources:

`background` (class `Background`)
: Specifies the color to use for the window background.

`borderWidth` (class `BorderWidth`)
: Specifies the width in pixels of the window border.

`borderColor` (class `BorderColor`)
: Specifies the color to use for the window border.

Most applications using the X Toolkit Intrinsics also have the resource `foreground` (class `Foreground`), specifying the color to use for text and graphics within the window.

By combining class and instance specifications, application preferences can be set quickly and easily. Users of color displays will frequently want to set `Background` and `Foreground` classes to particular defaults. Specific color instances such as text cursors can then be overridden without having to define all of the related resources. For example,

```
bitmap*Dashed:  off
XTerm*cursorColor:  gold
XTerm*multiScroll:  on
XTerm*jumpScroll:  on
XTerm*reverseWrap:  on
XTerm*curses:  on
XTerm*Font:  6x10
XTerm*scrollBar: on
XTerm*scrollbar*thickness: 5
XTerm*multiClickTime: 500
XTerm*charClass:  33:48,37:48,45-47:48,64:48
XTerm*cutNewline: off
XTerm*cutToBeginningOfLine: off
XTerm*titeInhibit:  on
XTerm*ttyModes:  intr ^c erase ^? kill ^u
XLoad*Background: gold
XLoad*Foreground: red
XLoad*highlight: black
XLoad*borderWidth: 0
emacs*Geometry:  80x65-0-0
emacs*Background:  #5b7686
emacs*Foreground:  white
emacs*Cursor:  white
emacs*BorderColor:  white
emacs*Font:  6x10
xmag*geometry: -0-0
xmag*borderColor:  white
```

If these resources were stored in a file called *Xresources* in your home directory, they could be added to any existing resources in the server with the following command:

```
% xrdb -merge $HOME/.Xresources
```

This is frequently how user-friendly startup scripts merge user-specific defaults into any site-wide defaults. All sites are encouraged to set up convenient ways of automatically loading resources.

Examples

The following is a collection of sample command lines for some of the more frequently used commands. For more information on a particular command, please refer to that command's manual page.

```
% xrdb -load $HOME/.Xresources
% xmodmap -e 'keysym BackSpace = Delete'
% mkfontdir /usr/local/lib/X11/otherfonts
% xset fp+ /usr/local/lib/X11/otherfonts
% xmodmap $HOME/.keymap.km
% xsetroot -solid '#888'
% xset b 100 400 c 50 s 1800 r on
% xset q
% twm
% xmag
% xclock -geometry 48x48-0+0 -bg blue -fg white
% xeyes -geometry 48x48-48+0
% xbiff -update 20
% xlsfonts '*helvetica*'
% xlswins -l
% xwininfo -root
% xdpyinfo -display joesworkstation:0
% xhost -joesworkstation
% xrefresh
% xwd | xwud
% bitmap companylogo.bm 32x32
% xcalc -bg blue -fg magenta
% xterm -geometry 80x66-0-0 -name myxterm
```

Diagnostics

A wide variety of error messages are generated from various programs. Various toolkits are encouraged to provide a common mechanism for locating error text so that applications can be tailored easily. Programs written to interface directly to the Xlib C language library are expected to do their own error checking.

The default error handler in Xlib (also used by many toolkits) uses standard resources to construct diagnostic messages when errors occur. The defaults for these messages are usually stored in */usr/lib/X11/XErrorDB*. If this file is not present, error messages will be rather terse and cryptic.

Reference Pages

When the X Toolkit Intrinsics encounter errors converting resource strings to the appropriate internal format, no error messages are printed. This is convenient when it is desirable to have one set of resources across a variety of displays (e.g., color versus monochrome, lots of fonts versus very few, etc.), although it can pose problems for trying to determine why an application might be failing. This behavior can be overridden by setting the `StringConversionsWarning` resource.

To force the X Toolkit Intrinsics to always print string conversion error messages, the following resource should be placed at the top of the file that gets loaded onto the RESOURCE_MANAGER property using the *xrdb* program (frequently called *.Xresources* or *.Xres* in the user's home directory):

```
*StringConversionWarnings: on
```

To have conversion messages printed for just a particular application, the appropriate instance name can be placed before the asterisk:

```
xterm*StringConversionWarnings: on
```

Bugs

If you encounter a *repeatable* bug, please contact your site administrator for instructions on how to submit an X Bug Report.

See Also

XConsortium(1), XStandards(1), Xau, Xserver, mkfontdir, bdftosnf, bitmap, bsdtosnf, oclock, showsnf, twm, uwm, x10tox11, xauth, xbiff, xcalc, xclock, xdpyinfo, xedit, xev, xfd, xfontsel, xhost, xinit, xkill, xload, xlogo, xlsclients, xlsfonts, xlswins, xmag, xman, xmh, xmodmap, xpr, xprop, xrdb, xrefresh, xset, xsetroot, resize, xterm, xwd, xwininfo, xwud, biff(1), mh(1), init(8), ttys(5); Volume One, *Xlib Programming Manual*; Volume Two, *Xlib Reference Manual*; Volume Four, *X Toolkit Intrinsics Programming Manual*; Volume Five, *X Toolkit Intrinsics Reference Manual*.

Copyright

The following copyright and permission notice outlines the rights and restrictions covering most parts of the standard distribution of the X Window System from MIT. Other parts have additional or different copyrights and permissions; see the individual source files.

Copyright 1984, 1985, 1986, 1987, 1988, 1989 Massachusetts Institute of Technology.

Permission to use, copy, modify, and distribute this software and its documentation for any purpose and without fee is hereby granted, provided that the above copyright notice appear in all copies and that both that copyright notice and this permission notice appear in supporting documentation, and that the name of M.I.T. not be used in advertising or publicity pertaining to distribution of the software without specific, written prior permission. M.I.T. makes no representations about the suitability of this software for any purpose. It is provided "as is" without express or implied warranty.

This software is not subject to any license of the American Telephone and Telegraph Company or of the Regents of the University of California.

Trademarks

UNIX and OPEN LOOK are trademarks of AT&T. X Window System is a trademark of MIT.

Authors

A cast of thousands. See the file *doc/contributors* in the standard sources for some of the names.

Reference Pages

Name

XauFileName, XauReadAuth, XauLockAuth,
XauUnlockAuth, XauWriteAuth, XauGetAuthByAddr – X authority database routines

Syntax

```
#include <X11/Xauth.h>
typedef struct xauth {
    unsigned short          family;
    unsigned short          address_length;
    char                    *address;
    unsigned short          number_length;
    char                    *number;
    unsigned short          name_length;
    char                    *name;
    unsigned short          data_length;
    char                    *data;
} Xauth;

char *XauFileName ()

Xauth *XauReadAuth (auth_file)
    FILE *auth_file;

int XauWriteAuth (auth_file, auth)
    FILE *auth_file;
    Xauth *auth;

Xauth *XauGetAuthByAddr (family, address_length, address,
        number_length, number)
    unsigned short family;
    unsigned short address_length;
    char *address;
    unsigned short number_length;
    char *number;

int XauLockAuth (file_name, retries, timeout, dead)
    char *file_name;
    int retries;
    int timeout;
    long dead;

int XauUnlockAuth (file_name)
    char *file_name;

XauDisposeAuth (auth)
    Xauth *auth;
```

Description

`XauFileName` generates the default authorization file name by first checking the XAUTHORITY environment variable if set, else it returns *$HOME/.Xauthority*. This name is statically allocated and should not be freed.

`XauReadAuth` reads the next entry from *`auth_file`*. The entry is *not* statically allocated and should be freed by calling `XauDisposeAuth`.

`XauWriteAuth` writes an authorization entry to *`auth_file`*. It returns 1 on success, 0 on failure.

`XauGetAuthByAddr` searches for an entry which matches the given network address/display number pair. The entry is not statically allocated and should be freed by calling `Xau-DisposeAuth`

`XauLockAuth` does the work necessary to synchronously update an authorization file. First it makes to file names, one with `-c` appended to *`file_name`*, the other with `-l` appended. If the `-c` file already exists and is more than *dead* seconds old, `XauLockAuth` removes it and the associated `-l` file. To prevent possible synchronization troubles with NFS, a *dead* value of zero forces the files to be removed. `XauLockAuth` makes *retries* attempts to create and link the file names, pausing *`timeout`* seconds between each attempt. `XauLockAuth` returns a collection of values depending on the results:

`LOCK_ERROR`	A system error occurred, either a *`file_name`* which is too long, or an unexpected failure from a system call. `errno` may prove useful.
`LOCK_TIMEOUT`	*`retries`* attempts failed.
`LOCK_SUCCESS`	The lock succeeded.

`XauUnlockAuth` undoes the work of `XauLockAuth` by unlinking both the `-c` and `-l` filenames.

`XauDisposeAuth` frees storage allocated to hold an authorization entry.

See Also

xauth, xdm

Author

Keith Packard, MIT X Consortium.

Reference Pages

Name

X – X Window System server.

Syntax

`X [:displaynumber] [options] [ttyname]`

Description

X is the generic name for the X Window System server. It is frequently a link or a copy of the appropriate server binary for driving the most frequently used server on a given machine. The sample server from MIT supports the following platforms:

Xqvss	Digital monochrome vaxstationII or II
Xqdss	Digital color vaxstationII or II
Xsun	Sun monochrome or color Sun 2, 3, or 4
Xhp	HP Topcat 9000s300
Xibm	IBM AED, APA and megapel PC/RT, 8514 and VGA PS/2 model 80
Xapollo	Apollo monochrome or color (Domain/OS SR10.1 or SR10.2)
XmacII	Apple monochrome Macintosh II
Xcfbpmax	Digital color DECstation 3100
Xmfbpmax	Digital monochrome DECstation 3100
Xtek	Tektronix 4319 (this is the only tested configuration)

Starting the Server

The server is usually started from the X Display Manager program, *xdm*. This utility is run from the system boot files and takes care of keeping the server running, prompting for usernames and passwords, and starting up the user sessions. It is easily configured for sites that wish to provide nice, consistent interfaces for novice users (loading convenient sets of resources, starting up a window manager, clock, and nice selection of terminal emulator windows).

Since *xdm* now handles automatic starting of the server in a portable way, the `-L` option to *xterm* is now considered obsolete. Support for starting a login window from BSD 4.3-derived */etc/ttys* files is no longer included as of Release 4.

Installations that run more than one window system will still need to use the *xinit* utility. However, *xinit* is to be considered a tool for building startup scripts and is not intended for use by end users. Site adminstrators are strongly urged to build nicer interfaces for novice users.

When the sample server starts up, it takes over the display. If you are running on a workstation whose console is the display, you cannot log into the console while the server is running.

Network Connections

The sample server supports connections made using the following reliable byte-streams:

TCP/IP The server listens on port htons(6000+***n***), where ***n*** is the display number.

UNIX Domain The sample server uses */tmp/.X11-unix/X**n*** as the filename for the socket, where ***n*** is the display number.

DECnet The server responds to connections to object *X$Xn*, where *n* is the display number.

Options

All of the sample servers accept the following command line options:

`-a` *number* Sets pointer acceleration (i.e., the ratio of how much is reported to how much the user actually moved the pointer).

`-auth` *authorization-file*
Specifies a file which contains a collection of authorization records used to authenticate access. (Available as of Release 4.)

`bc` Disables certain kinds of error checking, for bug compatibility with previous releases (e.g., to work around bugs in Release 2 and Release 3 versions of *xterm* and the toolkits). Use of this option is discouraged. (Available as of Release 4.)

`-bs` Disables backing store support on all screens.

`-c` Turns off key-click.

`c` *volume* Sets key-click volume (allowable range: 0-8).

`-cc` *class* Sets the visual class for the root window of color screens. The class numbers are as specified in the X protocol. Not obeyed by all servers. (Available as of Release 4.)

`-dpi` *resolution*
Sets the resolution of the screen, in dots per inch. To be used when the server cannot determine the screen size from the hardware. (Available as of Release 4.)

`-f` *volume* Sets beep (bell) volume (allowable range: 0-7).

`-I` Causes all remaining command line arguments to be ignored. (Available as of Release 4.)

`-ld` *kilobytes*
Sets the data space limit of the server to the specified number of kilobytes. The default value is zero, making the data size as large as possible. A value of –1 leaves the data space limit unchanged. (Available as of Release 4; not available in all operating systems.)

`-ls` *kilobytes*
Sets the stack space limit of the server to the specified number of kilobytes. The default value is zero, making the stack size as large as possible. A value of -1 leaves the stack space limit unchanged. This option is not available in all operating systems. (Available as of Release 4; not available in all operating systems.)

`-logo` Turns on the X Window System logo display in the screen-saver. There is currently no way to change this from a client.

`nologo` Turns off the X Window System logo display in the screen-saver. There is currently no way to change this from a client.

`-p` *`minutes`* Sets screen-saver pattern cycle time in minutes.

`-r` Turns off auto-repeat.

`r` Turns on auto-repeat.

`-s` *`minutes`* Sets screen-saver timeout in minutes.

`-su` Disables save under support on all screens.

`-t` *`numbers`* Sets pointer acceleration threshold in pixels (i.e., after how many pixels pointer acceleration should take effect).

`-to` *`seconds`* Sets default screen-saver timeout in seconds.

`v` Sets video-on screen-saver preference.

`-v` Sets video-off screen-saver preference.

`-co` *`filename`*
Sets the name of the RGB color database.

`-help` Prints a usage message.

`-fp` *`fontPath`*
Sets the search path for fonts. This path is a comma-separated list of directories the server searches for font databases.

`-fc` *`cursorFont`*
Sets the default cursor font.

`-fn` *`font`* Sets the default font.

`-wm` Forces the default backing-store of all windows to be `WhenMapped`; a cheap trick way of getting backing-store to apply to all windows.

`-x` *`extension`* Loads the specified extension at init. (Available as of Release 4; not supported in most implementations.)

XDMCP-specific Options (Release 4)

You can also have the X server connect to xdm using XDMCP. Although this is not typically useful as it doesn't allow xdm to manage the server process, it can be used to debug XDMCP implementations, and servers as a sample implementation of the server side of XDMCP. For more information on this protocol, see the XDMCP specification in *docs/XDMCP/xdmcp.ms*. The following options control the behavior of XDMCP:

`-query` *`host-name`*
Enables XDMCP and sends `Query` packets to the specified host.

`-broadcast` Enables XDMCP and broadcasts `BroadcastQuery` packets to the network. The first responding display manager will be chosen for the session.

`-indirect` *`host-name`*
Enables XDMCP and sends `IndirectQuery` packets to the specified host.

`-port` *port-num*
: Specifies an alternate port number for XDMCP packets. Must be specified before any `-query`, `-broadcast` or `-indirect` options.

`-once`
: Makes the server exit after the first session is over. Normally, the server keeps starting sessions, one after the other.

`-class` *display-class*
: XDMCP has an additional display qualifier used in resource lookup for display-specific options. This option sets that value; by default it is "MIT-Unspecified" (not a very useful value).

`-cookie` *xdm-auth-bits*
: When testing XDM-AUTHENTICATION-1, a private key is shared between the server and the manager. This option sets the value of that private data (not that it's very private, being on the command line).

`-displayID` *display-id*
: Yet another XDMCP-specific value, this one allows the display manager to identify each display so that it can locate the shared key.

Many servers also have device-specific command line options. See the manual pages for the individual servers for more details.

Security

As of Release 4, the sample server implements a simplistic authorization protocol, MIT-MAGIC-COOKIE-1, which uses data private to authorized clients and the server. This is a rather trivial scheme; if the client passes authorization data which is the same as the server has, it is allowed access. This scheme is worse than the host-based access control mechanisms in environments with unsecure networks as it allows any host to connect, given that it has discovered the private key. But in many environments, this level of security is better than the host-based scheme as it allows access control per-user instead of per-host.

In addition, the server provides support for a DES-based authorization scheme, XDM-AUTHORIZATION-1, which is more secure (given a secure key distribution mechanism), but as DES is not generally distributable, the implementation is missing routines to encrypt and decrypt the authorization data. This authorization scheme can be used in conjunction with XDMCP's authentication scheme, XDM-AUTHENTICATION-1 or in isolation.

The authorization data is passed to the server in a private file named with the `-auth` command line option. Each time the server is about to accept the first connection after a reset (or when the server is starting), it reads this file. If this file contains any authorization records, the local host is not automatically allowed access to the server, and only clients which send one of the authorization records contained in the file in the connection setup information will be allowed access. See the *Xau* manual page for a description of the binary format of this file. Maintenance of this file, and distribution of its contents to remote sites for use there, is left as an exercise for the reader.

The sample server also uses a host-based access control list for deciding whether or not to accept connections from clients on a particular machine. This list initially consists of the host on which the server is running as well as any machines listed in the file */etc/Xn.hosts*, where *n* is the display number of the server. Each line of the file should contain either an Internet hostname (e.g., expo.lcs.mit.edu) or a DECnet hostname in double colon format (e.g., hydra::). There should be no leading or trailing spaces on any lines. For example:

```
joesworkstation
corporate.company.com
star::
bigcpu::
```

Users can add or remove hosts from this list and enable or disable access control using the *xhost* command from the same machine as the server. For example:

```
% xhost +janesworkstation        janesworkstation added to access control list
% xhost -star::                  star:: removed from access control list
% xhost +                        all hosts allowed (access control disabled)
% xhost -                        all hosts restricted (access control enabled)
% xhost
access control enabled (only the following hosts are allowed)
joesworkstation
janesworkstation
corporate.company.com
bigcpu::
```

Unlike some window systems, X does not have any notion of window operation permissions or place any restrictions on what a client can do; if a program can connect to a display, it has full run of the screen. Sites that have authentication and authorization systems (such as Kerberos) might wish to make use of the hooks in the libraries and the server to provide additional security.

Signals

The sample server attaches special meaning to the following signals.

SIGHUP — Causes the server to close all existing connections, free all resources, and restore all defaults. It is sent by the display manager whenever the main user's primary application (usually an *xterm* or window manager) exits to force the server to clean up and prepare for the next user.

SIGTERM — Causes the server to exit cleanly.

SIGUSR1 — This signal is used quite differently from either of the above. When the server starts, it checks to see if it has inherited SIGUSR1 as SIG_IGN instead of the usual SIG_DFL. In this case, the server sends a SIGUSR1 to its parent process, after it has set up the various connection schemes. *xdm* uses this feature to recognize when connecting to the server is possible.

Fonts

Fonts are usually stored as individual files in directories. The list of directories in which the server looks when trying to open a font is controlled by the *font path*. Although most sites will choose to have the server start up with the appropriate font path (using the `-fp` option mentioned above), it can be overridden using the *xset* program.

The default font path for the sample server contains three directories:

/usr/lib/X11/fonts/misc
This directory contains several miscellaneous fonts that are useful on all systems. It contains a small family of fixed-width fonts in pixel heights 5 through 10, a family of fixed-width fonts from Dale Schumacher in similar pixel heights, several Kana fonts from Sony Corporation, a Kanji font, the standard cursor font, two cursor fonts from Digital Equipment Corporation, and OPEN LOOK cursor and glyph fonts from Sun Microsystems. It also has font name aliases for the fonts fixed and variable.

/usr/lib/X11/fonts/75dpi
This directory contains fonts contributed by Adobe Systems, Inc., Digital Equipment Corporation, Bitstream, Inc., Bigelow and Holmes, and Sun Microsystems, Inc. for 75 dots per inch displays. An integrated selection of sizes, styles, and weights is provided for each family.

/usr/lib/X11/fonts/100dpi
This directory contains versions of the fonts in the *75dpi* directory for 100 dots per inch displays.

Font databases are created by running the *mkfontdir* program in the directory containing the compiled versions of the fonts (the *.snf* files). Whenever fonts are added to a directory, *mkfontdir* should be rerun so that the server can find the new fonts. If *mkfontdir* is not run, the server will not be able to find any fonts in the directory.

Diagnostics

Too numerous to list them all. If run from *init*(8), errors are logged in the file */usr/adm/Xnmsgs*.

Files

/etc/Xn.hosts Initial access control list.

/usr/lib/X11/fonts/misc, /usr/lib/X11/fonts/75dpi, /usr/lib/X11/fonts/100dpi
Font directories.

/usr/lib/X11/rgb.txt Color database.

/tmp/.X11-unix/Xn UNIX domain socket.

/usr/adm/Xnmsgs Error log file.

See Also

X, Xqdss(1), Xqvss(1), Xsun(1), Xapollo(1), XmacII(1), Xau, mkfontdir, twm, uwm, xauth, xdm, xhost, xinit, xset, xsetroot, xterm, ttys(5), init(8); *X Window System Protocol; Definition of the Porting Layer for the X v11 Sample Server; Strategies for Porting the X v11 Sample Server; Godzilla's Guide to Porting the X V11 Sample Server.*

Bugs

The option syntax is inconsistent with itself and *xset*.

The acceleration option should take a numerator and a denominator like the protocol.

If *X* dies before its clients, new clients won't be able to connect until all existing connections have their TCP TIME_WAIT timers expire.

The color database is missing a large number of colors. However, there doesn't seem to be a better one available that can generate RGB values tailorable to particular displays.

Authors

The sample server was originally written by Susan Angebranndt, Raymond Drewry, Philip Karlton, and Todd Newman, of Digital Equipment Corporation, with support from a large cast. It has since been extensively rewritten by Keith Packard and Bob Scheifler of MIT.

appres

Name

appres – list application resource database.

Syntax

appres [[*classname* [*instancename*]] [**-xrm** *resource*]

Description

Available as of Release 4, the *appres* client prints the resources seen by an application of the specified classname and instancename. It is used to determine which resources a particular program would load. For example:

```
% appres XTerm
```

would list the resources that any *xterm* program would load. To also match particular instance names, you can enter both an instance and class name, as in the following:

```
% appres XTerm myxterm
```

If no application class is specified, the class -NoSuchClass- (which should have no defaults) is used.

Options

appres supports the following command line option:

-xrm *resource*

Specifies that, in addition to the current application resources, *appres* should return the *resource* specified as an argument to -xrm, if that resource would apply to the *classname* or *instancename*. You must specify both a *classname* and an *instancename* in order to use the -xrm option. (Note that -xrm does not actually load any resources.)

Without any arguments, *appres* returns those resources that might apply to any application (for example, those beginning with an asterisk in your *.Xresources* file).

See Also

X, xrdb, listres

Author

Jim Fulton, MIT X Consortium.

bdftosnf

Name

bdftosnf – BDF to SNF font compiler for X11.

Syntax

bdftosnf [*options*] *bdf_file*

Description

bdftosnf reads a Bitmap Distribution Format (BDF) font from the specified file (or from standard input if no file is specified) and writes an X11 Server Natural Format (SNF) font to standard output.

Options

-p*number*	Forces the glyph padding to a specific *number*. The legal values are 1, 2, 4, and 8.
-u*number*	Forces the scanline unit padding to a specific *number*. The legal values are 1, 2, and 4.
-m	Forces the bit order to most significant bit first.
-l	Forces the bit order to least significant bit first.
-M	Forces the byte order to most significant byte first.
-L	Forces the byte order to least significant byte first.
-w	Prints warnings if the character bitmaps have bits set to one outside of their defined widths.
-W	Prints warnings for characters with an encoding of -1; the default is to silently ignore such characters.
-t	Expands glyphs in "terminal-emulator" fonts to fill the bounding box.
-i	Suppresses computation of correct ink metrics for "terminal-emulator" fonts.

See Also

X, Xserver, *Bitmap Distribution Format 2.1*

Name

bitmap, bmtoa, atobm – system bitmap editor and conversion utilities.

Syntax

bitmap [*options*] *filename* [*WIDTHxHEIGHT*]

bmtoa [*options*] *filename*

atobm [*options*] *filename*

Description

bitmap allows you to create and edit small bitmaps which you can use to create backgrounds, icons, and pointers. A bitmap is a grid of pixels, or picture elements, each of which is white, black, or, in the case of color displays, a color.

The *bmtoa* and *atobm* filters convert *bitmap* files to and from ASCII strings. They are most commonly used to quickly print out bitmaps and to generate versions for inclusion in text. The *bmtoa* and *atobm* programs are available in the standard distribution of X as of Release 3.

The window that *bitmap* creates has three sections (see Figure 6-1 in Part One of this guide). The largest section is the checkerboard grid, which is a magnified version of the bitmap you are editing. Squares on the grid can be set, cleared, or inverted directly with the buttons on the pointer. A menu of higher level operations, such as drawing lines and circles, is provided to the right of the grid. You can invoke these menu commands by clicking with any mouse button. Beneath the menu commands is an actual size picture of the bitmap you are editing; below this is an inverted version of the same bitmap. Each time the grid changes, the same change occurs in the actual-size bitmap and its inverse.

If the bitmap is to be used for defining a cursor, one of the squares in the image may be designated as the *hot spot*. This determines where the cursor is actually pointing. For cursors with sharp tips (such as arrows or fingers), this is usually at the end of the tip; for symmetric cursors (such as crosses or bullseyes), this is usually at the center.

Bitmaps are stored as small C code fragments suitable for including in applications. They provide an array of bits as well as symbolic constants giving the width, height, and hot spot (if specified) that may be used in creating cursors, icons, and tiles.

The *WIDTHxHEIGHT* argument gives the size to use when creating a new bitmap (the default is 16x6). Existing bitmaps are always edited at their current size.

If the *bitmap* window is resized by the window manager, the size of the squares in the grid will shrink or enlarge to fit.

Options: bitmap

-display [*host*]:*server*[.*screen*]

Allows you to specify the host, server, and screen on which to create the *bitmap* window. `host` specifies which machine to create the *bitmap* window on, `server` specifies the server number, and `screen` specifies the screen number. For example:

Reference Pages

bitmap -display *your_node*:**0.1**

creates a *bitmap* window on screen 1 of server 0 on the machine *your_node*. If the host is omitted, the local machine is assumed. If the screen is omitted, screen 0 is assumed; the server and colon (:) are necessary in all cases.

-geometry *geometry*

The bitmap is created with the specified size and location determined by the supplied geometry specification. The -geometry option can be (and often is) abbreviated to -g, unless there is a conflicting option that begins with "g." The argument to the geometry option (*geometry*) has the form *widthx-height±xoff±yoff*. If you do not specify the geometry, *bitmap* asks you for window placement when it starts up. See *Window Geometry* in Chapter 8 of this guide for details.

-help Prints a brief description of the allowable options.

-bw *number* Specifies the border width in pixels of the *bitmap* window. Default is 3 pixels.

-fn *font* Specifies the font to be used in the command buttons (refer to the *Menu Commands* section below). Default is *fixed*, a 6x13 pixel, mono-spaced font.

-fg *color* Specifies the color to be used for the foreground. Default is black.

-bg *color* Specifies the color to be used for the background. Default is white.

-hl *color* Specifies the color to be used for highlighting.

-bd *color* Specifies the color to be used for the window border.

-ms *color* Specifies the color to be used for the pointer (mouse). Default is black.

-name *variable*

Specifies the variable name to be used when writing out the bitmap file. The default is to use the basename of the *filename* command line argument.

-nodashed Specifies that the grid lines in the *bitmap* window are drawn as solid lines not as dashed lines. Default is dashed lines. On some servers, dashed lines are significantly slower.

WIDTHxHEIGHT

Two numbers, separated by the letter "x", which specify the size of the checkerboard grid within the *bitmap* window (e.g., 9x13). The first number is the grid's width; the second number is its height. Default is 16x16.

Options: bmtoa

The *bmtoa* conversion program accepts the following options:

-chars *cc* Specifies the pair of characters to use in the string version of the bitmap. The first character is used for 0 bits and the second character is used for 1 bits. The default is to use dashes (–) for 0's and number signs (#) for 1's.

Options: atobm

The *atobm* conversion program accepts the following options:

`-chars cc` Specifies the pair of characters to use when converting string bitmaps into arrays of numbers. The first character represents a 0 bit and the second character represents a 1 bit. The default is to use dashes (–) for 0's and number signs (#) for 1's.

`-name variable`
Specifies the variable name to be used when writing out the bitmap file. The default is to use the basename of the *filename* command line argument or leave it blank if the standard input is read.

`-xhot number`
Specifies the X coordinate of the hot spot. Only positive values are allowed. By default, no hot spot information is included.

`-yhot number`
Specifies the Y coordinate of the hot spot. Only positive values are allowed. By default, no hot spot information is included.

Changing Grid Squares

Grid squares may be set, cleared, or inverted by pointing to them and clicking one of the buttons indicated below. Multiple squares can be changed at once by holding the button down and dragging the cursor across them. Set squares are filled and represent 1's in the bitmap; clear squares are empty and represent 0's.

Button 1 (usually the left)
Changes one or more grid squares to the foreground color and sets the corresponding bits in the bitmap to 1.

Button 2 (usually the middle)
Inverts one or more grid squares. The corresponding bit or bits in the bitmap are inverted (1's become 0's and 0's become 1's).

Button 3 (usually the right)
Changes one or more grid squares to the background color and sets the corresponding bits in the bitmap to 0.

Menu Commands

To make defining shapes easier, *bitmap* provides 13 commands for drawing whole sections of the grid at once, two commands for manipulating the hot spot, and two commands for updating the bitmap file and exiting. A command button for each of these operations is located to the right of the grid.

Several of the commands operate on rectangular portions of the grid. These areas are selected after the command button is pressed by moving the cursor to the upper left square of the desired area, pressing a pointer button, dragging the cursor to the lower right hand corner (with the button still pressed), and then releasing the button. The command may be aborted by pressing any other button while dragging or by releasing outside the grid.

To invoke a command, move the pointer over that command and click any button.

The following command descriptions assume that black is the foreground color and white is the background color (the defaults).

Clear All
: Turns all the grid squares white and sets all bitmap bits to 0. This is irreversible, so invoke it with caution.

Set All
: Turns all the grid squares black and sets all bitmap bits to 1. This is also irreversible, so invoke it with caution.

Clear Area
: Clears a rectangular area of the grid, turning it white and setting the corresponding bitmap to 0. After you click on this command, the cursor turns into a corner cursor representing the upper-left corner of the area you want to clear. Press and hold down any mouse button while moving the mouse to the lower-right corner of the area you want to clear, then release the button.

  While you are holding down the button, the selected area is covered with X's, and the cursor changes to a lower-right corner cursor. If you now wish to abort the command without clearing an area, either press another mouse button, move the cursor outside the grid, or move the cursor to the left of or above the left-corner.

Set Area
: Turns a rectangular area of the grid black and sets the corresponding bitmap bits to 1. It works the same way as the Clear Area command.

Invert Area
: Inverts rectangular area of the grid. It works the same way as the Clear Area command.

Copy Area
: Copies a rectangular area from one part of the grid to another. First, you select the rectangle to be copied, in the manner described under Clear Area above.

  Once you have selected the area to copy, the cursor changes to an upper-left corner cursor. When you press a mouse button, a destination rectangle overlays the grid; moving the mouse while holding down the button moves this destination rectangle. The copy occurs when you release the button. To cancel the copy, move the mouse outside the grid and then release the button.

Move Area
: Works identically to Copy Area, *except* it clears the source rectangle after copying to the destination.

Overlay Area
: Lays a rectangular area from one part of the grid over a rectangular area in another part of the grid. Select the area as described under Clear Area. Overlay is not a pixel for pixel replacement: those pixels that are clear (bitmap bits set to 0) allow those pixels that are set (bitmap bits set to 1) to show through the overlay.

Line — Draws a line between two points. When you select this menu option, the cursor changes to a dot shape. Position the cursor over the first point of the line you want to draw and click any mouse button. Then position the cursor over the end point of the line and click any mouse button. A black line is drawn between the two points.

Circle — Draws a circle. When you select this menu option, the cursor changes to a dot shape. First, position the cursor over the point you want to specify as the center and click any mouse button. Then position the cursor over a point you want to specify as the radius and click any mouse button. A black circle is drawn.

Filled Circle — Draws a filled circle when you specify the center and radius of the circle as with Circle.

Flood Fill — Fills all clear squares in a closed shape you specify. When you select this menu option, the cursor changes to a dot shape. Click on any clear square inside the shape you want to fill and all clear squares are filled out to the border of the closed shape. If the shape is not closed, the entire grid will be filled.

Set Hot Spot — Designates a point on the bitmap as the "hot spot." If a program is using your bitmap as a cursor, the hot spot indicates which point on the bitmap is the "actual" location of the cursor. For instance, if your cursor is an arrow, the hot spot could be the tip of the arrow; if your cursor is a cross, the hot spot should be where the perpendicular lines intersect.

Clear Hot Spot — Removes any hot spot that was defined for this bitmap.

Write Output — Writes the current bitmap value to the file specified in the command line. If the file already exists, the original file is first renamed to *filename~* (in the manner of *emacs*(1) and other text editors).

If either the renaming or the writing cause an error, a dialog box will appear asking if you want to write the file */tmp/filename* instead. If you say yes, all future Write Output commands are written to */tmp/filename* as well. See *File Format* below for the format of the output file.

Quit — Exits the *bitmap* program. If you have edited the bitmap and have not invoked Write Output, or you have edited since the last time you invoked Write Output, a dialog window appears, asking if you want to save changes before quitting. "Yes" does a Write Output before exiting. "No" just exits, losing the edits. "Cancel" means you decided not to quit after all and you can continue with your editing.

You can also terminate *bitmap* by typing Ctrl-C or q anywhere in the window. If you have edited the bitmap and have not invoked Write Output, a dialog window appears, asking if you want to save changes before quitting.

File Format

The Write Output command stores bitmaps as simple C program fragments that can be compiled into programs, referred to by X Toolkit pixmap resources, manipulated by other programs (see *xsetroot*), or read in using utility routines in the various programming libraries. The width and height of the bitmap as well as the hot spot, if specified, are written as preprocessor symbols at the start of the file. The bitmap image is then written out as an array of characters:

```
#define name_width 11
#define name_height 5
#define name_x_hot 5
#define name_y_hot 2

static char name_bits[] = {
    0x91, 0x04, 0xca, 0x06, 0x84,
    0x04, 0x8a, 0x04, 0x91, 0x04
};
```

The variables ending with `_x_hot` and `_y_hot` are optional; they must be present only if a hot spot has been defined for this bitmap. The other variables must be present.

In place of `name`, the five variables are prefixed with a string derived from the name of the file specified on the original command line. Any directories are stripped off the front of the `filename` and any suffix (including the preceding period) is stripped off the end. Any remaining non-alphabetic characters are replaced with underscores.

For example, invoking *bitmap* with filename */usr/include/bitmaps/cross.bitmap* produces a file with variable names `cross_width`, `cross_height`, and `cross_bits` (and `cross_x_hot` and `cross_y_hot`, if a hot spot is defined).

Each character in the the array contains 8 bits from one row of the image (rows are padded out at the end to a multiple of 8 to make this is possible). Rows are written out from left to right and top to bottom. The first character of the array holds the leftmost 8 bits of top line, and the last character holds the right most 8 bits (including padding) of the bottom line. Within each character, the leftmost bit in the bitmap is the least significant bit in the character.

This process can be demonstrated visually by splitting a row into words containing 8 bits each, reversing the bits each word (since Arabic numbers have the significant digit on the right and images have the least significant bit on the left), and translating each word from binary to hexadecimal.

In the following example, the array of 1's and 0's on the left represents a bitmap containing 5 rows and 11 columns that spells *X11*. To its right is is the same array split into 8 bit words with each row padded with 0's so that it is a multiple of 8 in length (16):

```
10001001001         10001001 00100000
01010011011         01010011 01100000
00100001001         00100001 00100000
01010001001         01010001 00100000
10001001001         10001001 00100000
```

Reversing the bits in each word of the padded, split version of the bitmap yields the left hand figure below. Interpreting each word as hexadecimal number yields the array of numbers on the right:

```
10010001 00000100                  0x91 0x04
11001010 00000110                  0xca 0x06
10000100 00000100                  0x84 0x04
10001010 00000100                  0x8a 0x04
10010001 00000100                  0x91 0x04
```

The character array can then be generated by reading each row from left to right, top to bottom:

```
static char name_bits[] = {
   0x91, 0x04, 0xca, 0x06, 0x84,
   0x04, 0x8a, 0x04, 0x91, 0x04
};
```

The *bmtoa* program may be used to convert *bitmap* files into arrays of characters for printing or including in text files. The *atobm* program can be used to convert strings back to *bitmap* format.

Using Bitmaps in Programs

To define a bitmap or pointer in an X program, include (*#include*) a bitmap file and refer to its variables. For instance, to use a pointer defined in the files *this.cursor* and *this_mask.cursor*, write:

```
#include "this.cursor"
#include "this_mask.cursor"
XColor foreground background;
Pixmap source = XCreateBitmapFromData (display, drawable, this_bits,
   this_width, this_height);
Pixmap mask = XCreateBitmapFromData (display, drawable, this_mask_bits,
   this_mask_width, this_mask_height);
Cursor cursor = XCreatePixmapCursor (display, source, mask, foreground,
   background, this_x_hot, this_y_hot);
```

where *foreground* and *background* are XColor values.

Additional routines are available for reading in *bitmap* files and returning the data in the file in Bitmap (single-plane Pixmap for use with routines that require stipples) or full depth Pixmaps (often used for window backgrounds and borders). Applications writers should be careful to understand the difference between Bitmaps and Pixmaps so that their programs function correctly on color and monochrome displays.

For backward compatibility, *bitmap* will also accept X10 format *bitmap* files. However, when the file is written out again it will be in X11 format.

Resources

The *bitmap* program accepts the following resources. The foreground, background, and highlight colors are ignored unless you specify new values for all three options.

`Background` Determines the window's background color. Bits which are 0 in the bitmap are displayed in this color. Default is white.

`BodyFont`	Determines the text font. Default is *fixed*, a 6x13 pixel mono-spaced font.
`BorderColor`	Determines the color of the border. Default is black.
`BorderWidth`	Determines the border width. Default is 2 pixels.
`Dashed`	Determines whether dashed or solid lines are used for the *bitmap* grid. (On specifies dashed lines, off specifies solid.) Default is on. (Available as of Release 4.)
`Foreground`	Determines the foreground color. Bits which are 1 in the bitmap are displayed in this color. Default is black.
`Highlight`	Determines the highlight color. *bitmap* uses this color to show the hot spot and to indicate rectangular areas that are affected by the **Move Area**, **Copy Area**, **Set Area**, **Clear Area**, and **Invert Area** commands. If a highlight color is not given, then *bitmap* highlights by inverting. For example, if you have a black rectangular area selected for a move, white X's appear in the rectangle.
`Mouse`	Determines the pointer's color. Default is black.
`Geometry`	Determines the size and location of the *bitmap* window.
`Dimensions`	Determines the *`WIDTHxHEIGHT`* of the checkerboard grid within the *bitmap* window. Default is 16x16.

Files

Many standard bitmaps can be found in the directory */usr/include/X11/bitmaps*.

Bugs

The old command line arguments aren't consistent with other X programs.

If you move the pointer too fast while holding a pointer button down, some squares may be missed. This is caused by limitations in how frequently the X server can sample the pointer location.

There is no way to write to a file other than the one specified on the command line.

There is no way to change the size of the bitmap once the program has started.

There is no **Undo** command.

Author

bitmap by Ron Newman, MIT Project Athena; *bmtoa* and *atobm* by Jim Fulton, MIT X Consortium.

See Also

Chapter 6 of this guide; Volume One, *Xlib Programmer's Guide*; *XmuReadBitmapDataFromFile*.

Name

listres – list resources in widgets.

Syntax

`listres` [*options*]

Description

Available as of Release 4, the *listres* program generates a list of a widget's resource database. The class in which each resource is first defined, the instance and class name, and the type of each resource is listed. If no specific widgets or the `-all` switch are given, a two-column list of widget names and their class hierarchies is printed.

Options

listres accepts all of the standard X Toolkit command line options, along with the following:

`-all` Indicates that *listres* should print information for all known widgets and objects.

`-nosuper` Indicates that resources that are inherited from a superclass should not be listed. This is useful for determining which resources are new to a subclass.

`-variable` Indicates that widgets should be identified by the names of the class record variables rather than the class name given in the variable. This is useful for distinguishing subclasses that have the same class name as their superclasses.

`-top` *name* Specifies the name of the widget to be treated as the top of the hierarchy. Case is not significant, and the name may match either the class variable name or the class name. The default is core.

`-format` *printf_string*
Specifies the printf-style format string to be used to print out the name, instance, class, and type of each resource.

See Also

X, xrdb; Volume Four, *X Toolkit Intrinsics Programming Manual*; Volume Five, *X Toolkit Intrinsics Reference Manual*; appropriate widget documents

Bugs

On operating systems that do not support dynamic linking of run-time routines, this program must have all of its known widgets compiled in. The sources provide several tools for automating this process for various widget sets.

Author

Jim Fulton, MIT X Consortium.

mkfontdir

Name

mkfontdir – creates a *fonts.dir* file for each specified directory of font files.

Syntax

mkfontdir *[directory-names]*

Description

For each directory argument, *mkfontdir* reads all of the font files in the directory and searches for properties named "FONT", or (failing that) the name of the file stripped of its suffix. These are used as font names, which are written out to the file *fonts.dir* in the directory, along with the name of the font file.

The kinds of font files read by *mkfontdir* depend on configuration parameters, but typically include SNF (suffix *.snf*), compressed SNF (suffix *.snf.Z*), BDF (suffix *.bdf*), and compressed BDF (suffix *.bdf.Z*). If a font exists in multiple formats, the most efficient format will be used.

Font Name Aliases

The file *fonts.alias*, which can be put in any directory of the font path, is used to map new names to existing fonts, and should be edited by hand. The format is straight forward enough, two white-space separated columns, the first containing aliases and the second containing font-name patterns.

When a font alias is used, the name it references is searched for in the normal manner, looking through each font directory in turn. This means that the aliases need not mention fonts in the same directory as the alias file.

To embed white-space in either name, simply enclose them in double-quote marks. To embed double-quote marks (or any other character), precede them with back-slash:

```
"magic-alias with spaces"     "\"fontname\" with quotes"
regular alias                 fontname
```

If the string FILE_NAMES_ALIASES stands alone on a line, each filename in the particular directory (stripped of it's *.snf* suffix) will be used as an alias for that font.

Usage

Xserver looks for both *fonts.dir* and *fonts.alias* in each directory in the font path each time the font path is set (see *xset*).

See Also

X, Xserver, xset

Name

oclock – display time of day in analog form.

Syntax

oclock [*options*]

Description

Available as of Release 4, *oclock* displays the current time on an analog display.

Options

-display *host*[:*server*][.*screen*]

Allows you to specify the host, server and screen on which to display the *oclock* window. *host* specifies the machine, *server* specifies the server number, and *screen* specifies the screen number. For example,

oclock -display *your_node*:**0.1**

specifies screen 1 of server 0 on the machine *your_node*. Either or both the *host* and *screen* elements to the display specification can be omitted. If *host* is omitted, the local machine is assumed. If *screen* is omitted, screen 0 is assumed (and the period is unnecessary). The colon and *server* are necessary in all cases.

-geometry *geometry*

The *oclock* window is created with the specified size and location determined by the supplied geometry specification. The -geometry option can be (and often is) abbreviated to -g, unless there is a conflicting option that begins with "g." The argument to the geometry option (*geometry*) is referred to as a "standard geometry string," and has the form *width*x*height*±*xoff*±*yoff*.

-fg *color* Specifies a color for both the hands and the jewel of the clock.

-bg *color* Specifies a color for the background.

-jewel *color*

Specifies a color for the jewel on the clock.

-minute *color*

Specifies a color for the minute hand of the clock.

-hour *color* Specifies a color for the hour hand of the clock.

-backing { *WhenMapped Always NotUseful* }

Selects an appropriate level of backing store.

-bd *color* Specifies a color for the window border.

-bw *pixels* Specifies a width in pixels for the window border. As the Clock widget changes its border around quite a bit, this is most usefully set to zero.

Reference Pages

`-noshape` Causes the clock not to reshape itself and ancestors to exactly fit the outline of the clock.

Colors

Although the default colors for the Clock widget are black and white, the widget was designed in color; unfortunately, the toolkit makes specifying these colors in a device-independent manner difficult. If you want to see the correct colors, add the following lines to your resource file:

```
Clock*Background: grey
Clock*BorderColor: light blue
Clock*hour: yellow
Clock*jewel: yellow
Clock*minute: yellow
```

See Also

X; Volume Four, *X Toolkit Intrinsics Programming Manual*; Volume Five, *X Toolkit Intrinsics Reference Manual*

Author

Keith Packard, MIT X Consortium.

Name

resize – utility to set TERMCAP and terminal settings to current window size.

Syntax

resize [*options*]

Description

resize prints a shell command for setting the TERM and TERMCAP environment variables to indicate the current size of the *xterm* window from which the command is run. For this output to take effect, *resize* must either be evaluated as part of the command line (usually done with a shell alias or function) or else redirected to a file which can then be read in. From the C shell (usually known as */bin/csh*), the following alias could be defined in the user's *.cshrc*:

```
%  alias rs 'set noglob; eval `resize`; unset noglob'
```

After resizing the window, the user would type:

```
%  rs
```

Users of versions of the Bourne shell (usually known as */bin/sh*) that don't have command functions will need to send the output to a temporary file and the read it back in with the "." command:

```
$  resize >/tmp/out
$  . /tmp/out
```

Options

The following options may be used with *resize*:

-u
: Indicates that Bourne shell commands should be generated even if the user's current shell isn't */bin/sh*.

-c
: Indicates that C shell commands should be generated even if the user's current shell isn't */bin/csh*.

-s [*rows columns*]
: Indicates that that Sun console escape sequences will be used instead of the special *xterm* escape code. If *rows* and *columns* are given, *resize* will ask the *xterm* to resize itself. However, the window manager may choose to disallow the change.

The -u or -c must appear to the left of -s if both are specified.

Files

/etc/termcap — for the base termcap entry to modify.

~/.cshrc — user's alias for the command.

See Also

csh(1), tset(1), xterm

Bugs

There should be some global notion of display size; *termcap* and *terminfo* need to be rethought in the context of window systems. (Fixed in 4.3BSD and Ultrix-32 1.2.)

Authors

Mark Vandevoorde (MIT-Athena), Edward Moy (Berkeley).

showsnf

Name

showsnf – print contents of an SNF file to standard output.

Syntax

showsnf [*options*] *snf_file*

Description

showsnf displays the contents of font files in the Server Natural Format produced by *bdftosnf*. It is usually only used to verify that a font file hasn't been corrupted or to convert the individual glyphs into arrays of characters for proofreading or for conversion to some other format.

Options

`-v`	Indicates that character bearings and sizes should be printed.
`-g`	Indicates that character glyph bitmaps should be printed.
`-m`	Indicates that the bit order of the font is most significant bit first.
`-l`	Indicates that the bit order of the font is least significant bit first.
`-M`	Indicates that the byte order of the font is most significant byte first.
`-L`	Indicates that the byte order of the font is least significant byte first.
`-p`*number*	Specifies the glyph padding of the font.
`-u`*number*	Specifies the scanline unit of the font.

See Also

X, Xserver, bdftosnf

Bugs

There is no way to just print out a single glyph.

twm

Name

twm – Tab Window Manager for the X Window System.

Syntax

twm [*options*]

Description

twm is a window manager for the X Window System. It has been made the official window manager in the standard distribution in Release 4. *twm* provides titlebars, shaped windows, several forms of icon management, user-defined macro functions, click-to-type and pointer-driven keyboard focus, and user-specified key and pointer button bindings.

This program is usually started by the user's session manager or startup script. When used from *xdm* or *xinit* without a session manager, *twm* is frequently executed in the foreground as the last client. When run this way, exiting *twm* causes the session to be terminated (i.e., logged out).

By default, application windows are surrounded by a "frame" with a titlebar at the top and a special border around the window. The titlebar contains the window's name, a rectangle that is lit when the window is receiving keyboard input, and function boxes known as "titlebuttons" at the left and right edges of the titlebar.

Pressing pointer Button1 (usually the left-most button unless it has been changed with *xmodmap*) on a titlebutton will invoke the function associated with the button. In the default interface, windows are iconified by clicking (pressing and then immediately releasing) the left titlebutton (which looks like a small X). Conversely, windows are deiconified by clicking in the associated icon or entry in the icon manager (see description of the variable `ShowIconManager` and of the function `f.showiconmgr`).

Windows are resized by pressing the right titlebutton (which resembles group of nested squares), dragging the pointer over edge that is to be moved, and releasing the pointer when the outline of the window is the desired size. Similarly, windows are moved by pressing in the title or highlight region, dragging a window outline to the new location, and then releasing when the outline is in the desired position. Just clicking in the title or highlight region raises the window without moving it.

When new windows are created, *twm* will honor any size and location information requested by the user (usually through `-geometry` command line argument or resources for the individual applications). Otherwise, an outline of the window's default size, its titlebar, and lines dividing the window into a 3x3 grid that track the pointer are displayed. Clicking pointer Button1 will position the window at the current position and give it the default size. Pressing pointer Button2 (usually the middle pointer button) and dragging the outline will give the window its current position but allow the sides to be resized as described above. Clicking pointer Button3 (usually the right pointer button) will give the window its current position but attempt to make it long enough to touch the bottom the screen.

Options

twm accepts the following command line options:

`-display` *host*`[:`*server*`][.`*screen*`]`
: Allows you to specify the host, server and screen to connect to. `host` specifies the machine, `server` specifies the server number, and `screen` specifies the screen number. For example,

  twm -display *your_node*:**0.0**

  specifies screen 0 of server 0 on the machine `your_node`. Either or both the `host` and `screen` elements to the display specification can be omitted. If `host` is omitted, the local machine is assumed. If `screen` is omitted, screen 0 is assumed (and the period is unnecessary). The colon and `server` are necessary in all cases.

`-s`
: Indicates that only the default screen (as specified by `-display` or by the DISPLAY environment variable) should be managed. By default, *twm* will attempt to manage all screens on the display.

`-f` *twmfile*
: Specifies the name of the startup file to use. By default, *twm* will look in the user's home directory for files named *.twmrc.num* (where *num* is a screen number) or *.twmrc*.

`-v`
: Indicates that *twm* should print error messages whenever an unexpected X Error event is received. This can be useful when debugging applications but can be distracting in regular use.

Customization

Much of *twm*'s appearance and behavior can be controlled by providing a startup file in one of the following locations (searched in order for each screen being managed when *twm* begins):

$HOME/.twmrc.screennumber
: The *screennumber* is a small positive number (e.g. 0, 1, etc.) representing the screen number (e.g. the last number in the DISPLAY environment variable *host:displaynum.screennum*) that would be used to contact that screen of the display. This is intended for displays with multiple screens of differing visual types.

$HOME/.twmrc
: This is the usual name for an individual user's startup file.

/usr/lib/X11/twm/system.twmrc
: If neither of the preceding files are found, *twm* will look in this file for a default configuration. This is often tailored by the site administrator to provide convenient menus or familiar bindings for novice users.

If no startup files are found, *twm* will use the built-in defaults described above. The only resource used by *twm* is `bitmapFilePath` for a colon-separated list of directories to search when looking for bitmap files. (For more information, see the *Athena Widgets* manual and *xrdb*).

twm startup files are logically broken up into three types of specifications: *variables*, *bindings*, and *menus*. The variables section must come first and is used to describe the fonts, colors, cursors, border widths, icon and window placement, highlighting, autoraising, layout of titles,

Reference Pages

warping, use of the icon manager. The bindings section usually comes second and is used to specify the functions that should be to be invoked when keyboard and pointer buttons are pressed in windows, icons, titles, and frames. The menus section gives any user-defined menus (containing functions to be invoked or commands to be executed).

Variable names and keywords are case-insensitive. Strings must be surrounded by double quote characters (e.g., "blue") and are case-sensitive. A pound sign (#) outside of a string causes the remainder of the line in which the character appears to be treated as a comment.

Variables

Many of the aspects of *twm*'s user interface are controlled by variables that may be set in the user's startup file. Some of the options are enabled or disabled simply by the presence of a particular keyword. Other options require keywords, numbers, strings, or lists of all of these.

Lists are surrounded by braces and are usually separated by whitespace or a newline. For example:

```
AutoRaise { "emacs" "XTerm" "Xmh" }
```

or

```
AutoRaise
{
    "emacs"
    "XTerm"
    "Xmh"
}
```

When a variable containing a list of strings representing windows is searched (e.g. to determine whether or not to enable autoraise as shown above), a string is considered to match a window if it is a case-sensitive prefix for the window's name name (given by the WM_NAME window property), resource name or class name (both given by the WM_CLASS window property). The preceding example would enable autoraise on windows named "emacs" as well as any *xterm* (since they are of class `XTerm`) or xmh windows (which are of class `Xmh`).

String arguments that are interpreted as filenames (see the `Pixmaps`, `Cursors`, and `IconDirectory` variables later in this reference page) will prepend the user's directory (specified by the HOME environment variable) if the first character is a tilde (~). If, instead, the first character is a colon (:), the name is assumed to refer to one of the internal bitmaps that are used to create the default titlebars symbols: :xlogo or :iconify (both refer to the X used for the iconify button), :resize (the nested squares used by the resize button), and :question (the question mark used for non-existent bitmap files).

The following variables may be specified at the top of a *twm* startup file. Lists of Window name prefix strings are indicated by *`win_list`*. Optional arguments are shown in square brackets:

`AutoRaise {` *`win_list`* `}`
: Specifies a list of windows that should automatically be raised whenever the pointer enters the window. This action can be interactively enabled or disabled on individual windows using the function `f.autoraise`.

`AutoRelativeResize`

Indicates that dragging out a window size (either when initially sizing the window with pointer Button2 or when resizing it) should not wait until the pointer has crossed the window edges. Instead, moving the pointer automatically causes the nearest edge or edges to move by the same amount. This allows allows the resizing windows that extend off the edge of the screen. If the pointer is in the center of the window, or if the resize is begun by pressing a titlebutton, *twm* will still wait for the pointer to cross a window edge (to prevent accidents). This option is particularly useful for people who like the press-drag-release method of sweeping out window sizes.

`BorderColor` *`string`*[{ *`win_color_list`* }]

Specifies the default color of the border to be placed around all non-iconified windows, and may only be given within a WColor or WMonochrome list. The optional *win_color_list* specifies a list of window and color name pairs for specifying particular border colors for different types of windows. For example:

```
BorderColor "gray50"
{
     "XTerm" "red"
     "xmh"   "green"
}
```

The default is black.

`BorderTileBackground` *`string`*[{ *`wincolorlist`* }]

Specifies the default background color in the gray pattern used in unhighlighted borders (only if `NoHighlight` hasn't been set), and may only be given within a `Color` or `Monochrome` list. The optional *`wincolorlist`* allows per-window colors to be specified. The default is black.

`BorderTileForeground` *`string`*[{ *`wincolorlist`* }]

Specifies the default foreground color in the gray pattern used in unhighlighted borders (only if `NoHighlight` hasn't been set), and may only be given within a `Color` or `Monochrome` list. The optional *`wincolorlist`* allows per-window colors to be specified. The default is white.

`BorderWidth` *`pixels`*

Specifies the width in pixels of the border surrounding all client window frames if `ClientBorderWidth` has not been specified. This value is also used to set the border size of windows created by *twm* (such as the icon manager). The default is 2.

`ButtonIndent` *`pixels`*

Specifies the amount by which titlebuttons should be indented on all sides. Positive values cause the buttons to be smaller than the window text and highlight area so that they stand out. Setting this and the `TitleButtonBorderWidth` variables to 0 makes titlebuttons be as tall and wide as possible. The default is 1.

`ClientBorderWidth`

Indicates that border width of a window's frame should be set to the initial border width of the window, rather than to the value of `BorderWidth`.

`Color {` *`colors_list`* `}`

Specifies a list of color assignments to be made if the default display is capable of displaying more than simple black and white. The *`colors_list`* is made up of the following color variables and their values: `DefaultBackground`, `DefaultForeground`, `MenuBackground`, `MenuForeground`, `MenuTitleBackground`, `MenuTitleForeground`, and `MenuShadowColor`.

The following color variables may also be given a list of window and color name pairs to allow per-window colors to be specified (see `BorderColor` for details): `BorderColor`, `IconManagerHighlight`, `BorderTitleBackground`, `BorderTitleForeground`, `TitleBackground`, `TitleForeground`, `IconBackground`, `IconForeground`, `IconBorderColor`, `IconManagerBackground`, and `IconManagerForeground`. For example:

```
Color
{
    MenuBackground          "gray50"
    MenuForeground          "blue"
    BorderColor             "red" { "XTerm" "yellow" }
    TitleForeground         "yellow"
    TitleBackground         "blue"
}
```

All of these color variables may also be specified for the `Monochrome` variable, allowing the same initialization file to be used on both color and monochrome displays.

`ConstrainedMoveTime` *`milliseconds`*

Specifies the length of time between button clicks needed to begin a constrained move operation. Double clicking within this amount of time when invoking `f.move` will cause the window only be moved in a horizontal or vertical direction. Setting this value to 0 will disable constrained moves. The default is 400 milliseconds.

`Cursors {` *`cursor_list`* `}`

Specifies the glyphs that *twm* should use for various pointer cursors. Each cursor may be defined either from the Cursor font or from two bitmap files. Shapes from the Cursor font may be specified directly as:

```
cursorname      "string"
```

where `cursorname` is one of the cursor names listed below, and *`string`* is the name of a glyph as found in the file /usr/include/X11/cursorfont.h (without the "XC_" prefix). If the cursor is to be defined from bitmap files, the following syntax is used instead:

```
cursorname          "image" "mask"
```

The *image* and *mask* strings specify the names of files containing the glyph image and mask in *bitmap* form. The bitmap files are located in the same manner as icon bitmap files. The following example shows the default cursor definitions:

```
Cursors
{
      Frame         "top_left_arrow"
      Title         "top_left_arrow"
      Icon          "top_left_arrow"
      IconMgr       "top_left_arrow"
      Move          "fleur"
      Resize        "fleur"
      Menu          "sb_left_arrow"
      Button        "hand2"
      Wait          "watch"
      Select        "dot"
      Destroy       "pirate"
}
```

`DecorateTransients`
Indicates that transient windows (those containing a WM_TRANSIENT_FOR property) should have titlebars. By default, transients are not reparented.

`DefaultBackground` *string*
Specifies the background color to be used for sizing and information windows. The default is white.

`DefaultForeground` *string*
Specifies the foreground color to be used for sizing and information windows. The default is black.

`DontIconifyByUnmapping` { *win_list* }
Specifies a list of windows that should not be iconified by simply unmapping the window (as would be the case if `IconifyByUnmapping` had been set). This is frequently used to force some windows to be treated as icons while other windows are handled by the icon manager.

`DontMoveOff` Indicates that windows should not be allowed to be moved off the screen. It can be overridden by the `f.forcemove` function.

`DontSqueezeTitle` [{ *win_list* }]
Indicates that titlebars should not be squeezed to their minimum size as described under `SqueezeTitle` below. If the optional window list is

Reference Pages

supplied, only those windows will be prevented from being squeezed.

`ForceIcons` Indicates that icon pixmaps specified in the `Icons` variable should override any client-supplied pixmaps.

`FramePadding` *`pixels`*

Specifies the distance between the titlebar decorations (the button and text) and the window frame. The default is 2 pixels.

`IconBackground` *`string`* [{ *`win_list`* }]

Specifies the background color of icons, and may only be specified inside of a `Color` or `Monochrome` list. The optional *`win_list`* is a list of window names and colors so that per-window colors may be specified. See the `BorderColor` variable for a complete description of the *`win_list`*. The default is white.

`IconBorderColor` *`string`* [{ *`win_list`* }]

Specifies the color of the border used for icon windows, and may only be specified inside of a `Color` or `Monochrome` list. The optional *`win_list`* is a list of window names and colors so that per-window colors may be specified. See the `BorderColor` variable for a complete description of the *`win_list`*. The default is black.

`IconBorderWidth` *`pixels`*

Specifies the width in pixels of the border surrounding icon windows. The default is 2.

`IconDirectory` *`string`*

Specifies the directory that should be searched if if a bitmap file cannot be found in any of the directories in the `bitmapFilePath` resource.

`IconFont` *`string`*

Specifies the font to be used to display icon names within icons. The default is 8x13.

`IconForeground` *`string`* [{ *`win_list`* }]

Specifies the foreground color to be used when displaying icons, and may only be specified inside of a `Color` or `Monochrome` list. The optional *`win_list`* is a list of window names and colors so that per-window colors may be specified. See the `BorderColor` variable for a complete description of the *`win_list`*. The default is black.

`IconifyByUnmapping` [{ *`win_list`* }]

Indicates that windows should be iconified by being unmapped without trying to map any icons. This assumes that the user is will remap the window through the icon manager, the `f.warpto` function, or the TwmWindows menu. If the optional *`win_list`* is provided, only those windows will be iconified by simply unmapping. Windows that have both this and the `IconManagerDontShow` options set may not be accessible if no binding to the TwmWindows menu is set in the user's startup file.

IconManagerBackground *string* [{ *win_list* }]
Specifies the background color to use for icon manager entries, and may only be specified inside of a Color or Monochrome list. The optional *win_list* is a list of window names and colors so that per-window colors may be specified. See the BorderColor variable for a complete description of the *win_list*. The default is white.

IconManagerDontShow [{ *win_list* }]
Indicates that the icon manager should not display any windows. If the optional *win_list* is given, only those windows will not be displayed. This variable is used to prevent windows that are rarely iconified (such as *xclock* or *xload*) from taking up space in the icon manager.

IconManagerFont *string*
Specifies the font to be used when displaying icon manager entries. The default is 8x13.

IconManagerForeground *string* [{ *win_list* }]
Specifies the foreground color to be used when displaying icon manager entries, and may only be specified inside of a Color or Monochrome list. The optional *win_list* is a list of window names and colors so that per-window colors may be specified. See the BorderColor variable for a complete description of the *win_list*. The default is black.

IconManagerGeometry *string* [*columns*]
Specifies the geometry of the icon manager window. The *string* argument is standard geometry specification that indicates the initial full size of the icon manager. The icon manager window is then broken into *columns* pieces and scaled according to the number of entries in the icon manager. Extra entries are wrapped to form additional rows. The default number of columns is 1.

IconManagerHighlight *string* [{ *win_list* }]
Specifies the border color to be used when highlighting the icon manager entry that currently has the focus, and can only be specified inside of a Color or Monochrome list. The optional *win_list* is a list of window names and colors so that per-window colors may be specified. See the BorderColor variable for a complete description of the *win_list*. The default is black.

IconManagers { *iconmgr_list* }
Specifies a list of icon managers to create. Each item in the *iconmgr_list* has the following format:

```
"winname" ["iconname"]   "geometry" columns
```

where *winname* is the name of the windows that should be put into this icon manager, *iconname* is the name of that icon manager window's icon, *geometry* is a standard geometry specification, and *columns* is the number of columns in this icon manager as described in

Reference Pages

`IconManagerGeometry`. For example:

```
IconManagers
{
    "XTerm"  "=300x5+800+5"5
    "myhost""=400x5+100+5"2
}
```

Clients whose name or class is "XTerm" will have an entry created in the "XTerm" icon manager. Clients whose name was "myhost" would be put into the "myhost" icon manager.

`IconManagerShow` { *`win_list`* }

Specifies a list of windows that should appear in the icon manager. When used in conjunction with the `IconManagerDontShow` variable, only the windows in this list will be shown in the icon manager.

`IconRegion` *`geomstring vgrav hgrav gridwidth gridheight`*

Specifies an area on the root window in which icons are placed if no specific icon location is provided by the client. The *`geomstring`* is a quoted string containing a standard geometry specification. If more than one `IconRegion` lines are given, icons will be put into the succeeding icon regions when the first is full. The *`vgrav`* argument should be either `North` or `South` and control and is used to control whether icons are first filled in from the top or bottom of the icon region. Similarly, the *`hgrav`* argument should be either `East` or `West` and is used to control whether icons should be filled in from left from the right. Icons are laid out within the region in a grid with cells *`gridwidth`* pixels wide and *`gridheight`* pixels high.

`Icons` { *`win_list`* }

Specifies a list of window names and the bitmap filenames that should be used as their icons. For example:

```
Icons
{
    "XTerm" "xterm.icon"
    "xfd"   "xfd_icon"
}
```

Windows that match "XTerm" and would not be iconified by unmapping, and would try to use the icon bitmap in the file "xterm.icon". If `ForceIcons` is specified, this bitmap will be used even if the client has requested its own icon pixmap.

`InterpolateMenuColors`

Indicates that menu entry colors should be interpolated between entry specified colors. In the example below:

```
Menu "mymenu"
{
    "Title"     ("black":"red")     f.title
```

```
        "entry1"                        f.nop
        "entry2"                        f.nop
        "entry3"   ("white":"green")    f.nop
        "entry4"                        f.nop
        "entry5"   ("red":"white")      f.nop
}
```

The foreground colors for "entry1" and "entry2" will be interpolated between black and white, and the background colors between red and green. Similarly, the foreground for "entry4" will be half-way between white and red, and the background will be half-way between green and white.

`MakeTitle` { *win_list* }

Specifies a list of windows on which a titlebar should be placed and is used to request titles on specific windows when WNoTitle has been set.

`MaxWindowSize` *string*

Specifies a geometry in which the width and height give the maximum size for a given window. This is typically used to restrict windows to the size of the screen. The default is 30000x30000.

`MenuBackground` *string*

Specifies the background color used for menus, and can only be specified inside of a `Color` or `Monochrome` list. The default is white.

`MenuFont` *string*

Specifies the font to use when displaying menus. The default is 8x13.

`MenuForeground` *string*

Specifies the foreground color used for menus, and can only be specified inside of a `Color` or `Monochrome` list. The default is black.

`MenuShadowColor` *string*

Specifies the color of the shadow behind pull-down menus and can only be specified inside of a `Color` or `Monochrome` list. The default is black.

`MenuTitleBackground` *string*

Specifies the background color for `f.title` entries in menus, and can only be specified inside of a `Color` or `Monochrome` list. The default is white.

`MenuTitleForeground` *string*

Specifies the foreground color for `f.title` entries in menus and can only be specified inside of a `Color` or `Monochrome` list. The default is black.

`Monochrome` { *colors* }

Specifies a list of color assignments that should be made if the screen has a depth of 1. See the description of `Colors`.

`MoveDelta` *pixels*

Specifies the number of pixels the pointer must move before the **f.move** function starts working. Also see the `f.deltastop` function. The default is zero pixels.

Reference Pages

`NoBackingStore`
: Indicates that *twm*'s menus should not request backing store to minimize repainting of menus. This is typically used with servers that can repaint faster than they can handle backing store.

`NoCaseSensitive`
: Indicates that case should be ignored when sorting icon names in an icon manager. This option is typically used with applications that capitalize the first letter of their icon name.

`NoDefaults`
: Indicates that *twm* should not supply the default titlebuttons and bindings. This option should only be used if the startup file contains a completely new set of bindings and definitions.

`NoGrabServer`
: Indicates that *twm* should not grab the server when popping up menus and moving opaque windows.

`NoHighlight` [{ *`win_list`* }]
: Indicates that borders should not be highlighted to track the location of the pointer. If the optional *`win_list`* is given, highlighting will only be disabled for those windows. When the border is highlighted, it will be drawn in the current `BorderColor`. When the border is not highlighted, it will be stippled with an gray pattern using the current `BorderTileForeground` and `BorderTileBackground` colors.

`NoIconManagers`
: Indicates that no icon manager should be created.

`NoMenuShadows`
: Indicates that menus should not have drop shadows drawn behind them. This is typically used with slower servers since it speeds up menu drawing at the expense of making the menu slightly harder to read.

`NoRaiseOnDeiconify`
: Indicates that windows that are deiconified should not be raised.

`NoRaiseOnMove`
: Indicates that windows should not be raised when moved. This is typically used to allow windows to slide underneath each other.

`NoRaiseOnResize`
: Indicates that windows should not be raised when resized. This is typically used to allow windows to be resized underneath each other.

`NoRaiseOnWarp`
: Indicates that windows should not be raised when the pointer is warped into them with the `f.warpto` function. If this option is set, warping to an occluded window may result in the pointer ending up in the occluding window instead the desired window (which causes unexpected behavior with `f.warpring`).

`NoSaveUnders`

Indicates that menus should not request save-unders to minimize window repainting following menu selection. It is typically used with displays that can repaint faster than they can handle save-unders.

`NoTitle [{ win_list }]`

Indicates that windows should not have titlebars. If the optional `win_list` is given, only those windows will not have titlebars. `MakeTitle` may be used with this option to force titlebars to be put on specific windows.

`NoTitleFocus`

Indicates that *twm* should not set keyboard input focus to each window as it is entered. Normally, *twm* sets the focus so that focus and key events from the titlebar and icon managers are delivered to the application. If the pointer is moved quickly and *twm* is slow to respond, input can be directed to the old window instead of the new. This option is typically used to prevent this "input lag" and to work around bugs in older applications that have problems with focus events.

`NoTitleHighlight [{ win_list }]`

Indicates that the highlight area of the titlebar, which is used to indicate the window that currently has the input focus, should not be displayed. If the optional `win_list` is given, only those windows will not have highlight areas. This and the `SqueezeTitle` options can be set to substantially reduce the amount of screen space required by titlebars.

`OpaqueMove` Indicates that the `f.move` function should actually move the window instead of just an outline so that the user can immediately see what the window will look like in the new position. This option is typically used on fast displays (particularly if `NoGrabServer` is set).

`Pixmaps { pixmaps }`

Specifies a list of pixmaps that define the appearance of various images. Each entry is a keyword indicating the pixmap to set, followed by a string giving the name of the bitmap file. The following pixmaps may be specified:

```
Pixmaps
{
        TitleHighlight   "gray1"
}
```

The default for `TitleHighlight` is to use an even stipple pattern.

`RandomPlacement`

Indicates that windows with no specified geometry should should be placed in a pseudo-random location instead of having the user drag out an outline.

`ResizeFont string`

Specifies the font to be used for in the dimensions window when resizing windows. The default is fixed.

Reference Pages

`RestartPreviousState`

Indicates that *twm* should attempt to use the WM_STATE property on client windows to tell which windows should be iconified and which should be left visible. This is typically used to make try to regenerate the state that the screen was in before the previous window manager was shutdown.

`ShowIconManager`

Indicates that the icon manager window should be displayed when *twm* is started. It can always be brought up using the `f.showiconmgr` function.

`SortIconManager`

Indicates that entries in the icon manager should be sorted alphabetically rather than by simply appending new windows to the end.

`SqueezeTitle` [{ *`squeeze_list`* }]

Indicates that *twm* should attempt to use the SHAPE extension to make titlebars occupy only as much screen space as they need, rather than extending all the way across the top of the window. The optional *`squeeze_list`* may be used to control the location of the squeezed titlebar along the top of the window. It contains entries of the form:

```
"name"      justification      num      denom
```

where *`name`* is a window name, *`justification`* is either *`left`*, *`center`*, or *`right`*, and *`num`* and *`denom`* are numbers specifying a ratio giving the relative position about which the titlebar is justified. The ratio is measured from left to right if the numerator is positive, and right to left if negative. A denominator of 0 indicates that the numerator should be measured in pixels. For convenience, the ratio 0/0 is the same as 1/2 for *`center`* and -1/1 for *`right`*. For example:

```
SqueezeTitle
{
      "XTerm"      left       0        0
      "xterm1"     left       1        3
      "xterm2"     left       2        3
      "oclock"     center              00
      "emacs"      right               00
}
```

The `DontSqueezeTitle` list can be used to turn off squeezing on certain titles.

`StartIconified` [{ *`win_list`* }]

Indicates that client windows should initially be left as icons until explicitly deiconified by the user. If the optional *`win_list`* is given, only those windows will be started iconic. This is useful for programs that do not support an `-iconic` command line option or resource.

`TitleBackground` *`string`* [{ *`win_list`* }]

Specifies the background color used in titlebars, and may only be specified inside of a Color or Monochrome list. The optional *win_list* is a list of window names and colors so that per-window colors may be specified. The default is white.

TitleButtonBorderWidth *pixels*

Specifies the width in pixels of the border surrounding titlebuttons. This is typically set to 0 to allow titlebuttons to take up as much space as possible and to not have a border. The default is 1.

TitleFont *string*

Specifies the font to used for displaying window names in titlebars. The default is 8x13.

TitleForeground *string* [{ *win_list* }]

Specifies the foreground color used in titlebars, and may only be specified inside of a Color or Monochrome list. The optional *win_list* is a list of window names and colors so that per-window colors may be specified. The default is black.

TitlePadding *pixels*

Specifies the distance between the various buttons, text, and highlight areas in the titlebar. The default is 8 pixels.

UnknownIcon *string*

Specifies the filename of a bitmap file to be used as the default icon. This bitmap will be used as the icon of all clients which do not provide an icon bitmap and are not listed in the Icons list.

UsePPosition *string*

Specifies whether or not *twm* should honor program-requested locations (given by the PPosition flag in the WM_NORMAL_HINTS property) in the absence of a user-specified position. The argument *string* may have one of three values: *off* (the default) indicating that *twm* should ignore the program-supplied position, *on* indicating that the position should be used, and *non-zero* indicating that the position should used if it is other than (0,0). The latter option is for working around a bug in older toolkits.

WarpCursor [{ *win_list* }]

Indicates that the pointer should be warped into windows when they are deiconified. If the optional *win_list* is given, the pointer will only be warped when those windows are deiconified.

WindowRing { *win_list* }

Specifies a list of windows along which the f.warpring function cycles.

WarpUnmapped

Indicates that that the f.warpto function should deiconify any iconified windows it encounters. This is typically used to make a key binding that will pop a particular window (such as *xmh*), no matter where it is. The default is for f.warpto to ignore iconified windows.

Reference Pages

`XorValue` *number*
: Specifies the value to use when drawing window outlines for moving and resizing. This should be set to a value that will result in a variety of of distinguishable colors when exclusive-or'ed with the contents of the user's typical screen. Setting this variable to 1 often gives nice results if adjacent colors in the default colormap are distinct. By default, *twm* will attempt to cause temporary lines to appear at the opposite end of the colormap from the graphics.

`Zoom [` *count* `]` Indicates that outlines suggesting movement of a window to and from its iconified state should be displayed whenever a window is iconified or deiconified. The optional *count* argument specifies the number of outlines to be drawn. The default count is 8.

The following variables must be set after the fonts have been assigned, so it is usually best to put them at the end of the variables or beginning of the bindings sections:

`DefaultFunction` *function*
: Specifies the function to be executed when a key or button event is received for which no binding is provided. This is typically bound to `f.nop`, `f.beep`, or a menu containing window operations.

`WindowFunction` *function*
: Specifies the function to execute when a window is selected from the `TwmWindows` menu. If this variable is not set, the window will be deiconified and raised.

Bindings

After the desired variables have been set, functions may be attached titlebuttons and key and pointer buttons. Titlebuttons may be added from the left or right side and appear in the titlebar from left-to-right according to the order in which they are specified. Key and pointer button bindings may be given in any order.

Titlebuttons specifications must include the name of the pixmap to use in the button box and the function to be invoked when a pointer button is pressed within them:

```
LeftTitleButton "bitmapname"= function
```

or:

```
RightTitleButton "bitmapname"= function
```

The *bitmapname* may refer to one of the built-in bitmaps (which are scaled to match `TitleFont`) by using the appropriate colon-prefixed name described above.

Key and pointer button specifications must give the modifiers that must be pressed, over which parts of the screen the pointer must be, and what function is to be invoked. Keys are given as strings containing the appropriate keysym name; buttons are given as the keywords `Button1-Button5`:

```
"FP1"       = modlist : context : function
Button1     = modlist : context : function
```

The modlist is any combination of the modifier names shift, control, and meta (which may be abbreviated as s, c, and m respectively) separated by a vertical bar (|). Similarly, the *context* is any combination of window, title, icon, root, frame, iconmgr, their first letters (iconmgr abbreviation is m), or all, separated by a vertical bar. The *function* is any of the f. keywords described below. For example, the default startup file contains the following bindings:

```
Button1  =   : root                : f.menu "TwmWindows"
Button1  = m : window | icon       : f.function "move-or-lower"
Button2  = m : window | icon       : f.iconify
Button3  = m : window | icon       : f.function "move-or-raise"
Button1  =   : title               : f.function "move-or-raise"
Button2  =   : title               : f.raiselower
Button1  =   : icon                : f.function "move-or-iconify"
Button2  =   : icon                : f.iconify
Button1  =   : iconmgr             : f.iconify
Button2  =   : iconmgr             : f.iconify
```

A user who wanted to be able to manipulate windows from the keyboard could use the following bindings:

```
"F1"     =         all         : f.iconify
"F2"     =         all         : f.raiselower
"F3"     =         all         : f.warpring "next"
"F4"     =         all         : f.warpto "xmh"
"F5"     =         all         : f.warpto "emacs"
"F6"     =         all         : f.colormap "next"
"F7"     =         all         : f.colormap "default"
"F20"    =         all         : f.warptoscreen "next"
"Left"   = m       all         : f.backiconmgr
"Right"  = m | s   all         : f.forwiconmgr
"Up"     = m       all         : f.upiconmgr
"Down"   = m | s   all         : f.downiconmgr
```

twm provides many more window manipulation primitives than can be conveniently stored in a titlebar, menu, or set of key bindings. Although a small set of defaults are supplied (unless the NoDefaults is specified), most users will want to have their most common operations bound to key and button strokes. To do this, *twm* associates names with each of the primitives and provides *user-defined functions* for building higher level primitives and *menus* for interactively selecting among groups of functions.

User-defined functions contain the name by which they are referenced in calls to f.function and a list of other functions to execute. For example:

```
Function "move-or-lower"       { f.move f.deltastop f.lower }
Function "move-or-raise"       { f.move f.deltastop f.raise }
Function "move-or-iconify"     { f.move f.deltastop f.iconify }
Function "restore-colormap"    { f.colormap "default" f.lower }
```

The function name must be used in f.function exactly as it appears in the function specification.

Reference Pages

In the descriptions below, if the function is said to operate on the selected window, but is invoked from a root menu, the cursor will be changed to the `Select` cursor and the next window to receive a button press will be chosen:

`! string` This is an abbreviation for `f.exec string`.

`f.autoraise` Toggles whether or not the selected window is raised whenever entered by the pointer. See the description of the variable `AutoRaise`.

`f.backiconmgr`
Warps the pointer to the previous column in the current icon manager, wrapping back to the previous row if necessary.

`f.beep` Sounds the keyboard bell.

`f.bottomzoom`
Similar to the `f.fullzoom` function, but resizes the window to fill only the bottom half of the screen.

`f.circledown`
Lowers the top-most window that occludes another window.

`f.circleup` Raises the bottom-most window that is occluded by another window.

`f.colormap string`
Rotates the colormaps (obtained from the WM_COLORMAP_WINDOWS property on the window) that *twm* will display when the pointer is in this window. The argument `string` may have one of the following values: `next`, `prev`, and `default`.

`f.deiconify` Deiconifies the selected window. If the window is not an icon, this function does nothing.

`f.delete` Sends the WM_DELETE_WINDOW message to the selected window if the client application has requested it through the WM_PROTOCOLS window property. The application is supposed to respond to the message by removing the indicated window. If the window has not requested WM_DELETE_WINDOW messages, the keyboard bell will be rung indicating that the user should choose an alternative method.

`f.deltastop` Allows a user-defined function to be aborted if the pointer has been moved more than *MoveDelta* pixels. See the example definition given for `Function "move-or-raise"` at the beginning of the section.

`f.destroy` Instructs the X server to close the display connection of the client that created the selected window. This should only be used as a last resort for shutting down runaway clients.

`f.downiconmgr`
Warps the pointer to the next row in the current icon manger, wrapping to the beginning of the next column if necessary.

`f.exec` *`string`*
: Passes the argument *`string`* to /bin/sh for execution. In multiscreen mode, if *`string`* starts a new X client without giving a display argument, the client will appear on the screen from which this function was invoked.

`f.focus` Toggles the keyboard focus of the server to the selected window, changing the focus rule from pointer-driven if necessary. If the selected window already was focused, this function executes an `f.unfocus`.

`f.forcemove` Like `f.move`, except that it ignores the `DontMoveOff` variable.

`f.forwiconmgr`
: Warps the pointer to the next column in the current icon manager, wrapping to the beginning of the next row if necessary.

`f.fullzoom` Resizes the selected window to the full size of the display or else restores the original size if the window was already zoomed.

`f.function` *`string`*
: Executes the user-defined function whose name is specified by the argument *`string`*.

`f.hbzoom` A synonym for `f.bottomzoom`.

`f.hideiconmgr`
: Unmaps the current icon manager.

`f.horizoom` Similar to the `f.zoom` function, except that the selected window is resized to the full width of the display.

`f.htzoom` A synonym for `f.topzoom`.

`f.hzoom` A synonym for `f.horizoom`.

`f.iconify` Iconifies or deiconifies the selected window or icon.

`f.identify` Displays a summary of the name and geometry of the selected window. Clicking the pointer or pressing a key in the window will dismiss it.

`f.lefticonmgr`
: Similar to `f.backiconmgr`, except that wrapping does not change rows.

`f.leftzoom` Similar to the `f.bottomzoom` function but causes the selected window is only resized to the left half of the display.

`f.lower` Lowers the selected window.

`f.menu` *`string`*
: Invokes the menu specified by the argument *`string`*. Cascaded menus may be built by nesting calls to `f.menu`.

`f.move` Drags an outline of the selected window (or the window itself if the `OpaqueMove` variable is set) until the invoking pointer button is released. Double clicking within the number of milliseconds given by `ConstrainedMoveTime` warps the pointer to the center of the window

Reference Pages

and constrains the move to be either horizontal or vertical depending on which grid line is crossed. To abort a move, press another button before releasing the first button.

`f.nexticonmgr`
Warps the pointer to the next icon manager containing any windows on the current or any succeeding screen.

`f.nop` Does nothing and is typically used with the `DefaultFunction` or `WindowFunction` variables or to introduce blank lines in menus.

`f.previconmgr`
Warps the pointer to the previous icon manager containing any windows on the current or preceding screens.

`f.quit` Causes *twm* to restore the window's borders and exit. If *twm* is the first client invoked from *xdm*, this will result in a server reset.

`f.raise` Raises the selected window.

`f.raiselower`
Raises the selected window to the top of the stacking order if it is occluded by any windows, otherwise the window will be lowered.

`f.refresh` Causes all windows to be refreshed.

`f.resize` Displays an outline of the selected window. Crossing a border (or setting `AutoRelativeResize`) will cause the outline to begin to rubber band until the invoking button is released. To abort a resize, press another button before releasing the first button.

`f.restart` Kills and restarts *twm*.

`f.righticonmgr`
Similar to `f.nexticonmgr`, except that wrapping does not change rows.

`f.rightzoom` Similar to the `f.bottomzoom` function, except that the selected window is only resized to the right half of the display.

`f.saveyourself`
Sends a WM_SAVEYOURSELF message to the selected window if it has requested the message in its WM_PROTOCOLS window property. Clients that accept this message are supposed to checkpoint all state associated with the window and update the WM_COMMAND property as specified in the ICCCM. If the selected window has not selected for this message, the keyboard bell will be rung.

`f.showiconmgr`
Maps the current icon manager.

`f.sorticonmgr`
Sorts the entries in the current icon manager alphabetically. See the variable `SortIconManager`.

`f.source` *string*
: Assumes *string* is a file name. The file is read and parsed as a *twm* startup file. This function is intended to be used only to re-build pull-down menus. None of the *twm* variables are changed.

`f.title` Provides a centered, unselectable item in a menu definition. It should not be used in any other context.

`f.topzoom` Similar to the `f.bottomzoom` function, except that the selected window is only resized to the top half of the display.

`f.twmrc` Causes the startup customization file to be re-read. This function is exactly like the `f.source` function without having to specify the filename.

`f.unfocus` Resets the focus back to pointer-driven. This should be used when a focused window is no longer desired.

`f.upiconmgr` Warps the pointer to the previous row in the current icon manager, wrapping to the last row in the same column if necessary.

`f.version` Causes the *twm* version window to be displayed. This window will be displayed until a pointer button is pressed or the pointer is moved from one window to another.

`f.vlzoom` A synonym for `f.leftzoom`.

`f.vrzoom` A synonym for `f.rightzoom`.

`f.warpring` *string*
: Warps the pointer to the next or previous window (as indicated by the argument *string*, which may be *next* or *prev*) specified in the `WindowRing` variable.

`f.warpto` *string*
: Warps the pointer to the window which has a name or class that matches *string*. If the window is iconified, it will be deiconified if the variable `WarpUnmapped` is set or else ignored.

`f.warptoiconmgr` *string*
: Warps the pointer to the icon manager entry associated with the window containing the pointer in the icon manager specified by the argument *string*. If *string* is empty, the current icon manager is chosen.

`f.warptoscreen` *string*
: Warps the pointer to the screen specified by the argument *string*. *String* may be a number (e.g., *0* or *1*), the word *next* (indicating the current screen plus 1, skipping over any unmanaged screens), the word *back* (indicating the current screen minus 1, skipping over any unmanaged screens), or the word *prev* (indicating the last screen visited).

`f.winrefresh`
: Similar to the `f.refresh` function, except that only the selected window is refreshed.

`f.zoom` Similar to the `f.fullzoom` function, except that the only the height of the selected window is changed.

Menus

Functions may be grouped and interactively selected using pop-up (when bound to a pointer button) or pull-down (when associated with a titiebutton) menus. Each menu specification contains the name of the menu as it will be referred to by `f.menu`, optional default foreground and background colors, the list of item names and the functions they should invoke, and optional foreground and background colors for individual items:

```
Menu "menuname" [ ("deffore":"defback") ]
{
     string1 [ ("fore1":"backn")]function1
     string2 [ ("fore2":"backn")]function2
          .
          .
          .
     stringN [ ("foreN":"backN")]functionN
}
```

The `menuname` is case-sensitive. The optional `deffore` and `defback` arguments specify the foreground and background colors used on a color display to highlight menu entries. The `string` portion of each menu entry will be the text which will appear in the menu. The optional `fore` and `back` arguments specify the foreground and background colors of the menu entry when the pointer is not in the entry. These colors will only be used on a color display. The default is to use the colors specified by the `MenuForeground` and `MenuBackground` variables. The *function* portion of the menu entry is one of the functions, including any user-defined functions, or additional menus.

There is a special menu named `TwmWindows` which contains the names of all of the client and *twm*-supplied windows. Selecting an entry will cause the `WindowFunction` to be executed on that window. If `WindowFunction` hasn't been set, the window will be deiconified and raised.

Icons

twm supports several different ways of manipulating iconified windows. The common pixmap-and-text style may be laid out by hand or automatically arranged as described by the `IconRegion` variable. In addition, a terse grid of icon names, called an icon manager, provides a more efficient use of screen space as well as the ability to navigate among windows from the keyboard.

Neither client-supplied icon windows nor dynamic setting of the icon pixmap are supported (icon name changes will be updated automatically).

An icon manager is a window that contains names of selected or all windows currently on the display. In addition to the window name, a small button using the default iconify symbol will be displayed to the left of the name when the window is iconified. By default, clicking on an entry in the icon manager performs `f.iconify`. To change the actions taken in the icon manager, use the the `iconmgr` context when specifying button and keyboard bindings.

Moving the pointer into the icon manager also directs keyboard focus to the indicated window (setting the focus explicitly or else sending synthetic events `NoTitleFocus` is set). Using the `f.upiconmgr`, `f.downiconmgr` `f.lefticonmgr`, and `f.righticonmgr` functions, the input focus can be changed between windows directly from the keyboard.

Bugs

Lock and Mod2 through Mod5 cannot be specified as modifier contexts. The correct fix is to add lock, 1, mod1 (for completeness), mod2, mod3, mod4, mod5 to the parse and grammar tables, and add a number as a valid key type (so long as it is 1-5).

The resource manager should have been used instead of all of the window lists.

The `IconRegion` variable should take a list.

Double clicking very fast to get the constrained move function will sometimes cause the window to move, even though the pointer is not moved.

If `IconifyByUnmapping` is on and windows are listed in `IconManagerDontShow` but not in `DontIconifyByUnmapping`, they may be lost if they are iconified and no bindings to `f.menu TwmWindows` or `f.warpto` are setup.

Files

*$HOME/.twmrc.**screen number***
$HOME/.twmrc
/usr/lib/X11/twm/system.twmrc

Environment Variables

DISPLAY — This variable is used to determine which X server to use. It is also set during `f.exec` so that programs come up on the proper screen.

HOME — This variable is used as the prefix for files that begin with a tilde and for locating the *twm* startup file.

See Also

X, Xserver, xdm, xrdb

Copyright

Authors

Tom LaStrange, Solbourne Computer;
Jim Fulton, MIT X Consortium;
Steve Pitschke, Stardent Computer;
Keith Packard, MIT X Consortium;
Dave Payne, Apple Computer.

Name

uwm – a window manager for X.

Syntax

uwm [*options*]

Description

The *uwm* program is a window manager client application of the window server. In releases prior to 4, *uwm* is the standard X window manager. As of Release 4, *uwm* has been moved to the user-contributed part of the distribution and replaced in the standard distribution by *twm*.

When *uwm* is invoked, it searches a predefined search path to locate any *uwm* startup files. If no startup files exist, *uwm* initializes its built-in defaults.

If startup files exist in any of the following locations, it adds the variables to the default variables. In the case of contention, the variables in the last file found override previous specifications. Files in the *uwm* search path are:

/usr/lib/X11/uwm/system.uwmrc
$HOME/.uwmrc

To use only the settings defined in a single startup file, include the variables, `resetbindings`, `resetmenus`, `resetvariables` at the top of that specific startup file.

Options

`-f` *filename* Names an alternate file as a *uwm* startup file.

`-display` [*host*]:*server*[.*screen*]

Allows you to specify the host, server, and screen on which to run the window manager. *host* specifies the machine, *server* specifies the server number, and *screen* specifies the screen number. For example,

uwm -display *your_node*:**0.1**

specifies screen 1 on server 0 on the machine *your_node*. If the host is omitted, the local machine is assumed. If the screen is omitted, the screen 0 is assumed; the server and colon (:) are necessary in all cases.

Startup File Variables

Variables are typically entered first, at the top of the startup file. By convention, `resetbindings`, `resetmenus`, and `resetvariables` head the list.

`autoselect/noautoselect`

Places the menu cursor in first menu item. If unspecified, the menu cursor is placed in the menu header when the menu is displayed.

`background=`*color*

Specifies the default background color for popup sizing windows, menus, and icons. The default is to use the `WhitePixel` for the current screen.

`bordercolor=`*color*
: Specifies the default border color for popup sizing windows, menus, and icons. The default is to use the `BlackPixel` for the current screen.

`borderwidth=`*pixels*
: Specifies the default width in pixels for borders surrounding icons.

`delta=`*pixels*
: Indicates the number of pixels the cursor is moved before the action is interpreted by the window manager as a command. (Also refer to the `delta` mouse action.)

`foreground=`*color*
: Specifies the default foreground color for popup sizing windows, menus, and icons. The default is to use the `BlackPixel` for the current screen.

`freeze/nofreeze`
: Locks all other client applications out of the server during certain window manager tasks, such as move and resize.

`grid/nogrid` Displays a finely-ruled grid to help you position an icon or window during resize or move operations.

`hiconpad=`*pixels*
: Indicates the number of pixels to pad an icon horizontally. The default is five pixels.

`hmenupad=`*pixels*
: Indicates the number of pixels to pad each menu item to the left and right of the text.

`iconfont=`*fontname*
: Names the font that is displayed within icons. Font names for a given server can be obtained using *xlsfonts*.

`maxcolors=`*n* Limits the number of colors the window manager can use in a given invocation. If set to zero, or not specified, *uwm* assumes no limit to the number of colors it can take from the color map. `maxcolors` counts colors as they are included in the file.

`mborderwidth=`*pixels*
: Indicates the width in pixels of the border surrounding menus.

`normali/nonormali`
: Places icons created with `f.newiconify` within the root window, even if they are placed partially off the screen. With `nonormali` the icon is placed exactly where the cursor leaves it.

`normalw/nonormalw`
: Places window created with `f.newiconify` within the root window, even if they are placed partially off the screen. With `nonormalw` the window is placed exactly where the cursor leaves it.

Reference Pages

`push=`*n* Moves a window *n* number of pixels or a 1/*n* times the size of the window, depending on whether `pushabsolute` or `pushrelative` is specified. Use this variable in conjunction with `f.pushup`, `f.pushdown`, `f.pushright`, or `f.pushleft`.

`pushabsolute/pushrelative`

`pushabsolute` indicates that the number entered with push is equivalent to pixels. When an `f.push` (left, right, up, or down) function is called, the window is moved exactly that number of pixels.

`pushrelative` indicates that the number entered with the push variable represents a relative number. When an `f.push` function is called, the window is invisibly divided into the number of parts you entered with the push variable, and the window is moved one part.

`resetbindings, resetmenus, resetvariables`

Resets all previous function bindings, menus, and variables entries, specified in any startup file in the *uwm* search path, including those in the default environment. By convention, these variables are entered first in the startup file.

`resizefont=`*fontname*

Identifies the font of the indicator that displays in the corner of the window as you resize windows. See *xlsfonts* for obtaining font names.

`resizerelative/noresizerelative`

Indicates whether or not resize operations should be done relative to a moving edge or edges. By default, the dynamic rectangle uses the actual pointer location to define the new size. (Available as of Release 3.)

`reverse/noreverse`

Defines the display as black characters on a white background for the window manager windows and icons.

`viconpad=`*pixels*

Indicates the number of pixels to pad an icon vertically. Default is five pixels.

`vmenupad=`*pixels*

Indicates the number of pixels to pad each menu item vertically (i.e., above and below the text).

`volume=`*n* Increases or decreases the base level volume set by the *xset*(1) command. Enter an integer from 0 to 7, 7 being the loudest.

`zap/nozap` Causes ghost lines to follow the window or icon from its previous default location to its new location during a move or resize operation.

Binding Syntax

function`=[`*control key(s)*`]:[`*context*`]:`*mouse events*`:` "*menu name*"

Function and mouse events are required input. Menu name is required with the `f.menu` function definition only.

Function

`f.beep` Emits a beep from the keyboard. Loudness is determined by the volume variable.

`f.circledown` Causes the top window that is obscuring another window to drop to the bottom of the stack of windows.

`f.circleup` Exposes the lowest window that is obscured by other windows.

`f.continue` Releases the window server display action after you stop action with the `f.pause` function.

`f.focus` Directs all keyboard input to the selected window. To reset the focus to all windows, invoke `f.focus` from the root window.

`f.iconify` When implemented from a window, this function converts the window to its respective icon. When implemented from an icon, `f.iconify` converts the icon to its respective window.

`f.kill` Kills the client that created a window.

`f.lower` Lowers a window that is obstructing a window below it.

`f.menu` Invokes a menu. Enclose 'menu name' in quotes if it contains blank characters or parentheses.

`f.move` Moves a window or icon to a new location, which becomes the default location.

`f.moveopaque` Moves a window or icon to a new screen location. When using this function, the entire window or icon is moved to the new screen location. The grid effect is not used with this function.

`f.newiconify` Allows you to create a window or icon and then position the window or icon in a new default location on the screen.

`f.pause` Temporarily stops all display action. To release the screen and immediately update all windows, use the `f.continue` function.

`f.pushdown` Moves a window down. The distance of the push is determined by the push variables.

`f.pushleft` Moves a window to the left. The distance of the push is determined by the push variables.

`f.pushright` Moves a window to the right. The distance of the push is determined by the push variables.

`f.pushup` Moves a window up. The distance of the push is determined by the push variables.

Reference Pages

`f.raise` Raises a window that is being obstructed by a window above it.

`f.refresh` Results in exposure events being sent to the window server clients for all unobscured or partially obscured windows. The windows will not refresh correctly if the exposure events are not handled properly.

`f.resize` Resizes an existing window. Note that some clients, notably editors, react unpredictably if you resize the window while the client is running.

`f.restart` Causes the window manager application to restart, retracing the *uwm* search path and initializing the variables it finds.

Control Keys

By default, the window manager uses meta as its control key. It can also use ctrl, shift, lock, or null (no control key). Control keys must be entered in lowercase, and can be abbreviated as: c, l, m, s for ctrl, lock, meta, and shift, respectively.

You can bind one, two, or no control keys to a function. Use the bar (|) character to combine control keys.

Note that client applications other than the window manager use the shift as a control key. If you bind the shift key to a window manager function, you can not use other client applications that require this key.

Context

The context refers to the screen location of the pointer when a command is initiated. When you include a context entry in a binding, the pointer must be in that context or the function will not be activated. The window manager recognizes the following four contexts: icon, window, root, (null).

The root context refers to the root, or background window, A (null) context is indicated when the context field is left blank, and allows a function to be invoked from any screen location. Combine contexts using the bar (|) character.

Mouse Buttons

Any of the following mouse buttons are accepted in lowercase and can be abbreviated as l, m, or r, respectively: left, middle, right.

With the specific button, you must identify the action of that button. Mouse actions can be:

`down` Function occurs when the specified button is pressed down.

`up` Function occurs when the specified button is released.

`delta` Indicates that the mouse must be moved the number of pixels specified with the delta variable before the specified function is invoked. The mouse can be moved in any direction to satisfy the delta requirement.

Menu Definition

After binding a set of function keys and a menu name to `f.menu`, you must define the menu to be invoked, using the following syntax:

```
menu = "menu name" {
"item name" : "action"
        .
        .
        .
}
```

Enter the menu name exactly the way it is entered with the `f.menu` function or the window manager will not recognize the link. If the menu name contains blank strings, tabs or parentheses, it must be quoted here and in the `f.menu` function entry. You can enter as many menu items as your screen is long. You cannot scroll within menus.

Any menu entry that contains quotes, special characters, parentheses, tabs, or strings of blanks must be enclosed in double quotes. Follow the item name by a colon (:).

Menu Action

Window manager functions
: Any function previously described (e.g., `f.move` or `f.iconify`).

Shell commands
: Begin with an exclamation point (!) and are set to run in the background. You cannot include a new line character within a shell command.

Text strings
: Text strings are placed in the window server's cut buffer.

: Strings starting with an up arrow (^) will have a new line character appended to the string after the up arrow (^) has been stripped from it.

: Strings starting with a bar character (|) will be copied as is after the bar character (|) has been stripped.

Color Menus

Use the following syntax to add color to menus:

```
menu = "menu name"(color1:color2:color3:color4) {
 "item name" :(color5 :color6)   :  "action"
        .
        .
        .
}
```

where:

color1 Foreground color of the header.

color2 Background color of the header.

color3 Foreground color of the highlighter, the horizontal band of color that moves with the cursor within the menu.

`color4`	Background color of the highlighter.
`color5`	Foreground color for the individual menu item.
`color6`	Background color for the individual menu item.

Color Defaults

Colors default to the colors of the root window under any of the following conditions:

If you run out of color map entries, either before or during an invocation of *uwm*. If you specify a foreground or background color that does not exist in the RGB color database of the server (see */usr/lib/X11/rgb.txt* for a sample) both the foreground and background colors default to the root window colors. If you omit a foreground or background color, both the foreground and background colors default to the root window colors. If the total number of colors specified in the startup file exceeds the number specified in the *maxcolors* variable. If you specify no colors in the startup file.

Sample .mwmrc File

The following sample startup file shows the use of window manager options:

```
# Global variables
#
resetbindings;resetvariables;resetmenus
autoselect
delta=25
freeze
grid
hiconpad=5
hmenupad=6
iconfont=oldeng
menufont=timrom12b
resizefont=9x15
viconpad=5
vmenupad=3
volume=7
#
# Mouse button/key maps
#
#FUNCTION        KEYS  CONTEXT    BUTTON          MENU(if any)
#========        ====  =======    ======          ============
f.menu =         meta  :          :left down      :"WINDOW OPS"
f.menu =         meta  :          :middle down    :"EXTENDED WINDOW OPS"
f.move =         meta  :w|i       :right down
f.circleup =     meta  :root      :right down
#
# Menu specifications
#
menu = "WINDOW OPS" {
"(De)Iconify":                f.iconify
Move:                         f.move
```

```
Resize:                        f.resize
Lower:                         f.lower
Raise:                         f.raise
}

menu = "EXTENDED WINDOW OPS" {
Create Window:                 !"xterm &"
Iconify at New Position:       f.lowericonify
Focus Keyboard on Window:      f.focus
Freeze All Windows:            f.pause
Unfreeze All Windows:          f.continue
Circulate Windows Up:          f.circleup
Circulate Windows Down:        f.circledown
}
```

Restrictions

The color specifications have no effect on a monochrome system.

Files

/usr/lib/X11/uwm/system.uwmrc
$HOME/.uwmrc

See Also

X, Xserver, xset, xlsfonts

Copyright

Copyright 1985, 1986, 1987, 1988 Digital Equipment Corporation, Maynard, MA.

Author

M. Gancarz, DEC Ultrix Engineering Group, Merrimack, New Hampshire, using some algorithms originally by Bob Scheifler, MIT Laboratory for Computer Science.

Reference Pages

Name

x10tox11 – X version 10 to version 11 protocol converter.

Syntax

x10tox11 [*options*]

Description

As of Release 4, this program is no longer included in the standard distribution of X.

x10tox11 masquerades as an X Window System Version 10 server. It enables an X Version 10 client to run unchanged under X Version 11 by converting Version 10 requests into appropriate Version 11 requests, and by converting all Version 11 events received from the server into Version 10 events. From the perspective of Version 10 clients, all Version 11 clients look like Version 10 clients; and from the perspective of Version 11 clients, all Version 10 clients look just like Version 11 clients. Hence, a Version 11 window manager can manipulate Version 10 clients.

This program does NOT use the X10 *libnest* ddX library. It does actual protocol translation, rather than simply using X11 graphics calls to implement X10 low level operations. As a result, it is both faster and more robust than the X10 Xnest server.

Typical Usage

The protocol converter must be run after the X11 server is running and should be run in the background:

```
% x10tox11 &
```

The program will continue to run until you intentionally kill it or the X11 server is shut down.

Options

-display [*host*]:*server*[.*screen*]

Allows you to specify the X11 display to which you want to be connected. *host* specifies the machine, *server* specifies the server number, and *screen* specifies the screen number. For example,

```
x10tox11 -display your_node:0.1
```

specifies screen 1 of server 0 on the machine *your_node*. Either or both of the *host* and *screen* elements to the display specification can be omitted. If *host* is omitted, the local machine is assumed. If *screen* is omitted, screen 0 is assumed (and the period is unnecessary). The colon and *server* are necessary in all cases.

Note that *x10tox11* will always pretend to be an X10 server with the same display number as the X11 server to which it connects. For example, if the DISPLAY environment variable or the -display option specifies your_node:1.0, then *x10tox11* will connect to the X11 server on *your_node* for display 1 and then will pretend to the the X10 server for display 1. Consequently, your X10 clients will expect to have the environment variable DISPLAY set to `your_node:1` (but they should still work even if your X10 clients use `your_node:1.0`).

`MinimumTileSize=`*n*

Sets minimum acceptable tile size to *n*. There is a difference in semantics between X10's `XQueryShape` and X11's `XQueryBestSize` such that X11 will allow any tile size but will return the optimum whereas X10 enforced a minimum tile size. Usually this minimum tile size was 16 and this is the default for *x10tox11*. If you find that this makes your X10 clients break, then you can override it with this option.

`help` Prints out a usage message and exits.

`NoOverrideRedirect`

Instructs *x10tox11* to make every effort not to use `OverrideRedirect` when creating and mapping windows. Normally, *x10tox11* creates all windows with the `OverrideRedirect` attribute set to true. Placing this option on the command line will cause *x10tox11* not to use `OverrideRedirect` except for windows that look like they might be menus. This will allow window managers that provide titlebars to do so. Unfortunately, it is impossible to determine ahead of time what an X10 client intends to do with windows. In addition, X10 clients are known to spontaneously unmap their windows which upsets X11 window managers unless the `OverrideRedirect` attribute is true. Further, some X11 window managers may refuse to resize or move windows that are marked with `OverrideRedirect`. This may be fixed to some extent when an Inter Client Communications Convention Manual (ICCCM) is adopted by the X11 community.

Reference Pages

See Also

X, Xserver

Bugs

There are limitations with respect to emulating Version 10 through a Version 11 server. See the file */usr/lib/X/x10tox11.help* for more details.

Some window managers may refuse to move, resize, or perform any operations on X10 client windows.

If the source is compiled with certain flags, there are significant debugging facilities available. Using the `help` option will tell you whether debugging facilities are available. *x10tox11* marks them with `OverrideRedirect`. See "Options" above.

Copyright

Copyright 1988, Tektronix Inc.

Author

Todd Brunhoff, Visual Systems Laboratory, Tektronix.

Name

xauth – X authority file utility

Syntax

`xauth` [*options*] [*command arguments*]

Description

Available as of Release 4, the *xauth* program is used to edit and display the authorization information used in connecting to the X server. This program is usually to extract authorization records from one machine and merge them in on another (as is the case when using remote logins or to grant access to other users). Commands (described below) may be entered interactively, on the *xauth* command line, or in scripts. Note that this program does *not* contact the X server.

Options

The following options may be used with *xauth*. They may be given individually (for example, `-q -i`) or may combined (for example, `-qi`):

`-f` *authfile* Specifies the name of the authority file to use. By default, *xauth* will use the file specified by the XAUTHORITY environment variable or *.Xauthority* in the user's home directory.

`-q` Indicates that *xauth* should operate quietly and not print unsolicited status messages. This is the default if an *xauth* command is is given on the command line or if the standard output is not directed to a terminal.

`-v` Indicates that *xauth* should operate verbosely and print status messages indicating the results of various operations (for example, how many records have been read in or written out). This is the default if *xauth* is reading commands from its standard input and its standard output is directed to a terminal.

`-i` Indicates that *xauth* should ignore any authority file locks. Normally, *xauth* will refuse to read or edit any authority files that have been locked by other programs (usually *xdm* or another *xauth*).

`-b` Indicates that *xauth* should attempt to break any authority file locks before proceeding and should only be used to clean up stale locks.

Commands

The following commands may be used to manipulate authority files:

`add` *displayname protocolname hexkey*

An authorization entry for the indicated display using the given protocol and key data is added to the authorization file. The data is specified as an even-lengthed string of hexadecimal digits, each pair representing one octet. The first digit gives the most significant 4 bits of the octet and the second digit gives the least significant 4 bits. A protocol name consisting of just a single period is treated as an abbreviation for *MIT-MAGIC-COOKIE-1*.

`[n]extract` *`filename displayname . . .`*
Authorization entries for each of the specified displays are written to the indicated file. If the `nextract` command is used, the entries are written in a numeric format suitable for non-binary transmission (such as secure electronic mail). The extracted entries can be read back in using the `merge` and `nmerge` commands. If the the filename consists of just a single dash, the entries will be written to the standard output.

`[n]list [`*`displayname...`*`]`
Authorization entries for each of the specified displays (or all if no displays are named) are printed on the standard output. If the `nlist` command is used, entries will be shown in the numeric format used by the `nextract` command; otherwise, they are shown in a textual format. Key data is always displayed in the hexadecimal format given in the description of the `add` command.

`[n]merge [`*`filename...`*`]`
Authorization entries are read from the specified files and are merged into the authorization database, superceding any matching existing entries. If the `nmerge` command is used, the numeric format given in the description of the `extract` command is used. If a filename consists of just a single dash, the standard input will be read if it hasn't been read before.

`remove` *`displayname...`*
Authorization entries matching the specified displays are removed from the authority file.

`source` *`filename`*
The specified file is treated as a script containing *xauth* commands to execute. Blank lines and lines beginning with a sharp sign (#) are ignored. A single dash may be used to indicate the standard input, if it hasn't already been read.

`info`
Information describing the authorization file, whether or not any changes have been made, and from where *xauth* commands are being read is printed on the standard output.

`exit`
If any modifications have been made, the authority file is written out (if allowed), and the program exits. An end of file is treated as an implicit exit command.

`quit`
The program exits, ignoring any modifications. This may also be accomplished by pressing the interrupt character.

`help [`*`string`*`]`
A description of all commands that begin with the given string (or all commands if no string is given) is printed on the standard output.

? A short list of the valid commands is printed on the standard output.

Display Names

Display names for the `add`, `[n]extract`, `[n]list`, `[n]merge`, and `remove` commands use the same format as the DISPLAY environment variable and the common `-display` command line option. Display-specific information (such as the screen number) is unnecessary and will be ignored. Same-machine connections (such as local-host sockets, shared memory, and the Internet Protocol hostname *localhost*) are referred to as *hostname*/unix:*displaynumber* so that local entries for different machines may be stored in one authority file.

Example

The most common use for *xauth* is to extract the entry for the current display, copy it to another machine, and merge it into the user's authority file on the remote machine:

```
% xauth extract - $DISPLAY | rsh other xauth merge -
```

Environment Variables

This *xauth* program uses the following environment variables:

XAUTHORITY To get the name of the authority file to use if the `-f` option isn't used. If this variable is not set, *xauth* will use *Xauthority* in the user's home directory.

HOME To get the user's home directory if XAUTHORITY isn't defined.

Bugs

Users that have unsecure networks should take care to use encrypted file transfer mechanisms to copy authorization entries between machines. Similarly, the *MIT-MAGIC-COOKIE-1* protocol is not very useful in unsecure environments. Sites that are interested in additional security may need to use encrypted authorization mechanisms such as Kerberos.

Spaces are currently not allowed in the protocol name. Quoting could be added for the truly perverse.

See Also

X, Xserver, Xau, xdm

Author

Jim Fulton, MIT X Consortium.

Name

xbiff – mail notification program for X.

Syntax

xbiff [*options*]

Description

The *xbiff* program displays a little image of a mailbox. When there is no mail, the flag on the mailbox is down. When mail arrives, the flag goes up and the mailbox beeps. By default, pressing any mouse button in the image forces *xbiff* to remember the current size of the mail file as being the "empty" size and to lower the flag.

This program is nothing more than a wrapper around the Athena Mailbox widget.

Options

xbiff accepts all of the standard X Toolkit command line options along with the additional options listed below:

`-help` Indicates that a brief summary of the allowed options should be printed on the standard error.

`-update` *seconds*
Specifies the frequency in seconds at which *xbiff* should update its display. If the mailbox is obscured and then exposed, it will be updated immediately. The default is 60 seconds.

`-file` *filename*
Specifies the name of the file which should be monitored. By default, it watches */usr/spool/mail/**username***, where ***username*** is your login name.

`-shape` Indicates that the mailbox window should be shaped if masks for the empty or full images are given. (Available as of Release 4.)

`-volume` *percentage*
Specifies how loud the bell should be rung when new mail comes in.

The following standard X Toolkit command line arguments are commonly used with *xbiff*:

`-bg` *color* Specifies he color to use for the background of the window. The default is white.

`-bd` *color* Specifies the color to use for the border of the window. The default is black.

`-bw` *pixels* Specifies the width in pixels of the border surrounding the window.

`-fg` *color* Specifies the color to use for the foreground of the window. The default is black.

`-rv` Indicates that reverse video should be simulated by swapping the foreground and background colors.

`-geometry` *`geometry`*
Specifies the size and location of the mailbox window. The `-geometry` option can be (and often is) abbreviated to `-g`, unless there is a conflicting option that begins with "g." The argument to the geometry option (*`geometry`*) is referred to as a "standard geometry string," and has the form *`widthxheight±xoff±yoff`*. If you do not specify the geometry, *xbiff* asks you for window placement. See "Window Geometry" in Chapter 8 of this guide for details. The default mailbox is 48 pixels on each side and is centered in the window.

`-display` [*`host`*]`:`*`server`*[`.`*`screen`*]
Allows you to specify the host, server, and screen on which to create the mailbox window. *`host`* specifies which machine to create the mailbox window on, *`server`* specifies the server number, and *`screen`* specifies the screen number. For example,

`xbiff -display` *`your_node`*`:`**`0.1`**

creates a mailbox on screen 1 of server 0 on the machine *`your_node`*. If the host is omitted, the local machine is assumed. If the screen is omitted, screen 0 is assumed; the server and colon (:) are necessary in all cases.

`-xrm` *`resourcestring`*
Specifies a resource string to be used. This is especially useful for setting resources that do not have separate command line options.

Resources

This program uses the Mailbox widget in the X Toolkit. It understands all of the core resource names and classes as well as:

`checkCommand` (class `CheckCommand`))
Specifies a shell command to be executed to check for new mail rather than examining the size of `file`. The specified string value is used as the argument to a *system*(3) call and may therefore contain I/O redirection. An exit status of zero indicates that new mail is waiting, 1 indicates that there has been no change in size, and 2 indicates that the mail has been cleared.

`file` (class `File`)
Specifies the name of the file to monitor. The default is to watch */usr/spool/mail/* ***username***, where ***username*** is your login name.

`flip` (class `Flip`)
Specifies whether or not the image that is shown when mail has arrived should be inverted. The default is true. (Available as of Release 4.)

Reference Pages

`fullPixmap` (class `Pixmap`)
Specifies a bitmap to be shown when new mail has arrived. (Available as of Release 4.)

`fullPixmapMask` (class `PixmapMask`)
Specifies a mask for the bitmap to be shown when new mail has arrived. (Available as of Release 4.)

`emptyPixmap` (class `Pixmap`)
Specifies a bitmap to be shown when no new mail is present. (Available as of Release 4.)

`emptyPixmapMask` (class `PixmapMask`)
Specifies a mask for the bitmap to be shown when no new mail is present. (Available as of Release 4.)

`width` (class `Width`)
Specifies the width of the mailbox.

`height` (class `Height`)
Specifies the height of the mailbox.

`onceOnly` (class `Boolean`)
Specifies that the bell is only rung the first time new mail is found and is not rung again until at least one interval has passed with no mail waiting. The window will continue to indicate the presence of new mail until it has been retrieved.

`shapeWindow` (class `ShapeWindow`)
Specifies whether or not the mailbox window should be shaped to the given `fullPixmapMask` and `emptyPixmapMask`. (Available as of Release 4.)

`update` (class `Interval`)
Specifies the frequency in seconds at which the mail should be checked.

`volume` (class `Volume`)
Specifies how loud the bell should be rung. The default is 33 percent.

`foreground` (class `Foreground`)
Specifies the color for the foreground. The default is black since the core default for background is white.

`reverseVideo` (class `ReverseVideo`)
Specifies that the foreground and background should be reversed.

Actions

The Mailbox widget provides the following actions for use in event translations:

`check()` Causes the widget to check for new mail and display the flag appropriately.

`unset()` Causes the widget to lower the flag until new mail comes in.

`set()` Causes the widget to raise the flag until user resets it.

The default translation is:

```
<ButtonPress>:unset()
```

See Also

X, xrdb, stat(2)

Author

Jim Fulton, MIT X Consortium;
Additional hacks by Ralph Swick, DEC/MIT Project Athena.

xcalc

Name

xcalc – scientific calculator for X.

Syntax

xcalc [*options*]

Description

xcalc is a scientific calculator desktop accessory that can emulate a TI-30 or an HP-10C. The Release 4 version of *xcalc* has been rewritten to use the X Toolkit. Also as of Release 4, the number in the calculator display can be selected, allowing you to paste the result of a calculation into text.

Versions of *xcalc* prior to Release 4 also emulate a slide rule.

Options

xcalc accepts all of the standard X Toolkit command line options, as well as the following:

`-stip`, `-stipple`
: Indicates that the background of the calculator should be drawn using a stipple of the foreground and background colors. On monochrome displays, this improves the appearance. The `-stipple` version of this option is available as of Release 4. The `-stip` option can also still be used.

`-rpn`
: Indicates that Reverse Polish Notation should be used. In this mode the calculator will look and behave like an HP-10C. Without this flag, it will emulate a TI-30.

`-analog`
: Indicates that a slide rule should be used. (Eliminated in Release 4.)

The following X Toolkit options are commonly used with *xcalc*:

`-bw` *pixels*
: Specifies the border width in pixels.

`-fg` *color*
: Specifies the foreground color in use.

`-bg` *color*
: Specifies the background color in use.

`-rv`
: Indicates that reverse video should be used.

`-geometry` *geometry*
: The *xcalc* window is created with the specified size and location determined by the supplied geometry specification. The `-geometry` option can be (and often is) abbreviated to `-g`, unless there is a conflicting option that begins with "g." The argument to the geometry option (*geometry*) is referred to as a "standard geometry string," and has the form *widthxheight±xoff±yoff*.

-display [*host*]:*server*[.*screen*]
Allows you to specify the host, server, and screen on which to create the *xcalc* window. `host` specifies the machine on which to create the *xcalc* window, `server` specifies the server number, and `screen` specifies the screen number. For example,

```
xcalc -display your_node:0.1
```

specifies screen 1 on server 0 on the machine `your_node`. If the host is omitted, the local machine is assumed. If the screen is omitted, the screen 0 is assumed; the server and colon (:) are necessary in all cases.

Calculator Operations

Pointer Usage

Operations may be performed with pointer button 1 (usually the leftmost button), or in many cases, with the keyboard. Many common calculator operations have keyboard equivalents, which are called accelerators, because they facilitate data entry. There are several ways to cause *xcalc* to exit: pressing the AC key of the TI calculator or the ON key of the HP calculator with pointer button 3 (usually the rightmost button); typing q, Q, or Ctrl-C while the pointer is in the *xcalc* window.

Calculator Key Usage (TI Mode)

The number keys, the +/- key, and the +, -, *, /, and = keys all do exactly what you would expect them to. It should be noted that the operators obey the standard rules of precedence. Thus, entering "`3+4*5=`" results in 23, not 35. Parentheses can be used to override this. For example, "`(1+2+3)*(4+5+6)=`" is evaluated as "`6*15=`" which results in 90.

The action associated with each function are given below. These are useful if you are interested in defining a custom calculator. The action used for all digit keys is `digit(n)`, where *n* is the corresponding digit, 0-9. (The actions are available as of Release 4).

The keys are described below.

1/x
Replaces the number in the display with its reciprocal. The corresponding action is `reciprocal()`.

x^2
Squares the number in the display. The corresponding action is `square()`.

SQRT
Evaluates the square root of the number in the display. The corresponding action is `squareRoot()`.

CE/C
When pressed once, clears the number in the display without clearing the state of the machine. Allows you to re-enter a number if you make a mistake. Pressing it twice clears the state also. The corresponding action is `clear()`.

AC
Clears everything: the display, the state, and the memory. Pressing it with the third (usually the right) button 'turns off' the calculator, in that it exits the program. The corresponding action to clear the state is `off()`; to quit, the action is `quit()`.

Reference Pages

INV — Inverts the meaning of the function keys. See the individual function keys for details. The corresponding action is `inverse()`.

sin — Computes the sine of the number in the display, as interpreted by the current DRG mode (see DRG, below). If inverted, it computes the arcsine. The corresponding action is `sine()`.

cos — Computes the cosine, or arccosine when inverted. The corresponding action is `cosine()`.

tan — Computes the tangent, or arctangent when inverted. The corresponding action is `tangent()`.

DRG — Changes the DRG mode, as indicated by 'DEG', 'RAD', or 'GRAD' at the bottom of the calculator "liquid crystal" display. When in 'DEG' mode, numbers in the display are taken as being degrees. In 'RAD' mode, numbers are in radians, and in 'GRAD' mode, numbers are in gradians. When inverted, the DRG key has the handy feature of converting degrees to radians to gradians and vice-versa. For example, put the calculator into 'DEG' mode, and type "`45 INV DRG`". The calculator should display approximately .785398, which is 45 degrees converted to radians. The corresponding action is `degree()`.

e — Is the constant 'e'. (2.7182818 . . .) The corresponding action is `e()`.

EE — Is used for entering exponential numbers. For example, to enter "`-2.3E-4`" you would type "`2 . 3 +/- EE 4 +/-`". The corresponding action is `scientific()`.

log — Calculates the log (base 10) of the number in the display. When inverted, it raises 10.0 to the number in the display. For example, entering "`3 INV log`" should result in 1000. The corresponding action is `logarithm()`.

ln — Calculates the log (base e) of the number in the display. When inverted, it raises "e" to the number in the display. For example, entering "`e ln`" should result in 1. The corresponding action is `naturalLog()`.

y^x — Raises the number on the left to the power of the number on the right. For example, "`2 y^x 3 =`" results in 8, which is 2^3. Also, "`(1+2+3) y^x (1+2)=`" is evaluated as "`6 y^x 3=`" which results in 216. The corresponding action is `power()`.

PI — The constant 'pi'. (3.1415927 . . . .) The corresponding action is `pi()`.

x! — Computes the factorial of the number in the display. The number in the display must be an integer in the range 0-500, though, depending on your math library, it might overflow long before that. The corresponding action is `factorial()`.

(— Left parenthesis. The corresponding action for TI calculators is `leftParen()`.

) Right parenthesis. The corresponding action for TI calculators is `rightParen()`.

/ Division. The corresponding action is `divide()`.

* Multiplication. The corresponding action is `multiply()`.

– Subtraction. The corresponding action is `subtract()`.

+ Addition. The corresponding action is `add()`.

= Perform calculation. The TI-specific action is `equal()`.

STO Copies the number in the display to the memory location. The corresponding action is `store()`.

RCL Copies the number from the memory location to the display. The corresponding action is `recall()`.

SUM Adds the number in the display to the number in the memory location. The corresponding action is `sum()`.

EXC Swaps the number in the display with the number in the memory location. The corresponding action is `exchange()`.

+/– Negate (change sign). The corresponding action is `negate()`.

. Decimal point. The corresponding action is `decimal()`.

Calculator Key Usage (RPN mode)

The number keys, CHS (change sign), +, -, *, /, and ENTR keys all do exactly what you would expect them to. Many of the remaining keys are the same as in TI (default) mode. The differences are detailed below. The action for the ENTR key is `enter()`.

<- Is a backspace key that can be used while entering a number. It will erase digits from the display. (See "Bugs.") Inverse backspace clears the X register. The corresponding action is `back()`.

ON Clears everything: the display, the state, and the memory. Pressing it with the third (usually the right) pointer button 'turns off' the calculator, in that it exits the program. The corresponding action to clear the state is `off()`; to quit, the action is `quit()`.

INV Inverts the meaning of the function keys. This would be the "f" key on an HP calculator, but *xcalc* does not display multiple legends on each key. See the individual function keys for details.

10^x Raises 10.0 to the number in the top of the stack. When inverted, it calculates the log (base 10) of the number in the display. The corresponding action is `tenpower()`.

e^x Raises "e" to the number in the top of the stack. When inverted, it calculates the log (base e) of the number in the display. The corresponding action is `epower()`.

STO — Copies the number in the top of the stack to one of ten memory locations. The desired memory is specified by pressing this key and then pressing a digit key.

RCL — Pushes the number from the specified memory location onto the stack.

SUM — Adds the number on top of the stack to the number in the specified memory location.

x:y — Exchanges the numbers in the top two stack positions, the X and Y registers. The corresponding action is `XexchangeY()`.

R v — Rolls the stack downward. When inverted, it rolls the stack upward. The corresponding action is `roll()`.

Blank keys were used for programming functions on the HP-10C. Their functionality has not been duplicated in *xcalc*.

Keyboard Equivalents (Accelerators)

If you have the pointer in the *xcalc* window, you can use the keyboard to enter numbers and other keys. Almost all of the calculator keys have keyboard equivalents, which are known as *accelerators* because they speed entry. The number keys, the operator keys, and the parentheses all have the obvious equivalents. The accelerators defined by *xcalc* are listed in the following table:

TI Key	HP Key	Keyboard Accelerator	TI Function	HP Function
SQRT	SQRT	r	`squareRoot()`	`squareRoot()`
AC	ON	space	`clear()`	`clear()`
AC	<-	Delete	`clear()`	`back()`
AC	<-	Backspace	`clear()`	`back()`
AC	<-	Control-H	`clear()`	`back()`
AC		Clear	`clear()`	
AC	ON	q	`quit()`	`quit()`
AC	ON	Control-C	`quit()`	`quit()`
INV	i	i	`inverse()`	`inverse()`
sin	s	s	`sine()`	`sine()`
cos	c	c	`cosine()`	`cosine()`
tan	t	t	`tangent()`	`tangent()`
DRG	DRG	d	`degree()`	`degree()`
e		e	`e()`	
ln	ln	l	`naturalLog()`	`naturalLog()`
y^x	y^x	^	`power()`	`power()`
PI	PI	p	`pi()`	`pi()`
x!	x!	!	`factorial()`	`factorial()`

TI Key	HP Key	Keyboard Accelerator	TI Function	HP Function
(		(	leftParen()	
)		)	rightParen()	
/	/	/	divide()	divide()
*	*	*	multiply()	multiply()
–	–	–	subtract()	subtract()
+	+	+	add()	add()
=		=	equal()	
0..9	0..9	0..9	digit()	digit()
.	.	.	decimal()	decimal()
+/-	CHS	n	negate()	negate()
	x:y	x		XexchangeY()
	ENTR	Return		enter()
	ENTR	Linefeed		enter()

Note that the use of the e keyboard accelerator to invoke the e calculator key is Release 4 specific. In the Release 3 version of *xcalc*, the e keyboard accelerator corresponds to the EE calculator key.

Resources (Release 4)

`rpn` (class `Rpn`)
: Specifies that the rpn mode should be used. The default is TI mode.

`stipple` (class `Stipple`)
: Indicates that the background should be stippled. The default is on for monochrome displays, and off for color displays.

`cursor` (class `Cursor`)
: The name of the symbol used to represent the pointer. The default is hand2.

Widget Hierarchy (Release 4)

In order to specify resources, it is useful to know the hierarchy of the widgets that compose *xcalc*. In the notation below, indentation indicates hierarchical structure. The widget class name is given first, followed by the widget instance name.

```
XCalc xcalc
      Form  ti  or  rpn    (the name depends on the mode)
            Form  bevel
                  Form  screen
                        Label  M
                        Toggle LCD
                        Label  INV
                        Label  DEG
                        Label  RAD
                        Label  GRAD
                        Label  P
```

```
Command  button1
Command  button2
Command  button3
```

and so on, ...

```
Command  button38
Command  button39
Command  button40
```

Customization (Release 4)

The application class name is `XCalc`.

As of Release 4, *xcalc* has an enormous application defaults file, which specifies the position, label, and function of each key on the calculator. It also gives translations to serve as keyboard accelerators. Because these resources are not specified in the source code, you can create a customized calculator by writing a private application defaults file, using the Athena Command and Form widget resources to specify the size and position of buttons, the label for each button, and the function of each button.

The foreground and background colors of each calculator key can be individually specified. For the TI calculator, a classical color resource specification might be:

```
XCalc.ti.Command.background:       gray50
XCalc.ti.Command.foreground:       white
```

For each of buttons 20, 25, 30, 35, and 40, specify:

```
XCalc.ti.button20.background:      black
XCalc.ti.button20.foreground:      white
```

For each of buttons 22, 23, 24, 27, 28, 29, 32, 33, 34, 37, 38, and 39:

```
XCalc.ti.button22.background:      white
XCalc.ti.button22.foreground:      black
```

Resources (Release 3)

The program uses the Xlib routine `XGetDefault`(3X) to read defaults, so its resource names are all capitalized.

`BorderWidth` Specifies the width of the border. The default is 2.

`ReverseVideo`
Indicates that reverse video should be used.

`Stipple` Indicates that the background should be stippled. The default is on for monochrome displays, and off for color displays.

`Mode` Specifies the default mode. Allowable values are are `rpn`, `analog`.

`Foreground` Specifies the default color used for borders and text.

`Background` Specifies the default color used for the background.

`NKeyFore, NKeyBack`
Specifies the colors used for the number keys.

`OKeyFore, OKeyBack`
Specifies the colors used for the operator keys.

`FKeyFore, FKeyBack`
Specifies the colors used for the function keys.

`DispFore, DispBack`
Specifies the colors used for the display.

`IconFore, IconBack`
Specifies the colors used for the icon.

Customization (Release 3)

If you're running on a monochrome display, you shouldn't need any resource file entries for *xcalc*. However, *xcalc* uses a lot of colors, given the opportunity. In the default case, it will just use two colors (`Foreground` and `Background`) for everything. This works out nicely. However, if you're a color fanatic you can specify the colors used for the number keys, the operator (+, -, *, /, =) keys, the function keys, the display, and the icon. On a color display, you might want to try the following in TI mode:

```
xcalc*Foreground:          black
xcalc*Background:          lightsteelblue
xcalc*NKeyFore:            black
xcalc*NKeyBack:            white
xcalc*OKeyFore:            aquamarine
xcalc*OKeyBack:            darkslategray
xcalc*FKeyFore:            white
xcalc*FKeyBack:            #900
xcalc*DispFore:            yellow
xcalc*DispBack:            #777
xcalc*IconFore:            red
xcalc*IconBack:            white
```

Bugs in Release 4

In HP mode, a bug report claims that the sequence of keys 5, ENTR, and <- should clear the display, but it doesn't.

Bugs in Release 3

The calculator doesn't resize.

The slide rule and HP mode may or may not work correctly.

Base conversions are not easily done.

See Also

X, xrdb, and for Release 4, the Athena Widget set

Authors

John Bradley, University of Pennsylvania;
Mark Rosenstein, MIT Project Athena.

Reference Pages

xclipboard

Name

xclipboard – X clipboard client.

Syntax

`xclipboard` [*options*]

Description

The *xclipboard* program is used to collect and display text selections that are sent to the CLIPBOARD by other clients. It is typically used to save CLIPBOARD selections for later use.

Since *xclipboard* uses a Text Widget to display the contents of the clipboard, text sent to the CLIPBOARD may be re-selected for use in other applications.

Release 4 Specifics

The Release 4 version of *xclipboard* stores each CLIPBOARD selection as a separate string, each of which can be selected. Each time CLIPBOARD is asserted by another application, *xclipboard* transfers the contents of that selection to a new buffer and displays it in the text window. Buffers are never automatically deleted, so you'll want to use the delete button to get rid of useless items.

xclipboard also responds to requests for the CLIPBOARD selection from other clients by sending the entire contents of the currently displayed buffer.

An *xclipboard* window has the following buttons across the top:

quit — When this button is pressed, *xclipboard* exits.

delete — When this button is pressed, the current buffer is deleted and the next one displayed.

new — Creates a new buffer with no contents. Useful in constructing a new CLIPBOARD selection by hand.

next — Displays the next buffer in the list.

previous — Displays the previous buffer.

Release 3 Specifics

The Release 3 version of *xclipboard* has the following buttons across the top:

quit — When this button is pressed, *xclipboard* exits.

erase — When this button is pressed, the contents of the text window are erased. (The erase button is not functional.)

Options

The *xclipboard* program accepts all of the standard X Toolkit command line options as well as the following:

`-w` — Indicates that lines of text that are too long to be displayed on one line in the clipboard should wrap around to the following lines.

`-nw` — Indicates that long lines of text should not wrap around. This is the default behavior.

Some of the more common Toolkit options used with *xclipboard* are:

`-display [host]:server[.screen]`

Allows you to specify the host, server and screen on which to create the *xclipboard* windows. *host* specifies the machine, *server* specifies the server number, and *screen* specifies the screen number. For example,

xclipboard -display *your_node*:**0.1**

specifies screen 1 of server 0 on the machine *your_node*. Either or both the *host* and *screen* elements to the display specification can be omitted. If *host* is omitted, the local machine is assumed. If *screen* is omitted, screen 0 is assumed (and the period is unnecessary). The colon and *server* are necessary in all cases.

`-geometry geometry`

The *xclipboard* window is created with the specified size and location determined by the supplied geometry specification. The `-geometry` option can be (and often is) abbreviated to `-g`, unless there is a conflicting option that begins with "g." The argument to the geometry option (*geometry*) is referred to as a "standard geometry string," and has the form *widthx-height±xoff±yoff*.

Sending and Retrieving Clipboard Contents

Text is copied *to* the clipboard whenever a client asserts ownership of the CLIPBOARD selection. Text is copied *from* the clipboard whenever a client requests the contents of the CLIPBOARD selection. Examples of event bindings that a user may wish to include in a resource configuration file to use the clipboard are:

```
*VT100.Translations: #override \
    Button1 <Btn3Down>:  select-end(CLIPBOARD) \n\
            <Btn2Up>:    insert-selection(PRIMARY,CLIPBOARD) \n\
```

Resources

This program accepts all of the standard X Toolkit resource names and classes as well as:

`wordWrap` (class `WordWrap`)

Specifies whether or not lines of text should wrap around to the following lines. The default is no. (Release 3 only.)

Widgets

In order to specify resources, it is useful to know the hierarchy of the widgets that compose *xclipboard*. In the notation below, indentation indicates hierarchical structure. The widget class name is given first, followed by the widget instance name.

```
XClipboard  xclipboard
        Form  form
              Command  quit
              Command  delete
```

```
Command   new
Command   next
Command   prev
Text      text
```

Bugs in Release 3

The erase button is not functional.

It would be nice to have a way of specifying the file in which the clipboard contents are saved.

Files

/usr/lib/X11/app-defaults/XClipboard Specifies required resources (as of Release 4).

See Also

X, xcutsel, xterm, individual client documentation for how to make a selection and send it to the CLIPBOARD.

Author

Ralph R. Swick, DEC/MIT Project Athena;
Chris Peterson, MIT X Consortium;
Keith Packard, MIT X Consortium.

Name

xclock – continuously display the time in either analog or digital form.

Syntax

xclock [*options*]

Description

xclock continuously displays the time of day, either in digital or analog form. In digital form, *xclock* displays the time using a 24-hour clock. It also displays the day, month, and year. In analog form, *xclock* displays a standard 12-hour clock face. You can set up more than one clock simultaneously.

The default clock is an analog clock with a black foreground on a white background. If you want to change the clock's appearance, type in the appropriate options. For example,

```
xclock -bd slateblue -fg navyblue -hl darkslategrey &
```

sets up a conventional 12-hour clock with a slate blue window border, navy blue tick marks, and dark slate grey hands.

By default, the clock is positioned in the upper-left corner of your background window. If you are running *twm*, you can place the clock using the pointer.

Options

xclock accepts all of the standard X Toolkit command line options along with the additional options listed below:

`-help` Displays a brief summary of *xclock*'s calling syntax and options.

`-analog` Draws a conventional 12-hour clock face with tick marks for each minute and stroke marks for each hour. This is the default.

`-digital` or `-d`
Displays the date and time in digital format. Note that `-display` must be used to specify a display.

`-chime` Indicates that the clock should chime once on the half hour and twice on the hour.

`-hd` *color* Specifies the color of the hands on an analog clock. The default is black.

`-hl` *color* Specifies the color of the edges of the hands on an analog clock. Only useful on color displays. The default is black.

`-padding` *pixels*
Specifies the width in pixels of the space between the window border and any portion of the *xclock* display. The default is 10 pixels in digital mode and 8 pixels in analog mode.

`-update` *seconds*
Specifies the frequency in seconds with which *xclock* updates its display. If the *xclock* window is obscured and then exposed, *xclock* overrides this setting

and redisplays immediately. A value of less than 30 seconds will enable a second hand on an analog clock. The default is 60 seconds.

The following standard X Toolkit options are commonly used with *xclock*:

`-bg` *`color`* Determines the background color of the window. The default is white.

`-bd` *`color`* Determines the border color of the window. The default is black.

`-bw` *`pixels`* Specifies the width in pixels of the border around the *xclock* window. The default is 2 pixels.

`-fg` *`color`* Determines the color of the text in digital mode, and the color of the tick and stroke marks in analog mode. The default is black.

`-fn` *`font`* Specifies the font to be used in digital mode. Any fixed width font may be used. The default is 6x10.

`-rv` Indicates that reverse video should be simulated by swapping the foreground and background colors.

`-geometry` *`geometry`*

Sets *xclock* window size and location according to the geometry specification. The `-geometry` option can be (and often is) abbreviated to `-g`, unless there is a conflicting option that begins with "g." The argument to the geometry option (*`geometry`*) is referred to as a "standard geometry string," and has the form *`widthxheight±xoff±yoff`*.

In digital mode, height and width are determined by the font in use, unless otherwise specified. In analog mode, width and height defaults are 164 pixels, unless otherwise specified. The default value for any unspecified x or y offset is -0. All values are in pixels. If you do not specify the geometry, *xclock* asks you for window window.

`-display` [*`host`*]`:`*`server`*[`.`*`screen`*]

Allows you to specify the host, server and screen on which to create the *xclock* window. *`host`* specifies which machine to create the *xclock* window on, *`server`* specifies the server number and *`screen`* specifies the screen number. For example,

```
xclock -display your_node:0.1
```

creates an *xclock* display on screen 1 on server 0 on the machine *`your_node`*. If the host is omitted, the local machine is assumed. If the screen is omitted, the screen 0 is assumed; the server and colon (:) are necessary in all cases.

Note that `-display` cannot be abbreviated to `-d`, which is shorthand for the `-digital` option.

`-xrm` *`resourcestring`*

Specifies a resource string to be used. This is especially useful for setting resources that do not have separate command line options.

Resources

xclock uses the Athena Clock widget. It understands all of the core resource names and classes as well as:

`width` (class `Width`)
: Specifies the width of the clock.

`height` (class `Height`)
: Specifies the height of the clock.

`update` (class `Interval`)
: Specifies the frequency in seconds at which the time should be redisplayed.

`background` (class `Background`)
: Determines the background color. The default is white.

`foreground` (class `Foreground`)
: Specifies the color for the tick marks and stroke marks. Using the class specifies the color for all things that normally would appear in the foreground color. The default is black since the core default for background is white.

`hands` (class `Foreground`)
: Specifies the color of the insides of the clock's hands. The default is the `foreground` color.

`highlight` (class `Foreground`)
: Specifies the color used to highlight the clock's hands. The default is the `foreground` color.

`analog` (class `Boolean`)
: Specifies whether or not an analog clock should be used instead of a digital one. The default is true.

`chime` (class `Boolean`)
: Specifies whether or not a bell should be rung on the hour and half hour. The default is false.

`padding` (class `Margin`)
: Specifies the amount of internal padding in pixels to be used. The default is 8.

`font` (class `Font`)
: Specifies the font to be used for the digital clock. Note that variable width fonts currently will not always display correctly.

`reverseVideo` (class `ReverseVideo`)
: Specifies that the foreground and background colors should be reversed.

Widgets (Release 4)

In order to specify resources, it is useful to know the hierarchy of the widgets which compose *xclock*. In the notation below, indentation indicates hierarchical structure. The widget class name is given first, followed by the widget instance name.

```
XClock  xclock
    Clock  clock
```

Files

/usr/lib/X11/app-defaults/XClock
Specifies default resources (as of Release 4).

Bugs

xclock believes the system clock.

When in digital mode, the string should be centered automatically.

No way to exit the program.

See Also

X, oclock, xrdb, time(3C), Athena Clock widget

Authors

Tony Della Fera (MIT-Athena, DEC);
Dave Mankins (MIT-Athena, BBN);
Ed Moy (UC Berkeley).

Name

xcutsel – interchange between cut buffer and selection.

Syntax

xcutsel [*options*]

Description

The *xcutsel* program is used to copy the current selection into a cut buffer and to make a selection that contains the current contents of the cut buffer. It acts as a bridge between applications that don't support selections and those that do.

By default, *xcutsel* will use the selection named PRIMARY and the cut buffer CUT_BUFFER0. Either or both of these can be overridden by command line arguments or by resources.

An *xcutsel* window has the following buttons:

quit
: When this button is pressed, *xcutsel* exits. Any selections held by *xcutsel* are automatically released.

copy PRIMARY to 0
: When this button is pressed, *xcutsel* copies the current selection into the cut buffer.

copy 0 to PRIMARY
: When this button is pressed, *xcutsel* converts the current contents of the cut buffer into the selection.

The button labels reflect the selection and cut buffer selected by command line options or through the resource database.

When the copy 0 to PRIMARY button is activated, the button will remain inverted as long as *xcutsel* remains the owner of the selection. This serves to remind you which client owns the current selection. Note that the value of the selection remains constant; if the cut buffer is changed, you must again activate the copy button to retrieve the new value when desired.

Options

xcutsel accepts all of the standard X Toolkit command line options as well as the following:

`-selection` *name*
: Specifies the name of the selection to use. The default is PRIMARY. The only supported abbreviations for this option are `-select`, `-sel` and `-s`, since the standard Toolkit option `-selectionTimeout` has a similar name.

`-cutbuffer` *number*
: Specifies the cut buffer to use. The default is cut buffer 0.

The following X Toolkit options are commonly used with *xcutsel*:

`-display [`*`host`*`]:`*`server`*`[.`*`screen`*`]`
Allows you to specify the host, server, and screen on which to create the *xcutsel* window. `host` specifies the machine, `server` specifies the server number, and `screen` specifies the screen number. For example,

xcutsel -display *your_node*:**0.1**

specifies screen 1 of server 0 on the machine `your_node`. Either or both the `host` and `screen` elements to the display specification can be omitted. If `host` is omitted, the local machine is assumed. If `screen` is omitted, screen 0 is assumed (and the period is unnecessary). The colon and `server` are necessary in all cases.

`-geometry` *`geometry`*
The *xcutsel* window is created with the specified size and location determined by the supplied geometry specification. The `-geometry` option can be (and often is) abbreviated to `-g`, unless there is a conflicting option that begins with "g." The argument to the geometry option (*`geometry`*) is referred to as a "standard geometry string," and has the form *`widthx-heightħxoffħyoff`*.

Resources

This program accepts all of the standard X Toolkit resource names and classes as well as:

`selection` (class `Selection`)
This resource specifies the name of the selection to use. The default is PRIMARY.

`cutBuffer` (class `CutBuffer`)
This resource specifies the number of the cut buffer to use. The default is 0.

Widget Names

The following instance names may be used when user configuration of the labels in them is desired:

`sel-cut` (class `Command`)
This is the copy selection to buffer button.

`cut-sel` (class `Command`)
This is the copy buffer to selection button.

`quit` (class `Command`)
This is the quit button.

Bugs

There is no way to change the name of the selection or the number of the cut buffer while the program is running.

See Also

X, xclipboard, xterm; Chapter 4 of this guide; text widget documentation, including Volume Four, *X Toolkit Intrinsics Programming Manual*

Author

Ralph R. Swick, DEC/MIT Project Athena.

xditview

Name

xditview – display *ditroff* DVI files.

Syntax

xditview [*options*]

Description

The *xditview* program displays *ditroff* output on an X display. It uses special font metrics that match the font set distributed with X11 Release 3, so it does not require access to the server machine for font loading.

Options

xditview accepts all of the standard X Toolkit command line options along with the additional options listed below:

`-help` Indicates that a brief summary of the allowed options should be printed.

`-page` Specifies the page number of the document to be displayed.

`-backingStore` *backing_store_type*
: Redisplay of the DVI window can take upto a second or so. This option causes the server to save the window contents so that when it is scrolled around the viewport, the window is painted from contents saved in backing store. *backing_store_type* can be one of `Always`, `WhenMapped` or `NotUseful`.

The following standard X Toolkit command line arguments are commonly used with *xditview*:

`-bg` *color* Specifies the color to use for the window background. The default is white.

`-bd` *color* Specifies the color to use for the window border. The default is black.

`-bw` *pixels* Specifies the width in pixels of the window border.

`-fg` *color* Specifies the color to use for displaying text. The default is black.

`-fn` *font* Specifies the font to be used for displaying widget text. The default is "fixed".

`-rv` Indicates that reverse video should be simulated by swapping the foreground and background colors.

`-display` *host*[:*server*][.*screen*]
: Allows you to specify the host, server and screen on which to display the *xditview* window. *host* specifies the machine, *server* specifies the server number, and *screen* specifies the screen number. For example,

xditview -display *your_node*:**0.1**

specifies screen 1 of server 0 on the machine *your_node*. Either or both the *host* and *screen* elements to the display specification can be omitted. If *host* is omitted, the local machine is assumed. If *screen* is omitted, screen 0 is assumed (and the period is unnecessary). The colon and *server* are necessary in all cases.

`-geometry` *geometry*
: The *xditview* window is created with the specified size and location determined by the supplied geometry specification. The `-geometry` option can be (and often is) abbreviated to `-g`, unless there is a conflicting option that begins with "g." The argument to the geometry option (*geometry*) is referred to as a "standard geometry string," and has the form *width*x*height*±*xoff*±*yoff*.

`-xrm` *resourcestring*
: Specifies a resource string to be used.

Resources

This program uses the Dvi widget in the X Toolkit. It understands all of the core resource names and classes as well as:

`width` (class `Width`)
: Specifies the width of the window.

`height` (class `Height`)
: Specifies the height of the window.

`foreground` (class `Foreground`)
: Specifies the default foreground color.

`font` (class `Font`)
: Specifies the font to be used for error messages.

Using xditview with ditroff

To build a DVI file suitable for use with *xditview*, use the device description in devX75:

```
$ cd devX75
$ makedev DESC
$ mkdir /usr/lib/font/devX75
$ cp *.out /usr/lib/font/devX75
$ ditroff -TX75 ditroff_input | xditview
```

See Also

X, xrdb, ditroff(1)

Bugs

xditview can be easily confused by attempting to display a DVI file constructed for the wrong device. Support for *pic* is not yet implemented.

Reference Pages

Authors

Portions of this program originated in *xtroff* which was derived from *suntroff*.

Keith Packard (MIT X Consortium);
Richard L. Hyde (Purdue);
David Slattengren (Berkeley);
Malcom Slaney (Schlumberger Palo Alto Research);
Mark Moraes (University of Toronto).

Name

xdm – X display manager.

Syntax

xdm [*options*]

Description

xdm manages a collection of X displays, both local and possibly remote — the emergence of X terminals guided the design of several parts of this system, along with the development of the X Consortium standard XDMCP, the X Display Manager Control Protocol (introduced in Release 4). It is designed to provide services similar to that provided by *init*, *getty* and *login* on character terminals: prompting for login/password, authenticating the user and running a "session."

A "session" is defined by the lifetime of a particular process; in the traditional character-based terminal world, it is the user's login shell process. In the *xdm* context, it is an arbitrary session manager. This is because in a windowing environment, a user's login shell process would not necessarily have any terminal-like interface with which to connect.

Until real session managers become widely available, the typical *xdm* substitute would be either a window manager with an exit option, or a terminal emulator running a shell - with the condition that the lifetime of the terminal emulator is the lifetime of the shell process that it is running — thus degenerating the X session to an emulation of the character-based terminal session.

When the session is terminated, *xdm* resets the X server and (optionally) restarts the whole process.

Because *xdm* provides the first interface that users will see, it is designed to be simple to use and easy to customize to the needs of a particular site. *xdm* has many options, most of which have reasonable defaults. Browse through the various sections, picking and choosing the things you want to change. Pay particular attention to "The Xsession File", which will describe how to set up the style of session desired.

Options

First, note that all of these options, except `-config`, specify values that can also be specified in the configuration file as resources.

`-config` *`configuration_file`*
: Specifies a resource file which specifies the remaining configuration parameters. If no file is specified and the file */usr/lib/X11/xdm/xdm-config* exists, *xdm* will use it.

`-daemon`
: Specifies true as the value for the `DisplayManager.daemonMode` resource. This makes *xdm* close all file descriptors, disassociate the controlling terminal and put itself in the background when it first starts up (just like the host of other daemons). It is the default behavior.

`-debug` *`debug_level`*
: Specifies the numeric value for the `DisplayManager.debugLevel` resource. A non-zero value causes *xdm* to print piles of debugging state-

ments to the terminal; it also disables the `DisplayManager.daemon-Mode` resource, forcing *xdm* to run synchronously. To interpret these debugging messages, a copy of the source code for xdm is almost a necessity. No attempt has been made to rationalize or standardize the output.

`-error` *`error_log_file`*
: Specifies the value for the `DisplayManager.errorLogFile` resource. This file contains errors from *xdm* as well as anything written to standard error by the various scripts and programs run during the progress of the session.

`-nodaemon`
: Specifies "false" as the value for the `DisplayManager.daemonMode` resource.

`-resources` *`resource_file`*
: Specifies the value for the `DisplayManager*resources` resource. This file is loaded using *xrdb* to specify configuration parameters for the authentication widget.

`-server` *`server_entry`*
: Specifies the value for the `DisplayManager.servers` resource. (See "Resources" below.)

`-udpPort` *`port_number`*
: Specifies the value for the `DisplayManager.requestPort` resource. This sets the port-number which XDM will monitor for XDMCP requests. As XDMCP uses the registered well-known udp port 177, this resource should probably not be changed except for debugging. (Available as of Release 4.)

`-session` *`session_program`*
: Specifies the value for the `DisplayManager*session` resource. This indicates the program to run when the user has logged in as the session. (Available as of Release 4.)

`-xrm` *`resource_specification`*
: Allows an arbitrary resource to be specified, just as most toolkit applications.

Resources

At many stages the actions of *xdm* can be controlled through the use of the configuration file, which is in the familiar X resource format. See Jim Fulton's article on resource files (*doc/tutorials/resources.txt*) for a description of the format. Some resources modify the behavior of *xdm* on all displays, while others modify its behavior on a single display. Where actions relate to a specific display, the display name is inserted into the resource name between "DisplayManager" and the final resource name segment. For example, `Display-Manager.expo_0.startup` is the name of the resource that defines the startup shell file on the "expo:0" display. Because the resource manager uses colons to separate the name of the resource from its value and dots to separate resource name parts, *xdm* substitutes underscores

scores for the dots and colons when generating the resource name. (If you are running Release 3, `DisplayManager.expo.0.startup` is the resource. In Release 3, *xdm* substitutes dots for the colons when generating the resource name.)

`DisplayManager.servers`

Specifies either a filename full of server entries, one per line, or a single server entry. Each entry indicates a display that should constantly be managed and that is not using XDMCP. (If the resource value begins with a slash, it is assumed to be the name of a file containing the list.) Each entry consists of at least three parts: a display name, a display class (Release 4 only), a display type, and (for local servers) a command line to start the server. (The program name should be an absolute UNIX pathname, since *xdm* does not search through the directories of the PATH environment variable.) Foreign servers can have a comment in place of the command line. A typical entry for local display number 0 would be:

```
:0 Digital-QV local /usr/bin/X11/X :0
```

The display types are:

`local`	A local display, i.e., one that has a server program to run
`foreign`	A remote display, i.e., one that has no server program to run

If you're running the Release 3 version of *xdm*, the following display types are also acceptable:

`localTransient`	A local display that has only one session run
`transient`	A remote display that has only one session run

The display name must be something that can be passed in the `-display` option to any X program. This string is used in the display-specific resources to specify the particular display, so be careful to match the names (e.g., use `:0 local /usr/bin/X11/X :0` instead of *`localhost`*`:0 local /usr/bin/X11/X :0` if your other resources are specified as `DisplayManager._0.session`).

The display class portion can also be used in display-specific resources, as the class portion of the resource. This is useful if you have a large collection of similar displays (perhaps several X terminals) and would like to set resources for groups of them. When using XDMCP, the display is required to specify the display class. Your X terminal documentation should describe a reasonably standard display class string for your device.

`DisplayManager.requestPort`

Indicates the UDP port number which *xdm* uses to listen for incoming XDMCP requests. Unless you need to debug the system, leave this with its default value of 177. (Available as of Release 4.)

`DisplayManager.errorLogFile`

Error output is normally directed at the system console. To redirect it simply set this resource to any filename. A method to send these messages to syslog should be developed for systems that support it; however the wide variety of "standard" interfaces precludes any system-independent implementation. This file also contains any output directed to standard error by *Xstartup*, *Xsession*, and *Xreset*, so it will contain descriptions of problems in those scripts as well.

`DisplayManager.debugLevel`

A non-zero value specified for this integer resource will enable reams of debugging information to be printed. It also disables daemon mode which would redirect the information into the bit-bucket. Specifying a non-zero debug level also allows non-root users to run *xdm* which would normally not be useful. (Available as of Release 4.)

`DisplayManager.daemonMode`

Normally, *xdm* attempts to make itself into an unassociated daemon process. This is accomplished by forking and leaving the parent process to exit, then closing file descriptors and mangling the controlling terminal. When attempting to debug *xdm*, this is quite bothersome. Setting this resource to false will disable this feature. (Available as of Release 4.)

`DisplayManager.pidFile`

The filename specified will be created to contain an ASCII representation of the process ID of the main *xdm* process. This is quite useful when reinitializing the system. *xdm* also uses file locking to attempt to eliminate multiple daemons running on the same machine, which would cause quite a bit of havoc. (Available as of Release 4.)

`DisplayManager.lockPidFile`

Controls whether *xdm* uses file locking to keep multiple *xdm* processes from running amok. On System V, this uses the *lockf* library call, while on BSD it uses *flock*. The default value is true. (Available as of Release 4.)

`DisplayManager.remoteAuthDir`

This is a directory name that *xdm* uses to temporarily store authorization files for displays using XDMCP. The default value is */usr/lib/X11/xdm*. (Available as of Release 4.)

`DisplayManager.autoRescan`

This boolean controls whether *xdm* rescans the configuration file and servers file after a session terminates and the files have changed. By default it is true. You can force *xdm* to reread these files by sending a SIGHUP to the main process. (Available as of Release 4.)

`DisplayManager.removeDomainname`

When computing the display name for XDMCP clients, the resolver will typically create a fully qualified host name for the terminal. Since this is sometimes confusing, *xdm* will remove the domain name portion of the host name if it is the same as the domain name for the local host when this variable is set. By default the value is true. (Available as of Release 4.)

`DisplayManager.keyFile`

XDM-AUTHENTICATION-1 style XDMCP authentication requires that a private key be shared between *xdm* and the terminal. This resource specifies the file containing those values. Each entry in the file consists of a display name and the shared key. By default, *xdm* does not include support for XDM-AUTHENTICATION-1 as it requires DES which is not generally distributable. (Available as of Release 4.)

`DisplayManager.DISPLAY.resources`

Specifies the name of the file to be loaded by *xrdb* as the resource database onto the root window of screen 0 of the display. This resource database is loaded just before the authentication procedure is started, so it can control the appearance of the "login" window. See "Authentication Widget Resources", which describes the various resources which are appropriate to place in this file. There is no default value for this resource, but the conventional name is */usr/lib/X11/xdm/Xresources*.

`DisplayManager.DISPLAY.xrdb`

Specifies the program used to load the resources. By default, *xdm* uses */usr/bin/X11/xrdb*.

`DisplayManager.DISPLAY.cpp`

Specifies the name of the C preprocessor used by *xrdb*. (Available as of Release 4.)

`DisplayManager.DISPLAY.startup`

Specifies a program which is run (as root) after the authentication process succeeds. By default, no program is run. The conventional name for a file used here is *Xstartup*. See "The Xstartup File" below.

`DisplayManager.DISPLAY.session`

Specifies the session to be executed (not running as root). By default, */usr/bin/X11/xterm* is run. The conventional name is *Xsession*. See "The Xsession File" below.

`DisplayManager.DISPLAY.reset`

Specifies a program which is run (as root) after the session terminates. Again, by default no program is run. The conventional name is *Xreset*. See "The Xreset File" below.

`DisplayManager.DISPLAY.openDelay`
`DisplayManager.DISPLAY.openRepeat`
`DisplayManager.DISPLAY.openTimeout`
`DisplayManager.DISPLAY.startAttempts`

Numeric resources control the behavior of *xdm* when attempting to open intransigent servers. `openDelay` is the length of the pause (in seconds) between successive attempts. `openRepeat` is the number of attempts to make. `openTimeout` is the amount of time to wait while actually attempting the open (i.e., the maximum time spent in the *connect* syscall). `startAttempts` (Release 4) is the number of times this entire process is done before giving up on the server. After `openRepeat` attempts have been made, or if `openTimeout` seconds elapse in any particular attempt, *xdm* terminates and restarts the server, attempting to connect again. This process is repeated `startAttempts` times, at which point the display is declared dead and disabled. Although this behaviour may seem arbitrary, it has been empirically developed and works quite well on most systems. The default values are 5 for `openDelay`, 5 for `openRepeat`, 30 for `openTimeout`, and 4 for `startAttempts`.

`DisplayManager.DISPLAY.pingInterval`
`DisplayManager.DISPLAY.pingTimeout`

To discover when remote displays disappear, *xdm* occasionally "pings" them, using an X connection and sending `XSync` requests. `pingInterval` specifies the time (in minutes) between each ping attempt, `pingTimeout` specifies the maximum amount of time (in minutes) to wait for the terminal to respond to the request. If the terminal does not respond, the session is declared dead and terminated. By default, both are set to 5 minutes. *xdm* will not ping local displays. Although it would seem harmless, it is unpleasant when the workstation session is terminated as a result of the server hanging for NFS service and not responding to the ping. (Available as of Release 4.)

`DisplayManager.DISPLAY.terminateServer`

Specifies whether the X server should be terminated when a session terminates (instead of resetting it). This option can be used when the server tends to grow without bound over time in order to limit the amount of time the server is run. The default value is false.

`DisplayManager.DISPLAY.userPath`

xdm sets the PATH environment variable for the session to this value. It should be a colon separated list of directories, see *sh*(1) for a full description. The default value can be specified in the X system configuration file with `DefUserPath`, frequently it is set to *:/bin:/usr/bin:/usr/bin/X11:/usr/ucb*.

`DisplayManager.DISPLAY.systemPath`

xdm sets the PATH environment variable for the startup and reset scripts to the value of this resource. The default for this resource is specified with the `DefaultSystemPath` entry in the system configuration file, but it is frequently */etc:/bin:/usr/bin:/usr/bin/X11:/usr/ucb*. Note the conspicuous absence of "." from this entry. This is a good practise to follow for root; it avoids many common trojan horse system penetration schemes.

`DisplayManager.DISPLAY.systemShell`

xdm sets the SHELL environment variable for the startup and reset scripts to the value of this resource. By default, it is */bin/sh*.

`DisplayManager.DISPLAY.failsafeClient`

If the default session fails to execute, *xdm* will fall back to this program. This program is executed with no arguments, but executes using the same environment variables as the session would have had. See "The Xsession File" below. By default, */usr/bin/X11/xterm* is used.

`DisplayManager.DISPLAY.grabServer`
`DisplayManager.DISPLAY.grabTimeout`

To eliminate obvious security shortcomings in the X protocol, *xdm* grabs the server and keyboard while reading the name/password. The `grabServer` resource specifies if the server should be held for the duration of the name/password reading, when FALSE, the server is ungrabbed after the keyboard grab succeeds, otherwise the server is grabbed until just before the session begins. The `grabTimeout` resource specifies the maximum time *xdm* will wait for the grab to succeed. The grab may fail if some other client has the server grabbed, or possibly if the network latencies are very high. This resource has a default value of 3 seconds; you should be cautious when raising it as a user can be spoofed by a look-alike window on the display. If the grab fails, *xdm* kills and restarts the server (if possible) and session. (Available as of Release 4.)

`DisplayManager.DISPLAY.authorize`
`DisplayManager.DISPLAY.authName`

`authorize` is a boolean resource that controls whether *xdm* generates and uses authorization for the server connections. If authorization is used, `authName` specifies the type to use. Currently, *xdm* supports only MIT-MAGIC-COOKIE-1 authorization, XDM-AUTHORIZATION-1 could be supported as well, but DES is not generally distributable. XDMCP connections specify which authorization types are supported dynamically, so `authName` is ignored in this case. When `authorize` is set for a display and authorization is not available, the user is informed by having a different message displayed in the login widget. By default, `authorize` is true; `authName` is MIT-MAGIC-COOKIE-1. (Available as of Release 4.)

`DisplayManager.DISPLAY.authFile`

This file is used to communicate the authorization data from *xdm* to the server, using the `-auth` server command line option. It should be kept in a directory which is not world-writable as it could easily be removed, disabling the authorization mechanism in the server. (Available as of Release 4.)

`DisplayManager.DISPLAY.resetForAuth`

The original implementation of authorization in the sample server reread the authorization file at server reset time, instead of when checking the initial connection. As *xdm* generates the authorization information just before connecting to the display, an old server would not get up-to-date authorization information. This resource causes *xdm* to send SIGHUP to the server after setting up the file, causing an additional server reset to occur, during which

Reference Pages

time the new authorization information will be read. (Available as of Release 4.)

`DisplayManager.DISPLAY.userAuthDir`
When *xdm* is unable to write to the usual user authorization file (*$HOME/.Xauthority*), it creates a unique file name in this directory and points the environment variable XAUTHORITY at the created file. By default it uses */tmp*. (Available as of Release 4.)

Controlling The Server

xdm controls local servers using POSIX signals. SIGHUP is expected to reset the server, closing all client connections and performing other clean up duties. SIGTERM is expected to terminate the server. If these signals do not perform the expected actions, *xdm* will not perform properly.

To control remote servers not using XDMCP, *xdm* searches the window hierarchy on the display and uses the protocol request `KillClient` in an attempt to clean up the terminal for the next session. This may not actually kill all of the clients, as only those which have created windows will be noticed. XDMCP provides a more sure mechanism; when xdm closes its initial connection, the session is over and the terminal is required to close all other connections.

Controlling xdm

xdm responds to two signals: SIGHUP and SIGTERM. When sent a SIGHUP, *xdm* rereads the file specified by the `DisplayManager.servers` resource and notices if entries have been added or removed. If a new entry has been added, *xdm* starts a session on the associated display. Entries that have been removed are disabled immediately, meaning that any session in progress will be terminated without notice, and no new session will be started.

When sent a SIGTERM, *xdm* terminates all sessions in progress and exits. This can be used when shutting down the system.

xdm attempts to mark the various sub-processes for *ps*(1) by editing the command line argument list in place. Because *xdm* can't allocate additional space for this task, it is useful to start *xdm* with a reasonably long command line (15 to 20 characters should be enough). Each process that is servicing a display is marked `-<Display_Name>`.

Authentication Widget Resources

The authentication widget is an application which reads a name/password pair from the keyboard. As this is a toolkit client, nearly every imaginable parameter can be controlled with a resource. Resources for this widget should be put into the file named by `DisplayManager.DISPLAY.resources`. All of these have reasonable default values, so it is not necessary to specify any of them.

`xlogin.Login.width, xlogin.Login.height, xlogin.Login.x, xlogin.Login.y`
The geometry of the login widget is normally computed automatically. If you wish to position it elsewhere, specify each of these resources.

`xlogin.Login.foreground`
The color used to display the typed-in user name.

`xlogin.Login.font`
The font used to display the typed-in user name.

`xlogin.Login.greeting`
A string which identifies this window. The default is "Welcome to the X Window System".

`xlogin.Login.unsecureGreeting`
When X authorization is requested in the configuration file for this display and none is in use, this greeting replaces the standard greeting. Its default value is "This is an unsecure session". (Available as of Release 4.)

`xlogin.Login.greetFont`
The font used to display the greeting.

`xlogin.Login.greetColor`
The color used to display the greeting.

`xlogin.Login.namePrompt`
The string displayed to prompt for a user name. *xrdb* strips trailing white space from resource values, so to add spaces at the end of the prompt (usually a nice thing), add spaces escaped with backslashes. (In Release 3, Control-A should work.) The default is "Login:".

`xlogin.Login.passwdPrompt`
The string displayed to prompt for a password. The default is "Password:".

`xlogin.Login.promptFont`
The font used to display both prompts.

`xlogin.Login.promptColor`
The color used to display both prompts.

`xlogin.Login.fail`
A message which is displayed when the authentication fails. The default is "Login Failed, please try again".

`xlogin.Login.failFont`
The font used to display the failure message.

`xlogin.Login.failColor`
The color used to display the failure message.

`xlogin.Login.failTimeout`
The time (in seconds) that the fail message is displayed. The default is 30 seconds.

`xlogin.Login.translations`

This specifies the translations used for the login widget. See Chapter 9, *Setting Resources*, and Appendix G, *Translation Table Syntax*, for more information on translations. The default translation table for *xdm* is:

```
Ctrl<Key>H:         delete-previous-character() \n\
Ctrl<Key>D:         delete-character() \n\
Ctrl<Key>B:         move-backward-character() \n\
Ctrl<Key>F:         move-forward-character() \n\
Ctrl<Key>A:         move-to-begining() \n\
Ctrl<Key>E:         move-to-end() \n\
Ctrl<Key>K:         erase-to-end-of-line() \n\
Ctrl<Key>U:         erase-line() \n\
Ctrl<Key>X:         erase-line() \n\
Ctrl<Key>C:         restart-session() \n\
Ctrl<Key>\\:        abort-session() \n\
<Key>BackSpace:     delete-previous-character() \n\
<Key>Delete:        delete-previous-character() \n\
<Key>Return:        finish-field() \n\
<Key>:              insert-char() \
```

The actions that are supported by the widget are:

delete-previous-character
: Erases the character before the cursor.

delete-character
: Erases the character after the cursor.

move-backward-character
: Moves the cursor backward.

move-forward-character
: Moves the cursor forward.

move-to-begining
: (Apologies about the spelling error.) Moves the cursor to the beginning of the editable text.

move-to-end
: Moves the cursor to the end of the editable text.

erase-to-end-of-line
: Erases all text after the cursor.

erase-line
: Erases the entire text.

finish-field
: If the cursor is in the name field, proceeds to the password field; if the cursor is in the password field, check the current name/password pair. If the name/password pair are valid, *xdm* starts the session. Otherwise the failure message is displayed and the user is prompted to try again.

abort-session
: Terminates and restarts the server.

abort-display
: Terminates the server, disabling it. This is a rash action and is not accessible in the default configuration. It can be used to stop *xdm* when shutting the system down, or when using xdmshell.

restart-session	Resets the X server and starts a new session. This can be used when the resources have been changed and you want to test them, or when the screen has been overwritten with system messages.
insert-char	Inserts the character typed.
set-session-argument	Specifies a single word argument which is passed to the session at startup. See "The Xsession File" and "Typical Usage" below.
allow-all-access	Disables access control in the server, this can be used when the *Xauthority* file cannot be created by xdm. Be very careful when using this; it might be better to disconnect the machine from the network first. (Available as of Release 4.)

The Xstartup File

This file is typically a shell script. It is run as "root" and should be very careful about security. This is the place to put commands which make fake entries in */etc/utmp*, mount users' home directories from file servers, display the message of the day, or abort the session if logins are not allowed. Various environment variables are set for the use of this script:

DISPLAY	is set to the associated display name.
HOME	is set to the home directory of the user.
USER	is set to the user name.
PATH	is set to the value of `DisplayManager.DISPLAY.systemPath`.
SHELL	is set to the value of `DisplayManager.DISPLAY.systemShell`.
XAUTHORITY	may be set to a non-standard authority file (Release 4).

No arguments of any kind are passed to the script. *xdm* waits until this script exits before starting the user session. If the exit value of this script is non-zero, *xdm* discontinues the session immediately and starts another authentication cycle.

The Xsession File

This is the script that is run as the user's session. It is run with the permissions of the authorized user, and has several environment variables specified:

DISPLAY	is set to the associated display name.
HOME	is set to the home directory of the user.
USER	is set to the user name.
PATH	is set to the value of `DisplayManager.DISPLAY.userPath`.
SHELL	is set to the user's default shell (from */etc/passwd*).
XAUTHORITY	may be set to a non-standard authority file (Release 4).

At most installations, *Xsession* should look in $HOME for a file *.xsession* which would contain commands that each user would like to use as a session. This would replace the system default session. *Xsession* should also implement the system default session if no user-specified session exists. See "Typical Usage" below.

An argument may be passed to this program from the authentication widget using the 'set-session-argument' action. This can be used to select different styles of session. One very good use of this feature is to allow the user to escape from the ordinary session when it fails. This would allow users to repair their own *.xsession* if it fails, without requiring administrative intervention. The section "Typical Usage" demonstrates this feature.

The Xreset File

Symmetrical with *Xstartup*, this script is run after the user session has terminated. Run as root, it should probably contain commands that undo the effects of commands in *Xstartup*, removing fake entries from */etc/utmp* or unmounting directories from file servers. The collection of environment variables that were passed to *Xstartup* are also given to *Xreset*.

Typical Usage

Actually, *xdm* is designed to operate in such a wide variety of environments that "typical" is probably a misnomer. However, this section will focus on making *xdm* a superior solution to traditional means of starting X from */etc/ttys* or manually.

First off, the *xdm* configuration file should be set up. A good thing to do is to make a directory (*/usr/lib/X11/xdm* comes immediately to mind) that will contain all of the relevant files. Here is a reasonable configuration file for Release 4, which could be named *xdm-config*:

```
DisplayManager.servers:          /usr/lib/X11/xdm/Xservers
DisplayManager.errorLogFile:     /usr/lib/X11/xdm/xdm-errors
DisplayManager.pidFile:          /usr/lib/X11/xdm/xdm-pid
DisplayManager*resources:        /usr/lib/X11/xdm/Xresources
DisplayManager*session:          /usr/lib/X11/xdm/Xsession
DisplayManager._0.authorize:     true
DisplayManager*authorize:        false
```

If you are running the Release 3 version of *xdm*, the default *xdm-config* file looks like this:

```
DisplayManager.servers:          /usr/lib/X11/xdm/Xservers
DisplayManager.errorLogFile:     /usr/lib/X11/xdm/xdm-errors
DisplayManager*resources:        /usr/lib/X11/xdm/Xresources
DisplayManager*startup:          /usr/lib/X11/xdm/Xstartup
DisplayManager*session:          /usr/lib/X11/xdm/Xsession
DisplayManager*reset:            /usr/lib/X11/xdm/Xreset
```

As you can see, the *xdm-config* file primarily contains references to other files. Note that some of the resources are specified with "*" separating the components. These resources can be made unique for each different display, by replacing the "*" with the display name, but normally this is not very useful. See the "Resources" section for a complete discussion.

The first file, */usr/lib/X11/xdm/Xservers*, contains the list of displays to manage. Most workstations have only one display, numbered 0, so the file will look like this:

```
:0 display_class local /usr/bin/X11/X :0
```

This will keep */usr/bin/X11/X* running on this display and manage a continuous cycle of sessions.

The file */usr/lib/X11/xdm/xdm-errors* will contain error messages from *xdm* and anything output to standard error by *Xstartup, Xsession or Xreset*. When you have trouble getting *xdm* working, check this file to see if *xdm* has any clues to the trouble.

The next configuration entry, */usr/lib/X11/xdm/Xresources*, is loaded onto the display as a resource database using *xrdb*. As the authentication widget reads this database before starting up, it usually contains parameters for that widget:

```
xlogin*login.translations: #override\\e
   <Key>F1: set-session-argument(failsafe) finish-field()\\en\\e
   <Key>Return: set-session-argument() finish-field()
xlogin*borderWidth: 3
#ifdef COLOR
xlogin*greetColor: #f63
xlogin*failColor: red
xlogin*Foreground: black
xlogin*Background: #fdc
#else
xlogin*Foreground: black
xlogin*Background: white
#endif
```

The various colors specified here look reasonable on several of the displays we have, but may look awful on other monitors. As X does not currently have any standard color naming scheme, you might need to tune these entries to avoid disgusting results. Please note the translations entry; it specifies a few new translations for the widget which allow users to escape from the default session (and avoid troubles that may occur in it). Note that if #override is not specified, the default translations are removed and replaced by the new value, not a very useful result as some of the default translations are quite useful (like *<Key>:* `insert-char()` which responds to normal typing).

The *Xstartup* file used here simply prevents login while the file */etc/nologin* exists. As there is no provision for displaying any messages here (there isn't any core X client which displays files), the user will probably be baffled by this behavior. I don't offer this as a complete example, but simply a demonstration of the available functionality.

Here is a sample *Xstartup* script:

```
#!/bin/sh
#
# Xstartup
#
# This program is run as root after the user is verified
#
if [ -f /etc/nologin ]; then
        exit 1
```

Reference Pages

```
fi
exit 0
```

The most interesting script is *Xsession*. This version recognizes the special "failsafe" mode, specified in the translations in the *Xresources* file above, to provide an escape from the ordinary session:

```
#!/bin/sh
#
# Xsession
#

# This is the program that is run as the client
# for the display manager.  This example is
# quite friendly as it attempts to run a per-user
# .xsession file instead of forcing a particular
# session layout

case $# in
1)
        case $1 in
        failsafe)
                exec xterm -geometry 80x24-0-0 -ls
                ;;
        esac
esac

startup=$HOME/.xsession
resources=$HOME/.Xresources

#
# check for a user-specific session and execute it
#
# Note: the -x flag to test is not supported in all versions of
        unix, check with local authorities before proceeding...
#
if [ -f $startup ]; then
        if [ -x $startup ]; then
                exec $startup
        else
                exec /bin/sh $startup
        fi
else
        #
        # a simple default session.  Check to see
        # if the user has created a default resource file
```

```
        # and load it, start the universal window manager
        # and use xterm as the session control process.
        #
        if [ -f $resources ]; then
                xrdb -load $resources
        fi
        twm &
        exec xterm -geometry 80x24+10+10 -ls
fi
```

No *Xreset* script is necessary, so none is provided in Release 4. (The Release 3 sample *Xreset* file contains nothing but a comment.)

Some Other Possibilities

You can also use *xdm* to run a single session at a time, using the 4.3 *init* options or other suitable daemon by specifying the server on the command line:

```
% xdm -server ":0 SUN-3/60CG4 local /usr/bin/X :0"
```

Or, you might have a file server and a collection of X terminals. The configuration for this could look identical to the sample above, except the *Xservers* file might look like:

```
extol:0 VISUAL-19 foreign
exalt:0 NCD-19 foreign
explode:0 NCR-TOWERVIEW3000 foreign
```

This would direct *xdm* to manage sessions on all three of these terminals. See "Controlling xdm" above for a description of using signals to enable and disable these terminals in a manner reminiscent of init.

One thing that *xdm* isn't very good at doing is coexisting with other window systems. To use multiple window systems on the same hardware, you'll probably be more interested in *xinit*.

See Also

X, xinit, and XDMCP

Author

Keith Packard, MIT X Consortium.

Reference Pages

xdpr

Name

xdpr – dump an X window directly to the printer.

Syntax

xdpr [*filename*] [*options*]

Description

xdpr runs the commands *xwd*, *xpr*, and *lpr*(1) to dump an X window, process it for a laser printer, and print it out. This is the easiest way to get a printout of a window. *xdpr* by default will print the largest possible representation of the window on the output page.

The options for *xdpr* are the same as those for *xpr*, *xwd*, and *lpr*(1). The most commonly used options are described below; see the reference pages for these commands for more detailed descriptions of the many options available.

Options

filename Specifies an existing file containing a window dump (created by xwd) to be printed instead of selecting an X window.

-P*printer* Specifies the name of the printer to be used. If a printer name is not specified here, *xdpr* (really, *lpr*(1)) will send your output to the printer specified by the PRINTER environment variable. Be sure that the type of the printer matches the type specified with the -device option.

-device *printer_device*

Specifies the device on which the file is to be printed. Currently the following printers are supported:

ln03	Digital LN03.
la100	Digital LA100.
ljet	HP LaserJet series and other monochrome PCL devices, such as ThinkJet, QuietJet, RuggedWriter, HP2560 series, and HP2930 series printers. (As of Release 4.)
pjet	HP PaintJet (color mode). (As of Release 4.)
pjetxl	HP PaintJet XL Color Graphics Printer (color mode). (As of Release 4.)
pp	IBM PP3812.
ps	PostScript printer.

-help Displays the list of options known to *xdpr*.

-display [*host*]:*server*[.*screen*]

Allows you to specify the server to connect to. *host* specifies the machine, *server* specifies the server number, and *screen* specifies the screen number. For example,

xdpr -display *your_node*:**0.1**

prints a dump of an X window from screen 1 of server 0 on the machine `your_node`. If the host is omitted, the local machine is assumed. If the screen is omitted, screen 0 is assumed; the server and colon (:) are necessary in all cases.

Any other arguments will be passed to the *xwd*, *xpr*, and *lpr*(1) commands as appropriate for each.

Environment Variables

PRINTER Specifies which printer to use by default.

See Also

X, xwd, xpr, xwud, lpr(1)

Authors

Paul Boutin, MIT Project Athena;
Michael R. Gretzinger, MIT Project Athena;
Jim Gettys, MIT Project Athena.

Reference Pages

xdpyinfo

Name

xdpyinfo – display information utility for X.

Syntax

xdpyinfo [*option*]

Description

xdpyinfo is a utility for displaying information about an X server. It is used to examine the capabilities of a server, the predefined values for various parameters used in communicating between clients and the server, and the different types of screens and visuals that are available.

Option

-display [*host*]:*server*[.*screen*]

Specifies the display about which *xdpyinfo* should display information. *host* specifies the machine, *server* specifies the server number, and *screen* specifies the screen number. By default, *xdpyinfo* displays information about all screens on the display. For example,

xdpyinfo -display *your_node*:**0.0**

displays information about all screens of server 0 of the machine *your_node*. If the hostname is omitted, the local node is assumed. If the screen is omitted, screen 0 is assumed. The server and colon (:) are necessary in all cases.

Sample Output (Release 4)

The following shows a sample produced by the Release 4 version of *xdpyinfo* when connected to a display that supports an 8 plane screen and a 1 plane screen.

```
name of display:    :0.0
version number:    11.0
vendor string:    MIT X Consortium
vendor release number:    4
maximum request size:  16384 longwords (65536 bytes)
motion buffer size:  0
bitmap unit, bit order, padding:    32, MSBFirst, 32
image byte order:    MSBFirst
number of supported pixmap formats:    2
supported pixmap formats:
    depth 1, bits_per_pixel 1, scanline_pad 32
    depth 8, bits_per_pixel 8, scanline_pad 32
keycode range:    minimum 8, maximum 129
number of extensions:    4
    SHAPE
    MIT-SHM
    Multi-Buffering
    MIT-SUNDRY-NONSTANDARD
default screen number:    0
number of screens:    2
```

```
screen #0:
  dimensions:    1152x900 pixels (325x254 millimeters)
  resolution:    90x90 dots per inch
  depths (2):    1, 8
  root window id:    0x8006e
  depth of root window:    8 planes
  number of colormaps:    minimum 1, maximum 1
  default colormap:    0x8006b
  default number of colormap cells:    256
  preallocated pixels:    black 1, white 0
  options:    backing-store YES, save-unders YES
  current input event mask:    0xd0801d
    KeyPressMask          ButtonPressMask       ButtonReleaseMask
    EnterWindowMask       ExposureMask          SubstructureRedirectMask
    PropertyChangeMask    ColormapChangeMask
  number of visuals:    6
  default visual id:  0x80065
  visual:
    visual id:    0x80065
    class:    PseudoColor
    depth:    8 planes
    size of colormap:    256 entries
    red, green, blue masks:    0x0, 0x0, 0x0
    significant bits in color specification:    8 bits
  visual:
    visual id:    0x80066
    class:    DirectColor
    depth:    8 planes
    size of colormap:    8 entries
    red, green, blue masks:    0x7, 0x38, 0xc0
    significant bits in color specification:    8 bits
  visual:
    visual id:    0x80067
    class:    GrayScale
    depth:    8 planes
    size of colormap:    256 entries
    red, green, blue masks:    0x0, 0x0, 0x0
    significant bits in color specification:    8 bits
  visual:
    visual id:    0x80068
    class:    StaticGray
    depth:    8 planes
    size of colormap:    256 entries
    red, green, blue masks:    0x0, 0x0, 0x0
    significant bits in color specification:    8 bits
  visual:
    visual id:    0x80069
    class:    StaticColor
    depth:    8 planes
    size of colormap:    256 entries
```

Reference Pages

```
    red, green, blue masks:    0x7, 0x38, 0xc0
    significant bits in color specification:    8 bits
  visual:
    visual id:    0x8006a
    class:    TrueColor
    depth:    8 planes
    size of colormap:    8 entries
    red, green, blue masks:    0x7, 0x38, 0xc0
    significant bits in color specification:    8 bits
  number of mono multibuffer types:    6
    visual id, max buffers, depth:    0x80065, 0, 8
    visual id, max buffers, depth:    0x80066, 0, 8
    visual id, max buffers, depth:    0x80067, 0, 8
    visual id, max buffers, depth:    0x80068, 0, 8
    visual id, max buffers, depth:    0x80069, 0, 8
    visual id, max buffers, depth:    0x8006a, 0, 8
  number of stereo multibuffer types:    0

screen #1:
  dimensions:    1152x900 pixels (325x254 millimeters)
  resolution:    90x90 dots per inch
  depths (1):    1
  root window id:    0x80070
  depth of root window:    1 plane
  number of colormaps:    minimum 1, maximum 1
  default colormap:    0x8006c
  default number of colormap cells:    2
  preallocated pixels:    black 1, white 0
  options:    backing-store YES, save-unders YES
  current input event mask:    0xd0801d
    KeyPressMask         ButtonPressMask       ButtonReleaseMask
    EnterWindowMask      ExposureMask          SubstructureRedirectMask
    PropertyChangeMask   ColormapChangeMask
  number of visuals:    1
  default visual id:  0x80064
  visual:
    visual id:    0x80064
    class:    StaticGray
    depth:    1 plane
    size of colormap:    2 entries
    red, green, blue masks:    0x0, 0x0, 0x0
    significant bits in color specification:    1 bits
  number of mono multibuffer types:    1
    visual id, max buffers, depth:    0x80064, 0, 1
  number of stereo multibuffer types:    0
```

Sample Output (Release 3)

The following shows a sample produced by the Release 3 version of *xdpyinfo* when connected to a display that supports an 8 plane Pseudocolor screen as well as a 1 plane (monochrome) screen.

```
name of display:    empire:0.0
version number:    11.0
vendor string:    MIT X Consortium
vendor release number:    3
maximum request size:  16384 longwords (65536 bytes)
motion buffer size:  0
bitmap unit, bit order, padding:    32, MSBFirst, 32
image byte order:    MSBFirst
keycode range:    minimum 8, maximum 129
default screen number:    0
number of screens:    2

screen #0:
  dimensions:    1152x900 pixels (325x254 millimeters)
  resolution:    90x90 dots per inch
  root window id:    0x8006d
  depth of root window:    1 plane
  number of colormaps:    minimum 1, maximum 1
  default colormap:    0x80065
  default number of colormap cells:    2
  preallocated pixels:    black 1, white 0
  options:    backing-store YES, save-unders YES
  current input event mask:    0x1b8003c
     ButtonPressMask    ButtonReleaseMask        EnterWindowMask
     LeaveWindowMask    SubstructureNotifyMask   SubstructureRedirectMask
     FocusChangeMask    ColormapChangeMask       OwnerGrabButtonMask
  number of visuals:    1
  default visual id:  0x80064
  visual:
     visual id:    0x80064
     class:    StaticGray
     depth:    1 plane
     size of colormap:    2 entries
     red, green, blue masks:    0x0, 0x0, 0x0
     significant bits in color specification:    1 bits

screen #1:
   dimensions:    1152x900 pixels (325x254 millimeters)
   resolution:    90x90 dots per inch
   root window id:    0x80070
   depth of root window:    8 planes
   number of colormaps:    minimum 1, maximum 1
   default colormap:    0x80067
   default number of colormap cells:    256
   preallocated pixels:    black 1, white 0
   options:    backing-store YES, save-unders YES
```

Reference Pages

```
current input event mask:     0x0
number of visuals:    1
default visual id:  0x80066
visual:
  visual id:      0x80066
  class:    PseudoColor
  depth:    8 planes
  size of colormap:     256 entries
  red, green, blue masks:    0x0, 0x0, 0x0
  significant bits in color specification:    8 bits
```

See Also

X, xwininfo, xprop, xrdb

Bugs in Release 3

Due to a bug in the Xlib interface, there is no portable way to determine the depths of pixmap images that are supported by the server.

Author

Jim Fulton, MIT X Consortium.

Name

xedit – simple text editor for X.

Syntax

xedit [*options*] [*filename*]

Description of the Release 4 Client

The Release 4 version of *xedit* provides a window consisting of the following four areas:

Commands Section
: A set of commands that allow you to exit *xedit*, save the file, or load a new file into the edit window.

Message Window
: Displays *xedit* messages. In addition, this window can be used as a scratch pad.

Filename Display
: Displays the name of the file currently being edited, and whether this file is *Read - Write* or *Read Only*.

Edit Window
: Displays the text of the file that you are editing or creating.

Editing (Release 4)

The Athena Text widget is used for the three sections of this application that allow text input. The characters typed will go to the Text widget that the pointer cursor is currently over. If the pointer cursor is not over a text widget then the keypresses will have no effect on the application. This is also true for the special key sequences that popup dialog widgets, so typing Control-S in the filename widget will enable searching in that widget, not the edit widget.

Both the message window and the edit window will create a scrollbar if the text to display is too large to fit in that window. Horizontal scrolling is not allowed by default, but can be turned on through the Text widget's resources, see Athena Widget set documentation for the exact resource definition.

Commands (Release 4)

Quit
: Quits the current editing session. If any changes have not been saved, *xedit* displays a warning message, allowing the user to save the file.

Save
: If file backups are enabled (see "Resources") *xedit* stores a copy of the original, unedited file in <prefix>*file*<suffix>, then overwrites the *file* with the contents of the edit window. The filename is retrieved from the Text widget directly to the right of the Load button.

Load
: Loads the file named in the text widget immediately to the right of the this button and displays it in the Edit Window. If the currently displayed file has been modified a warning message will ask the user to save the changes, or press Load again.

Description of the Release 3 Client

The Release 3 version of *xedit* provides a window consisting of the following three areas:

Commands Menu
: Lists editing commands (for example, Undo or Search).

Message Window
: Displays *xedit* messages. In addition, this window can be used as a scratch pad.

Edit Window
: Displays the text of the file that you are editing or creating.

Commands (Release 3)

Quit
: Quits the current editing session. If any changes have not been saved, *xedit* displays a warning message and allows you to save the file.

Save
: Stores a copy of the original, unedited file in *file*.BAK. Then, overwrites the original file with the edited contents.

Edit
: Allows the text displayed in the Edit window to be edited.

Load
: Loads the specified file and displays it in the Edit window.

Undo
: Undoes the last edit only.

More
: Undoes each edit previous to the last edit, which must first be undone with the Undo command.

Jump
: Advances the cursor from the beginning of the file to the text line that corresponds to the selected line number.

<<
: Searches from the cursor back to the beginning of the file for the string entered in the Search input box. If you do not enter a string in the Search input box, *xedit* automatically copies the last string that you selected from any X application into the Search input box and searches for that string.

Search >>
: Searches from the cursor forward to the end of the file for the string entered in the search input box. If you do not enter a string in the Search input box, *xedit* automatically copies the last string that you selected from any X application into the Search input box and searches for that string.

Replace
: Replaces the last searched-for string with the string specified in the Replace input box. If no string has been previously searched for, searches from the insert cursor to the end of the file for the next occurrence of the search string and highlights it.

All
: Repositions the cursor at the beginning of the file and replaces all occurrences of the search string with the string specified in the Replace input box.

Options

xedit accepts all of the standard X Toolkit command line options, as well as the following:

`filename`
: Specifies the file that is to be loaded during start-up. This is the file that will be edited. If a file is not specified, *xedit* lets you load a file or create a new file after it has started up.

Widgets (Release 4)

In order to specify resources, it is useful to know the hierarchy of the widgets which compose *xedit*. In the notation below, indentation indicates hierarchical structure. The widget class name is given first, followed by the widget instance name.

```
Xedit  xedit
       Paned  paned
              Paned  buttons
                     Command  quit
                     Command  save
                     Command  load
                     Text     filename
              Label  bc_label
              Text   messageWindow
              Label  labelWindow
              Text   editWindow
```

Resources (Release 4)

For the Release 4 version of *xedit*, the available resources are:

`enableBackups` (class `EnableBackups`)
: Specifies that, when edits made to an existing file are saved, *xedit* is to copy the original version of that file to <prefix>*file*<suffix> before it saves the changes. The default value for this resource is "off", stating that no backups should be created.

`backupNamePrefix` (class `BackupNamePrefix`)
: Specifies a string that is to be prepended to the backup filename. The default is that no string shall be prepended.

`backupNameSuffix` (class `BackupNameSuffix`)
: Specifies a string that is to be appended to the backup filename. The default is to append the string ".BAK".

Resources (Release 3)

For the Release 3 verion of *xedit*, the available class identifiers are:

`ButtonBox`	The two boxes containing command buttons.
`Command`	All command buttons.
`Scrollbar`	The two scroll bars.
`Text`	The two text areas.

The available name identifiers are:

```
All
Edit
EditWindow
Jump
```


Reference Pages

```
Load
MessageWindow
More
Quit
Replace
Save
Undo
xedit
```

The name identifiers for the various buttons are the same as the string on each button. The resources for individual buttons can be set using these names. All of the buttons can be affected by using the `Command` class. The resources for the two text windows can be modified using the names `EditWindow` and `MessageWindow`.

Beyond the standard resources, *xedit*'s resources are:

`EnableBackups`
: Specifies that, when edits made to an existing file are saved, *xedit* is to copy the original version of that file to *file*.BAK before it saves the changes. If the value of this option is specified as off, a backup file is not created.

`background`
: Specifies the background color to be displayed in command buttons. The default is white.

`border`
: Specifies the border color of the *xedit* window.

`borderWidth`
: Specifies the border width, in pixels, of the *xedit* window.

`font`
: Specifies the font displayed in the *xedit* window.

`foreground`
: Specifies the foreground color of the *xedit* window. The default is black.

`geometry`
: Specifies the geometry (window size and screen location) to be used as the default for the *xedit* window. For the format of the geometry specification, see *X*.

`internalHeight`
: Specifies the internal horizontal padding (spacing between text and button border) for command buttons.

`internalWidth`
: Specifies the internal vertical padding (spacing between text and button border) for command buttons.

Key Bindings (Release 3)

Each specification included in the *.XtActions* file modifies a key setting for the editor that *xedit* uses. When defining key specifications, you must use the following resource specification:

```
xedit*text.EventBindings:      .XtActions
```

Each key specification assigns an editor command to a named key and/or mouse combination and has the format:

`key:              function`

where

key	Specifies the key or mouse button that is used to invoke the named function.
function	Specifies the function to be invoked when the named key is pressed.

Files

/usr/lib/X11/app-defaults/Xedit - Specifies required resources (Release 4)
~/.XtActions (Release 3 only)
/usr/lib/X11/.XtActions (Release 3 only)

Restrictions in Release 4

There is no undo function.

Restrictions in Release 3

Large numbers of certain edit functions (for example, Undo or More) tend to degrade performance over time. If there is a noticeable decrease in response time, save and reload the file.

Bugs in Release 3

It is not clear how to select a line number for the Jump command.

The string searches do not work properly.

See Also

X, xrdb, Athena Widget set documentation

Copyright

Author

Chris D. Peterson, MIT X Consortium.

Reference Pages

Name

xev – print contents of X events.

Syntax

xev [*options*]

Description

xev creates a window and then asks the X server to send it notices called *events* whenever anything happens to the window (such as being moved, resized, typed in, clicked in, etc.). It is useful for seeing what causes events to occur and to display the information that they contain.

xev is included in the Release 3 standard distribution; in Release 4, it has been moved to *demos*.

Options

-display [*host*]:*server*[.*screen*]

Allows you to specify the host, server, and screen to connect to. *host* specifies the machine, *server* specifies the server number, and *screen* specifies the screen number. For example,

xev -display *your_node*:**0.1**

specifies screen 1 of server 0 on the machine *your_node*. Either or both the *host* and *screen* elements to the display specification can be omitted. If *host* is omitted, the local machine is assumed. If *screen* is omitted, screen 0 is assumed (and the period is unnecessary). The colon and *server* are necessary in all cases.

-geometry *geometry*

The *xev* window is created with the specified size and location determined by the supplied geometry specification. The -geometry option can be (and often is) abbreviated to -g, unless there is a conflicting option that begins with "g." The argument to the geometry option (*geometry*) is referred to as a "standard geometry string," and has the form *widthx-height±xoff±yoff*.

See Also

X, xwininfo, xdpyinfo; Volume One, *Xlib Programming Manual*; Volume Zero, *X Protocol Reference Manual*.

Author

Jim Fulton, MIT X Consortium.

Name

xfd – X window font displayer.

Syntax

xfd [*options*] **-fn** *fontname*

Description of the Release 4 Client

The Release 4 version of *xfd* creates a window containing the name of the font being displayed, a row of command buttons, several lines of text for displaying character metrics, and a grid containing one glyph per cell. The characters are shown in increasing order from left to right, top to bottom. The first character displayed at the top left will be character number 0 unless the `-start` option has been supplied in which case the character with the number given in the `-start` option will be used.

The characters are displayed in a grid of boxes, each large enough to hold any single character in the font. Each character glyph is drawn using the `PolyText16` request (used by the Xlib routine `XDrawString16`). If the `-box` option is given, a rectangle will be drawn around each character, showing where an `ImageText16` request (used by the Xlib routine `XDrawImageString16`) would cause background color to be displayed.

The origin of each glyph is normally set so that the character is drawn in the upper left hand corner of the grid cell. However, if a glyph has a negative left bearing or an unusually large ascent, descent, or right bearing (as is the case with the cursor font), some character may not appear in their own grid cells. The `-center` option may be used to force all glyphs to be centered in their respective cells.

All the characters in the font may not fit in the window at once. To see the next page of glyphs, press the Next button at the top of the window. To see the previous page, press Prev. To exit *xfd*, press Quit.

Individual character metrics (index, width, bearings, ascent and descent) can be displayed at the top of the window by pressing on the desired character.

The font name displayed at the top of the window is the full name of the font, as determined by the server. See *xlsfonts* for ways to generate lists of fonts, as well as more detailed summaries of their metrics and properties.

Description of the Release 3 Client

The Release 3 version of *xfd* creates a window in which the characters in the named font are displayed. The characters are shown in increasing order from left to right, top to bottom. The first character displayed at the top left will be character number 0 unless the `-start` option has been supplied in which case the character with the number given in the `-start` option will be used.

The characters are displayed in a grid of boxes, each large enough to hold any character in the font. If the `-gray` option has been supplied, the characters will be displayed using the Xlib routine `XDrawImageString` using the foreground and background colors on a gray background. This permits determining exactly how `XDrawImageString` will draw any given character. If `-gray` has not been supplied, the characters will simply be drawn using the foreground color on the background color.

All the characters in the font may not fit in the window at once. To see additional characters, click the right mouse button on the window. This will cause the next window full of characters to be displayed. Clicking the left mouse button on the window will cause the previous window full of characters to be displayed. *xfd* will beep if an attempt is made to go back past the 0th character.

Note that if the font is a 8 bit font, the characters 256-511 (0x100-0x1ff in hexidecimal), 512-767 (0x200-0x2ff), etc., will display exactly the same as the characters 0-255 (0x00-0xff). *xfd* by default creates a window big enough to display the first 256 characters using a 16 by 16 grid. In this case, there is no need to scroll forward or backward window fulls in order to see the entire contents of a 8 bit font. Of course, this window may very well not fit on the screen.

Clicking the middle button on a character will cause that character's number to be displayed in both decimal and hexidecimal at the bottom of the window. If verbose mode is selected, additional information about that particular character will be displayed as well. The displayed information includes the width of the character, its left bearing, right bearing, ascent, and descent. If verbose mode is selected, typing '<' or '>' into the window will display the minimum or maximum values respectively taken on by each of these fields over the entire font.

The fontname is interpreted by the X server. To obtain a list of all the fonts available, use *xlsfonts*.

The window stays around until the *xfd* process is killed or one of 'q', 'Q', ' ', or Control-C is typed into the *xfd* window.

Options (Release 4)

The Release 4 version of *xfd* accepts all of the standard X Toolkit command line options, as well as the following additional options. The option `-fn` *`font`* is required.

`-fn` *`font`* Specifies the font to be displayed.

`-box` Indicates that a box outlining the area that would be filled with background color by an `ImageText` request.

`-center` Indicates that each glyph should be centered in its grid.

`-start` *`char_num`*
Specifies that character number *`char_num`* should be the first character displayed. (It appears in the upper left hand corner of the grid.) This option is used to view characters at arbitrary locations in the font. The default is 0.

`-bc` *`color`* Specifies the color to be used if `ImageText` boxes are drawn.

Options (Release 3)

The Release 3 version of *xfd* accepts the following options. The option `-fn` *`font`* is required.

`-fn` *`font`* Specifies the font to be displayed.

`-bw` *pixels* Allows you to specify the width of the window border in pixels.

`-rv` Specifies that the foreground and background colors be switched. The default colors are black on white.

`-fw` Overrides a previous choice of reverse video. The foreground and background colors will not be switched.

`-fg` *color* On color displays, determines the foreground color (the color of the text).

`-bg` *color* On color displays, determines the background color.

`-bd` *color* On color displays, determines the color of the border.

`-bf` *fontname*
Specifies the font to be used for the messages at the bottom of the window.

`-tl` *title* Specifies that the title of the displayed window should be *title*.

`-in` *iconname*
Specifies that the name of the icon should be *iconname*.

`-icon` *filename*
Specifies that the bitmap in file *filename* should be used for the icon.

`-verbose` Specifies that verbose mode should be used (i.e., extra information about the font should be displayed).

`-gray` Specifies that a gray background should be used.

`-start` *char_num*
Specifies that character number *char_num* should be the first character displayed. (It appears in the upper left hand corner of the grid.) This option is used to view characters at arbitrary locations in the font. The default is 0.

`-geometry` *geometry*
Specifes the size and location of the *xfd* window. The `-geometry` option can be (and often is) abbreviated to `-g`, unless there is a conflicting option that begins with "g." The argument to the geometry option (*geometry*) is referred to as a "standard geometry string," and has the form *widthx-height±xoff±yoff*.

`-display` [*host*]:*server*[.*screen*]
Allows you to specify the host, server and screen on which to create the *xfd* window. *host* specifies the machine on which to create the *xfd* window, *server* specifies the server number, and *screen* specifies the screen number. For example,

xfd -display *your_node*:**0.1**

creates a window on screen 1 of server 0 on the machine *your_node*. If the host is omitted, the local machine is assumed. If the screen is omitted, the screen 0 is assumed; the server and colon (:) are necessary in all cases.

Resources (Release 4)

The Release 4 version of *xfd* was written with the X Toolkit Intrinsics. *xfd* accepts the following resources, which are accepted by most applications written with the Toolkit:

`background` (class `Background`)
Specifies the color to use for the window background.

`borderWidth` (class `BorderWidth`)
Specifies the width in pixels of the window border.

`borderColor` (class `BorderColor`)
Specifies the color to use for the window border.

`foreground` (class `Foreground`)
Specifies the color to use for text and graphics within the window.

Resources (Release 3)

The Release 3 *xfd* program uses the following resources:

`BorderWidth` Set the border width of the window in pixels.

`BorderColor` Set the border color of the window.

`ReverseVideo`
If "on", reverse the definition of foreground and background color.

`Foreground` Set the foreground color.

`Background` Set the background color.

`BodyFont` Set the font to be used in the body of the window (i.e., for messages). This is not the font that *xfd* displays; it is the font used to display information about the font being displayed.

`IconName` Set the name of the icon.

`IconBitmap` Set the file we should look in to get the bitmap for the icon.

`Title` Set the title to be used.

Bugs in Release 4

xfd should skip over pages full of non-existent characters.

Bugs in Release 3

Character information displayed in verbose mode is sometimes clipped to the window boundary hiding it from view.

xfd should skip over pages full of non-existent characters.

See Also

X, xfontsel, xlsfonts, xrdb

Author

Release 4 version by Jim Fulton, MIT X Consortium;
Release 3 version by Mark Lillibridge, MIT Project Athena.

Name

xfontsel – point and click interface for selecting display font names.

Syntax

xfontsel [*options*]

Description

Available as of Release 4, *xfontsel* provides a simple way to display the fonts known to your X server, examine samples of each, and retrieve the X Logical Font Description (XLFD) full name for a font.

If `-pattern` is not specified, all fonts with XLFD 14-part names will be selectable. To work with only a subset of the fonts, specify `-pattern` followed by a partially or fully qualified font name. For example,

```
% xfontsel -pattern *medium*
```

will select the subset of fonts that contain the string `medium` somewhere in their font name. Be careful about escaping wildcard characters in your shell.

If `-print` is specified on the command line the selected font specifier will be written to standard output when the quit button is activated. Regardless of whether or not `-print` was specified, the font specifier may be made the (text) selection by activating the select button.

Clicking any pointer button in one of the XLFD field names will pop up a menu of the currently-known possibilities for that field. If previous choices of other fields were made, only values for fonts which matched the previously selected fields will be selectable; to make other values selectable, you must deselect some other field(s) by choosing the "*" entry in that field. Unselectable values may be omitted from the menu entirely as a configuration option; see the `ShowUnselectable` resource, below. Whenever any change is made to a field value, *xfontsel* will assert ownership of the PRIMARY_FONT selection. Other applications (such as *xterm*) may then retrieve the selected font specification.

Clicking the left pointer button in the select widget will cause the currently selected font name to become the PRIMARY text selection as well as the PRIMARY_FONT selection. Then you can paste the string into other applications. The select button remains highlighted to remind you of this fact, and de-highlights when some other application takes the PRIMARY selection away. The select widget is a toggle; pressing it when it is highlighted will cause *xfontsel* to release the selection ownership and de-highlight the widget. Activating the select widget twice is the only way to cause *xfontsel* to release the PRIMARY_FONT selection.

Options

xfontsel accepts all of the standard X Toolkit command line options along with the additional options described below.

-display *host*[:*server*][.*screen*]
: Allows you to specify the host, server and screen on which to display the *xfontsel* window. *host* specifies the machine, *server* specifies the server number, and *screen* specifies the screen number. For example,

  xfontsel -display *your_node*:**0.1**

  specifies screen 1 of server 0 on the machine *your_node*. If the host is omitted, the local machine is assumed. If the screen is omitted, screen 0 is assumed; the colon (:) is necessary in either case.

-pattern *fontname*
: Specifies a subset of the available fonts, those with names that contain *fontname*, which can be a partial or full name.

-print
: Specifies that the selected font will be written to standard output when the quit button is activated.

-sample *text*
: Specifies the sample *text* to be used to display the selected font, overriding the default (the lower and uppercase alphabet and the digits 0 through 9).

Resources

The application class is XFontSel. Most of the user-interface is configured in the app-defaults file; if this file is missing a warning message will be printed to standard output and the resulting window will be nearly incomprehensible.

Most of the significant parts of the widget hierarchy are documented in the app-defaults file (normally */usr/lib/X11/app-defaults/XFontSel*).

Application specific resources:

cursor (class Cursor)
: Specifies the cursor for the application window.

pattern (class Pattern)
: Specifies the font name pattern for selecting a subset of available fonts. Equivalent to the -pattern option. Most useful patterns will contain at least one field delimiter, for example, *-m-* for monospaced fonts.

Reference Pages

`printOnQuit` (class `PrintOnQuit`)
If True, the currently selected font name is printed to standard output when the quit button is activated. Equivalent to the `-print` option.

Widget-specific resources:

`showUnselectable` (class `ShowUnselectable`)
For each field menu, specifies whether or not to show values that are not currently selectable, based upon previous field selections. If shown, the unselectable values are clearly identified as such and do not highlight when the pointer is moved down the menu. The full instance name of this resource is `field`*N*`.menu.options.showUnselectable`, class `MenuButton.SimpleMenu.Options.ShowUnselectable`; where *N* is replaced with the field number (starting with the left-most field numbered 0). The default is True for all but field 11 (average width of characters in font) and False for field 11. If you never want to see unselectable entries, `*menu.options.showUnselectable: False` is a reasonable thing to specify in a resource file.

Files

/usr/lib/X11/app-defaults/XFontSel - Specifies default resources.

See Also

xrdb

Bugs

Sufficiently ambiguous patterns can be misinterpreted and lead to an initial selection string which may not correspond to what the user intended and which may cause the initial sample text output to fail to match the proffered string. Selecting any new field value will correct the sample output, though possibly resulting in no matching font.

Should be able to return a font for the PRIMARY selection, not just a string.

Any change in a field value will cause *xfontsel* to assert ownership of the PRIMARY_FONT selection. Perhaps this should be parameterized.

When running on a slow machine, it is possible for the user to request a field menu before the font names have been completely parsed. An error message indicating a missing menu is printed to standard error, but otherwise nothing happens.

Author

Ralph R. Swick, Digital Equipment Corporation/MIT Project Athena.

Reference Pages

xhost

Name

xhost – server access control program for X.

Syntax

xhost [*options*]

Description

The *xhost* program is used to add and delete hosts to and from the list of machines that are allowed to make connections to the X server. This provides a rudimentary form of privacy control and security. It is only sufficient for a workstation (single user) environment, although it does limit the worst abuses. Environments that require more sophisticated measures should use the hooks in the protocol for passing authentication data to the server.

The server initially allows network connections only from programs running on the same machine or from machines listed in the file */etc/X**n**.hosts* (where ***n*** is the display number of the server). The *xhost* program is usually run either from a startup file or interactively to give access to other users.

Hostnames that are followed by two colons (::) are used in checking DECnet connections; all other hostnames are used for TCP/IP connections.

If no command line options are given, the list of hosts that are allowed to connect is printed on the standard output along with a message indicating whether or not access control is currently enabled. This is the only option that may be used from machines other than the one on which the server is running.

Options

xhost accepts the command line options described below. For security, the options that affect access control may only be run from the same machine as the server.

[+]*hostname* — The given *hostname* (the plus sign is optional) is added to the list of machines that are allowed to connect to the X server.

-*hostname* — The given *hostname* is removed from the list of machines that are allowed to connect to the server. Existing connections are not broken, but new connection attempts will be denied. Note that the current machine is allowed to be removed; however, further connections (including attempts to add it back) will not be permitted. Resetting the server (thereby breaking all connections) is the only way to allow local connections again.

\+ — Access is granted to everyone, even if they aren't on the list of allowed hosts (i.e., access control is turned off).

– — Access is restricted to only those machines on the list of allowed hosts (i.e., access control is turned on).

Files

*/etc/X**n**.hosts*

Bugs

You can't specify a display on the command line because `-display` indicates that you want to remove the machine named *display* from the access list.

See Also

X, Xserver

Authors

Bob Scheifler, MIT Laboratory for Computer Science;
Jim Gettys, MIT Project Athena (DEC).

xinit

Name

xinit – X Window System initializer.

Syntax

xinit [[*client*] *options*] [-- [*server_program*]
    [-display [*host*]:*server*[.*screen*]] *options*]

Description

The *xinit* program is used to start the X Window System server program and a first client program (usually a terminal emulator) on systems that cannot start X directly from */etc/init* or in environments that use multiple window systems. When this first client exits, *xinit* will kill the X server program and then terminate.

If no specific client program is given on the command line, *xinit* will look in the user's home directory for a file called *.xinitrc* to run as a shell script to start up other client programs. If no such file exists, *xinit* will use the following *xterm* command line as a default:

```
xterm -geometry +1+1 -n login -display :0
```

If no specific server program is given on the command line, *xinit* will look in the user's home directory for a file called *.xserverrc* to run as a shell script to start up the server. If no such file exists, *xinit* will use the following as a default server specification:

```
X :0
```

Note that this assumes that there is a server program called *X* in the current search path. However, servers are usually named *Xdisplaytype*, where *displaytype* is the type of graphics display which is driven by the server (for example, *Xsun*). The site administrator should therefore make a link to the appropriate type of server on the machine (see Chapter 2, *Getting Started*, in Part One of this guide for details), or create a shell script that runs *xinit* with the appropriate server.

Note that programs run by *.xinitrc* and by *.xserverrc* should be run in the background if they do not exit right away, so that they don't prevent other programs from starting up. However, the last long-lived program started (usually a window manager or terminal emulator) should be left in the foreground so that the script won't exit (which indicates that the user is done and that *xinit* should exit).

An alternate client and/or server may also be specified on the command line. The desired client program and its arguments should be given as the first command line arguments to *xinit*. To specify a particular server program, append a double dash (--) to the *xinit* command line (after any client and arguments) followed by the desired server program.

Both the client program name and the server program name must begin with a slash (/) or a period (.); otherwise, they are treated as an arguments to be appended to their respective startup lines. This makes it possible to add arguments (for example, foreground and background colors) without having to retype the whole command line.

If an explicit server name is not given and the first argument following the double dash (--) is a colon followed by a digit, *xinit* will use that number as the display number instead of zero. All remaining arguments are appended to the server command line.

Note that you can start X manually by running *xinit* from the command line or start it automatically by adding the *xinit* command line to your *.login* or *.profile* file. (See Appendix A, *System Management*, for more information.)

Options

`client` Specifies the client to be started with the server.

`server_program`
Specifies the server program to be used.

`-display [host]:server[.screen]`
Specifies the host, server and screen on which you are initializing the X Window System. For example,

```
xinit -display your_node:0.1
```

specifies screen 1 on server 0 on the machine *your_node*. If the host is omitted, the local machine is assumed. If the screen is omitted, the screen 0 is assumed; the server and colon (:) are necessary in any case.

Examples

`xinit` Will start up a server named *X* and run the user's *.xinitrc*, if it exists, or else start an *xterm*.

`xinit -- /usr/bin/X11/Xqdss :1`
Is how one could start a specific type of server on an alternate display.

`xinit -geometry 80x65+10+10 -fn 8x13 -j -fg white -bg navy`
Will start up a server named *X*, and will append the given arguments to the default *xterm* command. It will ignore *.xinitrc*.

`xinit -e widgets -- Xsun -l -c`
Will use the command *./Xsun -l -c* to start the server and will append the arguments *-e widgets* to the default *xterm* command.

`xinit rsh fasthost cpupig -display workstation:1 -- 1 -a 2 -t 5`
Will start a server named *X* on display 1 with the arguments *-a 2 -t 5*. It will then start a remote shell on the machine **fasthost** in which it will run the command *cpupig*, telling it to display back on the local workstation.

Below is a sample *.xinitrc* that starts a clock, several terminals, and leaves the window manager running as the "last" application. Assuming that the window manager has been configured properly, the user then chooses the Exit menu item to shut down X.

```
xrdb -load $HOME/.Xres
xsetroot -solid gray &
xclock -g 50x50-0+0 -bw 0 &
xload -g 50x50-50+0 -bw 0 &
xterm -g 80x24+0+0 &
xterm -g 80x24+0-0 &
twm
```

Sites that want to create a common startup environment could simply create a default *xinitrc* that references a site-wide startup file:

```
#!/bin/sh
./usr/local/lib/site.xinitrc
```

Another approach is to write a script that starts *xinit* with a specific shell script. Such scripts are usually named *x11*, *xstart*, or *startx* and are a convenient way to provide a simple interface for novice users:

```
#!/bin/sh
./xinit/usr/local/bin/startx -- /usr/bin/X11/Xhp :1
```

Environment Variables

XINITRC — Specifies an init file containing shell commands to start up the initial windows. By default, *xinitrc* in the home directory will be used.

See Also

X, Xserver, xterm

Author

Bob Scheifler, MIT Laboratory for Computer Science.

Name

xkill – kill a client by its X resource.

Syntax

xkill [*options*]

Description

xkill is a utility for forcing the X server to close connections to clients. This program is very dangerous, but is useful for aborting programs that have displayed undesired windows on a user's screen. If no resource identifier is given with `-id`, *xkill* will display a special cursor as a prompt for the user to select a window to be killed. If a pointer button is pressed over a non-root window, the server will close its connection to the client that created the window.

Options

`-display` [*host*]:*server*[.*screen*]

Allows you to specify the host, server and screen to connect to. *host* specifies the machine, *server* specifies the server number, and *screen* specifies the screen number. For example,

xkill -display *your_node*:**0.1**

specifies screen 1 of server 0 on the machine *your_node*. Either or both the *host* and *screen* elements to the display specification can be omitted. If *host* is omitted, the local machine is assumed. If *screen* is omitted, screen 0 is assumed (and the period is unnecessary). The colon and *server* are necessary in all cases.

`-id` *resource*

Specifies the X identifier for the resource whose creator is to be aborted. If no resource is specified, *xkill* will display a special cursor with which you should select a window to be killed.

`-button` *number*
`-button any`

Specifies the number of the pointer button that should be used to select the window to kill. If the word `any` is specified, any button on the pointer can be used. By default, the first button in the pointer map (which is usually the left-most button) is used.

`-all` Indicates that all clients with top-level windows on the screen should be killed. *xkill* will ask you to select the root window with each of the currently defined buttons to give you several chances to abort. Use of this option is highly discouraged.

`-frame` Indicates that *xkill* should ignore the standard conventions for finding top-level client windows (which are typically nested inside a window manager window), and simply believe that you want to kill direct children of the root. (Available as of Release 4.)

Resources

`Button` Specifies a pointer button number to use when selecting the window to be removed. If the word `any` is specified, any button on the pointer can be used.

See Also

X, xwininfo; Volume One, *Xlib Programming Manual*

Author

Jim Fulton, MIT X Consortium;
Dana Chee, Bellcore.

Name

xload – display system load average.

Syntax

`xload [options]`

Description

The *xload* program displays a periodically updating histogram of the system load average.

Options

xload accepts all of the standard X Toolkit command line options along with the additional options listed below:

`-scale integer`
: Specifies the minimum number of tick marks in the histogram, where one division represents one load average point. If the load goes above this number, *xload* will create more divisions, but it will never use fewer than this number. The default is 1.

`-update seconds`
: Specifies the frequency in seconds at which *xload* updates its display. If the load average window is uncovered (by moving windows with a window manager or by the *xrefresh* program), the graph will also be updated. In Release 4, the minimum amount of time allowed between updates is 1 second (the default is 5 seconds). In Release 3, the minimum amount of time allowed between updates is 5 seconds (which is also the default).

`-hl color` or
`-highlight color`
: Specifies the color of the scale lines in Release 4. Specifies the color of the label and scale lines in Release 3.

`-jumpscroll pixels`
: Specifies the number of pixels to shift the graph to the left when the graph reaches the right edge of the window. The default value is 1/2 the width of the current window. Smooth scrolling can be achieved by setting it to 1. (Available as of Release 4.)

`-label string`
: Specifies the text string for the label above the load average. (Available as of Release 4.)

`-nolabel`
: Specifies that no label be displayed above the load graph. (Available as of Release 4.)

The following standard X Toolkit options are commonly used with *xload*:

`-bd color`
: Specifies the border color. The default is black.

`-bg color`
: Specifies the background color. The default is white.

`-bw` *pixels* Specifies the width in pixels of the border around the window. The default is 2.

`-fg` *color* Specifies the graph color. The default is black.

`-fn` *fontname*

Specifies the font to be used in displaying the name of the host whose load is being monitored. The default is the 6x10 pixel, fixed-width font "fixed".

`-rv` Indicates that reverse video should be simulated by swapping the foreground and background colors.

`-geometry` *geometry*

Specifies the size and location of the window. The `-geometry` option can be (and often is) abbreviated to `-g`, unless there is a conflicting option that begins with "g." The argument to the geometry option (*geometry*) is referred to as a "standard geometry string," and has the form *width*x*height*±*xoff*±*yoff*.

`-display` [*host*]:*server*[.*screen*]

Allows you to specify the host, server and screen on which to create the *xload* window. *host* specifies on which machine to create the *xload* window, *server* specifies the server number, and *screen* specifies the screen number. For example,

xload -display *your_node*:**0.1**

creates an *xload* window on screen 1 of server 0 on the machine *your_node*. If the host is omitted, the local machine is assumed. If the screen is omitted, screen 0 is assumed; the server and colon (:) are necessary in all cases.

`-xrm` *resourcestring*

Specifies a resource string to be used. This is especially useful for setting resources that do not have separate command line options.

Resources (Release 4)

In addition to the resources available to each of the widgets used by *xload*, there is one resource defined by the application itself.

`showLabel` (class `Boolean`)

If False, then no label will be displayed.

Widgets (Release 4)

In order to specify resources, it is useful to know the hierarchy of the widgets that compose *xload*. In the notation below, indentation indicates hierarchical structure. The widget class name is given first, followed by the widget instance name.

```
XLoad  xload
       Paned  paned
              Label  label
              StripChart  load
```

Resources (Release 3)

The Release 3 version of *xload* uses the Load widget in the X Toolkit. It understands all of the core resource names and classes as well as:

`width` (class `Width`)
: Specifies the width of the load average graph.

`height` (class `Height`)
: Specifies the height of the load average graph.

`update` (class `Interval`)
: Specifies the frequency in seconds at which the load should be redisplayed.

`scale` (class `Scale`)
: Specifies the initial number of ticks on the graph. The default is 1.

`minScale` (class `Scale`)
: Specifies the minimum number of ticks that will be displayed. The default is 1.

`foreground` (class `Foreground`)
: Specifies the color for the graph. Using the class specifies the color for all things that normally would appear in the foreground color. The default is black since the core default for background is white.

`highlight` (class `Foreground`)
: Specifies the color for the text and scale lines. The default is the same as for the `foreground` resource.

`label` (class `Label`)
: Specifies the label to use on the graph. The default is the hostname.

`font` (class `Font`)
: Specifies the font to be used for the label. The default is "fixed."

`reverseVideo` (class `ReverseVideo`)
: Specifies that the foreground and background colors should be reversed.

See Also

X, xrdb, mem(4), Athena StripChart widget (Release 4), Athena Load widget (Release 3)

Diagnostics

Unable to open display or create window. Unable to open */dev/kmem*. Unable to query window for dimensions. Various X errors.

Bugs

This program requires the ability to open and read */dev/kmem*. Sites that do not allow general access to this file should make *xload* belong to the same group as */dev/kmem* and turn on the *set group id* permission flag.

Reading */dev/kmem* is inherently non-portable. Therefore, the routine used to read it (`get_load.c`) must be ported to each new operating system.

Border color has to be explicitly specified when reverse video is used.

Authors

K. Shane Hartman (MIT-LCS) and Stuart A. Malone (MIT-LCS);
with features added by Jim Gettys (MIT-Athena), Bob Scheifler (MIT-LCS), Tony Della Fera (MIT-Athena), and Chris Peterson (MIT-LCS).

xlogo

Name

xlogo – X Window System logo.

Synopsis

xlogo [*options*]

Description

The *xlogo* program displays the X Window System logo. This program is nothing more than a wrapper around the *undocumented* Athena Logo widget.

Options

xlogo accepts all of the standard X Toolkit command line options, of which the following are commonly used:

`-bg` *color* Specifies the color to use for the background of the window. The default is white. A correct color for the background is something like maroon.

`-bd` *color* Specifies the color to use for the border of the window. The default is black.

`-bw` *pixels* Specifies the width in pixels of the border surrounding the window.

`-fg` *color* Specifies the color to use for displaying the logo. The default is black. A correct color for the foreground is something like silver, which you can approximate with a shade of grey.

`-rv` Indicates that reverse video should be simulated by swapping the foreground and background colors.

`-geometry` *geometry*

The *xlogo* window is created with the specified size and location determined by the supplied geometry specification. The `-geometry` option can be (and often is) abbreviated to `-g`, unless there is a conflicting option that begins with "g." The argument to the geometry option (*geometry*) is referred to as a "standard geometry string," and has the form *widthxheight±xoff±yoff*.

`-display` [*host*]:*server*[.*screen*]

Allows you to specify the host, server and screen on which to create the *xlogo* window (see *X*). *host* specifies on which machine to create the *xlogo* window, *server* specifies the server number, and *screen* specifies the screen number. For example,

```
xlogo -display your_node:0.1
```

creates an *xlogo* window on screen 1 of server 0 on the machine *your_node*. If the host is omitted, the local machine is assumed. If the screen is omitted, screen 0 is assumed; the server and colon (:) are necessary in all cases.

Reference Pages

`-xrm` *`resourcestring`*

Specifies a resource string to be used. This is especially useful for setting resources that do not have separate command line options.

Resources

This program uses the Logo widget in the Athena widget set. It understands all of the core resource names and classes as well as:

`width` (class `Width`)

Specifies the width of the logo.

`height` (class `Height`)

Specifies the height of the logo.

`foreground` (class `Foreground`)

Specifies the foreground color for the logo. The default depends on whether `reverseVideo` is specified. If `reverseVideo` is specified, the default is white; otherwise, the default is black.

`reverseVideo` (class `ReverseVideo`)

Specifies that the foreground and background should be reversed.

Widgets

In order to specify resources, it is useful to know the hierarchy of the widgets that compose *xlogo*. In the notation below, indentation indicates hierarchical structure. The widget class name is given first, followed by widget instance name.

```
XLogo   xlogo
     Logo   xlogo
```

Files

/usr/lib/X11/app-defaults/XLogo – specifies required resources (as of Release 4).

See Also

X, xrdb

Authors

Ollie Jones of Apollo Computer and Jim Fulton of the X Consortium wrote the logo graphics routine, based on a graphic design by Danny Chong and Ross Chapman of Apollo Computer.

Name

xlsatoms – list interned atoms defined on server.

Syntax

xlsatoms [*options*]

Description

Available as of Release 4, *xlsatoms* lists the interned atoms. By default, all atoms starting from 1 (the lowest atom value defined by the protocol) are listed until unknown atom is found. If an explicit range is given, *xlsatoms* will try all atoms in the range, regardless of whether or not any are undefined.

Options

-display *host*[:*server*][.*screen*]

Allows you to specify the host, server and screen to connect to. *host* specifies the machine, *server* specifies the server number, and *screen* specifies the screen number. For example,

xlsatoms -display *your_node*:**0.1**

specifies screen 1 of server 0 on the machine *your_node*. Either or both the *host* and *screen* elements to the display specification can be omitted. If *host* is omitted, the local machine is assumed. If *screen* is omitted, screen 0 is assumed (and the period is unnecessary). The colon and *server* are necessary in all cases.

-format *printf_string*

Specifies a printf-style string used to list each atom <*value, name*> pair, printed in that order (*value* is an *unsigned long* and *name* is a *char* *). *xlsatoms* will supply a newline at the end of each line. The default is %ld\t%s.

-range [*low*]-[*high*]

Specifies the range of atom values to check. If *low* is not given, a value of 1 assumed. If *high* is not given, *xlsatoms* will stop at the first undefined atom at or above *low*.

-name *string*

Specifies the name of an atom to list. If the atom does not exist, a message will be printed on the standard error.

See Also

X, Xserver, xprop

Author

Jim Fulton, MIT X Consortium.

xlsclients

Name

xlsclients – list client applications running on a display.

Syntax

xlsclients [*options*]

Description

Available as of Release 4, *xlsclients* is a utility for listing information about the client applications running on a display. It may be used to generate scripts representing a snapshot of the the user's current session.

Options

`-display` *host*[:*server*][.*screen*]
: Allows you to specify the host, server and screen to connect to. *host* specifies the machine, *server* specifies the server number, and *screen* specifies the screen number. For example,

xlsclients -display *your_node*:**0.1**

specifies screen 1 of server 0 on the machine *your_node*. Either or both the *host* and *screen* elements to the display specification can be omitted. If *host* is omitted, the local machine is assumed. If *screen* is omitted, screen 0 is assumed (and the period is unnecessary). The colon and *server* are necessary in all cases.

`-a`
: Specifies that clients on all screens should be listed. By default, only those clients on the default screen are listed.

`-l`
: Requests a long listing showing the window name, icon name, and class hints in addition to the machine name and command string in the default listing.

`-m` *maxcmdlength*
: Specifies the maximum number of characters in a command to list. The default is 1000.

See Also

X, xprop, xwininfo

Author

Jim Fulton, MIT X Consortium.

xlsfonts

Name

xlsfonts – list available fonts.

Syntax

`xlsfonts [options] [-fn pattern]`

Description

xlsfonts lists the fonts that match the given `pattern`. The wildcard character "*" may be used to match any sequence of characters (including none), and "?" to match any single character. If no pattern is given, "*" is assumed.

The "*" and "?" characters must be quoted to prevent them from being expanded by the shell.

Options

`-display [host]:server[.screen]`
: Allows you to specify the host, server and screen. For example,

```
xlsfonts -display your_node:0.1
```

specifies screen 1 on server 0 on the machine `your_node`. If the host is omitted, the local machine is assumed. If the screen is omitted, the screen 0 is assumed; the server and colon are necessary in all cases.

`-fn pattern` Indicates that only fonts matching the specified `pattern` be listed.

`-l[l[l]]` Indicates that medium, long, and very long listings, respectively, should be generated for each font.

`-l` Indicates that a long listing should be generated for each font. (Release 3)

`-m` Indicates that long listings should also print the minimum and maximum bounds of each font.

`-C` Indicates that listings should use multiple columns. This is the same as `-n 0`.

`-1` Indicates that listings should use a single column. This is the same as `-n 1`.

`-w width` Specifies the width in characters that should be used in figuring out how many columns to print. The default is 79.

`-n columns` Specifies the number of columns to use in displaying the output. By default, it will attempt to fit as many columns of font names into the number of characters specified by `-w width`.

See Also

X, Xserver, xset, xfd, xfontsel

Bugs

Doing `xlsfonts -l` can tie up your server for a very long time. This is really a bug with single-threaded, non-preemptable servers, not with this program.

Author

Mark Lillibridge, MIT Project Athena;
Jim Fulton, MIT X Consortium;
Phil Karlton, SGI.

Name

xlswins – server window list displayer for X.

Syntax

xlswins [*options*] [*window_id*]

Description

xlswins lists the window tree. By default, the root window is used as the starting point, although another window may be specified using the *window_id* option.

Options

-display [*host*]:*server*[.*screen*]

Allows you to specify the host, server and screen to connect to. *host* specifies the machine, *server* specifies the server number, and *screen* specifies the screen number. For example,

xlswins -display *your_node*:**0.1**

specifies screen 1 of server 0 on the machine *your_node*. Either or both the *host* and *screen* elements to the display specification can be omitted. If *host* is omitted, the local machine is assumed. If *screen* is omitted, screen 0 is assumed (and the period is unnecessary). The colon and *server* are necessary in all cases.

-l

Indicates that a long listing should be generated for each window. This includes a number indicating the depth, the geometry relative to the parent as well as the location relative to the root window.

-format *radix*

Specifies the radix to use when printing out window IDs. Allowable values are: hex, octal, and decimal. The default is hex.

-indent *number*

Specifies the number of spaces that should be indented for each level in the window tree. The default is 2.

window_id

Specifies that the starting point for the window tree listing is the window *window_id*.

See Also

X, Xserver, xwininfo, xprop

Bugs

This should be integrated with *xwininfo* somehow.

Author

Jim Fulton, MIT X Consortium.

Name

xmag – magnify parts of the screen.

Syntax

xmag [*options*]

Description

The *xmag* program allows you to magnify portions of the screen. If no explicit region is specified, a square centered around the pointer is displayed indicating the area to be enlarged. Once a region has been selected, a window is popped up showing a blown up version of the region in which each pixel in the source image is represented by a small square of the same color. Pressing Button1 on the pointer in the enlargement window pops up a small window displaying the position, number, and RGB value of the pixel under the pointer until the button is released. Pressing the space bar or any other pointer button removes the enlarged image so that another region may be selected. Pressing q, Q, or Control-C in the enlargement window exits the program.

Options

-display *host*]:*server*[.*screen*]

Allows you to specify the host, server and screen to use for both reading the screen and displaying the enlarged version of the image. *host* specifies the machine, *server* specifies the server number, and *screen* specifies the screen number. For example,

xmag -display *your_node*:**0.1**

specifies screen 1 of server 0 on the machine *your_node*. Either or both the *host* and *screen* elements to the display specification can be omitted. If *host* is omitted, the local machine is assumed. If *screen* is omitted, screen 0 is assumed (and the period is unnecessary). The colon and *server* are necessary in all cases.

-geometry *geometry*

The enlargement window is created with the specified size and location determined by the supplied geometry specification. The -geometry option can be (and often is) abbreviated to -g, unless there is a conflicting option that begins with "g." The argument to the geometry option (*geometry*) is referred to as a "standard geometry string," and has the form *width*x*height*±*xoff*±*yoff*.

By default, the size is computed from the size of the source region and the desired magnification. Therefore, only one of -source *size* and -mag *magfactor* options may be specified if a window size is given with the -geometry option.

-source *geometry*

This option specifies the size and/or location of the source region on the screen. By default, a 64x64 square centered about the pointer is provided for the user to select an area of the screen. The size of the source is used with the desired magnification to compute the default enlargement window size. Therefore, only one of `-geometry` *size* and `-mag` *magfactor* options may be specified if a source size is given with this option.

`-mag` *magfactor*
: This option specifies an integral factor by which the source region should be enlarged. The default magnification is 5. This is used with the size of the source to compute the default enlargement window size. Therefore, only one of `-geometry` *size* and `-source` *geom* options may be specified if a magnification factor is given with this option.

`-bw` *pixels*
: This option specifies the width in pixels of the border surrounding the enlargement window.

`-bd` *color*
: This option specifies the color to use for the border surrounding the enlargement window.

`-bg` *color_or_pixel_value*
: This option specifies the name of the color to be used as the background of the enlargement window. If the name begins with a percent size (%), it is interpreted to be an absolute pixel value. This is useful when displaying large areas since pixels that are the same color as the background do not need to be painted in the enlargement. The default is to use the `BlackPixel` of the screen.

`-fn` *fontname*
: This option specifies the name of a font to use when displaying pixel values (used when button 1 is pressed in the enlargement window).

`-z`
: This option indicates that the server should be grabbed during the dynamics and the call to `XGetImage`. This is useful for ensuring that clients don't change their state as a result of entering or leaving them with the pointer.

Resources

The *xmag* program uses the following X resources:

`geometry` (class `Geometry`)
: Specifies the size and/or location of the enlargement window.

`source` (class `Source`)
: Specifies the size and/or location of the source region on the screen.

`magnification` (class `Magnification`)
: Specifies the enlargement factor.

`borderWidth` (class `BorderWidth`)
: Specifies the border width in pixels.

`borderColor` (class `BorderColor`)
: Specifies the color of the border.

`background` (class `Background`)

Specifies the color or pixel value to be used for the background of the enlargement window.

`font` (class `Font`)

Specifies the name of the font to use when displaying pixel values when the user presses button 1 in the enlargement window.

See Also

X, xwd

Bugs

This program will behave strangely on displays that support windows of different depths.

Because the window size equals the source size times the magnification, you only need to specify two of the three parameters. This can be confusing.

Being able to drag the pointer around and see a dynamic display would be very nice.

Another possible interface would be for the user to drag out the desired area to be enlarged.

Author

Jim Fulton, MIT X Consortium.

Name

xman – display manual pages.

Syntax

xman [*options*]

Description

xman is a manual page browser. The default size of the initial *xman* window is small so that you can leave it running throughout your entire login session. In the initial window there are three options: Help will pop up a window with on-line help, Quit will exit, and Manual Page will pop up a window with a manual page browser in it. You may pop up more than one manual page browser window from a single execution of *xman*.

For further information on using *xman* please read the on-line help information. The rest of this manual page will discuss customization of *xman*.

Customization (Release 4)

xman allows customization of both the directories to be searched for manual pages, and the name that each directory will map to in the Sections menu. *xman* determines which directories it will search by reading the MANPATH environment variable. If no MANPATH is found then the directory is */usr/man* is searched on POSIX systems. This environment is expected to be a colon-separated list of directories for xman to search.

```
setenv MANPATH /mit/kit/man:/usr/man
```

By default, *xman* will search each of the following directories (in each of the directories specified in the users MANPATH) for manual pages. If manual pages exist in that directory then they are added to list of manual pages for the corresponding menu item. A menu item is only displayed for those sections that actually contain manual pages.

Directory	Section Name
man1	(1) User Commands
man2	(2) System Calls
man3	(3) Subroutines
man4	(4) Devices
man5	(5) File Formats
man6	(6) Games
man7	(7) Miscellaneous
man8	(8) Sys. Administration
manl	(l) Local
mann	(n) New
mano	(o) Old

For instance, a user has three directories in her manual path and each contain a directory called *man3*. All these manual pages will appear alphabetically sorted when the user selects the menu item called (3) Subroutines. If there is no directory called *mano* in any of the directories in her

MANPATH, or there are no manual pages in any of the directories called *mano*, then no menu item will be displayed for the section called (o) Old.

By using the *mandesc* file a user or system manager is able to more closely control which manual pages will appear in each of the sections represented by menu items in the Sections menu. This functionality is only available on a section by section basis, and individual manual pages may not be handled in this manner (Although generous use of symbolic links, *ln*(1), will allow almost any configuration you can imagine).

The format of the *mandesc* file is a character followed by a label. The character determines which of the sections will be added under this label. For instance suppose that you would like to create an extra menu item that contains all programmer subroutines. This label should contain all manual pages in both sections two and three. The *mandesc* file would look like this:

```
2Programmer Subroutines
3Programmer Subroutines
```

This will add a menu item to the Sections menu that would bring up a listing of all manual pages in sections two and three of the UNIX Programmer's Manual. Since the label names are *exactly* the same they will be added to the same section. Note, however, that the original sections still exist.

If you want to completely ignore the default sections in a manual directory then add the line:

```
no default sections
```

anywhere in your *mandesc* file. This keeps *xman* from searching the default manual sections *in that directory only*. As an example, suppose you want to do the same thing as above, but you don't think that it is useful to have the System Calls or Subroutines sections any longer. You would need to duplicate the default entries, as well as adding your new one.

```
no default sections
1(1) User Commands
2Programmer Subroutines
3Programmer Subroutines
4(4) Devices
5(5) File Formats
6(6) Games
7(7) Miscellaneous
8(8) Sys. Administration
l(l) Local
n(n) New
o(o) Old
```

xman will read any section that is of the form `man<character>`, where `<character>` is an upper or lower case letter (they are treated distinctly) or a numeral (0-9). Be warned, however, that *man*(1) and *catman*(8) will not search directories that are non-standard.

Customization (Release 3)

xman accomodates new manual sections by the use of the environment variable MANPATH and by directory description files named *mandesc*. *xman* will search each directory specified in the environment variable MANPATH for the following subdirectories only: *man0*, *man1*, ..., *man8*, *manl* (local), and *mann* (new). (It usually ignores the information in *man0* unless there is a *mandesc* file that specifically tells it not to.) These subdirectories should contain man pages. Any manual section can be renamed by an optional *mandesc* file.

As an example, if MANPATH was set to */usr/man:/usr/sipb/man* and there was no *mandesc* file in */usr/man*, *xman* would put all of the files in the default section names (e.g., *manl* gets a section name of local). But if there were a *mandesc* file in */usr/sipb/man* which contained the line *lSIPB Programs*, then *xman* would put all files in the *manl* subdirectory in a new section called "SIPB Programs." *xman* will search the *mandesc* file until there are no more lines of information. This flexibility is ideal for courses that have their own manual pages.

xman creates temporary files in */tmp* for all unformatted man pages and all apropos searches.

Options

xman accepts all of the standard X Toolkit command line options, as well as the following additional options:

`-helpfile` *`filename`*
: Specifies a helpfile to use other than the default.

`-bothshown`
: Allows both the manual page and manual directory to be on the screen at the same time.

`-notopbox`
: Starts without the top menu with the three buttons in it.

`-pagesize` *`geometry`*
: Sets the size and location of all the Manual Pages.

The following X Toolkit options are commonly used with *xman*:

`-geometry` *`geometry`*
: Sets the size and location of the Top Menu with the three buttons in it. The top menu with the three buttons in it is created with the specified size and location determined by the supplied geometry specification. The `-geometry` option can be (and often is) abbreviated to `-g`, unless there is a conflicting option that begins with "g." The argument to the geometry option (*`geometry`*) is referred to as a "standard geometry string," and has the form *`widthxheight±xoff±yoff`*.

`-display [`*`host`*`]:`*`server`*`[.`*`screen`*`]`
: Allows you to specify the host, server and screen on which to display the *xman* window. *`host`* specifies the machine, *`server`* specifies the server number, and *`screen`* specifies the screen number. For example,

```
xman -display your_node:0.1
```

specifies screen 1 of server 0 on the machine *`your_node`*. Either or both the *`host`* and *`screen`* elements to the display specification can be omitted. If *`host`* is omitted, the local machine is assumed. If *`screen`* is omitted, screen 0 is assumed (and the period is unnecessary). The colon and *`server`* are necessary in all cases.

`-bw` *pixels* or `-borderwidth` *pixels*
: Specifies the width of the border for all windows in *xman*.

`-bd` *color* or `-bordercolor` *color*
: Specifies the color of the borders of all windows in *xman*.

`-fg` *color* or `-foreground` *color*
: Specifies the foreground color to be used.

`-bg` *color* or `-background` *color*
: Specifies the background color to be used.

`-fn` *font* or `-font` *font*
: Specifies the font to use for all buttons and labels.

`-name` *name* Specifies the name to use when retrieving resources.

`-title` *title* Specifies the title of this application.

`-xrm` *resources*
: Allows a resource to be specified on the command line.

Resources (Release 3 and Release 4)

The resources in this section are valid for both Release 3 and Release 4, unless otherwise indicated.

The *xman* program uses the following X Toolkit resources: `foreground`, `background`, `width`, `height`, `borderWidth`, and `borderColor`.

In addition, *xman* has application-specific resources that allow unique *xman* customizations.

`manualFontNormal` (class `Font`)
: The font to use for normal text in the manual pages.

`manualFontBold` (class `Font`)
: The font to use for bold text in the manual pages.

`manualFontItalic` (class `Font`)
: The font to use for italic text in the manual pages.

`directoryFontNormal` (class `Font`)
: The font to use for the directory text.

`bothShown` (class `Boolean`)
: Either true or false, specifies whether or not you want both the directory and the manual page shown at start up.

`directoryHeight` (class `DirectoryHeight`)
: The height in pixels of the directory, when the directory and the manual page are shown simultaneously.

`topCursor` (class `Cursor`)
: The cursor to use in the top box.

`helpCursor` (class `Cursor`)
The cursor to use in the help window.

`manpageCursor` (class `Cursor`)
The cursor to use in the manual page window.

`searchEntryCursor` (class `Cursor`)
The cursor to use in the search entry text widget.

`pointerColor` (class `Foreground`)
The color of all the cursors (pointers) listed above. The name was chosen to be compatible with *xterm*. (Available as of Release 4.)

`helpFile` (class `File`)
Use this rather than the system default helpfile.

`topBox` (class `Boolean`)
Either true or false, determines whether the top box (containing the Help, Quit and Manual Page buttons) or a manual page is put on the screen at start-up. The default is true.

`verticalList` (class `Boolean`)
Either true or false, determines whether the directory listing is vertically or horizontally organized. The default is horizontal (false).

Widgets (Release 4)

In order to specify resources, it is useful to know the hierarchy of the widgets that compose *xman*. In the notation below, indentation indicates hierarchical structure. The widget class name is given first, followed by the widget instance name.

```
Xman xman     (This widget is never used)
       TopLevelShell  topbox
              Form  form
                     Label  topLabel
                     Command  helpButton
                     Command  quitButton
                     Command  manpageButton
              TransientShell  search
                     DialogWidgetClass  dialog
                            Label  label
                            Text  value
                            Command  manualPage
                            Command  apropos
                            Command  cancel
              TransientShell  pleaseStandBy
                     Label  label
       TopLevelShell  manualBrowser
              Paned  Manpage_Vpane
                     Paned  horizPane
                            MenuButton  options
                            MenuButton  sections
```

Reference Pages

```
                    Label  manualBrowser
            Viewport  directory
                    List  directory
                    List  directory
                    .
                    .  (one for each section,
                    .   created "on the fly")
                    .
            ScrollByLine  manualPage
    SimpleMenu  optionMenu
            SmeBSB  displayDirectory
            SmeBSB  displayManualPage
            SmeBSB  help
            SmeBSB  search
            SmeBSB  showBothScreens
            SmeBSB  removeThisManpage
            SmeBSB  openNewManpage
            SmeBSB  showVersion
            SmeBSB  quit
    SimpleMenu  sectionMenu
            SmeBSB  <name of section>
                    .
                    .  (one for each section)
                    .
    TransientShell  search
            DialogWidgetClass  dialog
                    Label  label
                    Text  value
                    Command  manualPage
                    Command  apropos
                    Command  cancel
    TransientShell  pleaseStandBy
            Label  label
    TransientShell  likeToSave
            Dialog  dialog
                    Label  label
                    Text  value
                    Command  yes
                    Command  no
TopLevelShell  help
    Paned  Manpage_Vpane
            Paned  horizPane
                    MenuButton  options
                    MenuButton  sections
                    Label  manualBrowser
            ScrollByLine  manualPage
    SimpleMenu  optionMenu
            SmeBSB  displayDirectory
            SmeBSB  displayManualPage
            SmeBSB  help
```

```
SmeBSB  search
SmeBSB  showBothScreens
SmeBSB  removeThisManpage
SmeBSB  openNewManpage
SmeBSB  showVersion
SmeBSB  quit
```

Widgets (Release 3)

In order to change the default values for widget resources you need to know widget names. Below are the names of some of the most common widgets. You can also reference widgets by class. The most common classes are `Label`, `Command`, and `Text`.

`topBox` The top menu.

`help` The help window.

`manualBrowser`
The manual page display window.

`xmanCommands`
The manual page command popup menu.

`xmanSections`
The manual page section popup menu.

`xmanSearch` The manual page search popup menu.

Here are a few examples of how to string all this information together into a resource specification that can be used on the command line with the `-xrm` flag, or added to an *Xresources* or other resource file.

`xman*Command.foreground: blue`
All command buttons will be blue.

`xman*topBox*foreground: blue`
Everything in the top menu has a blue foreground.

`xman*Text.border: red`
All text widgets have a red border.

`xman*Label.font: 9x15`
All label buttons have a 9x15 font.

Global Actions (Release 4)

xman defines all user interaction through global actions. This allows the user to modify the translation table of any widget, and bind any event to the new user action. The list of actions supported by *xman* are:

`GotoPage(`*`page`*`)`
When used in a manual page display window, this action allows the user to move between a directory and manual page display. The *page* argument can be either `Directory` or `ManualPage`.

`Quit()` Can be used anywhere; exits *xman*.

`Search(type, action)`
Only useful when used in a search popup, this action will cause the search widget to perform the named search type on the string in the search popup's value widget. This action will also pop down the search widget. The `type` argument can be either `Apropos`, `Manpage` or `Cancel`. If an `action` of `Open` is specified then xman will open a new manual page to display the results of the search, otherwise xman will attempt to display the results in the parent of the search popup.

`PopupHelp()` Can be used anywhere; pops up the help widget.

`PopupSearch()`
Can be used anywhere, except in a help window. It will cause the search popup to become active and visible on the screen, allowing the user search for a manual page.

`CreateNewManpage()`
Can be used anywhere; creates a new manual page display window.

`RemoveThisManpage()`
Can be used in any manual page or help display window. When called it will remove the window, and clean up all resources associated with it.

`SaveFormattedPage(action)`
Can only be used in the `likeToSave` popup widget, and tells xman whether to **Save** or **Cancel** a save of the manual page that has just been formatted.

`ShowVersion()`
May be called from any manual page or help display window, and will cause the informational display line to show the current version of *xman*.

Files

<manpath directory>/man<character>
<manpath directory>/cat<character>
<manpath directory>/mandesc
/usr/lib/X11/app-defaults/Xman - specifies required resources (as of Release 4)
/tmp xman creates temporary files in */tmp* for all unformatted man pages and all apropos searches.

Environment Variables

MANPATH
The search path for manual pages. Directories are separated by colons (e.g., */usr/man:/mit/kit/man:/foo/bar/man*).

XAPPLRESDIR
A string that will have "Xman" appended to it. This string will be the full path name of a user *app-defaults* file to be merged into the resource database after the system *app-defaults* file, and before the resources that are attached to the display. (Available as of Release 4.)

Bugs In Release 3

The `-fn` and `-font` options only specify the fonts for the command button and not the text of the manpages or directories.

Protocol error upon selecting Remove This Manpage.

See Also

X, apropos(1), catman(8), man(1), Athena Widget set

Authors

Chris Peterson, MIT X Consortium from the V10 version written by Barry Shein formerly of Boston University.

Name

xmh – X window interface to the *mh* message handling system.

Syntax

xmh [**-path** *mailpath*] [**-initial** *foldername*] [**-flag**] [*-toolkitoption*]

Description

This reference page describes the Release 4 version of *xmh*, a window-oriented user interface to the Rand *mh* Message Handling System. The Release 3 version is described in the next reference page in this guide.

To actually do things with your mail, *xmh* makes calls to the *mh* package. Electronic mail messages may be composed, sent, received, replied to, forwarded, sorted, and stored in folders.

Please don't be misled by the size of this document. It introduces many aspects of the Athena Widget Set, and provides extensive mechanism for customization of the user interface. *xmh* really is easy to use.

Options

xmh accepts all of the standard X Toolkit command line options, as well as the following:

-path *mailpath*
: To specify an alternate collection of mail folders in which to process mail, use -path followed by the pathname of the alternate mail directory. The default mail path is the value of the Path component in *$HOME/.mh_profile*, or *$HOME/Mail* if the MH Path is not given.

-initial *foldername*
: Specifies an alternate folder that may receive new mail and is initially opened by *xmh*. The default initial folder is 'inbox'.

-flag
: Causes *xmh* to attempt to change the appearance of its icon when new mail arrives.

These three options have corresponding application-specific resources, named MailPath, InitialFolder, and MailWaitingFlag, which can be used in a resource file.

See *X* for a list of the standard Toolkit options.

Installation

The current version of *xmh* requires that the user is already set up to use *mh*, version 6. To do so, see if there is a file called *.mh_profile* in your home directory. If it exists, check to see if it contains a line that starts with Current-Folder. If it does, you've been using version 4 or earlier of *mh*; to convert to version 6, you must remove that line. (Failure to do so causes spurious output to standard error, which can hang *xmh* depending on your setup.)

If you do not already have a *.mh_profile*, you can create one (and everything else you need) by typing inc to the shell. You should do this before using *xmh* to incorporate new mail.

For more information, refer to the *mh*(1) documentation.

Basic Screen Layout

xmh starts out with a single window, divided into four main areas: Six buttons with pull-down command menus. A collection of buttons, one for each top level folder. New users of mh will have two folders, "drafts" and "inbox". A listing, or Table of Contents, of the messages in the open folder. Initially, this will show the messages in "inbox". A view of one of your messages. Initially this is blank.

xmh and the Athena Widget Set

xmh uses the X Toolkit Intrinsics and the Athena Widget Set. Many of the features described below (scrollbars, buttonboxes, etc.) are actually part of the Athena Widget Set, and are described here only for completeness. For more information, see the Athena Widget Set documentation.

Scrollbars

Some parts of the main window will have a vertical area on the left containing a grey bar. This area is a *scrollbar*. They are used whenever the data in a window takes up more space than can be displayed. The grey bar indicates what portion of your data is visible. Thus, if the entire length of the area is grey, then you are looking at all your data. If only the first half is grey, then you are looking at the top half of your data. The message viewing area will have a horizontal scrollbar if the text of the message is wider than the viewing area.

You can use the pointer in the scrollbar to change what part of the data is visible. If you click with the middle button, then the top of the grey area will move to where the pointer is, and the corresponding portion of data will be displayed. If you hold down the middle button, you can drag around the grey area. This makes it easy to get to the top of the data: just press with the middle, drag off the top of the scrollbar, and release.

If you click with button 1, then the data to the right of the pointer will scroll to the top of the window. If you click with pointer button 3, then the data at the top of the window will scroll down to where the pointer is.

Buttonboxes, Buttons, and Menus

Any area containing many words or short phrases, each enclosed in a rectangle or rounded boundary, is called a *buttonbox*. Each rectangle or rounded area is actually a button that you can press by moving the pointer onto it and pressing pointer button 1. If a given buttonbox has more buttons in it than can fit, it will be displayed with a scrollbar, so you can always scroll to the button you want.

Some buttons have pull-down menus. Pressing the pointer button while the pointer is over one of these buttons will pull down a menu. Holding the button down while moving the pointer over the menu, called dragging the pointer, will highlight each selectable item on the menu as the pointer passes over it. To select an item in the menu, release the pointer button while the item is highlighted.

Adjusting the Relative Sizes of Areas

If you're not satisfied with the sizes of the various areas of the main window, they can easily be changed. Near the right edge of the border between each region is a black box, called a *grip*. Simply point to that grip with the pointer, press a pointer button, drag up or down, and release. Exactly what happens depends on which pointer button you press.

If you drag with the middle button, then only that border will move. This mode is simplest to understand, but is the least useful.

If you drag with pointer button 1, then you are adjusting the size of the window above. *xmh* will attempt to compensate by adjusting some window below it.

If you drag with pointer button 3, then you are adjusting the size of the window below. *xmh* will attempt to compensate by adjusting some window above it.

All windows have a minimum and maximum size; you will never be allowed to move a border past the point where it would make a window have an invalid size.

Processing Your Mail

This section will define the concepts of the selected folder, current folder, selected message(s), current message, selected sequence, and current sequence. Each *xmh* command is introduced.

For use in customization, action procedures corresponding to each command are given; these action procedures can be used to customize the user interface, particularly the keyboard accelerators and the functionality of the buttons in the optional button box created by the application resource `CommandButtonCount`.

Selected Folder

A folder contains a collection of mail messages, or is empty.

The selected folder is whichever foldername appears in the bar above the folder buttons. Note that this is not necessarily the same folder that is being viewed. To change the selected folder, just press on the desired folder button; if that folder has subfolders, select a folder from the pull down menu.

The Table of Contents, or toc, lists the messages in the viewed folder. The title bar above the Table of Contents displays the name of the viewed folder.

The toc title bar also displays the name of the viewed sequence of messages within the viewed folder. Every folder has an "all" sequence, which contains all the messages in the folder, and initially the toc title bar will show "inbox:all".

Folder Commands

The Folder command menu contains commands of a global nature:

Open Folder — Displays the data in the selected folder. Thus, the selected folder also becomes the viewed folder. The action procedure corresponding to this command is `XmhOpenFolder([`*`foldername`*`])`. It takes an optional argument as the name of a folder to select and open; if no folder is specified, the selected folder is opened. It may be specified as part of an event translation from a folder menu button or from a folder menu, or as a binding of a keyboard accelerator to any widget other than the folder menu buttons or the folder menus.

Open Folder in New Window
: Displays the selected folder in an additional main window. Note, however, that you may not reliably display the same folder in more than one window at a time, although *xmh* will not prevent you from trying. The corresponding action is `XmhOpenFolderInNewWindow()`.

Create Folder
: Creates a new folder. You will be prompted for a name for the new folder; to enter the name, move the pointer to the blank box provided and type. Subfolders are created by specifying the parent folder, a slash, and the subfolder name. For example, to create a folder named "xmh" which is a subfolder of an existing folder named "clients", type "clients/xmh". Click on the Okay button when finished, or just press Return; click on Cancel to cancel this operation. The action corresponding to Create Folder is `XmhCreateFolder()`.

Delete Folder
: Destroys the selected folder. You will be asked to confirm this action (see "Confirmation Windows"). Destroying a folder will also destroy any subfolders of that folder. The corresponding action is `XmhDeleteFolder()`.

Close Window
: Exits *xmh*, after first confirming that you won't lose any changes; or, if selected from any additional *xmh* window, simply closes that window. The corresponding action is `XmhClose()`.

Highlighted and Selected Messages and the Current Message

It is possible to highlight a set of adjacent messages in the area of the Table of Contents. To highlight a message, click on it with pointer button 1. To highlight a range of messages, click on the first one with pointer button 1 and on the last one with pointer button 3; or press pointer button 1, drag, and release. To extend a range of selected messages, use pointer button 3. To highlight all messages in the table of contents, click rapidly three times with pointer button 1. To cancel any selection in the table of contents, click rapidly twice.

The selected messages are the same as the highlighted messages, if any. If no messages are highlighted, then the selected messages are considered the same as the current message.

The current message is indicated by a '+' next to the message number. It usually corresponds to the message currently being viewed. When a message is viewed, the title bar above the view will identify the message.

Table of Contents Commands

The Table of Contents command menu contains commands which operate on the open, or viewed folder.

Incorporate New Mail
: Adds any new mail received to your inbox folder, and set the current message to be the first new message. (This command is selectable only if "inbox" is the folder being viewed.) The corresponding action is `XmhIncorporateNewMail()`.

Reference Pages

Commit Changes
: Executes all deletions, moves, and copies that have been marked in this folder. The corresponding action is `XmhCommitChanges()`.

Pack Folder
: Renumbers the messages in this folder so they start with 1 and increment by 1. The corresponding action is `XmhPackFolder()`.

Sort Folder
: Sorts the messages in this folder in chronological order. As a side effect, this also packs the folder. The corresponding action is `XmhSortFolder()`.

Rescan Folder
: Rebuilds the list of messages. This can be used whenever you suspect that *xmh*'s idea of what messages you have is wrong. (In particular, this is necessary if you change things using straight *mh* commands without using *xmh*.) The corresponding action is `XmhForceRescan()`.

Message Commands

The Message command menu contains commands that operate on the selected message(s), or if there are no selected messages, the current message.

Compose Message
: Composes a new message. A new window will be brought up for composition; a description of it is given in the *Composition Windows* section below. This command does not affect the current message. The corresponding action is `XmhComposeMessage()`.

View Next Message
: Views the first selected message. If no messages are highlighted, view the current message. If current message is already being viewed, view the first unmarked message after the current message. The corresponding action is `XmhViewNextMessage()`.

View Previous
: Views the last selected message. If no messages are highlighted, view the current message. If current message is already being viewed, view the first unmarked message before the current message. The corresponding action is `XmhViewPrevious()`.

Mark Deleted
: Marks the selected messages for deletion. If no messages are highlighted, then this mark the current message for deletion and automatically display the next unmarked message. The corresponding action is `XmhMark-Deleted()`.

Mark Move
: Marks the selected messages to be moved into the current (selected) folder. (If the current folder is the same as the viewed folder, this command will just beep.) If no messages are highlighted, this will mark the current message to be moved and display the next unmarked message. The corresponding action is `XmhMarkMove()`.

Mark Copy
: Marks the selected messages to be copied into the current folder. (If the current folder is the same as the viewed folder, this command will just beep.) If no messages are highlighted, mark the current message to be copied. The corresponding action is `XmhMarkCopy()`.

Unmark Removes any of the above three marks from the selected messages, or the current message, if none are highlighted. The corresponding action is `XmhUnmark()`.

View in New Window
Creates a new window containing only a view of the first selected message, or the current message, if none are highlighted. The corresponding action is `XmhViewInNewWindow()`.

Reply Creates a composition window in reply to the first selected message, or the current message, if none are highlighted. The corresponding action is `XmhReply()`.

Forward Creates a composition window whose body is initialized to be the contents of the selected messages, or the current message if none are highlighted. The corresponding action is `XmhForward()`.

Use as Composition
Creates a composition window whose body is initialized to be the contents of the first selected message, or the current message if none are selected. Any changes you make in the composition will be saved in a new message in the ''drafts'' folder, and will not change the original message. However, this command was designed to be used within the ''drafts'' folder to compose message drafts, and there is an exception to this rule. If the message to be used as composition was selected from the ''drafts'' folder, the changes will be reflected in the original message (see "Composition Windows"). The action procedure corresponding to this command is `XmhUseAsComposition()`.

Print Prints the selected messages, or the current message if none are selected. *xmh* normally prints by invoking the *enscript*(1) command, but this can be customized with the application-specific resource `PrintCommand`. The action procedure corresponding to this command is `XmhPrint()`.

Sequence Commands

The **Sequence** command menu contains commands pertaining to message sequences (See "Message-Sequences"), and a list of the message-sequences defined for the currently viewed folder. The selected message-sequence is indicated by a check mark in its entry in the margin of the menu. To change the selected message-sequence, select a new message-sequence from the sequence menu.

Pick Messages Defines a new message-sequence. The corresponding action is `XmhPickMessages()`.

The following menu entries will be sensitive only if the current folder has any message-sequences other than the ''all'' message-sequence.

Open Sequence Changes the viewed sequence to be the same as the selected sequence. The corresponding action is `XmhOpenSequence()`.

Add to Sequence
Adds the selected messages to the selected sequence. The corresponding action is `XmhAddToSequence()`.

Remove from Sequence
Removes the selected messages from the selected sequence. The corresponding action is `XmhRemoveFromSequence()`.

Delete Sequence
Removes the selected sequence entirely. The messages themselves are not affected; they simply are no longer grouped together to define a message-sequence. The corresponding action is `XmhDeleteSequence()`.

View Commands

Commands in the View menu and in the buttonboxes of view windows (which result from the Message command View in New Window) correspond in functionality to commands of the same name in the Message menu, but they operate on the viewed message rather than the selected messages or current message.

Close Window When the viewed message is in a separate view window, this command will close the view, after confirming the status of any unsaved edits. The corresponding action procedure is `XmhCloseView()`.

Reply Creates a composition window in reply to the viewed message. The related action procedure is `XmhViewReply()`.

Forward Creates a composition window whose body is initialized to be the contents of the viewed message. The corresponding action is `XmhViewForward()`.

Use As Composition
Creates a composition window whose body is initialized to be the contents of the viewed message. Any changes made in the composition window will be saved in a new message in the "drafts" folder, and will not change the original message. An exception: if the viewed message was selected from the "drafts" folder, the original message is edited. The action procedure corresponding to this command is `XmhViewUseAsComposition()`.

Edit Message Enables the direct editing of the viewed message. The action procedure is `XmhEditView()`.

Save Message This command is insensitive until the message has been edited; when activated, edits will be saved to the original message in the view. The corresponding action is `XmhSaveView()`.

Print Prints the viewed message. *xmh* prints by invoking the *enscript*(1) command, but this can be customized with the application-specific resource `PrintCommand`. The corresponding action procedure is `XmhPrintView()`.

Options Menu

The Options menu contains one entry.

Read in Reverse When selected, a check mark appears in the margin of this menu entry. Read in Reverse will switch the meaning of the next and previous messages, and will increment in the opposite direction. This is useful if you want to read your messages in the order of most recent first. The option acts as a toggle; select it from the menu a second time to undo the effect. The check mark appears when the option is selected.

Composition Windows

Aside from the normal text editing functions, there are six command buttons associated with composition windows:

Close Window — Closes this composition window. If changes have been made since the most recent Save or Send, you will be asked to confirm losing them. The corresponding action is `XmhCloseView()`.

Send — Sends this composition. The corresponding action is `XmhSend()`.

New Headers — Replaces the current composition with an empty message. If changes have been made since the most recent Send or Save, you will be asked to confirm losing them. The corresponding action is `XmhResetCompose()`.

Compose Message — Brings up another new composition window. The corresponding action is `XmhComposeMessage()`.

Save Message — Saves this composition in your drafts folder. Then you can safely close the composition. At some future date, you can continue working on the composition by opening the drafts folder, selecting the message, and using the Use as Composition command. The corresponding action is `XmhSave()`.

Insert — Inserts a related message into the composition. If the composition window was created with a Reply command, the related message is the message being replied to, otherwise no related message is defined and this button is insensitive. The message may be filtered before being inserted; see `ReplyInsertFilter` under "Application-specific Resources" for more information. The corresponding action is `XmhInsert()`.

Accelerators

Accelerators are shortcuts. They allow you to invoke commands without using the menus, either from the keyboard or by using the pointer.

xmh defines pointer accelerators for common actions: To select and view a message with a single click, use pointer button 2 on the message's entry in the table of contents. To select and open a folder or a sequence in a single action, make the folder or sequence selection with pointer button 2.

To mark the highlighted messages to be moved in a single action, or current message if none have been highlighted, use pointer button 3 to select the target folder. Similarly, selecting a sequence with pointer button 3 will add the highlighted or current message(s) to that sequence.

Reference Pages

In both of these operations, the selected folder or sequence and the viewed folder or sequence are not changed.

xmh defines the following keyboard accelerators over the surface of the main window, except in the view area while editing a message:

Meta-I	Incorporate new mail.
Meta-C	Commit changes.
Meta-R	Rescan folder.
Meta-P	Pack folder.
Meta-S	Sort folder.
Meta-space	View next message.
Meta-c	Mark copy.
Meta-d	Mark deleted.
Meta-f	Forward the selected or current message.
Meta-m	Mark move.
Meta-n	View next message.
Meta-p	View previous message.
Meta-r	Reply to the selected or current message.
Meta-u	Unmark.
Control-V	Scroll the table of contents forward.
Meta-V	Scroll the table of contents backward.
Control-v	Scroll the view forward.
Meta-v	Scroll the view backward.

Text Editing Commands

All of the text editing commands are actually defined by the Text widget in the Athena Widget Set. The commands may be bound to different keys than the defaults described below through the X Toolkit Intrinsics key re-binding mechanisms. See the X Toolkit Intrinsics and the Athena Widget Set documentation for more details.

Whenever you are asked to enter any text, you will be using a standard text editing interface. Various control and meta keystroke combinations are bound to a somewhat Emacs-like set of commands. In addition, the pointer buttons may be used to select a portion of text or to move the insertion point in the text. Pressing pointer button 1 causes the insertion point to move to the pointer. Double-clicking button 1 selects a word, triple-clicking selects a line, quadruple-clicking selects a paragraph, and clicking rapidly five times selects everything. Any selection may be extended in either direction by using pointer button 3.

In the following, a *line* refers to one displayed row of characters in the window. A *paragraph* refers to the text between carriage returns. Text within a paragraph is broken into lines for display based on the current width of the window. When a message is sent, text is broken into lines based upon the values of the `SendBreakWidth` and `SendWidth` application-specific resources.

The following keystroke combinations are defined:

Control-a	Move to the beginning of the current line.
Control-b	Move backward one character.
Control-d	Delete the next character.
Control-e	Move to the end of the current line.
Control-f	Move forward one character.
Control-g	Multiply reset.
Control-h	Delete previous character.
Control-j	Create a new paragraph with the same indentation as the previous one.
Control-k	Kill the rest of the current line.
Control-l	Refresh window.
Control-m	New paragraph.
Control-n	Move down to the next line.
Control-o	Break this paragraph into two.
Control-p	Move up to the previous line.
Control-r	Search/replace backward.
Control-s	Search/replace forward.
Control-t	Transpose characters.
Control-u	Multiply by 4.
Control-v	Move down to the next screenful of text.
Control-w	Kill the selected text.
Control-y	Insert the last killed text.
Control-z	Scroll the text up one line.
Meta-B	Move backward one word.
Meta-d	Delete the next word.
Meta-D	Kill the next word.
Meta-f	Move forward one word.
Meta-h	Delete the previous word.
Meta-H	Kill the previous word.

Meta-i	Insert file.
Meta-k	Kill to end of paragraph.
Meta-q	Form paragraph.
Meta-v	Move up to the previous screenful of text.
Meta-y	Insert current text selection.
Meta-z	Scroll one line down.
Meta-<	Move to the beginning of the file.
Meta->	Move to the end of the file.
Meta-]	Move forward one paragraph.
Meta-[	Move backward one paragraph.
Meta-Delete	Delete previous word.
Meta-Shift Delete	Kill previous word.
Meta-Backspace	Delete previous word.
Meta-Shift Backspace	Kill previous word.

In addition, the pointer may be used to cut and paste text:

Button 1 Down	Start selection.
Button 1 Motion	Adjust selection.
Button 1 Up	End selection (cut).
Button 2 Down	Insert current selection (paste).
Button 3 Down	Extend current selection.
Button 3 Motion	Adjust selection.
Button 3 Up	End selection (cut).

Confirmation Dialog Boxes

Whenever you press a button that may cause you to lose some work or is otherwise dangerous, a popup dialog box will appear asking you to confirm the action. This window will contain an Abort or No button and a Confirm or Yes button. Pressing the No button cancels the operation, and pressing the Yes will proceed with the operation.

Some dialog boxes contain messages from *mh*. Clicking on the message field will cause the dialog box to resize so that you can read the entire message.

Message-Sequences

An *mh* message sequence is just a set of messages associated with some name. They are local to a particular folder; two different folders can have sequences with the same name. In all folders, the sequence ''all'' is predefined; it consists of the set of all messages in that folder. As many as nine sequences may be defined for each folder, including the predefined ''all'' sequence. (The sequence ''cur'' is also usually defined for every folder; it consists of only the current message. *xmh* hides ''cur'' from the user, instead placing a ''+'' by the current message. Also, *xmh* does not support the ''unseen'' sequence, so that one is also hidden from the user.)

The message sequences for a folder (including one for ''all'') are displayed in the Sequence menu, below the sequence commands. The table of contents (also known as the ''toc'') is at any one time displaying one message sequence. This is called the ''viewed sequence'', and its name will be displayed in the toc title bar just after the folder name. Also, at any time one of the sequences in the menu will have a check mark next to it. This is called the ''selected sequence''. Note that the viewed sequence and the selected sequence are not necessarily the same. (This all pretty much corresponds to the way the folders work.)

The Open Sequence, Add to Sequence, Remove from Sequence, and Delete Sequence commands are active only if the viewed folder contains message-sequences.

Note that none of the above actually affect whether a message is in the folder. Remember that a sequence is a set of messages within the folder; the above operations just affect what messages are in that set.

To create a new sequence, select the Pick menu entry. A new window will appear, with lots of places to enter text. Basically, you can describe the sequence's initial set of messages based on characteristics of the message. Thus, you can define a sequence to be all the messages that were from a particular person, or with a particular subject, and so on. You can also connect things up with boolean operators, so you can select all things from ''weissman'' with the subject ''xmh''.

Hopefully, the layout is fairly obvious. The simplest cases are the easiest: just point to the proper field and type. If you enter in more than one field, it will only select messages which match all non-empty fields.

The more complicated cases arise when you want things that match one field or another one, but not necessarily both. That's what all the ''or'' buttons are for. If you want all things with the subject ''xmh'' or ''xterm'', just press the ''or'' button next to the ''Subject:'' field. Another box will appear where you can enter another subject.

If you want all things either from ''weissman'' or with subject ''xmh'', but not necessarily both, select the ''-Or-'' button. This will essentially double the size of the form. You can then enter ''weissman'' in a from: box on the top half, and ''xmh'' in a subject: box on the lower part.

If you select the Skip button, then only those messages that *don't* match the fields on that row are included.

Finally, in the bottom part of the window will appear several more boxes. One is the name of the sequence you're defining. (It defaults to the name of the selected sequence when Pick was pressed, or to ''temp'' if ''all'' was the selected sequence.) Another box defines which sequence to look through for potential members of this sequence; it defaults to the viewed sequence when Pick was pressed.

Two more boxes define a date range; only messages within that date range will be considered. These dates must be entered in 822-style format: each date is of the form "dd mmm yy hh:mm:ss zzz", where dd is a one or two digit day of the month, mmm is the three-letter abbreviation for a month, and yy is a year. The remaining fields are optional: hh, mm, and ss specify a time of day, and zzz selects a time zone. Note that if the time is left out, it defaults to midnight; thus if you select a range of "7 nov 86" - "8 nov 86", you will only get messages from the 7th, as all messages on the 8th will have arrived after midnight.

Date field specifies which date field in the header to look at for this date range; it probably won't be useful to anyone. If the sequence you're defining already exists, you can optionally merge the old set with the new; that's what the Yes and No buttons are all about. Finally, you can OK the whole thing, or Cancel it.

In general, most people will rarely use these features. However, it's nice to occasionally use Pick to find some messages, look through them, and then hit Delete Sequence to put things back in their original state.

Widget Hierarchy

In order to specify resources, it is useful to know the hierarchy of widgets which compose *xmh*. In the notation below, indentation indicates hierarchical structure. The widget class name is given first, followed by the widget instance name. The application class name is `Xmh`.

The hierarchy of the main toc and view window is identical for additional toc and view windows, except that a `topLevelShell` widget is inserted in the hierarchy between the application shell and the `Paned` widget.

```
Xmh xmh
        Paned xmh
                SimpleMenu  folderMenu
                        SmeBSB  open
                        SmeBSB  openInNew
                        SmeBSB  create
                        SmeBSB  delete
                        SmeLine  line
                        SmeBSB  close
                SimpleMenu  tocMenu
                        SmeBSB  inc
                        SmeBSB  commit
                        SmeBSB  pack
                        SmeBSB  sort
                        SmeBSB  rescan
                SimpleMenu  messageMenu
                        SmeBSB  compose
                        SmeBSB  next
                        SmeBSB  prev
                        SmeBSB  delete
                        SmeBSB  move
                        SmeBSB  copy
                        SmeBSB  unmark
                        SmeBSB  viewNew
```

```
        SmeBSB  reply
        SmeBSB  forward
        SmeBSB  useAsComp
        SmeBSB  print
SimpleMenu  sequenceMenu
        SmeBSB  pick
        SmeBSB  openSeq
        SmeBSB  addToSeq
        SmeBSB  removeFromSeq
        SmeBSB  deleteSeq
        SmeLine  line
        SmeBSB  all
SimpleMenu  viewMenu
        SmeBSB  reply
        SmeBSB  forward
        SmeBSB  useAsComp
        SmeBSB  edit
        SmeBSB  save
        SmeBSB  print
SimpleMenu  optionMenu
        SmeBSB  reverse
Viewport.Core  menuBox.clip
        Box  menuBox
                MenuButton  folderButton
                MenuButton  tocButton
                MenuButton  messageButton
                MenuButton  sequenceButton
                MenuButton  viewButton
                MenuButton  optionButton
Grip  grip
Label folderTitlebar
Grip  grip
Viewport.Core  folders.clip
        Box  folders
                MenuButton  inbox
                MenuButton  drafts
                        SimpleMenu  menu
                                SmeBSB <folder_name>
                                        .
                                        .
                                        .

Grip  grip
Label  tocTitlebar
Grip  grip
Text toc
        Scrollbar  vScrollbar
Grip  grip
Label  viewTitlebar
Grip  grip
```

Reference Pages

```
        Text  view
                Scrollbar  vScrollbar
                Scrollbar  hScrollbar
```

The hierarchy of the Create Folder popup dialog box:

```
transientShell  prompt
        Dialog  dialog
                Label  label
                Text  value
                Command  okay
                Command  cancel
```

The hierarchy of the Notice dialog box, which reports messages from mh:

```
transientShell  notice
        Dialog  dialog
                Label  label
                Text  value
                Command  confirm
```

The hierarchy of the Confirmation dialog box:

```
transientShell  confirm
        Dialog  dialog
                Label  label
                Command  yes
                Command  no
```

The hierarchy of the dialog box which reports errors:

```
transientShell  error
        Dialog  dialog
                Label  label
                Command  OK
```

The hierarchy of the composition window:

```
topLevelShell  xmh
        Paned  xmh
                Label  composeTitlebar
                Text  comp
                Viewport.Core  compButtons.clip
                        Box  compButtons
                                Command  close
                                Command  send
                                Command  reset
                                Command  compose
                                Command  save
                                Command  insert
```

The hierarchy of the view window:

```
topLevelShell  xmh
      Paned  xmh
             Label  viewTitlebar
             Text  view
             Viewport.Core  viewButtons.clip
                    Box  viewButtons
                           Command  close
                           Command  reply
                           Command  forward
                           Command  useAsComp
                           Command  edit
                           Command  save
                           Command  print
```

The hierarchy of the pick window:
(Unnamed widgets have no name.)

```
topLevelShell  xmh
      Paned  xmh
             Label  pickTitlebar
             Viewport.core  pick.clip
                    Form  form
                           Form
```

The first 6 rows of the pick window have identical structure:

```
                                  Form
                                         Toggle
                                         Toggle
                                         Label
                                         Text
                                         Command
                                  Form
                                         Toggle
                                         Toggle
                                         Text
                                         Text
                                         Command
                                  Form
                                         Command
             Viewport.core  pick.clip
                    Form  form
                           From
                                  Form
                                         Label
                                         Text
                                         Label
                                         Text
```

```
                    Form
                            Label
                            Text
                            Label
                            Text
                            Label
                            Text
                    Form
                            Label
                            Toggle
                            Toggle
                    Form
                            Command
                            Command
```

Application-specific Resources

Resource instance names begin with a lower case letter but are otherwise identical to the class name.

If `TocGeometry`, `ViewGeometry`, `CompGeometry`, or `PickGeometry` are not specified, then the value of `Geometry` is used instead. If the resulting height is not specified (e.g., "", "=500", "+0-0"), then the default height of windows is calculated from fonts and line counts. If the width is not specified (e.g., "", "=x300", "-0+0), then half of the display width is used. If unspecified, the height of a pick window defaults to half the height of the display.

Any of these options may also be specified on the command line by using the X Toolkit Intrinsics resource specification mechanism. Thus, to run *xmh* showing all message headers,

```
% xmh -xrm '*HideBoringHeaders:off'
```

The following resources are defined:

`Banner` A short string that is the default label of the folder, Table of Contents, and view. The default is:

```
xmh    MIT X Consortium    R4
```

`BlockEventsOnBusy`
Whether to disallow user input and show a busy cursor while *xmh* is busy processing a command. Default is true.

`BusyCursor` The name of the symbol used to represent the position of the pointer, displayed if `BlockEventsOnBusy` is true, when *xmh* is processing a time-consuming command. The default is `watch`.

`BusyPointerColor`
The foreground color of the busy cursor. Default is `XtDefault-Foreground`.

`CheckFrequency`
: How often to check for new mail, make checkpoints, and rescan the Table of Contents, in minutes. If `CheckNewMail` is true, *xmh* checks to see if you have new mail each interval. If `MakeCheckpoints` is true, checkpoints are made every fifth interval. Also every fifth interval, the Table of Contents is checked for inconsistencies with the file system, and rescanned. To prevent all of these checks from occurring, set `CheckFrequency` to 0. The default is 1.

`CheckNewMail`
: If true, *xmh* will check at regular intervals to see if new mail has arrived for any of the folders. A visual indication will be given if new mail is waiting to be retrieved. Default is True. (See "Bugs"). The interval can be adjusted with the `CheckFrequency`.

`CommandButtonCount`
: The number of command buttons to create in a button box in between the toc and the view areas of the main window. *xmh* will create these buttons with the names *button1*, *button2* and so on, in a box with the name *commandBox*. The user can specify labels and actions for the buttons in a private resource file; see the section on "Actions". The default is 0.

`CompGeometry`
: Initial geometry for windows containing compositions.

`Cursor`
: The name of the symbol used to represent the pointer. Default is `left_ptr`.

`DraftsFolder`
: The folder used for message drafts. Default is `drafts`.

`Geometry`
: Default geometry to use. Default is none.

`HideBoringHeaders`
: If "on", then *xmh* will attempt to skip uninteresting header lines within messages by scrolling them off. Default is on.

`InitialFolder`
: Which folder to display on startup. Can also be set with the command-line option `-initial`. Default is `inbox`.

`InitialIncFile`
: The file name of your incoming mail drop. *xmh* tries to construct a filename for the `inc -file` command, but in some installations (e.g., those using the Post Office Protocol) no file is appropriate. In this case, `InitialIncFile` should be specified as the empty string, and *inc* will be invoked without a `-file` argument. The default is to use the value of the environment variable MAIL, or if that is not set, to append the value of the environment variable USER to */usr/spool/mail/*.

Reference Pages

`MailPath` The full path prefix for locating your mail folders. May also be set with the command-line option, `-path`. The default is the Path component in *$HOME/.mh_profile*, or *$HOME/Mail* if none.

`MailWaitingFlag`
If true, *xmh* will attempt to set an indication in its icon when new mail is waiting to be retrieved. If this option is true, then CheckNewMail is assumed to be true as well. The `-flag` command line option is a quick way to turn MailWaitingFlag on.

`MakeCheckpoints`
If true, *xmh* will attempt to save checkpoints of volatile information. The frequency of checkpointing is controlled by the resource `CheckFrequency`.

`MhPath` What directory in which to find the *mh* commands. If a command isn't found here, then the directories in the user's path are searched. Default is */usr/local/mh6*.

`PickGeometry`
Initial geometry for pick windows.

`PointerColor`
The foreground color of the pointer. Default is `XtDefaultForeground`.

`PrefixWmAndIconName`
Whether to prefix the window and icon name with "xmh: ". Default is true.

`PrintCommand`
What sh command to execute to print a message. Note that standard output and standard error must be specifically redirected! If a message or range of messages is selected for printing, the full file paths of each message file is appended to the specified print command. The default is ''enscript >/dev/null 2>/dev/null''.

`ReplyInsertFilter`
A shell command to be executed when the Insert button is activated in a composition window. The full path and filename of the source message is added to the end of the command before being passed to *sh*(1). The default filter is *cat*; i.e., it inserts the entire message into the composition. Interesting filters are: *awk -e* '{print "   " $0}' or *<mh directory>/lib/mhl -form mhl.body*.

`ReverseReadOrder`
When true, the next message will be the message prior to the current message in the table of contents, and the previous message will be the message after the current message in the table of contents. The default is false.

`SendBreakWidth`
When a message is sent from *xmh*, lines longer than this value will be split into multiple lines, each of which is no longer than `SendWidth`. This value may be overridden for a single message by inserting an additional line in the

message header of the form `SendBreakWidth: value`. This line will be removed from the header before the message is sent. The default is 85.

`SendWidth` When a message is sent from *xmh*, lines longer than `SendBreakWidth` characters will be split into multiple lines, each of which is no longer than this value. This value may be overridden for a single message by inserting an additional line in the message header of the form `SendWidth: value`. This line will be removed from the header before the message is sent. The default is 72.

`SkipCopied` Whether to skip over messages marked for copying when using View Next Message and View Previous Message. Default is true.

`SkipDeleted` Whether to skip over messages marked for deletion when using View Next Message and View Previous Message. Default is true.

`SkipMoved` Whether to skip over messages marked for moving to other folders when using View Next Message and View Previous Message. Default is true.

`StickyMenu` If true, when popup command menus are used, the most recently selected entry will be under the cursor when the menu pops up. Default is false. See the file *clients/xmh/Xmh.sample* for an example of how to specify resources for pop up command menus.

`TempDir` Directory for *xmh* to store temporary directories. For privacy, a user might want to change this to a private directory. Default is */tmp*.

`TocGeometry` Initial geometry for master *xmh* windows.

`TocPercentage`
The percentage of the main window that is used to display the Table of Contents. Default is 33.

`TocWidth` How many characters to generate for each message in a folder's table of contents. Default is 100. Use 80 if you plan to use *mhl* a lot, because it will be faster, and the extra 20 characters may not be useful.

`ViewGeometry`
Initial geometry for windows showing only a view of a message.

Actions

Because *xmh* provides action procedures which correspond to command functionality and installs accelerators, users can customize accelerators in a private resource file. *xmh* provides action procedures which correspond to entries in the command menus; these are given in the sections describing menu commmands. For examples of specifying customized resources, see the file *clients/xmh/Xmh.sample*. Unpredictable results can occur if actions are bound to events or widgets for which they were not designed.

In addition to the actions corresponding to commands, these action routines are defined:

Reference Pages

`XmhPushFolder([foldername, ...])`
Pushes each of its argument(s) onto a stack of foldernames. If no arguments are given, the selected folder is pushed onto the stack.

`XmhPopFolder()`
Pops one foldername from the stack and sets the selected folder.

`XmhPopupFolderMenu()`
Should always be taken when the user selects a folder button. A folder button represents a folder and zero or more subfolders. The menu of subfolders is built upon the first reference, by this routine. If there are no subfolders, this routine will mark the folder as having no subfolders, and no menu will be built. In that case the menu button emulates a toggle button. When subfolders exist, the menu will popup, using the menu button action `PopupMenu()`.

`XmhSetCurrentFolder()`
Allows menu buttons to emulate toggle buttons in the function of selecting a folder. This action is for menu button widgets only, and sets the selected folder.

`XmhLeaveFolderButton()`
Insures that the menu button behaves properly when the user moves the pointer out of the menu button window.

`XmhPushSequence([sequencename, ...])`
Pushes each of its arguments onto the stack of sequence names. If no arguments are given, the selected sequence is pushed onto the stack.

`XmhPopSequence()`
Pops one sequence name from the stack of sequence names, which then becomes the selected sequence.

`XmhPromptOkayAction()`
Equivalent to pressing the okay button in the Create Folder popup.

`XmhCancelPick()`
Equivalent to pressing the cancel button in the pick window.

Customization Using mh

The initial text displayed in a composition window is generated by executing the corresponding *mh* command; i.e., *comp*, *repl*, or *forw*, and therefore message components may be customized as specified for those commands. *comp* is executed only once per invocation of *xmh* and the message template is re-used for each successive new composition.

Files

~/Mail
~/.mh_profile - *mh* profile
/usr/local/mh6 - *mh* commands
~/Mail/<folder>/.xmhcache - scan folder

~/Mail/<folder>/.mh_sequences - sequence definitions
/tmp - temporary files

See Also

X, xrdb, mh(1), enscript(1); Athena Widget Set; Volume Four, *X Toolkit Intrinsics Programming Manual*; Volume Five, *X Toolkit Intrinsics Reference Manual*

Bugs

Printing support is minimal.

Should handle the "unseen" message-sequence.

Should determine by itself if the user hasn't used *mh* before, and offer to create the *.mh_profile*, instead of hanging on *inc*.

Still a few commands missing (rename folder, remail message).

A bug in *mh* limits the the number of characters in *.mh_sequences* to BUFSIZ. When the limit is reached, the *.mh_sequences* file often becomes corrupted, and sequence definitions may be lost.

Except for the icon, there isn't an indication that you have new mail.

There should be a resource, `ShowOnInc`, which when true, would show the current message in the view after incorporating new mail.

The `CheckFrequency` resource should be split into two separate resources.

WM_SAVE_YOURSELF protocol is ignored.

WM_DELETE_WINDOW protocol doesn't work right when requesting deletion of the first toc and view, while trying to keep other *xmh* windows around.

Doesn't support annotations when replying to messages.

Copyright

Author

Terry Weissman, Digital Western Research Laboratory;
Modified by Donna Converse, MIT X Consortium.

Name

xmh – X window interface to the *mh* message handling system.

Syntax

xmh [-path *mailpath*] [-initial *foldername*] [-flag] [-*toolkitoption*]

Description

This reference page describes the Release 3 version of *xmh*, a window-oriented user interface to the *mh* message handling system. The Release 4 version is described on the preceding reference page in this guide.

xmh consists of user-interface code only. To actually do things with your mail, it makes calls to the *mh* package.

Please don't be misled by the size of this document. *xmh* really is easy to use!

Options

xmh accepts all of the standard X Toolkit command line options, as well as the following:

`-path` *mailpath*
: To specify an alternate collection of mail folders in which to process mail, use `-path` followed by the pathname of the alternate mail directory. The default mail path is the value of the Path component in *$HOME/.mh_profile*, or *$HOME/Mail* if the MH Path is not given.

`-initial` *foldername*
: Specifies an alternate folder that may receive new mail and is initially opened by *xmh*. The default initial folder is 'inbox'.

`-flag`
: Causes *xmh* to attempt to change the appearance of its icon when new mail arrives.

These three options have corresponding application-specific resources, named `MailPath`, `InitialFolder`, and `MailWaitingFlag`, which can be used in a resource file.

See *X* for a list of the standard Toolkit options.

Installation

The current version of *xmh* requires that the user is already set up to use *mh*, Version 6. To do so, see if there is a file called *.mh_profile* in your home directory. If it exists, check to see if it contains a line that starts with `Current-Folder`. If it does, then you've been using version 4 or earlier of *mh*; to convert to version 6, you must remove that line. (Failure to do so causes spurious output to standard error, which can hang *xmh* depending on your setup.)

If you do not already have a *.mh_profile*, you can create one (and everything else you need) by typing `inc` to the shell.

For more information, refer to the *mh*(1) documentation.

Running xmh

Run *xmh* as you would any other X application (e.g., *xterm*). It will accept a command-line display (of the form `-display [host]:server[.screen]` the default display is specified in the environment variable DISPLAY.

The rest of this document will probably be rather hard to follow without actually running *xmh* and seeing the things being described.

Basic Screen Layout

xmh starts out with a single screen. There will be 6 or 7 areas on the screen:

- A list of your folders. (New users of *mh* will see only "inbox" here.)
- A list of the global and folder-oriented commands.
- A list of the messages in one of your folders (initially, this will show the messages in "inbox").
- A list of the message-oriented commands.
- A view of one of your messages. (Initially this is blank.)
- A list of commands for the message being viewed.

And, there will possibly be:

- A list of message-sequences defined for this folder. This appears just below the list of messages in this folder. (Message-sequences are discussed below; if you don't know what they are, then you won't have any.)

xmh and the Toolkit

xmh uses the X Toolkit. Many of the features described below (scrollbars, buttonboxes, etc.) are actually part of the Toolkit, and are described here only for completeness. For more information, see the Toolkit documentation.

Scrollbars

Some parts of the screen will have a vertical area on the left containing a grey bar. This area is a *scrollbar*. They are used whenever the data in a window takes up more space than can be displayed. The grey bar indicates what portion of your data is visible. Thus, if the entire length of the area is grey, then you are looking at all your data. If only the first half is grey, then you are looking at the top half of your data.

You can use the pointer in the scrollbar to change what part of the data is visible. If you click with the middle button, then the top of the grey area will move to where the pointer is, and the corresponding portion of data will be displayed. If you hold down the middle button, you can drag around the grey area. This makes it easy to get to the top of the data: just press with the middle, drag off the top of the scrollbar, and release.

If you click with button 1, then the data to the right of the pointer will scroll to the top of the window. If you click with pointer button 3, then the data at the top of the window will scroll down to where the pointer is.

Buttonboxes

Any area consisting of many words or short phrases, each enclosed in a box, is called a *buttonbox*. Each box is actually a button that you can press by moving the pointer onto it and pressing pointer button 1. If a given buttonbox has more buttons in it than can fit, it will be displayed with a scrollbar, so you can always scroll to the button you want.

Adjusting the Relative Sizes of Areas on the Screen

If you're not satisfied with the size of the various areas on the screen, they can easily be changed. Near the right edge of the border between each region is a black box, called a *grip*. Simply point to that grip with the pointer, press a pointer button, drag up or down, and release. Exactly what happens depends on which pointer button you press.

If you drag with the middle button, then only that border will move. This mode is simplest to understand, but is probably the least useful.

If you drag with pointer button 1, then you are adjusting the size of the window above. *xmh* will attempt to compensate by adjusting some window below it.

If you drag with pointer button 3, then you are adjusting the size of the window below. *xmh* will attempt to compensate by adjusting some window above it.

All windows have a mininum and maximum size; you will never be allowed to move a border past the point where it would make a window have an invalid size.

Selected Folder

The selected folder is whichever foldername is highlighted in the top buttonbox. Note that this is not necessarily the same folder that is being viewed. To change the selected folder, just press on the desired folder button.

General Commands and Folder Commands

The second buttonbox contains commands of a global nature:

Quit XMH — Exits *xmh*, after first checking that you won't lose any changes.

Compose Message — Composes a new message. A new window will be brought up; for a description of it, see "Composition Windows," below.

Open Folder — Displays the data in the selected folder. Thus, the selected folder also becomes the viewed folder.

Open Folder in New Window — Creates a new screen, and displays the selected folder in that screen. Note, however, that you may not display the same folder in more than one screen at a time.

Create Folder — Creates a new folder. You will be prompted for a name for the new folder; to enter the name, point the pointer at the blank box provided and type. Hit the Confirm button when finished, or hit Abort to cancel this operation.

Delete Folder — Destroys the selected folder. You will be asked to confirm this action (see "Confirmation Windows").

Highlighted Messages, Selected Messages and the Current Message

It is possible to highlight a set of messages in the list of messages for the viewed folder. To highlight a message, just click on it with pointer button 1. To highlight a range of messages, click on the first one with pointer button 1 and on the last one with pointer button 3.

The selected messages are the same as the highlighted messages, if any. If no messages are highlighted, then the selected messages are considered the same as the current message.

The current message is indicated by a ''+'' next to the message number. It usually corresponds to the message currently being viewed.

Message Commands

The third buttonbox (fourth if you have message-sequences displayed) contains commands to deal with messages:

Incorporate New Mail
: Adds any new mail received to your inbox folder, and set the current message to be the first new message. (This button is selectable only if ''inbox'' is the folder being viewed.)

View Next Message
: Views the first selected message. If no messages are highlighted, view the current message. If current message is already being viewed, view the first unmarked message after the current message.

View Previous Message
: Views the last selected message. If no messages are highlighted, view the current message. If current message is already being viewed, view the first unmarked message before the current message.

Mark Deleted — Marks the selected messages for deletion. If no messages are highlighted, then this will automatically display the next unmarked message.

Mark Move — Marks the selected messages to be moved into the current folder. (If the current folder is the same as the viewed folder, this command will just beep.) If no messages are highlighted, then this will automatically display the next unmarked message.

Mark Copy — Marks the selected messages to be copied into the current folder. (If the current folder is the same as the viewed folder, this command will just beep.)

Unmark — Removes any of the above three marks from the selected messages.

View in New Window
: Creates a new window containing only a view of the first selected message.

Reply — Creates a composition window in reply to the first selected message.

Forward
: Creates a composition window whose body is initialized to be the contents of the selected messages.

Use as Composition
: Creates a composition window whose body is initialized to be this message. Note that any changes you make in the composition will also be saved in this message. This function is meant to be used with the "drafts" folder. (See "Composition Windows.")

Commit Changes
: Executes any deletions, moves, and copies that have been marked in this folder.

Print
: Prints the selected messages. *xmh* normally prints by invoking the *enscript* command, but you may change the command it uses. (See "Resources" below).

Pack folder
: Renumbers the messages in this folder so they start with 1 and increment by 1.

Sort folder
: Sorts the messages in this folder in chronological order. As a side effect, this also packs the folder.

Force Rescan
: Rebuilds the list of messages. This can be used whenever you suspect *xmh*'s idea of what messages you have is wrong. (In particular, this is useful if you ever change things using straight mh commands without using *xmh*.)

Pick Messages
: Defines a new message-sequence. (See "Message-Sequences.")

The following buttons will appear but will be sensitive only if the current folder has any message-sequences defined. (See "Message-Sequences.")

Open Sequence
: Changes the viewed sequence to be the same as the selected sequence.

Add to Sequence
: Adds the selected messages to the selected sequence.

Remove from Sequence
: Removes the selected messages from the selected sequence.

Delete Sequence
: Removes the selected sequence entirely. Note the messages themselves are not affected; they simply are no longer grouped together as a message-sequence.

View Windows

The commands in these windows are the same as the message commands by the same name, except instead of affecting the selected messages, they affect the viewed message. In addition there is the Edit View button, which allows you to edit the message being viewed. While editing, the Edit View button will change to a Save View button, which should be pressed to save your edits.

Composition Windows

Aside from the normal text editing functions, there are six command buttons associated with composition windows:

Close — Closes this composition window. If changes have been made since the most recent Save or Send, you will be asked to confirm losing them.

Send — Sends this composition.

Reset — Replaces the current composition with an empty message. If changes have been made since the most recent Send or Save, you will be asked to confirm losing them.

Compose — Brings up another new composition window.

Save — Saves this composition in your drafts folder. (If you do not have a folder named "drafts", one will be created.) Then you can safely close the composition. At some future date, you can continue working on the composition by opening your drafts folder, selecting the message, and using the Use as Composition command.

Insert — Inserts a related message into the composition. If the composition window was created with a Reply button, the related message is the message being replied to, otherwise no related message is defined and this button is inactive. The message will be filtered before being inserted; see `ReplyInsertFilter` under "Resources" below.

Text Editing Commands

All of the text editing commands are actually defined by the Text widget in the X Toolkit. The commands may be bound to different keys than the defaults described below through the standard X Toolkit key re-binding mechanisms. See the X Toolkit and Athena Widgets documentation for more details.

Whenever you are asked to enter any text, you will be using a standard text editing interface. Various control and meta keystroke combinations are bound to a somewhat Emacs-like set of commands. In addition, the pointer buttons may be used to select a portion of text or to move the insertion point in the text. Pressing pointer button 1 causes the insertion point to move to the pointer. Double-clicking button 1 selects a word, triple-clicking selects a paragraph, and quadruple-clicking selects everything. Any selection may be extended in either direction by using pointer button 3.

In the following, a *line* refers to one displayed row of characters in the window. A *paragraph* refers to the text between carriage returns. Text within a paragraph is broken into lines based on the current width of the window.

The following keystroke combinations are defined:

Control-A — Move to the beginning of the current line.

Control-B, Control-H, Backspace
Move backward one character.

Reference Pages

Control-D Delete the next character.

Control-E Move to the end of the current line.

Control-F Move forward one character.

Control-J, LineFeed
Create a new paragraph with the same indentation as the previous one.

Control-K Kill the rest of this line.

Control-L Refresh window.

Control-M, Return
New paragraph.

Control-N Move down to the next line.

Control-O Break this paragraph into two.

Control-P Move up to the previous line.

Control-V Move down to the next screenful of text.

Control-W Kill the selected text.

Control-Y Insert the last killed text.

Control-Z Scroll the text one line up.

Meta-< Move to the beginning of the document.

Meta-> Move to the end of the document.

Meta-[Move backward one paragraph.

Meta-] Move forward one paragraph.

Meta-B Move backward one word.

Meta-D Kill the next word.

Meta-F Move forward one word.

Meta-H, Meta-Delete
Kill the previous word.

Meta-I Insert a file. If any text is selected, use the selected text as the filename. Otherwise, a box will appear in which you can type the desired filename.

Meta-V Move up to the previous screenful of text.

Meta-Y Stuff the last selected text here. Note that this can be text selected in some other text subwindow. Also, if you select some text in an xterm window, it may be inserted in an *xmh* window with this command. Pressing pointer button 2 is equivalent to this.

Meta-Z Scroll the text one line down.

Delete Delete the previous character.

Confirmation Windows

Whenever you press a button that may cause you to lose some work or is otherwise dangerous, a window will appear asking you to confirm the action. This window will contain an Abort or No button and a Confirm or Yes button. Pressing the Abort button cancels the operation, and pressing the "Confirm" will proceed with the operation. (A very handy shortcut exists: if you press the original, offending button again, it will be interpreted as a Confirm. If you press any other command button, it will be interpreted as an Abort.)

Message-Sequences

An *mh* message sequence is just a set of messages associated with some name. They are local to a particular folder; two different folders can have sequences with the same name. In all folders, the sequence "all" is predefined; it consists of the set of all messages in that folder. (The sequence "cur" is also usually defined for every folder; it consists of only the current message. *xmh* hides "cur" from the user, instead placing a "+" by the current message. Also, *xmh* does not support the "unseen" sequence, so that one is also hidden from the user.)

The message sequences for a folder are displayed as buttons containing the names of the sequences (including one for "all"). The table of contents (aka "toc") is at any one time displaying one message sequence. This is called the "viewed sequence"; if it's not "all", its name will be displayed in the title bar just after the folder name. Also, at any time one of the sequence buttons will be highlighted. This is called the "selected sequence". Note that the viewed sequence and the selected sequence are not necessarily the same. (This all pretty much corresponds to the way the folder buttons work.)

The Open Sequence, Add to Sequence, Remove from Sequence, and Delete Sequence buttons are active only if the viewed folder contains message-sequences.

Note that none of the above actually effect whether a message is in the folder. Remember that a sequence is a set of messages within the folder; the above operations just affect what messages are in that set.

To create a new sequence, press the Pick button. A new window will appear, with lots of places to enter text. Basically, you can describe the sequence's initial set of messages based on characteristics of the message. Thus, you can define a sequence to be all the messages that were from a particular person, or with a particular subject, and so on. You can also connect things up with boolean operators, so you can select all things from "weissman" with the subject "xmh".

Hopefully, the layout is fairly obvious. The simplest cases are the easiest: just point to the proper field and type. If you enter in more than one field, it will only select messages which match all non-empty fields.

The more complicated cases arise when you want things that match one field or another one, but not necessarily both. That's what all the "or" buttons are for. If you want all things with the subject "xmh" or "xterm", just press the "or" button next to the "Subject:" field. Another box will appear where you can enter another subject.

Reference Pages

If you want all things either from ''weissman'' or with subject ''xmh'', but not necessarily both, select the -Or- button. This will essentially double the size of the form. You can then enter ''weissman'' in a from: box on the top half, and ''xmh'' in a subject: box on the lower part.

If you ever select the Skip button, then only those messages that *don't* match the fields on that row are included.

Finally, in the bottom part of the window will appear several more boxes. One is the name of the sequence you're defining. (It defaults to the name of the selected sequence when Pick was pressed, or to ''temp'' if ''all'' was the selected sequence.) Another box defines which sequence to look through for potential members of this sequence; it defaults to the viewed sequence when Pick was pressed.

Two more boxes define a date range; only messages within that date range will be considered. These dates must be entered in 822-style format: each date is of the form ''dd mmm yy hh:mm:ss zzz'', where dd is a one or two digit day of the month, mmm is the three-letter abbreviation for a month, and yy is a year. The remaining fields are optional: hh, mm, and ss specify a time of day, and zzz selects a time zone. Note that if the time is left out, it defaults to midnight; thus if you select a range of ''7 nov 86'' - ''8 nov 86'', you will only get messages from the 7th, as all messages on the 8th will have arrived after midnight.

Date field specifies which date field in the header to look at for this date range; it probably won't be useful to anyone. If the sequence you're defining already exists, you can optionally merge the old set with the new; that's what the Yes and No buttons are all about. Finally, you can OK the whole thing, or Cancel it.

In general, most people will rarely use these features. However, it's nice to occasionally use Pick to find some messages, look through them, and then hit Delete Sequence to put things back in their original state.

Resources

As with all standard X applications, *xmh* may be customized through entries in the resource manager. The following resource manager entries are defined: [Note: the entry names must be entered in either all lower-case, or in the exact case shown below.]

`BackGround` Background color. Currently, this will effect only buttons. (Default is white.)

`ButtonFont` What font to use for button names. (Default is timrom10.)

`CheckNewMail`
If True, *xmh* will check at regular intervals to see if new mail has arrived for any of the folders. A visual indication will be given if new mail is waiting to be retrieved. (Default is true.)

`CompButtonLines`
How many rows of buttons to display under a composition. (Default is 1.)

`CompFont` What font to use when composing a message. (Default is 6x13.)

`CompGeometry`
Initial geometry for windows containing compositions.

`CompLines` How many lines of a composition to display. (Default is 20.)

`ConfirmFont` What font to use for confirmation windows. (Default is timrom10b.)

`FolderButtonLines`
How many rows of folder command buttons to display. (Default is 1.)

`FolderLines` How many rows of foldername buttons to display. (Default is 1.)

`ForeGround` Foreground color. Currently, this will effect only title bars and buttons. (Default is black.)

`Geometry` Default geometry to use. (Default is none.)

`HideBoringHeaders`
If on, then *xmh* will attempt to skip uninteresting header lines within messages by scrolling them off. (Default is on.)

`InitialFolder`
Which folder to display on startup. May also be set with the command-line option `-initial`. (Default is inbox.)

`InitialIncFile`
The filename of your incoming mail drop. *xmh* tries to construct a filename for the `inc -file` command, but in some installations (e.g., those using the Post Office Protocol) no file is appropriate. In this case, `InitialIncFile` should be specified as the empty string, and *inc* will be invoked without a `-file` argument.

`LabelFont` What font to use for the title bars. (Default is timrom10i.)

`MailPath` The full path prefix for locating your mail folders. May also be set with the command-line option, `-path`. (Default is the Path component in $HOME/.mh_profile, or $HOME/Mail if none.)

`MailWaitingFlag`
If True, *xmh* will attempt to set an indication in it's icon when new mail is waiting to be retrieved. If this option is True, then CheckNewMail is assumed to be True as well. The `-flag` command line option is a quick way to turn `MailWaitingFlag` on.

`MhPath` What directory in which to find the mh commands. If a command isn't found here, then the directories in the user's path are searched. (Default is */usr/local/mh6*.)

`PickGeometry`
Initial geometry for pick windows.

`PickEntryFont`
What font to use for user text fields in pick windows. (Default is timrom10.)

`PickTextFont`
What font to use for static text fields in pick windows. (Default is timrom10.)

Reference Pages

`PrintCommand`
What shell command to execute to print a message. Note that standard output and standard error must be specifically redirected! If a message or range of messages is selected for printing, the full file paths of each message file is appended to the specified print command. (Default is "enscript >*/dev/null* 2>*/dev/null*").

`ReplyInsertFilter`
A shell command to be executed when the Insert button is activated in a composition window. The full path and filename of the source message is added to the end of the command before being passed to *sh*(1). The default filter is *echo*; i.e., it merely inserts the name of the file into the composition. Other interesting filters are *awk -e* '{print "   " $0}' or */usr/new/mh.6.5/ lib/mhl -form mhl.body*.

`TempDir` Directory for *xmh* to store temporary directories. For privacy, a user might want to change this to a private directory. (Default is */tmp*.)

`TocButtonLines`
How many rows of message command buttons to display. (Default is 1.)

`TocFont` What font to use for a folder's table of contents. (Default is 6x13.)

`TocGeometry` Initial geometry for master *xmh* windows.

`TocLines` How many messages to display in a folder's table of contents. (Default is 10.)

`TocWidth` How many characters to generate for each message in a folder's table of contents. (Default is 100. Use 80 if you plan to use *mhl* a lot.)

`ViewButtonLines`
How many rows of buttons to display under a view of a message. (Default is 1.)

`ViewFont` What font to use for a view of a message. (Default is 6x13.)

`ViewGeometry`
Initial geometry for windows showing only a view of a message.

`ViewLines` How many lines of a message to display. (Default is 20.)

If `TocGeometry`, `ViewGeometry`, `CompGeometry`, or `PickGeometry` are not specified, then the value of `Geometry` is used instead. If the resulting height is not specified (e.g., "", "=500", "+0-0"), then the default height is calculated from the fonts and line counts specified above. If the width is not specified (e.g., "", "=x300", "-0+0"), then half of the display width is used. If unspecified, the height of a pick window defaults to half the height of the display.

Any of these options may also be specified on the command line by using the standard X Toolkit resource specification mechanism. Thus, to run *xmh* showing all message headers,

```
% xmh -xrm '*HideBoringHeaders:off'
```

The initial text displayed in a composition window is generated by executing the corresponding *mh* command; i.e., *comp*, *repl*, or *forw* and therefore message components may be customized as specified for those commands. *comp* is executed only once per invocation of *xmh* and the message template is re-used for each successive new composition.

Files

~/Mail
~/.mh_profile

See Also

X, xrdb, mh - the *mh* Message Handler

Bugs

Printing support is minimal.

Keyboard shortcuts for commands would be nice.

Should handle the ''unseen'' message-sequence.

Should determine by itself if the user hasn't used *mh* before, and offer to set things up for him or her.

Still a few commands missing (rename folder, remail message).

Needs sub-folder support.

Copyright

Author

Terry Weissman, Digital Western Research Laboratory.

xmodmap

Name

xmodmap – keyboard and pointer modifier utility.

Syntax

xmodmap [*options*] [*filename*]

Description

xmodmap is a utility for displaying and altering the X keyboard *modifier map* and *keymap table* on the specified server and host. It is intended to be run from a user's X startup script to setup the keyboard according to personal tastes.

With no arguments, *xmodmap* displays the current map.

Options

-display [*host*]:*server*[.*screen*]
: Allows you to specify the host, server and screen to use. For example,

    xmodmap -display *your_node*:**0.0**

    specifies the screen 0 on server 0 on the machine *your_node*. If the host is omitted, the local machine is assumed. If the screen is omitted, the screen 0 is assumed; the server and colon (:) are necessary in all cases.

-help
: Indicates that a brief description of the command line arguments should be printed on the standard error. This will be done whenever an unhandled argument is given to *xmodmap*.

-grammar
: Indicates that a help message describing the expression grammar used in files and with -e expressions should be printed on the standard error.

-verbose
: Indicates that *xmodmap* should print logging information as it parses its input.

-quiet
: Turns off the verbose logging. This is the default.

-n
: Indicates that *xmodmap* should not change the mappings, but should display what it would do, like *make*(1) does when given this option. (Cannot be used with expressions to change the pointer mapping.)

-e *expression*
: Specifies an expression to be executed. Any number of expressions may be specified from the command line.

-pm
: Indicates that the current modifier map should be printed on the standard output.

-pk
: Indicates that the current keymap table should be printed on the standard output.

-pp
: Indicates that the current pointer map should be printed on the standard output.

– A lone dash means that the standard input should be used as the input file.

The `filename` specifies a file containing *xmodmap* expressions to be executed. This file is usually kept in the user's home directory and has a name like *.xmodmaprc*.

For compatibility with an older version, *xmodmap* also accepts the following obsolete single letter options:

`-[SLC12345]`
: These options indicate that all current keys for the Shift, Lock, Control, or Mod modifier sets should be removed from the modifier map. These are equivalent to `clear` expressions.

`-[slc]` *`keysym`*
: These options specify a *keysym* to be removed from the Shift, Lock, or Control modifier sets. These are equivalent to `remove` expressions.

`+[slc12345]` *`keysym`*
: These options specify a *keysym* to be added to the Shift, Lock, or Control modifier sets. These are equivalent to `add` expressions.

Expression Grammar

The *xmodmap* program reads a list of expressions and parses them all before attempting to execute any of them. This makes it possible to refer to keysyms that are being redefined in a natural way without having to worry as much about name conflicts. Allowable expressions include:

`keycode` *`NUMBER`* `=` *`KEYSYMNAME`* `...`
: The list of keysyms is assigned to the indicated keycode (which may be specified in decimal, hex or octal and can be determined by running the *xev* program in the examples directory). Usually only one keysym is assigned to a given code.

`keysym` *`KEYSYMNAME`* `=` *`KEYSYMNAME`* `...`
: The *`KEYSYMNAME`* on the left hand side is looked up to find its current keycode and the line is replaced with the appropriate `keycode` expression. Note that if you have the same keysym bound to multiple keys, this might not work.

`clear` *`MODIFIERNAME`*
: This removes all entries in the modifier map for the given modifier, where valid name are: Shift, Lock, Control, Mod1, Mod2, Mod3, Mod4 and Mod5 (case does not matter in modifier names, although it does matter for all other names). For example, "clear Lock" will remove any keys that were bound to the lock modifier.

`add` *`MODIFIERNAME`* `=` *`KEYSYMNAME`* `...`
: This adds the given keysyms to the indicated modifier map. The keysym names are evaluated after all input expressions are read to make it easy to write expressions to swap keys.

`remove` *`MODIFIERNAME`* `=` *`KEYSYMNAME`* `...`
: This removes the given keysyms from the indicated modifier map. Unlike `add`, the keysym names are evaluated as the line is read in. This allows you to remove keys from a modifier without having to worry about whether or not they have been reassigned.

`pointer = default`
: This sets the pointer map back to its default settings (button 1 generates a code of 1, button 2 generates a 2, etc.).

`pointer =` *`X Y Z`*
: This sets the pointer map to contain the button codes *X*, *Y* and *Z*, where *X*, *Y* and *Z* are numbers. The list always starts with the first physical button.

Lines that begin with an exclamation mark (!) are taken as comments.

If you want to change the binding of a modifier key, you must also remove it from the appropriate modifier map.

Examples

Many pointers are designed such that the first button is pressed using the index finger of the right hand. People who are left handed frequently find that it is more comfortable to reverse the button codes that get generated so that the primary button is pressed using the index finger of the left hand. This could be done on a 3 button pointer as follows:

```
% xmodmap -e "pointer = 3 2 1"
```

Many editor applications support the notion of Meta keys (similar to Control keys except that Meta is held down instead of Control). However, some servers do not have a Meta keysym in the default keymap table, so one needs to be added by hand. The following command will attach Meta to the Multi-language key (sometimes labeled Compose Character). It also takes advantage of the fact that applications that need a Meta key simply need to get the keycode and don't require the keysym to be in the first column of the keymap table. This means that applications that are looking for a Multi_key (including the default modifier map) won't notice any change.

```
% keysym Multi_key = Multi_key Meta_L
```

One of the more simple, yet convenient, uses of *xmodmap* is to set the keyboard's "rubout" key to generate an alternate keysym. This frequently involves exchanging Backspace with Delete to be more comfortable to the user. If the `ttymodes` resource in *xterm* is set as well, all terminal emulator windows will use the same key for erasing characters:

```
% xmodmap -e "keysym BackSpace = Delete"
% echo "XTerm*ttyModes: erase ^?" | xrdb -merge
```

Some keyboards do not automatically generate less than and greater than characters when the comma and period keys are shifted. This can be remedied with *xmodmap* by resetting the bindings for the comma and period with the following scripts:

```
!
! make shift-, be < and shift-. be >
!
keysym comma = comma less
keysym period = period greater
```

One of the more irritating differences between keyboards is the location of the Control and Shift Lock keys. A common use of *xmodmap* is to swap these two keys as follows:

```
!
! Swap Caps_Lock and Control_L
!
remove Lock = Caps_Lock
remove Control = Control_L
keysym Control_L = Caps_Lock
keysym Caps_Lock = Control_L
add Lock = Caps_Lock
add Control = Control_L
```

The *keycode* command is useful for assigning the same keysym to multiple keycodes. Although unportable, it also makes possible to write scripts that can reset the keyboard to a known state. The following script sets the backspace key to generate Delete (as shown above), flushes all existing caps lock bindings, makes the CapsLock key a control key, makes F5 generate Escape, and makes Break/Reset be a shift lock.

```
!
! On the HP, the following keycodes have key caps as listed:
!
!      101  Backspace
!       55  Caps
!       14  Ctrl
!       15  Break/Reset
!       86  Stop
!       89  F5
!

keycode 101 = Delete
keycode 55 = Control_R
clear Lock
add Control = Control_R
keycode 89 = Escape
keycode 15 = Caps_Lock
add Lock = Caps_Lock
```

Reference Pages

See Also

X

Bugs

Every time a `keycode` expression is evaluated, the server generates a `MappingNotify` event on every client. This can cause some thrashing. All of the changes should be batched together and done at once. Clients that receive keyboard input and ignore `MappingNotify` events will not notice any changes made to keyboard mappings.

xmodmap should generate `add` and `remove` expressions automatically whenever a keycode that is already bound to a modifier is changed.

There should be a way to have the `remove` expression accept keycodes as well as keysyms for those times when you really mess up your mappings.

Authors

Rewritten by Jim Fulton, MIT X Consortium, from an earlier version by David Rosenthal of Sun Microsystems.

Name

xpr – print an X window dump.

Syntax

xpr [*options*] [*filename*]

Description

xpr takes as input a window dump file produced by *xwd* and formats it for output on PostScript printers, the DEC LN03 or LA100, the IBM PP3812 page printer, or, as of Release 4, the HP LaserJet (or other PCL printers), or the HP PaintJet. If you do not give a file option, standard input is used. By default, *xpr* prints the largest possible representation of the window on the output page. Options allow you to add headers and trailers, specify margins, adjust the scale and orientation, and append multiple window dumps to a single output file. Output is sent to standard output unless you specify `-output` *filename*.

Options

`-device` *printer_device*

Specifies the device on which the file is to be printed. Currently the following printers are supported:

`ln03`	Digital LN03.
`la100`	Digital LA100.
`ljet`	HP LaserJet series and other monochrome PCL devices, such as ThinkJet, QuietJet, RuggedWriter, HP2560 series, and HP2930 series printers. (As of Release 4.)
`pjet`	HP PaintJet (color mode). (As of Release 4.)
`pjetxl`	HP PaintJet XL Color Graphics Printer (color mode). (As of Release 4.)
`pp`	IBM PP3812.
`ps`	PostScript printer.

The default printer, for historical reasons, is the LN03. `-device lw` (Apple LaserWriter) is equivalent to `-device pp` and is provided only for backwards compatibility.

`-scale` *scale*

Affects the size of the window on the page. The PostScript, LN03, and HP printers are able to translate each bit in a window pixel map into a grid of a specified size. For example, each bit might translate into a 3x3 grid. This is specified by `-scale 3`. By default, a window is printed with the largest scale that fits onto the page for the specified orientation.

`-height` *inches*

Specifies the maximum height of the page.

`-width` *`inches`*
Specifies the maximum width of the page.

`-left` *`inches`*
Specifies the left margin in inches. Fractions are allowed. By default, the window is centered on the page.

`-top` *`inches`* Specifies the top margin for the picture in inches. Fractions are allowed. By default, the window is centered on the page.

`-header` *`header`*
Specifies a header string to be printed above the window. Default is no header.

`-trailer` *`trailer`*
Specifies a trailer string to be printed below the window. Default is no trailer.

`-landscape` Prints the window in landscape mode. By default, a window is printed such that its longest side follows the long side of the paper.

`-portrait` Prints the window in portrait mode. By default, a window is printed such that its longest side follows the long side of the paper.

`-rv` Reverses the foreground and background colors.

`-compact` Compresses white pixels on PostScript printers.

`-output` *`filename`*
Specifies an output filename. If this option is not specified, standard output is used.

`-append` *`filename`*
Specifies a filename previously produced by *xpr* to which the window contents are to be appended.

`-noff` When specified in conjunction with `-append`, the window appears on the same page as the previous window.

`-split` *`n`* Allows you to split a window onto several pages. This might be necessary for large windows that would otherwise cause the printer to overload and print the page in an obscure manner.

`-plane` *`number`*
Specifies which bit plane to use in an image. The default is to use the entire image and map values into black and white based on color intensities. (Available as of Release 4.)

`-gray 2|3|4`
Uses a simple 2x2, 3x3, or 4x4 gray scale conversion on a color image, rather than mapping to strictly black and white. This doubles, triples, or quadruples the effective width and height of the image. (Available as of Release 4.)

`-psfig` Suppress translation of the PostScript picture to the center of the page. (Available as of Release 4.)

`-density` *dpi* Indicates what dot-per-inch density should be used by the HP printer. (Available as of Release 4.)

`-cutoff` *level*
Changes the intensity level where colors are mapped to either black or white for monochrome output on a LaserJet printer. (Available as of Release 4.) The *level* is expressed as percentage of full brightness. Fractions are allowed. (Available as of Release 4.)

`-noposition` Causes header, trailer, and image positioning command generation to be bypassed for LaserJet, PaintJet and PaintJet XL printers. (Available as of Release 4.)

`-gamma` *correction*
Changes the intensity of the colors printed by PaintJet XL printer. The *correction* is a floating point value in the range 0.00 to 3.00. Consult the operator's manual to determine the correct value for the specific printer. (Available as of Release 4.)

`-render` *algorithm*
Allows PaintJet XL printer to render the image with the best quality versus performance tradeoff. Consult the operator's manual to determine which *algorithms* are available. (Available as of Release 4.)

`-slide` Allows overhead transparencies to be printed using the PaintJet and PaintJet XL printers. (Available as of Release 4.)

Limitations

The current version of *xpr* can generally print out on the LN03 most X windows that are not larger than two-thirds of the screen. For example, it will be able to print out a large *emacs* window, but it will usually fail when trying to print out the entire screen. The LN03 has memory limitations that can cause it to incorrectly print very large or complex windows. The two most common errors encountered are "band too complex" and "page memory exceeded." In the first case, a window may have a particular band (a row six pixels deep) that contains too many changes (from black to white to black). This will cause the printer to drop part of the line and possibly parts of the rest of the page. The printer will flash the number '1' on its front panel when this problem occurs. A possible solution to this problem is to increase the scale of the picture, or to split the picture onto two or more pages. The second problem, "page memory exceeded," will occur if the picture contains too much black, or if the picture contains complex half-tones such as the background color of a display. When this problem occurs the printer will automatically split the picture into two or more pages. It may flash the number '5' on its from panel. There is no easy solution to this problem. It will probably be necessary to either cut and paste, or rework the application to produce a less complex picture.

There are several limitations on the use of *xpr* with the LA100: the picture will always be printed in portrait mode, there is no scaling, and the aspect ratio will be slightly off.

Support for PostScript output currently cannot handle the `-append`, `-noff` or `-split` options.

The `-compact` option is *only* supported for PostScript output. It compresses white space but not black space, so it is not useful for reverse-video windows.

For color images, should map directly to PostScript image support.

HP Printer Specifics (Release 4)

If no `-density` is specified on the command line, 300 dots per inch will be assumed for `ljet` and 90 dots per inch for `pjet`. Allowable *`density`* values for a LaserJet printer are 300, 150, 100, and 75 dots per inch. Consult the operator's manual to determine densities supported by other printers.

If no `-scale` is specified the image will be expanded to fit the printable page area.

The default printable page area is 8x10.5 inches. Other paper sizes can be accommodated using the `-height` and `-width` options.

Note that a 1024x768 image fits the default printable area when processed at 100 dpi with scale=1, the same image can also be printed using 300 dpi with scale=3 but will require considerably more data be transferred to the printer.

xpr may be tailored for use with monochrome PCL printers other than the LaserJet. To print on a ThinkJet (HP2225A) *xpr* could be invoked as:

```
% xpr -density 96 -width 6.667 filename
```

or for black-and-white output to a PaintJet:

```
% xpr -density 180 filename
```

The monochrome intensity of a pixel is computed as 0.30*R + 0.59*G + 0.11*B. If a pixel's computed intensity is less than the `-cutoff` level it will print as white. This maps light-on-dark display images to black-on-white hardcopy. The default cutoff intensity is 50% of full brightness. Example: specifying `-cutoff 87.5` moves the white/black intensity point to 87.5% of full brightness.

A LaserJet printer must be configured with sufficient memory to handle the image. For a full page at 300 dots per inch approximately 2MB of printer memory is required.

Color images are produced on the PaintJet at 90 dots per inch. The PaintJet is limited to sixteen colors from its 330 color palette on each horizontal print line. *xpr* will issue a warning message if more than sixteen colors are encountered on a line. *xpr* will program the PaintJet for the first sixteen colors encountered on each line and use the nearest matching programmed value for other colors present on the line.

Specifying the `-rv`, reverse video, option for the PaintJet will cause black and white to be interchanged on the output image. No other colors are changed.

Multiplane images must be recorded by *xwd* in ZPixmap format. Single plane (monochrome) images may be in either XYPixmap or ZPixmap format.

Some PCL printers do not recognize image positioning commands. Output for these printers will not be centered on the page and header and trailer strings may not appear where expected.

The `-gamma` and `-render` options are supported only on the PaintJet XL printers.

The `-slide` option is not supported for LaserJet printers.

The `-split` option is not supported for HP printers.

See Also

xwd, xdpr, xwud, X

Copyright

Authors

Michael R. Gretzinger, MIT Project Athena;
Jose Capo, MIT Project Athena (PP3812 support);
Marvin Solomon (University of Wisconsin);
Bob Scheifler, MIT;
Angela Bock and E. Mike Durbin, Rich Inc. (grayscale);
Larry Rupp, Hewlett-Packard (HP printer support).

Reference Pages

xprop

Name

xprop – display window and font properties for X.

Syntax

xprop [*options*]

Description

The *xprop* utility is for displaying window and font properties in an X server. One window or font is selected using the command line arguments or in the case of a window, by clicking on the desired window. A list of properties is then given, possibly with formatting information.

For each of these properties, its value on the selected window or font is printed using the supplied formatting information if any. If no formatting information is supplied, internal defaults are used. If a property is not defined on the selected window or font, "not defined" is printed as the value for that property. If no property list is given, all the properties possessed by the selected window or font are printed.

A window may be selected in one of four ways. First, if the desired window is the root window, the `-root` option may be used. If the desired window is not the root window, it may be selected in two ways on the command line, either by id number such as might be obtained from *xwininfo*, or by name if the window possesses a name. The `-id` option selects a window by id number in either decimal or hex (must start with 0x) while the `-name` option selects a window by name.

The last way to select a window does not involve the command line at all. If none of `-font`, `-id`, `-name`, and `-root` are specified, a crosshair cursor is displayed and the user allowed to choose any visible window by pressing any pointer button in the desired window. If it is desired to display properties of a font as opposed to a window, the `-font` option must be used.

Other than the above four options, the `-help` option for obtaining help, and the `-grammar` option for listing the full grammar for the command line, all the other command line options are used in specifing both the format of the properties to be displayed and how to display them. The `-len` *n* option specifies that at most *n* bytes of any given property will be read and displayed. This is useful, for example, when displaying the cut buffer on the root window which could run to several pages if displayed in full.

Normally each property name is displayed by printing first the property name, then its type (if it has one) in parentheses, followed by its value. The `-notype` option specifies that property types should not be displayed. The `-fs` option is used to specify a file containing a list of formats for properties, while the `-f` option is used to specify the format for one property.

The formatting information for a property actually consists of two parts, a *format* and a *dformat*. The *format* specifies the actual formatting of the property (i.e., is it made up of words, bytes, or longs?, etc.) while the *dformat* specifies how the property should be displayed.

The following paragraphs describe how to construct *formats* and *dformats*. However, for the vast majority of users and uses, this should not be necessary as the built in defaults contain the *formats* and *dformats* necessary to display all the standard properties. It should only be necessary to specify *formats* and *dformats* if a new property is being dealt with or the user dislikes the standard display format. New users especially are encouraged to skip this part.

A *format* consists of one of 0, 8, 16, or 32 followed by a sequence of one or more format characters. The 0, 8, 16, or 32 specifies how many bits per field there are in the property. Zero is a special case meaning use the field size information associated with the property itself. (This is only needed for special cases like type INTEGER which is actually three different types depending on the size of the fields of the property.)

A value of 8 means that the property is a sequence of bytes while a value of 16 would mean that the property is a sequence of words. The difference between these two lies in the fact that the sequence of words will be byte swapped while the sequence of bytes will not be when read by a machine of the opposite byte order of the machine that orginally wrote the property. For more information on how properties are formatted and stored, consult Volume One, *Xlib Programming Manual*.

Once the size of the fields has been specified, it is necessary to specify the type of each field (i.e., is it an integer, a string, an atom, or what?). This is done using one format character per field. If there are more fields in the property than format characters supplied, the last character will be repeated as many times as necessary for the extra fields. The format characters and their meaning are as follows:

- `a` The field holds an atom number. A field of this type should be of size 32.
- `b` The field is an boolean. A 0 means false while anything else means true.
- `c` The field is an unsigned number, a cardinal.
- `i` The field is a signed integer.
- `m` The field is a set of bit flags, 1 meaning on.
- `s` This field and the next ones until either a 0 or the end of the property represent a sequence of bytes. This format character is only usable with a field size of 8 and is most often used to represent a string.
- `x` The field is a hex number (like 'c' but displayed in hex - most useful for displaying window ids and the like).

An example *format* is 32ica which is the format for a property of three fields of 32 bits each, the first holding a signed integer, the second an unsigned integer, and the third an atom.

The format of a *dformat* (unlike that of a *format*) is not so rigid. The only limitations on a *dformat* is that it may not start with a letter or a dash. This is so that it can be distinguished from a property name or an option. A *dformat* is a text string containing special characters instructing that various fields be printed at various points in a manner similar to the formatting string used by *printf*. For example, the *dformat* " is ($0, $1 \)\n" would render the POINT 3, -4 which has a *format* of 32ii as " is (3, -4)\n".

Any character other than a $, ?, \, or a (in a *dformat* prints as itself. To print out one of $, ?, \, or (preceed it by a \. For example, to print out a $, use \$. Several special backslash sequences are provided as shortcuts. \n will cause a newline to be displayed while \t will cause a tab to be displayed. \o where *o* is an octal number will display character number *o*.

A $ followed by a number *n* causes field number *n* to be displayed. The format of the displayed field depends on the formatting character used to describe it in the corrsponding *format*. For example, if a cardinal is described by 'c' it will print in decimal while if it is described by a 'x' it will be displayed in hex.

If the field is not present in the property (this is possible with some properties), <field not available> is displayed instead. $*n*+ will display field number *n* then a comma then field number *n*+1 then another comma then ... until the last field defined. If field *n* is not defined, nothing is displayed. This is useful for a property that is a list of values.

A ? is used to start a conditional expression, a kind of if-then statement. ?*exp*(*text*) will display *text* if and only if *exp* evaluates to non-zero. This is useful for two things. First, it allows fields to be displayed if and only if a flag is set. And second, it allows a value such as a state number to be displayed as a name rather than just as a number. The syntax of *exp* is as follows:

```
exp ::= term | term=exp | !exp
term::= n | $n | mn
```

The ! operator is a logical "not", changing 0 to 1 and any non-zero value to 0. = is an equality operator. Note that internally all expressions are evaluated as 32 bit numbers so -1 is not equal to 65535. = returns 1 if the two values are equal and 0 if not. *n* represents the constant value *n* while $*n* represents the value of field number *n*. m*n* is 1 if flag number *n* in the first field having format character 'm' in the corrsponding *format* is 1, 0 otherwise.

Examples: ?m3(count: $3\n) displays field 3 with a label of count if and only if flag number 3 (count starts at 0!) is on. ?$2=0(True)?!$2=0(False) displays the inverted value of field 2 as a boolean.

In order to display a property, *xprop* needs both a *format* and a *dformat*. Before *xprop* uses its default values of a *format* of 32x and a *dformat* of " = { $0+ }\n", it searches several places in an attempt to find more specific formats. First, a search is made using the name of the property. If this fails, a search is made using the type of the property. This allows type STRING to be defined with one set of formats while allowing property WM_NAME which is of type STRING to be defined with a different format. In this way, the display formats for a given type can be overridden for specific properties.

The locations searched are in order: the format if any specified with the property name (as in 8x WM_NAME), the formats defined by `-f` options in last to first order, the contents of the file specified by the `-fs` option if any, the contents of the file specified by the environment variable XPROPFORMATS if any, and finally *xprop*'s built in file of formats.

The format of the files refered to by the `-fs` option and the XPROPFORMATS variable is one or more lines of the following form:

```
name format [dformat]
```

Where *name* is either the name of a property or the name of a type, *format* is the *format* to be used with *name* and *dformat* is the *dformat* to be used with *name*. If *dformat* is not present, " = $0+\n" is assumed.

Options

`-help` Prints out a summary of command line options.

`-grammar` Prints out a detailed grammar for all command line options.

`-id` *id* Allows the user to select window *id* on the command line rather than using the pointer to select the target window. This is very useful in debugging X applications where the target window is not mapped to the screen or where the use of the pointer might be impossible or interfere with the application.

`-name` *name* Allows the user to specify that the window named *name* is the target window on the command line rather than using the pointer to select the target window.

`-font` *font* Allows the user to specify that the properties of font *font* should be displayed.

`-root` Specifies that X's root window is the target window. This is useful in situations where the root window is completely obscured.

`-display` [*host*]:*server*[.*screen*]
Allows you to specify the server to connect to. For example,

xprop -display *your_node*:**0.1**

specifies screen 1 on server 0 on the machine *your_node*. If the host is omitted, the local machine is assumed. If the screen is omitted, the screen 0 is assumed; the server and colon (:) are necessary in any case.

`-len` *n* Specifies that at most *n* bytes of any property should be read or displayed.

`-notype` Specifies that the type of each property should not be displayed.

`-fs` *file* Specifies that file *file* should be used as a source of more formats for properties.

`-remove` *propname*
Specifies the name of a property to be removed from the indicated window.

`-f` *name format* [*dformat*]
Specifies that the format for *name* should be *format* and that the dformat for *name* should be *dformat*. If *dformat* is missing, " = $0+\n" is assumed.

`-frame` Specifies that when selecting a window by hand (i.e., if none of `-name`, `-root`, or `-id` are given), *xprop* should look at the window manager frame (if any) instead of looking for the client window. (Available as of Release 4.)

`-spy` Indicates that *xprop* should examine window properties forever, looking for property change events. (Available as of Release 4.)

Reference Pages

Examples

To display the name of the root window: `prop -root WM_NAME`

To display the window manager hints for the clock: `xprop -name xclock WM_HINTS`

To display the start of the cut buffer: `xprop -root -len 100 CUT_BUFFER0`

To display the point size of the fixed font: `xprop -font fixed POINT_SIZE`

To display all the properties of window # 0x200007: `xprop -id 0x200007`

Environment Variables

XPROPFORMATS — Specifies the name of a file from which additional formats are to be obtained.

See Also

X, xwininfo

Author

Mark Lillibridge, MIT Project Athena.

Name

xpseudoroot – create a pseudo root window.

Syntax

xpseudoroot [*options*]

Description

This client is available in Release 3 only. It is experimental and should be used with caution. (Please see Warning below.) *xpseudoroot* has been removed from the X distribution as of Release 4.

The *xpseudoroot* program allows you to create pseudo root windows as outlined in the *Inter-Client Communications Conventions Manual*. By default it just makes a copy of the normal root window, but command line options may be used to alter much of the screen-related information.

The command line argument *property_name* specifies the name of a property on the screen's real root window in which to store the pseudo root information. Applications can be run within the pseudo root window by appending *.property_name* to the *server.screen* part of the display name; for example: expo:0.0.*property_name*.

Warning

This is experimental code for implementing pseudo root windows as specified by the *Inter-Client Communications Conventions Manual*. The interfaces that it provides should be considered private to the MIT implementation of Xlib and *will change in the next release*. The interfaces that it provides should not be incorporated into any toolkits or applications. No effort will be made to provide backward compatibility.

Reference Pages

Options

-display [*host*]:*server*[.*screen*]

Allows you to specify the host, server and screen to connect to. *host* specifies the machine, *server* specifies the server number, and *screen* specifies the screen number. For example,

xpseudoroot -display *your_node*:0.1

specifies screen 1 of server 0 on the machine *your_node*. Either or both the *host* and *screen* elements to the display specification can be omitted. If *host* is omitted, the local machine is assumed. If *screen* is omitted, screen 0 is assumed (and the period is unnecessary). The colon and *server* are necessary in all cases.

-geometry *geometry*

The *xpseudoroot* window is created with the specified size and location determined by the supplied geometry specification. The -geometry option can be (and often is) abbreviated to -g, unless there is a conflicting option that begins with "g." The argument to the geometry option (*geometry*) is referred to as a "standard geometry string," and has the form *widthx-height±xoff±yoff*.

`-visuals` *`visualid`*
: Specifies a list of visuals to support on the pseudo root window. Any number of numeric visual identifiers (in hex, octal, or decimal) may be supplied using the `-visuals` option.

`-colormap` *`colormapid`*
: Specifies the numeric colormap identifier to be associated with the pseudo root window.

`-Colormap` *`visualid`*
: Specifies a numeric visual identifier to be used in creating a new colormap for the pseudo root window. If this option is given, *xpseudoroot* will create a new colormap from the given visual and set the black and white pixel fields to the desired colors.

`-white` *`pixel`*
: Specifies the numeric pixel value to use for `WhitePixel` when creating a new colormap with `-Colormap`. The default is to copy the real screen's `WhitePixel`.

`-White` *`colorname`*
: Specifies the color to use when setting `WhitePixel` in newly created colormaps. It may be used with *`-white`* to create arbitrary `WhitePixels`.

`-black` *`pixel`*
: Specifies the numeric pixel value to use for `BlackPixel` when creating a new colormap with `-Colormap`. The default is to copy the real screen's `BlackPixel`.

`-Black` *`colorname`*
: Specifies the color to use when setting `BlackPixel` in newly created colormaps. It may be used with `-black` to create arbitrary `BlackPixels`.

`-empty`
: Indicates that any colormaps created with `-Colormap` should not have `BlackPixel` and `WhitePixel` preallocated (although the values may still be set with `-black` and `-white`). This leaves as much room as possible for running applications that would otherwise not find enough colors. This is not for general use as it guarantees that an application will be displayed in incorrect colors.

`-max` *`number`*
: Specifies the maximum number of installed colormaps that will be allowed on this screen. The default is to use the real screen's value.

`-min` *`number`*
: Specifies the minimum number of installed colormaps that will be allowed on this screen. The default is to use the real screen's value.

`-backingstore` *`when`*
: Specifies when backing store window attributes will be honored and takes one of the following arguments: `NotUseful`, `WhenMapped`, or `Always`. The default is to use the real screen's value.

`-saveunders` *boolean*

Specifies whether or not this screen supports save-unders and takes one of the following arguments: `yes` or `no`.

`-name` *string*

Specifies the name to be used for the pseudo root window.

See Also

X, xdpyinfo, xwininfo, xprop; Volume One, *Xlib Programming Manual*

Bugs

This is a sample program that is primarily intended as a testbed for ICCCM pseudo roots. It should not be incorporated into any toolkit or application.

Author

Jim Fulton, MIT X Consortium.

xrdb

Name

xrdb – X server resource database utility.

Syntax

xrdb [*options*] [*filename*]

Description

xrdb is used to get or set the contents of the RESOURCE_MANAGER property on the root window of screen 0. You would normally run this program from your X startup file.

The resource manager (used by the Xlib routine *XGetDefault*(3X) and the X Toolkit) uses the RESOURCE_MANAGER property to get user preferences about color, fonts, and so on for applications. Having this information in the server (where it is available to all clients) instead of on disk, solves the problem in previous versions of X that required you to maintain *defaults* files on every machine that you might use. It also allows for dynamic changing of defaults without editing files.

For compatibility, if there is no RESOURCE_MANAGER property defined (either because *xrdb* was not run or the property was removed), the resource manager will look for a file called *.Xdefaults* in your home directory.

The *filename* (or the standard input if – or no input file is given) is optionally passed through the C preprocessor with the following symbols defined, based on the capabilities of the server being used:

SERVERHOST=*hostname*
HOST=*hostname*
: The hostname portion of the display to which you are connected.

WIDTH=*number*
: The width of the default screen in pixels.

HEIGHT=*number*
: The height of the default screen in pixels.

X_RESOLUTION=*number*
: The x resolution of the default screen in pixels per meter.

Y_RESOLUTION=*number*
: The y resolution of the default screen in pixels per meter.

PLANES=*number*
: The number of bit planes (the depth) of the root window of the default screen.

CLASS=*visualclass*
: One of StaticGray, GrayScale, StaticColor, PsuedoColor, TrueColor, DirectColor. This is the visual class of the root window of the default screen.

COLOR
: Defined only if CLASS is one of StaticColor, PsuedoColor, TrueColor, or DirectColor.

`BITS_PER_RBG=`*`number`*
: The number of significant bits in an RGB color specification. This is the log base 2 of the number of distinct shades of each primary that the hardware can generate. Note that it is usually not related to the number of `PLANES`.

`CLIENTHOST=`*`hostname`*
: The name of the host on which *xrdb* is running. (Available as of Release 4.)

`RELEASE=`*`number`*
: The vendor release number for the server. The interpretation of this number will vary depending on `VENDOR`. (Available as of Release 4.)

`REVISION=`*`number`*
: The X protocol minor version supported by this server (currently 0).

`VERSION=`*`number`*
: The X protocol major version supported by this server (should always be 11).

`VENDOR=`*`number`*
: A string specifying the vendor of the server. (Available as of Release 4.)

Lines that begin with an exclamation mark (!) are ignored and may be used as comments.

Options

xrdb accepts the following options:

`-help`
: This option (or any unsupported option) will cause a brief description of the allowable options and parameters to be printed.

`-display [`*`host`*`]:`*`server`*`[.`*`screen`*`]`
: Allows you to specify the host, server and screen to connect to. *`host`* specifies the machine, *`server`* specifies the server number, and *`screen`* specifies the screen number. For example:

  `xrdb -display` *`your_node`***`:0.0`**

  specifies screen 0 of server 0 on the machine *`your_node`*. If the host is omitted, the local machine is assumed. If the screen is omitted, screen 0 is assumed; the server and colon (:) are necessary in all cases.

`-cpp `*`filename`*
: Specifies the pathname of the C preprocessor program to be used. Although *xrdb* was designed to use CPP, any program that acts as a filter and accepts the `-D`, `-I`, and `-U` options may be used.

`-nocpp`
: Indicates that *xrdb* should not run the input file through a preprocessor before loading it into the RESOURCE_MANAGER property.

`-symbols`
: Indicates that the symbols that are defined for the preprocessor should be printed onto the standard output. This option can be used in conjunction with `-query`, but not with the options that change the RESOURCE_MANAGER property.

`-query` Indicates that the current contents of the RESOURCE_MANAGER property should be printed onto the standard output. Note that since preprocessor commands in the input resource file are part of the input file, not part of the property, they won't appear in the output from this option. The `-edit` option can be used to merge the contents of the property back into the input resource file without damaging preprocessor commands.

`-load` Indicates that the input should be loaded as the new value of the RESOURCE_MANAGER property, replacing whatever was there (i.e., the old contents are removed). This is the default action.

`-merge` Indicates that the input should be merged with, instead of replacing, the current contents of the RESOURCE_MANAGER property. Since *xrdb* can read the standard input, this option can be used to the change the contents of the RESOURCE_MANAGER property directly from a terminal or from a shell script. Note that this option does a lexicographic sorted merge of the two inputs, which is almost certainly not what you want, but remains for backward compatibility.

`-n` Indicates that changes to the property (when used with `-load`) or to the resource file (when used with `-edit`) should be shown on the standard output, but should not be performed. (Available as of Release 4.)

`-quiet` Indicates that warning about duplicate entries should not be displayed. (Available as of Release 4.)

`-remove` Indicates that the RESOURCE_MANAGER property should be removed from its window.

`-retain` Indicates that the server should be instructed not to reset if *xrdb* is the first client. (Available as of Release 4.)

`-edit` *`filename`*

Indicates that the contents of the RESOURCE_MANAGER property should be edited into the given file, replacing any values already listed there. This allows you to put changes that you have made to your defaults back into your resource file, preserving any comments or preprocessor lines.

`-backup` *`string`*

Specifies a suffix to be appended to the filename used with `-edit` to generate a backup file.

`-D`*`name`*`[=`*`value`*`]`

Is passed through to the preprocessor and is used to define symbols for use with conditionals such as *#ifdef*.

`-U`*`name`* Is passed through to the preprocessor and is used to remove any definitions of this symbol.

`-I`*`directory`* Is passed through to the preprocessor and is used to specify a directory to search for files that are referenced with *#include*.

Files

Generalizes *~/.Xdefaults* files.

See Also

X, XGetDefault(3X), Xlib Resource Manager

Bugs

The default for no arguments should be to query, not to overwrite, so that it is consistent with other programs.

Authors

Phil Karlton, rewritten from the original by Jim Gettys. Copyright 1988, Digital Equipment Corporation.

xrefresh

Name

xrefresh – refresh all or part of an X screen.

Syntax

xrefresh [*options*]

Description

xrefresh is a simple X program that causes all or part of your screen to be repainted. This is useful when system messages have displayed on your screen. *xrefresh* maps a window on top of the desired area of the screen and then immediately unmaps it, causing refresh events to be sent to all applications. By default, a window with no background is used, causing all applications to repaint "smoothly." However, the various options can be used to indicate that a solid background (of any color) or the root window background should be used instead.

Options

`-white` Use a white background. The screen just appears to flash quickly, and then repaints.

`-black` Use a black background (in effect, turning off all of the electron guns to the tube). This can be somewhat disorienting as everything goes black for a moment.

`-solid` *color*
Use a solid background of the specified color. Try green.

`-root` Use the root window background.

`-none` This is the default. All of the windows simply repaint.

`-geometry` *geometry*
Specifies the portion of the screen to be repainted. The `-geometry` option can be (and often is) abbreviated to `-g`, unless there is a conflicting option that begins with "g." The argument to the geometry option (*geometry*) is referred to as a "standard geometry string," and has the form *widthx-height±xoff±yoff*.

`-display` [*host*]:*server*[.*screen*]
Allows you to specify the server and screen to refresh. For example, *host* specifies the machine, *server* specifies the server number, and *screen* specifies the screen number. For example,

xrefresh -display *your_node*:**0.1**

specifies screen 1 of server 0 on the machine *your_node*. If the host is omitted, the local machine is assumed. If the screen is omitted, screen 0 is assumed; the server and colon (:) are necessary in all cases.

Resources

The *xrefresh* program uses the routine *XGetDefault*(3X) to read defaults, so its resource names are all capitalized.

`Black`, `White`, `Solid`, `None`, `Root`
: Determines what sort of window background to use.

`Geometry`
: Determines the area to refresh. Not very useful.

See Also

X

Bugs

It should have just one default type for the background.

Author

Jim Gettys, Digital Equipment Corp., MIT Project Athena.

Reference Pages

xset

Name

xset – user preference utility for X.

Syntax

xset [*options*]

Description

xset is used to set various user preference options of the display and keyboard.

Options

Note that not all X implementations are guaranteed to honor all of these options.

`-display [host]:server[.screen]`

Allows you to specify the host, server, and screen for which to set preferences. *host* specifies the machine, *server* specifies the server number, and *screen* specifies the screen number. For example,

```
-display your_node:0.1 &
```

specifies screen 1 of server 0 on the machine *your_node*. If the host is omitted, the local machine is assumed. If the screen is omitted, screen 0 is assumed; the server and colon (:) are necessary in all cases.

`b`

Controls bell volume, pitch, and duration. The `b` option accepts up to three numerical parameters (*volume*, *pitch*, and *duration*), a preceding dash (–), or an `on/off` flag. If no parameters are given, or the `on` flag is used, the system defaults will be used. If the dash or `off` are given, the bell will be turned off. If only one numerical parameter is given, the bell *volume* will be set to that value, as a percentage of its maximum. Likewise, the second numerical parameter specifies the bell *pitch*, in hertz, and the third numerical parameter specifies the *duration* in milliseconds. Note that not all hardware can vary the bell characteristics. The X server will set the characteristics of the bell as closely as it can to the user's specifications.

`-bc`
`bc`

Controls *bug compatibility* mode in the server, if possible. The option with a preceding dash (-) disables the mode; the option alone enables the mode.

The need for this option is determined by the following circumstances. Various pre-R4 clients pass illegal values in some protocol requests, and pre-R4 servers did not correctly generate errors in these cases. Such clients, when run with an R4 server, will terminate abnormally or otherwise fail to operate correctly. Bug compatibility mode explicitly reintroduces certain bugs into the X server, so that many such clients can still be run.

This mode should be used with care; new application development should be done with this mode disabled. Be aware that the server must support the MIT-SUNDRY-NONSTANDARD protocol extension in order for this option to work.

`c` — Controls key click. The `c` option can take an optional value, a preceding dash (–), or an `on/off` flag. If no parameter or the `on` flag is given, the system defaults will be used. If the dash or `off` flag is used, the keyclick will be disabled. If a value from 0 to 100 is given, it is used to indicate volume, as a percentage of the maximum. The X server will set the volume to the nearest value that the hardware can support.

`fp=` *`path`* — Sets the font path used by the server. *`path`* must be a directory or a comma-separated list of directories. The directories are interpreted by the server, not the client, and are server-dependent. (Directories that do not contain font databases created by *mkfontdir* will be ignored by the server.)

`fp default` — Restores the default font path.

`fp rehash` — Causes the server to reread the font databases in the current font path. This is generally only used when adding new fonts to a font directory (after running *mkfontdir* to recreate the font database).

`-fp` *`path`* or `fp-` *`path`*

The `-fp` and `fp-` options remove elements from the current font path. *`path`* must be a directory or comma-separated list of directories.

`+fp` *`path`* or `fp+` *`path`*

The `+fp` and `fp+` options prepend and append elements to the current font path, respectively. *`path`* must be a directory or comma-separated list of directories.

`led` — Controls the turning on or off of one or all of the LEDs. The `led` option accepts an optional integer, a preceding dash (–) or an `on/off` flag. If no parameter or the `on` flag is given, all LEDs are turned on. If a preceding dash or the flag `off` is given, all LEDs are turned off. If a value between 1 and 32 is given, that LED will be turned on or off depending on the existence of a preceding dash. A common LED which can be controlled is the Caps Lock LED. `xset led 3` would turn led #3 on. `xset -led 3` would turn it off. The particular LED values may refer to different LEDs on different hardware.

`m` — Controls the mouse parameters. The parameters for the mouse are *`acceleration`* and *`threshold`*. The mouse, or whatever pointer the machine is connected to, will go *`acceleration`* times as fast when it travels more than *`threshold`* pixels in a short time. This way, the mouse can be used for precise alignment when it is moved slowly, yet it can be set to travel across the screen in a flick of the wrist when desired. One or both parameters for the `m` option can be omitted, but if only one is given, it will be interpreted as the acceleration. If no parameters or the flag `default` is used, the system defaults will be set.

`p` — Controls pixel color values. The parameters are the color map entry number in decimal, and a color specification. The root background colors may be changed on some servers by altering the entries for `BlackPixel` and

Reference Pages

WhitePixel. Although these are often 0 and 1, they need not be. Also, a server may choose to allocate those colors privately, in which case an error will be generated. The map entry must not be a read-only color, or an error will result.

r — Controls the autorepeat. If a preceding dash or the `off` flag is used, autorepeat will be disabled. If no parameters or the `on` flag is used, autorepeat will be enabled.

s — Controls the screen saver parameters. The `s` option accepts up to two numerical parameters (*`time`* and *`cycle`*), a `blank/noblank` flag, an `expose/noexpose` flag, an `on/off` flag, or the `default` flag. If no parameters or the `default` flag is used, the system will be set to its default screen saver characteristics. The `on/off` flags simply turn the screen saver functions on or off. The `blank` flag sets the preference to blank the video (if the hardware can do so) rather than display a background pattern, while `noblank` sets the preference to display a pattern rather than blank the video. The `expose` flag sets the preference to allow window exposures (the server can freely discard window contents), while `noexpose` sets the preference to disable screen saver unless the server can regenerate the screens without causing exposure events. The *`time`* and *`cycle`* parameters for the screen saver function determine how long the server must be inactive for screen saving to activate, and the period to change the background pattern to avoid burn in, respectively. The arguments are specified in seconds. If only one numerical parameter is given, it will be used for the *`time`*.

q — Gives you information on the current settings. (In Release 3, the `query` option can also be used.)

These settings will be reset to default values when you log out.

See Also

X, Xserver, xmodmap, xrdb, xsetroot

Authors

Bob Scheifler, MIT Laboratory for Computer Science;
David Krikorian, MIT Project Athena (X11 version).

Name

xsetroot – root window parameter setting utility.

Syntax

`xsetroot` [*`options`*]

Description

xsetroot allows you to tailor the appearance of the root (background) window on a display. You can experiment with *xsetroot* until you find a look that you like, then put the *xsetroot* command that produces it into your X startup file. If you do not specify any options or you specify `-def`, the window is reset to its defaults. The `-def` option can be specified along with other options and only the non-specified characteristics will be reset to the default state.

Options

xsetroot accepts the following options.

Only one of the background color/tile changing options (`-solid`, `-gray`, `-grey`, `-bitmap`, or `-mod`) may be specified at a time. *`color`* can be specified as a color name or an RGB value.

`-help` Displays a brief description of the allowable options.

`-def` Resets unspecified attributes to the default values; the background to the gray mesh background and the pointer to the hollow X pointer. If you specify def and other options, only the non-specified options are reset to their defaults.

`-cursor` *`cursorfile maskfile`*

Specifies the cursor shape to use as the root window pointer. The *`cursorfile`* and *`maskfile`* are bitmaps made with the *bitmap* client. Refer to Chapter 6, *Graphics Utilities*, for more information on creating bitmaps. The mask file may need to be all black until you are accustomed to the way masks work. The default root window pointer is an X cursor.

`-cursor_name` *`standard_cursor_name`*

Changes the root window cursor to one of the standard cursors from the cursor font. See Appendix D for a list and pictures of the *Standard Cursors*. To specify a cursor name as an argument to a command line option, the `XC_` prefix must be stripped from the name. (This option is available as of Release 4.)

`-bitmap` *`filename`*

Uses the bitmap specified in the file to set the window pattern. The entire background is made up of repeated tiles of the bitmap. You can make your own bitmap files using the *bitmap* client or you can use those available with X, in the directory */usr/include/X11/bitmaps*. The default is gray mesh.

`-mod` *`x y`* Makes a plaid-like grid pattern on your screen. *x* and *y* are integers ranging from 1 to 16. Zero and negative numbers are taken as 1.

`-gray` or `-grey`
: Creates a grey background.

`-fg` *`color`*
: Sets the foreground color of the root window. Foreground and background colors are meaningful only in combination with `-cursor`, `-bitmap`, or `-mod`. The default is black.

`-bg` *`color`*
: Sets the background color of the root window. Foreground and background colors are meaningful only in combination with `-cursor`, `-bitmap`, or `-mod`. The default is white.

`-rv`
: Reverses the foreground color and the background color when used with another option such as `-mod`. `-rv` without another specified option returns the root (background) window to the default state.

`-solid` *`color`*
: Sets the root window color. The default is gray mesh.

`-name` *`string`*
: Sets the name of the background window to *`string`*. There is no default value. Usually, a name is assigned to a window so that the window manager can use a text representation when the window is converted to an icon. This option also allows a client to refer to the root window by name.

`-display [`*`host`*`]:`*`server`*`[.`*`screen`*`]`
: Allows you to specify the host, server, and screen of the root window. *`host`* specifies the machine, *`server`* specifies the server number, and *`screen`* specifies the screen number. For example,

```
% xsetroot -display your_node:0.1
```

specifies screen 1 of server 0 on the machine *`your_node`*. If the host is omitted, the local machine is assumed. If the screen is omitted, screen 0 is assumed; the server and colon (:) are necessary in all cases.

See Also

X, xset, xrdb

Author

Mark Lillibridge, MIT Project Athena.

Name

xstdcmap – X standard colormap utility.

Syntax

xstdcmap [*options*]

Description

Available as of Release 4, the *xstdcmap* utility can be used to selectively define standard colormap properties. It is intended to be run from a user's X startup script to create standard colormap definitions in order to facilitate sharing of scarce colormap resources among clients. Where at all possible, colormaps are created with read-only allocations.

Options

The following options may be used with *xstdcmap*:

`-display` *host*[:*server*][.*screen*]
: Allows you to specify the host, server and screen to connect to. *host* specifies the machine, *server* specifies the server number, and *screen* specifies the screen number. For example,

xstdcmap -display *your_node*:**0.1**

specifies screen 1 of server 0 on the machine *your_node*. Either or both the *host* and *screen* elements to the display specification can be omitted. If *host* is omitted, the local machine is assumed. If *screen* is omitted, screen 0 is assumed (and the period is unnecessary). The colon and *server* are necessary in all cases.

`-all` Specifies that all six standard colormap properties should be defined on each screen of the display. Not all screens will support visuals under which all six standard colormap properties are meaningful. *xstdcmap* will determine the best allocations and visuals for the colormap properties of a screen. Any previously existing standard colormap properties will be replaced.

`-best` Specifies that the RGB_BEST_MAP should be defined.

`-blue` Specifies that the RGB_BLUE_MAP should be defined.

`-default` Specifies that the RGB_DEFAULT_MAP should be defined.

`-delete` *map* Specifies that a standard colormap property should be removed. *map* may be one of: default, best, red, green, blue, or gray.

`-gray` Specifies that the RGB_GRAY_MAP should be defined.

`-green` Specifies that the RGB_GREEN_MAP should be defined.

`-help` Specifies that a brief description of the command line arguments should be printed on the standard error. This will be done whenever an unhandled argument is given to *xstdcmap*.

`-red` Specifies that the RGB_RED_MAP should be defined.

`-verbose` Specifies that *xstdcmap* should print logging information as it parses its input and defines the standard colormap properties.

See Also

X

Author

Donna Converse, MIT X Consortium.

Name

xterm – window terminal emulator.

Syntax

xterm [*options*]

Description

The *xterm* program is a terminal emulator for the X Window System. It provides DEC VT102 and Tektronix 4014 compatible terminals for programs that can't use the window system directly. If the underlying operating system supports terminal resizing capabilities (for example, the SIGWINCH signal in systems derived from BSD 4.3), *xterm* will use the facilities to notify programs running in the window whenever it is resized.

The VT102 and Tektronix 4014 terminals each have their own window so that you can edit text in one and look at graphics in the other at the same time. To maintain the correct aspect ratio (height/width), Tektronix graphics will be restricted to the largest box with a 4014's aspect ratio that will fit in the window. This box is located in the upper left area of the window.

Although both windows can be displayed at the same time, one of them is considered the *active* window for receiving keyboard input and terminal output. This is the window that contains the text cursor and whose border highlights whenever the pointer is in either window. The active window can be chosen through escape sequences, the VT Options menu in the VT102 window, and the Tek Options menu in the 4014 window.

The Release 4 version of *xterm* provides four menus that allow you to manipulate the VT102 and Tektronix windows: Main Options, VT Options, Tek Options, and VT Fonts. The first three menus are available (with slight variations) in Release 3, but have the names xterm, Modes, and Tektronix. The VT Fonts menu is available as of Release 4.

Options

xterm accepts all of the standard X Toolkit command line options along with the additional options described below. Note that if the option begins with a + instead of a –, the option is restored to its default value. (Specifying the default with `+option` can be useful for overriding the opposite value in an *.Xresources* file or other prior resource specification.)

`-help` Causes *xterm* to print out a verbose message describing its options.

`-132` Causes the VT102 DECCOLM escape sequence, which switches between 80 and 132 column mode, to be recognized, enabling the *xterm* window to resize properly. By default, the DECCOLM escape sequence is ignored. (See Appendix C for more information on *xterm* escape sequences.)

(This option can be turned on and off from the *xterm* VT Options menu, described below.)

`-ah/+ah` `-ah` specifies that *xterm* should *always* highlight the text cursor and window borders. By default, *xterm* will display a hollow text cursor whenever the focus is lost or the pointer leaves the window. `+ah` sets the default.

`-b` *innerborder*
: Specifies the width of the inner border (the distance between the outer edge of the characters and the window border) in pixels. The default is two pixels.

`-C`
: Specifies that the *xterm* window should receive console output. This is not supported on all systems.

`-cc` *characterclassrange*`:`*value*[,...]
: Sets classes indicated by the given ranges for use in selecting by words. See "Specifying Character Classes" below.

`-cn/+cn`
: `-cn` indicates that newlines should not be cut in line mode selections.

`+cn` indicates that newlines should be cut in line mode selections. (`-cn` and `+cn` are available as of Release 4.)

`-cr` *color*
: Specifies the color to use for the text cursor. The default is to use the same foreground color that is used for text.

`-cu/+cu`
: `-cu` enables the *curses* fix. Several programs that use the *curses*(3x) cursor motion package have some difficulties with VT102-compatible terminals. The bug occurs when you run the `more` program on a file containing a line that is exactly the width of the window and which is followed by a line beginning with a tab. The leading tabs are not displayed. This option causes the tabs to be displayed correctly.

`+cu` indicates that *xterm* should not work around this *curses* bug.

(This option can be turned on and off from the VT Options menu, described below.)

`-e` *command* [*arguments*]
: Specifies the command (and its arguments) to be run in the *xterm* window. It also sets the window title and icon name to be the name of the program being executed if neither `-T` or `-n` are given on the command line. The `-e` option, command and the arguments must appear last on the *xterm* command line, for example, `xterm -rv -e more bigfile &`.

`-fb` *font*
: Uses the specified font as the bold font. This font must be the same height and width as the normal font. If only one of the normal or bold fonts is specified, it is used as the normal font and the bold font is produced by overstriking this font. The default is to overstrike the normal font.

`-j/+j`
: `-j` indicates that *xterm* should do jump scrolling. Normally, text is scrolled one line at a time; this option allows *xterm* to move multiple lines at a time so that it doesn't fall as far behind. The use of jump scrolling is strongly recommended since it makes *xterm* much faster when scanning through large amounts of text. The VT100 escape sequences for enabling and disabling smooth scroll and the Enable Jump Scroll item of the VT Options menu can also be used to toggle this feature.

The `+j` option specifies that *xterm* not do jump scrolling.

(This option can be turned on and off from the VT Options menu, described below.)

`-l/+l` `-l` logs *xterm* input/output into a file called *XtermLog.xxxx* where *xxxx* represents the process ID number. To display your data, turn off logging using the *xterm* menu, then type `cat XtermLog.xxxx` at the *xterm* window prompt and the output file is sent to your *xterm* window. Logging allows you to keep track of the sequence of data and is particularly helpful while debugging code.

`+l` specifies that *xterm* not do logging.

(This option can also be turned on and off from the VT Options menu, described below.)

`-lf file` Specifies the file in which the data is written to rather than the default *XtermLog.xxxx* where *xxxx* is the process identification of *xterm* (the file is created in the directory that *xterm* is started in or the home directory for a login *xterm*). If `file` begins with a "|", then the rest of the string is assumed to be a command to be executed by the shell and a pipe is opened to the process.

`-ls/+ls` `-ls` indicates that the shell that is started in the *xterm* window be a login shell (i.e., the first character of argv[0] will be a dash, indicating to the shell that it should read the user's *.login* or *.profile*).

`+ls` indicates that the shell that is started should not be a login shell (i.e., it will be a normal "subshell.")

`-mb/+mb` `-mb` turns on the margin bell. Default is bell off.

`+mb` indicates that the margin bell should not be rung.

(This option can be turned on and off from the VT Options menu, described below.)

`-mc milliseconds`

Specifies the maximum time between multi-click selections. (Available as of Release 4.)

`-ms color` Sets the color of the pointer. The default is to use the foreground color.

`-nb number` Sets the distance at which the margin bell rings for the right margin. Default is 10 characters.

`-rw/+rw` `-rw` turns on the reverse-wraparound mode that allows the cursor to wraparound from the leftmost column to the rightmost column of the previous line. Allows you to backspace to the previous line and overstrike data or erase data with the spacebar.

`+rw` indicates that reverse-wraparound should not be enabled.

(This option can be turned on and off from the VT Options menu, described below.)

`-Sccn` Specifies the last two letters of the name of a pseudo-terminal to use in slave mode, plus the number of the inherited file descriptor. The option is parsed "%c%c%d". This allows *xterm* to be used as an input and output channel for an existing program and is sometimes used in specialized applications.

`-s` Allows *xterm* to scroll asynchronously with the display, meaning that the screen does not have to be kept completely up to date while scrolling. *xterm* saves data in memory which is displayed later. This allows *xterm* to run faster when network latencies are high and is useful when running *xterm* across a large internet or many gateways.

`+s` indicates that *xterm* should scroll synchronously.

`-sb/+sb` `-sb` indicates that some number of lines that are scrolled off the top of the window should be saved and that a scrollbar should be displayed at startup so those lines can be viewed.

`+sb` indicates that a scrollbar should not be displayed at startup.

(This option can be turned on and off from the VT Options menu, described below.)

`-sf/+sf` `-sf` indicates that the Sun function key escape codes should be generated for function keys.

`+sb` indicates that the standard escape codes should be generated for function keys. This is the default.

`-si/+si` `-si` disables repositioning the cursor at the bottom of the scroll region when the process sends output.

`+si` indicates that the cursor should be repositioned at the bottom of the scroll region on output.

(This option can be turned on and off from the VT Options menu, described below.)

`-sk/+sk` `-sk` causes the cursor to be repositioned at the bottom of the scroll region when a key is pressed.

`+sk` indicates that pressing a key while using the scrollbar should not cause the cursor to be repositioned at the bottom of the scroll region.

(This option can be turned on and off from the VT Options menu, described below.)

`-sl` *`number`* Specifies the maximum number of lines to be saved that are scrolled off the top of the window. Default is 64 lines.

`-t/+t` `-t` causes the startup *xterm* window to be the Tektronix window rather than the VT102 window.

`+t` causes the startup window to be the VT102 window. This is the default.

`-tm` *string* Specifies a series of terminal setting keywords followed by the characters that should be bound to those functions, similar to the *stty* program. (In Release 3, this is ignored when `-L` is given since *getty* resets the terminal. The `-L` option is not supported in Release 4.) Allowable keywords include: intr, quit, erase, kill, eof, eol, swtch, start, stop, brk, susp, dsusp, rprnt, flush, weras, and lnext. Control characters may be specified as ^char (e.g., ^c or ^u), and ^? may be used to indicate delete.

`-tn` *name* Specifies the name of the terminal type to be set in the TERM environment variable. This terminal type must exist in the *termcap*(5) database and should have *li#* and *co#* entries.

`-ut/+ub` `-ut` indicates that *xterm* shouldn't write a record into the the system log file */etc/utmp*.

`+ut` indicates that *xterm* should write a record into the system log file */etc/utmp*.

`-vb/+vb` `-vb` causes your terminal window to flash whenever an event occurs that would ordinarily cause your terminal bell to ring.

`+vb` indicates that a visual bell should not be used.

(This option can be turned on and off from the Main Options menu, described below.)

`-wf/+wf` `-wf` indicates that *xterm* should wait for the window to be mapped the first time before starting the subprocess so that the initial terminal size settings and environment variables are correct. It is the application's responsibility to catch subsequent terminal size changes.

`+wf` indicates that *xterm* should not wait before starting the subprocess.

The following X Toolkit options are commonly used with *xterm*:

`-geometry` *geometry*

xterm takes this geometry specification for the VT102 window. The `-geometry` option can be (and often is) abbreviated to `-g`, unless there is a conflicting option that begins with "g." The argument to the geometry option (*geometry*) is referred to as a "standard geometry string," and has the form *widthxheight±xoff±yoff*.

`-display [`*host*`]:`*server*`[.`*screen*`]`

By default, *xterm* obtains the host, server, and screen to use from the environment variable DISPLAY. However, you can also specify them using the `-display` option. *host* specifies which machine to create the window on, *server* specifies the server number, and *screen* specifies the screen number. For example,

xterm -display *your_node*:**0.1**

Reference Pages

specifies that an *xterm* be created on screen 1 of server 0 on the machine `your_node`. If the host is omitted, the local machine is assumed. If the screen is omitted, screen 0 is assumed; the server and colon (:) are necessary in all cases.

`-bd` *color* Sets the color of the border. Default of the highlighted border is black. Default of the unhighlighted border is gray.

`-bg` *color* Sets the background color of the *xterm* window. Default is white.

`-bw` *pixels* Specifies the width of the *xterm* window border in pixels. Default is one pixel.

`-fg` *color* Sets the color of the text (foreground). Default is black.

`-fn` *font* Uses the specified font instead of the default font (*fixed*). You can use any fixed-width font.

`-iconic` Causes *xterm* to display an *xterm* icon rather than an *xterm* window when it starts up.

`-name` *name* Specifies the application name under which resources are to be obtained, rather than the default executable filename. *name* should not contain "." or "*" characters.

`-title` *string*

Specifies the window title string, which may be displayed by window managers if the user so chooses. The default title is the command line specified after the `-e` option, if any, otherwise the application name.

`-rv` Reverses the foreground and background colors.

(This option can be turned on and off from the VT Options menu, described below.)

`-xrm` *resourcestring*

Specifies a resource string to be used with this instance of the application. This is especially useful for setting resources that do not have command line option equivalents.

The following command line arguments are provided for compatibility with older versions (prior to Release 3). They may not be supported in the next release as the X Toolkit provides standard options that accomplish most of the same tasks. The `-L` option has been eliminated in Release 4.

`-L` Indicates that *xterm* is being started by *init*. In this mode, *xterm* does not try to allocate a new pseudo-terminal as *init* has already done so. (`xterm` presumes that its file descriptors are already open on a slave pseudo-terminal.) In addition, the system program *getty* is run rather than the user's shell. This option is only used by *init*.

This option has been superceded by the *xdm* program. Furthermore, `-L` should never be specified by users when starting terminal windows. This option has been eliminated in Release 4.

`%`*`geometry`* Specifies the preferred size and location of the Tektronix window. It is shorthand for specifying the `tekGeometry` resource.

`#`*`geometry`* Specifies the preferred position of the icon. It is shorthand for specifying the `iconGeometry` resource. The width and height values of the geometry string are optional.

`-n` *`string`* Specifies the icon name for the *xterm* window. It is shorthand for specifying the `*iconName` resource. Note that this is not equivalent to the Toolkit option `-name`. The default icon name is the name of a program run with the `-e` option, if any, otherwise the application name.

`-r` Indicates that reverse video should be simulated by swapping the foreground and background colors. It is equivalent to `-rv`.

`-w` *`pixels`* Specifies the width in pixels of the border surrounding the window. It is equivalent to `-bw`.

`-T` *`string`* Specifies the title for the *xterm* window. It is equivalent to `-title`.

Resources

The program understands all of the core X Toolkit resource names and classes as well as:

`iconGeometry` (class `IconGeometry`)
Specifies the preferred size and position of the application when iconified. It is not necessarily obeyed by all window managers.

`termName` (class `TermName`)
Specifies the terminal type name to be set in the TERM environment variable.

`title` (class `Title`)
Specifies a string that may be used by the window manager when displaying this application.

`ttyModes` (class `TtyModes`)
Specifies a string containing terminal setting keywords and the characters to which they may be bound. (In Release 3, this resource is ignored when `-L` is given since *getty* resets the terminal. The `-L` option has been eliminated in Release 4.) Allowable keywords include: intr, quit, erase, kill, eof, eol, swtch, start, stop, brk, susp, dsusp, rprnt, flush, weras, and lnext. Control characters may be specified as ^*char* (e.g., ^c or ^u), and ^? may be used to indicate delete. This is very useful for overriding the default terminal settings without having to do an *stty* every time an *xterm* is started.

`utmpInhibit` (class `UtmpInhibit`)
Specifies whether or not *xterm* should try to record the user's terminal in */etc/utmp*.

`sunFunctionKeys` (class `SunFunctionKeys`)
Specifies whether or not Sun Function Key escape codes should be generated for function keys instead of standard escape sequences.

The following resources are specified as part of the `vt100` widget (class `VT100`):

`allowSendEvents` (class `AllowSendEvents`)
Specifies whether or not synthetic key and button events (generated using the X protocol `SendEvent` request) should be interpreted or discarded. The default is false meaning they are discarded. Note that allowing such events creates a very large security hole. (Available as of Release 4.)

`alwaysHighlight` (class `AlwaysHighlight`)
Specifies whether or not *xterm* should always display a highlighted text cursor. By default, a hollow text cursor is displayed whenever the pointer moves out of the window or the window loses the input focus.

`boldFont` (class `Font`)
Specifies the name of the bold font to use instead of overstriking the normal font.

`c132` (class `C132`)
Specifies whether or not the VT102 DECCOLM escape sequence should be honored. The default is false.

`charClass` (class `CharClass`)
Specifies comma-separated lists of character class bindings of the form [*`low`*–]*`high`*:*`value`*. These are used in determining which sets of characters should be treated the same when doing cut and paste. See "Character Classes" below.

`curses` (class `Curses`)
Specifies whether or not the last column bug in the cursor should be worked around. The default is false.

`background` (class `Background`)
Specifies the color to use for the background of the window. The default is white.

`foreground` (class `Foreground`)
Specifies the color to use for displaying text in the window. Setting the class name instead of the instance name is an easy way to have everything that would normally appear in the "text" color change color. The default is black.

`cursorColor` (class `Foreground`)
Specifies the color to use for the text cursor. The default is black.

`eightBitInput` (class `EightBitInput`)
Specifies whether or not eight-bit characters should be accepted. The default is true. (Available as of Release 4.)

`font` (class `Font`)
Specifies the name of the normal font.

`font1` (class `Font1`)
Specifies the name of the first alternate font. This font is toggled using the Tiny menu item on the VT Fonts menu. (Available as of Release 4.)

`font2` (class `Font2`)
Specifies the name of the second alternate font. This font is toggled using the Small menu item on the VT Fonts menu. (Available as of Release 4.)

`font3` (class `Font3`)
Specifies the name of the third alternate font. This font is toggled using the Medium menu item on the VT Fonts menu. (Available as of Release 4.)

`font4` (class `Font4`)
Specifies the name of the fourth alternate font. This font is toggled using the Large menu item on the VT Fonts menu. (Available as of Release 4.)

`geometry` (class `Geometry`)
Specifies the preferred size and position of the VT102 window.

`internalBorder` (class `BorderWidth`)
Specifies the number of pixels between the characters and the window border. The default is 2.

`jumpScroll` (class `JumpScroll`)
Specifies whether or not jump scroll should be used. The default is true.

`logFile` (class `Logfile`)
Specifies the name of the file to which a terminal session is logged. The default is `XtermLog.`*`xxxx`* (where *xxxx* is the process ID of *xterm*).

`logging` (class `Logging`)
Specifies whether or not a terminal session should be logged. The default is false.

`logInhibit` (class `LogInhibit`)
Specifies whether or not terminal session logging should be inhibited. The default is false.

`loginShell` (class `LoginShell`)
Specifies whether or not the shell to be run in the window should be started as a login shell. The default is false.

`marginBell` (class `MarginBell`)
Specifies whether or not the bell should be run when the user types near the right margin. The default is false.

`multiClickTime` (class `MultiClickTime`)
Specifies the maximum time in milliseconds between multi-clock select events. The default is 250 milliseconds. (Available as of Release 4.)

Reference Pages

`multiScroll` (class `MultiScroll`)
Specifies whether or not scrolling should be done asynchronously. The default is false.

`nMarginBell` (class `Column`)
Specifies the number of characters from the right margin at which the margin bell should be run, when enabled.

`pointerColor` (class `Foreground`)
Specifies the color of the pointer. The default is `XtDefaultForeground` color.

`pointerColorBackground` (class `Background`)
Specifies the background color of the pointer. The default is `XtDefault-Background` color. (Available as of Release 4.)

`pointerShape` (class `Cursor`)
Specifies the name of the shape of the pointer. The default is "xterm."

`reverseVideo` (class `ReverseVideo`)
Specifies whether or not reverse video should be simulated. The default is false.

`reverseWrap` (class `ReverseWrap`)
Specifies whether or not reverse-wraparound should be enabled. The default is false.

`saveLines` (class `SaveLines`)
Specifies the number of lines to save beyond the top of the screen when a scrollbar is turned on. The default is 64.

`scrollBar` (class `ScrollBar`)
Specifies whether or not the scrollbar should be displayed. The default is false.

`scrollInput` (class `ScrollCond`)
Specifies whether or not output to the terminal should automatically cause the scrollbar to go to the bottom of the scrolling region. The default is true.

`scrollKey` (class `ScrollCond`)
Specifies whether or not pressing a key should automatically cause the scrollbar to go to the bottom of the scrolling region. The default is false.

`scrollLines` (class `ScrollLines`)
Specifies the number of lines that the `scroll-back` and `scroll-forw` actions should use as a default. The default value is 1. (Available as of Release 4.) (See "Actions.")

`signalInhibit` (class `SignalInhibit`)
Specifies whether or not the entries in the Main Options menu for sending signals to *xterm* should be disallowed. The default is false.

`tekGeometry` (class `Geometry`)
Specifies the preferred size and position of the Tektronix window.

`tekInhibit` (class `TekInhibit`)
Specifies whether or not Tektronix mode should be disallowed. The default is false.

`tekSmall` (class `TekSmall`)
Specifies whether or not the Tektronix mode window should start in its smallest size if no explicit geometry is given. This is useful when running *xterm* on displays with small screens. The default is false. (Available as of Release 4.)

`tekStartup` (class `TekStartup`)
Specifies whether or not *xterm* should start up in Tektronix mode. The default is false.

`titeInhibit` (class `TiteInhibit`)
Specifies whether or not *xterm* should remove `ti` or `te` termcap entries (used to switch between alternate screens on startup of many screen-oriented programs) from the TERMCAP string.

`translations` (class `Translations`)
Specifies the key and button bindings for menus, selections, "programmed strings," etc. See "Actions" below.

`visualBell` (class `VisualBell`)
Specifies whether or not a visible bell (i.e., flashing) should be used instead of an audible bell when Control-G is received. The default is false.

`waitForMap` (class `WaitForMap`)
Specifies whether or not *xterm* should wait for the initial window map before starting the subprocess. The default is false. (Available as of Release 4.)

The following resources are specified as part of the `tek4014` widget (class `Tek4014`):

`width` (class `Width`)
Specifies the width of the Tektronix window in pixels.

`height` (class `Height`)
Specifies the height of the Tektronix window in pixels.

`fontLarge` (class `Font`)
Specifies the large font to use in the Tektronix window. (Available as of Release 4.) This font is toggled using the Large Characters item on the Tek Options menu.

`font2` (class `Font`)
Specifies font number 2 to use in the Tektronix window. (Available as of Release 4.) This font is toggled using the #2 Size Characters item on the Tek Options menu.

`font3` (class `Font`)
: Specifies font number 3 font to use in the Tektronix window. (Available as of Release 4.) This font is toggled using the #3 Size Characters item on the Tek Options menu.

`fontSmall` (class `Font`)
: Specifies the small font to use in the Tektronix window. (Available as of Release 4.) This font is toggled using the Small Characters item on the Tek Options menu.

As of Release 4, the resources that can be specified for the various menus are described in the documentation for the Athena SimpleMenu widget. The name and classes of the entries in each of the menus are listed below.

The `mainMenu` (title Main Options) has the following entries:

`securekbd` (class `SmeBSB`)
: Invokes the `secure()` action.

`allowsends` (class `SmeBSB`)
: Invokes the `allow-send-events(toggle)` action.

`logging` (class `SmeBSB`)
: Invokes the `set-logging(toggle)` action.

`redraw` (class `SmeBSB`)
: Invokes the `redraw()` action.

`line1` (class `SmeLine`)
: A separator.

`suspend` (class `SmeBSB`)
: Invokes the `send-signal(suspend)` action on systems that support job control.

`continue` (class `SmeBSB`)
: Invokes the `send-signal(cont)` action on systems that support job control.

`interrupt` (class `SmeBSB`)
: Invokes the `send-signal(int)` action.

`hangup` (class `SmeBSB`)
: Invokes the `send-signal(hup)` action.

`terminate` (class `SmeBSB`)
: Invokes the `send-signal(term)` action.

`kill` (class `SmeBSB`)
: Invokes the `send-signal(kill)` action.

`line2` (class `SmeLine`)
: A separator.

`quit` (class `SmeBSB`)
: Invokes the `quit()` action.

The `vtMenu` (title VT Options) has the following entries:

`scrollbar` (class `SmeBSB`)
: Invokes the `set-scrollbar(toggle)` action.

`jumpscroll` (class `SmeBSB`)
: Invokes the `set-jumpscroll(toggle)` action.

`reversevideo` (class `SmeBSB`)
: Invokes the `set-reverse-video(toggle)` action.

`autowrap` (class `SmeBSB`)
: Invokes the `set-autowrap(toggle)` action.

`reversewrap` (class `SmeBSB`)
: Invokes the `set-reversewrap(toggle)` action.

`autolinefeed` (class `SmeBSB`)
: Invokes the `set-autolinefeed(toggle)` action.

`appcursor` (class `SmeBSB`)
: Invokes the `set-appcursor(toggle)` action.

`appkeypad` (class `SmeBSB`)
: Invokes the `set-appkeypad(toggle)` action.

`scrollkey` (class `SmeBSB`)
: Invokes the `set-scroll-on-key(toggle)` action.

`scrollttyoutput` (class `SmeBSB`)
: Invokes the `set-scroll-on-tty-output(toggle)` action.

`allow132` (class `SmeBSB`)
: Invokes the `set-allow132(toggle)` action.

`cursesemul` (class `SmeBSB`)
: Invokes the `set-cursesemul(toggle)` action.

`visualbell` (class `SmeBSB`)
: Invokes the `set-visualbell(toggle)` action.

`marginbell` (class `SmeBSB`)
: Invokes the `set-marginbell(toggle)` action.

`altscreen` (class `SmeBSB`)
: This entry is currently disabled.

`line1` (class `SmeLine`)
: A separator.

`softreset` (class `SmeBSB`)
: Invokes the `soft-reset()` action.

`hardreset` (class `SmeBSB`)
Invokes the `hard-reset()` action.

`line2` (class `SmeLine`)
A separator.

`tekshow` (class `SmeBSB`)
Invokes the `set-visibility(tek,toggle)` action.

`tekmode` (class `SmeBSB`)
Invokes the `set-terminal-type(tek)` action.

`vthide` (class `SmeBSB`)
Invokes the `set-visibility(vt,off)` action.

The `fontMenu` (title VT Fonts) has the following entries:

`fontdefault` (class `SmeBSB`)
Invokes the `set-vt-font(d)` action.

`font1` (class `SmeBSB`)
Invokes the `set-vt-font(1)` action.

`font2` (class `SmeBSB`)
Invokes the `set-vt-font(2)` action.

`font3` (class `SmeBSB`)
Invokes the `set-vt-font(3)` action.

`font4` (class `SmeBSB`)
Invokes the `set-vt-font(4)` action.

`fontescape` (class `SmeBSB`)
Invokes the `set-vt-font(e)` action.

`fontsel` (class `SmeBSB`)
Invokes the `set-vt-font(s)` action.

The `tekMenu` (title Tek Options) has the following entries:

`tektextlarge` (class `SmeBSB`)
Invokes the `set-tek-text(l)` action.

`tektext2` (class `SmeBSB`)
Invokes the `set-tek-text(2)` action.

`tektext3` (class `SmeBSB`)
Invokes the `set-tek-text(3)` action.

`tektextsmall` (class `SmeBSB`)
Invokes the `set-tek-text(s)` action.

`line1` (class `SmeLine`)
A separator.

`tekpage` (class `SmeBSB`)
Invokes the `tek-page()` action.

`tekreset` (class `SmeBSB`)
Invokes the `tek-reset()` action.

`tekcopy` (class `SmeBSB`)
Invokes the `tek-copy()` action.

`line2` (class `SmeLine`)
A separator.

`vtshow` (class `SmeBSB`)
Invokes the `set-visibility(vt,toggle)` action.

`vtmode` (class `SmeBSB`)
Invokes the `set-terminal-type(vt)` action.

`tekhide` (class `SmeBSB`)
Invokes the `set-visibility(tek,toggle)` action.

The following resources are useful when specified for the Athena Scrollbar widget (`scrollBar`, class `ScrollBar`):

`thickness` (class `Thickness`)
Specifies the width in pixels of the scrollbar.

`background` (class `Background`)
Specifies the color to use for the background of the scrollbar.

`foreground` (class `Foreground`)
Specifies the color to use for the foreground of the scrollbar. The "thumb" of the scrollbar is a simple checkerboard pattern alternating pixels for foreground and background color.

The Release 3 version of *xterm* uses the menu widget, which accepts the following resources:

`menuBorder` (class `MenuBorder`)
Specifies the size in pixels of the border surrounding menus. The default is 2.

`menuFont` (class `Font`)
Specifies the name of the font to use for displaying menu items.

`menuPad` (class `MenuPad`)
Specifies the number of pixels between menu items and the menu border. The default is 3.

Emulations

The VT102 emulation is fairly complete, but does not support the blinking character attribute nor the double-wide and double-size character sets. *termcap* entries that work with *xterm* include "xterm", "vt102", "vt100" and "ansi". *xterm* automatically searches the *termcap* file in this order for these entries and then sets the TERM and the TERMCAP environment variables. Note that the "xterm" *termcap* entry distributed with X is not automatically installed.

Reference Pages

You must add it to */etc/termcap* yourself.

Many of the special *xterm* features (like logging) may be modified under program control through a set of escape sequences different from the standard VT102 escape sequences. (See Appendix E, *xterm Control Sequences*, in this guide.)

The Tektronix 4014 emulation is also fairly good. Four different font sizes and five different line types are supported. The Tektronix text and graphics commands are recorded internally by *xterm* and may be written to a file by sending the COPY escape sequence (or through the Tektronix menu; see below). The name of the file will be ``COPY*yy-MM-dd.hh:mm:ss*'', where *yy*, *MM*, *dd*, *hh*, *mm* and *ss* are the year, month, day, hour, minute and second when the COPY was performed (the file is created in the directory *xterm* is started in, or the home directory for a login *xterm*).

Pointer Usage

Once the VT102 window is created, *xterm* allows you to select text and copy it within the same or other windows.

The selection functions are invoked when the pointer buttons are used with no modifiers, and when they are used with the Shift key. The assignment of the functions described below to keys and buttons may be changed through the resource database; see "Actions" below.

Pointer button one (usually the left) is used to save text into the cut buffer. Move the cursor to the beginning of the text, and then hold the button down while moving the cursor to the end of the region and release the button. The selected text is highlighted and is saved in the global cut buffer and made the PRIMARY selection when the button is released. Double-clicking selects by words. Triple-clicking selects by lines. Quadruple-clicking goes back to characters, etc. Multiple-click is determined by the time from button up to button down, so you can change the selection unit in the middle of a selection. If the key/button bindings specify that an X selection is to be made, *xterm* will leave the selected text highlighted for as long as it is the selection owner.

Pointer button two (usually the middle) 'types' (pastes) the text from the PRIMARY selection, if any, otherwise from the cut buffer, inserting it as keyboard input.

Pointer button three (usually the right) extends the current selection. (You can swap "right" and "left" everywhere in the rest of this paragraph.) If pressed while closer to the right edge of the selection than the left, it extends/contracts the right edge of the selection. If you contract the selection past the left edge of the selection, *xterm* assumes you really meant the left edge, restores the original selection, then extends/contracts the left edge of the selection. Extension starts in the selection unit mode that the last selection or extension was performed in; you can multiple-click to cycle through them.

By cutting and pasting pieces of text without trailing new lines, you can take text from several places in different windows and form a command to the shell, for example, or take output from a program and insert it into your favorite editor. Since the cut buffer is globally shared among different applications, you should regard it as a 'file' whose contents you know. The terminal emulator and other text programs should be treating it as if it were a text file, i.e., the text is delimited by new lines.

The scroll region displays the position and amount of text currently showing in the window (highlighted) relative to the amount of text actually saved. As more text is saved (up to the maximum), the size of the highlighted area decreases.

Clicking button one with the pointer in the scroll region moves the adjacent line to the top of the display window.

Clicking button three moves the top line of the display window down to the pointer position.

Clicking button two moves the display to a position in the saved text that corresponds to the pointer's position in the scrollbar.

Unlike the VT102 window, the Tektronix window does not allow the copying of text. It does allow Tektronix GIN mode, and in this mode the cursor will change from an arrow to a cross. Pressing any key will send that key and the current coordinate of the cross cursor. Pressing button one, two, or three will return the letters 'l', 'm', and 'r', respectively. If the Shift key is pressed when a pointer button is pressed, the corresponding upper case letter is sent. To distinguish a pointer button from a key, the high bit of the character is set (but this bit is normally stripped unless the terminal mode is RAW; see *tty*(4) for details).

Menus

The Release 4 version of *xterm* has four different menus, titled Main Options, VT Options, Tek Options, and VT Fonts. The first three menus are available in Release 3 under the names xterm, Modes, and Tektronix. The VT Fonts menu is available as of Release 4.

Many of the menu items have been also been renamed in Release 4; however, most items have not changed in functionality. The following sections describe the items available on the Release 3 and 4 menus. In the sections describing the various menu items, if an item has simply been renamed, the Release 3 name appears in parentheses after the Release 4 name.

Each menu pops up under the correct combinations of key and button presses. Most menus are divided into two sections, separated by a horizontal line. The top portion contains various modes that can be specified. A check mark appears next to a mode that is currently active. Selecting one of these modes toggles its state. The bottom portion contains command entries; selecting one of these performs the indicated function. The menus are described in detail in the following sections.

Main Options Menu (Release 3: xterm Menu)

The Main Options menu (formerly xterm) is displayed when the Control key and pointer button one are simultaneously pressed in an *xterm* window. The modes section contains items that apply to both the VT102 and Tektronix windows. The modes can also be set by command line options when invoking *xterm*, or by entries in a resource startup file like *.Xresources* (see Chapter 9, *Setting Resources*). The menu selections enable you to change your mind once *xterm* is running.

All of the commands on this menu (except for Redraw Window) send a signal that is intended to affect the *xterm* process (Send INT Signal, Send TERM Signal, etc.). Given that your operating system may recognize only certain signals, every menu item may not produce the intended function.

Reference Pages

Four of these commands (Send HUP Signal, Send TERM Signal, Send KILL Signal, and Quit) send signals that are intended to terminate the *xterm* window. In most cases, you can probably end an *xterm* process simply by typing some sequence (such as Control-D or `exit`) in the window. Of course, the menu options may be helpful if the more conventional ways of killing the window fail.

Main Options Menu Mode Toggles (On/Off)

Visual Bell
: Causes your terminal window to flash whenever an event occurs that would ordinarily cause your terminal bell to ring. This item appears on the equivalent Release 3 menu (the xterm menu) only. In Release 4, it has been renamed Enable Visual Bell and moved to the VT Options menu.

Secure Keyboard
: Ensures that all keyboard input is directed *only* to *xterm*. Used when typing in passwords or other sensitive data in an unsecure environment. (See "Security" later in this reference page.)

Allow SendEvents (Release 4 only)
: Causes synthetic key and button events (generated using the X protocol `SendEvent` request) to be interpreted. Note that allowing such events creates a very large security hole.

Log to File (Release 3: Logging)
: Logs *xterm* input/output into a file in your home directory called *XtermLog.xxxxx* where *xxxxx* represents the process ID number of the *xterm* process. Logging allows you to keep track of the sequence of data and, therefore, is particularly helpful while debugging code.

To display the data contained in the log file, at the *xterm* window prompt, type:

```
more XtermLog.xxxxx
```

The output file is sent to your *xterm* window.

Be sure to turn Log to File off before displaying the log file in the *xterm* window. When Log to File is on, anything in the window is appended to the end of the log file. If you display the log file while logging is on, you will get into a continuous loop, much as if you typed `cat * > file`.

To find out the exact name of the log file, list the contents of your home directory, looking for a log file with an appropriate time and date. Note that if you turn logging on in multiple *xterm* windows, there will be multiple log files.

Main Options Menu Commands

Redraw Window (Release 3: Redraw)
: Redraws the contents of the window. (If you are using the *uwm* window manager, you can also do this with the Redraw selection of the *uwm* WindowOps menu. Or you can refresh the entire screen with the

xrefresh client or the Refresh Screen selection of the WindowOps menu. See Appendix B, *Using the uwm Window Manager*.)

Send STOP Signal (Release 3: Suspend program)
: Suspends a process (sends the SIGTSTP signal to the process group of the process running under *xterm*, usually the shell). If your system supports job control, you may also be able to suspend the process by typing Control-Z. If your system does not support job control, this menu item won't work either.

Send CONT Signal (Release 3: Continue program)
: Continues a process that has been suspended (technically speaking, this menu item sends the SIGCONT signal to the process group of the process running under *xterm*, usually the shell). The Send CONT Signals item is especially useful on systems with job control if you accidentally type Control-Z and suspend a process.

Send INT Signal (Release 3: Interrupt program)
: Interrupts a process (sends the SIGINT signal to the process group of the process running under *xterm*, usually the shell).

Send HUP Signal (Release 3: Hangup program)
: Hangs up the process (sends the SIGHUP signal to the process group of the process running under *xterm*, usually the shell). This usually ends up killing the *xterm* process, and the window disappears from the screen.

Send TERM Signal (Release 3: Terminate program)
: Terminates the process (sends the SIGTERM signal to the process group of the process running under *xterm*, usually the shell). This usually ends up killing the *xterm* process, and the window disappears from the screen.

Send KILL Signal (Release 3: Kill program)
: Kills the process (sends the SIGKILL signal to the process group of the process running under *xterm*, usually the shell). This ends up killing the *xterm* process, and the window disappears from the screen.

Quit
: Like Send HUP Signal, Quit sends the SIGHUP signal to the process group of the process running under *xterm*, usually the shell. This usually ends up killing the *xterm* process, and the window disappears from the screen.

  Quit is separated from the earlier commands by a horizontal line, so it's easier to point at. Sending a SIGHUP signal with Quit is also slightly more gentle to the system than using Send KILL Signal.

See *signal*(3C) in the *UNIX Programmer's Manual* for more information on what each signal does.

Reference Pages

VT Options Menu (Release 3: Modes Menu)

The VT Options menu (formerly Modes) menu sets various modes in the VT102 emulation and is displayed when the Control key and pointer button two are pressed in the VT102 window.

In the command section of this menu, the soft reset entry will reset scroll regions. This can be convenient when some program has left the scroll regions set incorrectly (often a problem when using VMS or TOPS-20). The full reset entry will clear the screen, reset tabs to every eight columns, and reset the terminal modes (such as wrap and smooth scroll) to their initial states just after *xterm* has finish processing the command line options.

VT Options Menu Mode Toggles (On/Off)

Most of these modes can also be set by command line options when invoking *xterm*, or by entries in a resource startup file like *Xresources* (see Chapter 9, *Setting Resources*). The menu selections enable you to change your mind once *xterm* is running.

Enable Scrollbar (Release 3: Scrollbar)
: Causes a scrollbar to appear on the left-hand side of the *xterm* window. Off by default.

Enable Jump Scroll (Release 3: Jump Scroll)
: Causes the window to move text several lines at a time rather than line by line. On by default.

Enable Reverse Video (Release 3: Reverse Video)
: Reverses the foreground and background colors. Off by default.

Enable Auto Wraparound (Release 3: Auto Wraparound)
: Wraps the text or data to the next line automatically when the cursor reaches the window border on input. On by default.

Enable Reverse Wraparound (Release 3: Reverse Wraparound)
: Allows the cursor to wrap around from the leftmost column to the rightmost column of the previous line. Allows you to backspace to the previous line and overstrike data or erase data with the space bar. Off by default.

Enable Auto Linefeed (Release 3: Auto Linefeed)
: Generates a linefeed automatically. This is useful if you are using a program that generates a carriage return without dropping down a line on your screen. Off by default. (This option is usually not needed on UNIX systems.)

Enable Application Cursor Keys (Release 3: Application Cursor Mode)
: Generates ANSI escape sequences rather than standard cursor movement when you use the arrow keys. This option may be useful when working with certain applications. Off by default.

The following table lists the ANSI characters generated by application cursors.

Cursor Key (Arrow)	Reset (Cursor)	Set (Application)
Up	ESC [A	ESC O A
Down	ESC [B	ESC O B
Right	ESC [C	ESC O C
Left	ESC [D	ESC O D

Enable Application Keypad (Release 3: Application Keypad Mode)
Generates a control function rather than a numeric character when you use the numeric keypad. Off by default.

Scroll to Bottom on Key Press
Indicates that pressing a key while using the scrollbar causes the cursor to be repositioned at the bottom of the scroll region. For example, if you have scrolled up the window to see past history, as soon as you begin typing your next command the cursor jumps to the bottom of the screen. Off by default.

Scroll to Bottom on Tty Output
Indicates that receiving output to the window (or pressing a key, if `stty echo` has been specified), while using the scrollbar causes the cursor to be repositioned at the bottom of the scroll region. In Release 4, on by default. (In Release 3, off by default; on automatically if the window has a scrollbar.) This mode can be toggled off, but is generally desirable to have.

Allow 80/132 Column Switching (Release 3: Allow 80/132 switching)
Allows *xterm* to recognize the DECCOLM escape sequence, which switches the terminal between 80 and 132-column mode. The DECCOLM escape sequence can be included in a program (such as a spreadsheet) to allow the program to display in 132-column format. See Appendix E, *xterm Control Sequences*, for more information. Off by default.

Enable Curses Emulation (Release 3: Curses Emulation)
Enables the *curses* fix. Several programs that use the *curses* cursor motion package have some difficulties with VT102-compatible terminals. The bug occurs when you run the *more* program on a file containing a line that is exactly the width of the window and that is followed by a line beginning with a tab. The leading tabs may disappear. This mode causes the tabs to be displayed correctly. Off by default.

Enable Visual Bell
Causes your terminal window to flash whenever an event occurs that would ordinarily cause your terminal bell to ring. This item appears as

Visual Bell on the Release 3 xterm menu. In Release 4, it has been renamed Enable Visual Bell and moved to the VT Options menu.

Enable Margin Bell (Release 3: Margin Bell)
Turns on the margin bell. Off by default.

Tek Window Showing
Shows the current contents of the Tektronix window; you cannot input to that window until you choose Switch to Tek Mode. Off by default. This item is a mode toggle on the equivalent Release 3 menu (Modes). In
Release 4, it has been renamed and moved to the commands section, as described below.

Show Alternate Screen (Release 3: Alternate Screen)
Informs you that you are looking at the alternate screen. You cannot select this mode from the menu. If a check mark appears beside this mode, you are viewing the alternate screen. Off by default.

VT Options Menu Commands

These commands can only be invoked from the menu; there are no alternative ways to perform the same functions.

Do Soft Reset (Release 3: Soft Reset)
Resets the terminal scroll region from partial scroll (a portion of the window) to full scroll (the entire window). Use this command when a program has left the scroll region set incorrectly.

Do Full Reset (Release 3: Full Reset)
Clears the window, resets tabs to every eight columns, and resets the terminal modes such as auto wraparound and jump scroll to their initial states.

Show Tek Window (Release 3: Tek Window Showing)
Shows the current contents of the Tektronix window; you cannot input to that window until you choose Switch to Tek Mode. Off by default. The Release 3 item appeared in the mode toggles section of the menu; the item has been renamed and moved to the commands section in Release 4.

Switch to Tek Mode (Release 3: Select Tek Mode)
Brings up a Tektronix window. You can input to this window.

Hide VT Window
Removes the VT window but does not destroy it. It can be brought back by choosing Select VT Mode from the Tek Options menu.

Tek Options Menu (Release 3: Tektronix Menu)

The Tek Options menu (formerly Tektronix) sets various modes in the Tektronix emulation, and is displayed when the Control key and pointer button two are pressed in the Tektronix window. The current font size is checked in the modes section of the menu. The PAGE entry in the command section clears the Tektronix window.

Tek Options Menu Mode Toggles (On/Off)

These modes can only be set from the Tek Options menu.

Large Characters #2 Size Characters #3 Size Characters Small Characters	Selecting one of these four options sets the point size of text displayed in the Tektronix window. The four options are mutually exclusive.
VT Window Showing	Shows the current contents of the VT102 window; you cannot input to that window until you choose Switch to VT Mode. This item is a mode toggle on the equivalent Release 3 menu (Tektronix). In Release 4, it has been renamed and moved to the commands section, as described below.

Tek Options Menu Commands

PAGE	Clears the Tektronix window.
RESET	Closes down the Tektronix window.
COPY	Writes a file of the Tektronix text and graphics commands.

Show VT Window (Release 3: VT Window Showing)

Shows the current contents of the VT102 window; you cannot input to that window until you choose Switch to VT Mode. The Release 3 item appeared in the mode toggles section of the menu; the item has been renamed and moved to the commands section in Release 4.

Switch to VT Mode (Release 3: Select VT Mode)

Makes the associated VT102 window active for input.

Hide Tek Window	Removes the Tektronix window but does not destroy it. It can be brought back by choosing Switch to Tek Mode from the VT Options Menu menu.

VT Fonts Menu (Release 4)

Added in Release 4, the VT Fonts menu enables you to change the VT102 display font dynamically. The menu is displayed when the Control key and pointer button three are pressed in the VT102 window. All items on the menu toggle different display fonts. The items are mutually exclusive. A checkmark appears on the menu next to the current font.

Default Tiny Small Medium Large	Selecting one of these five options sets the point size of text displayed in the VT102 window. The Default font is the font specified when the *xterm* was run.
Escape Sequence	Allows you to select a font previously toggled using an escape sequence. See Chapter 5, *Font Specification*, for the escape sequence to use.

Selection — Allows you to toggle a font whose name you've previously selected with the pointer or using the select button of the *xfontsel* client. See Chapter 5, *Font Specification*, for more information.

Security

X environments differ in their security consciousness. MIT servers, run under *xdm*, are capable of using a ''magic cookie'' authorization scheme that can provide a reasonable level of security for many people. If your server is only using a host-based mechanism to control access to the server (see *xhost*), then if you enable access for a host and other users are also permitted to run clients on that same host, there is every possibility that someone can run an application that will use the basic services of the X protocol to snoop on your activities, potentially capturing a transcript of everything you type at the keyboard. This is of particular concern when you want to type in a password or other sensitive data. The best solution to this problem is to use a better authorization mechanism that host-based control, but a simple mechanism exists for protecting keyboard input in *xterm*.

The Main Options menu (see "Menus" above) contains a Secure Keyboard entry which, when enabled, ensures that all keyboard input is directed *only* to *xterm* (using the `GrabKeyboard` protocol request). When an application prompts you for a password (or other sensitive data), you can enable Secure Keyboard using the menu, type in the data, and then disable Secure Keyboard using the menu again. Only one X client at a time can secure the keyboard, so when you attempt to enable Secure Keyboard it may fail. In this case, the bell will sound. If the Secure Keyboard succeeds, the foreground and background colors will be exchanged (as if you selected the Enable Reverse Video entry in the VT Options menu); they will be exchanged again when you exit secure mode. If the colors do *not* switch, then you should be *very* suspicious that you are being spoofed. If the application you are running displays a prompt before asking for the password, it is safest to enter secure mode *before* the prompt gets displayed, and to make sure that the prompt gets displayed correctly (in the new colors), to minimize the probability of spoofing. You can also bring up the menu again and make sure that a check mark appears next to the entry.

Secure Keyboard mode will be disabled automatically if your xterm window becomes iconified (or otherwise unmapped), or if you start up a reparenting window manager (that places a title bar or other decoration around the window) while in Secure Keyboard mode. (This is a feature of the X protocol not easily overcome.) When this happens, the foreground and background colors will be switched back and the bell will sound in warning.

Character Classes

Clicking the middle mouse button twice in rapid succession will cause all characters of the same class (e.g., letters, white space, punctuation) to be selected. Since different people have different preferences for what should be selected (for example, should filenames be selected as a whole or only the separate subnames), the default mapping can be overridden through the use of the `charClass` (class `CharClass`) resource.

This resource is simply a list of `range:value` pairs where the range is either a single number or *low-high* in the range of 0 to 127, corresponding to the ASCII code for the character or characters to be set. The `value` is arbitrary, although the default table uses the character number of the first character occurring in the set.

The default table is:

```
static int charClass[128] = {
/* NUL  SOH  STX  ETX  EOT  ENQ  ACK  BEL */
    32,   1,   1,   1,   1,   1,   1,   1,
/*  BS   HT   NL   VT   NP   CR   SO   SI */
     1,  32,   1,   1,   1,   1,   1,   1,
/* DLE  DC1  DC2  DC3  DC4  NAK  SYN  ETB */
     1,   1,   1,   1,   1,   1,   1,   1,
/* CAN   EM  SUB  ESC   FS   GS   RS   US */
     1,   1,   1,   1,   1,   1,   1,   1,
/*  SP    !    "    #    $    %    &    ' */
    32,  33,  34,  35,  36,  37,  38,  39,
/*   (    )    *    +    ,    -    .    / */
    40,  41,  42,  43,  44,  45,  46,  47,
/*   0    1    2    3    4    5    6    7 */
    48,  48,  48,  48,  48,  48,  48,  48,
/*   8    9    :    ;    <    =    >    ? */
    48,  48,  58,  59,  60,  61,  62,  63,
/*   @    A    B    C    D    E    F    G */
    64,  48,  48,  48,  48,  48,  48,  48,
/*   H    I    J    K    L    M    N    O */
    48,  48,  48,  48,  48,  48,  48,  48,
/*   P    Q    R    S    T    U    V    W */
    48,  48,  48,  48,  48,  48,  48,  48,
/*   X    Y    Z    [    \    ]    ^    _ */
    48,  48,  48,  91,  92,  93,  94,  48,
/*   `    a    b    c    d    e    f    g */
    96,  48,  48,  48,  48,  48,  48,  48,
/*   h    i    j    k    l    m    n    o */
    48,  48,  48,  48,  48,  48,  48,  48,
/*   p    q    r    s    t    u    v    w */
    48,  48,  48,  48,  48,  48,  48,  48,
/*   x    y    z    {    |    }    ~  DEL */
    48,  48,  48, 123, 124, 125, 126,   1};
```

For example, the string "33:48,37:48,45-47:48,64:48" indicates that the exclamation mark, percent sign, dash, period, slash, and ampersand characters should be treated the same way as characters and numbers. This is very useful for cutting and pasting electronic mailing addresses and UNIX filenames.

Actions (Release 4)

It is possible to rebind keys (or sequences of keys) to arbitrary strings for input, by changing the translations for the `vt100` or `tek4014` widgets. Changing the translations for events other than key and button events is not expected, and will cause unpredictable behavior. In Release 4, the following actions are provided for using with the vt100 or tek4014 `translations` resource:

`bell([percent])`
: Rings the keyboard bell at the specified percentage above or below the base volume.

`ignore()`
: Ignores the event but checks for special pointer position escape sequences.

`insert()`
: A synonym for `insert-seven-bit()`.

`insert-seven-bit()`
: Inserts the 7-bit USASCII character or string associated with the keysym that was pressed.

`insert-eight-bit()`
: Inserts the 8-bit ISO Latin-1 character or string associated with the keysym that was pressed.

`insert-selection(sourcename [, ...])`
: Inserts the string found in the selection or cut buffer indicated by *sourcename*. Sources are checked in the order given (case is significant) until one is found. Commonly-used selections include: PRIMARY, SECONDARY, and CLIPBOARD. Cut buffers are typically named CUT_BUFFER0 through CUT_BUFFER7.

`keymap(name)`
: Dynamically defines a new translation table whose resource name is *name* with the suffix `Keymap` (case is significant). The keymap name `None` restores the original translation table.

`popup-menu(menuname)`
: Displays the specified popup menu. Valid names (case is significant) include: `mainMenu`, `vtMenu`, `fontMenu`, and `tekMenu`.

`secure()`
: Toggles the secure keyboard mode described in the *Security* section, and is invoked from the Secure Keyboard entry in `mainMenu`.

`select-start()`
: Begins text selection at the current pointer location. See the section on "Pointer Usage" for information on making selections.

`select-extend()`
: Tracks the pointer and extends the selection. It should only be bound to motion events.

`select-end(destname [, ...])`
: Puts the currently selected text into all of the selections or cutbuffers specified by *destname*.

`select-cursor-start()`
: Similar to `select-start`, except that it begins the selection at the current text cursor position.

`select-cursor-end(`*`destname`*` [, ...])`
Similar to `select-end`, except that it should be used with `select-cursor-start`.

`set-vt-font(d/1/2/3/4/e/s [,`*`normalfont`*` [, `*`boldfont`*`]])`
Sets the font or fonts currently being used in the VT102 window. The first argument is a single character that specifies the font to be used: `d` or `D` indicates the default font (the font initially used when *xterm* was started); `1` through `4` indicate the fonts specified by the `font1` through `font4` resources; `e` or `E` indicates the normal and bold fonts that may be set through escape codes (or specified as the second and third action arguments, respectively); and `i` or `I` indicates the font selection (as made by programs such as *xfontsel*) indicated by the second action argument.

`start-extend()`
Similar to `select-start` except that the selection is extended to the current pointer location.

`start-cursor-extend()`
Similar to `select-extend` except that the selection is extended to the current text cursor position.

`string(`*`string`*`)`
Inserts the specified text string as if it had been typed. Quotation is necessary if the string contains whitespace or non-alphanumeric characters. If the string argument begins with the characters "0x", it is interpreted as a hex character constant.

`scroll-back(`*`count`*` [,`*`units`*`])`
Scrolls the text window backward so that text that had previously scrolled off the top of the screen is now visible. The *`count`* argument indicates the number of *`units`* (which may be `page`, `halfpage`, `pixel`, or `line`) by which to scroll.

`scroll-forw(`*`count`*` [,`*`units`*`])`
Scrolls is similar to `scroll-back` except that it scrolls the other direction.

`allow-send-events(`*`on/off/toggle`*`)`
Sets or toggles the `allowSendEvents` resource and is also invoked by the `allowsends` entry in `mainMenu`.

`set-logging(`*`on/off/toggle`*`)`
Toggles the `logging` resource and is also invoked by the `logging` entry in the `mainMenu`.

`redraw()`
Redraws the window and is also invoked by the `redraw` entry in `mainMenu`.

`send-signal(`*`signame`*`)`
Sends the signal named by *signame* (which may also be a number) to the *xterm* subprocess (the shell or program specified with the `-e` command line option) and is also invoked by the `suspend`, `continue`, `interrupt`, `hangup`, `terminate`, and `kill` entries in `mainMenu`. Allowable signal names are (case is not significant): suspend, tstp (if supported by the operating system), cont (if supported by the operating system), int, hup, term, and kill.

`quit()`
Sends a SIGHUP to the subprogram and exits. It is also invoked by the `quit` entry in `mainMenu`.

`set-scrollbar(`*on/off/toggle*`)`
Toggles the `scrollbar` resource and is also invoked by the `scrollbar` entry in `vtMenu`.

`set-jumpscroll(`*on/off/toggle*`)`
Toggles the `jumpscroll` resource and is also invoked by the `jumpscroll` entry in `vtMenu`.

`set-reverse-video(`*on/off/toggle*`)`
Toggles the `reverseVideo` resource and is also invoked by the `reversevideo` entry in `vtMenu`.

`set-autowrap(`*on/off/toggle*`)`
Toggles automatic wrapping of long lines and is also invoked by the `autowrap` entry in `vtMenu`.

`set-reversewrap(`*on/off/toggle*`)`
Toggles the `reverseWrap` resource and is also invoked by the `reversewrap` entry in `vtMenu`.

`set-autolinefeed(`*on/off/toggle*`)`
Toggles automatic insertion of linefeeds and is also invoked by the `autolinefeed` entry in `vtMenu`.

`set-appcursor(`*on/off/toggle*`)`
Toggles the application cursor key mode and is also invoked by the `appcursor` entry in `vtMenu`.

`set-appkeypad(`*on/off/toggle*`)`
Toggles the application keypad mode and is also invoked by the `appkeypad` entry in `vtMenu`.

`set-scroll-on-key(`*on/off/toggle*`)`
Toggles the `scrollKey` resource and is also invoked from the `scrollkey` entry in `vtMenu`.

`set-scroll-on-tty-output(`*on/off/toggle*`)`
Toggles the `scrollTtyOutput` resource and is also invoked from the `scrollttyoutput` entry in `vtMenu`.

`set-allow132(`*on/off/toggle*`)`
Toggles the `c132` resource and is also invoked from the `allow132` entry in `vtMenu`.

`set-cursesemul(`*on/off/toggle*`)`
Toggles the `curses` resource and is also invoked from the `cursesemul` entry in `vtMenu`.

`set-visual-bell(`*`on/off/toggle`*`)`
: Toggles the `visualBell` resource and is also invoked by the `visualbell` entry in `vtMenu`.

`set-marginbell(`*`on/off/toggle`*`)`
: Toggles the `marginBell` resource and is also invoked from the `marginbell` entry in `vtMenu`.

`set-altscreen(`*`on/off/toggle`*`)`
: Toggles between the alternative and current screens.

`soft-reset()`
: Resets the scrolling region and is also invoked from the `softreset` entry in `vtMenu`.

`hard-reset()`
: Resets the scrolling region, tabs, window size, and cursor keys and clears the screen. It is also invoked from the `hardreset` entry in `vtMenu`.

`set-terminal-type(`*`type`*`)`
: Directs output to either the `vt` or `tek` windows, according to the `type` string. It is also invoked by the `tekmode` entry in `vtMenu` and the `vtmode` entry in `tekMenu`.

`set-visibility(`*`vt/tek,on/off/toggle`*`)`
: Controls whether or not the `vt` or `tek` windows are visible. It is also invoked from the `tekshow` and `vthide` entries in `vtMenu` and the `vtshow` and `tekhide` entries in `tekMenu`.

`set-tek-text(`*`large/2/3/small`*`)`
: Sets font used in the Tektronix window to the value of the resources `tektextlarge`, `tektext2`, `tektext3`, and `tektextsmall` according to the argument. It is also by the entries of the same names as the resources in `tekMenu`.

`tek-page()`
: Clears the Tektronix window and is also invoked by the `tekpage` entry in `tekMenu`.

`tek-reset()`
: Resets the Tektronix window and is also invoked by the `tekreset` entry in `tekMenu`.

`tek-copy()`
: Copies the escape codes used to generate the current window contents to a file in the current directory beginning with the name COPY. It is also invoked from the `tekcopy` entry in `tekMenu`.

The Tektronix window also has the following action:

`gin-press(l/L/m/M/r/R)`
: Sends the indicated graphics input code.

The default bindings in the VT102 window are:

Reference Pages

```
Shift   <KeyPress>   Prior:          scroll-back(1,halfpage)\n\
Shift   <KeyPress>   Next:           scroll-forw(1,halfpage)\n\
Shift   <KeyPress>   Select:         select-cursor-start()\
                                     select-cursor-end(PRIMARY,CUT_BUFFER0)\n\
Shift   <KeyPress>   Insert:         insert-selection(PRIMARY,CUT_BUFFER0)\n\
        ~Meta        <KeyPress>:     insert-seven-bit()\n\
        Meta         <KeyPress>:     insert-eight-bit()\n\
Ctrl    ~Meta        <Btn1Down>:     popup-menu(mainMenu)\n\
        ~Meta        <Btn1Down>:     select-start()\n\
        ~Meta        <Btn1Motion>:   select-extend()\n\
Ctrl    ~Meta        <Btn2Down>:     popup-menu(vtMenu)\n\
~Ctrl   ~Meta        <Btn2Down>:     ignore()\n\
~Ctrl   ~Meta        <Btn2Up>:       insert-selection(PRIMARY,CUT_BUFFER0)\n\
Ctrl    ~Meta        <Btn3Down>:     popup-menu(fontMenu)\n\
~Ctrl   ~Meta        <Btn3Down>:     start-extend()\n\
        ~Meta        <Btn3Motion>:   select-extend()\n\
        ~Ctrl        ~Meta           <BtnUp>:
                     <BtnDown>:      bell(0)
```

The default bindings in the Tektronix window are:

```
        ~Meta   <KeyPress>:   insert-seven-bit()\n\
        Meta    <KeyPress>:   insert-eight-bit()\n\
Ctrl    ~Meta   <Btn1Down>:   popup-menu(mainMenu)\n\
Ctrl    ~Meta   <Btn2Down>:   popup-menu(tekMenu)\n\
Shift   ~Meta   <Btn1Down>:   gin-press(L)\n\
        ~Meta   <Btn1Down>:   gin-press(l)\n\
Shift   ~Meta   <Btn2Down>:   gin-press(M)\n\
        ~Meta   <Btn2Down>:   gin-press(m)\n\
Shift   ~Meta   <Btn3Down>:   gin-press(R)\n\
        ~Meta   <Btn3Down>:   gin-press(r)
```

Below is a sample how of the `keymap()` action is used to add special keys for entering commonly-typed works:

```
*VT100.Translations: #override <Key>F13: keymap(dbx)
*VT100.dbxKeymap.translations: \

<Key>   F14:   keymap(None)\n\
<Key>   F17:   string("next") string(0x0d)\n\
<Key>   F18:   string("step") string(0x0d)\n\
<Key>   F19:   string("continue") string(0x0d)\n\
<Key>   F20:   string("print ") insert-selection(PRIMARY,CUT_BUFFER0)
```

Actions (Release 3)

It is possible to rebind keys (or sequences of keys) to arbitrary strings for input, by changing the translations for the `vt100` or `tek4014` widgets. Changing the translations for events other than key and button events is not expected, and will cause unpredictable behavior.

The actions available for key translations are:

`insert()` Processes the key in the normal way; i.e., inserts the ASCII character code corresponding to the keysym found in the keyboard mapping table into the input stream.

`string(`*string*`)`
Rebinds the key or key sequence to the string value; that is, inserts the string argument into the input stream. Quotation is necessary if the string contains whitespace or non-alphanumeric characters. If the string argument begins with the characters "0x", it is interpreted as a hex character constant and the corresponding character is sent in the normal way.

`keymap(`*name*`)`
Takes a single string argument naming a resource to be used to dynamically define a new translation table; the name of the resource is obtained by appending the string `Keymap` to *name*. The keymap name `None` restores the original translation table (the very first one; a stack is not maintained). Upper/lower case is significant.

`insert-selection(`*name*[,*name*]`...)`
Retrieves the value of the first (leftmost) named selection that exists or cut buffer that is non-empty and inserts the value into the input stream. *name* is the name of any selection, for example, PRIMARY or SECONDARY, or the name of a cut buffer: CUT_BUFFER0, ..., CUT_BUFFER7. Upper/lower case is significant.

For example, a debugging session might benefit from the following bindings:

```
*VT100.Translations: #override <Key>F13: keymap(dbx)
*VT100.dbxKeymap.translations: \
    <Key>F14: keymap(None) \n\
    <Key>F17: string("next") string(0x0d) \n\
    <Key>F18: string("step") string(0x0d) \n\
    <Key>F19: string("continue") string(0x0d) \n\
    <Key>F20: string("print") insert-selection(PRIMARY, CUT_BUFFER0)
```

Within the VT100 widget the key and button bindings for selecting text, pasting text, and activating the menus are controlled by the translation bindings. In addition to the actions listed above under *Key Translations*, the following actions are available:

`mode-menu()` Posts one of the two mode menus, depending on which button is pressed.

`select-start()`
Unselects any previously selected text and begins selecting new text.

`select-extend()`
Continues selecting text from the previous starting position.

`start-extend()`
Begins extending the selection from the farthest (left or right) edge.

`select-end(`*name*`[,`*name*`]...)`
: Ends the text selection. *name* is the name of a selection, or the name of a cut buffer into which the text is to be copied. *xterm* will assert ownership of all the selections named and will copy the text into each of the cut buffers. Upper/lower case is significant.

`ignore()` Quietly discards the key or button event.

`bell([`*volume*`])`
: Rings the bell at the specified *volume* increment above/below the base volume.

The default bindings are:

```
                <KeyPress>:        insert()\n\
Ctrl    ~Meta   <Btn1Down>:        mode-menu()\n\
        ~Meta   <Btn1Down>:        select-start()\n\
        ~Meta   <Btn1Motion>:      select-extend()\n\
Ctrl    ~Meta   <Btn2Down>:        mode-menu()\n\
~Ctrl   ~Meta   <Btn2Down>:        ignore()\n\
        ~Meta   <Btn2Up>:          insert-selection(PRIMARY,CUT_BUFFER0)\n\
~Ctrl   ~Meta   <Btn3Down>:        start-extend()\n\
        ~Meta   <Btn3Motion>:      select-extend()\n\
        ~Meta   <BtnUp>:           select-end(PRIMARY,CUT_BUFFER0)\n\
                <BtnDown>:         bell(0)
```

An Obsolete Feature: Starting xterm from Init

Warning: *This feature is now obsolete. It is not supported in Release 4. If Release 3 is running at your site, this method may still be in use. However, sites using this method should switch to* xdm *instead.*

On operating systems such as BSD 4.3 and Ultrix, the server and initial login window are normally started automatically by *init*(8).

By convention, the pseudo-terminal with the highest minor device number (e.g., *devttyqf* and *devptyqf*) is renamed for the lowest display number (e.g., *devttyv0* and *devptyv0*). Machines that have more than one display can repeat this process using *ttyqe* for *ttyv1*, and so on.

Once the pseudo-terminals are in place, a line similar to the following may be added to */etc/ttys* (replacing *Xqvss* with the appropriate server and putting it all on one line):

```
ttyv0 "/usr/bin/X11/xterm -L -geom 80x24+1+1 -display :0"
   xterm on secure window="/usr/bin/X11/Xqvss :0"
```

Sites that used to run X10 should note that the colon in the server display number is required.

Although the release will install both the X server and *xterm* in */usr/bin/X11* by default, many sites choose to make a copy of both of these programs on the root partition (usually in */etc*) so that they may still be used even if the partition containing */usr/bin/X11* isn't mounted.

Some versions of *init* have relatively small program name buffer sizes and treat all sharp signs as comment delimiters. Sites that wish to list large numbers of options on the *xterm* line will need to write a small shell script to execute the long *xterm* line. The best solution, of course, is to use *xdm*.

Other Features

xterm automatically highlights the window border and text cursor when the pointer enters the window (selected) and unhighlights them when the pointer leaves the window (unselected). If the window is the focus window, then the window is highlighted no matter where the pointer is.

In VT102 mode, there are escape sequences to activate and deactivate an alternate screen buffer, which is the same size as the display area of the window. When activated, the current screen is saved and replaced with the alternate screen. Saving of lines scrolled off the top of the window is disabled until the normal screen is restored. The *termcap* entry for *xterm* allows the visual editor *vi* to switch to the alternate screen for editing, and restore the screen on exit.

In either VT102 or Tektronix mode, there are escape sequences to change the name of the windows and to specify a new log file name.

Environment

xterm sets the environment variables TERM and TERMCAP properly for the size window you have created. It also uses and sets the environment variable DISPLAY to specify which bitmap display terminal to use. The environment variable WINDOWID is set to the X window ID number of the *xterm* window.

Bugs

The class name is `XTerm` instead of `Xterm`.

The `-L` option is no longer needed since the display manager, *xdm*, handles logging in much more cleanly. No more trying to match colors in */etc/ttys* or worrying about an unwanted login window. (The `-L` option has been removed in Release 4.)

xterm will hang forever if you try to paste too much text at one time. It is both producer and consumer for the *pty* and can deadlock.

Variable-width fonts are not handled reasonably.

This program still needs to be rewritten. It should be split into very modular sections, with the various emulators being completely separate widgets that don't know about each other. Ideally, you'd like to be able to pick and choose emulator widgets and stick them into a single control widget.

The focus is considered lost if some other client (e.g., the window manager) grabs the pointer; it is difficult to do better without an addition to the protocol.

There needs to be a dialog box to allow entry of the log file name and the COPY filename.

Many of the options are not resettable after *xterm* starts.

The Tek widget does not support key/button re-binding.

See Also

X, resize, pty(4), tty(4); Appendix E, *xterm Control Sequences*

Authors

Far too many people, including:

Loretta Guarino Reid (DEC-UEG-WSL), Joel McCormack (DEC-UEG-WSL), Terry Weissman (DEC-UEG-WSL), Edward Moy (Berkeley), Ralph R. Swick (MIT-Athena), Mark Vandevoorde (MIT-Athena), Bob McNamara (DEC-MAD), Jim Gettys (MIT-Athena), Bob Scheifler (MIT X Consortium), Doug Mink (SAO), Steve Pitschke (Stellar), Ron Newman (MIT-Athena), Jim Fulton (MIT X Consortium), Dave Serisky (HP).

Name

xwd – place window images in a dump file.

Syntax

xwd [*options*]

Description

xwd stores window images in a specially formatted window dump file. This file can then be read by various other X utilities for redisplay, printing, editing, formatting, archiving, image processing, etc. The target window is selected by clicking the mouse in the desired window. The keyboard bell is rung once at the beginning of the dump and twice when the dump is completed.

Options

`-help` Prints out the 'Usage:' command syntax summary.

`-nobdrs` Specifies that the window dump should not include the pixels that compose the X window border. This is useful when the window contents are included in a document as an illustration.

`-out` *file* Allows you to specify the output file on the command line. The default outputs to the standard output (*stdout*).

`-xy` Applies to color displays only. The `-xy` option selects 'XY' pixmap format dumping instead of the default 'Z' pixmap format.

`-root` Makes a dump of the entire root window.

`-add` *value* Specifies a signed value to be added to every pixel.

`-frame` Indicates that the window manager frame should be included when manually selecting a window. (Available as of Release 4.)

`-display` [*host*]:*server*[.*screen*]

Allows you to specify the host, server and screen to connect to. *host* is the machine, *server* is the server number and *screen* is the screen number. For example,

xwd -display *your_node*:**0.1 &**

specifies screen 1 on server 0 on the machine *your_node*. If the host is omitted, the local machine is assumed. If the screen is omitted, the screen 0 is assumed; the server and colon (:) are necessary in all cases.

Files

XWDFile.h X Window Dump File format definition file.

See Also

X, xdpr, xpr, xwud

Author

Tony Della Fera, Digital Equipment Corp., MIT Project Athena;
William F. Wyatt, Smithsonian Astrophysical Observatory.

xwininfo

Name

xwininfo – window information utility for X.

Syntax

xwininfo [*options*]

Description

xwininfo is a utility for displaying information about windows. Depending on which options are choosen, various information is displayed. If no options are choosen, -stats is assumed.

The user has the option of selecting the target window with the mouse (by clicking any mouse button in the desired window) or by specifying its window id on the command line with the -id option. Or instead of specifying the window by its id number, the -name option may be used to specify the window by name. There is also a special -root option to quickly obtain information on the root window.

Options

-display [*host*]:*server*[.*screen*]
: Allows you to specify the host, server and screen to connect to. *host* specifies the machine, *server* specifies the server number, and *screen* specifies the screen number. For example,

xwininfo -display *your_node*:**0.1 &**

specifies screen 1 of server 0 on the machine *your_node*. If the host is omitted, the local machine is assumed. If the screen is omitted, screen 0 is assumed; the server and colon (:) are necessary in all cases.

-help
: Prints out the 'Usage:' command syntax summary.

-id *id*
: Allows the user to specify a target window *id* on the command line rather than using the mouse to select the target window. This is very useful in debugging X applications where the target window is not mapped to the screen or where the use of the mouse might be impossible or interfere with the application.

-name *name*
: Allows the user to specify that the window named *name* is the target window on the command line rather than using the mouse to select the target window.

-root
: Specifies that the root window is the target window. This is useful in situations where the root window is completely obscured.

-frame
: Causes window manager frames not to be ignored when manually selecting windows. (Available as of Release 4.)

-int
: Specifies that all X window ids should be displayed as integer values. The default is to display them as hexadecimal values.

-tree
: Causes the root, parent, and children windows' ids and names of the selected window to be displayed.

-stats Causes various attributes of the selected window having to do with its location and appearence to be displayed. Information displayed includes the location of the window, its width, height, depth, border width, class, and map state, colormap ID (if any), backing-store hint, and the location of its corners. If *xwininfo* is run with no options, `-stats` is assumed.

-bits Causes the display of various attributes pertaining to the selected window's raw bits and how the selected window is to be stored to be displayed. Information displayed includes the selected window's bit gravity, window gravity, backing store hint, backing planes value, backing pixel, and whether or not the window has save-under set.

-events Causes the selected window's event masks to be displayed. Both the event mask of events wanted by some client and the event mask of events not to propagate are displayed.

-size Causes the selected window's sizing hints to be displayed. Information displayed includes: for both the normal size hints and the zoom size hints the user supplied location if any; the program supplied location if any; the user supplied size if any; the program supplied size if any; the minimum size if any; the maximum size if any; the resize increments if any; and the minimum and maximum aspect ratios if any.

-wm Causes the selected window's window manager hints to be displayed. Information displayed may include whether or not the application accepts input, what the window's icon window # and name is, where the window's icon should go, and what the window's initial state should be.

-metric Causes all individual height, width, and x and y positions to be displayed in millimeters, as well as number of pixels, based on what the server thinks the resolution is. Geometry specifications that are in *+x+y* form are not changed.

-english Causes all individual height, width, and x and y positions to be displayed in inches (and feet, yards, and miles if necessary), as well as number of pixels. `-metric` and `-english` may be used at the same time.

-all A quick way to ask for all information possible.

Examples

The following is a sample summary taken with no options specified.

```
xwininfo ==> Please select the window you wish
         ==> information on by clicking the
         ==> mouse in that window.

xwininfo ==> Window id: 0x30000f (xterm)

         ==> Upper left X: 0
         ==> Upper left Y: 0
```

```
==> Width: 578
==> Height: 316
==> Depth: 1
==> Border width: 1
==> Window class: InputOutput
==> Colormap: 0x80065
==> Window Bit Gravity State: NorthWestGravity
==> Window Window Gravity State: NorthWestGravity
==> Window Backing Store State: NotUseful
==> Window Save Under State: no
==> Window Map State: IsUnviewable
==> Window Override Redirect State: no
==> Corners:  +0+0  -572+0  -572-582  +0-582
```

Bugs

Using `-stats` and `-bits` together shows some redundant information.

See Also

X, xprop

Author

Mark Lillibridge, MIT Project Athena.

Reference Pages

Name

xwud – X window image displayer.

Syntax

xwud [*options*]

Description

xwud is an X Window System window image undumping utility. *xwud* allows X users to display a window image saved in a specially formatted dump file, such as one produced by *xwd*.

The Release 4 version of *xwud* allows you to specify the coordinates at which this image is displayed using the -geometry option. If you are using the Release 3 version of *xwud*, the window image will appear at the coordinates of the original window from which the dump was taken.

Options

-help Prints out a short description of the allowable options.

-in *file* Allows the user to explicitly specify the input file on the command line. The default is to take input from standard input.

-display [*host*]:*server*[.*screen*]

Allows you to specify the host, server and screen to connect to. *host* specifies the machine, *server* specifies the server number, and *screen* specifies the screen number. For example,

xwud -display *your_node*:**0.1**

specifies screen 1 on server 0 on the machine *your_node*. If the host is omitted, the local machine is assumed. If the screen is omitted, the screen 0 is assumed; the server and colon (:) are necessary in all cases.

-geometry *geometry*

The *xwud* window is created with the specified size and location determined by the supplied geometry specification. The -geometry option can be (and often is) abbreviated to -g, unless there is a conflicting option that begins with "g." The argument to the geometry option (*geometry*) is referred to as a "standard geometry string," and has the form *widthx-height±xoff±yoff*. (This option is available for use with *xwud* as of Release 4.)

Typically, you will only want to specify the position and let the size default to the actual size of the image.

-bg *color* If a bitmap image (or a single plane of an image) is displayed, this option can be used to specify the color to display for the "0" bits in the image. (Available as of Release 4.)

-fg *color* If a bitmap image (or a single plane of an image) is displayed, this option can be used to specify the color to display for the "1" bits in the image. (Available as of Release 4.)

`-new` Forces creation of a new colormap for displaying the image. If the image characteristics happen to match those of the display, this can get the image on the screen faster, but at the cost of using a new colormap (which on most displays will cause other windows to go technicolor). (Available as of Release 4.)

`-noclick` Clicking any button in the window will terminate the application, unless this option is specified. Termination can always be achieved by typing 'q', 'Q', or Ctrl-c. (Available as of Release 4.)

`-plane` *`number`*

Selects a single bit plane of the image to display. Planes are numbered with zero being the least significant bit. This option can be used to figure out which plane to pass to *xpr* for printing. (Available as of Release 4.)

`-raw` Forces the image to be displayed with whatever color values happen to currently exist on the screen. This option is mostly useful when undumping an image back onto the same screen that the image originally came from, while the original windows are still on the screen, and results in getting the image on the screen faster. (Available as of Release 4.)

`-rv` If a bitmap image (or a single plane of an image) is displayed, this option forces the foreground and background colors to be swapped. This may be needed when displaying a bitmap image which has the color sense of pixel values "0" and "1" reversed from what they are on your display. (Available as of Release 4.)

`-std` *`map_type`*

Causes the image to be displayed using the specified Standard Colormap. The property name is obtained by converting the type to upper case, prepending "RGB_", and appending "_MAP". Typical types are `best`, `default`, and `gray`. See *xstdcmap* for one way of creating Standard Colormaps. (Available as of Release 4.)

`-vis` *`vis_type_or_ID`*

Allows you to specify a particular visual or visual class. The default is to pick the "best" one. A particular class can be specified: `StaticGray`, `GrayScale`, `StaticColor`, `PseudoColor`, `DirectColor`, or `TrueColor`. Or `Match` can be specified, meaning use the same class as the source image. Alternatively, an exact visual ID (specific to the server) can be specified, either as a hexadecimal number (prefixed with "0x") or as a decimal number. Finally, "default" can be specified, meaning to use the same class as the colormap of the root window. Case is not significant in any of these strings. (Available as of Release 4.)

`-inverse` Applies to monochrome window dump files only. If selected, the window is undumped in reverse video. This is mainly needed because the display is 'write white', whereas dump files intended eventually to be written to a printer are generally 'write black'. (Available in Release 3 only.)

Files

XWDFile.h X Window Dump File format definition file.

Bugs in Release 3

Does not attempt to do color translation when the destination screen does not have a colormap exactly matching that of the original window.

See Also

X, xdpr, xpr, xstdcmap, xwd

Author

Release 4 version by Bob Scheifler, MIT X Consortium;

Release 3 version by Tony Della Fera, Digital Equipment Corp. and MIT Project Athena, and William F. Wyatt, Smithsonian Astrophysical Observatory.

Part Four:

Appendices

This part of the book contains useful reference information.

A

System Management

This appendix discusses various tasks involved in X Window System management, mostly from the UNIX point of view.

In This Chapter:

A
System Management

X exists in so many incarnations and runs on so many different versions of UNIX (not to mention other operating systems) that it is difficult to be definitive about system management. This appendix discusses several topics relevant to setting up the standard version of X (with UNIX) and keeping it running smoothly. The range of subjects discussed is somewhat broad. Here's an overview.

This appendix primarily focuses on ways in which you can set up X to run automatically:

- *xdm*, the display manager.
- *xinit*.
- By an older (and now obsolete) method, running *xterm* from */etc/ttys*.

In addition to information relating to starting X, we've also included brief discussions of other topics relevant to X system management:

- Including X in your search path.
- Setting the terminal type for *xterm*.
- Managing fonts.
- Addressing security issues and access control.
- Redirecting console messages.
- Maintaining log files.
- Changing the color name database.

Given the various incarnations of X and UNIX, you should be sure to check your system's documentation for additional (or contrary) details.

Including X in Your Search Path

The various X clients are normally stored in the directory */usr/bin/X11*. In order to invoke them by name like any other UNIX program, you need to make this directory part of your search path.*

This is normally done from your *.cshrc* (C shell) or *.profile* (Bourne shell) file, using a command similar to the following:

Bourne Shell:

```
PATH=.:/usr/ucb:/bin:/usr/bin:/usr/bin/X11:Other directories;
        export PATH
```

C Shell:

```
set path=(. /usr/ucb /bin /usr/bin /usr/bin/X11 Other directories)
```

The exact list of directories will differ from system to system. You should be aware that directories are searched in order from left to right, so a command with the same name in an earlier directory will be found and used before one in a later directory. Many users take advantage of this fact to run customized versions of programs by putting "." (the current directory) or a local tools directory first in their search path. This works fine, but you should be aware that this provides a security loophole that can be taken advantage of by an experienced system cracker. It's much safer to put "." at the end of your path, or eliminate it entirely.

If you have already logged in before adding the above line to your *.profile* or *.cshrc* file, you should log out and log in again, or type in the path-setting command at your prompt, so that it takes effect for your current session.

Setting the Terminal Type

Several *termcap* entries work with *xterm*, including "xterm," "vt102," "vt100," and "ansi." The *xterm* program automatically searches the *termcap* file for these entries (in this order) and sets the TERM and TERMCAP environment variables according to the entry it finds.

We've found that the *termcap* entry called "xterm," which comes with the standard X distribution, provides very reliable emulation. We suggest you copy this entry from the *xterm* source directory (the file is called *termcap*) and add it as the first entry in the */etc/termcap* file on your system. This will allow you to set your terminal type to xterm.

*This topic isn't really part of system management, but since we assume most people know how to do it, we didn't want to clutter up Chapter 2 with unnecessary discussion. On the other hand, the information is critical for those who don't already know it, so we wanted to put it somewhere!

A Startup Shell Script

It's a basic principle of UNIX to "let the computer do the work." Accordingly, you'd no doubt like to run various X clients automatically whenever you log in.

The best way to do this is to create a script that runs the clients you want. Depending on how X is set up on your system, you can execute this script in one of two ways:*

- If *xdm* is running X, name the script *.xsession* and put it in your home directory. When you log in, *xdm* will automatically execute your *.xsession* script.
- If you are starting X with *xinit*, name the script *.xinitrc* and put it in your home directory. Then put the command *xinit* at the end of your *.login* file. *xinit* normally starts the server and runs a single *xterm* as a client, but if a file called *.xinitrc* exists in your home directory, *xinit* starts the server and executes *.xinitrc*.

Methods of starting X automatically with *xinit* or *xdm* are discussed later in this appendix.

What Should Go in the Script

With some variation depending on the specific environment, in most cases your startup script should:

- Set the DISPLAY environment variable.
- Load your resources file with *xrdb*.
- Start the window manager.
- Start other clients you want on your default display, such as *xterm*, *oclock*, *xload*, etc.
- Run a console *xterm* process in the foreground; terminating this process will terminate the login session.

The script can be either a C shell or Bourne shell script. We've included a sample script in Bourne shell syntax.†

In writing a script, keep in mind this limitation: running *xterm* from inside a shell script only works if the script executes quickly—or does not terminate at all.

The problem involves the way that *xterm* sets up its controlling terminal (*/dev/tty*). If the *xterm*'s parent process has died by the time the *xterm* gets around to doing this, then */dev/tty* is redefined properly. If the parent has not died, however, *xterm* uses the parent's controlling terminal as its own. If the parent dies at any time after that, */dev/tty* will become undefined for that *xterm* (and all processes spawned by it).

---

*If you are still starting the X server from the */etc/ttys* file, as described later in this appendix, this will bring up an *xterm* window with a login prompt. In this case, you can run the script to start other clients from your *.login* file. Note, however, that this method of starting the X server is not supported in Release 4.

†Thanks to Dave Curry for his help in preparing this sample.

A C shell script that starts up a few *xterms* and then exits will probably work because the *xterm*'s parent process (the script) has exited by the time the *xterms* start defining their */dev/tty*. If, however, there is a sleep or another command that takes a long time in the script after the line invoking the *xterm*, the parent may still be around when the *xterm* defines */dev/tty*. Then, when the script finally exits, */dev/tty* becomes undefined for those *xterms*.

If you want to use a C shell script, this problem can be avoided by enclosing commands in parentheses. This causes the shell to fork an extra time before executing the command, and thus disassociates the process from the controlling terminal before the process begins.

Whether you are using a C shell or Bourne shell script, you should make the last command in the script be one that opens a window, and run that command in the foreground. Then the script will not terminate until that final foreground command terminates—that is, when you kill the window. In this case, all the *xterms* will have the script's controlling tty, but since the script is guaranteed to hang around, this causes no problem.

Regardless of how and in what environment you're starting X, it is advisable to set the DISPLAY variable inside the script, since otherwise the clients won't know which display to connect to. (Normally, *xterm* sets the DISPLAY variable. Since you are invoking the other clients not from a shell in an *xterm* window, but from a standard shell, it will not automatically be set.)

Though without explicit settings, both *xdm* and *xinit* will automatically set DISPLAY to `unix:0.0` (or some variation thereof), this default setting limits the remote hosts that can connect to the local system. (If every system has the same DISPLAY variable, it becomes rather difficult to run programs on a remote host!) We suggest you set the DISPLAY explicitly, determining the appropriate host name with the *hostname* command, as shown in the script below.

Note that the *hostname* command is a BSD command. For a System V equivalent, see your UNIX documentation. Note also that in this script, *sed* is used to strip domained-based hostnames such as *isla.ora.com* back to their initial term, the actual system name. If you are running in a standalone environment, this is not necessary.

Example A-1 shows a startup Bourne shell script, which would open windows on the display, as shown in Figure A-1. You can use this script even if you normally use the C shell for interactive use. Note that the comments should probably not be present in the working script. While they are ignored, they do slow down execution, and on a loaded system can cause X to start up improperly.

Example A-1. Startup Bourne shell script

```
#!/bin/sh

# Get hostname, strip the domain name if there is one

cpu=`hostname | sed -e 's/\..*//'`

# If no DISPLAY is set, set one.

if [ -z $DISPLAY ]
then
     DISPLAY=$cpu:0
fi
```

Example A-1. Startup Bourne shell script (continued)

```
# Special-case the "bogus" non-network display names and
# make sure can always execute remote clients

case $DISPLAY in
    unix:0.0|unix:0|:0.0|:0)DISPLAY="$cpu:0";;
esac
export DISPLAY

# Load resource definitions from .Xresources

xrdb -Dhostname=$cpu $HOME/.Xresources

# Set keyclick off and invoke the screen saver after
# seven minutes of idleness

xset c off s 420

# Start the twm window manager

twm &

# Now start up some xterms

# Start an xterm in bottom left corner

xterm -geometry 80x35+0-0 -display $DISPLAY &

# xterm next to it across the bottom

xterm -geometry 80x35+500-0 -display $DISPLAY &

# remote xterm in regular size just above, but below console xterm
# at top

rsh ora xterm -geometry -0-0 -display $DISPLAY &

# Now start up other clients

# digital xclock in upper right corner

xclock -digital -update 1 -geometry -0+0 &

# xcalc just below it; xclock 30 pixels high on sun, so offset by 30

xcalc -geometry -0+30 &

#xload 235 pixels below that, at bottom of xcalc

xload -geometry -0+265 &

#xbiff down another 120 pixels

xbiff -geometry -0+385 &

# Start a console xterm window.
# This is the only xterm that should be run in the foreground.
# Killing this window will shut down X.

# Use the following line with xinit; comment out if you use xdm

exec xterm -C -display $DISPLAY -geometry 80x5+0+0

# Uncomment this line if you use xdm
# exec xterm -C -ls -display $DISPLAY -geometry 80x5+0+0
```

System Management

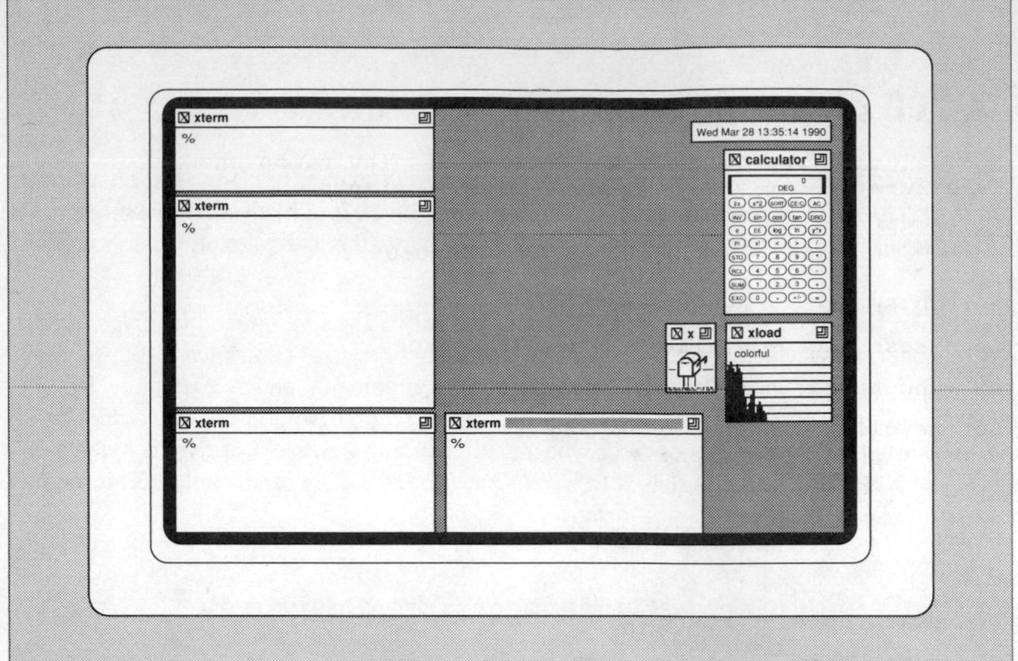

Figure A-1. Display after running sample script

Note that all programs that create windows (and hence don't run quickly and then go away) are run in the background, with the exception of the final *xterm* window. This will cause the script to simulate the behavior of the console *xterm* normally started by *xinit* or *xdm*.

The `-C` option specified with the console *xterm* window redirects messages sent to */dev/console* to that *xterm* window. This option is only supported in some implementations of X; see your documentation. For additional information, see the section "Console Messages" later in this appendix.

You may want to start the console *xterm* window as an icon, using the `-iconic` option, so you're less likely to terminate the window inadvertently and end the session. If you do this, you should specify the position of the icon in your resource file. The following resource entry would place the icon at coordinates 50,50:

```
xterm*iconGeometry: +50+50
```

In the example, though, we simply make the window only five lines high, so that we can still see console messages, but won't be tempted to use it for most purposes.

Note that if you are using *xdm*, you want to run the final *xterm* with the `-ls` option, to make that window be your login shell. If you are using *xinit*, you should definitely *not* use this option! Since *xinit* is invoked from the end of the *.login* file (instead of directly by *xdm* before login), you will end up in an infinite loop.

Note that windows are actually arranged in a "tiled" fashion, with two large xterms side by side on the bottom of the screen, a smaller one (connected to a remote system) above, and the "desk accessories" lined up in the upper left corner. This leaves some room free for new windows or for invoking the Twm menu on the root window. This is ideal for our purposes, which are mainly editing, formatting, and testing examples for books. Depending on what you do, another arrangement might be better.*

*Note that this file was developed for and run on a Sun workstation. Differences in pixel sizes may make the coordinates and sizes of various windows come out differently on other hardware.

Starting X

In Chapter 2 *Getting Started*, we described how to start X manually. However, on a single-user workstation (or perhaps on several connected displays), it is likely that you might want X to come up automatically. In many commercial X ports, this may already have been done for you.

This section describes three ways to run X automatically. The first method involves the display manager, *xdm*, which can run X on a single display or several connected displays. Since the display manager is the recommended method of running X and is extremely flexible, we're including a fairly detailed discussion of it. The second method is to use *xinit*, which was introduced in Chapter 2. For those who are still running Release 3, we've included a discussion of a third method that runs X from */etc/ttys* (on BSD 4.3 systems only). This method has been phased out in Release 4.

Starting X with the Display Manager, xdm (Release 4)

Introduced in Release 3, the display manager, *xdm*, offers an alternative to running X with *xinit* (or by the obsolete method, from */etc/ttys*). *xdm* is designed to run the X server from the */etc/rc* system startup file. In its most basic implementation, the display manager emulates a *login* or *getty* on a standard terminal, keeping the server running, prompting for a user's name and password, and managing a standard login session.

However, *xdm* has far more powerful and versatile capabilities. Users can design their own login sessions, using *.xsession* files. You can also customize special *xdm* files to manage several connected displays (both local and remote), and to set system-wide and user-specific X resources.

A not so obvious limitation of *xdm* is that it does not work well if you are using other window systems (in addition to X). If you want to use multiple window systems on the same hardware, you should continue to use *xinit* for the time being. Future releases of *xdm* should overcome these limitations.

The functionality of *xdm* has been expanded in Release 4, though many features have not changed since Release 3. The following sections describe the Release 4 version of *xdm*. Release 4 specific features are noted. If you are running Release 3, also read the section "Release 3 xdm" later in this appendix.

First, we'll give you the basics of using *xdm* to run X on a single display and then give you some tips on how to design your own user session and manage multiple displays.

Getting Started with xdm on a Single Display

To have *xdm* run X on a single display, the system administrator should perform three simple tasks:

1. Set up the *xdm* configuration file and other special files, as described in the next section.
2. Put the line */usr/bin/X11/xdm* at the end of */etc/rc* or other similar system startup file.
3. It's also a good idea to turn off the "console" in */etc/ttys* on a single-user workstation, although this is discretionary. (As we'll see, the display manager provides its own login window. Turning off the console prevents the standard UNIX prompt from being simultaneously displayed on the full screen when *xdm* is started. Keep in mind this will also prevent system messages from being sent to the console but they should still be saved in */usr/adm/messages*.) How you'd turn off the "console" depends on the version of UNIX you are running. The procedure and the system file you edit may differ from system to system. See the *getty*(8) and *init*(8) reference pages in your UNIX documentation for details.

Once you perform these steps, as long as UNIX is running, *xdm* should keep the X server running, allow users to log on and off, and manage a simple login session.

The following sections describe the steps you need to get started with *xdm* in greater detail.

Setting Up the Configuration File and Other Special Files

In order to run X, *xdm* uses a configuration file and several special files that specify such things as the server, basic login session, and an error log file.

Be aware that *xdm should* be able to work in a very rudimentary fashion *without any* special files. However, a problem with Release 4 may require that at least two of the special files be present (namely, *xdm-config* and *Xservers*). These limitations should be removed by patches to the release. If this bug has been patched and *xdm* finds no special files, it will still start the server and a login *xterm* window. This default action can be very helpful, because it allows you to log in even if the special files have been inadvertently removed or corrupted.

Despite the potential to work in a rudimentary fashion without special files, *xdm* was not intended to be run in this way. For most purposes, system administrators will want to use and very likely customize the special files to have *xdm* run X in a manner more suitable for the particular system.

The configuration file and some prototypical special files can be found in the *config* directory under the *xdm* source directory. (Starting from the top of the X11 source tree, the directory is *mit/clients/xdm/config*.) Table A-1 lists some of the more commonly used special files for Release 4:

Table A-1. xdm Special Files

File	What it specifies
xdm-config	Configuration parameters.
Xservers	List of displays to manage.
xdm-errors	*xdm* error log file.
xdm-pid	Contains ID of the *xdm* parent process (Release 4 only).
Xresources	Resources to load (with xrdb).
Xsession	Default login session.
Xstartup	Startup procedure.
Xreset	Reset procedure.

As you can see, the file *xdm-pid* has been added in Release 4; it represents new functionality. The *Xstartup* and *Xreset* files can still be used to affect *xdm* in Release 4, but there are no default files. We'll discuss these and some of the other special files in greater detail later in this appendix.

Each of the special files can be specified by an *xdm* command line option. However, it's more efficient to specify the files—other than the single *xdm* configuration file—as resources and put those resources in the configuration file itself. The configuration file shipped with the standard version of X is called *xdm-config*. The Release 4 version of this file is shown in Figure A-2:

```
DisplayManager.servers:            /usr/lib/X11/xdm/Xservers
DisplayManager.errorLogFile:       /usr/lib/X11/xdm/xdm-errors
DisplayManager.pidFile:            /usr/lib/X11/xdm/xdm-pid
DisplayManager*resources:          /usr/lib/X11/xdm/Xresources
DisplayManager*session:            /usr/lib/X11/xdm/Xsession
DisplayManager._0.authorize:       true
DisplayManager*authorize:          false
```

Figure A-2. Default xdm-config file, Release 4

The following three *xdm-config* file entries have been added in Release 4:

```
DisplayManager.pidFile:            /usr/lib/X11/xdm/xdm-pid
DisplayManager._0.authorize:       true
DisplayManager*authorize:          false
```

These entries represent new *xdm* functionality, which will be discussed later in this appendix. If you are using Release 3, these entries are not applicable. (See "Release 3 xdm" for the appropriate *xdm-config* file.)

In effect, most of the entries in the default configuration file are just pointers to the other special files *xdm* uses. Notice also that, in most cases, the configuration file has the same syntax as any resource file. Release 4 introduces a variation from traditional resource syntax, which appears in the following line:

```
DisplayManager._0.authorize:       true
```

System Management

when you specify a display name on the command line). This is because dots and colons have special meaning for the resource manager. (Dots separate resource variable components; a colon signals the end of the variable and the beginning of the value field. See Chapter 9, *Command Line Options* for more information.) Underscores allow a display name to be treated as a single resource variable component. This syntax variance is applicable only to Release 4. The Release 3 version of *xdm* compensates for resource syntax anomalies—display name components are separated by dots.

In addition to the variables set in the default *xdm-config* file, you can specify several other display manager resources in the configuration file. See the *xdm* reference page in Part Three of this guide for a complete list of resource variables.

To get started using *xdm*, the system administrator should make a directory (*/usr/lib/X11/xdm* is suggested) and copy these default special files into it:

- *xdm-config*.
- *Xresources*.
- *Xsession*.

As we'll see later, each of the standard files can be customized but in many cases the defaults will be sufficient to run X on a single display.*

Next, the system administrator should create an *Xservers* file containing an entry for the local display. As we've said, if the Release 4 *xdm* has been updated with all relevant patches, the *Xservers* file is not necessary for *xdm* to run X on a single display. However, if you are running Release 4 without the relevant patches, *xdm* has a bug that requires you to set up an *Xservers* file before *xdm* can work properly. (The bug also requires an *xdm-config* file be present.) Since setting up an *Xservers* file is fairly simple to do and a good way to avoid potential problems, we recommend that you do so before placing the *xdm* command in one of the system startup files.

Most workstations can be run using an *Xservers* file made up of this line:

```
:0 local /usr/bin/X11/X
```

This *Xservers* file is probably adequate for most workstations. However, if X does not run properly on your single display, you should edit the *Xservers* file. See "The Xservers File" later in this appendix and the *xdm* reference page in Part Three of this guide for more information about file syntax.

*For our purposes, we are talking about the default special files provided with the standard release of X. Keep in mind that you can rewrite the resource definitions in the *xdm-config* file to specify files of any name (in any directory) as the so-called special files. (The configuration file also can have any name you like and be stored in any directory). If you use a filename other than *xdm-config*, you need to specify that filename (and its explicit path) with the `-config` option after the *xdm* command. See the *xdm* reference page in Part Three of this guide for more information.)

The Standard Login Session

Once you copy the special files to */usr/lib/X11/xdm* and create a single-entry *Xservers* file, if you want *xdm* simply to run the X server on the local display, prompt for username and password, and run a simple login session, you should be able simply to add this line to the end of the */etc/rc* file:

```
/usr/bin/X11/xdm
```

(Depending on your version of UNIX, you may want to add this line to */etc/rc.local*, */etc/rc2* or some other file. Consult your operating system documentation. Regardless of the file to which it is added, the display manager should be the last process run.)

After this simple modification, when UNIX is put into multi-user mode, *xdm* automatically starts the X server and keeps it running.

xdm also takes over the login procedure for displays specified in the *Xservers* file, supplying username and password prompts normally provided by the *getty* and *login* programs. Without modification, *xdm* provides the login window pictured in Figure 2-2 of Chapter 2, *Getting Started*.

This login procedure is controlled by the authentication widget (part of the *xdm* program), which in effect "authenticates" the user and password. You can customize the login window by setting resources for the authentication widget in the *Xresources* file. (These resources must be set in the *Xresources* file in the directory */usr/lib/X11/xdm* to take effect. They cannot be set in a resources file in a user's home directory, since that file is not loaded into the resource manager until after the login procedure.) Among the customizable features are the login greeting (by default, *Welcome to the X Window System*), the size and position of the window, and colors and fonts of the text displayed or typed in the window. See the *xdm* reference page in Part Three of this guide for a complete list of resources.

Each time a user successfully logs on, *xdm* looks for a file called *.xsession* in the user's home directory. If that file exists and is an executable script, *xdm* runs it as the user's login session. The *.xsession* file should follow the general guidelines for startup scripts described earlier in this appendix.

If you've just set up *xdm*, users may not have written *.xsession* scripts. If *xdm* finds no *.xsession* file in a user's home directory, it provides a default session, consisting of the following commands (excerpted from the standard *Xsession* file):

```
resources=$HOME/.Xresources
xrdb -load $resources
twm &
exec xterm -geometry 80x24+10+10 -ls
```

This default session has three elements: First, *xdm* checks the user's home directory for a file called *Xresources*. If that file exists, it is loaded into the resource manager with *xrdb*. Second, the window manager, *twm*, is started. Third, the console *xterm* window is started with a login shell (`-ls`) in the foreground.

After this basic session has been started, the screen looks something like Figure 2-3 and the user is ready to work.

System
Management

Customizing xdm

The display manager can do far more than run the simple session described above. Any of the special files can be edited to customize the display manager for your site. For example, by editing the *Xservers* file, you can set up *xdm* to run multiple displays, such as X terminals.*

Remember that, if *xdm* has been modified with the proper Release 4 patches, *none* of the special files (not even the *xdm-config* file) is *absolutely necessary* to run X on a single display. In a worst case scenario—if all the special files are removed or corrupted—*xdm* has reasonable defaults that will allow you to log in and work. Depending on your system configuration, you may elect not to use some of the special files. For example, the Release 4 *xdm* works well without *Xstartup* and *Xreset* files in many environments. As we've said, if no *Xsession* is specified, *xterm* is executed, etc. (If you decide not to use one of the special files listed in the default *xdm-config* file, remember to remove the pointer to it from the file!)

What the special files provide is the flexibility to configure *xdm* for your site, perhaps running X on several displays, each possibly with a different default session, different resources for the authentication widget, etc.

If you examine the default configuration file, you'll notice most of the resources are specified with loose bindings. This means that the specified resource (for example, *Xsession*) will apply to all displays being run by *xdm*. By using tight bindings in the configuration file, you can also specify resources that only take effect on a specific display. To specify a resource for a particular display, just insert the name of the display between `DisplayManager` and the final resource variable. For example, say *xdm* is running X on a workstation (named `:0`) and a connected X terminal (`visual:0`). You could specify two different default sessions by using resource definitions (in the configuration file) similar to the following:

```
DisplayManager._0.session:        /usr/lib/X11/xdm/Xsession.ws
DisplayManager.visual_0.session: /usr/lib/X11/xdm/Xsession.visual
```

Note that an *xdm* resource specification uses an underscore in place of the colon in a display name. (As discussed earlier, the use of underscores has been introduced in Release 4. The Release 3 syntax is discussed in the section "Release 3 xdm" later in this appendix.) You should match the display name syntax for resources intended to be used on the same display. For example, you might have the following `resources` variable settings to match the `session` resource specifications above:

```
DisplayManager._0.resources: /usr/lib/X11/xdm/Xresources.ws
DisplayManager.visual_0.resources: /usr/lib/X11/xdm/Xresources.visual
```

The following sections discuss some possible customizations of the default special files. With the vast number of possible system configurations and user preferences, you should consult the *xdm* reference page in Part Three of this guide for more information.

---

*Generally, this modification is *required* for *xdm* to run sessions on X terminals. However, as we'll see, an increasing number of X terminals do not require an *Xservers* file entry in order to be controlled by *xdm*. See "X Terminals and the XDM Control Protocol (Release 4)" later in this appendix.

The Xservers File

The Release 4 *xdm* source directory contains two sample *Xservers* files, *Xservers.ws* and *Xservers.fs*, which illustrate file entries for workstations and file servers (such as X terminals), respectively. To run *xdm* on a single workstation, you should create an *Xservers* file using the *Xservers.ws* file as a guide. As we'll see later, in most circumstances, you must edit the *Xservers* file to specify additional displays for *xdm* to manage.

Each entry in the *Xservers* file usually has three or four elements: the display name, an optional display class, the display type, and the server program name (and its arguments, typically the display number). (Since an X terminal runs its own server, the final argument can be a comment, such as "Joe's X terminal.") Possible display types are described on the *xdm* reference page in Part Three of this guide.

Most workstations have a single display numbered 0 of the type *local*, as illustrated by the typical *Xservers* file entry for a workstation:

```
:0 local /usr/bin/X11/X
```

The display class part of the *Xservers* entry is new as of Release 4. The sample entry above does not contain a display class, but it would normally be the second part, between the display name and type, as in the following:

```
:0 display_class local /usr/bin/X11/X
```

The display class is determined by the machine you are using and should be provided by the hardware vendor. The use of the display class is related to an underlying feature of the Release 4 *xdm*, the X Display Manager Control Protocol (XDMCP), which is described later in this appendix. For now, suffice it to say that, in most circumstances, you do not have to supply a class name within an *Xservers* file entry.

For *xdm* to run sessions on most X terminals, you must add specifications for these displays to the *Xservers* file, using the sample file *Xservers.fs* from the *xdm* source directory as a template. For instance, say you have two X terminals hooked up to a workstation. (As of Release 4, most X terminals are of the display type *foreign*. In Release 3, most X terminals are of the display type *transient*.) Your *Xservers* file might look like this:

```
:0  local  /usr/bin/X11/X
visual:0  foreign  Lucy's Visual
ncd:0  foreign  Ricky's NCD16
```

Notice that the final element of each X terminal entry is a comment. Using this *Xservers* file, *xdm* provides login windows on the two X terminals, as well as the workstation, and runs a session for any user who logs on.

If you edit the *Xservers* file while the server is running, *xdm* will not be aware of the changes. You can make *xdm* reread the *Xservers* file (or another file specified by the resource `DisplayManager.servers`) by sending the *xdm* parent process a SIGHUP. Use the UNIX *kill* command with the `-HUP` option (for SIGHUP) and the process ID number of *xdm*.

It's likely there will be multiple *xdm* processes, since the program forks a child process for every display it's managing. As of Release 4, the ID of the parent process is stored in the file specified by the resource `DisplayManager.pidFile`—usually */usr/lib/X11/xdm/xdm-pid*.

```
% kill -HUP process-ID
```

If a new entry has been added, the display manager starts a session on that display. If an entry has been removed, the display manager terminates any session on that display without notice and no new sessions will be started.

Once you edit the *Xservers* file to reflect the different displays you want to manage, you can enter other display-specific resources in the configuration file.

Be aware that communication problems can arise between the display manager and many autonomous displays (primarily X terminals). If the main display is powered off or reset, *xdm* may not detect that the server has been stopped and restarted, and thus may not send new login windows to connected displays. In the spring of 1989, the X Consortium proposed a standard protocol between displays and display managers that would avert these problems. The X Display Manager Control Protocol (XDMCP) has been adopted and is implemented by the Release 4 *xdm*, but not all X terminals implement it yet. We'll discuss the goals of this protocol at greater length in "X Terminals and the XDM Control Protocol" later in this appendix. For now, be aware that the XDMCP will eventually eliminate the need for *Xservers* file entries for X terminals. Currently, however, chances are that your X terminal does not understand the XDMCP and requires an *Xservers* file entry.

The Xsession File and .xsession Scripts

Depending on the needs of your site, you can edit the *Xsession* file to make the default session anything you want. You can specify an alternative window manager, perhaps even use another program to load resources, and execute any combination of clients.

Another strength of *xdm* is that it provides for each user to design his own *.xsession* file. See "A Startup Shell Script" earlier in this appendix for more information on writing a *.xsession* file.

Be aware that if you're testing a *.xsession* script and it doesn't work, by default *xdm* will not let you log in (using the normal method) to fix it. However, *xdm* does provide an escape hatch for these situations, which is explained in "The Xresources File" below.

The Xresources File

The *Xresources* file is where you should specify resources for the authentication widget. See the *xdm* reference page in Part Three of this guide for a complete list of resource variables.

As of Release 4, the default *Xresources* file contains the following event translations, which allow users to log in if a *.xsession* script doesn't work:

```
xlogin*login.translations: #override\
        <Key>F1: set-session-argument(failsafe) finish-field()\n\
        <Key>Return: set-session-argument() finish-field()
```

This translation table specifies that if you type the F1 key (rather than Return) after your password when logging in, a "failsafe" session, consisting of a simple login *xterm* window, will be executed. This will enable you to edit the non-functioning *.xsession* file. See the *xdm* reference page in Part Three of this guide for more information. (See Chapter 9, *Setting Resources*, and Appendix H, *Translation Table Syntax*, for a discussion of event translations.)

The Error Log File

xdm errors are normally printed to the console. It's wise to redirect them to a file. The default configuration file sets the resource `DisplayManager.errorLogFile` to */usr/lib/X11/xdm/xdm-errors*. The *xdm-errors* file can be very helpful if you are testing various *xdm* configurations.

The xdm-pid File (Release 4 Only)

Added to *xdm* as of Release 4, the *xdm-pid* file stores the ID number of the *xdm* parent process. If you edit the *Xservers* file while the server is running, *xdm* will not be aware of the changes. You can make *xdm* reread the *xdm-config* file and the *Xservers* file (or another file specified by the resource `DisplayManager.servers`) by sending the *xdm* parent process a SIGHUP.

To make *xdm* aware of changes to the *Xservers* file, use the UNIX *kill* command with the `-HUP` option (for SIGHUP) and the process ID number of *xdm* stored in the *xdm-pid* file. (See "The Xservers File" earlier in this appendix for an example.)

Xstartup and Xreset

As stated previously, the *Xstartup* and *Xreset* files mentioned in Table A-1 can still be used to affect *xdm* in Release 4, but there are no default files; thus, they are not specified in the default configuration file.

The *Xstartup* file is intended to be a script that is run as root before starting the user session. You might want to write a script containing commands to make fake entries in */etc/utmp*, mount users' home directories from file servers, display a message of the day, or abort the session if logins are not currently allowed.

The *Xreset* file is intended to be a script that is run as root after a user session has been ended. You might want to write a script to undo the effects of commands in *Xstartup*, perhaps removing fake entries from */etc/utmp*, or unmounting directories from file servers.

See the *xdm* reference page for more information about the *Xstartup* and *Xreset* files.

Security and the authorize Resource (Release 4 Only)

In addition to pointers to several special files, the *xdm-config* file contains the following resource specifications:

```
DisplayManager._0.authorize:    true
DisplayManager*authorize:    false
```

Available as of Release 4, the `authorize` resource represents a new method of security for X, which *xdm* can be set up to provide. The first resource specification above sets a user-based server access scheme to work on the local display. The second one turns the scheme off on all other displays. These defaults should be compatible with running X on the local display and most X terminals that might be connected to it. See "User-based Access: xdm and the .Xauthority File" later in this appendix and the *xdm* reference page in Part Three of this guide for more about authorization.

System Management

Stopping xdm and the Server

By default, *xdm* automatically restarts the server if the server is killed. If you don't want this boomerang effect, set the following resource in the *xdm-config* file:

```
DisplayManager.DISPLAY.terminateServer: true
```

Then if you kill the server and all *xdm* processes, X will exit.

X Terminals and the XDM Control Protocol (Release 4)

The X Display Manager Control Protocol (XDMCP), introduced at Release 4, facilitates the connection of X terminals to remote hosts via *xdm*. From a user's standpoint, the main advantage of XDMCP is that it allows you to turn an X terminal off and on again, while maintaining the connection to the remote host. When you turn on an X terminal, *xdm* should automatically display a login window. The exchange of information between the X terminal and the remote host is invisible to the user. In fact, XDMCP and *xdm* are intended to make X terminals as easy to use as traditional character terminals. Under the X Display Manager Control Protocol, an X terminal basically requests a connection to a remote host, is recognized by the host, and is sent a login prompt by *xdm*.

Prior to the adoption of this protocol, *xdm* was not equipped to reconnect to X terminals that had been turned off and on again. In most cases, X terminals had to be left on at all times. If a terminal was turned off, it was often necessary to kill the associated *xdm* process; *xdm* would then restart itself and reestablish the connection, again displaying the login window.

XDMCP is intended to solve problems like this. Be aware, however, that the X terminals in question must be programmed to interpret XDMCP or modified to do so. At the time of Release 4, virtually no X terminals in the market supported XDMCP. Protocol-compatible X terminals should become available in increasing numbers by the fall of 1990. If you're using an older X terminal, chances are that the programs controlling it must be upgraded to communicate via XDMCP.

If you are using X terminals at your site, the way you set up *xdm* partially depends on whether the terminals can communicate via the XDMCP. If a terminal *can't* communicate in this way, the *Xservers* file must include an entry for it and the terminal must be left on at all times to maintain the connection to the host via *xdm*. If a terminal *can* communicate via the protocol, no *Xservers* file entry is necessary and the terminal can be turned on and off, while still maintaining the connection to the host. Refer your X terminal documentation to find out whether it's XDMCP compatible.

The XDMCP helps clarify the actual purpose of the *Xservers* file. The file is actually a list of displays to which *xdm* must perpetually maintain a connection. By contrast, the XDMCP is a dynamic mechanism whereby connections are made when requested by a display, such as a workstation or a newer X terminal, that can communicate via the protocol.

XDMCP also affects the *Xservers* file entry for the host. If you are running Release 4, it is recommended that the *Xservers* file entry for the host include a display class name, which should be provided by the hardware manufacturer. You can use this name in the *xdm-config* file to specify resources by display class, rather than by individual display.

Release 3 xdm

The Release 3 version of *xdm* is somewhat simpler to get started with, albeit somewhat less powerful, than the Release 4 version. This section highlights the Release 3 specifics. We assume you have already read the preceding sections describing the Release 4 version.

The Release 3 *xdm* provides sample files that are probably adequate to run X on most workstations. (A sample *Xservers* file intended for use on a workstation is included in the Release 3 *xdm* source directory.) In order to have *xdm* run X on a single display, simply perform the following three steps:

1. Create a directory called */usr/lib/X11/xdm*. Copy the default versions of the files from the *config* directory under the *xdm* source directory into the new directory.
2. Put the line */usr/bin/X11/xdm* at the end of */etc/rc* or other similar system startup file.
3. It's also a good idea to turn off the "console" in */etc/ttys* on a single-user workstation, although this is discretionary. (Since the display manager provides its own login window, turning off the "console" prevents the standard UNIX prompt from being simultaneously displayed on the full screen when *xdm* is started. Keep in mind this will also prevent system messages from being sent to the console, but they should still be saved in */usr/adm/messages*.) How you'd turn off the "console" depends on the version of UNIX you are running. The procedure and the system file you edit may differ from system to system. See the *getty*(8) and *init*(8) reference pages in your UNIX documentation for details.

Once you perform these steps, so long as UNIX is running, *xdm* should keep the X server running, allow users to log on and off, and manage a simple login session.

The Release 3 *xdm* should be able to run X on a single workstation without any special files, though it was not intended to be used in this manner. If *xdm* finds no special files, it will still start the server and a login *xterm* window. This default action can be very helpful, because it allows you to log in even if the special files have been inadvertently removed or corrupted. For most purposes, however, system administrators will want to use and very likely customize the special files to have *xdm* run X in a manner more suitable for the particular system.

Release 3 Special Files and the Config File

The Release 3 *xdm* recognizes most of the same special files and resources as the Release 4 version (see Table A-1), with the following exceptions: the *xdm-pid* file and the `authorization` resource setting are available in Release 4 only.

The Release 3 version of the *xdm-config* file is shown in Figure A-3:

```
DisplayManager.servers:             /usr/lib/X11/xdm/Xservers
DisplayManager.errorLogFile:        /usr/lib/X11/xdm/xdm-errors
DisplayManager*resources:           /usr/lib/X11/xdm/Xresources
DisplayManager*startup:             /usr/lib/X11/xdm/Xstartup
DisplayManager*reset:               /usr/lib/X11/xdm/Xreset
DisplayManager*session:             /usr/lib/X11/xdm/Xsession
```

Figure A-3. Default xdm-config file, Release 3

The Release 3 default *Xservers* file, in Figure A-4, is probably adequate for most workstations.

```
:0 local /usr/bin/X11/X :0
```

Figure A-4. Typical Xservers file for a workstation, Release 3

However, if X does not run properly on your single display, you should edit the *Xservers* file to reflect the local display name. You must also edit the *Xservers* file to specify additional displays for *xdm* to manage. See "Managing Multiple Displays: the Release 3 *Xservers* File" later in this appendix.

Customizing the Release 3 xdm

Like the Release 4 version, the Release 3 version special files provide the flexibility to configure *xdm* for your site, perhaps running X on several displays, each possibly with a different default session, different resources for the authentication widget, etc. (If you decide not to use one of the special files listed in the default *xdm-config* file, remember to remove the pointer to it from the file!)

Most of the resources specified in the default configuration file have loose bindings, indicating that the resource applies to all displays being run by *xdm*. By using tight bindings in the configuration file, you can also specify resources that only take effect on a particular display. To specify a resource for a particular display, just insert the name of the display between `DisplayManager` and the final resource variable. For example, say *xdm* is running X on a workstation (`:0`) and a connected X terminal (`visual:0`). You could specify two different default sessions by using resource definitions (in the configuration file) similar to the following:

```
DisplayManager..0.session:  /usr/lib/X11/xdm/Xsession.ws
DisplayManager.visual.0.session:     /usr/lib/X11/xdm/Xsession.visual
```

Note that an *xdm* resource specification uses a dot in place of the colon in a display name. (This is different from the syntax expected by Release 4, in which underscores are used between the parts of a display name.) You should match the display name syntax for resources intended to be used on the same display. For example, you might have the following `resources` variable settings to match the `session` resource specifications above:

```
DisplayManager..0.resources: /usr/lib/X11/xdm/Xresources.ws
DisplayManager.visual.0.resources: /usr/lib/X11/xdm/Xresources.visual
```

The following sections describe Release 3 specific features that may affect customization and discuss possible customizations of some of the default special files. You should first have read the sections on customizing the Release 4 version of *xdm* earlier in this appendix. With the vast number of possible system configurations and user preferences, you should also consult the *xdm* reference page in Part Three of this guide for more information.

Managing Multiple Displays: the Release 3 Xservers File

If you are running Release 3, you must edit the *Xservers* file to specify additional displays for *xdm* to manage.

In Release 3, each entry in the *Xservers* file has three elements: the display name, the display type, and the server program name (and its arguments, in most cases the display number). (Since an X terminal uses a remote server, the third argument can be a comment, such as "Ethel's X terminal.")

Most workstations have a display numbered 0 of the type *local*, so the *Xservers* file should look like this:

```
:0  local  /usr/bin/X11/X  :0
```

You can also add specifications for additional displays, such as X terminals. In Release 3, X terminals have the display type *transient*. (In Release 4, this has been changed to *foreign*.) To add a single X terminal, you might create a file similar to the following:

```
:0 local   /usr/bin/X11/X  :0
visual:0  transient  Andy's Visual
```

Notice that the third element of the X terminal entry is a comment. Using this *Xservers* file, *xdm* provides login windows on the workstation and the X terminal, and runs login sessions for any users who log in.

Be aware that communication problems can arise between the display manager and many displays. If the main display is powered off or reset, *xdm* may not detect that the server has been stopped and restarted, and thus may not send new login windows to connected displays. The X Display Manager Control Protocol, introduced in Release 4, is designed to avert these problems. (See "X Terminals and the XDM Control Protocol (Release 4)" earlier in this appendix for more information.) However, if you are still running Release 3, the safest way to keep *xdm* running X on an X terminal is to leave the terminal on.

If you edit the *Xservers* file while the server is running, *xdm* will not be aware of the changes. You can make *xdm* reread the *Xservers* file (or another file specified by the resource `DisplayManager.servers`) by sending the *xdm* parent process a SIGHUP. Use the UNIX *kill* command with the `-HUP` option (for SIGHUP) and the ID number of *xdm*'s parent process, as in the following example:

```
% kill -HUP process-ID
```

It's likely there will be multiple *xdm* processes, since the program forks a child process for every display it's managing. As a general rule, send the signal to the lowest numbered *xdm* process. (As we've seen, in Release 4, the *xdm-pid* special file contains the relevant process ID number.)

If a new entry has been added, the display manager starts a session on that display. If an entry has been removed, the display manager terminates any session on that display without notice and no new sessions will be started.

If the *xdm* connection to an X terminal is interrupted, you should also be able to reestablish it by sending a SIGHUP to the *xdm* parent process.

Once you edit the *Xservers* file to reflect the different displays you want to manage, you can enter other display-specific resources in the configuration file.

Release 3 .xsession Scripts

Be warned that if you're testing a *.xsession* script and it doesn't work, by default *xdm* will not let you log in (under the same login name) to fix it. While the default Release 4 version of *xdm* provides an escape hatch for these situation, the Release 3 version does not. We strongly suggest that you set one up using "The Xresources File."

Release 3 Xresources File

To give users a way to log in if a *.xsession* script doesn't work, place the following event translations in the *Xresources* file:

```
xlogin*login.translations: #override\
        <Key>F1: set-session-argument(failsafe) finish-field()\n\
        <Key>Return: set-session-argument() finish-field()
```

This translation specifies that if you type the F1 key (rather than Return) after your password when logging in, a "failsafe" session, consisting of a simple login *xterm* window, will be executed. This will enable you to edit the non-functioning *.xsession* file. [This translation table has been added to the default *Xresources* file in Release 4.]

The *Xresources* file is also where you should specify resources for the authentication widget. See the *xdm* reference page in Part Three of this guide for a complete list of resource variables. (See Chapter 9, *Setting Resources*, and Appendix H, *Translation Table Syntax*, for a discussion of event translations.)

Release 3 Xstartup and Xreset

The Release 3 version of *xdm* includes default *Xstartup* and *Xreset* files that contain nothing more than a comment. You can use these files to specify custom startup and reset procedures. See "Xstartup and Xreset" under the discussion of the Release 4 *xdm*, earlier in this appendix. Also see the *xdm* reference page in Part Three of this guide for more information about the *Xstartup* and *Xreset* files.

Starting X with xinit

The *xinit* program is used to start the server and a first client program, by default an *xterm* window. Starting X manually with *xinit* is described in Chapter 2, *Getting Started*. You can also use *xinit* to start X automatically.

The easiest way to do this is to run *xinit* from your *.login* or *.profile* file. (If you are using System V, this may be the only reliable way to run *xinit*.)

xinit will look in your home directory for a file called *.xserverrc* to run as a shell script to start up the server. If there is no such script, *xinit* will start the server X on the display :0.

xinit will also look in your home directory for a file called *.xinitrc* to run as a login script, such as the one described earlier in this appendix. If no such script is found, it will execute a login *xterm* window.

With System V only, you might try to run *xinit* from the terminal initialization file */etc/inittab*. This file is analogous to the BSD 4.3 */etc/ttys*. The */etc/inittab* file normally has an entry for each serial port on a system, plus several entries that are used during the boot process. Note that the concept of pseudo-terminals, or ptys (which X relies on) is foreign to System V. All System V servers will have had to do some system hacking to add support for ptys. How this is done will vary from system to system. As a result, we're going to beg off on describing *inittab* in detail, and refer you to your system documentation. Again, it is also possible that there will be problems with the controlling tty.

See the *xinit* reference page in Part Three of this guide for more information.

An Older Method of Starting X: /etc/ttys

For Release 3, this method was supported only for backwards compatibility with older releases of X. As of Release 4, it is not supported. In either case, system administrators should switch to *xinit* or *xdm*.

On BSD 4.3-derived systems, you can start X automatically from the */etc/ttys* terminal initialization file.* This file normally contains a list of terminals on which a login prompt should be printed by the *getty* program. For X, this file can be used instead to start *xterm* for a pseudo-terminal. A typical line to start X from the */etc/ttys* file might have the following format:

*Note that the technique described here will not work on earlier BSD systems, Xenix, or other systems which use the pre-BSD 4.3 *ttys* format.

BSD 4.3 */etc/ttys*

```
devname                        command                     ttytype
   |                              |                           |
ttyv0 "/etc/xterm -L -geometry -1+1 -display :0"  xterm
            on secure window="/usr/bin/X11/X :0 -c -l"   #Start X
                    |                                         |
                  status                                    comment
```

Field	*Function in /etc/ttys*
devname	The name of the special file in the *dev* directory that corresponds to the device. For X, the pseudo-terminal with the highest minor device number (e.g. */dev/ttyqf* and */dev/ptyqf*) is normally renamed */dev/ttyv0* and */dev/ptyv0*. For systems with more than one display, the next highest pty is used for the second display, and so on.
command	The command to be run by *init*. This is normally *getty*, but can be another command, such as the command to start a window system. In this example, *xterm* is run with the `-L` option, which causes *getty* to be run in the *xterm* window rather than the shell. (The `-L` option is not supported in Release 4.) The window is placed in the top right corner of the screen. Since spaces and tabs are used to separate fields in */etc/ttys*, the entire command must be quoted. Note that some implementations of *init* have relatively small program name buffer sizes, so you may find you can't list many *xterm* options. In addition, because the # character is used as a comment symbol in */etc/ttys*, you may have difficulty specifying colors (say for an *xterm* window background) using the hexadecimal color syntax. If you run into either of these problems, you may want to write a small program that runs *xterm* with the desired arguments, and have *init* run that instead.
ttytype	The name of the terminal attached to the line. This should be the name as defined in the */etc/termcap* terminal database. In the example above, it is specified as *xterm*. Note that the presence of the terminal type field in the BSD 4.3 *ttys* replaces the */etc/ttytype* file that was used for this purpose in earlier BSD versions.
status	The word **on** if the *command* is to be executed, or **off** if it is not. Additional flags may be specified after **on** or **off**. The word **secure** must be present to allow root to log in on a particular terminal. The flag **window="***command***"** specifies a window system command to be executed by *init* before it starts *xterm*. This should be the command to start the X server, as shown in the example.
comment	Comments can appear anywhere in the file. They are introduced by #, and are terminated by a newline.

Server Access Control

X runs in a networked environment. Because of X's design, your workstation is no longer your private preserve, but hypothetically, can be accessed by any other host on the network. This is the true meaning of the server concept: your display can serve clients on any system, and clients on your system can display on any other screen.

The possibilities for abuse are considerable. However, there are two access control mechanisms, one host-based and one user-based. The host-based scheme involves a system file (*/etc/Xn.hosts*) and can be controlled using the *xhost* client. The user-based scheme involves authorization capabilities provided by the display manager, *xdm*, as of Release 4, and depends upon the newly introduced X Display Manager Control Protocol (XDMCP). As we'll see, since most X terminals cannot interpret the XDMCP at this time, the usefulness of this latter access control mechanism is currently somewhat limited.

These two access control methods are discussed briefly in the following sections. For more information, see the *Xserver*, *xhost*, *xdm*, and *xauth* reference pages in Part Three of this guide.

Host-based Access and the xhost Client

The */etc/Xn.hosts* file (where ***n*** is the number of the display) contains a list of systems that are allowed to access the server. By default, this file contains only the name of the local host. Edit this file so that it contains the list of systems you want to have access to your server on a regular basis.

The *xhost* client can be used to give (or deny) systems access to the server interactively, possibly overriding the contents of */etc/Xn.hosts*. (The *xhost* client can also be run from a startup script.) Note that this is really only sufficient for a single-user workstation environment, however.

Specifying a host name (with an optional leading plus sign) allows the host to access the server, and specifying a host name with a leading minus sign prevents a previously allowed host from accessing the server. Multiple hosts can be specified on the same line. Running *xhost* without any arguments prints the current hosts allowed to access your display.

For example, to add the hosts jupiter and saturn, and remove neptune:

```
% xhost +jupiter saturn -neptune
```

It is possible to remove the current host from the access list. Be warned that you can't undo this without logging out.

Note that when a remote system is denied access to your display, it means two things: that a person working on the remote system can't display on your screen, and that you can't use that remote system for running clients you want displayed on your screen.

System Management

User-based Access: xdm and the .Xauthority File (Release 4)

As of Release 4, the display manager and its control protocol (XDMCP) provide a user-based access control mechanism, which can be used to supplement or replace the host-based access mechanism discussed in the previous section. The Release 4 *xdm* can be set up to provide user authorization on a particular display (see "Security and the authorize Resource" earlier in this appendix). If authorization is enabled, when you log in, *xdm* places a machine-readable access code, known as a *magic cookie*, in a file called *Xauthority* in your home directory. *xdm* also makes this magic cookie available to the server.

The magic cookie defined in a user's *Xauthority* file is basically a secret code shared by the server and a particular user logged in on a particular display. When the user runs a client on the local display, the server checks to see whether the client program has access to the magic cookie. All processes started by the user in question have that access, and thus the server allows the client to be run on the display. Basically, under the magic cookie authorization scheme, a display becomes user-controlled. (Once *xdm* creates an *Xauthority* file for a user, each time the user logs on, *xdm* merges in authorization codes (magic cookies).)

The access afforded by magic cookies is not as broad as that afforded by the host-based mechanism. When a system relies entirely on host-based access, any machine on the list of approved hosts can connect to the system. Thus, generally, any user logged on to an approved host can access any display connected to the system. This is somewhat feeble security. User-based access control is a little safer.

Be aware, however, that, currently, user-based access control cannot provide security for all X terminal users. This method of access control relies on the X Display Manager Control Protocol and few X terminals in the current market are programmed to understand the protocol. However, user-based access *can* be used effectively on workstations running Release 4 and on many of the newer X terminals.

The security mechanism provided by the magic cookie is evident in a situation in which another user tries to run a client on your machine. The server requires the client run by the other user to have access to the magic cookie shared exclusively between you and the server. The other user cannot provide the proper authorization code, and thus cannot run a client on your host.

Of course, in many cases, users in a network will want to run clients on several machines (while displaying the client window on their local displays). This can be done if a user supplies authorization information associated with his local machine (or X terminal display) to the remote host. X developers have provided a new client, *xauth*, to allow users to transfer this information. Basically, *xauth* is a utility to manipulate *Xauthority* files.

The most common use for *xauth* is to extract a user's authorization information for the current display, copy it to another machine, and merge it into the server's authorization records on the remote machine, as in the following:

```
% xauth extract - $DISPLAY | rsh host2 xauth merge -
```

The dash (-) arguments indicate that extracted authorization records should be written to the standard output and that the *xauth* merge function should accept records from standard input. This command supplies the remote server with authorization information, allowing the user to run a remote shell on that host. See the *xauth* reference page in Part Three of this guide for more information.

If an installation is using remote file sharing, such as NFS, then sharing authorization records may not be an issue. If every user has a single home directory that is accessible to all machines, the machines have access to the necessary *.Xauthority* files at all times. In such an environment, users should be able to run programs on any of the networked machines without using *xauth*.

When user-based access control fails (for example, when a null or invalid magic cookie is offered to the server), host-based access takes over. To be more specific, say for example a user is logged on at an X terminal that is not XDMCP compatible, and thus the user has no *.Xauthority* file (i.e., magic cookie). If that user tries to open a window on the remote console display, the client window cannot access a magic cookie. (The host interprets this as a null cookie.) Then host-based access control takes over. If the user in question is working on a system authorized in the */etc/Xn.hosts* file, he should be authorized to run a client on the console display.

Font Management

In Release 3, the X Consortium adopted the Bitmap Display Format (BDF) as the (non-exclusive) standard font format. BDF font files must be compiled to produce SNF (Server Natural Format) font files, which can be used by the server. (These font files have a *.snf* extension.)

The standard fonts shipped with X should already be compiled. If you add BDF font files to the system, the files must be converted to SNF format using the program *bdftosnf*. The *showsnf* program displays the SNF font file so you can check that it compiled properly. See the *bdftosnf* and *showsnf* reference pages in Part Three of this guide for details.

Once a new font is moved to the directory you want (perhaps */usr/lib/X11/fonts/misc*), you must add the font to the font database (*fonts.dir* file) used by the server. To do this, run *mkfontdir* with the directory as an argument, as in the following:

```
% mkfontdir /usr/lib/X11/fonts/misc
```

An entry for the new font is added to the *fonts.dir* file. You should also edit the *fonts.alias* file if you want to add an alias for the new font.

Then the server must be made aware of the new font. The command:

```
% xset fp rehash
```

makes the server reread the font databases and alias files in the current font path.

If you are using a server other than the standard release, the server developer should provide a program to convert BDF font files to a format appropriate for the server.

Console Messages

On a single-user workstation, it is likely that the screen used for running X is also used as the system console.

If X is started manually, the console will be the first window to appear on the screen. But if X is started from your *.login* file, console messages from the kernel may sometimes appear on the screen, overlaying the X windows. They make a nasty mess of the screen, but the display can be refreshed and the console message erased by running the client *xrefresh* (described in Part Three).

Some implementations of X support a `-C` option to *xterm* that redirects messages sent to */dev/console* to that *xterm* window. If this option is supported, you should add the `-C` option to the console *xterm* in your startup file. After this window is mapped (displayed on the screen), all such messages are displayed there.

Log Files

The X server creates log files useful in fixing a problem that might occur. These files are located in */usr/adm*.

You should make provisions to trim these files periodically. As with all log files, you can do this automatically with an entry in the *crontab* file.

Changing the Color Name Database

The X Window System comes with a predefined set of colors, listed in the file */usr/lib/X11/rgb.txt*. You can use these color names to specify colors either on the command line or in a resources file. If you have the X sources, you can customize the color name database using the following procedure.

1. Edit the *rgb.txt* source file, which is located in the *mit/rgb* directory, to change or add colors. The format of a line in the *rgb.txt* file is:

   ```
   red green blue color_name
   ```

   The red, green, and blue values are integers in the range 0 to 255; the color name is case insensitive, but must not include any special symbols. A typical entry in the *rgb.txt* file is:

   ```
   127 255 212aquamarine
   ```

   See Chapter 8, *Command Line Options*, for more about color specifications.

2. Run the *rgb* program using the makefile also located in the *mit/rgb* directory. This program converts the text file (*rgb.txt*) to a UNIX *dbm*(1) format file (*rgb.dir*), which is used as the color database. Just type:

   ```
   % make
   ```

3. Then install the new *rgb.dir* file in */usr/lib/X11* by typing:

   ```
   % make install
   ```

If the color name database gets corrupted in some way (e.g., written to accidentally), the server may not be able to find any colors with which to display. On a black and white workstation, you may get error messages similar to the following:

```
X Toolkit Warning:  Cannot allocate colormap entry for White
X Toolkit Warning:  Cannot allocate colormap entry for Black
X Toolkit Warning:  Cannot allocate colormap entry for white
X Toolkit Warning:  Cannot allocate colormap entry for black
```

If you get errors of this sort, perform steps 2 and 3 in the procedure described above. This will overwrite the corrupted *rgb.dir* file.

B

The uwm Window Manager

This appendix describes uwm, *the Release 3 standard window manager, which has been moved to the user-contributed distribution in Release 4. It covers both the basics of using* uwm and how to customize it.

In This Chapter:

B
The uwm Window Manager

If you are running Release 3 of X (or an earlier release), the standard window manager is *uwm*, the *u*niversal *w*indow *m*anager. *uwm* allows you to perform all of the basic window manipulation functions, such as:

- Sizing and positioning client windows on the screen interactively.
- Creating additional *xterm* terminal windows.
- Refreshing your screen.
- Moving windows around the screen.
- Changing the size of windows.
- Lowering windows (sending them to the back of others).
- Raising windows (bringing them to the front of others).
- Converting windows to icons and icons to windows.
- Removing windows.

The *uwm* window manipulation functions can be invoked in three ways:

- Using the WindowOps menu.
- By combinations of keyboard keys and pointer buttons.
- Automatically, when a client is started (to allow you to size and place the client window on the screen).

The window manager also has a second menu, the Preferences menu, that allows you to set various keyboard and pointer preferences.

Be aware also that you can customize nearly every feature of *uwm* by modifying a window manager startup file called *.uwmrc*, kept in your home directory. You can change the keystroke and pointer button combinations used to invoke window manager functions, modify the default *uwm* menus, create new menus, etc.

The first half of this appendix discusses the default window manipulation functions provided by *uwm*. The second half discusses how to customize the window manager to suit your needs. First, however, let's take a look at starting *uwm*.

Starting the Window Manager

You start *uwm* from the command line by typing:

```
% uwm &
```

in an *xterm* window. If *xdm* (the display manager) is starting X on your system, the *uwm* window manager is probably started automatically when you log on. (See the discussions of *xdm* in Chapter 2, *Getting Started*, and Appendix A, *System Management*.) When *uwm* is started, nothing visible will happen, but your terminal will beep once to indicate that *uwm* is running on the current screen.

Note also that you can run *xterm* or other X clients without running a window manager. *uwm* allows you to size and place client windows on the screen, but you can also use command line options to do this. However, there is no way to change the size or location of windows on the screen without a window manager.

The WindowOps Menu

The *uwm* WindowOps menu gives you access to many of the most frequently used window manipulation functions. In the standard version of *uwm* shipped by MIT, you bring up this menu by moving the pointer to the root window and holding down the middle pointer button. The WindowOps menu and the menu pointer appear as shown in Figure B-1.

Note that the last two items, KillWindow and Exit, appear on the menu as of Release 3. If you are running Release 2, your menu will not include these items. (However, the items that appear on both Release 2 and Release 3 menus are identical in functionality; our discussions of these common menu items apply to either release.)

Another Release 3 feature is that the "hand" pointer is used to indicate the window to be acted upon (resized, refreshed, etc.). In Release 2, this function was performed by the "target circle" pointer. The figures in this appendix depict Release 3 pointers, but the Release 2 and 3 pointers function in the same way.

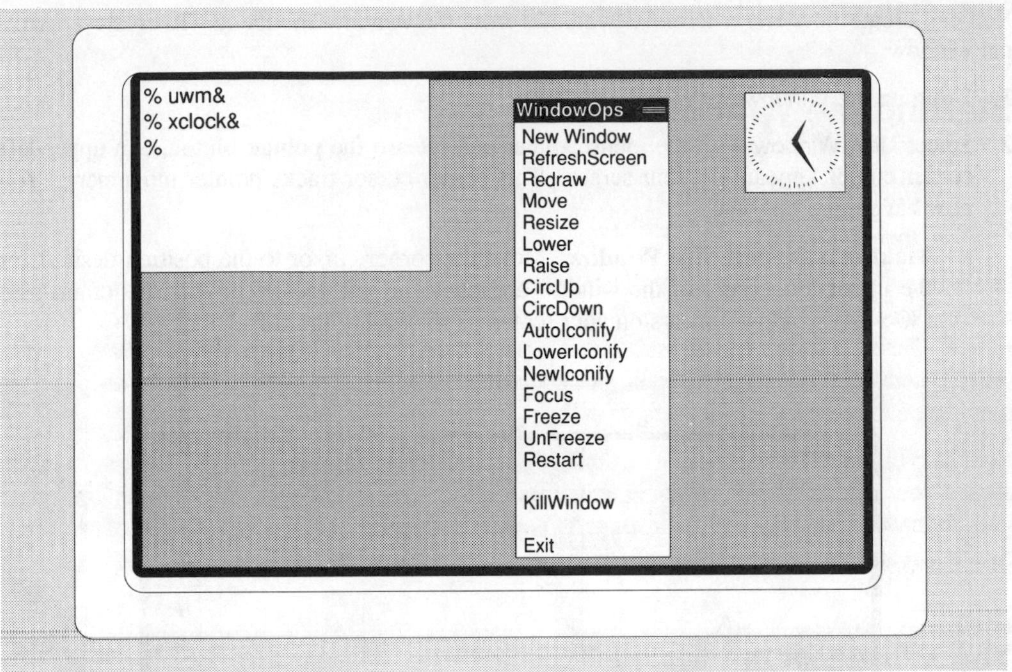

Figure B-1. WindowOps menu

The following pages explain the functions of the *uwm* WindowOps menu. Remember that all of the window manager functions are customizable. Items can be added to or deleted from this menu (and the Preferences menu) by modifying the *.uwmrc* window manager startup file, as described in the section "Customizing uwm" later in this appendix. This appendix describes the window manager as it is shipped with the standard release of the X Window System from the MIT X Consortium.

To bring up the WindowOps menu, move the pointer to the root window and hold down the middle button on the pointer. To *select* a menu item, continue to hold down the middle button and move the pointer to the desired menu item. A horizontal band, or *highlighting bar*, follows the pointer. When you've highlighted the desired menu item, release the button. The selected function will be executed. Note that you must keep the pointer within the menu as you drag down to make a choice, or the menu will disappear and you'll have to start over.

Some of the functions on the menus can be invoked simply by pressing a combination of pointer buttons and keyboard keys. We discuss these "keyboard shortcuts" as appropriate when discussing each menu function, and summarize them in Table B-1 later in this appendix. These shortcuts all make use of the "Meta" modifier key. See Chapter 11, *Setup Clients*, for a discussion of how to determine which key on your keyboard serves as the Meta key. (For the Sun-3 keyboard, for example, Meta is either of the keys labeled "Left" or "Right.")

Creating New Terminal Windows

You can create new *xterm* terminal windows from the WindowOps menu. To create a terminal window:

1. Bring up the WindowOps menu.
2. Select New Window with the menu pointer and release the pointer button. An upper-left corner cursor appears on your screen. This corner cursor tracks pointer movement. You now have three options:

   - **Making a Default-Size Window.** Move the corner cursor to the position desired for the upper-left corner of the window and click the left pointer button. A default-size (80 x 24) window appears on your screen as shown in Figure B-2.

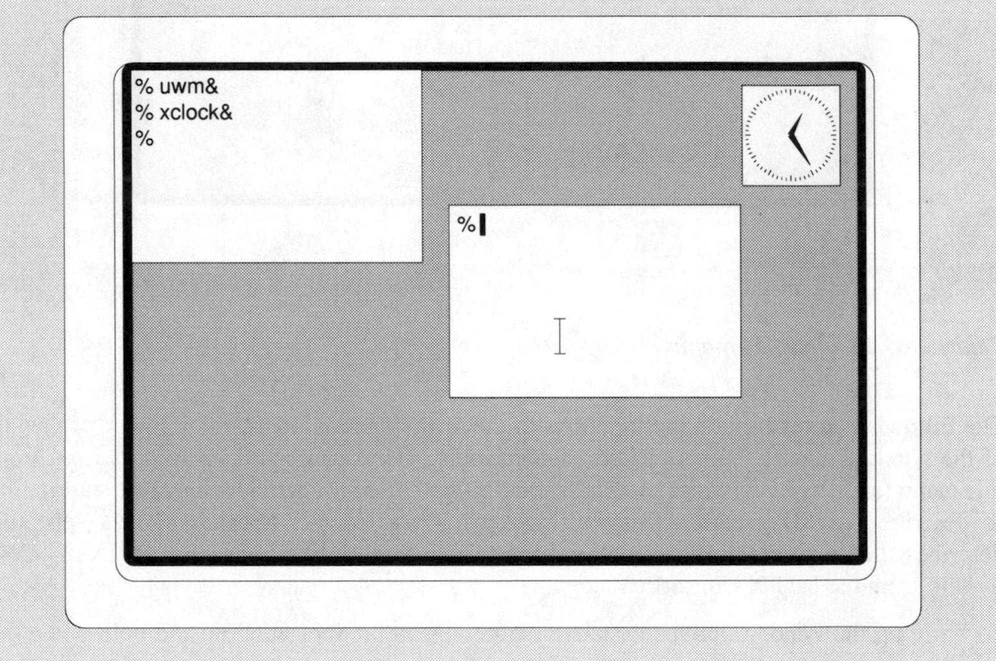

Figure B-2. A default-size xterm window

   - **Making a Custom-Size Window.** Move the corner cursor to the desired position for the upper-left corner of the new window. Press and hold down the middle pointer button. Notice that the upper-left corner cursor is now fixed at that position and that a lower-right corner cursor appears.

     While holding down the middle button, move the corner cursor to the desired position for the lower-right corner of the window. The window size, as you change it, appears in the upper-left corner of your screen. Release the button. A window of the width and height you specified with the pointer appears. See Figure B-3.

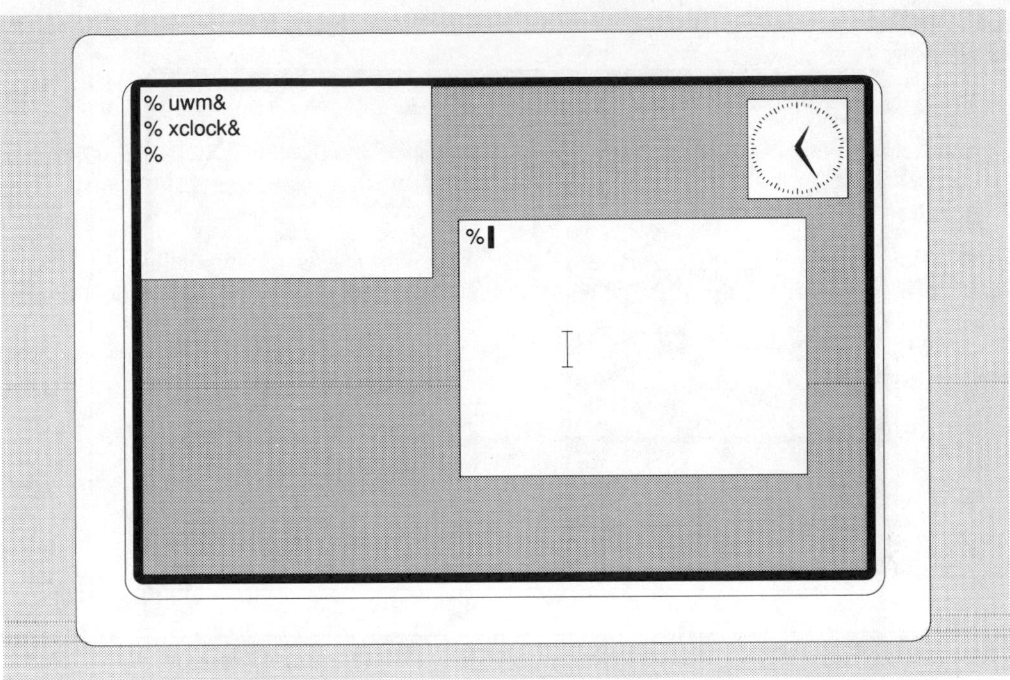

Figure B-3. A custom-size xterm window

- **Making a Maximum-Height Window**. Move the corner to the desired position and click the right button. A default-width by maximum-height (to the bottom of the screen) window appears. See Figure B-4.

Refreshing the Screen

Refreshing your screen means redrawing its contents. This is useful if system messages from outside the X window system appear on the screen, overlaying its contents. To refresh your screen:

1. Bring up the WindowOps menu.
2. Select RefreshScreen with the menu pointer. The screen redraws itself. You can use the *xrefresh* client to achieve the same effect. Simply type `xrefresh` at the prompt in any *xterm* window.

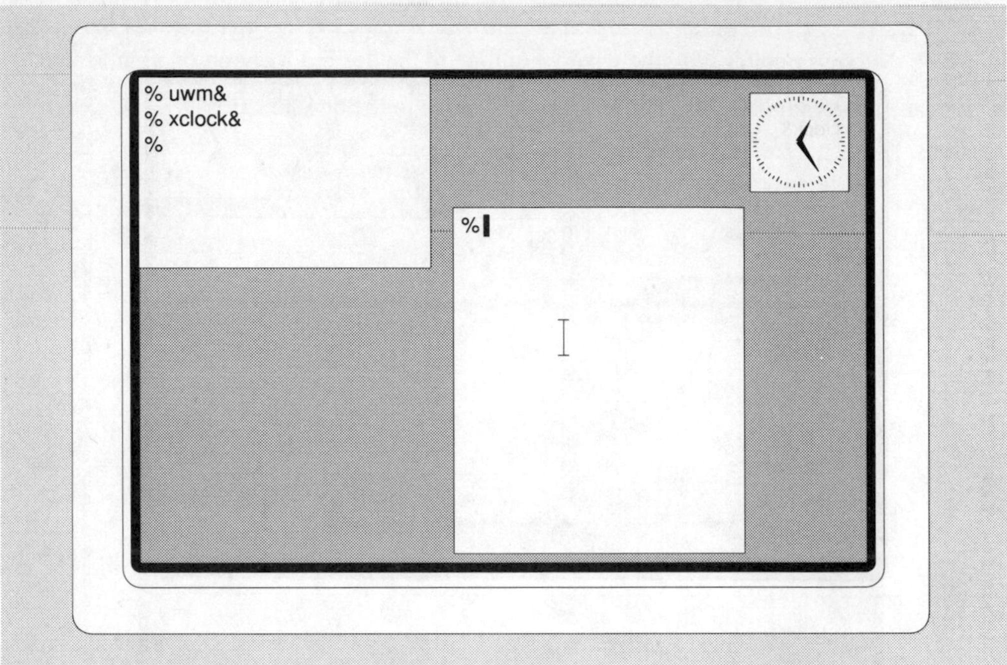

Figure B-4. A maximum-height xterm window

Redrawing a Window

The Redraw menu item redraws (or refreshes) an individual window. To redraw a window:

1. Bring up the WindowOps menu.
2. Select Redraw with the menu pointer. The pointer changes to the hand pointer.
3. Move the hand pointer to the window you want to redraw.
4. Click the left or middle button to redraw the window.

Moving Windows and Icons

The Move menu item moves a window or icon to a new location. When you use this function, an outline, not the entire window or icon, tracks the pointer movement to the new location. See Figure B-5. To move a window:

1. Bring up the WindowOps menu.
2. Select Move with the menu pointer. The pointer changes to the hand pointer.

3. Move the hand pointer to the desired window or icon. Hold down the middle button. The pointer changes to the cross pointer and a window outline appears. This outline tracks the pointer movement.
4. Move the cross pointer with the window outline to the desired location on your screen.
5. Release the middle button. The window will move to the new location.

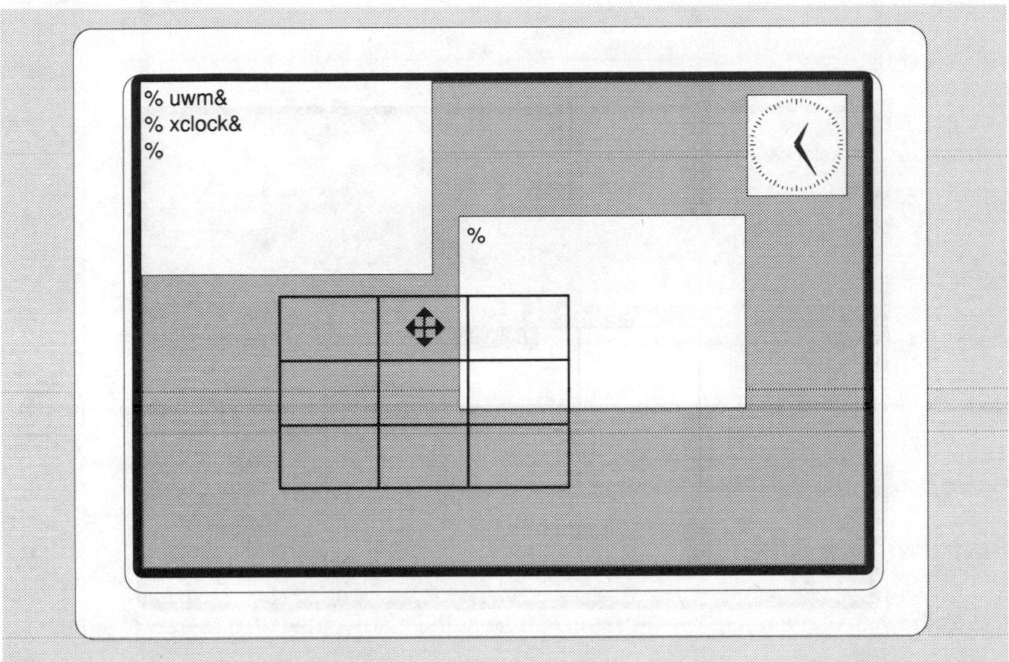

Figure B-5. Moving windows or icons

You can also move a window or icon simply by moving the pointer to the window or icon you want to move, then pressing the right pointer button while holding down the Meta key. The pointer at first changes to a small image of an icon. You can now let go of the Meta key. Then, as you drag the pointer while holding down the button, the pointer changes to a cross, while the window or icon changes to outline form. Drag the outline to the new location, and let go of the right button. The window will be redrawn in the new location.

Resizing Windows

The Resize menu item resizes an existing window. See Figure B-6. To resize a window:

1. Bring up the WindowOps menu.
2. Select Resize with the menu pointer. The pointer changes to the hand pointer.

3. Move the hand pointer to the window you want to resize. Place it near the border you want to move. The opposite border remains in its current position.
4. Hold down the middle button. The pointer changes to the cross pointer.
5. Move the window's border to obtain the desired window size. As you resize the window, a digital readout appears opposite the pointer showing the window size in pixels. (For the *xterm* client, size is in characters and lines.) Release the middle button.

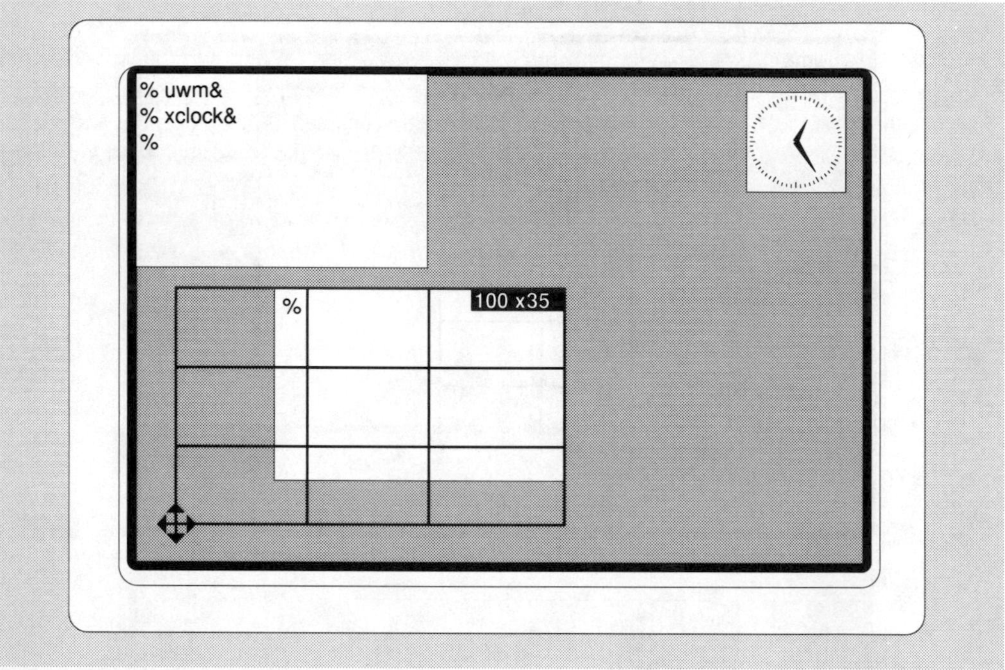

Figure B-6. Resizing a window

You can also resize a window without using the menu. Move the pointer so that it is within the window you want to resize, placing the pointer near the window border you want to change. With one hand, press and hold down the Meta key on the keyboard. With the other hand, press and hold down the middle pointer button. The pointer starts as an icon pointer, but as you drag the pointer, it changes to a cross and a window outline appears. Move the pointer to resize the window. When the window is the proper size, release the middle button and the Meta key.

Resizing an *xterm* window will not change the dimensions of the text currently in the window. (If you make the window smaller, for instance, some of the text may be obscured.) However, if the operating system supports terminal resizing capabilities (for example, the SIGWINCH signal in systems derived from BSD 4.3), *xterm* will use these facilities to notify programs running in the window whenever it is resized. As you continue to work, perhaps starting an editing session, the program will use the entire window. If you resize *during* an editing session, the text editing program may not know about the new size, and may operate incorrectly. Simply quitting out of the editor and starting another session should solve this problem.

If your resized *xterm* window does not seem to know its new size, you may be working with an operating system that does not support terminal resizing capabilities. Refer to the discussion of the *resize* client in Chapter 4, *The xterm Terminal Emulator*, (and to the *resize* reference page in Part Three of this guide) for alternative solutions.

Shuffling the Window Stack: Raise, Lower, CircUp, CircDown

Under the X Window System, windows can overlap each other. When windows overlap, one or more windows may be fully or partially hidden behind other windows (see Figure B-7). You can think of these windows as being stacked on top of each other much the way papers are stacked on a desk. *uwm* can control the stacking order of the windows. Stacking functions include: raising a window to the top of the stack, making all of it visible; lowering a window to the bottom of the stack (possibly obscuring it by other windows); circulating the bottom window to the top and lowering every other window one level; or circulating the top window to the bottom and raising every other window one level.

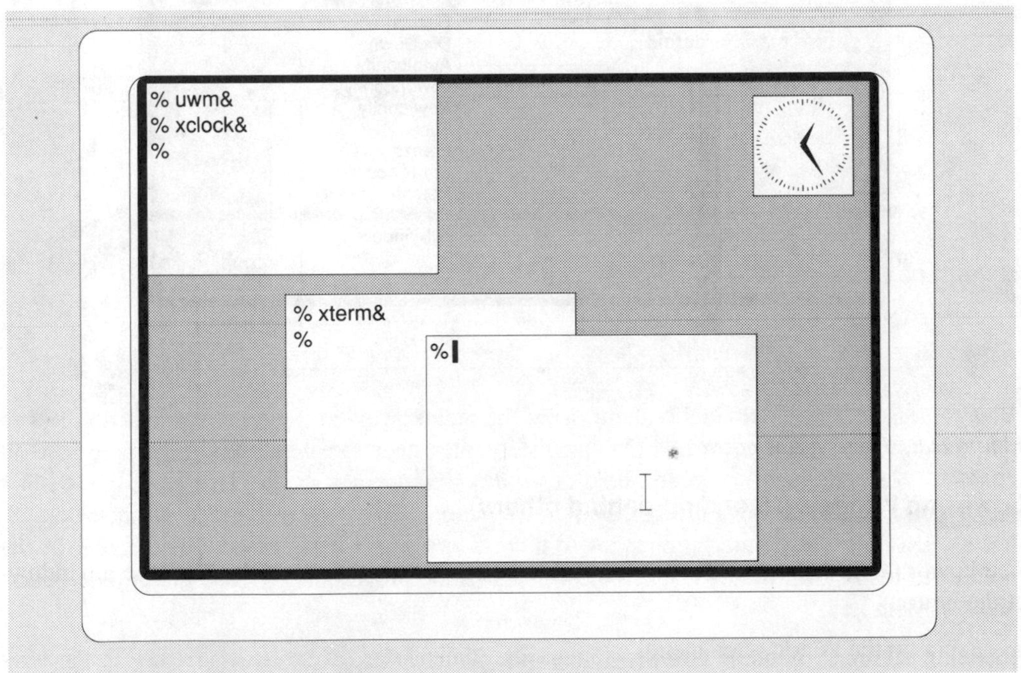

Figure B-7. One xterm window overlapping another

Raising Windows (bringing in front of others)

The Raise menu item places a window at the top of a window stack. See Figure B-8. To bring a window to the front:

1. Bring up the WindowOps menu.
2. Select Raise with the menu pointer. The pointer changes to the hand pointer.
3. Move the hand pointer to the desired window.
4. Click the left or middle button. The window is raised to the top of the stack.

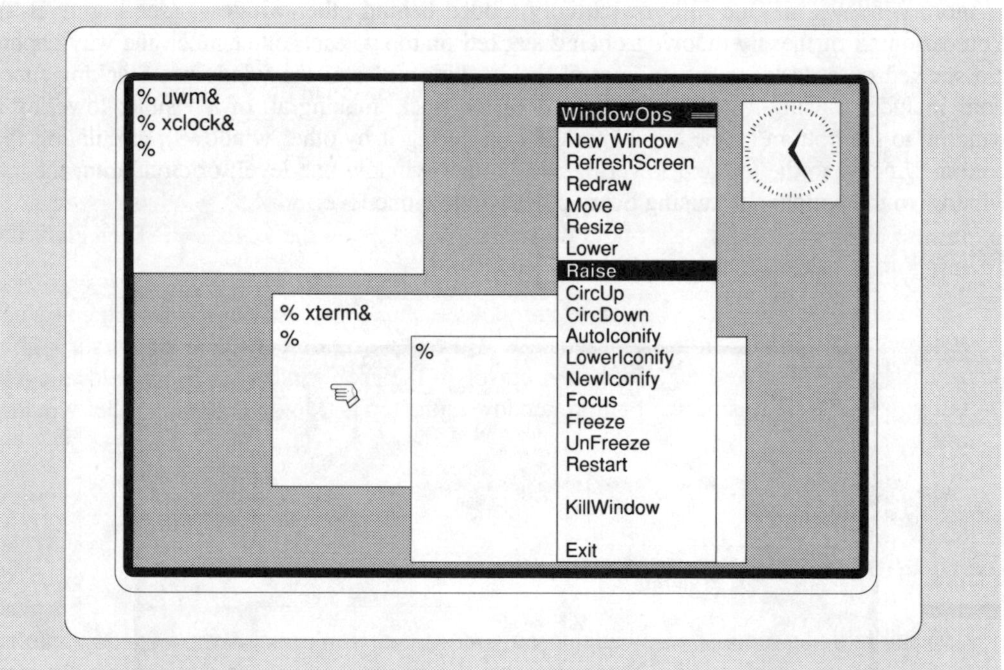

Figure B-8. Raising a window

Lowering Windows (sending behind others)

The Lower menu item places a window at the bottom of a window stack. To place a window at the bottom:

1. Bring up the WindowOps menu.
2. Select Lower with the menu pointer. The pointer changes to the hand pointer.
3. Move the hand pointer to the appropriate window.
4. Click the left or middle button. The desired window is placed behind all windows except the root window.

Circulating Windows

The CircUp and CircDown menu items circulate the windows in a stack. CircUp raises the bottom window to the top and lowers every other one by one level. CircDown lowers the top window to the bottom and raises every other window by one level. CircUp and CircDown only affect overlapping windows.

To circulate the windows in a stack:

1. Bring up the WindowOps menu.
2. Select CircUp or CircDown.

Note that both CircUp and CircDown circulate *every* window stack if there is more than one stack of windows on the screen.

Here's how to change the stacking order using keyboard shortcuts:

- To raise a window, move the pointer so that the cursor is within the window you want to raise. With your other hand, hold down the Meta key on the keyboard. Then click the right pointer button. The window is raised.
- To lower a window, move the pointer so that the cursor is within the window you want to lower. With your other hand, hold down the Meta key on the keyboard. Then click the left pointer button. The window is lowered.
- To circulate all windows, you can use any of the above key and pointer button combinations with the pointer in the root window. However, you do not place the cursor within any particular window (e.g., leave the cursor in the root window). The windows cycle through the stack, raising the bottom window to the top and lowering every other window one level.

Displaying Windows as Icons

If you want to make more space available on your screen, you can convert a window into an icon. An *icon* is a small symbol that represents the window. You also can convert the icon back into a window.

There are three menu items on the default WindowOps menu used to iconify and deiconify: AutoIconify, LowerIconify, and NewIconify. All three iconify a window or deiconify an icon. In addition, LowerIconify and NewIconify interactively move the icon or window to a new location. See Figure B-9 and Figure B-10.

To convert a window to an icon or an icon to a window:

1. Bring up the WindowOps menu.
2. Select NewIconify with the menu pointer. The pointer changes to the hand pointer.
3. Move the hand pointer to the desired window or icon.

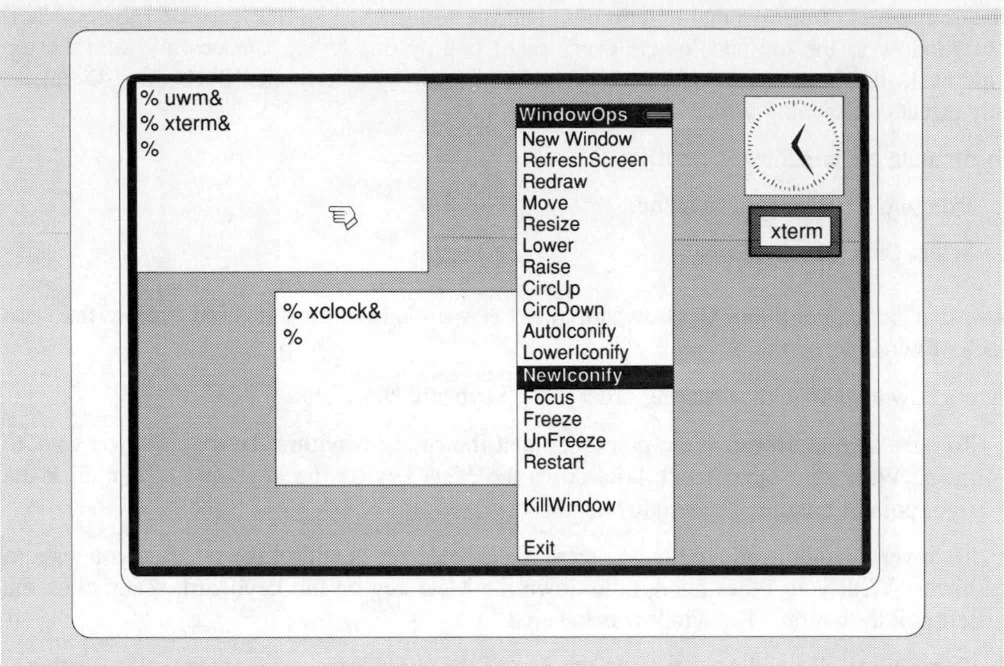

Figure B-9. The login window is about to become an icon

4. Hold down the left button and move the pointer to the desired location. The window or icon tracks the pointer to the new location.
5. Release the left button. The window is converted to an icon or the icon to a window in the new location.

While the pointer rests in the icon, you can edit the icon name by typing in the appropriate name or characters. Use the Delete key to delete unwanted characters.

NewIconify can also be used to display an icon as its original window. Follow the same procedure as to iconify a window, but start with an icon, and turn it into a window.

To iconify or deiconify a window using keyboard shortcuts, move the pointer so that the cursor is within the window you want to iconify. With one hand, press and hold down the Meta key on the keyboard. With the other hand, press and hold the left pointer button and drag the window. The window converts to an icon-sized outline. Drag the outline to the desired position, and then release the pointer button and the Meta key. The full icon appears in the specified position.

To bring back the window (deiconify it), move the pointer so that the cursor is within the icon. Then hold down the Meta key and click the middle pointer button. The window appears back in its original position. Or hold down the Meta key and use the left pointer button while dragging the window outline to a new location, just as you did to iconify the window in the first place.

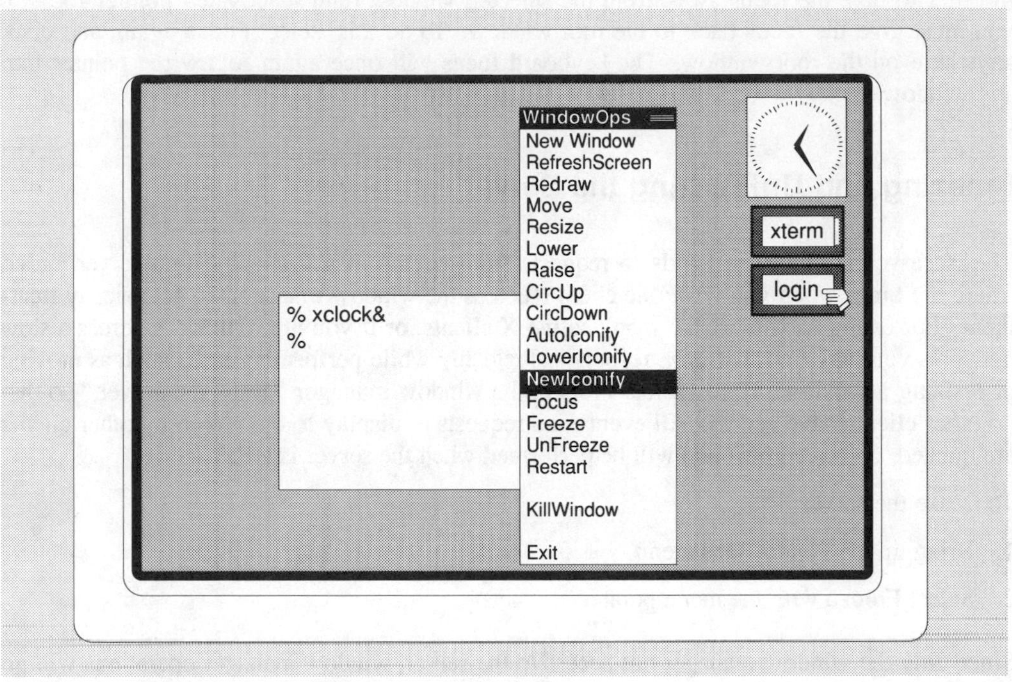

Figure B-10. The login window is about to be deiconified

Changing Keyboard Focus

Normally, keyboard input goes to whichever window the pointer is currently in. The Focus option causes keyboard input to go only to a selected window (the *focus* window) regardless of the position of the pointer.

Focusing can be useful if you are working in one window for an extended period of time, and want to move the pointer out of the way. It also prevents the annoying situation in which you inadvertently knock the pointer out of the window while typing. (This can be very important for touch typists who look infrequently at the screen while typing!)

To choose a focus window:

1. Bring up the WindowOps menu.
2. Select Focus with the menu pointer. The pointer changes to the hand pointer.
3. Move the hand pointer to the window you want to choose as the focus window.
4. Click the middle button to choose the window.

The focus window becomes highlighted with a dark border.

In order to take the focus away from the selected window (and reactivate "pointer focus"), you must give the focus back to the root window. To do this, select Focus again, and click anywhere on the root window. The keyboard focus will once again follow the pointer into any window.

Freezing and UnFreezing the Server

The X server normally responds to requests from clients in a first-come first-served order. There are times when you want one client (such as the window manager) to get priority treatment. For example, if there are many active X clients, or if you are running X across a slow network, you may find that *uwm* responds sluggishly while performing tasks such as moving or resizing a window. If you select Freeze, the window manager "grabs the server," so that no other clients have access. All events and requests to display to the screen by other clients are queued, or "saved up," and will be performed when the server is unfrozen.

To freeze the server:

1. Bring up the WindowOps menu.
2. Select Freeze with the menu pointer.

Since only the window manager has access to the server, window manager operations will go much more quickly. When you are finished moving or resizing windows (or whatever it was you wanted the window manager to do more quickly), select Unfreeze to resume normal operation.

Restarting the Window Manager

The Restart menu item restarts the window manager. This may occasionally become necessary if the window manager functions improperly. To stop and restart the window manager:

1. Bring up the WindowOps menu.
2. Select Restart with the menu pointer.

You may also want to restart the window manager if you edit your *.uwmrc* configuration file to change the functionality of *uwm*. For more information, see the section "Customizing uwm" later in this appendix.

Note that when the window manager is stopped, all icons revert to windows. This happens because the window manager is what allows windows to be iconified. When the window manager is restarted, you can iconify the windows again.

Removing a Window

The KillWindow menu item terminates a client window. Like other methods of 'killing' a program (such as the *xkill* client), the KillWindow menu item can adversely affect underlying processes.

Most windows can be removed in ways that do not harm relevant processes. For example, you can generally remove an *xterm* window by typing the same command you use to log off the system. KillWindow is intended to be used primarily after more conventional methods to remove a window have failed.

To remove a stubborn window:

1. Bring up the WindowOps menu.
2. Select KillWindow with the menu pointer. The pointer changes to the hand pointer.
3. Move the hand pointer into the window you want to terminate.
4. Click any pointer button.

The window is removed.

Refer to the section on *xkill* in Chapter 7, *Other Clients*, for a more complete discussion of the hazards of killing a client and a summary of alternatives.

Exiting the Window Manager

The Exit menu item stops the window manager. You may want to stop *uwm* in order to start another window manager. To stop *uwm*:

1. Bring up the WindowOps menu.
2. Select Exit with the menu pointer.

The window manager is stopped. All icons revert to windows.

Button Control of Window Manager Functions

Table B-1 summarizes the keyboard shortcuts for window management functions. The first column lists the desired function; the second, the required location for the pointer; and the third, the button-key combination. In this column, "click" means to press and immediately release the specified pointer button; "down" means to press and hold the pointer button, and "drag" means to move the pointer while holding down the pointer button. In all cases, you can let go of the keyboard key as soon as you have pressed the appropriate pointer button.

Note that these key "bindings" can be changed in your *.uwmrc* file as described later in this appendix. The combinations described in Table B-1 work for the *default.uwmrc* file.

Table B-1. Keyboard Shortcuts for Window Manager Functions

Function	Pointer Location	Keyboard Shortcut
Move	Window or icon	Meta key, right pointer button down and drag.
Resize	Window	Meta key, middle pointer button down and drag.
Raise	Window or icon	Meta key, right pointer button click .
Lower	Window or icon	Meta key, left pointer button click.
Circulate up	Root	Meta key, right pointer button click.
Circulate down	Root	Meta key, left pointer button click.
Circulate down	Anywhere	Meta-Shift key combination, left pointer button click.
Iconify and move	Window or icon	Meta key, left pointer button down and drag.
Deiconify and move	Icon	Meta key, middle pointer button click.
WindowOps menu	Root	Meta key, middle pointer button down.
WindowOps menu	Anywhere	Meta-Shift key combination, middle pointer button down.
Preferences menu	Anywhere	Meta-Shift key combination, middle pointer button down (must display WindowOps with Meta-Shift middle down and slip off).

Using uwm to Place Other Clients

As described in Chapter 2, *Getting Started*, you can start another client simply by typing its name at the command line prompt in an *xterm* window. Some clients have a default size and/or location. A preferred size and location can also be specified in your *.Xresources* file, as described in Chapter 9, *Setting Resources*.

When you start a client, you can also use the `-geometry` command line option described in Chapter 8, *Command Line Options*, to size and locate the window, overriding any defaults that the client has.

If none of these geometry specifications has been provided, *uwm* steps in and requires you to interactively size and locate the windows. You have already seen the process of interactively sizing and positioning a window in Chapter 2, when we discussed how to start a second *xterm* or an *xclock* window.

First, the pointer turns into a corner shape and the name of the client appears in the upper-left corner of the screen followed by the digital size readout `0x0`.

To place the default-size client, move the pointer to the desired upper-left corner position for the new client. Click the left pointer button.

To both size and place the client, move the pointer to the desired upper-left corner position; press and hold down the middle pointer button. The pointer changes to a lower-right corner shape. Move the pointer to the desired window size. Release the pointer button.

The Preferences Menu

The Preferences menu is generally included in the version of *uwm* provided with most systems. The Preferences menu lists options for setting bell volume, keyclick volume, whether or not the Caps Lock key works, and the pointer tracking speed.* See Figure B-11.

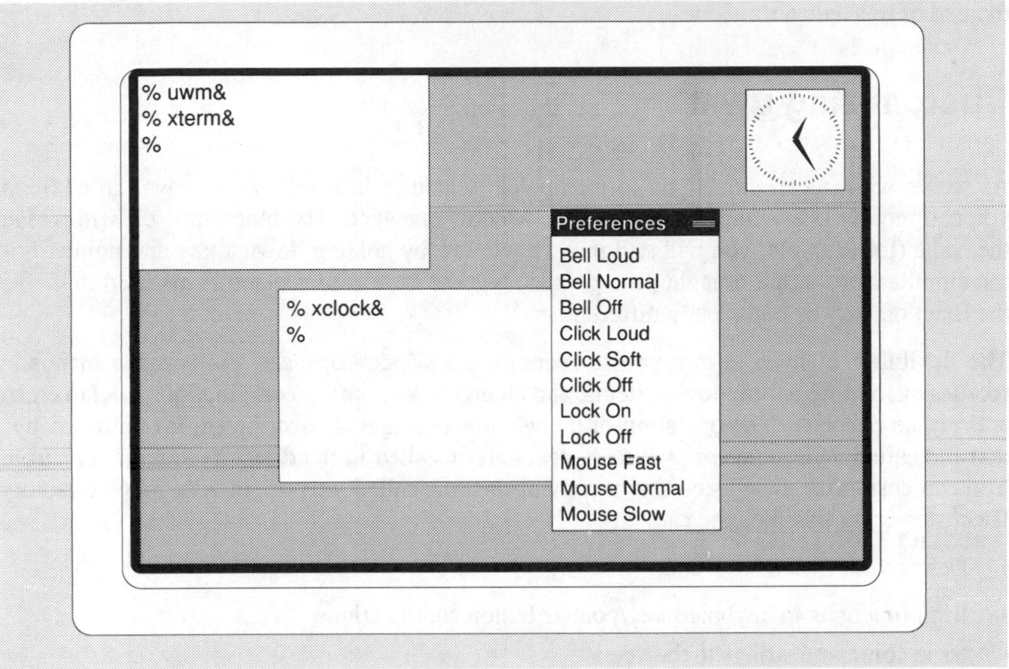

Figure B-11. Preferences menu

Without customizing the window manager, the only way to display the Preferences menu is to first display the WindowOps menu by an alternative method. Instead of placing the pointer on the root window and holding down the middle pointer button, place the pointer anywhere on the screen, hold down both the Shift and Meta keys, and press the middle pointer button. (See Chapter 11, *Setup Clients*, for a discussion of how to determine which key on your keyboard serves as the Meta key.) The WindowOps menu is displayed.

You can let go of the Shift and Meta keys, but keep holding down the middle pointer button. Then drag the pointer off the right or left side of the WindowOps menu and the Preferences menu will be displayed.

*The pointer tracking speed controls how much the pointer moves on the screen when you move the pointer. Experiment with each setting and see which you are most comfortable with.

Menus displayed in this way are called *slip off* menus and are discussed in greater detail in the section "Customizing uwm." This section also describes how to set up the window manager to display the Preferences menu more easily.

To make selections on the Preferences menu, bring up the menu and select a setting with the menu pointer. There is no visible change to the menu, but the new setting is made. Note that another button or combination might be used to display the Prefences menu at your site. If you cannot access the Preferences menu, this menu is included in the sample *.uwmrc* file at the end of this appendix.

Customizing uwm

As we've seen, *uwm* allows you to manipulate windows in a variety of ways. In addition, you can modify every function of the *uwm* window manager. The function itself will remain the same (for example, you will still move a window by holding down a key and pointer button simultaneously and dragging the pointer), but the keys and/or menu items used to invoke the function may be completely different.

The flexibility of *uwm* allows you to redesign the WindowOps and Preferences menus by reordering, adding and removing items, and changing key/button combinations, *and* to create entirely new menus. The operation of the window manager, as distributed, is controlled by a text file called *default.uwmrc*, which is generally installed in the directory */usr/lib/X11/uwm*. You can customize *uwm* by editing a copy of this file, called *.uwmrc*, in your home directory. By customizing this file, you can:

- Define your own *uwm* menus.
- Bind functions to keyboard key/pointer button combinations.
- Issue command strings to the shell.

The *.uwmrc* file has three parts:

- A variables section, which contains various settings, such as the font with which menus should be displayed, the volume of the keyboard bell, and so on.
- A key bindings section, which defines the keys, pointer buttons, and key and pointer button combinations that will be used to invoke each window manager function (including the display of menus).
- A menus section, which defines the contents of the menus.

As users gain experience with the window manager, each can create a file called *.uwmrc* in his or her home directory. This file can extend *default.uwmrc*, resetting variables, changing a key binding or adding a menu item—or it can replace it completely, changing the way the window manager operates. As one of its creators remarked, this flexibility makes *uwm* "the bane of trade show demonstrators and the joy of experienced users."*

*Joel Gancarz, "UWM: A User Interface for X Windows," in *USENIX Conference Proceedings*, Summer 1986, p. 431.

Rather than abstractly explaining the syntax of these various sections in a *.uwmrc* file, let's plunge right in, by looking at the *default.uwmrc* file from the MIT X11 distribution. This is shown in Example B-1. (Note that if you are using a commercial version of X, this file may be significantly different. However, in that case, you most likely have a user's guide specific to your system—perhaps even a customized version of this one!)

Example B-1. The default.uwmrc file from the MIT distribution

```
# Copyright (c) 1987 by the Massachusetts Institute of Technology.
#
# This is a startup file for uwm that produces an xwm lookalike,
# but adds two useful menus.  It is patterned on the public
# distribution ../lib/X/uwm/jg.uwmrc file by Jim Gettys.
#
resetbindings
resetvariables
resetmenus
noautoselect
delta=5
freeze
grid
zap
pushabsolute
push=1
hiconpad=5
viconpad=5
hmenupad=3
vmenupad=0
iconfont=fixed
menufont=fixed
resizefont=fixed
volume=0

# FUNCTION      KEYS CONTEXT        MOUSE BUTTON      ACTIONS
f.newiconify=   meta :window|icon:  delta left
f.raise=        meta :window|icon:  delta left
f.lower=        meta :window|icon:  left up
f.raise=        meta :window:       middle down
f.resize=       meta :window:       delta middle
f.iconify=      meta :icon:         middle up
f.raise=        meta :window|icon:  right down
f.move=         meta :window|icon:  delta right
f.circledown=   meta :root:         left down
f.circleup=     meta :root:         right down
f.circledown=   m|s  ::             left down
f.menu=              :root:         middle down      : "WindowOps"
f.menu=         m|s  ::             middle down      : "WindowOps"
f.menu=         m|s  ::             middle down      : "Preferences"
f.circleup=     m|s  ::             right down
f.iconify=      m|c  :window|icon:  left down
f.newiconify=   m|l  :window|icon:  left down
f.raise=        m|l  :window|icon:  left up
f.pushright=    m|l  :window|icon:  right down
f.pushleft=     m|c  :window|icon:  right down
f.pushup=       m|l  :window|icon:  middle down
f.pushdown=     m|c  :window|icon:  middle down
```

Example B-1. The default.uwmrc file from the MIT distribution (continued)

```
f.raise=        m|l   :window|icon: left up
f.pushright=    m|l   :window|icon: right down
f.pushleft=     m|c   :window|icon: right down
f.pushup=       m|l   :window|icon: middle down
f.pushdown=     m|c   :window|icon: middle down

menu = "WindowOps" {
New Window:    !"xterm&"
RefreshScreen: f.refresh
Redraw:        f.redraw
Move:          f.move
Resize:        f.resize
Lower:         f.lower
Raise:         f.raise
CircUp:        f.circleup
CircDown:      f.circledown
AutoIconify:   f.iconify
LowerIconify:  f.newiconify
NewIconify:    f.newiconify
Focus:         f.focus
Freeze:        f.pause
UnFreeze:      f.continue
Restart:       f.restart
" ":           f.beep
KillWindow:    f.kill
" ":           f.beep
Exit:          f.exit
}
menu = "Preferences" {
Bell Loud:     !"xset b 7&"
Bell Normal:   !"xset b 3&"
Bell Off:      !"xset b off&"
Click Loud:    !"xset c 8&"
Click Soft:    !"xset c on&"
Click Off:     !"xset c off&"
Lock On:       !"xset led on&"
Lock Off:      !"xset led off&"
Mouse Fast:    !"xset m 4 2&"
Mouse Normal:  !"xset m 2 5&"
Mouse Slow:    !"xset m 1 1&"
}
```

If you wish to change the operation of the window manager, you shouldn't change the *default.uwmrc* file. Instead, copy it to your home directory, under the name *.uwmrc*, and make changes to that copy. Or else, if you are planning only small changes, you can create a *.uwmrc* file from scratch. Settings in *default.uwmrc* and your own local *.uwmrc* file are cumulative (unless you explicitly override *default.uwmrc* as explained in the next section), so all you need to enter in your *.uwmrc* are values you wish to change.

Setting .uwmrc Variables

The first section of the file sets global variables. Some variables are Boolean—that is, their presence or absence "toggles" some attribute of the window manager—while others have the form:

```
variable=value
```

where *value* is either a number or a text string.

An example of a Boolean variable is `autoselect`, which, if present, causes the pointer to automatically appear in the first menu item whenever a menu is invoked. Note however that there are inconsistencies in the way *uwm* specifies Boolean variables. Some, like `resetvariables`, take effect if present; they must be deleted from the file or commented out by placing a sharp sign (#) at the start of the line if you don't want them to take effect. Others, such as `normali` (which makes sure that icons aren't placed partially offscreen when created), have an opposite toggle (`nonormali`), which must be used if you want the opposite effect. If two corresponding on/off toggles are both mistakenly placed in a file, whichever is specified later in the file takes effect.

An example of a text string variable is:

```
menufont=fixed
```

which names the font that should be used in all menus. (See Appendix E, *Release 3 and 4 Standard Fonts*, for lists and illustrations of fonts in the standard X11 distribution.)

An example of a numeric variable is:

```
volume=4
```

which sets the volume of the keyboard bell on a scale ranging from 0 to 7.

The available variables are described in detail on the *uwm* reference page in Part Three of this guide, so we won't go into detail on each of them here. Three variables that are worthy of note, though, are `resetvariables`, `resetbindings`, and `resetmenus`. You may recall that settings in your local *.uwmrc* file are cumulative with those in the *default.uwmrc* file. That is, you need define only changed or added variable values, function bindings or menus if you are happy with the basic operations set forth in *default.uwmrc*. If, however, you want to start with a clean slate, you should use one or more of the three *reset* variables which reset, respectively, the three sections of the *.uwmrc* file. If specified, these variables should always head the list of variables.

One additional note of syntax that is not obvious from the *default.uwmrc* example shown above: variable definitions need not be written on separate lines; instead, they can be separated by a semicolon and space. For example:

```
resetvariables; resetbindings; resetmenus
```

Button/Key Bindings

The second section of the *.uwmrc* file specifies which combination of keys and buttons (and in which context) will be used to invoke each predefined *uwm* function. Let's see how this works, by looking at the first two lines of the function binding section of *default.uwmrc*.

```
# FUNCTION      KEYS CONTEXT          MOUSE BUTTON   ACTIONS
f.newiconify= meta :window|icon: delta left
```

The first line we've shown is just a comment line, which labels each of the fields in the line below. The first field is separated from the others by an equals sign; subsequent fields are separated by colons. In *default.uwmrc*, fields are separated by tabs for clarity, making the colons (falsely) appear to be delimiters only for the context field; they could instead follow each other without intervening whitespace.

Let's talk about each of the fields in turn.

Function Names

The first field in a key binding contains the name of a function, followed by an equals sign.

uwm has a number of predefined functions. Each of these functions has a name beginning with "`f.`". The meaning of most of these functions should be fairly obvious to you from the name, if not from your experience using the window manager. For example, `f.resize` is used to resize a window, `f.move` to move a window, or `f.iconify` to change a window to an icon.

Others are less obvious. The function shown in the example, `f.newiconify`, is used to turn a window into an icon, or an icon into a window, and then to move it to a new location. Notice the function `f.beep`, which appears coupled with a set of empty quotes rather than a menu selection. This line in the *.uwmrc* creates a blank line on the WindowOps menu, to isolate the KillWindow and Exit selections from the others. If you select the blank line, the keyboard beeps.

Each of the functions is described in detail on the reference page for *uwm* in Part Three of this guide.

Keys

The second field lists keys, if any, which must be held down while invoking the specified function. *uwm* recognizes a small number of keys (discussed more fully in Chapter 11, *Setup Clients*), the most common of which are shift, control, lock and meta. These names must be entered in the *.uwmrc* file in lower case, and can be abbreviated s, c, l, and m.

If two keys must be held down at once, the names should be separated by a vertical bar (|). For example, `c|s` would mean that the Control and Shift keys should be pressed simultaneously. It is not permissible to bind a function to three keys at once. If the field is left blank, no key needs to be pressed while invoking the function.

Control, Shift and Lock should be familiar to most users. But what is a "Meta" key? There isn't a key by that name on many keyboards—instead, Meta is a user-definable Control key that can be mapped to an actual key on the physical keyboard using the *xmodmap* client as described in Chapter 11. Most implementations of X will include a mapped Meta key. Type *xmodmap* without any arguments to display the map. The *default.uwmrc* specifies the Meta key in many keyboard bindings. On workstations without a special key corresponding to Meta, you will have to use *xmodmap* to find out or change the definition of Meta to something reasonable.

Meta could be mapped to the Control key, although this could potentially lead to conflicts with applications that want to use the Control key. In particular, certain functions of *xedit* will operate strangely or not at all if Meta is mapped to Control.

If you want to map the Meta key, it is best to choose a keyboard key that's within easy reach and is not used frequently for other applications (perhaps an Alt or Funct key). Left- or right-handedness could also be a factor in choosing a Meta key.

The developers of *uwm* warn against binding functions to the Shift key alone, since they say certain applications use it as a Control key. If you use it in *uwm*, it will perform both functions simultaneously, which is likely to be confusing. For the same reason, you should not bind functions to buttons without modifier keys, except in the context of the root window.

Context

The third field defines the context—the location the pointer must be in before the function can be invoked. This field may be blank, or may contain one or more of: window, icon, or root. Multiple context specifications should be separated by vertical bars.

If the context is blank, it means that the pointer can be anywhere. If root is specified, it means that the pointer must be in the root (background) window, and not in any other window or icon. If the context is window or icon, the pointer must be in a window or icon for the function to be invoked.

The context field makes perfect sense if you consider our sample function binding:

```
f.newiconify= meta :window|icon: delta left
```

`f.newiconify` turns a window into an icon, or an icon into a window, and then moves it to a new location. The pointer must be in a window or an icon for the function to be used.

Mouse Buttons

The fourth field defines the state of the pointer buttons used to invoke the function.

uwm is designed to be used with a three-button pointer, and keeps separate track of when the button is pressed and when it is released. It can also tell when the pointer is moved.

Accordingly, a button specification has two parts:

- The name of a button: left, middle or right. These must be in lower case, and can be abbreviated l, m and r.
- The state of the button: down, up (just released), or delta (held down while the pointer is moving). The distance in pixels the pointer must be moved in order to trigger the delta state is set by the `delta` variable, and is set to 5 in *default.uwmrc*. The actual translation of pixels to distance will vary from system to system, and you will probably want to experiment to find a value that you are comfortable with. The context for the delta state is the context at the point the button was first pressed, not its position at the time it has moved a *delta* number of pixels.

The button name and state can be specified in either order.

Going back to our sample function binding:

```
f.newiconify= meta :window|icon: delta left
```

you can now understand that the `f.newiconify` function is invoked by moving the pointer to either a window or an icon, pressing the Meta key and the left pointer button, and dragging the pointer in any direction.

All of the other function definitions should be equally readable to you. Go back for a moment and review the bindings shown in the *default.uwmrc* file in Example B-1.

You'll notice that it is possible to bind the same function to more than one set of keys, buttons and/or contexts. For example, the WindowOps menu can be invoked anywhere by pressing the Meta and Shift keys together with the middle button on the pointer. But when the pointer is in the root window, the WindowOps menu can be invoked by pressing only the middle button on the pointer. The reason for this becomes obvious if you realize that when the pointer is on a window or an icon, the middle pointer button alone might have some other meaning to the application running in that window. In order to avoid conflict with other applications, *uwm* uses the more complex key/button combination. But when the pointer is in the root window, there is no possibility of conflict, and it can take a more forgiving approach.

Action

The fifth field, labeled "Action," is typically used only for the `f.menu` function, which allows you to invoke menus. The fifth field specifies the name of a menu, whose contents are defined in the third section of the *.uwmrc* file. If the menu name contains quotes, special characters, parentheses, tabs, or blanks, it must be enclosed in double quotes. For consistency, you may want to always quote menu names. For example:

```
f.menu=            :root:     middle down: "WindowOps"
f.menu=       m|s  ::         middle down: "WindowOps"
f.menu=       m|s  ::         middle down: "Preferences"
```

Defining Menus

The third section of a *.uwmrc* file contains menu definitions. These definitions have the format:

```
menu = menu_name {
item_name : action
          .
          .
          .
}
```

The menu name must exactly match a name specified with the `f.menu` function.

Each item on the menu is given a label (*`item_name`*), which will appear on the menu. This is followed by a colon and the action to be performed. The action may be one of *uwm*'s functions, or if prefixed by a ! character, it can be a system command to be executed, as if in an *xterm* window. As shown in Example B-2, the WindowOps menu defined in *default.uwmrc* shows both types of action.

Example B-2. The WindowOps menu

```
menu = "WindowOps" {
New Window:       !"xterm&"
RefreshScreen:    f.refresh
Redraw:           f.redraw
Move:             f.move
Resize:           f.resize
Lower:            f.lower
Raise:            f.raise
CircUp:           f.circleup
CircDown:         f.circledown
AutoIconify:      f.iconify
LowerIconify:     f.newiconify
NewIconify:       f.newiconify
Focus:            f.focus
Freeze:           f.pause
UnFreeze:         f.continue
Restart:          f.restart
" ":              f.beep
KillWindow:       f.kill
" ":              f.beep
Exit:             f.exit
}
```

New Window is accomplished by running another instance of *xterm*. The other functions are accomplished simply by invoking one of *uwm*'s predefined functions.

The Preferences menu shown in Example B-3 simply invokes *xset* with a number of different options:

The uwm Window Manager

Example B-3. The Preferences menu

```
menu = "Preferences" {
Bell Loud:     !"xset b 7&"
Bell Normal: !"xset b 3&"
Bell Off:      !"xset b off&"
Click Loud:   !"xset c 8&"
Click Soft:   !"xset c on&"
Click Off:    !"xset c off&"
Lock On:      !"xset led on&"
Lock Off:     !"xset led off&"
Mouse Fast:   !"xset m 4 2&"
Mouse Normal:!"xset m 2 5&"
Mouse Slow:   !"xset m 1 1&"
}
```

Submenus

Frankly, we consider the menus defined by the *default.uwmrc* file to be rather awkward and far from complete. Among other things, the WindowOps menu has too many infrequently-used functions mixed right in with those you need all the time.

For the moment, let's assume that we want to leave the variable definitions and function key bindings alone, but want to redefine the menus. We might create a local *.uwmrc* file that contained a menu definition like the one shown in Example B-4.

Example B-4. Window operations divided into two menus

```
resetmenus
menu = "WindowOps" {
Move:                          f.move
Resize:                        f.resize
Raise:                         f.raise
Lower:                         f.lower
(De)Iconify:                   f.iconify
New window:                    !"xterm -sb&"
Refresh screen:                f.refresh
Restart window manager:        f.restart
" ":                           f.beep
KillWindow:                    f.kill
" ":                           f.beep
More Window Operations:        f.menu:"More Window Operations"
}

menu = "More Window Operations" {
(De)Iconify and move:          f.newiconify
Circulate windows up:          f.circleup
Circulate windows down:        f.circledown
Focus keyboard on window:      f.focus
Freeze server:                 f.pause
Unfreeze server:               f.continue
" ":                           f.beep
Exit:                          f.exit
}
```

We've consolidated the three original menu items to iconify and deiconify into two, called (De)Iconify and (De)Iconify and Move. The latter corresponds to the NewIconify choice on the standard *uwm* menu.

To get from one menu to another, we simply define `f.menu` as the action for one item on the menu. No key, button or context is defined, so we go right to the next menu when selecting that item.

Slip off menus

In Example B-4, there was no keyboard binding for the More Window Operations menu. That menu could only be invoked by selecting it from the WindowOps menu. Another way to divide the window into two would be to give both the same key/button/context binding, as shown in Example B-5.

Example B-5. Window operations as two pull-right menus

```
resetbindings
# Note that if you resetbindings, you must recreate all desired
# operations.  If you are doing this kind of thing, you'd best copy
# the entire default.uwmrc to your home .uwmrc and edit it

f.menu=         :root:      middle down  : "WindowOps"
f.menu=         :root:      middle down  : "More Window Operations"
f.menu=   m|s   ::          middle down  : "WindowOps"
f.menu=   m|s   ::          middle down  : "More Window Operations"
```

If two menus have the same context and buttons, you can cause the second (or third, if more than two are defined) to appear simply by selecting nothing from the first, and, while continuing to hold down the specified pointer button (you can let go of the key), sliding the pointer off the menu to the right or left. The first menu will be replaced by the second.

Slip off menus may be awkward to control. If the labels of menu items are short, the menu can be too narrow, and hence difficult to use: you spend much more time sliding off menus unintentionally than you do selecting items. You can either train yourself to make pointer movements exactly perpendicular, or you can add horizontal menu padding as suggested in the revamp of *uwm* at the end of this appendix.

Executing System Commands from a Menu

We mentioned above that it is possible to specify a system command as a menu action simply by placing an exclamation point in front of the string to be executed. As we saw, the menus defined in *default.uwmrc* use this mechanism to create a new *xterm* window.

It is easy to cook up a menu that contains a miscellany of useful commands, as shown in Example B-6.

Example B-6. A Useful Commands menu

```
f.menu=        :root:    middle down        : "Useful Commands"
                .
                .
                .
menu = "Useful Commands" {
Analog clock:                  !"xclock -geometry 162x162-10+10&"
Digital clock:                 !"xclock -digital -geometry 162x37-10+174&"
Edit File:                     !"xterm -e vi"
Calculator:                    !"xcalc -geometry 126x230-180+10&"
Mailbox:                       !"xbiff -geometry 65x65-353+10&"
Display keyboard mappings:     !"xmodmap&"
}
```

As you can quickly see, you can run any window-based programs directly, but you need to run other programs using *xterm*'s `-e` option (discussed in Chapter 4, *The xterm Terminal Emulator*). You are limited only by your imagination in what commands you might want to put on a menu. Each command runs in its own window, but that isn't necessarily the case, as we'll see in a moment.

Cut Buffer Strings

Another useful feature of *uwm*'s menus is that you can define the action for a menu item to be the insertion of a string into the server's cut buffer. As discussed in Chapter 4, *The xterm Terminal Emulator*, you can use this cut buffer to cut and paste text between certain client windows. (See Chapter 4 for a more complete discussion of cut buffers.) You can also use the cut buffer from within *uwm* to define strings that will be placed in the cut buffer, ready for pasting into a window.

This feature is useful for specifying command strings that you want to have executed in an existing *xterm* window.

A string prefixed with a vertical bar will be loaded into the cut buffer with no trailing newline. This means that you can paste the string into a window and keep typing to add to the command line.

A string prefixed with a caret will be terminated with a newline, which means that if it is a command, and you paste it at the shell prompt in an *xterm* window, it will be executed immediately.

For example, we could add the following lines to our "Useful Commands" menu, as shown in Example B-7.

Example B-7. Useful commands using cut buffer strings

```
menu = "Useful Commands" {
    .
    .
    .
Check disk space: ^"df"
Remote login:     |"rlogin"
}
```

The last item on the menu uses | instead of ^, so that when the string is pasted into an *xterm* window, you can type in the name of the system to connect to. (If you tended to connect to a number of different systems on a regular basis, you could also just create a submenu with the names of various systems as menu items, and execute the correct command to log in to each system from there.)

Of course, cut buffer strings are not just useful for pasting in commands at the shell prompt. You could also associate editing macros or frequently-used text with menu items for use with a text editor.

Unfortunately, as of Release 3, there is a serious limitation to pasting strings from a *uwm* menu, related to the discussion of cut buffers versus text "selections" in Chapter 4. The window manager uses a cut buffer only; most Release 3 clients, notably *xterm*, use selections. With the default keyboard translations (Chapter 9), the contents of a selection are pasted *before* the contents of a cut buffer. Thus, if you've been copying and pasting text from an *xterm* window, the PRIMARY (default) selection probably contains text. If you then choose the Check disk space item from the *uwm* menu, that menu item is stored in the cut buffer, but does not replace the PRIMARY selection. When you go to paste Check disk space into an *xterm* window, you get the text from the PRIMARY selection instead (previously cut from an *xterm* window).

To solve this problem, you can use the *xcutsel* client to copy the text from the *cut* buffer into the *sel*ection. In an *xterm* window, type:

```
% xcutsel &
```

and then position the *xcutsel* window using the pointer. When you are having trouble pasting text yanked from a window manager menu because of a previous text selection, click on the Copy 0 to Primary command button in the *xcutsel* window. This command copies text in the cut buffer (specifically CUT_BUFFER "0") to the PRIMARY selection. You should then be able to paste the text yanked from the *uwm* menu successfully.

Note that if the PRIMARY selection is currently empty, the text in the cut buffer will be pasted instead, and this problem will not occur. For more information on the *xcutsel* client, see Chapter 4, *The xterm Terminal Emulator*, and the *xcutsel* reference page in Part Three of this guide.

Color Menus

So far, we've assumed that all menus are black and white. But you can also create color menus. You can even assign different colors to the menu title, the highlighting bar (the horizontal band that follows the pointer within the menu and shows which item is selected) and the individual selections on the menu.

Colors are added to menus using the following syntax:

```
menu = "menu name" (title_fg:title_bg:highlight_fg: highlight_bg) {
"item name": (item_fg:item_bg):   "action"
    .
    .
    .
}
```

Up to four different colors can be defined for the overall menu:

title_fg — The foreground color of the menu title (i.e., the color of the lettering).

title_bg — The background color of the menu title.

highlight_fg — The foreground color of the highlighting bar (i.e., the color of the lettering within the bar).

highlight_bg — The background color of the highlighting bar.

Two colors can be defined for each menu item:

item_fg — The foreground color of the item (i.e., the color of the lettering).

item_bg — The background color of the item.

Colors can be specified either with color names or hex strings, as described in Chapter 8, *Command Line Options*.

Here's a color menu that works well on a Sun-3 workstation. Keep in mind that the colors in the color database may look different on different servers.

```
menu = "WindowOps" (darkslategrey:plum:darkslategrey:plum) {
   Move:                        (slateblue:lightblue):f.move
   Resize:                      (slateblue:lightblue):f.resize
   Raise:                       (slateblue:lightblue):f.raise
   Lower:                       (slateblue:lightblue):f.lower
   (De)Iconify:                 (slateblue:lightblue):f.iconify
   New window:                  (slateblue:lightblue):!"xterm&"
   Refresh screen:              (slateblue:lightblue):f.refresh
   Restart window manager:      (slateblue:lightblue):f.restart
}
```

The total number of colors that can be allocated by the window manager for its own use is specified by the maxcolors variable. If you try to use more than maxcolors colors, the additional colors will default to the colors of the root window. This can also happen if the server runs out of free colormap entries.

Some releases of *uwm* include a color menu bug. If all menu items in the file are specified in color, all menus default to black and white. One quick fix is to leave the final item on the final menu in the file in black and white. More recent versions of *uwm* have corrected the problem.

A Complete Revamp of uwm

Using the various techniques described in this appendix, we've modified the *default.uwmrc* file to create an interface we think is more helpful to the average user.

Our modified *.uwmrc* file, shown in Example B-8, sets up four slip off menus, each with a slightly different focus. In effect, we've split the original WindowOps menu into two, called WindowOps and More Window Operations, renaming and modifying many of the selections, adding a few of our own, and putting the less frequently used ones on the second menu. The third menu offers some Useful Commands to place other clients, including *xclock* and *xcalc*, and to execute system commands, such as *df* and *rlogin*. The final menu is a slightly modified Preferences menu, which sets different keyclick volumes, leds, and pointer speeds than the default.

You can test our *.uwmrc* (following) or just use it as a touchstone to create your own.

Example B-8. Modified .uwmrc file

```
resetbindings; resetvariables; resetmenus
noautoselect
delta=5
freeze
grid
zap
pushabsolute
push=1
hiconpad=16
viconpad=16
hmenupad=22
vmenupad=1
iconfont=fg-16
menufont=fixed
resizefont=fixed
volume=0

# FUNCTION      KEYS    CONTEXT         MOUSE BUTTON ACTIONS
f.newiconify=   meta    :window|icon:   delta left
f.raise=        meta    :window|icon:   delta left
f.lower=        meta    :window|icon:   left up
f.raise=        meta    :window:        middle down
f.resize=       meta    :window:        delta middle
f.iconify=      meta    :icon:          middle up
f.raise=        meta    :window|icon:   right down
f.move=         meta    :window|icon:   delta right
f.circledown=   m|s     ::              left down
```

The uwm Window Manager

Example B-8. Modified .uwmrc file (continued)

```
f.circledown=   meta    :root:            left down
f.circleup=     meta    :root:            right down
f.menu=                 :root:            middle down  :"WindowOps"
f.menu=                 :root:            middle down  :"More Window Operations"
f.menu=                 :root:            middle down  :"Useful Commands"
f.menu=                 :root:            middle down  :"Preferences"
f.menu=         m|s     ::                middle down  :"WindowOps"
f.menu=         m|s     ::                middle down  :"More Window Operations"
f.menu=         m|s     ::                middle down  :"Useful Commands"
f.menu=         m|s     ::                middle down  :"Preferences"
f.circleup=     m|s     ::                right down
f.iconify=      m|c     :window|icon:     left down
f.newiconify=   m|l     :window|icon:     left down
f.raise=        m|l     :window|icon:     left up
f.pushright=    m|l     :window|icon:     right down
f.pushleft=     m|c     :window|icon:     right down
f.pushup=       m|l     :window|icon:     middle down
f.pushdown=     m|c     :window|icon:     middle down

menu = "WindowOps" {
  Move:                               f.move
  Resize:                             f.resize
  Raise:                              f.raise
  Lower:                              f.lower
  (De)Iconify:                        f.iconify
  New window:                         !"xterm -sb &"
  Refresh screen:                     f.refresh
  Restart window manager:             f.restart
  " ":                                f.beep
  Kill window:                        f.kill
}

menu = "More Window Operations" {
  Iconify and move:                   f.newiconify
  Circulate windows up:               f.circleup
  Circulate windows down:             f.circledown
  Focus keyboard on window:           f.focus
  Freeze server:                      f.pause
  Unfreeze server:                    f.continue
  Create color window:                !"xterm -d unix:0.1 -fg darkslategrey
                                      -bg lightblue -bd plum -bw 5&"
  " ":                                f.beep
  Exit:                               f.exit
}

menu = "Useful Commands" {
  Analog clock: !"xclock -hd darkslategrey -hl darkslategrey
                  -fg mediumorchid -bg lightblue -bd plum -bw 5
                  -geometry 162x162-10+10&"
  Digital clock:  !"xclock -digital -fg darkslategrey  -bg lightblue
                  -bd plum -bw 5 -geometry 162x37-10+174&"
  Calculator:     !"xcalc -geometry 126x230-180+10&"
  Mailbox:        !"xbiff -bg lightblue -fg lightslategrey -bd plum
                  -bw 3 -geometry 65x65-353+10&"
  Display keyboard mappings:          !"xmodmap&"
  Check disk space:  ^"df"
  Remote login: |"rlogin"
```

Example B-8. Modified .uwmrc file (continued)

```
}

menu = "Preferences" {
  Bell Loud:          !"xset b 7&"
  Bell Normal:        !"xset b 3&"
  Bell Off:           !"xset b off&"
  Click Loud:         !"xset c 9&"
  Click Soft:         !"xset c 2&"
  Click Off:          !"xset c off&"
  Lock On:            !"xset led 1&"
  Lock Off:           !"xset -led 1&"
  Mouse Fast:         !"xset m 4 5&"
  Mouse Normal:       !"xset m 2 5&"
  Mouse Slow:         !"xset m 1 1&"
}
```

C

The OSF/Motif Window Manager

This appendix describes the OSF/Motif™ window manager, mwm, *one of the more popular window managers in the X market today. It describes both the basics of using* mwm *and how to customize it.*

In This Chapter:

C
The OSF/Motif Window Manager

Getting Started with mwm

The Motif window manager (*mwm*) is one of the more popular window managers available in the X market. Developed by Ellis Cohen of the Open Software Foundation, *mwm* is the window manager component of OSF/Motif, OSF's graphical user interface (GUI). *mwm* allows you to perform all of the standard window manipulation functions. You can:

- Create additional *xterm* windows.
- Change the size of windows.
- Move windows around the screen.
- Raise windows (move them to the front of others).
- Lower windows (move them to the back of others).
- Convert windows to icons and icons to windows.
- Refresh your screen.
- Remove windows.

Like *twm*, the Motif window manager allows you to invoke window manipulation functions in a variety of ways:

- Using the window "frame" and various features available on it: the Minimize (iconify) button, Maximize button, title area, Window Menu, etc.
- Using the Root Menu.
- Using keyboard keys, pointer buttons, and key and button combinations.

mwm attempts to create a three-dimensional appearance, which is somewhat more aesthetic than the look provided by many other window managers. You'll probably notice that window frames, various command buttons, icons, etc., appear to be raised to varying heights above screen level. This illusion is created by subtle shading and gives many display features a "beveled" look, similar to the beveled style of some mirrors.

This appendix is intended primarily for those using the default version of *mwm*, Release 1.0. If *mwm* has been customized at your site or you are running a different version, the principles should be basically the same, but the window manipulation functions may be invoked in different ways. From time to time, we'll mention how commands or functionality might vary, depending on your version of *mwm*.

If you have never used a window manager before, first read Chapter 1, *An Introduction to the X Window System*, for a conceptual overview of what a window manager does.

In this appendix, we'll take a look at the standard window manipulation functions provided by *mwm* and the wide variety of methods for invoking them. Then we'll consider how to customize various features of *mwm*. Perhaps the most useful customization that can be performed involves selecting a keyboard focus policy, either *pointer* focus or click-to-type (referred to as *explicit*) focus. (Keyboard focus is described in Chapter 1, *An Introduction to the X Window System*.) By default, *mwm* uses explicit (click-to-type) focus.

First, however, let's start with some basics: how to start *mwm*; and how to select the window to receive input, also known as the active window. Then we'll take a look at perhaps the most distinguishing feature of *mwm*: the frame it places around all windows on the display.

Starting mwm

As described in Chapter 2, *Getting Started*, you can start a window manager from the command line in an *xterm* window. The following command line starts *mwm*:

```
% mwm &
```

If *xdm* (the display manager) or another session manager is starting X on your system, *mwm* is probably started automatically when you log on. If *mwm* is already running, all windows will be surrounded by the characteristic window frame, pictured in Figure C-1.

If *mwm* is not running, start it using the command line above. While *mwm* is starting up, the root window pointer changes to an hour glass that appears to be filling up with sand. When the hour glass is full, all windows will become framed, indicating that *mwm* is running.

Selecting the Window to Receive Input

By default, you select the window to receive input (the active window) by clicking the first pointer button anywhere within the window. As we've said, this focus policy is called click-to-type, or explicit. Whether *mwm* is started automatically or you started it by typing in an *xterm* window, you must then click in a window in order to enter text.

Once you focus input to a window, all text typed appears in that window, regardless of where you move the pointer. In order to type in another window, you must transfer focus to that window by clicking the first pointer button within it. Later in this appendix, we'll describe how to make the keyboard focus follow pointer movement.

Figure C-1. mwm is running on the display

When you focus input on a window, the window frame changes color. Depending on the version of *mwm* you are running and the color resources specified for your system, the frame may change from black to white, from grey to white, etc. In any case, the active window's frame will be a different color than the frames of all other windows on the display. (In some versions, be aware that the black window frame of non-active windows obscures the titlebar text, which also appears in black. Only the title of the active window is visible in these cases.)

Notice that if you are working with a stack of windows that overlap, selecting a window as the active window automatically raises that window to the top of the stack. (As we'll see when we look at customization, this behavior is controlled by an *mwm* resource variable called `autoFocusRaise`, which is true by default.)

Manipulating Windows with the mwm Window Frame

Figure C-2 shows an *xterm* window "framed" by *mwm*. The window frame itself and several features of it are tools that allow you to manipulate the window using the pointer.

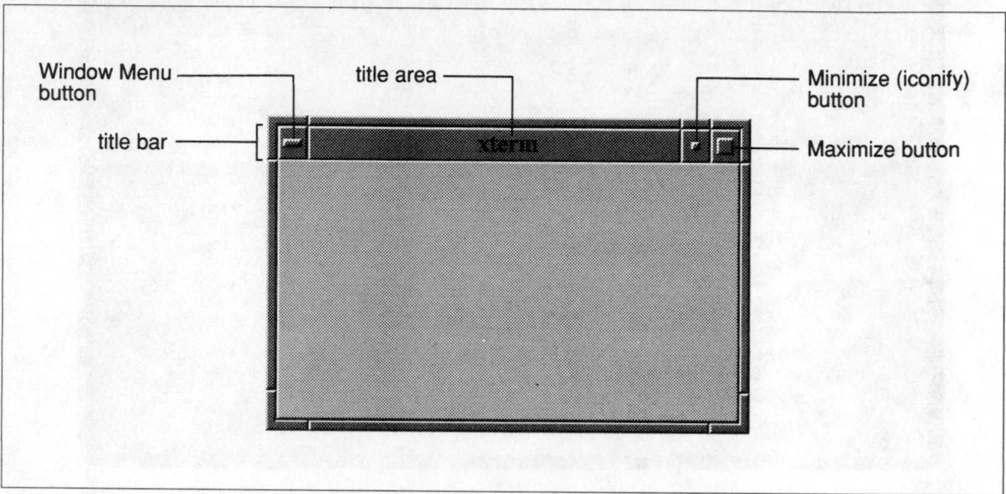

Figure C-2. An xterm window running with the OSF/Motif window manager

The following sections describe the features of the *mwm* window frame and the functions they perform. Later, we'll take a look at menu items and keyboard shortcuts that also perform these functions.

Be aware that *mwm* also allows you to manipulate *icons* using simple pointer actions, menu items, and keyboard shortcuts. An icon is a small symbol that (generally) represents a window in an inactive state. (See Chapter 1, *Introduction to the X Window System*, for more information about icons.) After we learn the various window manipulation functions, we'll look at the section "Manipulating Icons."

Moving a Window: The Title Area

When you select a window as the focus window, the name of the application is displayed within the *title area*. The title area allows you to move the window, using the following steps:

1. Place the pointer within the title area. The pointer changes to the arrow cursor.
2. Press and hold down the first pointer button.
3. Move the window by dragging the pointer. Figure C-3 shows one being moved in this way. When you begin to move the window, the pointer changes to a cross arrow pointer

and a window outline appears. This outline tracks the pointer's movement. In the center of the screen, a small, rectangular box also appears, displaying the x and y coordinates of the window as you move it.

4. Drag the cross arrow pointer with the window outline to the desired location on your screen.

5. Release the first pointer button. The window will move to the selected location.

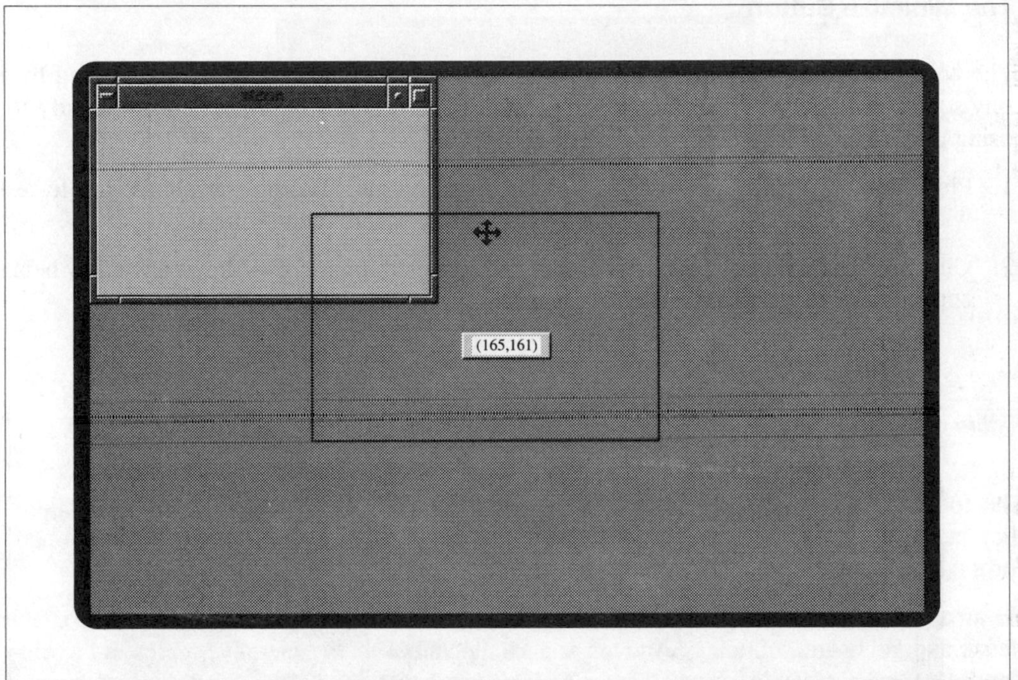

Figure C-3. Moving a window by dragging the title area

The title area is the largest section of the horizontal bar that spans the top of the window frame. This horizontal bar is known as the *titlebar*. Notice that whenever you move the pointer into the titlebar, the pointer changes to the arrow cursor.

In addition to the title area, the titlebar features three command buttons: one on the left and two on the right. These command buttons are described in the following sections.

Minimizing (Iconifying) and Maximizing a Window

The two command buttons on the right side of the titlebar are the Minimize and Maximize buttons. The Minimize command button converts a window to an icon. As mentioned previously, an icon is a small symbol that represents a window in an inactive state.

The Maximize command button can be used to enlarge a window to the size of the root window, and once the window has been enlarged, to convert it back to its original size.

The Minimize Button

The Minimize command button, immediately to the right of the title area, is identified by a tiny square in its center. This button allows you to convert the window to an icon (iconify it), using the following steps:

1. Place the pointer within the Minimize command button. The pointer simply has to rest within the button's outer border, not within the tiny square identifying it.
2. Click the first pointer button. The window is iconified. Figure C-4 shows a window being converted to an icon in this way.

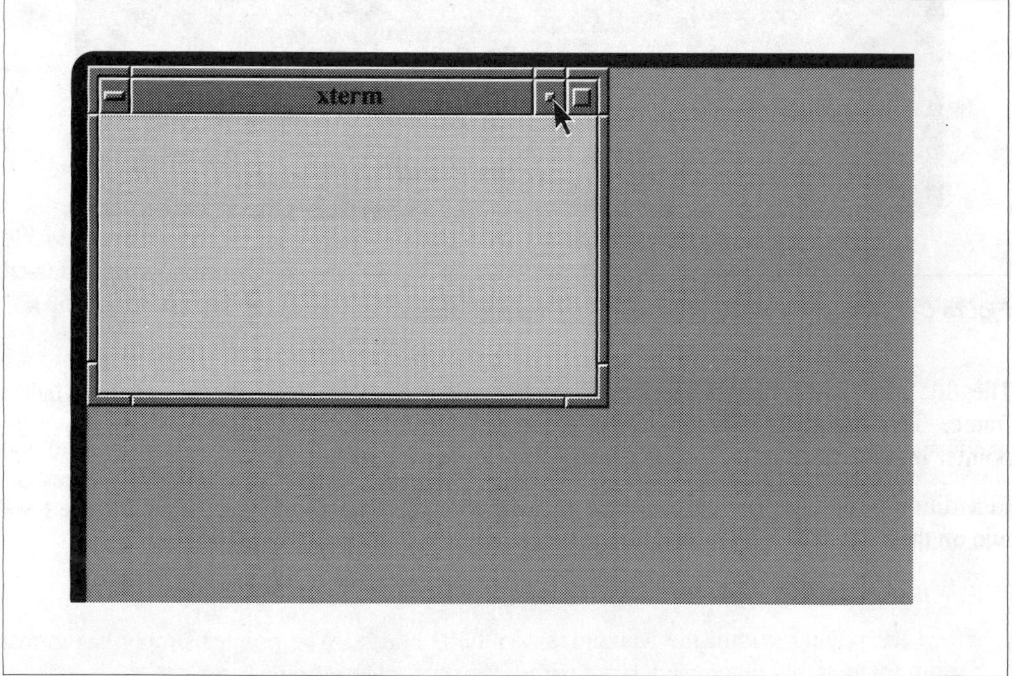

Figure C-4. Converting a window to an icon with the Minimize button

By default, icons are displayed in the bottom left corner of the root window. *mwm* can also be set up to place icons in another location, to allow you to place them interactively using the pointer, or to organize icons within a window known as an *icon box*. Later in this appendix, we'll discuss the specifications necessary to set up an icon box.

If you've used other window managers, you may notice that icon symbols generated by *mwm* are larger and more decorated than those generated by many other window mangers. This is one of the aesthetic advantages of *mwm*. Figure C-5 shows an example.

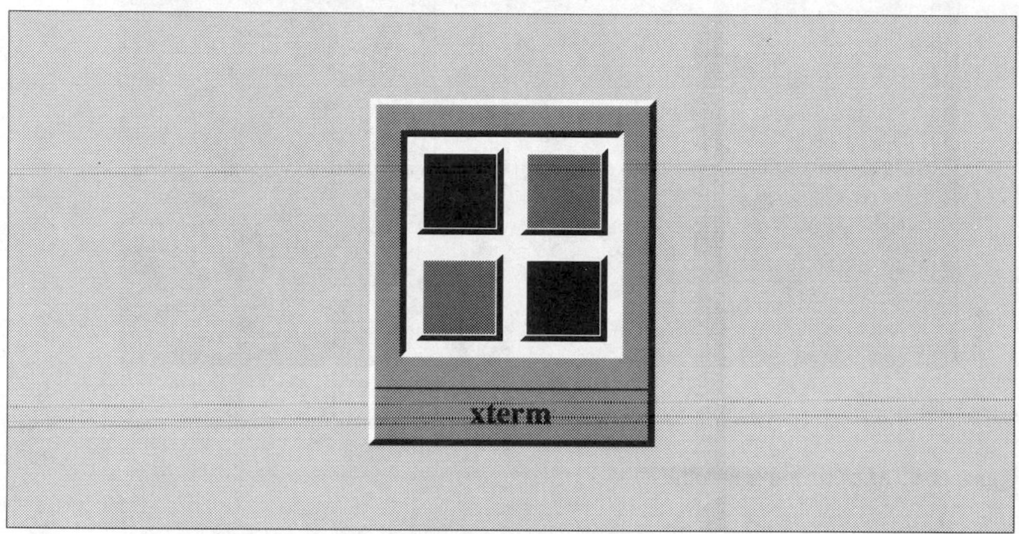

Figure C-5. xterm window icon under mwm

To convert the icon back to a window (deiconify it), place the pointer on the icon and double click, using the first pointer button. The window is redisplayed in the position it appeared before it was iconfied. (See the section "Manipulating Icons" for a summary of functions.)

The Maximize Button

To the right of the Minimize command button (in the upper right corner of the window), the Maximize command button is identified by a larger square in its center. The Maximize button allows you to enlarge the window to the size of the root window, and once it has been enlarged, to convert it back to its original size.

To maximize a window, use the following steps:

1. Place the pointer within the Maximize command button. The pointer simply has to rest within the button's outer border, not within the square identifying it.
2. Click the first pointer button. The window is maximized. Figure C-6 shows how it's done.

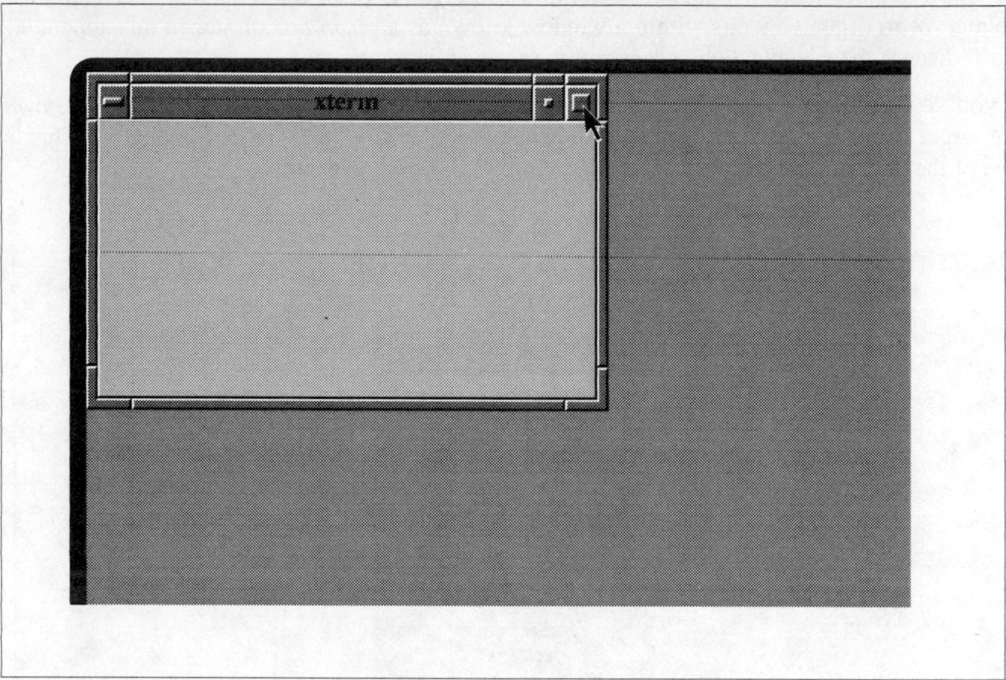

Figure C-6. Maximizing a window

The large window should function in the same way it did before it was maximized. Theoretically, you can maximize an *xterm* window to have a single, very large terminal screen. However, be aware that certain programs you may run within an *xterm*, such as the *vi* text editor, do not always work properly within a window of this size (even if you've used the *resize* client, as described in Chapter 4, *The xterm Terminal Emulator*). The Maximize function is more safely used with an application that displays a graphic image or performs a simple function, such as *xclock*.

Also, some client programs that do not support resizing, such as the Release 3 version of *xcalc*, cannot be maximized correctly. In the case of *xcalc*, the frame surrounding the calculator application is maximized, but the actual calculator remains the same size.

The Maximize button is a toggle. To convert a maximized window back to its original size, click on the Maximize button again with the first pointer button.

Raising a Window

Windows often overlap on the screen. You can raise a window that is obscured by other windows to the top of the stack using the *mwm* frame. To raise a window:

1. Place the pointer on any part of the window frame, except the command buttons (Minimize, Maximize, and the button in the upper left corner of the titlebar, which as we'll see, brings up the Window Menu).
2. Click the first pointer button. The window is raised to the top of the stack.

When you are using explicit (click-to-type) focus and the other default *mwm* resources, this action also selects the window to receive input, i.e., makes the window the active window.

Resizing a Window

One of the most distinctive and useful features of the *mwm* window frame is not at all obvious. The entire frame (other than the title area and the command buttons) is designed to allow you to resize the window using the pointer. Notice that the frame is divided by small lines into eight sections: four long borders (two horizontal and two vertical) and four corners. Figure C-7 shows these sections of the window frame.

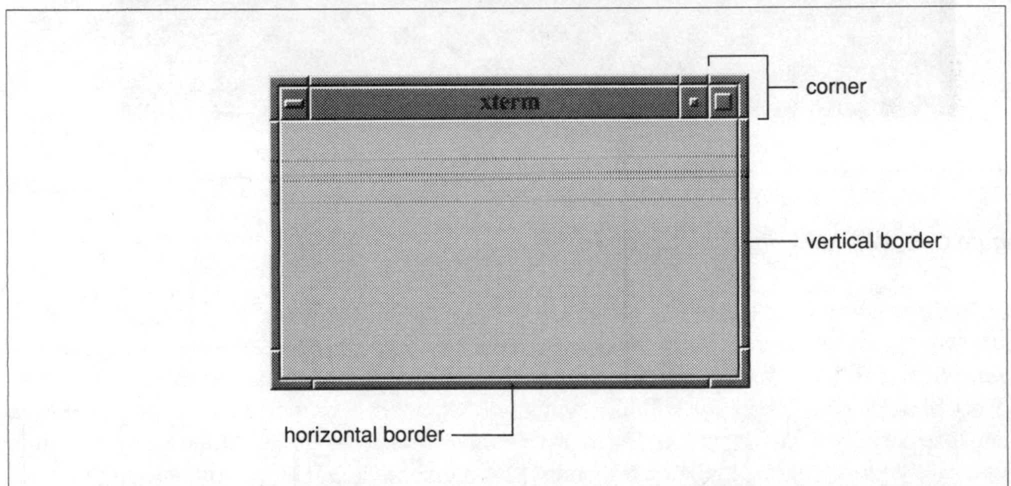

Figure C-7. The outer frame is divided into four long borders and four corners

If you place the pointer within a window and then move it into one of the long horizontal or vertical borders, you'll notice the pointer changes to a new shape: an arrow (pointing toward the window border), with a short line perpendicular to it. This short line represents the window border. Try moving the pointer in this fashion in one of the windows on your display to get a better idea of what the pointer looks like. If you move the pointer from within a window into the outer border at one of the corners, the pointer will become an arrow pointing diagonally at a small corner symbol, as pictured in Figure C-8. Figure C-9 shows all of the possible resize pointers.

Once the pointer changes to one of these shapes, you can move the border (or corner) of the window. Resizing from one of the long borders only allows you to change one dimension of the window: a horizontal border can only be moved up or down, changing the height; a vertical border can only be moved left or right, changing the width.

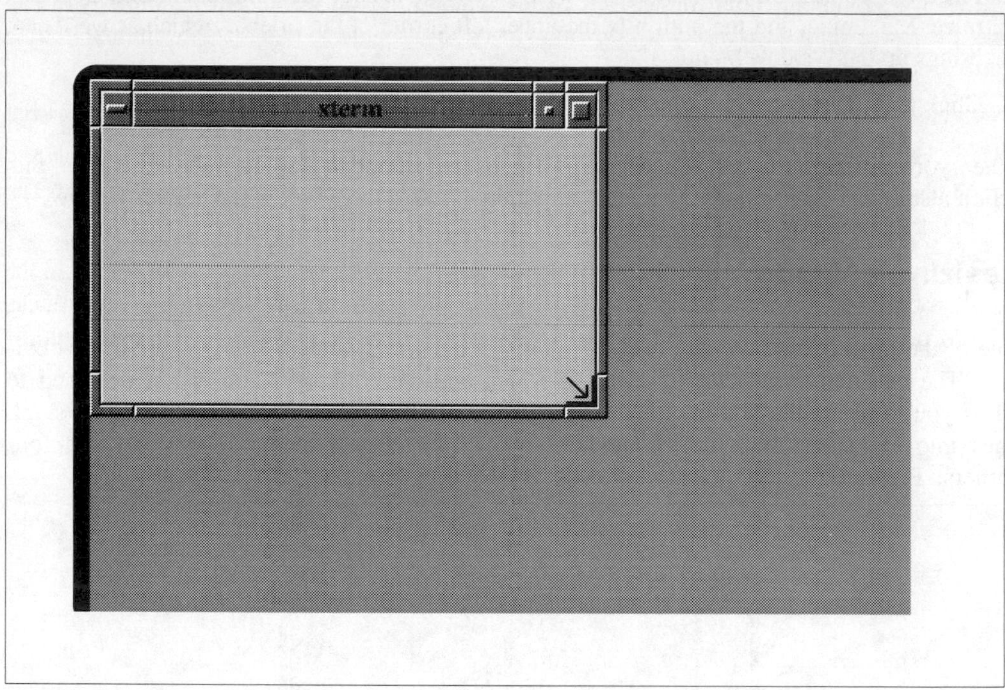

Figure C-8. Window with resizing pointer

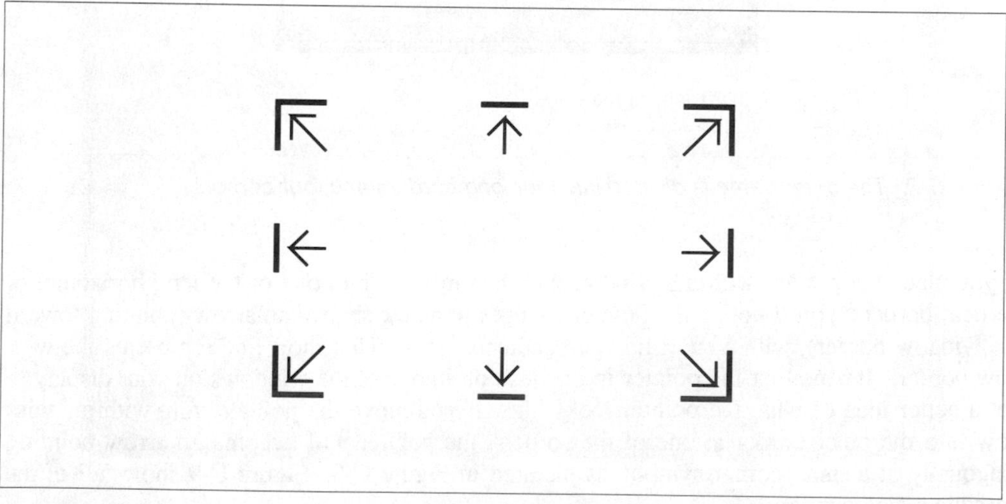

Figure C-9. Resizing pointer symbols

Resizing from a corner offers the most flexibility. You can move a corner in any direction you choose, changing both dimensions of the window if you want. For example, you can drag the lower right corner of a window down and to the right to enlarge the window in both dimensions.

You determine the size and shape of the window by choosing the border or corner you want to extend (or contract) and moving it the desired amount using the following steps:

1. Move the pointer from within the window to the border or corner you want to move. The pointer changes to one of the symbols pictured in Figure C-9.
2. Press and hold down the first pointer button and drag the window border or corner in the direction you want. As you resize the window, an image of the moving border(s) tracks the pointer movement. Also, in the center of the display, a small rectangular window shows the dimensions of the window as they change (in characters and lines for *xterm* windows, in pixels for most other clients).
3. Resize the window as desired.
4. Release the first pointer button. The window is redisplayed in the new shape. (The border image and window geometry tracking box disappear.)

Figure C-10 shows a window being "stretched" from the lower right corner.

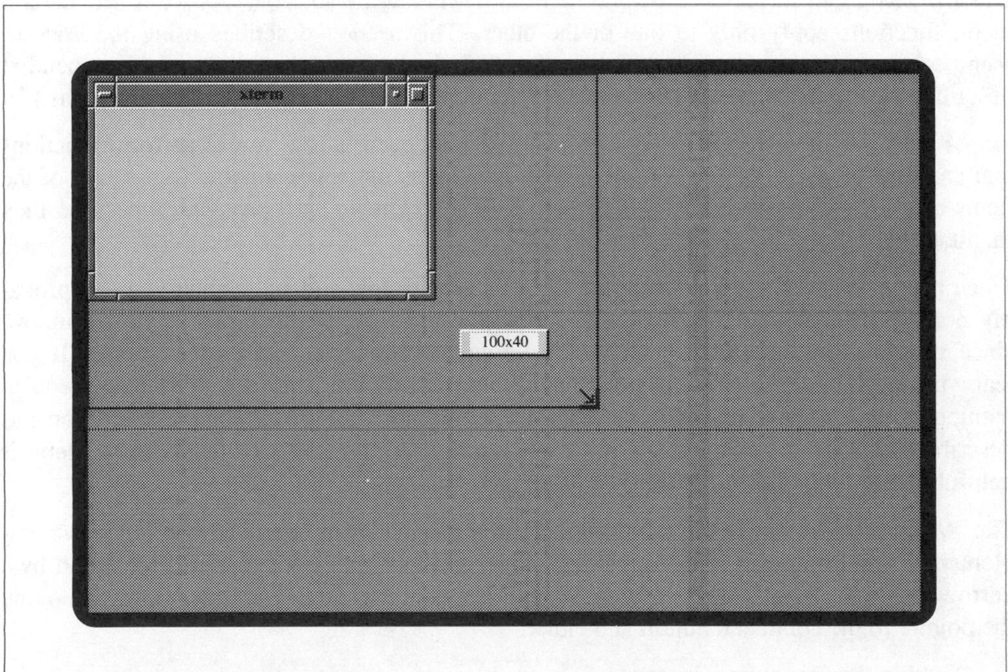

Figure C-10. Dragging the corner to make a window larger

The Window Menu Button: Display a Menu or Close the Window

The command button on the left side of the titlebar is used to bring up the Window Menu, which provides seven items that manipulate the window and its icon. The following sections describe how to bring up the Window Menu and invoke its various functions.

This command button also has another function. Double-clicking the first pointer button on the Window Menu command button kills the client program and closes the window. Be aware that, like other methods of 'killing' a program (such as the *xkill* client), double-clicking on the Window menu item can adversely affect underlying processes. Refer to the section on *xkill* in Chapter 7, *Other Clients*, for a more complete discussion of the hazards of killing a client and a summary of alternatives.

You can customize *mwm* so that double-clicking performs no function by setting a resource variable, `wMenuButtonClick2`, to false. See the sections "Setting mwm Resources" and "mwm-Specific Appearance and Behavior Resources" later in this appendix, and the *mwm* reference page in your OSF/Motif documentation for details.

Manipulating Windows Using the Window Menu

The command button on the left side of the titlebar is used to display the Window Menu. The Window Menu can actually be displayed from a window *or* an icon. As we'll see, certain menu functions apply only to one or the other. This section describes using the Window Menu to manipulate a window. (The section "Manipulating Icons," later in this appendix, describes the use of Window Menu items, pointer commands, and other shortcuts on icons.)

Six of the seven items on the Window Menu (all but Lower) allow you to perform functions that can also be performed by simple pointer actions on the *mwm* window frame. All of the items can also be requested using keyboard shortcuts, known as *accelerators*, because they facilitate the action.

Since manipulating a window using the frame is very simple and accessible, you will probably not use the Window Menu often. You may want to use the menu to Lower a window, since this function cannot be performed by a simple pointer action on the frame. (If you learn the keyboard shortcuts for this menu item, you may not need the Window Menu to manipulate windows at all.) You may find the menu more helpful in manipulating icons, as described later in this chapter. In any case, learning the functions of the Window Menu is helpful in orienting yourself within the Motif environment.

The Window Menu can be displayed either from a window or from its icon. The Window Menu command button is in the upper left corner of the window frame and is identified by a narrow rectangle in its center. You can display the Window Menu from a window by moving the pointer to the command button and either:

- Clicking the first pointer button.
- Pressing and holding down the first pointer button.

(You can also display the menu using keyboard shortcuts described at the end of this section.) The menu is displayed. If you've clicked the first pointer button to display the menu (the easier method), the first item that is available for selection is highlighted by a box. Figure C-11 shows the default Window Menu, which has been displayed by clicking the first pointer button in the menu command button.

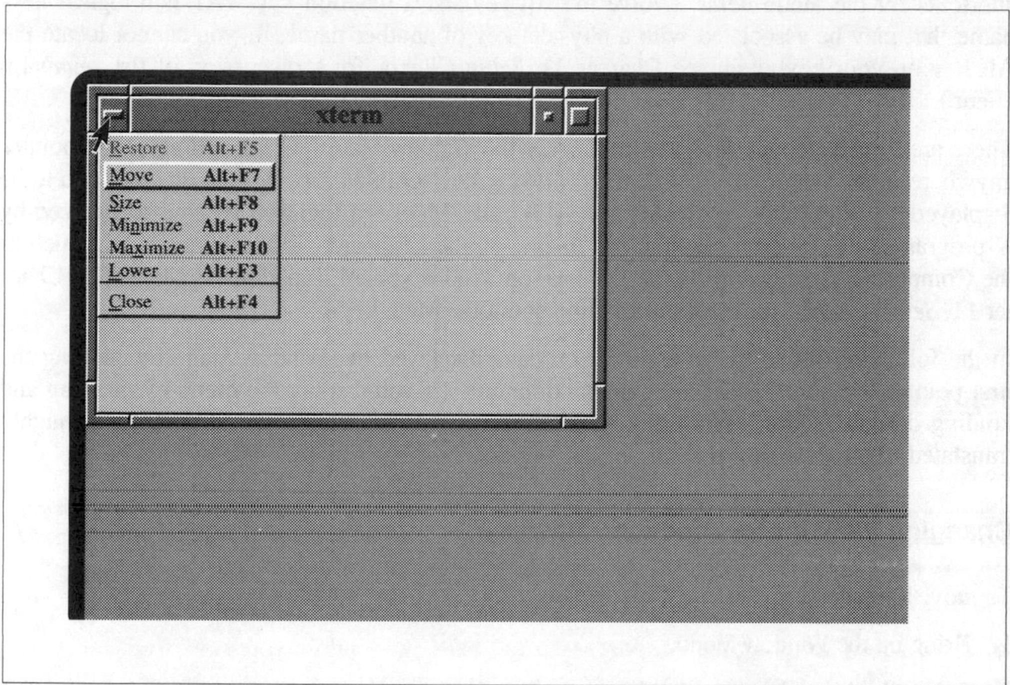

Figure C-11. The Window Menu

Notice that the first item available for selection (indicated by the surrounding box) is Move. The first item on the menu, Restore, is used to change an icon back into a window or a maximized window back to its original size; therefore, it is not useful at this time. The fact that Restore is not selectable is also indicated by the fact that it appears in a lighter typeface.

Notice also that one letter of each menu item is underlined. This letter represents a unique abbreviation for the menu item, called a *mnemonic*, and is useful in selecting the item.

Once the menu is displayed, you can select an item in the following ways:

- If you displayed the menu by pressing and holding down the first pointer button, drag the pointer down the menu to the desired item and release the first button.
- If you displayed the menu by clicking the first pointer button, either:

  —Move the pointer onto the item and click the first button.

  —Type the unique abbreviation (the underlined letter). (Though several of the abbreviations are capital letters, you should type the lower-case equivalent.)

The following sections explain how each of the Window Menu items works.

To remove the menu without making a selection, move the pointer off of the menu and release or click the first pointer button, as appropriate.

Notice also that a keyboard shortcut follows each command. The keyboard shortcuts allow you to perform all of the functions without having to display the menu. All of the keyboard shortcuts for the menu items involve the Alt key and a function key. (Alt is a logical keyname that may be associated with a physical key of another name. If you cannot locate the Alt key on your keyboard, see Chapter 11, *Setup Clients*, for a discussion of the *xmodmap* client.)

There are also keyboard shortcuts to display the Window Menu. Once you place the pointer anywhere in the window, either of the following key combinations will cause the menu to be displayed: Shift-Escape or Meta-space. (Like Alt, Meta is a logical keyname recognized by X programs. There is no key marked "meta" on the keyboard. Rather another key, such as the Compose Character key on the DECstation 3100 keyboard, functions as Meta. See Chapter 11, *Setup Clients*, for more information about the Meta key.)

In the following sections, we assume you have displayed the Window Menu by clicking the first pointer button on the menu command button. (If you display the menu by pressing and holding down the first pointer button, instructions to click a pointer button can be roughly translated to mean release the button.)

Changing the Window Location: Move

To move a window:

1. Bring up the Window Menu.
2. Select the Move item by clicking on it with the first pointer button, or by typing the letter m. The menu disappears. The pointer changes to the cross arrow pointer and appears in the center of the window.
3. Move the window by dragging the pointer. When you begin to move the window, a window outline appears. This outline tracks the pointer's movement. In the center of the screen, a small rectangular box also appears, displaying the x and y coordinates of the window as you move it.
4. Drag the cross arrow pointer with the window outline to the desired location on your screen.
5. Click the first pointer button. The window will move to the selected location.

To cancel the Move function, keep the pointer stationary and click the first button.

The Move function can also be invoked using the keyboard shortcut Alt-F7.

Resizing the Window: Size

To resize a window:

1. Bring up the Window Menu.
2. Select the Size item by clicking on it with the first pointer button, or by typing the letter s. The menu disappears. The pointer changes to the cross arrow pointer and appears in the center of the window.
3. Move the pointer from within the window to the border or corner you want to move. The pointer changes to one of the symbols pictured in Figure C-9.
4. Once the pointer has become one of the resize pointers, you can drag the window border or corner in the direction you want. As you resize the window, an image of the moving border(s) tracks the pointer movement. Also, in the center of the display, a small rectangular window shows the dimensions of the window as they change (in characters and lines for *xterm* windows, in pixels for most other clients).
5. Resize the window as desired.
6. Click the first pointer button. The window is redisplayed in the new shape. (The border image and window geometry tracking box disappear.)

The Size function can also be invoked using the keyboard shortcut Alt-F8.

To cancel the Size function, don't move the pointer near any of the borders; just click the first pointer button.

Iconifying the Window: Minimize

To iconify a window:

1. Bring up the Window Menu.
2. Select the Minimize item by clicking on it with the first pointer button, or typing the letter n.
3. The window is converted to an icon.

The Minimize function can also be invoked using the keyboard shortcut Alt-F9.

The easiest way to convert an icon back to a window is to place the pointer on the icon and double click with the first button.

Changing to the Maximum Size: Maximize

To make a window as large as the root window:

1. Bring up the Window Menu.
2. Select the Maximize item by clicking on it with the first pointer button, or typing the letter x.
3. The window is enlarged to the size of the root window.

The Maximize function can also be invoked using the keyboard shortcut Alt-F10.

Moving a Window to the Bottom of the Stack: Lower

The Lower menu item allows you to send a window to the bottom of the window stack. This is the only Window Menu function that cannot be performed simply by clicking the pointer on the window frame. To lower a window:

1. Bring up the Window Menu.
2. Select the Lower item by clicking on it with the first pointer button, or typing the letter l.
3. The window is moved behind others on the display to the bottom of the window stack.

Though this function cannot be performed by clicking the pointer on the frame, it *can* be invoked using the keyboard shortcut Alt-F3.

Removing a Window: Close

The Close menu item terminates the client window and the window is removed from the display. This powerful command is separated from the other menu items by a horizontal line to prevent you from inadvertently closing a window.

Be aware that, like other methods of 'killing' a program (such as the *xkill* client), the Close menu item can adversely affect underlying processes. Most windows can be removed in ways that do not harm relevant processes. For example, you can generally remove an *xterm* window by typing the same command you use to log off the system. Refer to the section on *xkill* in Chapter 7, *Other Clients*, for a more complete discussion of the hazards of killing a client and a summary of alternatives.

Like *xkill*, Close is intended to be used primarily after more conventional methods to remove a window have failed.

To remove a stubborn window:

1. Bring up the Window Menu.
2. Select the Close item by clicking on it with the first pointer button, or typing the letter c.
3. The window is removed.

The Close function can also be invoked using the keyboard shortcut Alt-F4.

Restoring a Maximized Window or an Icon: Restore

The Restore menu item allows you to restore an icon to a window or a maximized window to its original size. To restore a maximized window:

1. Bring up the Window Menu.
2. Select the Restore item by clicking on it with the first pointer button, or by typing the letter `r`.
3. The window is restored to its original size.

The Restore function can also be invoked using the keyboard shortcut Alt-F5.

Restore can also be used to convert an icon back to a window, as described in the section "Manipulating Icons Using the Window Menu" below.

Manipulating Icons

In addition to manipulating windows, *mwm* provides several easy methods for manipulating icons. The following functions can be invoked using simple pointer button actions on an icon:

Move	Hold down the first pointer button and drag the icon to the desired position. Then release the button.
Raise	Click on the obscured icon with the first pointer button. The icon is raised to the top of the stack.
Restore (Deiconify)	To convert an icon back to a window, double-click on the icon with the first pointer button.

Manipulating Icons Using the Window Menu

You can also display the Window Menu from an icon and invoke menu items that affect it. To display the menu, just place the pointer on the icon and click the first button. (You can also use either of these keyboard shortcuts: Shift-Escape or Meta-space.)

The Window Menu displayed from an icon is virtually identical to the menu displayed from a window; it contains all of the same items, but only five of the seven are selectable. (When displayed from a window, six of the seven items are selectable.) The five selectable items are: Restore, Move, Maximize, Lower, and Close. These items perform manipulations on an icon analogous to those performed on a window (see "Manipulating Windows Using the Window Menu" earlier in this appendix).

Two menu items, Size and Minimize, appear in a lighter typeface, indicating they are not available for selection. Size cannot be selected because, unlike a window, an icon cannot be resized. Obviously, Minimize cannot be used to iconify an icon.

Table C-1 summarizes the Window Menu functions when invoked from an icon. For instructions on selecting an item and performing the various functions, read "Manipulating Windows Using the Window Menu" earlier in this appendix. Note that the keyboard shortcuts (accelerators) for the commands are also the same as those described for windows.

Table C-1. Window Menu Actions on an Icon

Menu Item	Function	Shortcut
Restore	Converts the icon back to a window.	Alt+F5
Move	Moves the icon on the display.	Alt+F7
Size	Not available for selection.	n/a
Minimize	Not available for selection.	n/a
Maximize	Converts an icon to a window the size of the root window.	Alt+F10
Lower	Sends an icon to the bottom of the window/icon stack.	Alt+F3
Close	Exits the client, removing the icon.	Alt+F4

Later in this appendix, we'll discuss using *mwm* resources to set up an icon box, a window for organizing icons on the display. Using an icon box changes the way you work with the Window Menu from an icon and introduces another menu item, PackIcons, which reorganizes icons in the icon box. See "Using an Icon Box" later in this chapter for details.

The Root Menu

The Root Menu is *mwm*'s main menu. It provides commands that can be thought of as affecting the entire display and is analogous to the Twm menu describe in Chapter 3. To display the Root Menu, move the pointer to the root window and press and hold down the first pointer button. The default Root Menu appears in Figure C-12.

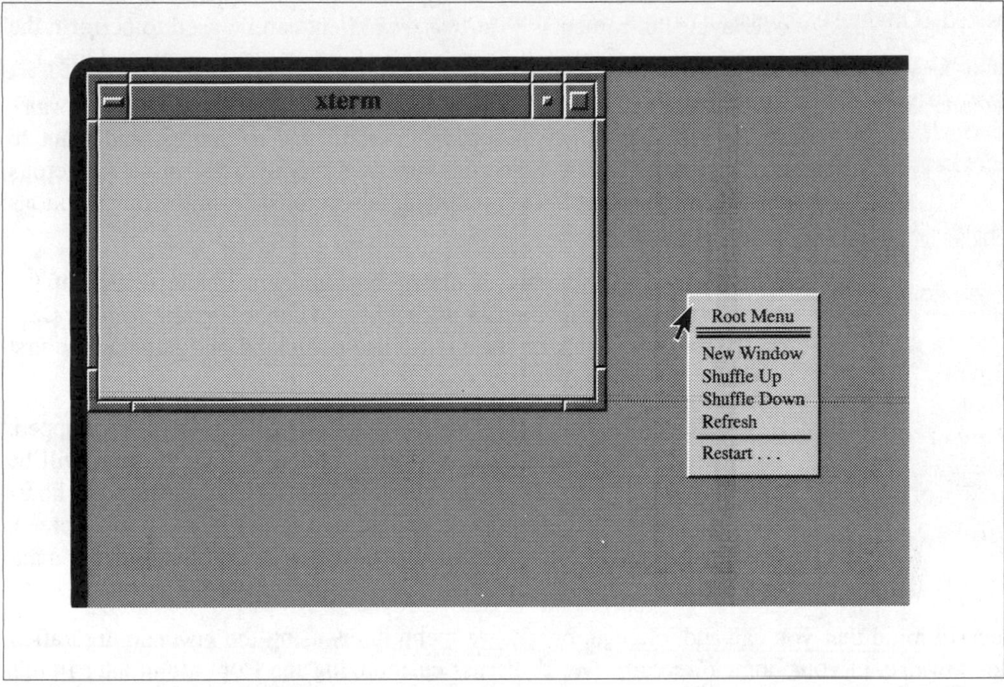

Figure C-12. The mwm Root Menu

When you display the Root Menu, the pointer changes to the arrow pointer. As you can see, the default Root Menu offers only five items. To select an item, use the following steps:

1. As you continue to hold down the first pointer button, move the pointer onto the the desired item name. (If you accidentally move the pointer off the menu, it will still remain displayed, as long as you continue to hold the first button down.) As you move the pointer onto an item, notice that a rectangular box is displayed around the item to highlight it.
2. Once the pointer is positioned on the item you want, release pointer button one. The action is performed.

The functions performed by the default Root Menu are described below.

New Window — By default, this command runs an *xterm* window on the display specified by the DISPLAY environment variable, generally the local display. When you create a new window (by using the menu or typing the command in an *xterm*), the new window automatically becomes the active window.

Shuffle Up — If windows and/or icons are stacked on your display, this command moves the bottom window or icon in the stack to the top (raises it).

Shuffle Down — If windows and/or icons are stacked on your display, this command moves the top window or icon in the stack to the bottom (lowers it).

Refresh — This command is used to *refresh* the display screen, that is, redraw its contents. Refresh is useful if system messages appear on the screen, overlaying its contents. (The *xrefresh* client can be used to perform the same function. Simply type `xrefresh` on an *xterm* command line.)

Restart... — Stops and restarts *mwm*. This is useful when you've edited the *.mwmrc* configuration file, which specifies certain *mwm* features, and want to activate the changes. Since this function is potentially more dangerous than the other Root Menu options, it is separated from the other options by a horizontal line.

When you select Restart, a dialog box appears in the center of the screen with command buttons asking you to either Restart mwm or Cancel the request. Click on the appropriate command button using the first pointer button.

If you select Restart mwm, the window manager process is stopped. The screen will momentarily go blank. The new *mwm* process will be started immediately. While the new *mwm* process is starting, an hourglass symbol is displayed in the center of the otherwise blank screen. The hourglass appears to be filling up with sand until the window manager is running and the windows again are displayed on the screen.

Keep in mind that you can add, change, or remove menu items using the *mwm* configuration file, *.mwmrc*, in your home directory. We'll discuss customizing the Root Menu later in this appendix.

Customizing mwm

The Motif window manager is one of the more flexible window managers available in the X market today. As we've seen, *mwm* provides a wide variety of methods for manipulating windows. In addition, virtually every feature of *mwm* can be customized. You can change the appearance of window frames, icons, and menus, the functions available on the Root Menu and the Window Menu, the keyboard focus policy, how icons are arranged on the display, as well as the appearance of client applications running under OSF/Motif. As we'll see, you can also create additional menus, displayed from the root window, to perform manipulations on the display as a whole.

Customization of *mwm* is controlled in two ways:

- Through a special file, called *.mwmrc*, in your home directory.
- Through *mwm* resources you can enter in your *.Xresources* file.

The default operation of *mwm* is largely controlled by a system-wide file, called *system.mwmrc*, which establishes the contents of the Root Menu and Window Menu, how menu functions are invoked, and what key and button combinations can be used to manipulate windows. To modify the behavior of *mwm*, you can edit a copy of this file in your home directory. The version of this file in your home directory should be called *.mwmrc*. We'll take a look at the *system.mwmrc* and ways to edit your own *.mwmrc* file to make the window manager work more effectively for you.

In addition to the flexibility provided by the *.mwmrc* file, *mwm* provides dozens of application resources that you can set! It's neither practical or necessary to discuss all of those resources here. (You could spend quite a long time customizing *mwm*, if you had the time and inclination.) We'll just consider some basic categories into which *mwm* resources can be divided and also look at some of the more useful resources. See Chapter 9, *Setting Resources*, for syntax rules and information about loading resources into the server so that they will be accessible to client programs. See the *mwm* reference page in your OSF/Motif documentation for descriptions of all available resources.

In the remainder of this appendix, we're going to demonstrate the *basics* of customizing *mwm* and suggest what we think are helpful modifications. (This is still quite a lot to absorb.) To illustrate, we'll discuss how to customize the following features of *mwm*:

- The menus and how menu functions are invoked.
- The keyboard focus policy.
- How icons are organized (namely, how to set up a window known as an *icon box*, in which icons on the display can be organized).

Before we can customize the *mwm* menus or the ways in which their functions are invoked, we need to take a closer look at the *system.mwmrc* file. First, however, let's consider an important topic: how to make the window manager aware of customizations.

Activating Changes to the Window Manager

Be aware that if you edit your *.mwmrc* or *Xresources* file to change the way *mwm* works, the changes will not take effect automatically. Whether you change resource settings, edit your *.mwmrc* file, or both, you must restart *mwm* for the changes to take effect.

If you edit your resources file, you must first make the server aware of the new resource specifications by using the *xrdb* client. Generally, you will enter the following command at the prompt in an *xterm* window:

```
% xrdb -load .Xresources
```

The settings in the current version of your *Xresources* file will replace the resource settings previously stored in the resource database. You can merely append new settings to the old ones using the *xrdb* `-merge` option. See Chapter 9, *Setting Resources*, for more information.

Once you've loaded the new resource settings, you can restart *mwm*. This can be done using the Restart item of the Root Menu, as described earlier in this appendix. When *mwm* has been restarted, it should reflect any changes made to the *.mwmrc* and *Xresources* files.

The system.mwmrc File

The following example shows the *system.mwmrc* file shipped with OSF/Motif Release 1.0. If you've used other window managers, this file may seem a bit more complicated than other configuration files, but the complexity is deceptive.

If you wish to change the operation of *mwm*, you shouldn't change the *system.mwmrc* file. Instead, copy it to your home directory, under the name *.mwmrc*, and make changes to that copy.

Example C-1. The system.mwmrc file, Release 1.0

```
#
#  DEFAULT mwm RESOURCE DESCRIPTION FILE (system.mwmrc)
#

#
# menu pane descriptions
#

# Root Menu Description
Menu RootMenu
{
    "Root Menu"          f.title
    No-label             f.separator
    "New Window"         f.exec "xterm &"
    "Shuffle Up"         f.circle_up
    "Shuffle Down"       f.circle_down
    "Refresh"            f.refresh
    no-label             f.separator
    "Restart..."         f.restart
}

# Default Window Menu Description

Menu DefaultWindowMenu MwmWindowMenu
{
    "Restore"       _R        Alt<Key>F5         f.normalize
    "Move"          _M        Alt<Key>F7         f.move
    "Size"          _S        Alt<Key>F8         f.resize
    "Minimize"      _n        Alt<Key>F9         f.minimize
    "Maximize"      _x        Alt<Key>F10        f.maximize
    "Lower"         _L        Alt<Key>F3         f.lower
    no-label                                     f.separator
    "Close"         _C        Alt<Key>F4         f.kill
}

#
# key binding descriptions
#

Keys DefaultKeyBindings
{
  Shift<Key>Escape          icon|window           f.post_wmenu
  Meta<Key>space            icon|window           f.post_wmenu
  Meta<Key>Tab              root|icon|window      f.next_key
  Meta Shift<Key>Tab        root|icon|window      f.prev_key
```

Example C-1. The system.mwmrc file, Release 1.0 (continued)

```
  Meta<Key>Escape            root|icon|window  f.next_key
  Meta Shift<Key>Escape      root|icon|window  f.prev_key
  Meta Ctrl Shift<Key>exclam root|icon|window  f.set_behavior
  Meta<Key>F6                window            f.next_key transient
# Meta<Key>Down              root|icon|window  f.circle_down
# Meta<Key>Up                root|icon|window  f.circle_up
}

#
# button binding descriptions
#

Buttons DefaultButtonBindings
{
    <Btn1Down>          frame|icon          f.raise
    <Btn2Down>          frame|icon          f.post_wmenu
    <Btn1Down>          root                f.menu      RootMenu
    Meta<Btn1Down>      window|icon         f.lower
    Meta<Btn2Down>      window|icon         f.resize
    Meta<Btn3Down>      window|icon         f.move
}

Buttons ExplicitButtonBindings
{
    <Btn1Down>          frame|icon          f.raise
    <Btn2Down>          frame|icon          f.post_wmenu
    <Btn3Down>          frame|icon          f.lower
    <Btn1Down>          root                f.menu      RootMenu
    Meta<Btn1Down>      window|icon         f.lower
    Meta<Btn2Down>      window|icon         f.resize
    Meta<Btn3Down>      window|icon         f.move
}

Buttons PointerButtonBindings
{
    <Btn1Down>          frame|icon          f.raise
    <Btn2Down>          frame|icon          f.post_wmenu
    <Btn3Down>          frame|icon          f.lower
    <Btn1Down>          root                f.menu      RootMenu
# If (Mwm*passButtons == False)
    Meta<Btn1Down>      window|icon         f.raise
# Else
#   <Btn1Down>          window              f.raise
#   Meta<Btn1Down>      window|icon         f.lower
    Meta<Btn2Down>      window|icon         f.resize
    Meta<Btn3Down>      window|icon         f.move
}

#
#  END OF mwm RESOURCE DESCRIPTION FILE
#
```

The *system.mwmrc* file can be divided into three sections:

- Menu specifications.
- Key bindings.
- Button bindings.

Comment lines are introduced by the number sign (#).

The menu section of the *system.mwmrc* file defines the contents of the Root Menu and the Window Menu. Menu item labels are paired with predefined *mwm* functions.

A *binding* is a mapping between a user action (such as a keystroke) and a function, in this case a window manager function. The key bindings section specifies keyboard keys that can be used to invoke some of the pre-defined window manager functions. The button bindings section specifies pointer buttons or key/button combinations that can be used to invoke various functions.

Each section of the *system.mwmrc* file matches the following basic template:

```
Section_Type  Section_Title
{
definitions
}
```

For example, the basic syntax of a menu specification is as follows:

```
Menu menu_name . . .
{
menu items defined
}
```

`Menu` is the *`Section_Type`*. The other possible section types are `Keys` and `Buttons`. The *`Section_Title`* is somewhat arbitrary. In this case, it corresponds to the title of a menu. In the key and button sections, it is simply a title assigned to a group of bindings.

However, the *`Section_Title`* can be very significant. As we'll see, a section title can be used as the value of a resource variable in your *.Xresources* file. Menu titles are often referenced elsewhere in the *.mwmrc* file. The *`menu_name`* is generally paired with a pointer button action (in the button bindings section of the *.mwmrc* file) to allow you to use a particular button to display the menu.

The syntax of the actual menu items, key bindings, and button bindings requires further explanation. But first, let's take a look at some of the predefined window manager functions.

mwm Functions

mwm has a number of predefined functions. Each of these functions has a name beginning with "`f.`". Several functions appear in the *system.mwmrc* file, paired with the method by which the function can be invoked: by menu item, pointer button action, keystroke(s), or key and pointer button combinations.

The meaning of most of these functions should be fairly obvious to you from the name, if not from your experience using the window manager. For example, `f.resize` is used to resize a window, `f.move` to move a window, or `f.minimize` to change a window to an icon.

Others are less obvious. The function `f.post_wmenu` is used to display (or post) the Window Menu. Notice the function `f.separator`, which appears in the menu definition coupled with the instruction `no-label` rather than with a menu item. This line in the

.mwmrc creates a divider line on a menu. For example, such a divider line is used to isolate the Restart ... item from the other items on the Root Menu.

As we'll see, the function `f.menu` is used to associate a menu with the key or button binding that is used to display it. The `f.menu` function takes a required argument: the menu name. This function can also be used to define a submenu.

Each of the functions is described in detail on the reference page for *mwm* in your OSF/Motif documentation.

Menu Specifications

The first section of the *system.mwmrc* file contains specifications for the Root Menu and Window Menu. As we've said, the basic syntax of a menu specification is as follows:

```
Menu menu_name . . .
{
menu items defined
}
```

Menu items are defined in slightly different ways for the Root Menu and the Window Menu. The following text in the *system.mwmrc* file creates the Root Menu:

```
# Root Menu Description
Menu RootMenu
{
    "Root Menu"         f.title
    No-label            f.separator
    "New Window"        f.exec "xterm &"
    "Shuffle Up"        f.circle_up
    "Shuffle Down"      f.circle_down
    "Refresh"           f.refresh
    no-label            f.separator
    "Restart..."        f.restart
}
```

The syntax for defining Root Menu items is very simple. Each item is defined by a line of this format:

> *"label"* *function*

When you pair a label with a menu function, that label appears as a menu item. You can invoke the function by selecting the item from the menu using the pointer. For example, the line:

```
"Refresh"    f.refresh
```

sets up the Refresh menu item, which can be selected from the Root Menu as discussed earlier in this appendix. (Again, the function performed is obvious from the function name.) As we'll see later, it's easy to add items to the Root Menu by adding lines of label/function pairs.

Because Window Menu items can be invoked in a variety of ways, the syntax for defining items is more complicated. The following text defines the Window Menu:

```
# Default Window Menu Description
Menu DefaultWindowMenu MwmWindowMenu
{
    "Restore"       _R          Alt<Key>F5       f.normalize
    "Move"          _M          Alt<Key>F7       f.move
    "Size"          _S          Alt<Key>F8       f.resize
    "Minimize"      _n          Alt<Key>F9       f.minimize
    "Maximize"      _x          Alt<Key>F10      f.maximize
    "Lower"         _L          Alt<Key>F3       f.lower
    no-label                                     f.separator
    "Close"         _C          Alt<Key>F4       f.kill
}
```

The syntax of each menu item is as follows:

"label" *mnemonic* *accelerator* *function*

(The *mnemonic* and *accelerator* fields are optional.) Like the Root Menu, each item on the Window Menu can be invoked by selecting its label with the pointer. In addition, there are two shortcuts defined for invoking the function, a mnemonic and an accelerator. As you may recall, a mnemonic is a unique letter abbreviation for the menu item label. On the menu, mnemonic abbreviations are underlined; thus an underscore precedes each mnemonic definition in the *system.mwmrc* file. Once the Window Menu is displayed, you can select an item by typing its mnemonic abbreviation. Similarly, you can invoke the function without displaying the menu, simply by typing the accelerator keys (by default, the Alt key plus a function key).

Now let's see how one of the Window Menu definition lines fits this template:

```
"Move"    _M   Alt<Key>F7     f.move
```

The menu item label is Move. Selecting the item invokes the `f.move` function. The mnemonic "m" or the accelerator key combination Alt-F7 can also be used to invoke the function.

Key Bindings

The second section of the *system.mwmrc* file binds keystroke combinations to window manager functions.

Like the menu definintion section, the key bindings section of the file is titled and bracketed:

```
Keys Section_Title
{
key bindings defined
}
```

The section type is `Keys`. The section title in the *system.mwmrc* file is `DefaultKeyBindings`. This title can also be specified as the value of the *mwm* resource `keyBindings` in your *Xresources* file. However, since these bindings are used by default, this is not necessary.

Using the section title as a resource becomes significant when you want to create an alternative set of bindings. Hypothetically, you could add another set of bindings with a different title to your *.mwmrc* file. Then specify this title as the value of the `keyBindings` resource in your *Xresources* file. If you add the following resource specification to your *Xresources* file, `MyButtonBindings` replace `DefaultButtonBindings` for all client applications running with *mwm*:

```
Mwm*keyBindings:    MyButtonBindings
```

If you want to use different sets of bindings for different applications, you can add an application name between the parts of the resource specification. For example, if you want `MyButtonBindings` to apply only to *xterm* windows running with *mwm*, you could enter the following resource line:

```
Mwm*xterm*keyBindings:    MyButtonBindings
```

Then `DefaultButtonBindings` would still apply to all applications other than *xterm*.

A non-obvious principle behind a key/function (or button/function) binding is that in order for the keys (or buttons) to invoke the function, the pointer must be in a certain location. This location is known as the *context*. For *mwm*, the most commonly used contexts are: `root`, `frame`, `window`, and `icon`. The `window` context refers to the entire window, including the frame. (There are a few more specific contexts, such as `border`, but they are not used in the *system.mwmrc* file. See the *mwm* reference page in your OSF/Motif documentation for details.)

Some functions can be invoked if the pointer is in more than one context. For example, as we've seen, you can display the Window Menu from either a window or an icon using the keyboard shortcuts Meta-space or Shift-Escape. The action involved is `f.post_wmenu` and the window and the icon are the pointer contexts from which this action can be performed. These keyboard shortcuts are defined in the key bindings section of the *system.mwmrc* file as follows:

```
Shift<Key>Escape   icon|window   f.post_wmenu
Meta<Key>space     icon|window   f.post_wmenu
```

Upon examining these lines, we can discern the template for a key binding:

[*modifier_keys*]<Key>*key_name* *context* *function*

Each binding can have one or more modifier keys (modifiers are optional) and *must* have a single primary key (signaled by the word <Key> in angle brackets) to invoke the function. In the first specification, Shift is the modifier and Escape is the primary key. In the second specification, Meta is the modifier and space is the primary key. Both specifications have two acceptable pointer contexts: either a window or an icon. And both bindings are mapped to the same action, `f.post_wmenu`, which displays the Window Menu.

Button Bindings

The key bindings section of the file is also titled and bracketed:

```
Buttons Section_Title
{
button bindings defined
}
```

The section type is `Buttons`. The *system.mwmrc* file contains three sets of button bindings with the section titles:

```
DefaultButtonBindings
ExplicitButtonBindings
PointerButtonBindings
```

Button bindings clearly illustrate the need to coordinate your *.Xresources* and *.mwmrc* files. The three sets of button bindings correspond to three possible settings for the resource `buttonBindings`. The default setting for the resource is:

```
Mwm*buttonBindings:     DefaultButtonBindings
```

specifying that the `DefaultButtonBindings` are used.

You can specify that one of the other sets of button bindings is to be used by setting this resource in your *.Xresources* file. For example, if you add the following specification to your resource file:

```
Mwm*buttonBindings:     ExplicitButtonBindings
```

mwm will use those bindings that come under the heading `ExplicitButtonBindings` in the *.mwmrc* file.

Be aware that if you do specify different button bindings, the value of the resource must exactly match the title associated with the bindings, or the bindings will not take effect.

The syntax for a button binding specification is very similar to that of a key binding:

[*modifier_key*]<*button_event*>   *context*   *function*

Each binding can have one or more modifier keys (modifiers are optional) and *must* have a single button event (enclosed in angle brackets) to invoke the function. The motion that comprises each button event should be fairly obvious. (A list of acceptable button events appears on the *mwm* reference page in your OSF/Motif documentation.)

Now let's see how the button binding syntax relates to the default button bindings in the *system.mwmrc* file:

```
Buttons DefaultButtonBindings
{
     <Btn1Down>          frame|icon        f.raise
     <Btn2Down>          frame|icon        f.post_wmenu
     <Btn1Down>          root              f.menu    RootMenu
     Meta<Btn1Down>      window|icon       f.lower
     Meta<Btn2Down>      window|icon       f.resize
     Meta<Btn3Down>      window|icon       f.move
}
```

The first specification is familiar. It indicates that the event of pressing down the first pointer button while the pointer is in a window frame or an icon performs the action of raising the window or icon, respectively.

Most of the other default button bindings reveal ways to perform *mwm* functions that were not covered in the first half of this appendix. Upon closer examination, you should be able to figure out these bindings and what they do. The second binding reveals *still another* way to display the Window Menu, by pressing the second pointer button on a window frame or an icon.

The third binding is also familiar. and illustrates the use of the `f.menu` function. As previously mentioned, the `f.menu` function is used to associate a menu with the key or button binding that is used to display it. The following binding specifies that the Root Menu is displayed by pressing and holding down the first pointer button on the root window:

```
<Btn1Down>           root           f.menu           RootMenu
```

Notice that the function requires an argument, the menu name (RootMenu), which also appears in the first line of the menu definition. This correspondence is required—`f.menu` needs to know which menu to display.

The other default button bindings perform useful (though not obvious) functions. Each specifies holding down the Meta key and simultaneously pressing a different pointer button while the pointer is on a window or icon. Holding down the Meta key and pressing the first pointer button on a window or icon lowers the window or icon to the bottom of the stack. Holding down the Meta key and pressing the second or third pointer button enables you to resize or move the object, respectively.

Customizing the Root Menu

You can add items to the Root Menu simply by adding lines of the format:

"*label*"   *function*

within the menu definition section of your *.mwmrc* file.

The `f.exec` function allows you to execute system commands from a menu. In the default Root Menu, the New Window command uses the `f.exec` function to execute the system command `xterm &`.

```
# Root Menu Description
Menu RootMenu
{
    "Root Menu"          f.title
    No-label             f.separator
    "New Window"         f.exec "xterm &"
    "Shuffle Up"         f.circle_up
    "Shuffle Down"       f.circle_down
    "Refresh"            f.refresh
    no-label             f.separator
    "Restart..."         f.restart
}
```

To create a menu item labeled Clock that opens an *xclock* window on your display, simply add a line to your *.mwmrc* file, as shown here:

```
# Root Menu Description
Menu RootMenu
{
    "Root Menu"          f.title
    No-label             f.separator
    "New Window"         f.exec "xterm &"
    "Clock"              f.exec "xclock &"
    "Shuffle Up"         f.circle_up
    "Shuffle Down"       f.circle_down
    "Refresh"            f.refresh
```

```
    no-label            f.separator
    "Restart..."        f.restart
}
```

You can also edit (or remove) existing menu items. For example, if you want to run a terminal emulator program other than *xterm*, you can edit the menu item definition in your *.mwmrc* file. Say you want to run the *hpterm* terminal emulator (developed by Hewlett-Packard), you would edit your menu specification to look like this:

```
# Root Menu Description
Menu RootMenu
{
    "Root Menu"         f.title
    No-label            f.separator
    "New Window"        f.exec "hpterm &"
    "Shuffle Up"        f.circle_up
    "Shuffle Down"      f.circle_down
    "Refresh"           f.refresh
    no-label            f.separator
    "Restart..."        f.restart
}
```

Creating New Menus

Keep in mind that *mwm* also allows you to specify entirely new menus in your *.mwmrc* file. A new menu can be separate from all existing menus, or it can be a submenu of an existing menu. (Submenus are described in the following section, "Cascading Menus.")

If you want to create a new, independent menu, it must conform to the menu specification syntax discussed earlier. Items must invoke predefined window manager functions.

The *.mwmrc* file must also specify how the menu will be displayed and in what context. This involves associating a key or button with the `f.menu` function. Say you've specified a new menu, titled GamesMenu, that runs various game programs, each in its own window. (The `f.exec` function would be used to define each item.) The following button binding specifies that pressing the second pointer button on the root window causes the Games Menu to be displayed:

```
<Btn2Down>          root        f.menu    GamesMenu
```

Cascading Menus

mwm also allows you to create submenus, generally known as *cascading* menus because they are displayed to the right side of (and slightly lower than) another menu. You define a submenu just as you would any other, using the syntax rules discussed earlier. The following lines create a Utilities Menu that invokes several "desktop" clients and one game:

```
Menu UtilitiesMenu
{
    "Utilities Menu"    f.title
    No-label            f.separator
    "Clock"             f.exec "xclock &"
    "System Load"       f.exec "xload &"
```

```
        "Calculator"          f.exec "xcalc &"
        "Manpage Browser"     f.exec "xman &"
        "Tetris"              f.exec "xtetris &"
    }
```

In order to make this a submenu of the Root Menu, you need to add an `f.menu` function to the Root Menu. This `f.menu` function must be coupled with the correct submenu title:

```
    # Root Menu Description
    Menu RootMenu
    {
        "Root Menu"           f.title
        No-label              f.separator
        "New Window"          f.exec "xterm &"
        "Shuffle Up"          f.circle_up
        "Shuffle Down"        f.circle_down
        "Refresh"             f.refresh
        "Utilities"           f.menu              UtilitiesMenu
        no-label              f.separator
        "Restart..."          f.restart
    }
```

After you specify the preceding menus in your *.mwmrc* file (and restart *mwm*), display the Root Menu. It will feature a new item, labeled Utilities. Since this item is actually a pointer to a submenu, it will be followed by an arrow pointing to the right, as in Figure C-13.

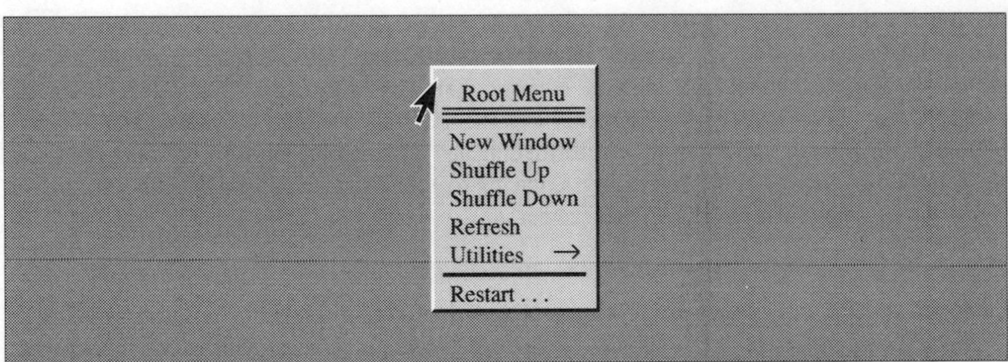

Figure C-13. An arrow pointing to the right indicates a submenu

If you drag the pointer down the Root Menu to the Utilities item, the submenu will appear to cascade to the right. Figure C-14 shows it appearing.

If you release the pointer button, both menus will remain displayed and the Utilities item and the first item on the Utilities Menu will be highlighted by a box. You can then select an item from the Utilities Menu by moving the pointer to the item and clicking the first button.

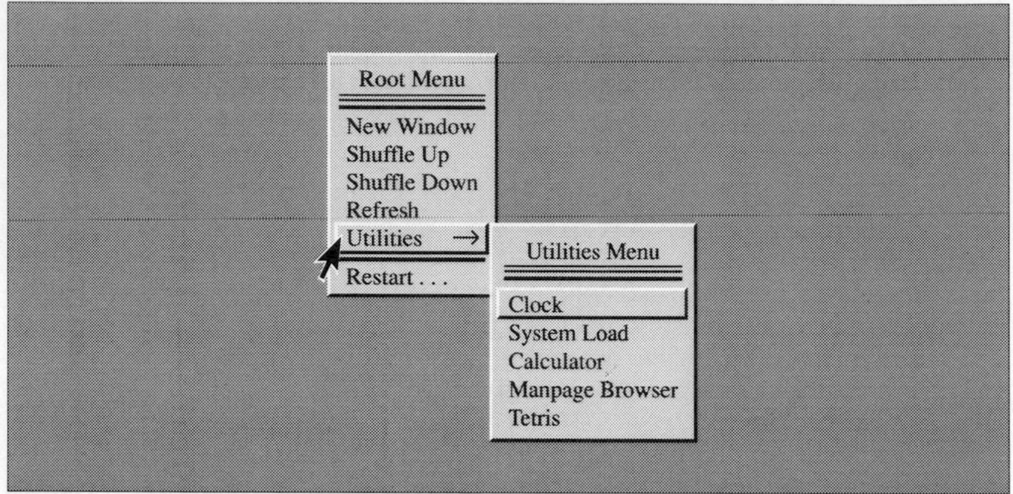

Figure C-14. Utilities submenu of the Root Menu

Keep in mind that you can create several submenus beneath a single menu and that menus can cascade several levels, though such complexity is not necessarily desirable.

Setting mwm Resources

The Motif window manager provides dozens of resources that control the appearance and functionality of the window manager, its component features, and other clients running with it. *mwm* resources should be entered in your *.Xresources* file and take effect when the resources have been loaded into the server and *mwm* has been started or restarted. See Chapter 9, *Setting Resources*, for syntax information and instructions on how to load resources using the *xrdb* client. See "Activating Changes to the Window Manager" for information about running *mwm* with the new resource settings.

mwm resources are considered to fall into three categories:

1. ***mwm* component appearance resources.** These resources set the characteristics of *mwm*'s component features, such as the window frame, menus, and icons.
2. ***mwm*-specific appearance and behavior resources**. These resources set characteristics of the window manager client, such as focus policy, key and button bindings, and so forth.
3. **Client-specific resources**. These *mwm* resources can be used to set the appearance and behavior of a particular client or class of clients.

Under these categories fall dozens of *mwm* resources. The sheer number of resources makes it impractical for all of them to be discussed here. (You could spend quite a long time customizing *mwm* in this way, if you had the time and inclination!) In the following sections, we discuss the three categories of resources in somewhat greater detail. We'll then take a look at two of the more powerful and useful resources, `keyboardFocusPolicy` and `useIconBox`, which set the focus policy and set up *mwm* to use an icon box, respectively. For a comprehensive list of available resources, see the *mwm* reference page in your OSF/Motif documentation.

Component Appearance Resources

The Motif window manager can be considered to be made up of components: client window frames, menus, icons, and what are known as *feedback boxes*. An example of a feedback box is the box that appears so that you can confirm or cancel a Restart command from the Root Menu. (See "The Root Menu" earlier in this appendix.)

Certain resources allow you to specify the appearance of one or all of these *mwm* component features. In specifying the resource setting, you can use the name of one of the features as part of the resource name. For example, one of the most useful component appearance resources is `background`, which, as we know from Chapter 8, specifies the background color. You can specify a resource that sets the background color of any of the *mwm* components. The following resource specification sets the background color of all client window frames to light blue:

```
Mwm*client*background:      lightblue
```

Table C-2 summarizes the resource name that corresponds to each of the *mwm* components:

Table C-2. Resource Names Corresponding to mwm Components

Component	Resource name
Menu	`menu`
Icon	`icon`
Client window frame	`client`
Feedback box	`feedback`

Thus, to set the background color of feedback boxes to sea green, you'd use the following resource:

```
Mwm*feedback*foreground:    seagreen
```

Of course, if you omit any specific component from the resource specification, it applies to *all* components. Thus, the following specification sets the background color of all window frames, feedback boxes, icons, and menus to light grey:

```
Mwm*foreground:   lightgrey
```

mwm-Specific Appearance and Behavior Resources

The *mwm*-specific resources control aspects of what you probably think of as the window manager application itself, features such as the focus policy, whether windows are placed on the display automatically or interactively, which set(s) of button and key bindings are used, whether an icon box is used, and so forth.

The syntax of *mwm*-specific resource specifications is very simple: the *mwm* class name connected by a loose binding to the resource variable name,* shown here:

```
Mwm*clientAutoPlace:    false
```

This resource establishes the behavior that the user will interactively place client windows on the display. (The default is true, meaning *mwm* places them automatically.)

Two of the *mwm*-specific resources bring up an issue of coordination between the *.Xresources* and *.mwmrc* files. Remember, the default *.mwmrc* file contains three sets of button bindings:

```
DefaultButtonBindings
ExplicitButtonBindings
PointerButtonBindings
```

These three sets of button bindings correspond to three possible settings for the resource variable `buttonBindings`. If your resource file contains the following setting:

```
Mwm*buttonBindings:    ExplicitButtonBindings
```

mwm will use those bindings that come under the heading `ExplicitButtonBindings` in the *.mwmrc* file.

Similarly, the resource variable `keyBindings` should be coordinated to match the key bindings in the *.mwmrc* file. Since the default *.mwmrc* file has only one set of key bindings, named `DefaultKeyBindings`, and the `keyBindings` resource also sets this by default, coordination should not be an issue unless you create a new set of key bindings with a different name.

Two of the most useful and powerful *mwm*-specific resources set the keyboard focus policy and specify that icons be stored in an icon box. We'll discuss the use and advantages of these resources later in this appendix.

Client-Specific Resources

Some *mwm* resources can be set to apply to certain client applications or classes of applications. These resources generally have the form:

```
Mwm*application*resource_variable:
```

where *`application`* can be an instance name or a class name.† Be aware that the application name is optional. If you omit an application name, the resource applies to all clients.

---

*Loose and tight bindings are described in Chapter 9, *Setting Resources*.

†Instance and class names are described in Chapter 9, *Setting Resources*.

Many of the client-specific resources provide what might be considered advanced customization. For example, a combination of resources allows you to specify your own bitmap as the image for a client icon. The average user will probably not need most of these resources.

One client-specific resource users might be interested in is called `focusAutoRaise`. This resource, true by default, causes the active window (the window receiving input focus) to be raised to the top of the stack. If you are using explicit (click-to-type) focus (also the default), this behavior is clearly very desirable. However, if you change the focus policy to pointer focus (as we'll describe in the following section), having `focusAutoRaise` on can make the display seem chaotic.

When pointer focus is active, as you move the pointer across the display, the focus changes from window to window based on the location of the pointer, often a desirable feature. However, if `focusAutoRaise` is still true, each time the pointer moves into a window, the window will be moved to the front of the display. Simply moving the pointer across a screenful of windows can create a distracting shuffling effect! If you set the focus policy to pointer, we suggest you also set `focusAutoRaise` to false, as in the following example:

```
Mwm*focusAutoRaise:     false
```

Since an application name is omitted from this resource specification, it applies to all clients. To change the behavior only for the class of *xterm* windows, you could specify:

```
Mwm*XTerm*focusAutoRaise:   false
```

Of course, suppressing `focusAutoRaise` with pointer focus is just our preference. You may want to experiment a while to see how you like working *with* it.

Setting the Focus Policy

The most common resource users will probably want to set controls *mwm*'s keyboard focus policy. By default, *mwm* has explicit (or click-to-type) focus, which is set using the following resource:

```
Mwm*keyboardFocusPolicy:    explicit
```

To change the keyboard focus policy from explicit to pointer focus (that is, focus follows the movement of the pointer), enter the following line in your *Xresources* file:

```
Mwm*keyboardFocusPolicy:    pointer
```

Using an Icon Box

One of the most interesting (and desirable) features *mwm* can provide is a window in which icons can be organized on the display. This window is known as an *icon box*, and is pictured in Figure C-15 below.

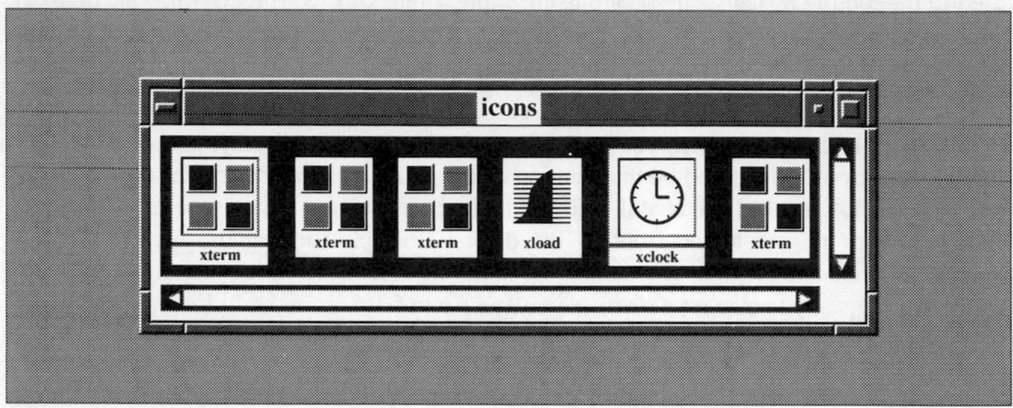

Figure C-15. An icon box

As we'll see, in addition to organizing icons neatly on the display, the icon box also provides a few window manipulation functions.

You can set up *mwm* to provide an icon box automatically by specifying the following resource in your *.Xresources* file:

```
Mwm*useIconBox:    true
```

If this resource is included in your *.Xresources* file (and the resources have been loaded as described in Chapter 9, *Setting Resources*), *mwm* will provide an icon box when it is started (or restarted). Other resources can be used to customize the size, appearance and location of the icon box, as well as the window's title. By default, the icon box is six icons wide by one icon high (the size of individual icons depends on other *mwm* resources) and is located in the lower left hand corner of the display.

The horizontal and vertical scrollbars within the icon box suggest a significant, albeit non-obvious, feature. Icons can extend beyond the visible bounds of the icon box. If more than six icons are present in the default size box, you can view them using the scrollbars. (See Chapter 4, *The xterm Terminal Emulator*, for instructions on using scrollbars.) Keep in mind that if icons do extend beyond the visible bounds of the box, the appearance of the scrollbars will indicate it.

The presence of an icon box changes the way icons are used on the display. If you are using *mwm* without an icon box, only those windows that have been iconified are represented by icons on the display. If you are using *mwm* with an icon box, *all* windows on the display are represented by icons that are stored in the box, whether or not the windows are in an iconfied state.

When a client window is started, the window appears on the display *and* a corresponding icon appears in the icon box. However, an icon that represents a window currently visible on the display has a different appearance than an actual icon (that is, an iconified window). An icon corresponding to a window currently on the display appears flatter and less defined than the image of an iconified window. The former probably has fewer lines in its outer border. If you set up *mwm* to use an icon box, the differing appearance of these two types of icons should be obvious.

Somewhat similar to a menu item in a lighter typeface, the flatter, less defined icon suggests that it is not available to be chosen. In a sense, this is true. Since the flat icon is not an iconified window, but merely an image, it is not available to be converted back to a window. The icon box in Figure C-15 contains two iconified windows (*xclock* and the first *xterm*) and four icons representing windows currently visible on the display.

You can perform some manipulations by clicking on icons in the icon box. If you double click on an iconified window using the first pointer button, the icon is converted back to a window. If you double click on an icon representing an active window on the display, the corresponding window is raised to the front of the display.

However, an icon box limits the way you can work with the Window Menu. (It also changes one of the menu's options.) If you are using an icon box, you cannot display the Window Menu from an individual icon and manipulate that icon.* Instead, when you display the menu from the icon box, the menu commands apply to the box itself (which is actually a window). You can display the menu from the icon box using any of the methods described in the section "Manipulating Windows Using the Window Menu" earlier in this appendix. For example, if you use the keyboard shortcut Meta-space, the menu is displayed above the Window Menu command button in the upper left hand corner of the icon box frame.

When displayed from the icon box, the Window Menu Close item is replaced by an item called PackIcons (mnemonic "p", accelerator Alt+F12†). PackIcons rearranges the icons in the box to fill in empty slots. This is useful when icons are removed from the box or the box is resized.

When you remove a window, the corresponding icon is removed from the box, leaving an empty slot. PackIcons will move any icons that are to the right of the slot one space to the left to fill the hole. If you resize the icon box, PackIcons will arrange the icons to fit the new window in an optimal way. For instance, say we resize the icon box in Figure C-15 so that it is only three icons wide, but twice as high, as in Figure C-16. The first three icons from the box appear; the second three are obscured.††

**mwm* is documented to display the Window Menu from an icon if you press the *third* pointer button. However, this does not seem to work according to the specifications. The 1.1 version of *mwm*, scheduled for release in June of 1990, may provide this functionality.

†Obviously, if your keyboard has only ten function keys, you cannot use the Alt+F12 accelerator.

††When you resize the icon box, you'll notice the resize action has a tendency to jump the width or height of an icon at a time. The box must be resized exactly to fit a number of icons wide and a number high, though there are no obvious limitations as to the numbers. Basically, you can have an icon box of any size, even one icon high and wid and display the other icons using the scrollbars.

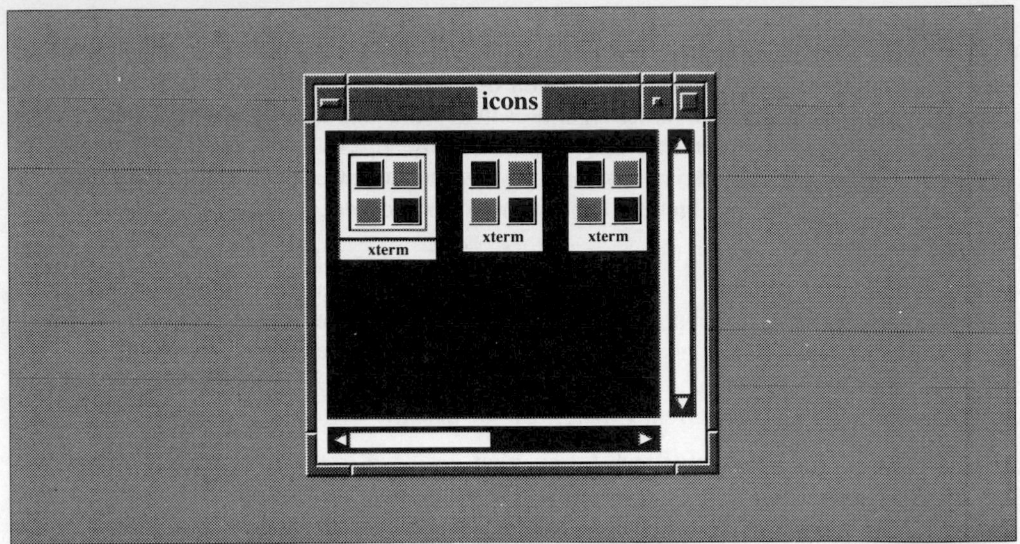

Figure C-16. In the resized icon box, only three icons are visible

Notice the horizontal scrollbar at the bottom of the window, indicating that the other three icons are still to the right of these and thus not viewable in the resized box. If you place the pointer on the scrollbar, hold down the first button and drag the scrollbar to the right, the hidden icons will be revealed.

In order to rearrange the icons to better fill the new shape box, use the PackIcons menu item. Figure C-17 shows the icon box after you've selected PackIcons.

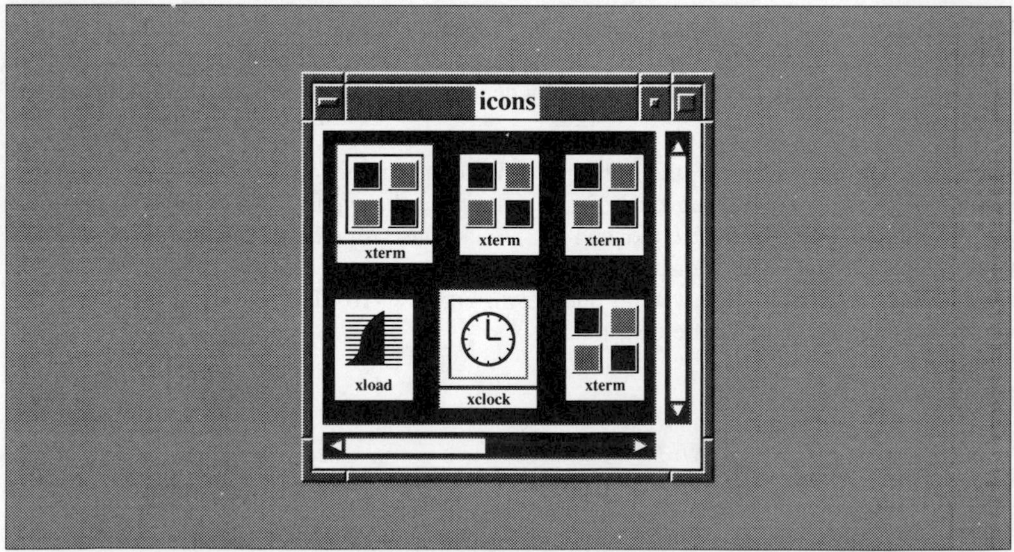

Figure C-17. PackIcons menu item rearranges icons in resized box

If you want to reorganize icons in the box yourself, without PackIcons, this is also possible. You can actually move icons into adjacent empty slots using the pointer. Just hold down the first pointer button on the icon and drag it into the next slot. If you first make the icon box larger, so that there are several empty spaces, you'll find you can radically reorganize icons. Once you've arranged them as you like, you resize the box to fit the icons—or perhaps make it even smaller and view the obscured icons using the scrollbars.

D

Standard Cursors

This appendix shows the standard cursor images that can be used by X programs.

D
Standard Cursors

Table D-1 lists the cursors available in the standard distribution of X from MIT; the cursor shapes themselves are pictured in Figure D-1. The cursor shapes in the standard distribution are the same in Release 3 and Release 4.

To specify a cursor as an argument to a command line option, as the value of a resource variable, etc., strip the `XC_` prefix from the symbol name. For example, to specify the `XC_sailboat` cursor as the *xterm* pointer, you could enter the command:

```
% xterm -xrm 'xterm*pointerShape: sailboat'
```

Each cursor has an associated numeric value (to the right of the symbol name in the table). You may notice that the values skip the odd numbers. Each cursor is actually comprised of two font characters: the character that defines the shape (pictured in Figure D-1), and a mask character (not shown) that sets the cursor shape off from the root (or other) window. (More precisely, the mask selects which pixels in the screen around the cursor are disturbed by the cursor.) The mask is generally the same shape as the character it underlies, but is one pixel wider in all directions.

To get an idea of what masks look like, display the entire cursor font using the command:

```
% xfd -fn cursor
```

Table D-1. Standard Cursor Symbols

Symbol	Value	Symbol	Value
XC_X_cursor	0	XC_ll_angle	76
XC_arrow	2	XC_lr_angle	78
XC_based_arrow_down	4	XC_man	80
XC_based_arrow_up	6	XC_middlebutton	82
XC_boat	8	XC_mouse	84
XC_bogosity	10	XC_pencil	86
XC_bottom_left_corner	12	XC_pirate	88
XC_bottom_right_corner	14	XC_plus	90
XC_bottom_side	16	XC_question_arrow	92
XC_bottom_tee	18	XC_right_ptr	94
XC_box_spiral	20	XC_right_side	96
XC_center_ptr	22	XC_right_tee	98
XC_circle	24	XC_rightbutton	100
XC_clock	26	XC_rtl_logo	102
XC_coffee_mug	28	XC_sailboat	104
XC_cross	30	XC_sb_down_arrow	106
XC_cross_reverse	32	XC_sb_h_double_arrow	108
XC_crosshair	34	XC_sb_left_arrow	110
XC_diamond_cross	36	XC_sb_right_arrow	112
XC_dot	38	XC_sb_up_arrow	114
XC_dotbox	40	XC_sb_v_double_arrow	116
XC_double_arrow	42	XC_shuttle	118
XC_draft_large	44	XC_sizing	120
XC_draft_small	46	XC_spider	122
XC_draped_box	48	XC_spraycan	124
XC_exchange	50	XC_star	126
XC_fleur	52	XC_target	128
XC_gobbler	54	XC_tcross	130
XC_gumby	56	XC_top_left_arrow	132
XC_hand1	58	XC_top_left_corner	134
XC_hand2	60	XC_top_right_corner	136
XC_heart	62	XC_top_side	138
XC_icon	64	XC_top_tee	140
XC_iron_cross	66	XC_trek	142
XC_left_ptr	68	XC_ul_angle	144
XC_left_side	70	XC_umbrella	146
XC_left_tee	72	XC_ur_angle	148
XC_leftbutton	74	XC_watch	150
		XC_xterm	152

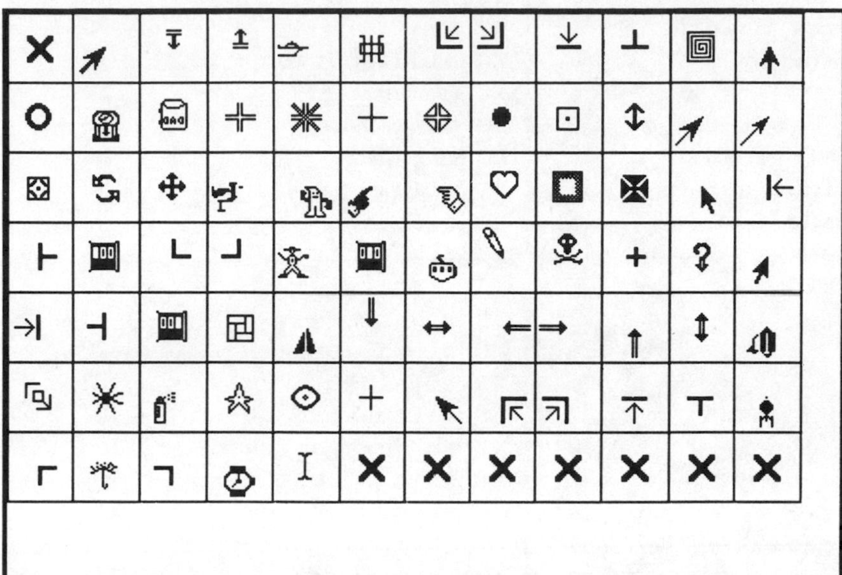

Figure D-1. The Standard Cursors

Standard Cursors

E

Release 3 and 4 Standard Fonts

This appendix shows the standard display fonts available in Release 4 of the MIT X distribution. The images contained in this appendix are window dumps created with our own program, called xshowfonts, *the code for which is included.*

E
Release 3 and 4 Standard Fonts

This appendix includes pictures of some representative fonts from the standard X distribution in Releases 3 and 4. Not every font may be supported by particular server vendors, and some vendors may supplement the set.

The standard Release 3 and 4 fonts are stored in three directories:

Directory	Contents
/usr/lib/X11/fonts/misc	Six fixed-width fonts (also available in Release 2), the cursor font, other miscellaneous fonts.
/usr/lib/X11/fonts/75dpi	Fixed- and variable-width fonts, 75 dots per inch.
/usr/lib/X11/fonts/100dpi	Fixed- and variable-width fonts, 100 dots per inch.

Tables E-1 through E-3 list the fonts in each of the three Release 4 font directories. Tables E-4 through E-6 list the fonts in each of the three Release 3 font directories. The first column lists the name of the file in which the font is stored (without the *.snf* extension); the second column lists the actual font name. See Chapter 5, *Font Specification*, for information about font naming conventions.

PICTURES of the different font families supplied in the MIT X11 distribution appear on subsequent pages. We show just the fonts in the *75dpi* directory. The *100dpi* directory contains the same fonts stored in the *75dpi* directory, but for 100 dots per inch monitors. Keep in mind that all of the fonts in the *75dpi* and *100dpi* directories are available in 8, 10, 12, 14, 18 and 24-point sizes. Each page shows fonts of various sizes, weights, and styles. We include the source for *xshowfonts.c*, the program we wrote to make these displays, at the end of the chapter.* We also show you, using *xfd*, one example of each of the unique character sets available.

All of the characters in each font are shown actual size, as they would appear on a 900 × 1180 pixel, 10" × 13.5" screen (Sun). On a screen with different pixel density, these fonts would appear a different size.

---

*If you don't want to type this program in, you can obtain the source from uunet.uu.net via anonymous *ftp* or *uucp*. See the Preface for more information.

Fonts that begin with many blank characters are shown with most leading blanks removed. Therefore, you can't always get the character number of each cell in the font by counting from the first cell we have shown. Use *xfd* to quickly determine the code for a particular cell.

Table E-1. Fonts in the misc Directory, Release 4

Filename	Font name
7x13B.snf	-misc-fixed-bold-r-normal—13-120-75-75-c-70-iso8859-1
8x13B.snf	-misc-fixed-bold-r-normal—13-120-75-75-c-80-iso8859-1
9x15B.snf	-misc-fixed-bold-r-normal—15-140-75-75-c-90-iso8859-1
6x13B.snf	-misc-fixed-bold-r-semicondensed—13-120-75-75-c-60-iso8859-1
6x10.snf	-misc-fixed-medium-r-normal—10-100-75-75-c-60-iso8859-1
7x13.snf	-misc-fixed-medium-r-normal—13-120-75-75-c-70-iso8859-1
8x13.snf	-misc-fixed-medium-r-normal—13-120-75-75-c-80-iso8859-1
k14.snf	-misc-fixed-medium-r-normal—14-130-75-75-c-140-jisx0208.1983-0
7x14.snf	-misc-fixed-medium-r-normal—14-130-75-75-c-70-iso8859-1
7x14rk.snf	-misc-fixed-medium-r-normal—14-130-75-75-c-70-jisx0201.1976-0
9x15.snf	-misc-fixed-medium-r-normal—15-140-75-75-c-90-iso8859-1
10x20.snf	-misc-fixed-medium-r-normal—20-200-75-75-c-100-iso8859-1
5x8.snf	-misc-fixed-medium-r-normal—8-80-75-75-c-50-iso8859-1
6x9.snf	-misc-fixed-medium-r-normal—9-90-75-75-c-60-iso8859-1
6x12.snf	-misc-fixed-medium-r-semicondensed—12-110-75-75-c-60-iso8859-1
6x13.snf	-misc-fixed-medium-r-semicondensed—13-120-75-75-c-60-iso8859-1
clB6x10.snf	-schumacher-clean-bold-r-normal—10-100-75-75-c-60-iso8859-1
clB8x10.snf	-schumacher-clean-bold-r-normal—10-100-75-75-c-80-iso8859-1
clB6x12.snf	-schumacher-clean-bold-r-normal—12-120-75-75-c-60-iso8859-1
clB8x12.snf	-schumacher-clean-bold-r-normal—12-120-75-75-c-80-iso8859-1
clB8x13.snf	-schumacher-clean-bold-r-normal—13-130-75-75-c-80-iso8859-1
clB8x14.snf	-schumacher-clean-bold-r-normal—14-140-75-75-c-80-iso8859-1
clB9x15.snf	-schumacher-clean-bold-r-normal—15-150-75-75-c-90-iso8859-1
clB8x16.snf	-schumacher-clean-bold-r-normal—16-160-75-75-c-80-iso8859-1
clB8x8.snf	-schumacher-clean-bold-r-normal—8-80-75-75-c-80-iso8859-1
clI6x12.snf	-schumacher-clean-medium-i-normal—12-120-75-75-c-60-iso8859-1
clI8x8.snf	-schumacher-clean-medium-i-normal—8-80-75-75-c-80-iso8859-1
clR5x10.snf	-schumacher-clean-medium-r-normal—10-100-75-75-c-50-iso8859-1
clR6x10.snf	-schumacher-clean-medium-r-normal—10-100-75-75-c-60-iso8859-1
clR7x10.snf	-schumacher-clean-medium-r-normal—10-100-75-75-c-70-iso8859-1
clR8x10.snf	-schumacher-clean-medium-r-normal—10-100-75-75-c-80-iso8859-1
clR6x12.snf	-schumacher-clean-medium-r-normal—12-120-75-75-c-60-iso8859-1
clR7x12.snf	-schumacher-clean-medium-r-normal—12-120-75-75-c-70-iso8859-1
clR8x12.snf	-schumacher-clean-medium-r-normal—12-120-75-75-c-80-iso8859-1
clR6x13.snf	-schumacher-clean-medium-r-normal—13-130-75-75-c-60-iso8859-1
clR8x13.snf	-schumacher-clean-medium-r-normal—13-130-75-75-c-80-iso8859-1
clR7x14.snf	-schumacher-clean-medium-r-normal—14-140-75-75-c-70-iso8859-1
clR8x14.snf	-schumacher-clean-medium-r-normal—14-140-75-75-c-80-iso8859-1
clR9x15.snf	-schumacher-clean-medium-r-normal—15-150-75-75-c-90-iso8859-1
clR8x16.snf	-schumacher-clean-medium-r-normal—16-160-75-75-c-80-iso8859-1

Table E-1. Fonts in the misc Directory, Release 4 (continued)

Filename	Font name
clR4x6.snf	-schumacher-clean-medium-r-normal—6-60-75-75-c-40-iso8859-1
clR5x6.snf	-schumacher-clean-medium-r-normal—6-60-75-75-c-50-iso8859-1
clR6x6.snf	-schumacher-clean-medium-r-normal—6-60-75-75-c-60-iso8859-1
clR5x8.snf	-schumacher-clean-medium-r-normal—8-80-75-75-c-50-iso8859-1
clR6x8.snf	-schumacher-clean-medium-r-normal—8-80-75-75-c-60-iso8859-1
clR7x8.snf	-schumacher-clean-medium-r-normal—8-80-75-75-c-70-iso8859-1
clR8x8.snf	-schumacher-clean-medium-r-normal—8-80-75-75-c-80-iso8859-1
8x16.snf	-sony-fixed-medium-r-normal—16-120-100-100-c-80-iso8859-1
8x16rk.snf	-sony-fixed-medium-r-normal—16-120-100-100-c-80-jisx0201.1976-0
12x24.snf	-sony-fixed-medium-r-normal—24-170-100-100-c-120-iso8859-1
12x24rk.snf	-sony-fixed-medium-r-normal—24-170-100-100-c-120-jisx0201.1976-0
olcursor.snf	-sun-open look cursor-----12-120-75-75-p-160-sunolcursor-1
olgl10.snf	-sun-open look glyph-----10-100-75-75-p-101-sunolglyph-1
olgl12.snf	-sun-open look glyph-----12-120-75-75-p-113-sunolglyph-1
olgl14.snf	-sun-open look glyph-----14-140-75-75-p-128-sunolglyph-1
olgl19.snf	-sun-open look glyph-----19-190-75-75-p-154-sunolglyph-1
cursor.snf	cursor
deccurs.snf	decw$cursor
decsess.snf	decw$session
nil2.snf	nil2

Table E-2. Fonts in the 75dpi Directory, Release 4

Filename	Font name
courBO10.snf	-adobe-courier-bold-o-normal—10-100-75-75-m-60-iso8859-1
courBO12.snf	-adobe-courier-bold-o-normal—12-120-75-75-m-70-iso8859-1
courBO14.snf	-adobe-courier-bold-o-normal—14-140-75-75-m-90-iso8859-1
courBO18.snf	-adobe-courier-bold-o-normal—18-180-75-75-m-110-iso8859-1
courBO24.snf	-adobe-courier-bold-o-normal—24-240-75-75-m-150-iso8859-1
courBO08.snf	-adobe-courier-bold-o-normal—8-80-75-75-m-50-iso8859-1
courB10.snf	-adobe-courier-bold-r-normal—10-100-75-75-m-60-iso8859-1
courB12.snf	-adobe-courier-bold-r-normal—12-120-75-75-m-70-iso8859-1
courB14.snf	-adobe-courier-bold-r-normal—14-140-75-75-m-90-iso8859-1
courB18.snf	-adobe-courier-bold-r-normal—18-180-75-75-m-110-iso8859-1
courB24.snf	-adobe-courier-bold-r-normal—24-240-75-75-m-150-iso8859-1
courB08.snf	-adobe-courier-bold-r-normal—8-80-75-75-m-50-iso8859-1
courO10.snf	-adobe-courier-medium-o-normal—10-100-75-75-m-60-iso8859-1
courO12.snf	-adobe-courier-medium-o-normal—12-120-75-75-m-70-iso8859-1
courO14.snf	-adobe-courier-medium-o-normal—14-140-75-75-m-90-iso8859-1
courO18.snf	-adobe-courier-medium-o-normal—18-180-75-75-m-110-iso8859-1
courO24.snf	-adobe-courier-medium-o-normal—24-240-75-75-m-150-iso8859-1

Table E-2. Fonts in the 75dpi Directory, Release 4 (continued)

Filename	Font name
courO08.snf	-adobe-courier-medium-o-normal—8-80-75-75-m-50-iso8859-1
courR10.snf	-adobe-courier-medium-r-normal—10-100-75-75-m-60-iso8859-1
courR12.snf	-adobe-courier-medium-r-normal—12-120-75-75-m-70-iso8859-1
courR14.snf	-adobe-courier-medium-r-normal—14-140-75-75-m-90-iso8859-1
courR18.snf	-adobe-courier-medium-r-normal—18-180-75-75-m-110-iso8859-1
courR24.snf	-adobe-courier-medium-r-normal—24-240-75-75-m-150-iso8859-1
courR08.snf	-adobe-courier-medium-r-normal—8-80-75-75-m-50-iso8859-1
helvBO10.snf	-adobe-helvetica-bold-o-normal—10-100-75-75-p-60-iso8859-1
helvBO12.snf	-adobe-helvetica-bold-o-normal—12-120-75-75-p-69-iso8859-1
helvBO14.snf	-adobe-helvetica-bold-o-normal—14-140-75-75-p-82-iso8859-1
helvBO18.snf	-adobe-helvetica-bold-o-normal—18-180-75-75-p-104-iso8859-1
helvBO24.snf	-adobe-helvetica-bold-o-normal—24-240-75-75-p-138-iso8859-1
helvBO08.snf	-adobe-helvetica-bold-o-normal—8-80-75-75-p-50-iso8859-1
helvB10.snf	-adobe-helvetica-bold-r-normal—10-100-75-75-p-60-iso8859-1
helvB12.snf	-adobe-helvetica-bold-r-normal—12-120-75-75-p-70-iso8859-1
helvB14.snf	-adobe-helvetica-bold-r-normal—14-140-75-75-p-82-iso8859-1
helvB18.snf	-adobe-helvetica-bold-r-normal—18-180-75-75-p-103-iso8859-1
helvB24.snf	-adobe-helvetica-bold-r-normal—24-240-75-75-p-138-iso8859-1
helvB08.snf	-adobe-helvetica-bold-r-normal—8-80-75-75-p-50-iso8859-1
helvO10.snf	-adobe-helvetica-medium-o-normal—10-100-75-75-p-57-iso8859-1
helvO12.snf	-adobe-helvetica-medium-o-normal—12-120-75-75-p-67-iso8859-1
helvO14.snf	-adobe-helvetica-medium-o-normal—14-140-75-75-p-78-iso8859-1
helvO18.snf	-adobe-helvetica-medium-o-normal—18-180-75-75-p-98-iso8859-1
helvO24.snf	-adobe-helvetica-medium-o-normal—24-240-75-75-p-130-iso8859-1
helvO08.snf	-adobe-helvetica-medium-o-normal—8-80-75-75-p-47-iso8859-1
helvR10.snf	-adobe-helvetica-medium-r-normal—10-100-75-75-p-56-iso8859-1
helvR12.snf	-adobe-helvetica-medium-r-normal—12-120-75-75-p-67-iso8859-1
helvR14.snf	-adobe-helvetica-medium-r-normal—14-140-75-75-p-77-iso8859-1
helvR18.snf	-adobe-helvetica-medium-r-normal—18-180-75-75-p-98-iso8859-1
helvR24.snf	-adobe-helvetica-medium-r-normal—24-240-75-75-p-130-iso8859-1
helvR08.snf	-adobe-helvetica-medium-r-normal—8-80-75-75-p-46-iso8859-1
ncenBI10.snf	-adobe-new century schoolbook-bold-i-normal—10-100-75-75-p-66-iso8859-1
ncenBI12.snf	-adobe-new century schoolbook-bold-i-normal—12-120-75-75-p-76-iso8859-1
ncenBI14.snf	-adobe-new century schoolbook-bold-i-normal—14-140-75-75-p-88-iso8859-1
ncenBI18.snf	-adobe-new century schoolbook-bold-i-normal—18-180-75-75-p-111-iso8859-1
ncenBI24.snf	-adobe-new century schoolbook-bold-i-normal—24-240-75-75-p-148-iso8859-1
ncenBI08.snf	-adobe-new century schoolbook-bold-i-normal—8-80-75-75-p-56-iso8859-1
ncenB10.snf	-adobe-new century schoolbook-bold-r-normal—10-100-75-75-p-66-iso8859-1
ncenB12.snf	-adobe-new century schoolbook-bold-r-normal—12-120-75-75-p-77-iso8859-1
ncenB14.snf	-adobe-new century schoolbook-bold-r-normal—14-140-75-75-p-87-iso8859-1
ncenB18.snf	-adobe-new century schoolbook-bold-r-normal—18-180-75-75-p-113-iso8859-1
ncenB24.snf	-adobe-new century schoolbook-bold-r-normal—24-240-75-75-p-149-iso8859-1
ncenB08.snf	-adobe-new century schoolbook-bold-r-normal—8-80-75-75-p-56-iso8859-1
ncenI10.snf	-adobe-new century schoolbook-medium-i-normal—10-100-75-75-p-60-iso8859-1

Table E-2. Fonts in the 75dpi Directory, Release 4 (continued)

Filename	Font name
ncenI12.snf	-adobe-new century schoolbook-medium-i-normal—12-120-75-75-p-70-iso8859-1
ncenI14.snf	-adobe-new century schoolbook-medium-i-normal—14-140-75-75-p-81-iso8859-1
ncenI18.snf	-adobe-new century schoolbook-medium-i-normal—18-180-75-75-p-104-iso8859-1
ncenI24.snf	-adobe-new century schoolbook-medium-i-normal—24-240-75-75-p-136-iso8859-1
ncenI08.snf	-adobe-new century schoolbook-medium-i-normal—8-80-75-75-p-50-iso8859-1
ncenR10.snf	-adobe-new century schoolbook-medium-r-normal—10-100-75-75-p-60-iso8859-1
ncenR12.snf	-adobe-new century schoolbook-medium-r-normal—12-120-75-75-p-70-iso8859-1
ncenR14.snf	-adobe-new century schoolbook-medium-r-normal—14-140-75-75-p-82-iso8859-1
ncenR18.snf	-adobe-new century schoolbook-medium-r-normal—18-180-75-75-p-103-iso8859-1
ncenR24.snf	-adobe-new century schoolbook-medium-r-normal—24-240-75-75-p-137-iso8859-1
ncenR08.snf	-adobe-new century schoolbook-medium-r-normal—8-80-75-75-p-50-iso8859-1
symb10.snf	-adobe-symbol-medium-r-normal—10-100-75-75-p-61-adobe-fontspecific
symb12.snf	-adobe-symbol-medium-r-normal—12-120-75-75-p-74-adobe-fontspecific
symb14.snf	-adobe-symbol-medium-r-normal—14-140-75-75-p-85-adobe-fontspecific
symb18.snf	-adobe-symbol-medium-r-normal—18-180-75-75-p-107-adobe-fontspecific
symb24.snf	-adobe-symbol-medium-r-normal—24-240-75-75-p-142-adobe-fontspecific
symb08.snf	-adobe-symbol-medium-r-normal—8-80-75-75-p-51-adobe-fontspecific
timBI10.snf	-adobe-times-bold-i-normal—10-100-75-75-p-57-iso8859-1
timBI12.snf	-adobe-times-bold-i-normal—12-120-75-75-p-68-iso8859-1
timBI14.snf	-adobe-times-bold-i-normal—14-140-75-75-p-77-iso8859-1
timBI18.snf	-adobe-times-bold-i-normal—18-180-75-75-p-98-iso8859-1
timBI24.snf	-adobe-times-bold-i-normal—24-240-75-75-p-128-iso8859-1
timBI08.snf	-adobe-times-bold-i-normal—8-80-75-75-p-47-iso8859-1
timB10.snf	-adobe-times-bold-r-normal—10-100-75-75-p-57-iso8859-1
timB12.snf	-adobe-times-bold-r-normal—12-120-75-75-p-67-iso8859-1
timB14.snf	-adobe-times-bold-r-normal—14-140-75-75-p-77-iso8859-1
timB18.snf	-adobe-times-bold-r-normal—18-180-75-75-p-99-iso8859-1
timB24.snf	-adobe-times-bold-r-normal—24-240-75-75-p-132-iso8859-1
timB08.snf	-adobe-times-bold-r-normal—8-80-75-75-p-47-iso8859-1
timI10.snf	-adobe-times-medium-i-normal—10-100-75-75-p-52-iso8859-1
timI12.snf	-adobe-times-medium-i-normal—12-120-75-75-p-63-iso8859-1
timI14.snf	-adobe-times-medium-i-normal—14-140-75-75-p-73-iso8859-1
timI18.snf	-adobe-times-medium-i-normal—18-180-75-75-p-94-iso8859-1
timI24.snf	-adobe-times-medium-i-normal—24-240-75-75-p-125-iso8859-1
timI08.snf	-adobe-times-medium-i-normal—8-80-75-75-p-42-iso8859-1
timR10.snf	-adobe-times-medium-r-normal—10-100-75-75-p-54-iso8859-1
timR12.snf	-adobe-times-medium-r-normal—12-120-75-75-p-64-iso8859-1
timR14.snf	-adobe-times-medium-r-normal—14-140-75-75-p-74-iso8859-1
timR18.snf	-adobe-times-medium-r-normal—18-180-75-75-p-94-iso8859-1
timR24.snf	-adobe-times-medium-r-normal—24-240-75-75-p-124-iso8859-1
timR08.snf	-adobe-times-medium-r-normal—8-80-75-75-p-44-iso8859-1
luBIS10.snf	-b&h-lucida-bold-i-normal-sans-10-100-75-75-p-67-iso8859-1
luBIS12.snf	-b&h-lucida-bold-i-normal-sans-12-120-75-75-p-79-iso8859-1
luBIS14.snf	-b&h-lucida-bold-i-normal-sans-14-140-75-75-p-92-iso8859-1

Table E-2. Fonts in the 75dpi Directory, Release 4 (continued)

Filename	Font name
luBIS18.snf	-b&h-lucida-bold-i-normal-sans-18-180-75-75-p-119-iso8859-1
luBIS19.snf	-b&h-lucida-bold-i-normal-sans-19-190-75-75-p-122-iso8859-1
luBIS24.snf	-b&h-lucida-bold-i-normal-sans-24-240-75-75-p-151-iso8859-1
luBIS08.snf	-b&h-lucida-bold-i-normal-sans-8-80-75-75-p-49-iso8859-1
luBS10.snf	-b&h-lucida-bold-r-normal-sans-10-100-75-75-p-66-iso8859-1
luBS12.snf	-b&h-lucida-bold-r-normal-sans-12-120-75-75-p-79-iso8859-1
luBS14.snf	-b&h-lucida-bold-r-normal-sans-14-140-75-75-p-92-iso8859-1
luBS18.snf	-b&h-lucida-bold-r-normal-sans-18-180-75-75-p-120-iso8859-1
luBS19.snf	-b&h-lucida-bold-r-normal-sans-19-190-75-75-p-122-iso8859-1
luBS24.snf	-b&h-lucida-bold-r-normal-sans-24-240-75-75-p-152-iso8859-1
luBS08.snf	-b&h-lucida-bold-r-normal-sans-8-80-75-75-p-50-iso8859-1
luIS10.snf	-b&h-lucida-medium-i-normal-sans-10-100-75-75-p-59-iso8859-1
luIS12.snf	-b&h-lucida-medium-i-normal-sans-12-120-75-75-p-71-iso8859-1
luIS14.snf	-b&h-lucida-medium-i-normal-sans-14-140-75-75-p-82-iso8859-1
luIS18.snf	-b&h-lucida-medium-i-normal-sans-18-180-75-75-p-105-iso8859-1
luIS19.snf	-b&h-lucida-medium-i-normal-sans-19-190-75-75-p-108-iso8859-1
luIS24.snf	-b&h-lucida-medium-i-normal-sans-24-240-75-75-p-136-iso8859-1
luIS08.snf	-b&h-lucida-medium-i-normal-sans-8-80-75-75-p-45-iso8859-1
luRS10.snf	-b&h-lucida-medium-r-normal-sans-10-100-75-75-p-58-iso8859-1
luRS12.snf	-b&h-lucida-medium-r-normal-sans-12-120-75-75-p-71-iso8859-1
luRS14.snf	-b&h-lucida-medium-r-normal-sans-14-140-75-75-p-81-iso8859-1
luRS18.snf	-b&h-lucida-medium-r-normal-sans-18-180-75-75-p-106-iso8859-1
luRS19.snf	-b&h-lucida-medium-r-normal-sans-19-190-75-75-p-108-iso8859-1
luRS24.snf	-b&h-lucida-medium-r-normal-sans-24-240-75-75-p-136-iso8859-1
luRS08.snf	-b&h-lucida-medium-r-normal-sans-8-80-75-75-p-45-iso8859-1
lubBI10.snf	-b&h-lucidabright-demibold-i-normal—10-100-75-75-p-59-iso8859-1
lubBI12.snf	-b&h-lucidabright-demibold-i-normal—12-120-75-75-p-72-iso8859-1
lubBI14.snf	-b&h-lucidabright-demibold-i-normal—14-140-75-75-p-84-iso8859-1
lubBI18.snf	-b&h-lucidabright-demibold-i-normal—18-180-75-75-p-107-iso8859-1
lubBI19.snf	-b&h-lucidabright-demibold-i-normal—19-190-75-75-p-114-iso8859-1
lubBI24.snf	-b&h-lucidabright-demibold-i-normal—24-240-75-75-p-143-iso8859-1
lubBI08.snf	-b&h-lucidabright-demibold-i-normal—8-80-75-75-p-48-iso8859-1
lubB10.snf	-b&h-lucidabright-demibold-r-normal—10-100-75-75-p-59-iso8859-1
lubB12.snf	-b&h-lucidabright-demibold-r-normal—12-120-75-75-p-71-iso8859-1
lubB14.snf	-b&h-lucidabright-demibold-r-normal—14-140-75-75-p-84-iso8859-1
lubB18.snf	-b&h-lucidabright-demibold-r-normal—18-180-75-75-p-107-iso8859-1
lubB19.snf	-b&h-lucidabright-demibold-r-normal—19-190-75-75-p-114-iso8859-1
lubB24.snf	-b&h-lucidabright-demibold-r-normal—24-240-75-75-p-143-iso8859-1
lubB08.snf	-b&h-lucidabright-demibold-r-normal—8-80-75-75-p-47-iso8859-1
lubI10.snf	-b&h-lucidabright-medium-i-normal—10-100-75-75-p-57-iso8859-1
lubI12.snf	-b&h-lucidabright-medium-i-normal—12-120-75-75-p-67-iso8859-1
lubI14.snf	-b&h-lucidabright-medium-i-normal—14-140-75-75-p-80-iso8859-1
lubI18.snf	-b&h-lucidabright-medium-i-normal—18-180-75-75-p-102-iso8859-1
lubI19.snf	-b&h-lucidabright-medium-i-normal—19-190-75-75-p-109-iso8859-1

Table E-2. Fonts in the 75dpi Directory, Release 4 (continued)

Filename	Font name
lubI24.snf	-b&h-lucidabright-medium-i-normal—24-240-75-75-p-136-iso8859-1
lubI08.snf	-b&h-lucidabright-medium-i-normal—8-80-75-75-p-45-iso8859-1
lubR10.snf	-b&h-lucidabright-medium-r-normal—10-100-75-75-p-56-iso8859-1
lubR12.snf	-b&h-lucidabright-medium-r-normal—12-120-75-75-p-68-iso8859-1
lubR14.snf	-b&h-lucidabright-medium-r-normal—14-140-75-75-p-80-iso8859-1
lubR18.snf	-b&h-lucidabright-medium-r-normal—18-180-75-75-p-103-iso8859-1
lubR19.snf	-b&h-lucidabright-medium-r-normal—19-190-75-75-p-109-iso8859-1
lubR24.snf	-b&h-lucidabright-medium-r-normal—24-240-75-75-p-137-iso8859-1
lubR08.snf	-b&h-lucidabright-medium-r-normal—8-80-75-75-p-45-iso8859-1
lutBS10.snf	-b&h-lucidatypewriter-bold-r-normal-sans-10-100-75-75-m-60-iso8859-1
lutBS12.snf	-b&h-lucidatypewriter-bold-r-normal-sans-12-120-75-75-m-70-iso8859-1
lutBS14.snf	-b&h-lucidatypewriter-bold-r-normal-sans-14-140-75-75-m-90-iso8859-1
lutBS18.snf	-b&h-lucidatypewriter-bold-r-normal-sans-18-180-75-75-m-110-iso8859-1
lutBS19.snf	-b&h-lucidatypewriter-bold-r-normal-sans-19-190-75-75-m-110-iso8859-1
lutBS24.snf	-b&h-lucidatypewriter-bold-r-normal-sans-24-240-75-75-m-140-iso8859-1
lutBS08.snf	-b&h-lucidatypewriter-bold-r-normal-sans-8-80-75-75-m-50-iso8859-1
lutRS10.snf	-b&h-lucidatypewriter-medium-r-normal-sans-10-100-75-75-m-60-iso8859-1
lutRS12.snf	-b&h-lucidatypewriter-medium-r-normal-sans-12-120-75-75-m-70-iso8859-1
lutRS14.snf	-b&h-lucidatypewriter-medium-r-normal-sans-14-140-75-75-m-90-iso8859-1
lutRS18.snf	-b&h-lucidatypewriter-medium-r-normal-sans-18-180-75-75-m-110-iso8859-1
lutRS19.snf	-b&h-lucidatypewriter-medium-r-normal-sans-19-190-75-75-m-110-iso8859-1
lutRS24.snf	-b&h-lucidatypewriter-medium-r-normal-sans-24-240-75-75-m-140-iso8859-1
lutRS08.snf	-b&h-lucidatypewriter-medium-r-normal-sans-8-80-75-75-m-50-iso8859-1
charBI10.snf	-bitstream-charter-bold-i-normal—10-100-75-75-p-62-iso8859-1
charBI12.snf	-bitstream-charter-bold-i-normal—12-120-75-75-p-74-iso8859-1
charBI14.snf	-bitstream-charter-bold-i-normal—15-140-75-75-p-93-iso8859-1
charBI18.snf	-bitstream-charter-bold-i-normal—19-180-75-75-p-117-iso8859-1
charBI24.snf	-bitstream-charter-bold-i-normal—25-240-75-75-p-154-iso8859-1
charBI08.snf	-bitstream-charter-bold-i-normal—8-80-75-75-p-50-iso8859-1
charB10.snf	-bitstream-charter-bold-r-normal—10-100-75-75-p-63-iso8859-1
charB12.snf	-bitstream-charter-bold-r-normal—12-120-75-75-p-75-iso8859-1
charB14.snf	-bitstream-charter-bold-r-normal—15-140-75-75-p-94-iso8859-1
charB18.snf	-bitstream-charter-bold-r-normal—19-180-75-75-p-119-iso8859-1
charB24.snf	-bitstream-charter-bold-r-normal—25-240-75-75-p-157-iso8859-1
charB08.snf	-bitstream-charter-bold-r-normal—8-80-75-75-p-50-iso8859-1
charI10.snf	-bitstream-charter-medium-i-normal—10-100-75-75-p-55-iso8859-1
charI12.snf	-bitstream-charter-medium-i-normal—12-120-75-75-p-65-iso8859-1
charI14.snf	-bitstream-charter-medium-i-normal—15-140-75-75-p-82-iso8859-1
charI18.snf	-bitstream-charter-medium-i-normal—19-180-75-75-p-103-iso8859-1
charI24.snf	-bitstream-charter-medium-i-normal—25-240-75-75-p-136-iso8859-1
charI08.snf	-bitstream-charter-medium-i-normal—8-80-75-75-p-44-iso8859-1
charR10.snf	-bitstream-charter-medium-r-normal—10-100-75-75-p-56-iso8859-1
charR12.snf	-bitstream-charter-medium-r-normal—12-120-75-75-p-67-iso8859-1
charR14.snf	-bitstream-charter-medium-r-normal—15-140-75-75-p-84-iso8859-1

Table E-2. Fonts in the 75dpi Directory, Release 4 (continued)

Filename	Font name
charR18.snf	-bitstream-charter-medium-r-normal—19-180-75-75-p-106-iso8859-1
charR24.snf	-bitstream-charter-medium-r-normal—25-240-75-75-p-139-iso8859-1
charR08.snf	-bitstream-charter-medium-r-normal—8-80-75-75-p-45-iso8859-1
techB14.snf	-dec-terminal-bold-r-normal—14-140-75-75-c-80-dec-dectech
termB14.snf	-dec-terminal-bold-r-normal—14-140-75-75-c-80-iso8859-1
tech14.snf	-dec-terminal-medium-r-normal—14-140-75-75-c-80-dec-dectech
term14.snf	-dec-terminal-medium-r-normal—14-140-75-75-c-80-iso8859-1

Table E-3. Fonts in the 100dpi Directory, Release 4

Filename	Font name
courBO08.snf	-adobe-courier-bold-o-normal—11-80-100-100-m-60-iso8859-1
courBO10.snf	-adobe-courier-bold-o-normal—14-100-100-100-m-90-iso8859-1
courBO12.snf	-adobe-courier-bold-o-normal—17-120-100-100-m-100-iso8859-1
courBO14.snf	-adobe-courier-bold-o-normal—20-140-100-100-m-110-iso8859-1
courBO18.snf	-adobe-courier-bold-o-normal—25-180-100-100-m-150-iso8859-1
courBO24.snf	-adobe-courier-bold-o-normal—34-240-100-100-m-200-iso8859-1
courB08.snf	-adobe-courier-bold-r-normal—11-80-100-100-m-60-iso8859-1
courB10.snf	-adobe-courier-bold-r-normal—14-100-100-100-m-90-iso8859-1
courB12.snf	-adobe-courier-bold-r-normal—17-120-100-100-m-100-iso8859-1
courB14.snf	-adobe-courier-bold-r-normal—20-140-100-100-m-110-iso8859-1
courB18.snf	-adobe-courier-bold-r-normal—25-180-100-100-m-150-iso8859-1
courB24.snf	-adobe-courier-bold-r-normal—34-240-100-100-m-200-iso8859-1
courO08.snf	-adobe-courier-medium-o-normal—11-80-100-100-m-60-iso8859-1
courO10.snf	-adobe-courier-medium-o-normal—14-100-100-100-m-90-iso8859-1
courO12.snf	-adobe-courier-medium-o-normal—17-120-100-100-m-100-iso8859-1
courO14.snf	-adobe-courier-medium-o-normal—20-140-100-100-m-110-iso8859-1
courO18.snf	-adobe-courier-medium-o-normal—25-180-100-100-m-150-iso8859-1
courO24.snf	-adobe-courier-medium-o-normal—34-240-100-100-m-200-iso8859-1
courR08.snf	-adobe-courier-medium-r-normal—11-80-100-100-m-60-iso8859-1
courR10.snf	-adobe-courier-medium-r-normal—14-100-100-100-m-90-iso8859-1
courR12.snf	-adobe-courier-medium-r-normal—17-120-100-100-m-100-iso8859-1
courR14.snf	-adobe-courier-medium-r-normal—20-140-100-100-m-110-iso8859-1
courR18.snf	-adobe-courier-medium-r-normal—25-180-100-100-m-150-iso8859-1
courR24.snf	-adobe-courier-medium-r-normal—34-240-100-100-m-200-iso8859-1
helvBO08.snf	-adobe-helvetica-bold-o-normal—11-80-100-100-p-60-iso8859-1
helvBO10.snf	-adobe-helvetica-bold-o-normal—14-100-100-100-p-82-iso8859-1
helvBO12.snf	-adobe-helvetica-bold-o-normal—17-120-100-100-p-92-iso8859-1
helvBO14.snf	-adobe-helvetica-bold-o-normal—20-140-100-100-p-103-iso8859-1
helvBO18.snf	-adobe-helvetica-bold-o-normal—25-180-100-100-p-138-iso8859-1
helvBO24.snf	-adobe-helvetica-bold-o-normal—34-240-100-100-p-182-iso8859-1

Table E-3. Fonts in the 100dpi Directory, Release 4 (continued)

Filename	Font name
helvB08.snf	-adobe-helvetica-bold-r-normal—11-80-100-100-p-60-iso8859-1
helvB10.snf	-adobe-helvetica-bold-r-normal—14-100-100-100-p-82-iso8859-1
helvB12.snf	-adobe-helvetica-bold-r-normal—17-120-100-100-p-92-iso8859-1
helvB14.snf	-adobe-helvetica-bold-r-normal—20-140-100-100-p-105-iso8859-1
helvB18.snf	-adobe-helvetica-bold-r-normal—25-180-100-100-p-138-iso8859-1
helvB24.snf	-adobe-helvetica-bold-r-normal—34-240-100-100-p-182-iso8859-1
helvO08.snf	-adobe-helvetica-medium-o-normal—11-80-100-100-p-57-iso8859-1
helvO10.snf	-adobe-helvetica-medium-o-normal—14-100-100-100-p-78-iso8859-1
helvO12.snf	-adobe-helvetica-medium-o-normal—17-120-100-100-p-88-iso8859-1
helvO14.snf	-adobe-helvetica-medium-o-normal—20-140-100-100-p-98-iso8859-1
helvO18.snf	-adobe-helvetica-medium-o-normal—25-180-100-100-p-130-iso8859-1
helvO24.snf	-adobe-helvetica-medium-o-normal—34-240-100-100-p-176-iso8859-1
helvR08.snf	-adobe-helvetica-medium-r-normal—11-80-100-100-p-56-iso8859-1
helvR10.snf	-adobe-helvetica-medium-r-normal—14-100-100-100-p-76-iso8859-1
helvR12.snf	-adobe-helvetica-medium-r-normal—17-120-100-100-p-88-iso8859-1
helvR14.snf	-adobe-helvetica-medium-r-normal—20-140-100-100-p-100-iso8859-1
helvR18.snf	-adobe-helvetica-medium-r-normal—25-180-100-100-p-130-iso8859-1
helvR24.snf	-adobe-helvetica-medium-r-normal—34-240-100-100-p-176-iso8859-1
ncenBI08.snf	-adobe-new century schoolbook-bold-i-normal—11-80-100-100-p-66-iso8859-1
ncenBI10.snf	-adobe-new century schoolbook-bold-i-normal—14-100-100-100-p-88-iso8859-1
ncenBI12.snf	-adobe-new century schoolbook-bold-i-normal—17-120-100-100-p-99-iso8859-1
ncenBI14.snf	-adobe-new century schoolbook-bold-i-normal—20-140-100-100-p-111-iso8859-1
ncenBI18.snf	-adobe-new century schoolbook-bold-i-normal—25-180-100-100-p-148-iso8859-1
ncenBI24.snf	-adobe-new century schoolbook-bold-i-normal—34-240-100-100-p-193-iso8859-1
ncenB08.snf	-adobe-new century schoolbook-bold-r-normal—11-80-100-100-p-66-iso8859-1
ncenB10.snf	-adobe-new century schoolbook-bold-r-normal—14-100-100-100-p-87-iso8859-1
ncenB12.snf	-adobe-new century schoolbook-bold-r-normal—17-120-100-100-p-99-iso8859-1
ncenB14.snf	-adobe-new century schoolbook-bold-r-normal—20-140-100-100-p-113-iso8859-1
ncenB18.snf	-adobe-new century schoolbook-bold-r-normal—25-180-100-100-p-149-iso8859-1
ncenB24.snf	-adobe-new century schoolbook-bold-r-normal—34-240-100-100-p-193-iso8859-1
ncenI08.snf	-adobe-new century schoolbook-medium-i-normal—11-80-100-100-p-60-iso8859-1
ncenI10.snf	-adobe-new century schoolbook-medium-i-normal—14-100-100-100-p-81-iso8859-1
ncenI12.snf	-adobe-new century schoolbook-medium-i-normal—17-120-100-100-p-92-iso8859-1
ncenI14.snf	-adobe-new century schoolbook-medium-i-normal—20-140-100-100-p-104-iso8859-1
ncenI18.snf	-adobe-new century schoolbook-medium-i-normal—25-180-100-100-p-136-iso8859-1
ncenI24.snf	-adobe-new century schoolbook-medium-i-normal—34-240-100-100-p-182-iso8859-1
ncenR08.snf	-adobe-new century schoolbook-medium-r-normal—11-80-100-100-p-60-iso8859-1
ncenR10.snf	-adobe-new century schoolbook-medium-r-normal—14-100-100-100-p-82-iso8859-1
ncenR12.snf	-adobe-new century schoolbook-medium-r-normal—17-120-100-100-p-91-iso8859-1
ncenR14.snf	-adobe-new century schoolbook-medium-r-normal—20-140-100-100-p-103-iso8859-1
ncenR18.snf	-adobe-new century schoolbook-medium-r-normal—25-180-100-100-p-136-iso8859-1
ncenR24.snf	-adobe-new century schoolbook-medium-r-normal—34-240-100-100-p-181-iso8859-1
symb08.snf	-adobe-symbol-medium-r-normal—11-80-100-100-p-61-adobe-fontspecific
symb10.snf	-adobe-symbol-medium-r-normal—14-100-100-100-p-85-adobe-fontspecific

Table E-3. Fonts in the 100dpi Directory, Release 4 (continued)

Filename	Font name
symb12.snf	-adobe-symbol-medium-r-normal—17-120-100-100-p-95-adobe-fontspecific
symb14.snf	-adobe-symbol-medium-r-normal—20-140-100-100-p-107-adobe-fontspecific
symb18.snf	-adobe-symbol-medium-r-normal—25-180-100-100-p-142-adobe-fontspecific
symb24.snf	-adobe-symbol-medium-r-normal—34-240-100-100-p-191-adobe-fontspecific
timBI08.snf	-adobe-times-bold-i-normal—11-80-100-100-p-57-iso8859-1
timBI10.snf	-adobe-times-bold-i-normal—14-100-100-100-p-77-iso8859-1
timBI12.snf	-adobe-times-bold-i-normal—17-120-100-100-p-86-iso8859-1
timBI14.snf	-adobe-times-bold-i-normal—20-140-100-100-p-98-iso8859-1
timBI18.snf	-adobe-times-bold-i-normal—25-180-100-100-p-128-iso8859-1
timBI24.snf	-adobe-times-bold-i-normal—34-240-100-100-p-170-iso8859-1
timB08.snf	-adobe-times-bold-r-normal—11-80-100-100-p-57-iso8859-1
timB10.snf	-adobe-times-bold-r-normal—14-100-100-100-p-76-iso8859-1
timB12.snf	-adobe-times-bold-r-normal—17-120-100-100-p-88-iso8859-1
timB14.snf	-adobe-times-bold-r-normal—20-140-100-100-p-100-iso8859-1
timB18.snf	-adobe-times-bold-r-normal—25-180-100-100-p-132-iso8859-1
timB24.snf	-adobe-times-bold-r-normal—34-240-100-100-p-177-iso8859-1
timI08.snf	-adobe-times-medium-i-normal—11-80-100-100-p-52-iso8859-1
timI10.snf	-adobe-times-medium-i-normal—14-100-100-100-p-73-iso8859-1
timI12.snf	-adobe-times-medium-i-normal—17-120-100-100-p-84-iso8859-1
timI14.snf	-adobe-times-medium-i-normal—20-140-100-100-p-94-iso8859-1
timI18.snf	-adobe-times-medium-i-normal—25-180-100-100-p-125-iso8859-1
timI24.snf	-adobe-times-medium-i-normal—34-240-100-100-p-168-iso8859-1
timR08.snf	-adobe-times-medium-r-normal—11-80-100-100-p-54-iso8859-1
timR10.snf	-adobe-times-medium-r-normal—14-100-100-100-p-74-iso8859-1
timR12.snf	-adobe-times-medium-r-normal—17-120-100-100-p-84-iso8859-1
timR14.snf	-adobe-times-medium-r-normal—20-140-100-100-p-96-iso8859-1
timR18.snf	-adobe-times-medium-r-normal—25-180-100-100-p-125-iso8859-1
timR24.snf	-adobe-times-medium-r-normal—34-240-100-100-p-170-iso8859-1
luBIS08.snf	-b&h-lucida-bold-i-normal-sans-11-80-100-100-p-69-iso8859-1
luBIS10.snf	-b&h-lucida-bold-i-normal-sans-14-100-100-100-p-90-iso8859-1
luBIS12.snf	-b&h-lucida-bold-i-normal-sans-17-120-100-100-p-108-iso8859-1
luBIS14.snf	-b&h-lucida-bold-i-normal-sans-20-140-100-100-p-127-iso8859-1
luBIS18.snf	-b&h-lucida-bold-i-normal-sans-25-180-100-100-p-159-iso8859-1
luBIS19.snf	-b&h-lucida-bold-i-normal-sans-26-190-100-100-p-166-iso8859-1
luBIS24.snf	-b&h-lucida-bold-i-normal-sans-34-240-100-100-p-215-iso8859-1
luBS08.snf	-b&h-lucida-bold-r-normal-sans-11-80-100-100-p-70-iso8859-1
luBS10.snf	-b&h-lucida-bold-r-normal-sans-14-100-100-100-p-89-iso8859-1
luBS12.snf	-b&h-lucida-bold-r-normal-sans-17-120-100-100-p-108-iso8859-1
luBS14.snf	-b&h-lucida-bold-r-normal-sans-20-140-100-100-p-127-iso8859-1
luBS18.snf	-b&h-lucida-bold-r-normal-sans-25-180-100-100-p-158-iso8859-1
luBS19.snf	-b&h-lucida-bold-r-normal-sans-26-190-100-100-p-166-iso8859-1
luBS24.snf	-b&h-lucida-bold-r-normal-sans-34-240-100-100-p-216-iso8859-1
luIS08.snf	-b&h-lucida-medium-i-normal-sans-11-80-100-100-p-62-iso8859-1
luIS10.snf	-b&h-lucida-medium-i-normal-sans-14-100-100-100-p-80-iso8859-1

Table E-3. Fonts in the 100dpi Directory, Release 4 (continued)

Filename	Font name
luIS12.snf	-b&h-lucida-medium-i-normal-sans-17-120-100-100-p-97-iso8859-1
luIS14.snf	-b&h-lucida-medium-i-normal-sans-20-140-100-100-p-114-iso8859-1
luIS18.snf	-b&h-lucida-medium-i-normal-sans-25-180-100-100-p-141-iso8859-1
luIS19.snf	-b&h-lucida-medium-i-normal-sans-26-190-100-100-p-147-iso8859-1
luIS24.snf	-b&h-lucida-medium-i-normal-sans-34-240-100-100-p-192-iso8859-1
luRS08.snf	-b&h-lucida-medium-r-normal-sans-11-80-100-100-p-63-iso8859-1
luRS10.snf	-b&h-lucida-medium-r-normal-sans-14-100-100-100-p-80-iso8859-1
luRS12.snf	-b&h-lucida-medium-r-normal-sans-17-120-100-100-p-96-iso8859-1
luRS14.snf	-b&h-lucida-medium-r-normal-sans-20-140-100-100-p-114-iso8859-1
luRS18.snf	-b&h-lucida-medium-r-normal-sans-25-180-100-100-p-142-iso8859-1
luRS19.snf	-b&h-lucida-medium-r-normal-sans-26-190-100-100-p-147-iso8859-1
luRS24.snf	-b&h-lucida-medium-r-normal-sans-34-240-100-100-p-191-iso8859-1
lubBI08.snf	-b&h-lucidabright-demibold-i-normal—11-80-100-100-p-66-iso8859-1
lubBI10.snf	-b&h-lucidabright-demibold-i-normal—14-100-100-100-p-84-iso8859-1
lubBI12.snf	-b&h-lucidabright-demibold-i-normal—17-120-100-100-p-101-iso8859-1
lubBI14.snf	-b&h-lucidabright-demibold-i-normal—20-140-100-100-p-119-iso8859-1
lubBI18.snf	-b&h-lucidabright-demibold-i-normal—25-180-100-100-p-149-iso8859-1
lubBI19.snf	-b&h-lucidabright-demibold-i-normal—26-190-100-100-p-156-iso8859-1
lubBI24.snf	-b&h-lucidabright-demibold-i-normal—34-240-100-100-p-203-iso8859-1
lubB08.snf	-b&h-lucidabright-demibold-r-normal—11-80-100-100-p-66-iso8859-1
lubB10.snf	-b&h-lucidabright-demibold-r-normal—14-100-100-100-p-84-iso8859-1
lubB12.snf	-b&h-lucidabright-demibold-r-normal—17-120-100-100-p-101-iso8859-1
lubB14.snf	-b&h-lucidabright-demibold-r-normal—20-140-100-100-p-118-iso8859-1
lubB18.snf	-b&h-lucidabright-demibold-r-normal—25-180-100-100-p-149-iso8859-1
lubB19.snf	-b&h-lucidabright-demibold-r-normal—26-190-100-100-p-155-iso8859-1
lubB24.snf	-b&h-lucidabright-demibold-r-normal—34-240-100-100-p-202-iso8859-1
lubI08.snf	-b&h-lucidabright-medium-i-normal—11-80-100-100-p-63-iso8859-1
lubI10.snf	-b&h-lucidabright-medium-i-normal—14-100-100-100-p-80-iso8859-1
lubI12.snf	-b&h-lucidabright-medium-i-normal—17-120-100-100-p-96-iso8859-1
lubI14.snf	-b&h-lucidabright-medium-i-normal—20-140-100-100-p-113-iso8859-1
lubI18.snf	-b&h-lucidabright-medium-i-normal—25-180-100-100-p-142-iso8859-1
lubI19.snf	-b&h-lucidabright-medium-i-normal—26-190-100-100-p-148-iso8859-1
lubI24.snf	-b&h-lucidabright-medium-i-normal—34-240-100-100-p-194-iso8859-1
lubR08.snf	-b&h-lucidabright-medium-r-normal—11-80-100-100-p-63-iso8859-1
lubR10.snf	-b&h-lucidabright-medium-r-normal—14-100-100-100-p-80-iso8859-1
lubR12.snf	-b&h-lucidabright-medium-r-normal—17-120-100-100-p-96-iso8859-1
lubR14.snf	-b&h-lucidabright-medium-r-normal—20-140-100-100-p-114-iso8859-1
lubR18.snf	-b&h-lucidabright-medium-r-normal—25-180-100-100-p-142-iso8859-1
lubR19.snf	-b&h-lucidabright-medium-r-normal—26-190-100-100-p-149-iso8859-1
lubR24.snf	-b&h-lucidabright-medium-r-normal—34-240-100-100-p-193-iso8859-1
lutBS08.snf	-b&h-lucidatypewriter-bold-r-normal-sans-11-80-100-100-m-70-iso8859-1
lutBS10.snf	-b&h-lucidatypewriter-bold-r-normal-sans-14-100-100-100-m-80-iso8859-1
lutBS12.snf	-b&h-lucidatypewriter-bold-r-normal-sans-17-120-100-100-m-100-iso8859-1
lutBS14.snf	-b&h-lucidatypewriter-bold-r-normal-sans-20-140-100-100-m-120-iso8859-1

Table E-3. Fonts in the 100dpi Directory, Release 4 (continued)

Filename	Font name
lutBS18.snf	-b&h-lucidatypewriter-bold-r-normal-sans-25-180-100-100-m-150-iso8859-1
lutBS19.snf	-b&h-lucidatypewriter-bold-r-normal-sans-26-190-100-100-m-159-iso8859-1
lutBS24.snf	-b&h-lucidatypewriter-bold-r-normal-sans-34-240-100-100-m-200-iso8859-1
lutRS08.snf	-b&h-lucidatypewriter-medium-r-normal-sans-11-80-100-100-m-70-iso8859-1
lutRS10.snf	-b&h-lucidatypewriter-medium-r-normal-sans-14-100-100-100-m-80-iso8859-1
lutRS12.snf	-b&h-lucidatypewriter-medium-r-normal-sans-17-120-100-100-m-100-iso8859-1
lutRS14.snf	-b&h-lucidatypewriter-medium-r-normal-sans-20-140-100-100-m-120-iso8859-1
lutRS18.snf	-b&h-lucidatypewriter-medium-r-normal-sans-25-180-100-100-m-150-iso8859-1
lutRS19.snf	-b&h-lucidatypewriter-medium-r-normal-sans-26-190-100-100-m-159-iso8859-1
lutRS24.snf	-b&h-lucidatypewriter-medium-r-normal-sans-34-240-100-100-m-200-iso8859-1
charBI08.snf	-bitstream-charter-bold-i-normal—11-80-100-100-p-68-iso8859-1
charBI10.snf	-bitstream-charter-bold-i-normal—14-100-100-100-p-86-iso8859-1
charBI12.snf	-bitstream-charter-bold-i-normal—17-120-100-100-p-105-iso8859-1
charBI14.snf	-bitstream-charter-bold-i-normal—19-140-100-100-p-117-iso8859-1
charBI18.snf	-bitstream-charter-bold-i-normal—25-180-100-100-p-154-iso8859-1
charBI24.snf	-bitstream-charter-bold-i-normal—33-240-100-100-p-203-iso8859-1
charB08.snf	-bitstream-charter-bold-r-normal—11-80-100-100-p-69-iso8859-1
charB10.snf	-bitstream-charter-bold-r-normal—14-100-100-100-p-88-iso8859-1
charB12.snf	-bitstream-charter-bold-r-normal—17-120-100-100-p-107-iso8859-1
charB14.snf	-bitstream-charter-bold-r-normal—19-140-100-100-p-119-iso8859-1
charB18.snf	-bitstream-charter-bold-r-normal—25-180-100-100-p-157-iso8859-1
charB24.snf	-bitstream-charter-bold-r-normal—33-240-100-100-p-206-iso8859-1
charI08.snf	-bitstream-charter-medium-i-normal—11-80-100-100-p-60-iso8859-1
charI10.snf	-bitstream-charter-medium-i-normal—14-100-100-100-p-76-iso8859-1
charI12.snf	-bitstream-charter-medium-i-normal—17-120-100-100-p-92-iso8859-1
charI14.snf	-bitstream-charter-medium-i-normal—19-140-100-100-p-103-iso8859-1
charI18.snf	-bitstream-charter-medium-i-normal—25-180-100-100-p-136-iso8859-1
charI24.snf	-bitstream-charter-medium-i-normal—33-240-100-100-p-179-iso8859-1
charR08.snf	-bitstream-charter-medium-r-normal—11-80-100-100-p-61-iso8859-1
charR10.snf	-bitstream-charter-medium-r-normal—14-100-100-100-p-78-iso8859-1
charR12.snf	-bitstream-charter-medium-r-normal—17-120-100-100-p-95-iso8859-1
charR14.snf	-bitstream-charter-medium-r-normal—19-140-100-100-p-106-iso8859-1
charR18.snf	-bitstream-charter-medium-r-normal—25-180-100-100-p-139-iso8859-1
charR24.snf	-bitstream-charter-medium-r-normal—33-240-100-100-p-183-iso8859-1
techB14.snf	-bitstream-terminal-bold-r-normal—18-140-100-100-c-110-dec-dectech
termB14.snf	-bitstream-terminal-bold-r-normal—18-140-100-100-c-110-iso8859-1
tech14.snf	-bitstream-terminal-medium-r-normal—18-140-100-100-c-110-dec-dectech
term14.snf	-bitstream-terminal-medium-r-normal—18-140-100-100-c-110-iso8859-1

Table E-4. Fonts in the misc Directory, Release 3

Filename	Font name
6x10	6x10
6x12	6x12
8x13	8x13
8x13B	8x13bold
9x15	9x15
cursor	cursor
6x13	fixed

Table E-5. Fonts in the 75dpi Directory, Release 3

Filename	Font name
courBO10	-adobe-courier-bold-o-normal- -10-100-75-75-m-60-iso8859-1
courBO12	-adobe-courier-bold-o-normal- -12-120-75-75-m-70-iso8859-1
courBO14	-adobe-courier-bold-o-normal- -14-140-75-75-m-90-iso8859-1
courBO18	-adobe-courier-bold-o-normal- -18-180-75-75-m-110-iso8859-1
courBO24	-adobe-courier-bold-o-normal- -24-240-75-75-m-150-iso8859-1
courBO08	-adobe-courier-bold-o-normal- -8-80-75-75-m-50-iso8859-1
courB10	-adobe-courier-bold-r-normal- -10-100-75-75-m-60-iso8859-1
courB12	-adobe-courier-bold-r-normal- -12-120-75-75-m-70-iso8859-1
courB14	-adobe-courier-bold-r-normal- -14-140-75-75-m-90-iso8859-1
courB18	-adobe-courier-bold-r-normal- -18-180-75-75-m-110-iso8859-1
courB24	-adobe-courier-bold-r-normal- -24-240-75-75-m-150-iso8859-1
courB08	-adobe-courier-bold-r-normal- -8-80-75-75-m-50-iso8859-1
courO10	-adobe-courier-medium-o-normal- -10-100-75-75-m-60-iso8859-1
courO12	-adobe-courier-medium-o-normal- -12-120-75-75-m-70-iso8859-1
courO14	-adobe-courier-medium-o-normal- -14-140-75-75-m-90-iso8859-1
courO18	-adobe-courier-medium-o-normal- -18-180-75-75-m-110-iso8859-1
courO24	-adobe-courier-medium-o-normal- -24-240-75-75-m-150-iso8859-1
courO08	-adobe-courier-medium-o-normal- -8-80-75-75-m-50-iso8859-1
courR10	-adobe-courier-medium-r-normal- -10-100-75-75-m-60-iso8859-1
courR12	-adobe-courier-medium-r-normal- -12-120-75-75-m-70-iso8859-1
courR14	-adobe-courier-medium-r-normal- -14-140-75-75-m-90-iso8859-1
courR18	-adobe-courier-medium-r-normal- -18-180-75-75-m-110-iso8859-1
courR24	-adobe-courier-medium-r-normal- -24-240-75-75-m-150-iso8859-1
courR08	-adobe-courier-medium-r-normal- -8-80-75-75-m-50-iso8859-1
helvBO10	-adobe-helvetica-bold-o-normal- -10-100-75-75-p-60-iso8859-1
helvBO12	-adobe-helvetica-bold-o-normal- -12-120-75-75-p-69-iso8859-1
helvBO14	-adobe-helvetica-bold-o-normal- -14-140-75-75-p-82-iso8859-1
helvBO18	-adobe-helvetica-bold-o-normal- -18-180-75-75-p-104-iso8859-1
helvBO24	-adobe-helvetica-bold-o-normal- -24-240-75-75-p-138-iso8859-1
helvBO08	-adobe-helvetica-bold-o-normal- -8-80-75-75-p-50-iso8859-1

Table E-5. Fonts in the 75dpi Directory, Release 3 (continued)

Filename	Font name
helvB10	-adobe-helvetica-bold-r-normal- -10-100-75-75-p-60-iso8859-1
helvB12	-adobe-helvetica-bold-r-normal- -12-120-75-75-p-70-iso8859-1
helvB14	-adobe-helvetica-bold-r-normal- -14-140-75-75-p-82-iso8859-1
helvB18	-adobe-helvetica-bold-r-normal- -18-180-75-75-p-103-iso8859-1
helvB24	-adobe-helvetica-bold-r-normal- -24-240-75-75-p-138-iso8859-1
helvB08	-adobe-helvetica-bold-r-normal- -8-80-75-75-p-50-iso8859-1
helvO10	-adobe-helvetica-medium-o-normal- -10-100-75-75-p-57-iso8859-1
helvO12	-adobe-helvetica-medium-o-normal- -12-120-75-75-p-67-iso8859-1
helvO14	-adobe-helvetica-medium-o-normal- -14-140-75-75-p-78-iso8859-1
helvO18	-adobe-helvetica-medium-o-normal- -18-180-75-75-p-98-iso8859-1
helvO24	-adobe-helvetica-medium-o-normal- -24-240-75-75-p-130-iso8859-1
helvO08	-adobe-helvetica-medium-o-normal- -8-80-75-75-p-47-iso8859-1
helvR10	-adobe-helvetica-medium-r-normal- -10-100-75-75-p-56-iso8859-1
helvR12	-adobe-helvetica-medium-r-normal- -12-120-75-75-p-67-iso8859-1
helvR14	-adobe-helvetica-medium-r-normal- -14-140-75-75-p-77-iso8859-1
helvR18	-adobe-helvetica-medium-r-normal- -18-180-75-75-p-98-iso8859-1
helvR24	-adobe-helvetica-medium-r-normal- -24-240-75-75-p-130-iso8859-1
helvR08	-adobe-helvetica-medium-r-normal- -8-80-75-75-p-46-iso8859-1
ncenBI10	-adobe-new century schoolbook-bold-i-normal- -10-100-75-75-p-66-iso8859-1
ncenBI12	-adobe-new century schoolbook-bold-i-normal- -12-120-75-75-p-76-iso8859-1
ncenBI14	-adobe-new century schoolbook-bold-i-normal- -14-140-75-75-p-88-iso8859-1
ncenBI18	-adobe-new century schoolbook-bold-i-normal- -18-180-75-75-p-111-iso8859-1
ncenBI24	-adobe-new century schoolbook-bold-i-normal- -24-240-75-75-p-148-iso8859-1
ncenBI08	-adobe-new century schoolbook-bold-i-normal- -8-80-75-75-p-56-iso8859-1
ncenB10	-adobe-new century schoolbook-bold-r-normal- -10-100-75-75-p-66-iso8859-1
ncenB12	-adobe-new century schoolbook-bold-r-normal- -12-120-75-75-p-77-iso8859-1
ncenB14	-adobe-new century schoolbook-bold-r-normal- -14-140-75-75-p-87-iso8859-1
ncenB18	-adobe-new century schoolbook-bold-r-normal- -18-180-75-75-p-113-iso8859-1
ncenB24	-adobe-new century schoolbook-bold-r-normal- -24-240-75-75-p-149-iso8859-1
ncenB08	-adobe-new century schoolbook-bold-r-normal- -8-80-75-75-p-56-iso8859-1
ncenI10	-adobe-new century schoolbook-medium-i-normal- -10-100-75-75-p-60-iso8859-1
ncenI12	-adobe-new century schoolbook-medium-i-normal- -12-120-75-75-p-70-iso8859-1
ncenI14	-adobe-new century schoolbook-medium-i-normal- -14-140-75-75-p-81-iso8859-1
ncenI18	-adobe-new century schoolbook-medium-i-normal- -18-180-75-75-p-104-iso8859-1
ncenI24	-adobe-new century schoolbook-medium-i-normal- -24-240-75-75-p-136-iso8859-1
ncenI08	-adobe-new century schoolbook-medium-i-normal- -8-80-75-75-p-50-iso8859-1
ncenR10	-adobe-new century schoolbook-medium-r-normal- -10-100-75-75-p-60-iso8859-1
ncenR12	-adobe-new century schoolbook-medium-r-normal- -12-120-75-75-p-70-iso8859-1
ncenR14	-adobe-new century schoolbook-medium-r-normal- -14-140-75-75-p-82-iso8859-1
ncenR18	-adobe-new century schoolbook-medium-r-normal- -18-180-75-75-p-103-iso8859-1
ncenR24	-adobe-new century schoolbook-medium-r-normal- -24-240-75-75-p-137-iso8859-1
ncenR08	-adobe-new century schoolbook-medium-r-normal- -8-80-75-75-p-50-iso8859-1
timBI10	-adobe-times-bold-i-normal- -10-100-75-75-p-57-iso8859-1
timBI12	-adobe-times-bold-i-normal- -12-120-75-75-p-68-iso8859-1

Table E-5. Fonts in the 75dpi Directory, Release 3 (continued)

Filename	Font name
timBI14	-adobe-times-bold-i-normal- -14-140-75-75-p-77-iso8859-1
timBI18	-adobe-times-bold-i-normal- -18-180-75-75-p-98-iso8859-1
timBI24	-adobe-times-bold-i-normal- -24-240-75-75-p-128-iso8859-1
timBI08	-adobe-times-bold-i-normal- -8-80-75-75-p-47-iso8859-1
timB10	-adobe-times-bold-r-normal- -10-100-75-75-p-57-iso8859-1
timB12	-adobe-times-bold-r-normal- -12-120-75-75-p-67-iso8859-1
timB14	-adobe-times-bold-r-normal- -14-140-75-75-p-77-iso8859-1
timB18	-adobe-times-bold-r-normal- -18-180-75-75-p-99-iso8859-1
timB24	-adobe-times-bold-r-normal- -24-240-75-75-p-132-iso8859-1
timB08	-adobe-times-bold-r-normal- -8-80-75-75-p-47-iso8859-1
timI10	-adobe-times-medium-i-normal- -10-100-75-75-p-52-iso8859-1
timI12	-adobe-times-medium-i-normal- -12-120-75-75-p-63-iso8859-1
timI14	-adobe-times-medium-i-normal- -14-140-75-75-p-73-iso8859-1
timI18	-adobe-times-medium-i-normal- -18-180-75-75-p-94-iso8859-1
timI24	-adobe-times-medium-i-normal- -24-240-75-75-p-125-iso8859-1
timI08	-adobe-times-medium-i-normal- -8-80-75-75-p-42-iso8859-1
timR10	-adobe-times-medium-r-normal- -10-100-75-75-p-54-iso8859-1
timR12	-adobe-times-medium-r-normal- -12-120-75-75-p-64-iso8859-1
timR14	-adobe-times-medium-r-normal- -14-140-75-75-p-74-iso8859-1
timR18	-adobe-times-medium-r-normal- -18-180-75-75-p-94-iso8859-1
timR24	-adobe-times-medium-r-normal- -24-240-75-75-p-124-iso8859-1
timR08	-adobe-times-medium-r-normal- -8-80-75-75-p-44-iso8859-1
charBI10	-bitstream-charter-bold-i-normal- -10-100-75-75-p-62-iso8859-1
charBI12	-bitstream-charter-bold-i-normal- -12-120-75-75-p-74-iso8859-1
charBI14	-bitstream-charter-bold-i-normal- -15-140-75-75-p-93-iso8859-1
charBI18	-bitstream-charter-bold-i-normal- -19-180-75-75-p-117-iso8859-1
charBI24	-bitstream-charter-bold-i-normal- -25-240-75-75-p-154-iso8859-1
charBI08	-bitstream-charter-bold-i-normal- -8-80-75-75-p-50-iso8859-1
charB10	-bitstream-charter-bold-r-normal- -10-100-75-75-p-63-iso8859-1
charB12	-bitstream-charter-bold-r-normal- -12-120-75-75-p-75-iso8859-1
charB14	-bitstream-charter-bold-r-normal- -15-140-75-75-p-94-iso8859-1
charB18	-bitstream-charter-bold-r-normal- -19-180-75-75-p-119-iso8859-1
charB24	-bitstream-charter-bold-r-normal- -25-240-75-75-p-157-iso8859-1
charB08	-bitstream-charter-bold-r-normal- -8-80-75-75-p-50-iso8859-1
charI10	-bitstream-charter-medium-i-normal- -10-100-75-75-p-55-iso8859-1
charI12	-bitstream-charter-medium-i-normal- -12-120-75-75-p-65-iso8859-1
charI14	-bitstream-charter-medium-i-normal- -15-140-75-75-p-82-iso8859-1
charI18	-bitstream-charter-medium-i-normal- -19-180-75-75-p-103-iso8859-1
charI24	-bitstream-charter-medium-i-normal- -25-240-75-75-p-136-iso8859-1
charI08	-bitstream-charter-medium-i-normal- -8-80-75-75-p-44-iso8859-1
charR10	-bitstream-charter-medium-r-normal- -10-100-75-75-p-56-iso8859-1
charR12	-bitstream-charter-medium-r-normal- -12-120-75-75-p-67-iso8859-1
charR14	-bitstream-charter-medium-r-normal- -15-140-75-75-p-84-iso8859-1
charR18	-bitstream-charter-medium-r-normal- -19-180-75-75-p-106-iso8859-1

Table E-5. Fonts in the 75dpi Directory, Release 3 (continued)

Filename	Font name
charR24	-bitstream-charter-medium-r-normal- -25-240-75-75-p-139-iso8859-1
charR08	-bitstream-charter-medium-r-normal- -8-80-75-75-p-45-iso8859-1
symb10	dec-adobe-symbol-medium-r-normal- -10-100-75-75-p-61-adobe-fontspecific
symb12	dec-adobe-symbol-medium-r-normal- -12-120-75-75-p-74-adobe-fontspecific
symb14	dec-adobe-symbol-medium-r-normal- -14-140-75-75-p-85-adobe-fontspecific
symb18	dec-adobe-symbol-medium-r-normal- -18-180-75-75-p-107-adobe-fontspecific
symb24	dec-adobe-symbol-medium-r-normal- -24-240-75-75-p-142-adobe-fontspecific
symb08	dec-adobe-symbol-medium-r-normal- -8-80-75-75-p-51-adobe-fontspecific

Table E-6. Fonts in the 100dpi Directory, Release 3

Filename	Font name
charBI08	-bitstream-charter-bold-i-normal- -11-80-100-100-p-68-iso8859-1
charBI10	-bitstream-charter-bold-i-normal- -14-100-100-100-p-86-iso8859-1
charBI12	-bitstream-charter-bold-i-normal- -17-120-100-100-p-105-iso8859-1
charBI14	-bitstream-charter-bold-i-normal- -19-140-100-100-p-117-iso8859-1
charBI18	-bitstream-charter-bold-i-normal- -25-180-100-100-p-154-iso8859-1
charBI24	-bitstream-charter-bold-i-normal- -33-240-100-100-p-203-iso8859-1
charB08	-bitstream-charter-bold-r-normal- -11-80-100-100-p-69-iso8859-1
charB10	-bitstream-charter-bold-r-normal- -14-100-100-100-p-88-iso8859-1
charB12	-bitstream-charter-bold-r-normal- -17-120-100-100-p-107-iso8859-1
charB14	-bitstream-charter-bold-r-normal- -19-140-100-100-p-119-iso8859-1
charB18	-bitstream-charter-bold-r-normal- -25-180-100-100-p-157-iso8859-1
charB24	-bitstream-charter-bold-r-normal- -33-240-100-100-p-206-iso8859-1
charI08	-bitstream-charter-medium-i-normal- -11-80-100-100-p-60-iso8859-1
charI10	-bitstream-charter-medium-i-normal- -14-100-100-100-p-76-iso8859-1
charI12	-bitstream-charter-medium-i-normal- -17-120-100-100-p-92-iso8859-1
charI14	-bitstream-charter-medium-i-normal- -19-140-100-100-p-103-iso8859-1
charI18	-bitstream-charter-medium-i-normal- -25-180-100-100-p-136-iso8859-1
charI24	-bitstream-charter-medium-i-normal- -33-240-100-100-p-179-iso8859-1
charR08	-bitstream-charter-medium-r-normal- -11-80-100-100-p-61-iso8859-1
charR10	-bitstream-charter-medium-r-normal- -14-100-100-100-p-78-iso8859-1
charR12	-bitstream-charter-medium-r-normal- -17-120-100-100-p-95-iso8859-1
charR14	-bitstream-charter-medium-r-normal- -19-140-100-100-p-106-iso8859-1
charR18	-bitstream-charter-medium-r-normal- -25-180-100-100-p-139-iso8859-1
charR24	-bitstream-charter-medium-r-normal- -33-240-100-100-p-183-iso8859-1

-adobe-courier-medium-o-normal--8-80-75-75-m-50-iso8859-1
-adobe-courier-medium-o-normal--10-100-75-75-m-60-iso8859-1
-adobe-courier-medium-o-normal--12-120-75-75-m-70-iso8859-1
-adobe-courier-medium-o-normal--14-140-75-75-m-90-iso8859-1
-adobe-courier-medium-o-normal--18-180-75-75-m-110-iso8859-1
-adobe-courier-medium-o-normal--24-240-75-75-m
-adobe-courier-medium-r-normal--8-80-75-75-m-50-iso8859-1
-adobe-courier-medium-r-normal--10-100-75-75-m-60-iso8859-1
-adobe-courier-medium-r-normal--12-120-75-75-m-70-iso8859-1
-adobe-courier-medium-r-normal--14-140-75-75-m-90-iso8859-1
-adobe-courier-medium-r-normal--18-180-75-75-m-110-iso8859-1
-adobe-courier-medium-r-normal--24-240-75-75-m
-adobe-courier-bold-o-normal--8-80-75-75-m-50-iso8859-1
-adobe-courier-bold-o-normal--10-100-75-75-m-60-iso8859-1
-adobe-courier-bold-o-normal--12-120-75-75-m-70-iso8859-1
-adobe-courier-bold-o-normal--14-140-75-75-m-90-iso8859-1
-adobe-courier-bold-o-normal--18-180-75-75-m-110-iso8859-1
-adobe-courier-bold-o-normal--24-240-75-75-m-1
-adobe-courier-bold-r-normal--8-80-75-75-m-50-iso8859-1
-adobe-courier-bold-r-normal--10-100-75-75-m-60-iso8859-1
-adobe-courier-bold-r-normal--12-120-75-75-m-70-iso8859-1
-adobe-courier-bold-r-normal--14-140-75-75-m-90-iso8859-1
-adobe-courier-bold-r-normal--18-180-75-75-m-110-iso8859-1
-adobe-courier-bold-r-normal--24-240-75-75-m-1

Foundry: *adobe*
Family: *courier*

Release 3 and 4 Standard Fonts

-adobe-helvetica-medium-o-normal--8-80-75-75-p-47-iso8859-1
-adobe-helvetica-medium-o-normal--10-100-75-75-p-57-iso8859-1
-adobe-helvetica-medium-o-normal--12-120-75-75-p-67-iso8859-1
-adobe-helvetica-medium-o-normal--14-140-75-75-p-78-iso8859-1
-adobe-helvetica-medium-o-normal--18-180-75-75-p-98-iso8859-1
-adobe-helvetica-medium-o-normal--24-240-75-75-p-130
-adobe-helvetica-medium-r-normal--8-80-75-75-p-46-iso8859-1
-adobe-helvetica-medium-r-normal--10-100-75-75-p-56-iso8859-1
-adobe-helvetica-medium-r-normal--12-120-75-75-p-67-iso8859-1
-adobe-helvetica-medium-r-normal--14-140-75-75-p-77-iso8859-1
-adobe-helvetica-medium-r-normal--18-180-75-75-p-98-iso8859-1
-adobe-helvetica-medium-r-normal--24-240-75-75-p-130-
-adobe-helvetica-bold-o-normal--8-80-75-75-p-50-iso8859-1
-adobe-helvetica-bold-o-normal--10-100-75-75-p-60-iso8859-1
-adobe-helvetica-bold-o-normal--12-120-75-75-p-69-iso8859-1
-adobe-helvetica-bold-o-normal--14-140-75-75-p-82-iso8859-1
-adobe-helvetica-bold-o-normal--18-180-75-75-p-104-iso8859-1
-adobe-helvetica-bold-o-normal--24-240-75-75-p-138-
-adobe-helvetica-bold-r-normal--8-80-75-75-p-50-iso8859-1
-adobe-helvetica-bold-r-normal--10-100-75-75-p-60-iso8859-1
-adobe-helvetica-bold-r-normal--12-120-75-75-p-70-iso8859-1
-adobe-helvetica-bold-r-normal--14-140-75-75-p-82-iso8859-1
-adobe-helvetica-bold-r-normal--18-180-75-75-p-103-iso8859-1
-adobe-helvetica-bold-r-normal--24-240-75-75-p-138-i

Foundry: adobe
Family: helvetica

-adobe-new century schoolbook-medium-i-normal--8-80-75-75-p-50-iso8859-1
-adobe-new century schoolbook-medium-i-normal--10-100-75-75-p-60-iso8859-1
-adobe-new century schoolbook-medium-i-normal--12-120-75-75-p-70-iso8859-1
-adobe-new century schoolbook-medium-i-normal--14-140-75-75-p-81-iso8859-1
-adobe-new century schoolbook-medium-i-normal--18-180-75-75-p-104-iso8859-1
-adobe-new century schoolbook-medium-i-normal--24-240-75-75-p-136-iso8859-1
-adobe-new century schoolbook-medium-r-normal--8-80-75-75-p-50-iso8859-1
-adobe-new century schoolbook-medium-r-normal--10-100-75-75-p-60-iso8859-1
-adobe-new century schoolbook-medium-r-normal--12-120-75-75-p-70-iso8859-1
-adobe-new century schoolbook-medium-r-normal--14-140-75-75-p-82-iso8859-1
-adobe-new century schoolbook-medium-r-normal--18-180-75-75-p-103-iso8859-1
-adobe-new century schoolbook-medium-r-normal--24-240-75-75-p-137-iso8859-1
-adobe-new century schoolbook-bold-i-normal--8-80-75-75-p-56-iso8859-1
-adobe-new century schoolbook-bold-i-normal--10-100-75-75-p-66-iso8859-1
-adobe-new century schoolbook-bold-i-normal--12-120-75-75-p-76-iso8859-1
-adobe-new century schoolbook-bold-i-normal--14-140-75-75-p-88-iso8859-1
-adobe-new century schoolbook-bold-i-normal--18-180-75-75-p-111-iso8859-1
-adobe-new century schoolbook-bold-i-normal--24-240-75-75-p-148-iso8859-1
-adobe-new century schoolbook-bold-r-normal--8-80-75-75-p-56-iso8859-1
-adobe-new century schoolbook-bold-r-normal--10-100-75-75-p-66-iso8859-1
-adobe-new century schoolbook-bold-r-normal--12-120-75-75-p-77-iso8859-1
-adobe-new century schoolbook-bold-r-normal--14-140-75-75-p-87-iso8859-1
-adobe-new century schoolbook-bold-r-normal--18-180-75-75-p-113-iso8859-1
-adobe-new century schoolbook-bold-r-normal--24-240-75-75-p-149-iso8859-1

Foundry: *adobe*
Family: *new century schoolbook*

-b&h-lucida-medium-i-normal-sans-8-80-75-75-p-45-iso8859-1
-b&h-lucida-medium-i-normal-sans-10-100-75-75-p-59-iso8859-1
-b&h-lucida-medium-i-normal-sans-12-120-75-75-p-71-iso8859-1
-b&h-lucida-medium-i-normal-sans-14-140-75-75-p-82-iso8859-1
-b&h-lucida-medium-i-normal-sans-18-180-75-75-p-105-iso8859-1
-b&h-lucida-medium-i-normal-sans-19-190-75-75-p-108-iso8859-1
-b&h-lucida-medium-i-normal-sans-24-240-75-75-p-
-b&h-lucida-medium-r-normal-sans-8-80-75-75-p-45-iso8859-1
-b&h-lucida-medium-r-normal-sans-10-100-75-75-p-58-iso8859-1
-b&h-lucida-medium-r-normal-sans-12-120-75-75-p-71-iso8859-1
-b&h-lucida-medium-r-normal-sans-14-140-75-75-p-81-iso8859-1
-b&h-lucida-medium-r-normal-sans-18-180-75-75-p-106-iso8859-1
-b&h-lucida-medium-r-normal-sans-19-190-75-75-p-108-iso8859-1
-b&h-lucida-medium-r-normal-sans-24-240-75-75-p-1
-b&h-lucida-bold-i-normal-sans-8-80-75-75-p-49-iso8859-1
-b&h-lucida-bold-i-normal-sans-10-100-75-75-p-67-iso8859-1
-b&h-lucida-bold-i-normal-sans-12-120-75-75-p-79-iso8859-1
-b&h-lucida-bold-i-normal-sans-14-140-75-75-p-92-iso8859-1
-b&h-lucida-bold-i-normal-sans-18-180-75-75-p-119-iso8859
-b&h-lucida-bold-i-normal-sans-19-190-75-75-p-122-iso885
-b&h-lucida-bold-i-normal-sans-24-240-75-75-p-
-b&h-lucida-bold-r-normal-sans-8-80-75-75-p-50-iso8859-1
-b&h-lucida-bold-r-normal-sans-10-100-75-75-p-66-iso8859-1
-b&h-lucida-bold-r-normal-sans-12-120-75-75-p-79-iso8859-1
-b&h-lucida-bold-r-normal-sans-14-140-75-75-p-92-iso8859-1
-b&h-lucida-bold-r-normal-sans-18-180-75-75-p-120-iso885
-b&h-lucida-bold-r-normal-sans-19-190-75-75-p-122-iso885
-b&h-lucida-bold-r-normal-sans-24-240-75-75-p

Foundry: b&h
Family: lucida

```
-b&h-lucidabright-medium-i-normal--8-80-75-75-p-45-iso8859-1
-b&h-lucidabright-medium-i-normal--10-100-75-75-p-57-iso8859-1
-b&h-lucidabright-medium-i-normal--12-120-75-75-p-67-iso8859-1
-b&h-lucidabright-medium-i-normal--14-140-75-75-p-80-iso8859-1
-b&h-lucidabright-medium-i-normal--18-180-75-75-p-102-iso8859-1
-b&h-lucidabright-medium-i-normal--19-190-75-75-p-109-iso8859-
-b&h-lucidabright-medium-i-normal--24-240-75-75-p-
-b&h-lucidabright-medium-r-normal--8-80-75-75-p-45-iso8859-1
-b&h-lucidabright-medium-r-normal--10-100-75-75-p-56-iso8859-1
-b&h-lucidabright-medium-r-normal--12-120-75-75-p-68-iso8859-1
-b&h-lucidabright-medium-r-normal--14-140-75-75-p-80-iso8859-1
-b&h-lucidabright-medium-r-normal--18-180-75-75-p-103-iso8859-1
-b&h-lucidabright-medium-r-normal--19-190-75-75-p-109-iso8859-
-b&h-lucidabright-medium-r-normal--24-240-75-75-p-
-b&h-lucidabright-demibold-i-normal--8-80-75-75-p-48-iso8859-1
-b&h-lucidabright-demibold-i-normal--10-100-75-75-p-59-iso8859-1
-b&h-lucidabright-demibold-i-normal--12-120-75-75-p-72-iso8859-1
-b&h-lucidabright-demibold-i-normal--14-140-75-75-p-84-iso8859-1
-b&h-lucidabright-demibold-i-normal--18-180-75-75-p-107-iso8859-1
-b&h-lucidabright-demibold-i-normal--19-190-75-75-p-114-iso885
-b&h-lucidabright-demibold-i-normal--24-240-75-75-
-b&h-lucidabright-demibold-r-normal--8-80-75-75-p-47-iso8859-1
-b&h-lucidabright-demibold-r-normal--10-100-75-75-p-59-iso8859-1
-b&h-lucidabright-demibold-r-normal--12-120-75-75-p-71-iso8859-1
-b&h-lucidabright-demibold-r-normal--14-140-75-75-p-84-iso8859-1
-b&h-lucidabright-demibold-r-normal--18-180-75-75-p-107-iso8859-1
-b&h-lucidabright-demibold-r-normal--19-190-75-75-p-114-iso885
-b&h-lucidabright-demibold-r-normal--24-240-75-75-
```

Foundry: *b&h*
Family: *lucidabright*

-adobe-times-medium-i-normal--8-80-75-75-p-42-iso8859-1
-adobe-times-medium-i-normal--10-100-75-75-p-52-iso8859-1
-adobe-times-medium-i-normal--12-120-75-75-p-63-iso8859-1
-adobe-times-medium-i-normal--14-140-75-75-p-73-iso8859-1
-adobe-times-medium-i-normal--18-180-75-75-p-94-iso8859-1
-adobe-times-medium-i-normal--24-240-75-75-p-125-iso885
-adobe-times-medium-r-normal--8-80-75-75-p-44-iso8859-1
-adobe-times-medium-r-normal--10-100-75-75-p-54-iso8859-1
-adobe-times-medium-r-normal--12-120-75-75-p-64-iso8859-1
-adobe-times-medium-r-normal--14-140-75-75-p-74-iso8859-1
-adobe-times-medium-r-normal--18-180-75-75-p-94-iso8859-1
-adobe-times-medium-r-normal--24-240-75-75-p-124-iso885
-adobe-times-bold-i-normal--8-80-75-75-p-47-iso8859-1
-adobe-times-bold-i-normal--10-100-75-75-p-57-iso8859-1
-adobe-times-bold-i-normal--12-120-75-75-p-68-iso8859-1
-adobe-times-bold-i-normal--14-140-75-75-p-77-iso8859-1
-adobe-times-bold-i-normal--18-180-75-75-p-98-iso8859-1
-adobe-times-bold-i-normal--24-240-75-75-p-128-iso8859-1
-adobe-times-bold-r-normal--8-80-75-75-p-47-iso8859-1
-adobe-times-bold-r-normal--10-100-75-75-p-57-iso8859-1
-adobe-times-bold-r-normal--12-120-75-75-p-67-iso8859-1
-adobe-times-bold-r-normal--14-140-75-75-p-77-iso8859-1
-adobe-times-bold-r-normal--18-180-75-75-p-99-iso8859-1
-adobe-times-bold-r-normal--24-240-75-75-p-132-iso8859-

Foundry: *adobe*
Family: *times*

```
-αδοβε-συμβολ-μεδιυμ-ρ-νορμαλ--8-80-75-75-π-51-αδοβε-φοντσπεχιφιχ
-αδοβε-συμβολ-μεδιυμ-ρ-νορμαλ--10-100-75-75-π-61-αδοβε-φοντσπεχιφιχ
-αδοβε-συμβολ-μεδιυμ-ρ-νορμαλ--12-120-75-75-π-74-αδοβε-φοντσπεχιφιχ
-αδοβε-συμβολ-μεδιυμ-ρ-νορμαλ--14-140-75-75-π-85-αδοβε-φοντσπεχιφιχ
-αδοβε-συμβολ-μεδιυμ-ρ-νορμαλ--18-180-75-75-π-107-αδοβε-φοντσπεχιφιχ
-αδοβε-συμβολ-μεδιυμ-ρ-νορμαλ--24-240-75-75-π-142-αδοβ
```

Foundry: *adobe*
Family: *symbol*

```
-b&h-lucidatypewriter-medium-r-normal-sans-8-80-75-75-m-50-iso8859-1
-b&h-lucidatypewriter-medium-r-normal-sans-10-100-75-75-m-60-iso8859-1
-b&h-lucidatypewriter-medium-r-normal-sans-12-120-75-75-m-70-iso8859-1
-b&h-lucidatypewriter-medium-r-normal-sans-14-140-75-75-m-90-iso8859-1
-b&h-lucidatypewriter-medium-r-normal-sans-18-180-75-75-m-110-i
-b&h-lucidatypewriter-medium-r-normal-sans-19-190-75-75-m-110-i
-b&h-lucidatypewriter-medium-r-normal-sans-24-240-
-b&h-lucidatypewriter-bold-r-normal-sans-8-80-75-75-m-50-iso8859-1
-b&h-lucidatypewriter-bold-r-normal-sans-10-100-75-75-m-60-iso8859-1
-b&h-lucidatypewriter-bold-r-normal-sans-12-120-75-75-m-70-iso8859-1
-b&h-lucidatypewriter-bold-r-normal-sans-14-140-75-75-m-90-iso8859-1
-b&h-lucidatypewriter-bold-r-normal-sans-18-180-75-75-m-110-iso
-b&h-lucidatypewriter-bold-r-normal-sans-19-190-75-75-m-110-iso
-b&h-lucidatypewriter-bold-r-normal-sans-24-240-75
```

Foundry: *b&h*
Family: *lucidatypewriter*

-bitstream-charter-medium-i-normal--8-80-75-75-p-44-iso8859-1
-bitstream-charter-medium-i-normal--10-100-75-75-p-55-iso8859-1
-bitstream-charter-medium-i-normal--12-120-75-75-p-65-iso8859-1
-bitstream-charter-medium-i-normal--15-140-75-75-p-82-iso8859-1
-bitstream-charter-medium-i-normal--19-180-75-75-p-103-iso8859-1
-bitstream-charter-medium-i-normal--25-240-75-75-p-136-iso88
-bitstream-charter-medium-r-normal--8-80-75-75-p-45-iso8859-1
-bitstream-charter-medium-r-normal--10-100-75-75-p-56-iso8859-1
-bitstream-charter-medium-r-normal--12-120-75-75-p-67-iso8859-1
-bitstream-charter-medium-r-normal--15-140-75-75-p-84-iso8859-1
-bitstream-charter-medium-r-normal--19-180-75-75-p-106-iso8859-1
-bitstream-charter-medium-r-normal--25-240-75-75-p-139-iso8
-bitstream-charter-bold-i-normal--8-80-75-75-p-50-iso8859-1
-bitstream-charter-bold-i-normal--10-100-75-75-p-62-iso8859-1
-bitstream-charter-bold-i-normal--12-120-75-75-p-74-iso8859-1
-bitstream-charter-bold-i-normal--15-140-75-75-p-93-iso8859-1
-bitstream-charter-bold-i-normal--19-180-75-75-p-117-iso8859-1
-bitstream-charter-bold-i-normal--25-240-75-75-p-154-i
-bitstream-charter-bold-r-normal--8-80-75-75-p-50-iso8859-1
-bitstream-charter-bold-r-normal--10-100-75-75-p-63-iso8859-1
-bitstream-charter-bold-r-normal--12-120-75-75-p-75-iso8859-1
-bitstream-charter-bold-r-normal--15-140-75-75-p-94-iso8859-1
-bitstream-charter-bold-r-normal--19-180-75-75-p-119-iso8859-1
-bitstream-charter-bold-r-normal--25-240-75-75-p-157-

Foundry: *bitstream*
Family: *charter*

-bitstream-terminal-medium-r-normal--18-140-100

-bitstream-terminal-bold-r-normal--18-140-100-1

Foundry: *bitstream*
Family: *terminal*

-dec-terminal-medium-r-normal--14-140-75-75-c-80-iso8859-1

-dec-terminal-bold-r-normal--14-140-75-75-c-80-iso8859-1

Foundry: *dec*
Family: *terminal*

```
-misc-fixed-medium-r-normal--8-80-75-75-c-50-iso8859-1
-misc-fixed-medium-r-normal--9-90-75-75-c-60-iso8859-1
-misc-fixed-medium-r-normal--10-100-75-75-c-60-iso8859-1
-misc-fixed-medium-r-semicondensed--12-110-75-75-c-60-iso8859-1
-misc-fixed-medium-r-semicondensed--13-120-75-75-c-60-iso8859-1
-misc-fixed-medium-r-normal--13-120-75-75-c-70-iso8859-1
-misc-fixed-medium-r-normal--13-120-75-75-c-80-iso8859-1
-misc-fixed-medium-r-normal--14-130-75-75-c-70-iso8859-1
-misc-fixed-medium-r-normal--15-140-75-75-c-90-iso8859-1
-misc-fixed-medium-r-normal--20-200-75-75-c-100-iso8
-misc-fixed-bold-r-semicondensed--13-120-75-75-c-60-iso8859-1
-misc-fixed-bold-r-normal--13-120-75-75-c-70-iso8859-1
-misc-fixed-bold-r-normal--13-120-75-75-c-80-iso8859-1
-misc-fixed-bold-r-normal--15-140-75-75-c-90-iso8859-1
```

Foundry: *misc*
Family: *fixed*

```
-schumacher-clean-medium-i-normal--8-80-75-75-c-80-iso8859-1
-schumacher-clean-medium-i-normal--12-120-75-75-c-60-iso8859-1
-schumacher-clean-medium-r-normal--6-60-75-75-c-60-iso8859-1
-schumacher-clean-medium-r-normal--6-60-75-75-c-40-iso8859-1
-schumacher-clean-medium-r-normal--6-60-75-75-c-50-iso8859-1
-schumacher-clean-medium-r-normal--8-80-75-75-c-50-iso8859-1
-schumacher-clean-medium-r-normal--8-80-75-75-c-60-iso8859-1
-schumacher-clean-medium-r-normal--8-80-75-75-c-70-iso8859-1
-schumacher-clean-medium-r-normal--8-80-75-75-c-80-iso8859-1
-schumacher-clean-medium-r-normal--10-100-75-75-c-70-iso8859-1
-schumacher-clean-medium-r-normal--10-100-75-75-c-80-iso8859-1
-schumacher-clean-medium-r-normal--10-100-75-75-c-50-iso8859-1
-schumacher-clean-medium-r-normal--10-100-75-75-c-60-iso8859-1
-schumacher-clean-medium-r-normal--12-120-75-75-c-60-iso8859-1
-schumacher-clean-medium-r-normal--12-120-75-75-c-70-iso8859-1
-schumacher-clean-medium-r-normal--12-120-75-75-c-80-iso8859-1
-schumacher-clean-medium-r-normal--13-130-75-75-c-80-iso8859-1
-schumacher-clean-medium-r-normal--13-130-75-75-c-60-iso8859-1
-schumacher-clean-medium-r-normal--14-140-75-75-c-80-iso8859-1
-schumacher-clean-medium-r-normal--14-140-75-75-c-70-iso8859-1
-schumacher-clean-medium-r-normal--15-150-75-75-c-90-iso88
-schumacher-clean-medium-r-normal--16-160-75-75-c-80-iso8859-1
-schumacher-clean-bold-r-normal--8-80-75-75-c-80-iso8859-1
-schumacher-clean-bold-r-normal--10-100-75-75-c-60-iso8859-1
-schumacher-clean-bold-r-normal--10-100-75-75-c-80-iso8859-1
-schumacher-clean-bold-r-normal--12-120-75-75-c-80-iso8859-1
-schumacher-clean-bold-r-normal--12-120-75-75-c-60-iso8859-1
-schumacher-clean-bold-r-normal--13-130-75-75-c-80-iso8859-1
-schumacher-clean-bold-r-normal--14-140-75-75-c-80-iso8859-1
-schumacher-clean-bold-r-normal--15-150-75-75-c-90-iso8859
-schumacher-clean-bold-r-normal--16-160-75-75-c-80-iso8859-1
```

Foundry: *schumacher*
Family: *clean*

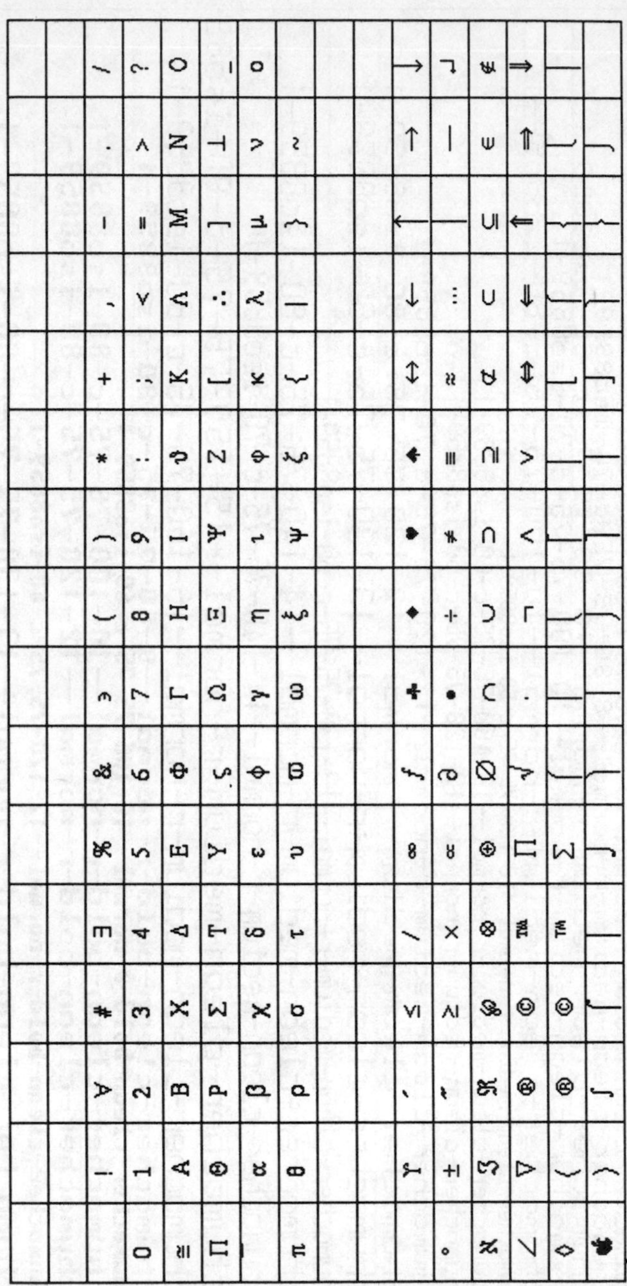

Encoding: adobe-fontspecific

	!	"	#	$	%	&	'	(	)	*	+	,	-	.	/
0	1	2	3	4	5	6	7	8	9	:	;	<	=	>	?
@	A	B	C	D	E	F	G	H	I	J	K	L	M	N	O
P	Q	R	S	T	U	V	W	X	Y	Z	[	\	]	^	
◆	▒	␉	␌	␍	␊	°	±	␤	␋	┘	┐	┌	└	┼	⎺
⎻	─	⎼	⎽	├	┤	┴	┬	│	≤	≥	π	≠	£	·	
	⎷	┌	─	⌠	⌡	│	⎡	⎣	⎤	⎦	⎛	⎝	⎞	⎠	⎨
⎬	⎲	⎳	╲	╱	┐	┘	〉					≤	≠	≥	∫
∴	∝	∞	÷	Δ	∇	Φ	Γ	∼	≃	Θ	×	Λ	⇔	⇒	≡
Π	Ψ		Σ			√	Ω	Ξ	Υ	⊂	⊃	∩	∪	∧	∨
¬	α	β	χ	δ	ε	φ	γ	η	ι	θ	κ	λ		ν	∂
π	ψ	ρ	σ	τ		ƒ	ω	ξ	υ	ζ	←	↑	→	↓	

Encoding: dec-dectech

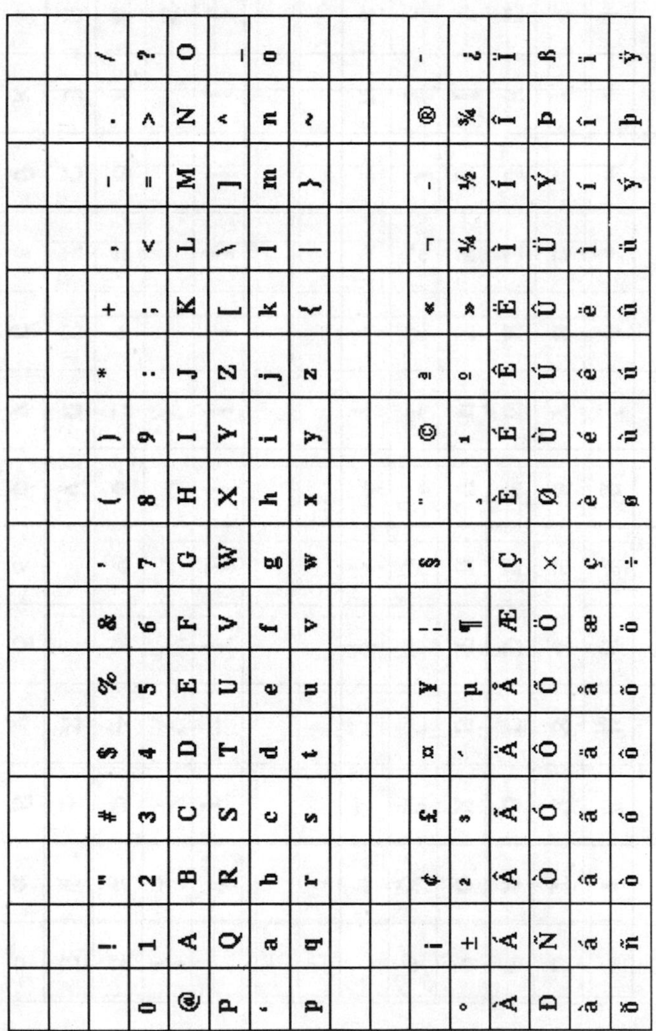

Encoding: iso8859

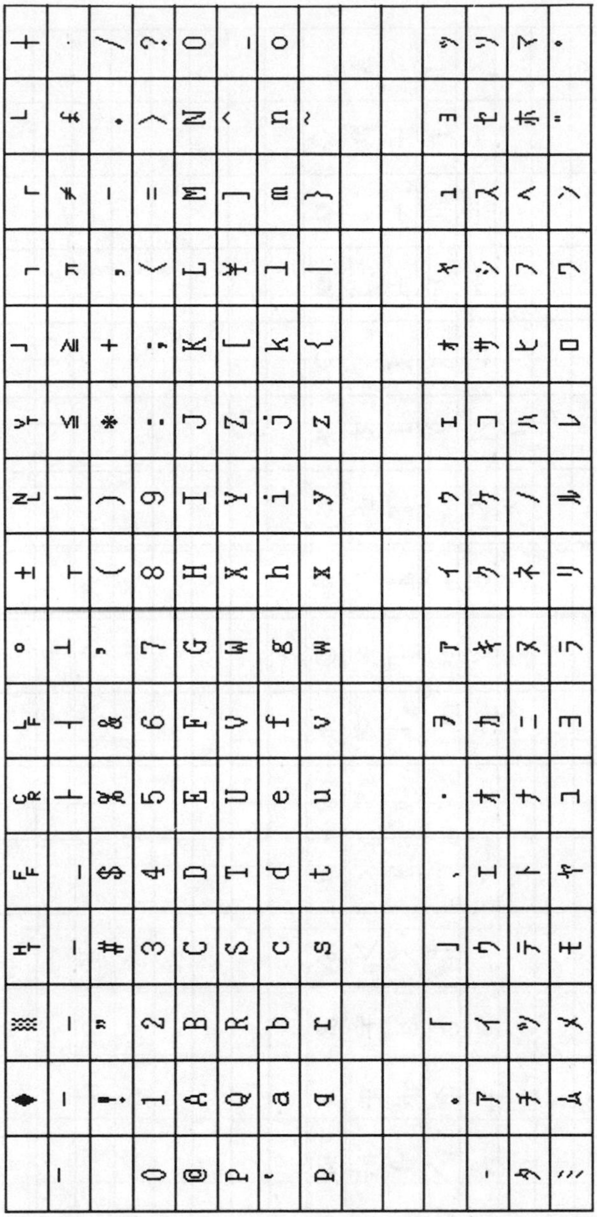

	◆	▒	HT	FF	CR	LF	°	±	NL	VT	┘	┐	┌	└	┼
─	─	─	─	_	├	┤	┴	┬	│	≤	≥	π	≠	£	·
	!	"	#	$	%	&	'	(	)	*	+	,	-	.	/
0	1	2	3	4	5	6	7	8	9	:	;	<	=	>	?
@	A	B	C	D	E	F	G	H	I	J	K	L	M	N	O
P	Q	R	S	T	U	V	W	X	Y	Z	[	¥	]	^	_
`	a	b	c	d	e	f	g	h	i	j	k	l	m	n	o
p	q	r	s	t	u	v	w	x	y	z	{	|	}	~	
	｡	｢	｣	､	･	ｦ	ｧ	ｨ	ｩ	ｪ	ｫ	ｬ	ｭ	ｮ	ｯ
ｰ	ｱ	ｲ	ｳ	ｴ	ｵ	ｶ	ｷ	ｸ	ｹ	ｺ	ｻ	ｼ	ｽ	ｾ	ｿ
ﾀ	ﾁ	ﾂ	ﾃ	ﾄ	ﾅ	ﾆ	ﾇ	ﾈ	ﾉ	ﾊ	ﾋ	ﾌ	ﾍ	ﾎ	ﾏ
ﾐ	ﾑ	ﾒ	ﾓ	ﾔ	ﾕ	ﾖ	ﾗ	ﾘ	ﾙ	ﾚ	ﾛ	ﾜ	ﾝ	ﾞ	ﾟ

Encoding: jisx0201.1976

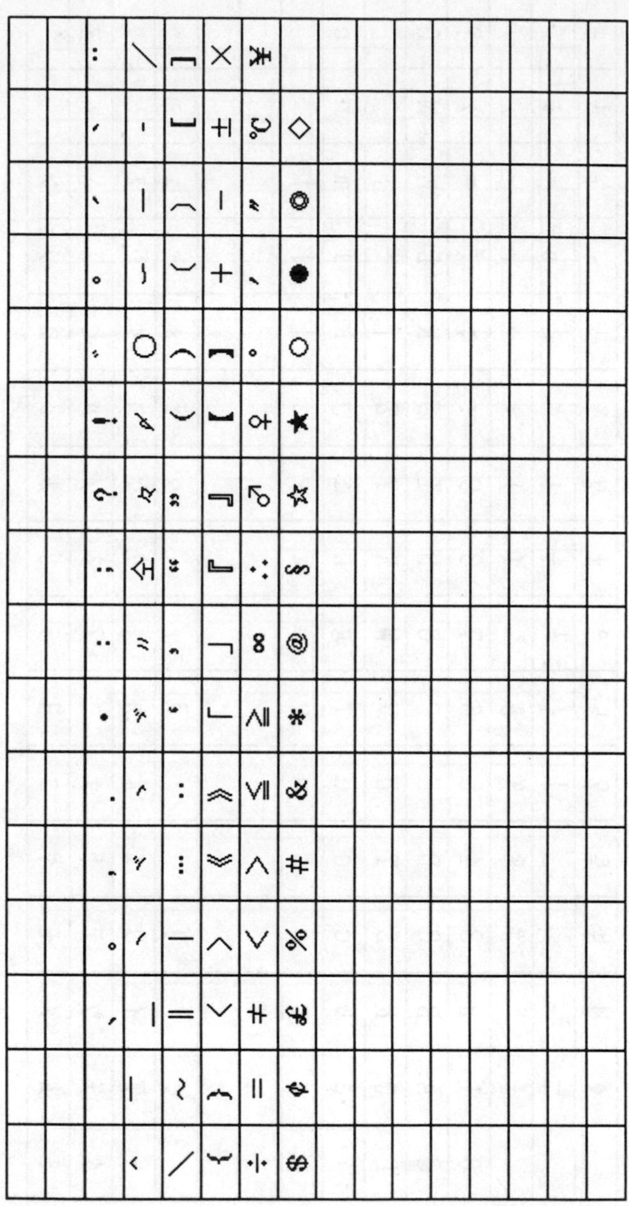

Encoding: jisx0208.1983

<table>
<tr><td></td><td>◆</td><td>▒</td><td></td><td></td><td></td><td></td><td></td><td></td><td></td><td></td><td>┘</td><td>┐</td><td>┌</td><td>└</td><td>┼</td></tr>
<tr><td>⎺</td><td>⎻</td><td>─</td><td>⎼</td><td>⎽</td><td>├</td><td>┤</td><td>┴</td><td>┬</td><td>│</td><td></td><td></td><td></td><td></td><td></td><td></td></tr>
<tr><td></td><td>!</td><td>"</td><td>#</td><td>$</td><td>%</td><td>&</td><td>'</td><td>(</td><td>)</td><td>*</td><td>+</td><td>,</td><td>-</td><td>.</td><td>/</td></tr>
<tr><td>0</td><td>1</td><td>2</td><td>3</td><td>4</td><td>5</td><td>6</td><td>7</td><td>8</td><td>9</td><td>:</td><td>;</td><td><</td><td>=</td><td>></td><td>?</td></tr>
<tr><td>@</td><td>A</td><td>B</td><td>C</td><td>D</td><td>E</td><td>F</td><td>G</td><td>H</td><td>I</td><td>J</td><td>K</td><td>L</td><td>M</td><td>N</td><td>O</td></tr>
<tr><td>P</td><td>Q</td><td>R</td><td>S</td><td>T</td><td>U</td><td>V</td><td>W</td><td>X</td><td>Y</td><td>Z</td><td>[</td><td>¥</td><td>]</td><td>^</td><td>_</td></tr>
<tr><td>`</td><td>a</td><td>b</td><td>c</td><td>d</td><td>e</td><td>f</td><td>g</td><td>h</td><td>i</td><td>j</td><td>k</td><td>l</td><td>m</td><td>n</td><td>o</td></tr>
<tr><td>p</td><td>q</td><td>r</td><td>s</td><td>t</td><td>u</td><td>v</td><td>w</td><td>x</td><td>y</td><td>z</td><td>{</td><td>|</td><td>}</td><td>‾</td><td></td></tr>
<tr><td></td><td></td><td></td><td></td><td></td><td></td><td></td><td></td><td></td><td></td><td></td><td></td><td></td><td></td><td></td><td></td></tr>
<tr><td></td><td></td><td></td><td></td><td></td><td></td><td></td><td></td><td></td><td></td><td></td><td></td><td></td><td></td><td></td><td></td></tr>
<tr><td></td><td>｡</td><td>｢</td><td>｣</td><td>､</td><td>･</td><td>ｦ</td><td>ｧ</td><td>ｨ</td><td>ｩ</td><td>ｪ</td><td>ｫ</td><td>ｬ</td><td>ｭ</td><td>ｮ</td><td>ｯ</td></tr>
<tr><td>ｰ</td><td>ｱ</td><td>ｲ</td><td>ｳ</td><td>ｴ</td><td>ｵ</td><td>ｶ</td><td>ｷ</td><td>ｸ</td><td>ｹ</td><td>ｺ</td><td>ｻ</td><td>ｼ</td><td>ｽ</td><td>ｾ</td><td>ｿ</td></tr>
<tr><td>ﾀ</td><td>ﾁ</td><td>ﾂ</td><td>ﾃ</td><td>ﾄ</td><td>ﾅ</td><td>ﾆ</td><td>ﾇ</td><td>ﾈ</td><td>ﾉ</td><td>ﾊ</td><td>ﾋ</td><td>ﾌ</td><td>ﾍ</td><td>ﾎ</td><td>ﾏ</td></tr>
<tr><td>ﾐ</td><td>ﾑ</td><td>ﾒ</td><td>ﾓ</td><td>ﾔ</td><td>ﾕ</td><td>ﾖ</td><td>ﾗ</td><td>ﾘ</td><td>ﾙ</td><td>ﾚ</td><td>ﾛ</td><td>ﾜ</td><td>ﾝ</td><td>ﾞ</td><td>ﾟ</td></tr>
</table>

Encoding: jisx0201.1976

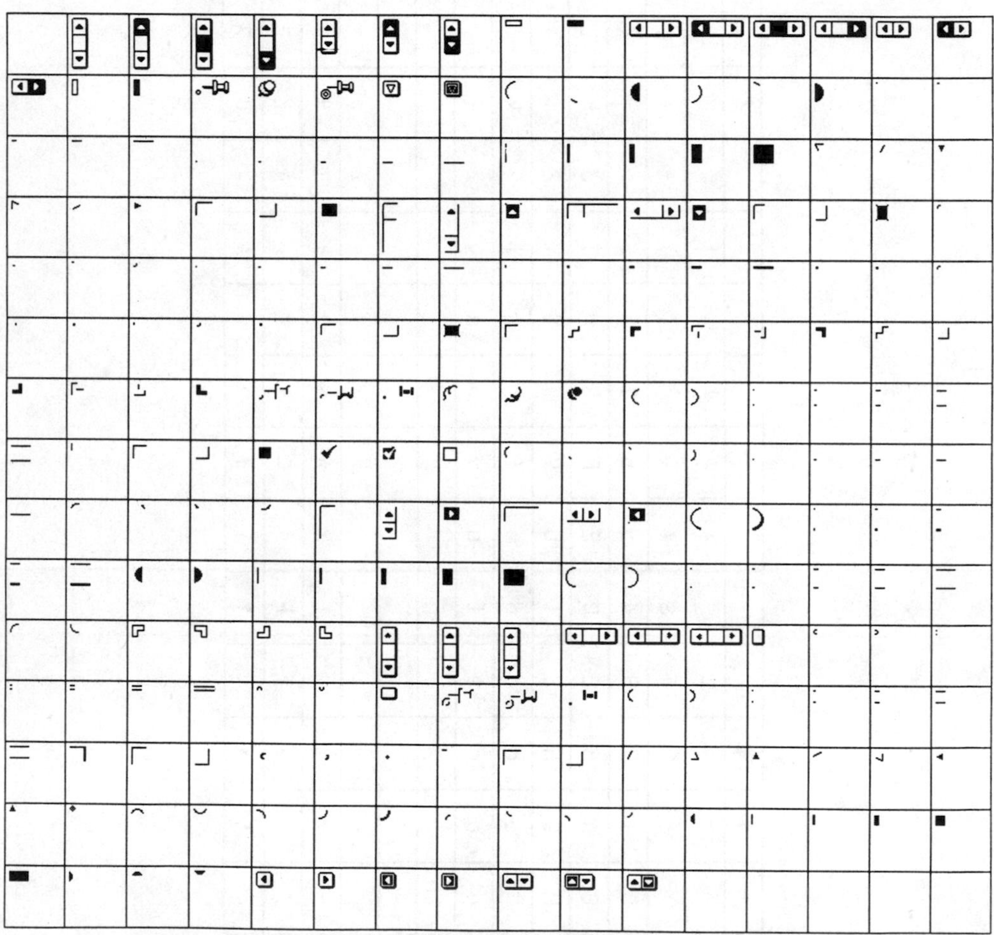

Encoding: sunolglyph

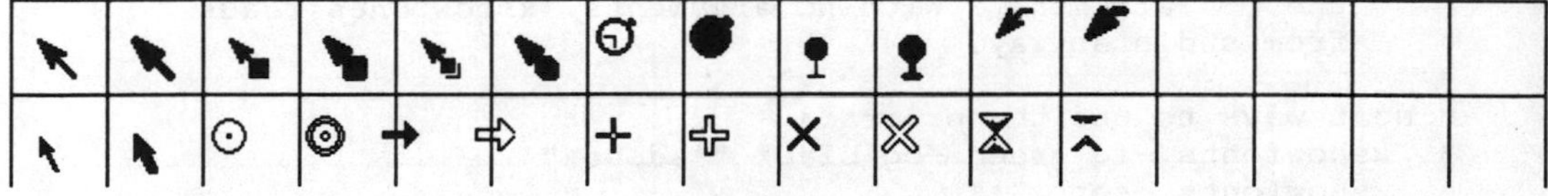

Encoding: SunOLcursor

Example E-1 is the source code for the *xshowfonts* program, which we used to create most of the illustrations in this appendix. If you don't want to type it in, you can find instructions for getting it online in the *Preface*.

Example E-1. xshowfont source listing

```
/* Dan Heller <argv@sun.com>, based on a design by Tim O'Reilly
 *
 * xshowfonts.c -
 *   Displays a set of fonts specified on the command line, from
 * a pipe, or typed into stdin.  Fonts can be specified as specific
 * fonts or as wildcard character strings.  A pixmap is created to
 * display all the fonts.  This is done by using the pixmap as the
 * pixmap image for a label widget.  Each font prints its own name
 * in its own font style -- the -phrase option prints the phrase
 * instead.
 *
 * All fonts are loaded first and scanned to determine the total
 * width and height of the pixmap first.  Then the fonts are
 * reopened again to actually render the fonts into the pixmap.
 * All this could be avoided by using XListFontsWithInfo()
 * rather than XListFonts(), but since the list is potentially
 * very large, I didn't want to overload the server and client
 * with all those fonts + a very large pixmap.
 *
 * Usage: xshowfonts
 *    -s sorts the fonts in alphabetical order before displaying
        them.
 *    -v verbose mode for when input is redirected to stdin.
 *    -w width of viewport window
 *    -h height of viewport window
 *    -fg foreground_color
 *    -bg background_color
 *    -phrase "text string" (otherwise, name of font is used)
 *    -indicates to read from stdin.  Piping doesn't require
      the '-' argument.  With no arguments, xshowfonts reads
 *    from stdin anyway.
 *
 * Neat ways to use the program:
 *  xshowfonts -fg green -bg black "*adobe*"
 *  xshowfonts -sort "*"
 *  xshowfonts -phrase "The quick brown fox jumps over the lazy
 *             dog" "*times*"
 *  xlsfonts | xshowfonts -sort
 *  xshowfonts "*helvetica*"
 *
 * compile: (triple click and paste next line)
     cc -O -s xshowfonts.c -lXaw -lXt -lXmu -lX11 -o xshowfonts
 */
#include <stdio.h>
#include <X11/Intrinsic.h>
#include <X11/StringDefs.h>
#include <X11/Xaw/Label.h>
#include <X11/Xaw/Viewport.h>

struct _resrcs {
    int sort;
```

Example E-1. xshowfont source listing (continued)

```
    int verbose;
    Pixel fg, bg;
    char *phrase;
    int view_width, view_height;
} Resrcs;

static XtResource resources[] = {
    { "sort", "Sort", XtRBoolean, sizeof (int),
     XtOffsetOf(struct _resrcs,sort), XtRImmediate,
        False },
    { "verbose", "Verbose", XtRBoolean, sizeof (int),
     XtOffsetOf(struct _resrcs,verbose), XtRImmediate,
        False },
    { "foreground", "Foreground", XtRPixel, sizeof (Pixel),
     XtOffsetOf(struct _resrcs,fg), XtRString,
        XtDefaultForeground },
    { "background", "Background", XtRPixel, sizeof (Pixel),
     XtOffsetOf(struct _resrcs,bg), XtRString,
        XtDefaultBackground },
    { "phrase", "Phrase", XtRString, sizeof (String),
     XtOffsetOf(struct _resrcs,phrase), XtRImmediate, NULL },
    { "view-width", "View-width", XtRInt, sizeof (int),
     XtOffsetOf(struct _resrcs,view_width), XtRImmediate,
        (char *)500 },
    { "view-height", "View-height", XtRInt, sizeof (int),
     XtOffsetOf(struct _resrcs,view_height), XtRImmediate,
        (char *)300 },
};

static XrmOptionDescRec options[] = {
    { "-sort", "sort", XrmoptionNoArg, "True" },
    { "-v", "verbose", XrmoptionNoArg, "True" },
    { "-fg", "foreground", XrmoptionSepArg, NULL },
    { "-bg", "background", XrmoptionSepArg, NULL },
    { "-phrase", "phrase", XrmoptionSepArg, NULL },
    { "-w", "view-width", XrmoptionSepArg, NULL },
    { "-h", "view-height", XrmoptionSepArg, NULL },
};

/* sort font according to the following parameters.
 * font specs we're interested in:
 *     -fndry-fmly-wght-slant-*swdth-*adstyl-*pxlsz-ptsz- ....
 * foundry -- sort by foundry first; similar ones are always
 *            grouped together
 * weight -- medium, demi-bold, bold
 * slant -- roman, italic/oblique, reverse italic/oblique
 *          (i or o, r, ri, ro)
 * ptsize -- increase numerical order
 */
font_cmp(f1, f2)
char **f1, **f2;
{
    char fndry1[16], fmly1[64], wght1[32], slant1[3];
    char fndry2[16], fmly2[64], wght2[32], slant2[3];
    int n, m, ptsize1, ptsize2;
    char *font_fmt_str = "-%[^-]-%[^-]-%[^-]-%[^-]-%*[^0-9]%
        *d-%d-";
```

Example E-1. xshowfont source listing (continued)

```
    n = sscanf(*f1, font_fmt_str, fndry1, fmly1, wght1, slant1,
              &ptsize1);
    m = sscanf(*f2, font_fmt_str, fndry2, fmly2, wght2, slant2,
              &ptsize2);
    if (m < 5 || n < 5)
     /* font not in correct format -- just return font names
      * in order */
     return strcmp(*f1, *f2);
    if (n = strcmp(fndry1, fndry2))
     return n; /* different foundries -- return alphabetical
                * order */
    if (n = strcmp(fmly1, fmly2))
     return n; /* different families -- return alphabetical
                * order */
    if (n = strcmp(wght1, wght2))
     return -n; /* weight happens to be correct in reverse
                 * alpha order */
    if (n = strcmp(slant1, slant2))
     return n; /* slants happen to be correct in alphabetical
                * order */
    /* sort according to point size */
    return ptsize1 - ptsize2;
}

main(argc, argv)
int argc;
char *argv[];
{
    Widget topLevel, vp;
    char **list = (char **)NULL, **tmp;
    char buf[128];
    extern char **XListFonts();
    extern int strcmp();
    XFontStruct *font;
    Pixmap pixmap;
    GC gc;
    Display *dpy;
    int istty = isatty(0), redirect = !istty, i, j, total = 0;
    unsigned int w, width = 0, height = 0;

    topLevel = XtInitialize(argv[0], argv[0], options,
        XtNumber(options), &argc, argv);
    dpy = XtDisplay(topLevel);

    XtGetApplicationResources(topLevel, &Resrcs,
     resources, XtNumber(resources), NULL, 0);

    if (!argv[1] || !strcmp(argv[1], "-")) {
     printf("Loading fonts from input. ");
     if (istty) {
         puts("End with EOF or .");
         redirect++;
     } else
         puts("Use -v to view font names being loaded.");
    } else if (!istty && strcmp(argv[1], "-"))
     printf("%s: either use pipes or specify font names --
              not both.\n",
```

Example E-1. xshowfont source listing (continued)

```
        argv[0]), exit(1);
    while (*++argv || redirect) {
     if (!redirect)
        if (!strcmp(*argv, "-"))
         redirect++;
        else
         strcpy(buf, *argv);
     if (redirect) {
        if (istty)
         printf("Fontname: "), fflush(stdout);
        if (!fgets(buf, sizeof buf, stdin) ||
              !strcmp(buf, ".\n"))
         break;
        buf[strlen(buf)-1] = 0;
     }
     if (!buf[0])
        continue;
     if (istty || Resrcs.verbose)
        printf("Loading
     tmp = XListFonts(dpy, buf, 32767, &i);
     if (i == 0) {
        printf("couldn't load font ");
        if (!istty && !Resrcs.verbose)
         printf("
        putchar('\n');
        continue;
     }
     if (istty || Resrcs.verbose)
        printf("%d font%s\n", i, i == 1? "" : "s");
     if (!list) {
        list = tmp;
        total = i;
     } else {
        i += total;
        if (!(list = (char **)XtRealloc(list, i *
                     sizeof (char *))))
         XtError("Not enough memory for font names");
        for (j = 0; total < i; j++, total++)
         list[total] = tmp[j];
     }
     }
    if (total == 0)
     puts("No fonts?!"), exit(1);
    printf("Total fonts loaded: %d\n", total);
    if (Resrcs.sort) {
     printf("Sorting fonts..."), fflush(stdout);
     qsort(list, total, sizeof (char *), font_cmp);
     putchar('\n');
     }
    /* calculate size for pixmap by getting the dimensions
     * of each font */
    puts("Calculating sizes for pixmap.");
    for (i = 0; i < total; i++) {
     if (!(font = XLoadQueryFont(dpy, list[i]))) {
        printf("Can't load font: %s\n", list[i]);
        continue;
```

Example E-1. xshowfont source listing (continued)

```
        }
        if ((w = XTextWidth(font, list[i],
              strlen(list[i]))) > width)
             width = w;
        height += font->ascent + font->descent;
        XFreeFont(dpy, font);
       }
       width += 6;
       height += 6;
       /* Create pixmap + GC */
       printf("Creating pixmap of size %dx%d\n", width, height);
       if (!(pixmap = XCreatePixmap(dpy, DefaultRootWindow(dpy),
        width, height, DefaultDepth(dpy, DefaultScreen(dpy)))))
        XtError("Can't Create pixmap");
       if (!(gc = XCreateGC(dpy, pixmap, NULL, 0)))
        XtError("Can't create gc");
       XSetForeground(dpy, gc, Resrcs.bg);
       XFillRectangle(dpy, pixmap, gc, 0, 0, width, height);
       XSetForeground(dpy, gc, Resrcs.fg);
       XSetBackground(dpy, gc, Resrcs.bg);
       height = 0;
       for (i = 0; i < total; i++) {
        if (!(font = XLoadQueryFont(dpy, list[i])))
            continue; /* it's already been reported */
        XSetFont(dpy, gc, font->fid);
        height += font->ascent;
        if (Resrcs.phrase)
            XDrawString(dpy, pixmap, gc, 0, height,
             Resrcs.phrase, strlen(Resrcs.phrase));
        else
            XDrawString(dpy, pixmap, gc, 5, height, list[i],
                      strlen(list[i]));
        height += font->descent;
        XFreeFont(dpy, font);
       }
       vp = XtVaCreateManagedWidget("viewport", viewportWidgetClass,
            topLevel,
        XtNallowHoriz,     True,
        XtNallowVert, True,
        XtNwidth,Resrcs.view_width,
        XtNheight,    Resrcs.view_height,
        NULL);
       XtVaCreateManagedWidget("_foo", labelWidgetClass, vp,
        XtNbitmap,    pixmap,
        NULL);

       if (!redirect)
        XFreeFontNames(list);

       XtRealizeWidget(topLevel);
       XtMainLoop();
}
```

F

xterm Control Sequences

This appendix list the escape sequences that can be used to control features of an xterm *window or its terminal emulation.*

In This Chapter:

F
xterm Control Sequences

A standard terminal performs many operations in response to escape sequences sent out by a program. In emulating a terminal, *xterm* responds to those same terminal escape sequences. Under UNIX, programs use the *termcap* or *terminfo* database to determine which escape sequences to send out. For more information, see the standard UNIX man pages *termcap*(5) or *terminfo*(5), or the Nutshell Handbook *Termcap and Terminfo*, available from O'Reilly & Associates, Inc.

xterm Control Sequences

This appendix is based on two sources: the "Xterm Control Sequences" document, written by Edward Moy, University of California, Berkeley, for the X10 *xterm*; and X11 updates provided to the X Consortium by Skip Montanaro, GE Corporate Research & Development.

Definitions

C A single (required) character.

P_s A single (usually optional) numeric parameter, composed of one of more digits.

P_m A multiple numeric parameter composed of any number of single numeric parameters, separated by ; character(s).

P_t A text parameter composed of printable characters.

VT102 Mode

Most of these control sequences are standard VT102 control sequences. There are, however, additional ones to provide control of *xterm*-dependent functions, like the scrollbar or window size.

BEL	Bell (Ctrl-G)
BS	Backspace (Ctrl-H)
TAB	Horizontal Tab (Ctrl-I)
LF	Line Feed or New Line (Ctrl-J)
VT	Vertical Tab (Ctrl-K)
FF	Form Feed or New Page (Ctrl-L)
CR	Carriage Return (Ctrl-M)
SO	Shift Out (Ctrl-N) → Switch to Alternate Character Set
SI	Shift In (Ctrl-O) → Switch to Standard Character Set
ESC BEL	Same as non-escaped BEL
ESC BS	Same as non-escaped BS
ESC HT	Same as non-escaped HT
ESC NL	Same as non-escaped NL
ESC VT	Same as non-escaped VT
ESC NP	Same as non-escaped NP
ESC CR	Same as non-escaped CR
ESC SO	Same as non-escaped SO
ESC SI	Same as non-escaped SI
ESC # BEL	Same as non-escaped BEL
ESC # BS	Same as non-escaped BS
ESC # HT	Same as non-escaped HT
ESC # NL	Same as non-escaped NL
ESC # VT	Same as non-escaped VT
ESC # NP	Same as non-escaped NP
ESC # CR	Same as non-escaped CR
ESC # SO	Same as non-escaped SO
ESC # SI	Same as non-escaped SI
ESC # 8	DEC Screen Alignment Test (DECALN)
ESC (BEL	Same as non-escaped BEL
ESC (BS	Same as non-escaped BS
ESC (HT	Same as non-escaped HT
ESC (NL	Same as non-escaped NL
ESC (VT	Same as non-escaped VT
ESC (NP	Same as non-escaped NP
ESC (CR	Same as non-escaped CR
ESC (SO	Same as non-escaped SO

ESC (SI	Same as non-escaped SI
ESC (*C*	Select G0 Character Set (SCS) *C* = 0 → Special Character and Line Drawing Set *C* = 1 → Alternate Character ROM Standard Set *C* = 2 → Alternate Character ROM Special Set *C* = A → United Kingdom (UK) *C* = B → United States (USASCII)
ESC) *C*	Select G1 Character Set (SCS) *C* = 0 → Special Character and Line Drawing Set *C* = 1 → Alternate Character ROM Standard Set *C* = 2 → Alternate Character ROM Special Set *C* = A → United Kingdom (UK) *C* = B → United States (USASCII)
ESC * *C*	Select G2 Character Set (SCS) *C* = 0 → Special Character and Line Drawing Set *C* = 1 → Alternate Character ROM Standard Set *C* = 2 → Alternate Character ROM Special Set *C* = A → United Kingdom (UK) *C* = B → United States (USASCII)
ESC + *C*	Select G3 Character Set (SCS) *C* = 0 → Special Character and Line Drawing Set *C* = 1 → Alternate Character ROM Standard Set *C* = 2 → Alternate Character ROM Special Set *C* = A → United Kingdom (UK) *C* = B → United States (USASCII)
ESC 7	Save Cursor (DECSC)
ESC 8	Restore Cursor (DECRC)
ESC =	Application Keypad (DECPAM)
ESC >	Normal Keypad (DECPNM)
ESC D	Index (IND)
ESC E	Next Line (NEL)
ESC H	Tab Set (HTS)
ESC M	Reverse Index (RI)
ESC N	Single Shift Select of G2 Character Set (SS2)
ESC O	Single Shift Select of G3 Character Set (SS3)
ESC	Return Terminal ID (DECID)

ESC [BEL	Same as non-escaped BEL
ESC [BS	Same as non-escaped BS
ESC [HT	Same as non-escaped HT
ESC [NL	Same as non-escaped NL
ESC [VT	Same as non-escaped VT
ESC [NP	Same as non-escaped NP
ESC [CR	Same as non-escaped CR
ESC [SO	Same as non-escaped SO
ESC [SI	Same as non-escaped SI
ESC [? BEL	Same as non-escaped BEL
ESC [? BS	Same as non-escaped BS
ESC [? HT	Same as non-escaped HT
ESC [? NL	Same as non-escaped NL
ESC [? VT	Same as non-escaped VT
ESC [? NP	Same as non-escaped NP
ESC [? CR	Same as non-escaped CR
ESC [? SO	Same as non-escaped SO
ESC [? SI	Same as non-escaped SI
ESC [P_s @	Insert P_s (Blank) Character(s) (default = 1) (ICH)
ESC [P_s A	Cursor Up P_s Times (default = 1) (CUU)
ESC [P_s B	Cursor Down P_s Times (default = 1) (CUD)
ESC [P_s C	Cursor Forward P_s Times (default = 1) (CUF)
ESC [P_s D	Cursor Backward P_s Times (default = 1) (CUB)
ESC [P_s ; P_s H	Cursor Position [row;column] (default = [1,1]) (CUP)
ESC [P_s J	Erase in Display (ED)
	P_s = 0 → Clear Below (default)
	P_s = 1 → Clear Above
	P_s = 2 → Clear All
ESC [P_s K	Erase in Line (EL)
	P_s = 0 → Clear to Right (default)
	P_s = 1 → Clear to Left
	P_s = 2 → Clear All
ESC [P_s L	Insert P_s Line(s) (default = 1) (IL)
ESC [P_s M	Delete P_s Line(s) (default = 1) (DL)
ESC [P_s P	Delete P_s Character(s) (default = 1) (DCH)
ESC [T	Track mouse

ESC [P_s c	Device Attributes (DA1)
ESC [P_s ; P_s f	Cursor Position [row;column] (default = [1,1]) (HVP)
ESC [P_s g	Tab Clear
	P_s = 0 → Clear Current Column (default)
	P_s = 3 → Clear All
ESC [P_s h	Mode Set (SET)
	P_s = 4 → Insert Mode (IRM)
	P_s = 2 0 → Automatic Linefeed (LNM)
ESC [P_s l	Mode Reset (RST)
	P_s = 4 → Insert Mode (IRM)
	P_s = 2 0 → Automatic Linefeed (LNM)
ESC [P_m m	Character Attributes (SGR)
	P_m = 0 → Normal (default)
	P_m = 1 → Blink (appears as Bold)
	P_m = 4 → Underscore
	P_m = 5 → Bold
	P_m = 7 → Inverse
ESC [P_s n	Device Status Report (DSR)
	P_s = 5 → Status Report ESC [0 n → OK
	P_s = 6 → Report Cursor Position (CPR) [row;column] as ESC [*r* ; *c* R
ESC [P_s ; P_s r	Set Scrolling Region [top;bottom] (default = full size of window) (DECSTBM)
ESC [P_s x	Request Terminal Parameters (DECREQTPARM)
ESC P_s *ND string NP*	OSC Mode
	ND can be any non-digit Character (it's discarded)
	NP can be any non-printing Character (it's discarded)
	string can be any ASCII printable string (max 511 characters)
	P_s = 0 → use string as a new icon name and title
	P_s = 1 → use string as a new icon name only
	P_s = 2 → use string as a new title only
	P_s = 4 6 → use string as a new log file name
ESC [? P_s h	DEC Private Mode Set (DECSET)
	P_s = 1 → Application Cursor Keys (DECCKM)
	P_s = 2 → Set VT52 Mode
	P_s = 3 → 132 Column Mode (DECCOLM)

P_s = [4] → Smooth (Slow) Scroll (DECSCLM)
P_s = [5] → Reverse Video (DECSCNM)
P_s = [6] → Origin Mode (DECOM)
P_s = [7] → Wraparound Mode (DECAWM)
P_s = [8] → Auto-repeat Keys (DECARM)
P_s = [9] → Send MIT Mouse Row & Column on Button Press
P_s = [3][8] → Enter TekTronix Mode (DECTEK)
P_s = [4][0] → Allow 80 ↔ 132 Mode
P_s = [4][1] → *curses*(5) fix
P_s = [4][4] → Turn On Margin Bell
P_s = [4][5] → Reverse-wraparound Mode
P_s = [4][6] → Start Logging
P_s = [4][7] → Use Alternate Screen Buffer
P_s = [1][0][0][0] → send VT200 Mouse Row & Column on Button Press
P_s = [1][0][0][3] → send VT200 Hilite Mouse Row & Column on Button Press

[ESC][[][?]P_s[l] DEC Private Mode Reset (DECRST)
P_s = [1] → Normal Cursor Keys (DECCKM)
P_s = [3] → 80 Column Mode (DECCOLM)
P_s = [4] → Jump (Fast) Scroll (DECSCLM)
P_s = [5] → Normal Video (DECSCNM)
P_s = [6] → Normal Cursor Mode (DECOM)
P_s = [7] → No Wraparound Mode (DECAWM)
P_s = [8] → No Auto-repeat Keys (DECARM)
P_s = [9] → Don't Send MIT Mouse Row & Column on Button Press
P_s = [4][0] → Disallow 80 ↔ 132 Mode
P_s = [4][1] → No *curses*(5) fix
P_s = [4][4] → Turn Off Margin Bell
P_s = [4][5] → No Reverse-wraparound Mode
P_s = [4][6] → Stop Logging
P_s = [4][7] → Use Normal Screen Buffer
P_s = [1][0][0][0] → Don't send Mouse Row & Column on Button Press
P_s = [1][0][0][3] → Don't send Hilite Mouse Row & Column on Button Press

ESC [? P_s r — Restore DEC Private Mode

P_s = 1 → Normal/Application Cursor Keys (DECCKM)
P_s = 3 → 80/132 Column Mode (DECCOLM)
P_s = 4 → Jump (Fast)/Smooth (Slow) Scroll (DECSCLM)
P_s = 5 → Normal/Reverse Video (DECSCNM)
P_s = 6 → Normal/Origin Cursor Mode (DECOM)
P_s = 7 → No Wraparound/Wraparound Mode (DECAWM)
P_s = 8 → Auto-repeat/No Auto-repeat Keys (DECARM)
P_s = 9 → Don't Send/Send MIT Mouse Row & Column on Button Press
P_s = 4 0 → Disallow/Allow 80 ↔ 132 Mode
P_s = 4 1 → Off/On *curses*(5) fix
P_s = 4 4 → Turn Off/On Margin Bell
P_s = 4 5 → No Reverse-wraparound/Reverse-wraparound Mode
P_s = 4 6 → Stop/Start Logging
P_s = 4 7 → Use Normal/Alternate Screen Buffer
P_s = 1 0 0 0 → Don't send/send VT200 Mouse Row & Column on Button Press
P_s = 1 0 0 3 → Don't send/send VT200 Hilite Mouse Row & Column on Button Press

ESC [? P_s s — Save DEC Private Mode

P_s = 1 → Normal/Application Cursor Keys (DECCKM)
P_s = 3 → 80/132 Column Mode (DECCOLM)
P_s = 4 → Jump (Fast)/Smooth (Slow) Scroll (DECSCLM)
P_s = 5 → Normal/Reverse Video (DECSCNM)
P_s = 6 → Normal/Origin Cursor Mode (DECOM)
P_s = 7 → No Wraparound/Wraparound Mode (DECAWM)
P_s = 8 → Auto-repeat/No Auto-repeat Keys (DECARM)
P_s = 9 → Don't Send/Send MIT Mouse Row & Column on Button Press
P_s = 4 0 → Disallow/Allow 80 ↔ 132 Mode
P_s = 4 1 → Off/On *curses*(5) fix
P_s = 4 4 → Turn Off/On Margin Bell
P_s = 4 5 → No Reverse-wraparound/Reverse-wraparound Mode
P_s = 4 6 → Stop/Start Logging
P_s = 4 7 → Use Normal/Alternate Screen Buffer

P_s = [1][0][0][0] → Don't send/send VT200 Mouse Row & Column on Button Press

P_s = [1][0][0][3] → Don't send/send VT200 Hilite Mouse Row & Column on Button Press

[ESC][]]P_s[;]P_t[BEL]	Set Text Parameters
	P_s = [0] → Change Window Name and Title to P_t
	P_s = [1] → Change Window Name to P_t
	P_s = [2] → Change Window Title to P_t
	P_s = [4][6] → Change Log File to P_t
	P_s = [5][0] → Change Font to P_t
[ESC][c]	Full Reset (RIS)
[ESC][n]	Locking Shift Select of G2 Character Set (LS2)
[ESC]	Locking Shift Select of G3 Character Set (LS3)

Tektronix 4014 Mode

Most of these sequences are standard Tektronix 4014 control sequences. The major features missing are the alternate (APL) character set and the write-thru and defocused modes.

[BEL]	Bell (Ctrl-G)
[BS]	Backspace (Ctrl-H)
[TAB]	Horizontal Tab (Ctrl-I)
[LF]	Line Feed or New Line (Ctrl-J)
[VT]	Vertical Tab (Ctrl-K)
[FF]	Form Feed or New Page (Ctrl-L)
[CR]	Carriage Return (Ctrl-M)
[ESC][ETX]	Switch to VT102 Mode
[ESC][ENQ]	Return Terminal Status
[ESC][LF]	PAGE (Clear Screen)
[ESC][ETB]	COPY (Save Tektronix Codes to File)
[ESC][CAN]	Bypass Condition
[ESC][SUB]	GIN mode
[ESC][FS]	Special Point Plot Mode
[ESC][GS]	Graph Mode (same as [GS])
[ESC][RS]	Incremental Plot Mode (same as [RS])
[ESC][US]	Alpha Mode (same as [US])
[ESC][8]	Select Large Character Set

ESC 9	Select #2 Character Set
ESC :	Select #3 Character Set
ESC ;	Select Small Character Set
ESC] P_s ; P_t BEL	Set Text Parameters
	P_s = 0 → Change Window Name and Title to P_t
	P_s = 1 → Change Icon Name to P_t
	P_s = 2 → Change Window Title to P_t
	P_s = 4 6 → Change Log File to P_t
ESC `	Normal Z Axis and Normal (solid) Vectors
ESC a	Normal Z Axis and Dotted Line Vectors
ESC b	Normal Z Axis and Dot-Dashed Vectors
ESC c	Normal Z Axis and Short-Dashed Vectors
ESC d	Normal Z Axis and Long-Dashed Vectors
ESC h	Defocused Z Axis and Normal (solid) Vectors
ESC i	Defocused Z Axis and Dotted Line Vectors
ESC j	Defocused Z Axis and Dot-Dashed Vectors
ESC k	Defocused Z Axis and Short-Dashed Vectors
ESC l	Defocused Z Axis and Long-Dashed Vectors
ESC p	Write-Thru Mode and Normal (solid) Vectors
ESC q	Write-Thru Mode and Dotted Line Vectors
ESC r	Write-Thru Mode and Dot-Dashed Vectors
ESC s	Write-Thru Mode and Short-Dashed Vectors
ESC t	Write-Thru Mode and Long-Dashed Vectors
FS	Point Plot Mode
GS	Graph Mode
RS	Incremental Plot Mode
US	Alpha Mode

G

Standard Bitmaps

This appendix shows the bitmaps included with the standard distribution of the X Window System. These can be used for setting window background, cursor symbols, pixmaps, and possibly for application icon pixmaps.

G
Standard Bitmaps

A number of bitmaps are included with the standard distribution of the X Window System. These bitmaps can be used for setting window background pixmaps and possibly for application icon pixmaps.

By default, the standard bitmaps are located in the directory */usr/include/X11/bitmaps*. Each bitmap is in standard X11 bitmap format in its own file. The *bitmap* application can be used to view these bitmaps in larger scale and to edit them (though their permissions normally do not allow overwriting).

You can use these bitmaps to set the background pattern of a window in any application that allows it. For example, if you wanted to change the root window background pixmap, you could do so using *xsetroot* as follows:

```
xsetroot -bitmap /usr/include/X11/bitmaps/wide_weave
```

Note that the bitmaps that come in pairs, such as `cntr_ptr` and `cntr_ptrmsk`, are intended for creating pointer shapes. See Chapter 11, *Setup Clients*, for information on specifying a bitmap as the root window pointer.

The 63 bitmaps pictured on the following pages are included in the Release 4 standard distribution of X. Forty-one of these bitmaps are also available in the Release 3 standard distribution. Table G-1 lists those bitmaps that have been added to the standard distribution in Release 4.

Table G-1. Standard Bitmaps Available as of Release 4

calculator	dropbar7	dropbar8
escherknot	hlines2	hlines3
keyboard16	letters	mailempty
mailemptymsk	mailfull	mailfullmsk
menu10	menu12	menu16
menu8	noletters	plaid
terminal	vlines2	vlines3
xlogo11		

1x1	2x2	black	boxes	calculator
cntr_ptr	cntr_ptrmsk	cross_weave	dimple1	dimple3
dot	dropbar7	dropbar8	flagdown	flagup
flipped_gray	gray	gray1	gray3	hlines2
hlines3	icon	keyboard16	left_ptr	left_ptrmsk
letters	light_gray	mailempty	mailemptymsk	mailfull
mailfullmsk	menu10	menu12	menu16	menu8
noletters	opendot	opendotMask	plaid	right_ptr
right_ptrmsk	root_weave	scales	sipb	star
starMask	stipple	target	terminal	tie_fighter
vlines2	vlines3	weird_size	wide_weave	wingdogs
xfd_icon	xlogo11	xlogo16	xlogo32	xlogo64

Figure G-1. The Standard Bitmaps

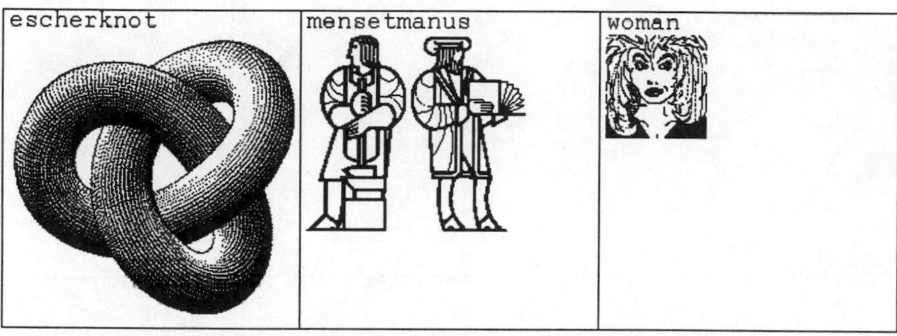

Figure G-1. The Standard Bitmaps (continued)

H

Translation Table Syntax

This appendix describes the basic syntax of translation table resources, described in Chapter 9, Setting Resources.

In This Chapter:

H
Translation Table Syntax

This appendix explains some of the more complex aspects of translation table syntax. It probably gives more detail than the average user will need, but we've included it to help clarify this rather complicated topic.

Event Types and Modifiers

The syntax of the translation table is sufficiently general to encompass a wide variety of events and circumstances. Event translations can be specified to handle characteristic user interface idioms like double clicking, dragging, or combining keyboard modifiers with pointer button input. To specify translations that use these features, it is necessary to learn more about the detailed syntax used to specify translations.

An activity susceptible to translation is a sequence of events and modifiers (that perform an action). Events are specified in angle brackets and modifiers precede the event they modify. The legal events that can be specified in a translation are as shown in Table H-1.

Table H-1. Event Types and Their Abbreviations

Event Name	Event Type	Abbreviations/Synonyms
KeyPress	Keyboard	Key, KeyDown
KeyUp	Keyboard	KeyRelease
ButtonPress	Mouse Button	BtnDown
ButtonRelease	Mouse Button	BtnUp
Btn1Down	Mouse Button Press	
.		
.		
Btn5Down		
Btn1Up	Mouse Button Release	
.		
.		
Btn5Up		

Table H-1. Event Types and Their Abbreviations (continued)

Event Name	Event Type	Abbreviations/Synonyms
MotionNotify	Mouse Motion	Motion, MouseMoved, PtrMoved
ButtonMotion	Motion w/any Button Down	BtnMotion
Button1Motion	Motion w/Button Down	Btn1Motion
.		.
.		.
Button5Motion		Btn5Motion
EnterNotify	Mouse in Window	Enter, EnterWindow
LeaveNotify		LeaveWindow, Leave
FocusIn	Keyboard Input Focus	
FocusOut		
KeymapNotify	Changed Key Map	Keymap
ColormapNotify	Changed Color Map	Clrmap
Expose	Related Exposure Events	
GraphicsExpose		GrExp
NoExpose		NoExp
VisibilityNotify		Visible
CreateNotify	Window Management	Create
DestroyNotify		Destroy
UnmapNotify		Unmap
MapNotify		Map
MapRequest		MapReq
ReparentNotify		Reparent
ConfigureNotify		Configure
ConfigureRequest		ConfigureReq
GravityNotify		Grav
ResizeRequest		ResReq
CirculateNotify		Circ
CirculateRequest		CircReq
PropertyNotify		Prop
SelectionClear	Intra-client Selection	SelClr
SelectionRequest		SelReq
SelectionNotify		Select

The possible modifiers of an event are listed in the table. The modifiers Mod1 through Mod5 are highly system-dependent, and may not be implemented by all servers.

Table H-2. Key Modifiers

Event Modifiers	Abbreviation
Ctrl	c
Meta	m
Shift	s
Lock	l
Any	
ANY	
None	
Mod1	1
.	.
.	.
Mod5	5

Detail Field

To provide finer control over the translation process, the event part of the translation can include an additional "detail." For example, if you want the event to require an additional keystroke, for instance, an A key, or a Ctrl-T, then that keystroke can be specified as a translation detail. The default detail field is *ANY*.

The valid translation details are event-dependent. For example, to specify the above example for keypress events, you would use:

```
<Key>A
```

and:

```
Ctrl<Key>T
```

respectively.

Key fields can be specified by the keysym value, as well as by the keysym symbolic name. For example, the keysym value of the Delete key is 0xffff. Keysym values can be determined by examining the file *<X11/keysymdef.h>* or by using the *xmodmap* client. (See Chapter 11, *Setup Clients*, for information about *xmodmap*.) Unfortunately, with some translations the keysym value may actually be required, since not all keysym symbolic names may be properly interpreted.

Modifiers

Modifiers can be closely controlled to define exactly which events can be specified. For example, if you want the action to be performed by pointer button clicks, but not by pointer button clicks with the Control or Shift key down, these limitations can be specified. Similarly, if you don't care if there are modifiers present, this can also be specified.

Table H-3 lists the available event modifiers.

Table H-3. Event Modifiers and their Meanings

Modifier	Meaning
None *<event>*	No modifiers allowed.
<event>	Doesn't care. Any modifiers ok.
Mod1 Mod	Mod1 and Mod2, plus any others (i.e., anything that includes m1 and m2).
!Mod1 Mod2*<event>*	Mod1 and Mod2 but nothing else.
Mod1 ~Mod2*<event>*	Mod1 and not Mod2.

Complex Translation Examples

The following translation specifies that function *f* is to be invoked when both the Shift key and the third pointer button are pressed.

```
Shift<Btn3Down>: f()
```

To specify that both the Control and Shift keys are to be pressed use:

```
Ctrl Shift<Btn3Down>: f()
```

To specify an optional repeat count for an activity, put a number in parentheses after the action. The number refers to the whole translation. To make the last example require a double-click, with both Control and Shift keys pressed, use:

```
Ctrl Shift<Btn3Down>(2): f()
```

The server distinguishes between single-clicks and double-clicks based on a pre-programmed timing interval. If a second click occurs before the interval expires, then the event is interpreted as a double-click; otherwise the event is interpreted as two single-clicks. The variable `clickTime` is maintained deep in the internals of X. Unfortunately, thus far there is no way to set this time interval to match user preference. Currently it is set to be 200 milliseconds.

A translation involving two or more clicks can be specified as (2+) in the previous example. In general, a plus sign following the number *n* would mean *n* or more occurrences of the event.

Multiple events can be specified by separating them with commas on the translation line. To indicate pressing button 1, pressing button 2, then releasing button 1, and finally releasing button 2, use:

```
<Btn1Down>,<Btn2Down>,<Btn1Up>,<Btn2Up>: f()
```

Another way to describe this action in English would be to say "while button 1 is down, click button 2." "Meaningless" pointer movement is generally ignored. In the previous case, for example, if pointer motion occurred while the buttons were down, it would not interfere with detection of the event. Thus, inadvertent pointer jiggling will not thwart even the most complex user-input sequences.

Glossary

X uses many common terms in unique ways. A good example is "children." While most, if not all, of these terms are defined where they are first used in this book, you will undoubtedly find it easier to refresh your memory by looking for them here.

Glossary

access control list — X maintains lists of hosts that are allowed access to each server controlling a display. By default, only the local host may use the display, plus any hosts specified in the *access control list* for that display. The list is found in */etc/X**n**.hosts* where ***n*** is the number of the display. The access control list is also known as the host access list.

active window — The window where the input is directed. With a "pointer focus" window manager such as *twm*, you must put the pointer in a window to make it the active window. The *active window* is sometimes called the **focus window.**

ASCII — American Standard Code for Information Interchange. This standard for data transmission assigns individual 7-bit codes to represent each of a specific set of 128 numerals, letters, and control characters.

background — Windows may have a *background*, consisting of either a solid color or a tile pattern. If a window has a background, it will be repainted automatically by the server whenever there is an `Expose` event on the window. If a window does not have a background, it will be transparent. See also **foreground**.

background color — The color that determines the backdrop of a window, for example, on monochrome displays, the root window background color is gray.

background window — A shaded area (also called the **root window**) that covers the entire screen and upon which other windows are displayed.

binding — An association between a function and a key and/or pointer button. *twm* allows you to bind its functions to any key(s) on the keyboard, or to a combination of keys and pointer button (e.g., the Control key and the middle button on a 3-button pointer).

bitmap — A grid of pixels or picture elements, each of which is white, black, or, in the case of color displays, a color. The *bitmap* client allows you to edit bitmaps, which you can use as pointers, icons, and background window patterns.

border A window can have a border that is zero or more pixels wide. If a window has a border, the border can have a solid color or a tile pattern, and it will be repainted automatically by the server whenever its color or pattern is changed or an `Expose` event occurs on the window.

client An X application program. There are *client* programs to perform a variety of tasks, including terminal emulation and window management. Clients need not run on the same system as the display server program.

colorcell An entry in a colormap is known as a *colorcell.* An entry contains three values specifying red, green, and blue intensities. These values are always 16-bit unsigned numbers, with zero being minimum intensity. The values are truncated or scaled by the server to match the display hardware. See also **colormap**.

colormap A *colormap* consists of a set of colorcells. A pixel value indexes into the colormap to produce intensities of red, green, and blue to be displayed. Depending on hardware limitations, one or more colormaps may be installed at one time, such that windows associated with those maps display with true colors. Regardless of the number of installable colormaps, any number of virtual colormaps can be created. When needed, a virtual colormap can be installed and the existing installed colormap may have to be uninstalled. The colormap on most systems is a limited resource that should be conserved by allocating read-only colorcells whenever possible, and selecting RGB values from the predefined color database. Read-only cells may be shared between clients. See also **RGB**.

console xterm window

This *xterm* window is the first window to appear on your display. Exiting the console window kills the X server program and any associated applications. Also called the login *xterm* window.

default A function-dependent value assigned when you do not specify a value. For example, specifying the `-rv` option with *xterm* reverses the foreground and background colors for the *xterm* window. If you do not specify this option, the default foreground and background colors are used.

depth The *depth* of a window or pixmap is the number of bits per pixel.

device-dependent Aspects of a system that vary depending on the hardware. For example, the number of colors available on the screen (or whether color is available at all) is a *device-dependent* feature of X.

display A set of one or more screens driven by a single X server. The DISPLAY environment variable tells programs which servers to connect to, unless it is overridden by the `-display` command line option. The default is always screen 0 of (display) server 0 on the local node.

event Something that must happen before an action can occur.

exposure Window *exposure* occurs when a window is first mapped, or when another window that obscures it is unmapped, resized, or moved. Servers do not guarantee to preserve the contents of windows when windows are obscured or reconfigured. `Expose` events are sent to clients to inform them when contents of regions of windows have been lost and need to be regenerated.

focus window The window to which keyboard input is directed. By default, the keyboard focus belongs to the root, which has the effect of sending input to whichever window has the pointer in it (if you are using a "pointer focus" window manager, such as *twm*). However, some clients may automatically take the focus, which means they may send input to a particular window regardless of the position of the pointer.

font A style of text characters. Fonts and X font naming conventions are described in Chapter 5, *Font Specification*. Samples of Release 3 and 4 screen fonts are pictured in Appendix E.

font directory By default, Release 3 and Release 4 fonts are stored in three subdirectories of */usr/lib/X11/fonts*: called *misc*, *75dpi*, and *100dpi*. (Release 2 fonts are stored in the directory */usr/lib/X11/fonts*.) You can specify an alternative font search path for the server with the *xset* client.

foreground The pixel value that will actually be used for drawing pictures or text is referred to as the *foreground*.

foreground color The color in which the text in windows and menus, or graphics output are displayed.

geometry The specification for the size and placement of a window, which can be specified with the `-geometry` option. This option takes an argument of the form: *`widthxheight±xoff±yoff`*.

hexadecimal A base-16 arithmetic system, which uses the digits A through F to represent the base-10 numbers 10 through 15. *Hexadecimal* notation (called hex for short) is frequently used with computers because a single hex digit can represent four binary digits (bits). The table below shows the equivalence between hex digits and binary numbers.

Hex	Binary	Hex	Binary	Hex	Binary	Hex	Binary
0	0000	4	0100	8	1000	C	1100
1	0001	5	0101	9	1001	D	1101
2	0010	6	0110	A	1010	E	1110
3	0011	7	0111	B	1011	F	1111

X clients accept a special hexadecimal notation (prefixed by a # character) in all command line options relating to color. See Chapter 8, *Command Line Options*, for more information.

highlighter The horizontal band of color that moves with the pointer within a menu.

hot spot The reference point of a pointer that corresponds to its specified position on the display. In the case of an arrow, an appropriate *hot spot* is its tip. In the case of a cross, an appropriate hot spot might be its center.

icon A small symbol that represents a window but uses little space on the display. Converting windows to *icons* allows you to keep your display uncluttered.

input device Hardware device that allows you to input information to the system. For a window-based system, a keyboard and pointer are the most common input devices.

keyboard focus See **focus window**.

menu A list of commands or functions, listed in a small window, which can be selected with the pointer.

modifier keys Keys on the keyboard such as Control, Alt, and Shift. X programs recognize a set of "logical" *modifier key* functions that can be mapped to physical keys. The most frequently used of these logical keys is called the "meta" key.

mouse An input device that, when moved across a flat surface, moves the pointer symbol correspondingly across the display. The mouse usually has buttons that can be pressed to send signals that in turn accomplish certain functions. The mouse is one type of pointer device; the representation of the mouse on the screen is also called the **pointer**. (See **pointer**.)

occluding In a windowing system, windows may be stacked on top of each other much like a deck of cards. The window that overlays another window is said to *occlude* that window. A window need not completely conceal another window to be occluding it.

padding Space inserted to maintain alignment within the borders of windows and menus.

parameter A value required before a client can perform a function. Also called an argument.

pixel The smallest element of a display surface that can be addressed.

pointer A generic name for an input device that, when moved across a flat surface, moves the pointer symbol correspondingly across the display. A *pointer* usually has buttons that can be pressed to send signals that in turn accomplish certain functions. A mouse is one type of pointer device.

The pointer also refers to the symbol on your display that tracks pointer movement on your desk. Pointers allow you to make selections in menus, size and position windows and icons, and select the window where you want to focus input. A pointer can be represented by a variety of symbols. (See **text cursor**.) Some typical X pointer symbols are the I-beam and the skull and crossbones.

property Windows have associated *properties*, each consisting of a name, a type, a data format, and some data. The X protocol places no interpretation on properties; they are intended as a general-purpose data storage and intercommunication mechanism for clients. There is, however, a list of predefined properties and property types so that clients can share information such as resize hints, program names, and icon formats with a window manager. In order to avoid passing arbitrary length property-name strings, each property name is associated with a corresponding integer value known as an atom.

reverse video Reversing the default foreground and background colors.

RGB An additive method for defining color in which tenths of percentages of the primaries red, green, and blue are combined to form other colors.

root window A shaded area (also called the **background window**) that covers the entire screen and upon which other windows are displayed.

screen A server may provide several independent *screens*, which may or may not have physically independent monitors. For instance, it is sometimes possible to treat a color monitor as if it were two screens, one color and one black and white.

scrollbar A bar on the side of an *xterm* window that allows you to use the pointer to scroll up and down through the text saved in the window. The number of lines saved is usually greater than the number of lines displayed and can be controlled by the `saveLines` resource variable.

select A process in which you move the pointer to the desired menu item or window and click or hold down a pointer button in order to perform some action.

selection *Selections* are a means of communication between clients using properties and events. From the user's perspective, a selection is an item of data that can be highlighted in one instance of an application and pasted into another instance of the same or a different application. The client that highlights the data is the owner, and the client into which the data is pasted is the requestor. Properties are used to store the selection data and the type of the data, while events are used to synchronize the transaction and to allow the requestor to indicate the type of data it prefers and to allow the owner to convert the data to the indicated type if possible.

server — The combination of graphics display, hardware, and X server software that provides display services for clients. The *server* also handles keyboard and pointer input.

text cursor — The standard underscore or block cursor that appears on the command line or in a text editor running an *xterm* window. To make the distinction clearer, the cursor that tracks the movement of a mouse or other pointing device is referred to as the **pointer**. The pointer may be associated with any number of cursor shapes, and may change shape as it moves from window to window.

tile — A pattern that is replicated (as if laying a tile) to form the background of a window or other area. This term is also used to refer to a style of window manager or application that places windows side by side instead of allowing them to overlap.

window — A region on your display created by a client. For example, the *xterm* terminal emulator, the *xcalc* calculator, and the *bitmap* graphics editor all create windows. You can manipulate windows on your display using a window manager.

window manager — A client that allows you to move, resize, circulate, and iconify windows on your display.

Index

C

N

O

P

Q

R

T

U

V

W

X

Books That Help People Get More Out of Computers

If you want more information about our books, or want to know where to buy them, we're happy to send it.

- ❑ Send me a free catalog of titles.
- ❑ What bookstores in my area carry your books (U.S. and Canada only)?
- ❑ Where can I buy your books outside the U.S. and Canada?
- ❑ Send me information about consulting services for documentation or programming.
- ❑ Send me information about bundling books with my product.

Name____________________

Address____________________

____

City____________________

State, ZIP____________________

Country____________________

Phone____________________

Email Address____________________

Books That Help People Get More Out of Computers

If you want more information about our books, or want to know where to buy them, we're happy to send it.

- ❑ Send me a free catalog of titles.
- ❑ What bookstores in my area carry your books (U.S. and Canada only)?
- ❑ Where can I buy your books outside the U.S. and Canada?
- ❑ Send me information about consulting services for documentation or programming.
- ❑ Send me information about bundling books with my product.

Name____________________

Address____________________

____

City____________________

State, ZIP____________________

Country____________________

Phone____________________

Email Address____________________

NAME ____________________

COMPANY ____________________

ADDRESS ____________________

CITY __________ STATE _____ ZIP __________

NO POSTAGE NECESSARY IF MAILED IN THE UNITED STATES

BUSINESS REPLY MAIL

FIRST CLASS MAIL PERMIT NO. 80 SEBASTOPOL, CA

POSTAGE WILL BE PAID BY ADDRESSEE

O'Reilly & Associates, Inc.

632 Petaluma Avenue
Sebastopol, CA 95472-9902

NAME ____________________

COMPANY ____________________

ADDRESS ____________________

CITY __________ STATE _____ ZIP __________

NO POSTAGE NECESSARY IF MAILED IN THE UNITED STATES

BUSINESS REPLY MAIL

FIRST CLASS MAIL PERMIT NO. 80 SEBASTOPOL, CA

POSTAGE WILL BE PAID BY ADDRESSEE

O'Reilly & Associates, Inc.

632 Petaluma Avenue
Sebastopol, CA 95472-9902